Sixtieth issue

YEARBOOK OF AMERICAN & CANADIAN CHURCHES 1992

Edited by Kenneth Bedell and Alice M. Jones

Prepared and edited for the Education, Communication and
Discipleship Unit of the National Council of Churches of Christ
in the U.S.A., 475 Riverside Drive, New York, NY 10115-0050

**Published and Distributed
by Abingdon Press
Nashville**

Yearbook of American and
Canadian Churches
1992

Joan Brown Campbell
Publisher

J. Martin Bailey
Editorial Director

Kenneth Bedell
Editor

Alice Jones
Editorial Associate

Candace Murrell
Larry Ramey
Assistant Editors

Emmanuel Giddings
Scott Reed
Computer Programmers

Kathryn Bedell
Freda Brown
Gerald Crutcher
Jeffrey Christian
Production Assistants

Printed in the United States of America
ISBN 0687-46647-4
ISSN 0195-9034
Library of Congress catalog card number:
16-5726

Preparation of this Year-
book is an annual project of
the National Council of
Churches of Christ in the
United States of America.

This is the sixtieth edition
of a yearbook that was first
published in 1916. Previous
editions have been entitled,
Federal Council Yearbook
(1916-1917), Yearbook of the
Churches (1918-1925), The
Handbook of the Churches
(1927), The New Handbook
of the Churches (1928), Yearbook of American Churches
(1933-1972) and Yearbook of
American and Canadian
Churches (1973-present).

INTRODUCTION

This edition of the **Yearbook of American and Canadian Churches** is the 60th in a series that began in 1916. Although it is a project of the National Council of Churches of Christ in the U.S.A., it is intended to be a general report on religious life in North America. Therefore, this yearbook contains information about many different faiths, not only Christian bodies, which the term *churches* implies.

This edition represents the first step in an evolution from a manual process of collecting and recording data to an electronic process. One of the first benefits of this transition is the index of names of people listed in directories 3 and 4 (Religious Bodies). Once the records were computerized the computer extracted names and organized the index.

Organizing all the information into a form that could be computerized presented several problems. Many of these problems were the result of the diversity of organizational structures and styles of religious bodies in Canada and the United States. In all cases an attempt was made to present information about organizations in a form that accurately reflects the structure of their organization.

Another change that computerization made possible was a reorganization of the way that religious periodicals are listed. Directories 3 and 4 which are religious bodies in Canada and the United States now only include the names of periodicals published by each organization. The editor's name, address and telephone number is listed in directories 13 and 14.

A new directory is included in this edition. It is directory 15, International Congregations. The material found in directory 16, Depositories of Church History Materials, has been expanded and is now included as a directory.

Regular users of this yearbook will notice several changes in the statistical section. Previous editions have included summaries of statistics for comparative purposes. The statistics collected this year do not lend themselves to comparisons with previous years without distortions. Rather than publish information that will misrepresent the changing nature of religious life in North America, the comparisons are not included. Two examples will illustrate the difficulty. This year the Church of God in Christ reported membership statistics for the first time since 1982. They reported an increase of 1,790,214. To include this increase in membership as if it happened in one year gives the wrong impression. A second example is the Presbyterian Church (U.S.A.). This denomination changed the way that it counts its members. The result is that between 1989 and 1990 they indicate an increase of 1,101,527 members.

Please refer to the introduction to the statistical section for more information about using the statistical tables.

Kenneth Bedell
Editor

CONTENTS

I. The Church in the '90s: Trends and Developments

II. Directories

III. Statistical Section

IV. A Calendar for Church Use

Indexes

I
THE CHURCH IN THE '90s:
TRENDS AND DEVELOPMENTS

THE STATE OF THE ECUMENICAL MOVEMENT

Joan Brown Campbell
General Secretary of the National Council of Churches of Christ in the USA

In recent years the ecumenical movement has been challenged on numerous occasions. Some commentators describe these events and conditions as threats to the conciliar efforts of the churches. Some say that the ecumenical reality has been seriously inhibited or even irreparably damaged.

The Meaning of Ecumenism

That analysis is based on an understanding of ecumenism that views its goals in only proximate terms. The goals are measured as projects successfully undertaken and as dollars easily raised and spent.

A more faithful understanding of ecumenism is that it is a gift from God to the people of God and for the sake of the world. This understanding would evaluate ecumenism not only in terms of particular meetings and accomplishments but also in terms of its contributions to the lives of persons and churches. This evaluation would test the commitments of persons and churches to each other.

To be sure, the late 1980s and early 1990s have been difficult years. The churches in the United States and elsewhere have attempted to respond to enormous problems and urgent needs with limited means. Like other organizations the churches have struggled with the impact of inflation at a time when hunger, homelessness, natural disasters and wars have taken heavy tolls. The valiant efforts of the churches have eased the pain of the poor, but solutions to the inequities of our society can only be addressed through social policy change.

One ecumenical barometer in our time is the National Council of the Churches of Christ in the USA. The health of the NCCC can be discussed only in the light of the state of the communions themselves. When the churches hurt, their Council hurts. As one wag said, "When the churches—any one of them—gets a cold, the NCCC gets pneumonia." That is true, especially if several communions have trouble at the same time, and particularly if the trouble is financial. The Council's financial condition is affected by the financial circumstances of the 32 member communions.

The National Council of Churches was therefore particularly fortunate that in 1991 contributions by the denominations to the Ecumenical Commitment Fund (which supports the basic work of the Council) slightly exceeded the support received in 1990. Admittedly, these contributions failed to match the "askings." Nevertheless, several churches which were forced to make significant cuts in their own budgets did not make commensurate reductions in contributions toward their ecumenical commitments. That must be seen as a positive indicator.

Positive Tensions

Tensions within the denominations are often reflected in the ecumenical community. When the churches argue over issues of human sexuality, when there are debates between so-called liberals and so-called conservatives, when the churches struggle with efforts to maintain the bonds of unity and over come issues of diversity, their divisions are played out within ecumenical agencies. Turf wars within the denominations repeat themselves within the National Council of Churches.

Often these are perceived as negative factors, but even such strains can be seen in a positive light. It is natural for the NCCC to share the same difficulties, the same joys and the same problems that the communions experience. The Council, after all, is an ecclesial body and not a collection of agencies. It is a council of churches. It is a community of communions.

1991 saw the five Eastern Orthodox bodies first suspend and then nine months later renew their membership in the National Council of Churches. Their concern was that "the NCCC identifies too strongly with its most liberal churches." In that action the Orthodox bodies saw the NCCC in its highest ecclesial form. They were, in effect, expressing a shared identity along with the most liberal of the denominations. They were saying that their Council is not separate from the Presbyterian Church, the United Methodist Church, the Episcopal Church or the United Church of Christ—or any of the 32 communions that together make up the National Council of the Churches of Christ in the USA.

One of the things that will surely result from the questions raised by the Eastern Orthodox churches is a renewed self- understanding that the Council is, in fact, a council of the churches. That renewed understanding almost certainly will press the churches in the NCCC to review their ecumenical priorities and to reorder their common life.

The "struggle" with the Orthodox communions, therefore, is not a struggle between the Orthodox and the NCCC, but a struggle between and among the churches. Taken seriously, this struggle has transforming power for the ecumenical movement in the United States, where a remarkable contradiction is already occurring within the churches. Local congregations are vibrant and fiscally strong while national denominations struggle and face retrenchments.

There are a host of reasons for this contradictory situation. There have been analyses, surveys, accusations and contentions, all seeking to explain or even explain away the present circumstances. Yet one paramount factor is omitted or ignored: the ecumenical reality.

The Influence of Ecumenism

It has become increasingly apparent that the "ecumenical movement" has significantly influenced what is occurring. An ecumenical understanding of what it means to be Christian, individually and socially, has impacted the life of the churches at their deepest level.

For example, ecumenism has reshaped the way ordinary members in the churches understand the phrase "Christian living." The typical church member lives ecumenically—and without apology. Neighborhoods are ecumenical and so are workplaces. Professions, company boards, labor unions, and community agencies function ecumenically. Religious ministries in the military services and hospital chaplaincies long have been ecumenical in their operating style and, perhaps more importantly, in their impact. Increasingly, marriage and family life is ecumenical. The baptism of a baby with full complement of grandparents often is a celebration of the ecumenical reality. In this context, baptizing a child into the Church of Jesus Christ is all that makes sense. Even to the average person, the issues that confront our common life require an ecumenical response.

Freeing Ecumenism

The ecumenical movement in our lifetime, with now a full century of history, needs to be understood as one of the great movements in the history of the Christian pilgrimage. Robert Bilheimer has suggested that it can take its rightful place alongside the Reformation and the monastic movement. The ecumenical reality has freed the Christian community in its understanding of itself from a debilitating narrowness of thought, experience and witness. It is apparent in local congregations which now, more often than not, understand both their character and mission in broader and more inclusive terms.

One of the major breakthroughs in the last half-century is the deepened religious interaction between and among Protestant, Roman Catholic, and Orthodox

Christians. Although the Roman Catholic Church is not a member of either the National Council of Churches or the World Council of Churches, there are many points of significant participation. Many local Roman Catholic dioceses in the USA are full participants in local councils of churches. During 1991, the U.S. Roman Catholic Bishops granted an imprimatur to the New Revised Standard Version of the Bible. No single event since the Second Vatican Council will do more to strengthen ecumenical ties than the use of the same Bible by faithful men and women in the cities and rural areas of our country.

Recently, when Edward Cardinal Cassidy visited the National Council of Churches offices in New York, he was asked by several journalists whether the Vatican has been underplaying or resisting its own ecumenical commitments. In his response, Cardinal Cassidy, president of the Pontifical Council for Promoting Christian Unity, borrowed a metaphor from Pope John Paul II. "Ecumenical work is like the ascent of a mountain," he said. "At the start, you make rapid progress. But as you climb it gets more difficult and you need greater skill." He testified that "in 25 years the Roman Catholic Church has come an enormous distance. Now we are looking at the great problems that have divided the Church for a thousand years."

Cardinal Cassidy stressed that "we must dig deep into our theological and doctrinal roots. In the present situation, that makes the going more difficult—but no less important."

As the churches work together and get to know one another better they are not bound to struggle together over issues of faith and practice. In almost every church assembly, including those of the National and World Councils of Churches, issues surface that are understood differently by representatives of differing traditions. These issues are themselves important and quite naturally call forth strong opinions and reactions. As Christians deal with one another honestly and directly across the ecumenical spectrum, they begin to appreciate each other's histories, worship patterns, commitments and practices. That fact alone is a promising part of the ecumenical reality in the 1990s.

Several years ago, after the Episcopal

Cardinal Cassidy

Church consecrated Barbara Clementine Harris as the Suffragan Bishop of Massachusetts, one expression of concern came from His Holiness Pope Shenouda, the head of the Coptic Orthodox Church in Egypt and a president of the World Council of Churches. He indicated that, while the ordination of women was not a relevant issue for the Orthodox, "the consecration of Barbara Harris put the issue of the ordination of women to the priesthood on the agenda again. We cannot ignore what is taking place in the Anglican communion," he said. An Episcopal priest from the Diocese of New York had raised the same issue at the consecration ceremony itself. The Rev. James Hopkinson Cupid, Jr., insisted that Bishop Harris' "consecration and election were contrary to sound doctrine and the consecration was an intractable impediment to the realization of that visible unity of the church for which Christ prayed."

I happen to disagree with the content of Father Cupid's concerns, but I agree completely that the consecration of Barbara Harris challenged our understanding of church unity. From my perspective, the unity of the church is inseparably bound to the renewal of our broken human community. To have refused her ordination and consecration also would have been an impediment to Christian unity. The Faith and Order Commission of the World Council of Churches has tried to clarify the meaning of Christian unity by saying that the visible unity of Christ's church may never be considered apart from concern for Christian proclamation, witness, and service in a world crying out for renewal. To separate those two ecumenical themes is to forget that Jesus' prayer for the unity of the church was for the sake of the world.

Continuing the Tradition

The current debates within the ecumenical movement are not a departure from ecumenical tradition. In the pursuit of visible expressions of Christian unity, the churches engage each other candidly, speaking the truth in love. Konrad Raiser, former Deputy General Secretary of the World Council of Churches, once said that "Ecumenism can no longer be toyed with as a mere possibility. It has become a test case of faith." It is true that the Christian churches are struggling with one another—but there is a remarkable openness to serious dialogue.

In August 1991, Billy Graham's visit to the General Secretary of the National Council of Churches is an example of the hope and promise of ecumenical dialogue. He took the initiative, despite the fact that he had nothing to gain and possibly much to lose, to publicly identify himself with the National Council. Many fundamentalists already discount him because of his involvement with persons they describe as "unbelievers." But he came to the NCCC to express solidarity with fellow Christians who call Jesus Lord and Savior and who witness in his name to the needs of the poor and who work for justice and peace.

"I want to thank the National Council of Churches," he said, "and particularly Jesse Bader, then the NCCC secretary for evangelism, for the integrity of my own ministry." He spoke of his conversion to ecumenism and quoted directly from the Roman Catholic Decree on Ecumenism, saying, "There can be no ecumenism worthy of the name without an interior conversion. The faithful should remember that they promote union among Christians better, and indeed they live it better, when they try to lead lives according to the Gospel. The closer their union with God, with the Word and the Spirit, the more closely and easily they will be able to grow in mutual love. This change of heart and holiness of life, along with public and private prayer for Christian unity and for all Christians, should be regarded as the soul of the whole ecumenical movement." And, he added, "This is how I understand ecumenism."

Billy Graham expressed a desire to work more closely with the churches in the NCCC, especially in Eastern Europe. He is one of those persons we call bridge persons—not ideologically bound, but God's man seeking to be faithful. The ecumenical movement needs more persons like Billy Graham to guide it through troubled times.

Ecumenical Education

One of the major ecumenical challenges facing us in the decade of the 1990s is the ecumenical education of God's people. There is a serious temptation to leave ecumenism to the professionals and to those institutions that have been created as our ecumenical voices. Support for those visible signs of unity is an urgent matter. But equally urgent is the "ecumenizing" of the people of God. We need to find a way to teach ecumenism. We need to deepen the base of commitment to the ecumenical movement, and that involves congregations. Neither ecumenical organizations nor member churches have taken seriously the education of people in the pews.

Perhaps one of the reasons for the controversies over the ecumenical institutions is that we have failed to create a climate for understanding their work and witness. Perhaps we have hesitated to create this climate because we understand that a call for the reunion of the creation and of all God's children is a radical word. The quest for Christian unity is a response to the Gospel of Jesus Christ. It is a recognition that God is on the side of what unites, integrates, heals and makes whole. When the mystery of God's grace is at work in our midst one must conclude that there are, indeed, many signs of hope and promise.

SOCIAL IDEOLOGY AND COMMUNITY MINISTRIES
Implications from Church Membership Surveys

Carl S. Dudley and Thomas Van Eck
Center for Church & Community Ministries

Which churches will launch social ministries in their communities? Conservative or liberal? Big or small? City or country? Black or white?

We studied approximately 100 congregations of 14 denominations, involved in social ministries in Illinois and Indiana. We found that everything from theology to geography affected churches' attitudes toward social action and community ministry. But because of the complex interaction of all those factors in each church, many churches defied stereotypes. Among them:

- Many conservative churches felt just as strongly about social justice as liberal churches;
- Rich churches support social justice ministries as much as low-income congregations; and
- Socially conservative lay members were more inclined to support social justice ministries than their more liberal pastors thought they were.
- The social attitudes of most congregations favor and support social ministries, but attitudes alone don't accurately predict project success.

Previous research shows that a variety of factors help shape members' attitudes toward social justice issues and the action their churches take.

We explored the effects of:

- Denominational affiliation;
- Socioeconomic status;
- Congregational size and geographic location;
- Theological orientation and social posture;
- Congregational self-images of social ministry;
- Stability and change
- Members' attitudes on their projects' success; and
- Pastor-laity differences and perceptions.

The question is: What makes the difference for each church?

1. Denominational Comparisons

Generally, denominational breakdowns do not show significant differences in membership responses.

Initially we examined our data for relationships between members' scores on the scales and their denominational affiliation. Although other researchers using national data have found differences between liberal, moderate, and conservative Protestants on various measures of social and political ideology (Roof and McKinney, 1987), we do not find striking differences between the more conservative, moderate, and liberal Protestants in our sample. On certain scales, some theologically liberal denominations are more socially liberal (e.g. United Church of Christ on the Systemic and Social Ideology scale), while on other scales they are less supportive of social ministry than some more typically conservative groups (e.g. Priority on Local Social Ministry).

Catholics in our survey lean slightly more toward favoring local social ministry; however, they are not significantly more liberal on the justice and social ideology scales. Although we explored the position that more hierarchial or connectional denominational structures (e.g. Catholics, Lutherans, Presbyterians, Methodists, and Disciples of Christ) may contribute to more support of social ministry (Davidson, et al. 1990; cf. Lincoln and Mamiya 1990), we found little support for that thesis in comparing these particular congregations.

We do find consistent differences in two areas, however.

Black churches in our study were significantly more liberal on social issues and orientation to working for justice (as anticipated by Roof and McKinney, cf. Lincoln and Mamiya, 1990).

In addition, the two Church of the Brethren congregations were also significantly more liberal than other Euro-American

TABLE 1, Denominational Contrasts on Scales   CCPI -I

Scale Measuring:	R.C.	UCC	Presb	UMC	Luth	DOC	Bapt	Breth	Black	EvCov
Causes of Poverty:										
Systemic	10.0	10.5	9.5	9.7	9.6	9.8	10.1	10.4	11.8	10.5
Individual	9.9	10.7	10.5	11.1	10.7	10.1	10.3	9.2	9.5	9.7
Social Justice	10.2	9.9	9.8	10.1	9.6	10.2	9.8	10.9	10.7	10.3
Social Ideol.	9.3	9.8	8.8	8.7	8.9	9.2	9.6	11.3	11.2	9.9
Priority on										
Local Soc Min	11.3	10.6	11.0	10.9	10.8	10.8	10.8	11.5	12.1	10.6
Church should work										
for justice (%)	27	26	23	20	32	26	23	55	41	41
# Churches	9	5	10	11	5	6	4	2	5	4

See the following article for an explanation of the tables

respondents. Since our field studies and other survey questions show that both the African American and Brethren churches express a more conservative theology and maintain habits of cultural distinctiveness, we might speculate that this combination of theological views and social uniqueness contributes to these "denominational" differences in their social attitudes.

In general, we found that the attitudes of most congregations toward social justice issues were congenial and even supportive of the development of social ministries.

2. Socio-economic Effects

Attitudes cross socio-economic lines.

The influence of education, income, and employment have often been associated with particular ideological perspectives. When we compared members' attitudes among different educational levels, we found more liberal views among the more highly educated (cf. Roof and McKinney, 1987). But when we included education with other socio-economic factors such as income and occupation (Table 2), the combined socio-economic status effect does not show significant differences in the churches of our study, with two important exceptions.

Churches of lower socio-economic status, as compared with moderate and higher status groups, place uniquely strong emphasis on personal responsibility (failure) for situations of poverty. Churches with higher socio-economic status do not place as much blame on the individual for being in poverty, but they also resist blaming the system—poverty just is. At the same time, churches of higher socio-economic status are signifi-

cantly more likely to support an active role for the church in developing justice ministries.

Throughout all the congregational responses, however, only one-fourth favor the church's involvement in justice ministries. In general, congregations may be more congenial with ministries of care and service than ministries of justice that seek changes in systems.

3. Church Location and Size

Urban churches are more involved in social action. Congregational size doesn't seem to be a factor.

Beyond the pre-existing conditions of denominational affiliation and socio-economic status, we explored the influences on members' attitudes based on community location and congregational size.

Geographic location of the church seems to have a strong influence on social attitudes. When we defined congregations in social locations from the inner city and urban areas to the small town and rural communities (see Table 3), significant differences are evident: Urban areas are more liberal and supportive of church involvement in community and justice ministries, while towns and rural communities are more conservative and less supportive.

In examining the influence of congregational size, these data do not support the thesis that large rather than small churches are more likely to support community ministries. Our data show that our smallest churches were nearly as likely as the largest to be in favor of church involvement in the local community, and were much more supportive of the view that the church should work for justice (See Table 3). The greater resources of

TRENDS AND DEVELOPMENTS

6

TABLE 2 Congregational SES Contrasts on Scales

SES:	LOW	MED	HIGH
Scale Measuring:			
Causes of Poverty:			
Systemic	10.3	10.2	9.7
Individual	11.0	10.2	9.6
Social Justice	10.0	10.1	10.2
Social Ideol.	9.3	9.4	9.6
Priority on			
Local Soc Min	11.1	11.0	11.0
Church should work			
for justice (%)	25	23	36
# Churches	25	16	20

See the following article for an explanation
of the tables

larger churches account for their reported higher levels of involvement in social ministries, not a greater predisposition to become involved on the part of members (Davidson, et al., 1990; Lincoln and Mamiya, 1991). As we examined possible reasons for the effect of location on social attitudes, our small urban congregations most frequently reported feelings of being threatened and made vulnerable by massive social ills surrounding them that greatly increased their social consciousness.

4. Congregational Theology and Orientation to Society

Attitudes defy Evangelical or Liberal labels.

Apart from denominational affiliation, we examined the distribution of theological views of the members of each congregation. In developing a theological typology (Mock, forthcoming), we categorized churches as:

- ■ **Evangelical** — when they showed a strong conversionist approach to salvation and a high percentage of members who take a literal interpretation of the Bible;
- ■ **Liberal** — when they reflect a strong gradualist approach to salvation and a low percentage of members with a literal interpretation of the Bible.
- ■ **Moderate** — when they have a blend of conversionist and gradualist approaches and a moderate percentage of members with a literal interpretation.

When we divided the churches into these categories, we found a spread of 11 evangelical, 27 moderate and 22 liberal churches. Churches of different denominations were distributed in several categories, but generally in the expected direction. We found, however, a few Evangelical congregations in traditionally moderate denominations (American Baptist, United Methodist), and a moderate congregation in a traditionally Conservative denomination (Lutheran Church-Missouri Synod).

To determine the individual congregations' orientation to society we also developed three categories of community posture based on members' views of how the church approaches social issues, community involvement, and focus of ministry:

- ■ **Sanctuary** has an emphasis on an educational approach to social issues, low community involvement, and an emphasis on serving current church members;
- ■ **Civic** has a mix of education and activism on social issues, moderate involvement in the community, and a blend of serving both members and the world;
- ■ **Activist** has an avowed activist approach to social issues, support for community involvement and an emphasis on the church serving the world.

We found Evangelical churches with a conservative theology that supported strong Civic and Activist attitudes, and the opposite, congregations with Liberal theology that were inclined toward Sanctuary attitudes of social ministry. About half of these "unexpected" combinations were partners with contract congregations, drawn into the program through trusted working relationships in their communities.

But together they suggest that an Evangelical theology does not automatically restrict a congregation from engaging in community ministries, nor does a Liberal theology inevitably lead to attitudes that support social ministries.

As shown in Table 4, we found the theological orientation of congregations did vary with members' social justice ideologies, but not consistently in the direc-

TABLE 3   Urban/Rural and Congregational Size Contrasts

Scales Measuring:	Inner Urban	Outer Urban/ Suburb	Small City	Small Town/ Rural	Number of Members:			
					LT 125	125 to 249	250 to 499	Over 500
Causes of Poverty:								
Systemic	10.5	9.8	9.8	9.8	10.3	10.1	10.0	9.8
Individual	10.4	9.7	10.6	11.0	10.5	10.3	10.5	10.0
Social Justice	10.2	10.2	9.9	9.9	10.3	10.0	10.0	10.1
Social Ideol.	9.9	9.5	9.0	8.8	9.7	9.4	9.2	9.3
Priority on								
Local Soc Min	11.3	11.2	10.8	10.7	11.1	10.9	10.8	11.3
Church should work								
for justice (%)	35	32	23	16	37	27	21	27
# Churches	20	17	13	11	14	17	14	16

See the following article for an explanation of the tables

tion anticipated from earlier studies (e.g., Hoge, 1976; Roozen, et al. 1984). Evangelical churches, when compared with Moderate and Liberal churches, indicated higher priorities on local social ministry, a greater concern for how systems cause poverty, and more liberal social ideology—all significant and in the direction opposite to the traditional expectations.

These differences reaffirm our field experience that Evangelical churches cannot be categorically consigned to conservative social views, or liberal churches to liberal socio-political positions.

Also in Table 4, the scores on members' attitudes strongly support the clustering of congregations according to their community posture. Sanctuary congregations were significantly more conservative in all the questions of priorities, causes, social justice and social ideology, while members of Activist congregations were more liberal. These differences are particularly dramatic in responses to the questions of the church's involvement in social justice.

These categories cut across denominational lines and are not limited by theological orientations. Members' view of their church's orientation to the community appears to have a very strong correlation with members' personal social ideology and justice views. This suggests that congregational self-awareness might both reflect and shape the social attitudes of its members.

5. Congregational Self-images of Social Ministry

Self-image affects a congregation's understanding of its mission.

Another approach to attitudes toward social ministry can be found by reviewing the history and specific stories by which congregations recall their relationships with their communities. In reading narrative materials we looked for images that seem to guide or dominate congregational attitudes. The congregational images focus the way that the church feels about its

TABLE 4   Contrasts on Scales by Mock Types CCPI-I

Scale Measuring	Sanct.	Civic	Activist	Evang	Moderate	Liberal
Causes of Poverty:						
Systemic	9.5	10.2	10.4	10.6	10.3	9.6
Individual	10.9	10.3	9.8	10.6	10.4	10.1
Social Justice	9.7	10.1	10.4	10.3	10.1	10.0
Social Ideol.	8.5	9.4	10.3	9.7	9.4	9.2
Priority on						
Local Soc Min	10.3	11.1	11.4	11.2	11.1	10.9
Church should work						
for justice (%)	18	25	40	27	26	28
# Churches	12	35	13	11	27	22

See the following article for an explanation of the tables

TABLE 5   IMAGES Contrasts on Scales   CCPI-I

Scales Measuring:	Survivor	Prophet	Pillar	Pilgrim	Servant
Causes of Poverty					
Systemic	10.5	10.6	9.6	11.3	9.9
Individual	9.8	10.3	10.2	10.3	10.5
Social Ideol.	9.8	10.1	9.0	10.6	9.1
Priority on					
Local Soc Min	11.4	11.7	11.0	11.5	11.1
Church should work					
for justice (%)	32	32	22	33	22
Activism *	3.9	4.4	3.5	3.7	3.6
Advocacy **	10.7	11.0	10.3	11.0	10.6
# Churches	9	6	11	6	8

* Individual conscience vs. corporate congregational action on social issues. Scale from 1.0=individual to 7.0=corporate.
** Scale measuring priority given to church's advocacy for social justice issues. Higher score = greater priority.
See the following article for an explanation of the tables

role in the community, often reflected in program activities, membership recruitment, fund raising, social conflict, and other experiences in their community settings. We identified five patterned self-images by which churches tell their stories (Dudley and Johnson, 1991):

- **Pillar Churches** provide the anchor for their communities and have strong feelings of responsibility for it.

- **Pilgrim churches**, rather than focusing on place, provide spiritual and cultural shelter for racial and ethnic groups.

- **Survivor churches** have a lifestyle of weathering crises, and, although constantly on the verge of disaster, they will endure.

- **Prophet churches**, when they see evil, take a pro-active stance to transform the condition.

- **Servant churches** seek to live their faith in quiet service to help particular individuals in their time of need.

Although we identify these images through content analysis of congregational stories, differences are also evident in members' attitudes toward social ministries. As can be seen in Table 5, Prophet congregations are significantly more inclined toward corporate congregational action on social issues (Activism item), and they share with Pilgrim churches in their priority on local social ministry and an emphasis on advocacy for social justice issues (Advocacy scale). By contrast,

Pillar and Servant churches have a more conservative social ideology, fewer members who support the church's involvement in local justice ministries, and fewer who agree the church should be working for justice. Survivor and Pilgrim churches, perhaps feeling trapped and punished by circumstances beyond their control, see poverty caused more by systemic problems than individual failures; Pillar and Servant churches place more responsibility on the individual and less on the system. In short, how churches "read" their history directly affects their present perceptions and future preparations for ministry.

6. Continuity and Change, 1987-1991

Participation in social action ministries have a slight effect on members' attitudes.

Since we have data drawn from the same

TABLE 6   1987 compared to 1991

Scales Measuring:	CCPI-1	CCPI-2
Causes of Poverty:		
Systemic	10.0	10.0
Individual	10.4	10.5
Social Justice	10.1	10.4
Social Ideol.	9.3	9.7
Priority on		
Local Soc Min	11.0	11.0
Church should work		
for justice (%)	25	28
# Churches *	44	44

* Only Churches who took both surveys are included in this table.
See the following article for an explanation of the tables

TABLE 7   SUCCESS Contrasts on Scales

Scales Measuring:	Viable 18 mos. after seed funding	Viable 12 mos. after seed funding	Lasted through seed funding period	Lasted less than one year
Causes of Poverty				
Systemic	10.0	10.3	10.5	10.5
Individual	10.3	9.8	10.3	10.2
Social Justice	10.2	10.2	10.0	10.0
Social Ideol.	9.4	9.8	9.6	9.8
Priority on				
Local Soc Min	11.2	11.0	11.3	11.4
Church should work				
for justice (%)	27	28	23	31
# Churches *	18	6	8	8

* Contract Churches Only
See the following article for an explanation of the tables

congregations in two samples taken in September, 1987 and January, 1991, we can observe the continuity or change in response to each item, possibly as a result of their participation in a program of social ministry. As seen in Table 6, three of the items showed no substantial change. Since these results reflect the views of different membership samples from congregations, the stability of these figures suggests that we have tapped the strong, solid continuity of social attitudes in these congregations.

Also in Table 6, we see a barely significant move toward more socially conscious ministry as reflected in the scales for both social justice and social ideology. Further, members of participating congregations were somewhat more likely to feel that the church should work for social justice. The slight movement in these measures and the intervention of many additional factors prevents us from claiming a direct, causal relationship between social ministries and attitude change. But at least the changes are in the direction of increased social sensitivity. Further, when compared with the stability of responses to most survey questions, these data suggest that ministry participation may have a liberalizing effect on members' social ideology and justice views.

7. Social Attitudes and Project Success

Most congregations have sufficiently liberal attitudes toward social action to make ministries work, but attitudes don't accurately predict project success.

To measure the relationship between members' attitudes toward social minis-

try and the church's development of a social ministry project, we defined project success as the ability to continue the ministry after the conclusion of seed funding in June, 1991. Our results are calculated in April, 1992, nine months beyond seed funding. Of the 40 original ministry projects, 18 seemed well organized and solidly funded and would be viable 18 months after seed funding; six additional will survive at least 12 months after seed funding; eight closed or were absorbed back into their congregational life when the seed funding was no longer available; and eight others never got started or ceased operation within the first year.

In Table 7 we see that members' attitudes and priorities are not useful predictors of project success. As we noted at the outset, these congregations showed strong support for social ministry. If there is a threshold of liberal social attitudes that is necessary to develop a program of social ministries, these churches seem to have sufficient strength. With that foundation, project success was more dependent upon other factors, such as the nature of the ministry that was chosen, the skills of available leaders, and the mobilization of essential resources.

Since our sample of churches was chosen to be typical of the Midwest, and is comparable in responses to similar questions in other regional studies, our data suggest that most mainline congregations' members have sufficiently liberal social attitudes and positive views of the church's role in promoting justice to support programs of social ministry.

TABLE 8   Pastor/Laity Differences   CCPI-I

Scales Measuring:	Pastors' Scores	Actual Laity Scores	Pastors' Expectation of Laity
Causes of Poverty			
Systemic	11.4	10.0	9.8
Individual	7.7	10.3	10.4
Social Justice	12.4	10.1	9.9
Social Ideol.	11.9	9.5	8.9
Priority on			
Local Soc Min	12.0	11.1	9.9
Church should work			
for justice (%)	93	29	*
# Churches	42	42	42

* Pastors were not asked to rate congregations on this question
See the following article for an explanation of the tables

8. Pastor/Laity Differences and Misperceptions

Lay members are more supportive than many pastors perceive.

The first two columns of Table 8 show that pastors are significantly more liberal in their social attitudes than church members, as has been demonstrated in other studies (Hadden, 1969 and Wood, 1981). Pastors were also asked to estimate where they thought their laity, on average, would respond on the attitude and priority questions. We did not anticipate that pastors believed their church members to be substantially more conservative than the members reported about themselves. The consistent, comprehensive character of these differences suggests that clergy frequently overestimate the distance between themselves and their members and underestimate member support for social ministries. Pastors may consequently exaggerate the difficulties in gaining support for social ministries in the congregations they serve.

Since we have already seen the broad base of attitudes that support social ministries in most churches, this apparent misunderstanding between clergy and laity may inhibit the development of many social ministries by clergy who mistakenly believe that their members would not support such a program simply because they do not hold similar social views.

9. Summary of Findings

Positive social justice attitudes show a remarkably stable, broad base in Catholic, Mainline and Evangelical Protestant congregations. Since these churches appear to be typical, then we expect that most similar congregations have attitudes sufficiently supportive to provide a foundation for developing strong community ministries.

The church's location has more to do with members' support for such ministries than do denominational affiliations, popular theological categories, or members' socio-economic characteristics. While the broader culture provides the base for members' attitudes, the specific profile of these attitudes depends on congregational experiences.

The congregational self-image plays a crucial role in shaping the social ministry that is chosen, and in guiding how it is developed. The stories people tell of who they are as a congregation are a thread of continuity supporting their new ventures in ministry.

Clergy can also be significant. Although they hold more liberal views than their members on social justice issues, pastors tend to exaggerate these differences, which may be a barrier to developing social ministries. There appears to be more grass roots support for social ministries in typical situations than most leaders expected.

Because of this existing base of support, church leaders can give priority to encouraging members' involvement in ministry and can nurture and affirm the resulting attitude changes.

The Church and Community Project

Carl S. Dudley and Thomas Van Eck

When the Reagan Administration reduced federal funding for community services, many congregations showed renewed interest in their historic role as catalysts for local social ministries. With a grant from Lilly Endowment, the Center for Church and Community Ministries (affiliated with McCormick Seminary in Chicago) provided leadership training and seed money for 40 church-sponsored social ministries throughout the four areas of Chicago, central Illinois, Indianapolis, and northern Indiana.

In our study, we examine some of the attitudes of church members and clergy that are thought to be related to the development of community ministries and social action involvement. We compare responses of congregations of most major mainline denominations in a variety of social settings. We examine their beliefs and priorities, their attitudes and performance, and how all of that might change or stabilize during an extended period of time.

Between 1987 and 1991, we encouraged and studied the development of 40 social ministries involving more than 100 congregations of 14 denominations. Although the study is more limited than a national survey, the focus of these data allows us to both confirm and raise questions about other research.

Contract congregations were selected by denominational leaders who recommended typical congregations that were not heavily engaged in social ministries, but might be willing to try. In the course of developing community ministries, participating churches invited other congregations and social agencies to join as partners. These ministries were located in a range of communities from inner city to open country, with an ethnic, racial, cultural and ecumenical distribution that roughly reflects a regional demographic profile of Catholic and mainline churches, along with a small number of evangelical churches. With funding and strong volunteer participation, these churches developed a variety of community programs including transitional and rehab housing, youth education and employment, con-flict resolution and resources for teen parents, adult literacy and elderly care, neighborhood centers and community development.

In September, 1987, 61 congregations participated in a membership survey. In addition, most pastors of these congregations completed surveys on their personal views and also gave estimates of their church members' average responses. Individual congregations used the survey information for project development and interpretation. The Center used it for comparative research. In January, 1991, near the conclusion of seed funding for projects, 50 congregations (along with most pastors) participated in a second membership survey.

Previous research has explored in detail the relationship between members' and clergy attitudes toward social issues and their congregations' social action activity (see Hadden, 1969 and Wood, 1981). In addition, a recent work by Davidson, Johnson, and Mock (1990) explores the relationship between faith and social ministry from 10 different denominational perspectives. Lincoln and Mamiya (1991) have provided us with important insights into social ministry and community involvement in the church experience of African Americans. These works suggest that a variety of factors (denominational affiliation, theology, congregational setting and size, socio-economic elements) are important in determining members' attitudes toward social justice issues and activity related to social ministry on the part of churches.

In this study, we begin by exploring the differences in members' ideological views by denominational affiliation and socio-economic status, and the effect of congregational size and geographic location. With this background, we examine more complex relationships by grouping churches into categories of theological orientation, social posture, and congregational self-image. We note the stability and the changes in members' attitudes between 1987 and 1991, and we observe the relation between project success and the members' survey scores. Finally, we look at pastoral leadership by exploring differences between clergy responses, membership responses, and clergy perceptions of their members.

The Sample

The responses come from congregations selected for the Church and Community Project developed by the Center for Church and Community Ministries. The ministries in this project were located in a range of communities from inner city to open country, with an ethnic, racial, cultural and ecumenical distribution that roughly reflects a regional demographic profile of Catholic and mainline Protestant churches, along with a small number of evangelical churches. With funding and strong volunteer participation, these churches developed a variety of community programs including transitional and rehab housing, youth education and employment, conflict resolution and resources for teen parents, adult literacy and elderly care, neighborhood centers and community development.

At the beginning of a year-long planning phase in September, 1987, 61 congregations participated in a membership survey using questions drawn from the Parish Profile Inventory (Carroll, et al. 1986) and other sources (Feagin, 1975 and Wood, 1981). In addition, most pastors of these congregations completed surveys on their personal views, and also gave estimates of their church members' average responses. While individual congregations used these data for project development and interpretation, the Center gathered the data for comparative research. In January, 1991, near the conclusion of seed funding for projects, 50 congregations (along with most pastors) participated in a second membership survey. Although the survey data represent only a small part of the information we gathered from the reports of participants and observers throughout the development of these ministries, they provide the primary basis for this discussion.

Data and Measures

For our comparisons, we will be using selected questions and scales we've constructed from a number of survey items which provide slightly different, yet related, views on members' social ideology, their views on poverty, and their ideas about the role of the church in community and justice ministries. A brief description of each scale is given here.

Social Ideology Scale

This scale measures members' general orientation to selected social and political issues. Its four items measure attitudes toward welfare spending, affirmative action, obligations to the poor, and nuclear freeze.

Range: 3 (most conservative) to 15 (most liberal).

Causes of Poverty Scales:

Systemic - This scale measures the belief that poverty is the result of structural or systemic barriers blocking some groups from success such as government cutbacks, discrimination, low wages, and failures of industry.

Range: 3 (least blaming of the system) to 15 (most blaming of the system).

Individual - This scale measures the belief that poverty is the result of inadequacies of individuals such as lack of effort, lack of skills, and loose morals.

Range: 3 (least blaming of the individual) to 15 (most blaming of the individual).

Social Justice Scale

Measures how much one's faith calls one to work for social justice or to relieve injustices in society.

Range: 3 (least oriented to faith and social justice perspective) to 15 (most supportive).

Priority on Local Social Ministry Scale

Measures one's priority on the church being involved in local community ministry activities such as helping the needy, supporting local reform efforts, and developing programs to educate people on local problems and issues.

Range: 3 (least oriented to involvement in local efforts) to 15 (most supportive of local social ministry).

One additional survey question included in the tables for comparison asks members how they interpret the Biblical notion of God being a "God of Justice." In the tables, we report the percent of members' saying it means that the Church should work for justice and should support groups that are working to end inequality and oppression.

BIBLIOGRAPHY

Carroll, Jackson W., Carl S. Dudley and William McKinney, ed. *Handbook for Congregational Studies*. Nashville: Abingdon Press, 1986.

Davidson, James D., C. Lincoln Johnson, and Alan K. Mock. *Faith and Social Ministry: Ten Christian Perspectives*. Chicago: Loyola University Press, 1990.

Dudley, Carl S. and Sally A. Johnson. "Congregational Self-Images for Social Ministry." In *Carriers of Faith: Lessons from Congregational Studies*, ed. Carl S. Dudley, Jackson W. Carroll and James P. Wind. Louisville, KY: Westminster/John Knox Press, 1991.

Feagin, Joe R. *Subordinating the Poor: Welfare and American Beliefs*. Lexington, MA: Lexington Books, 1975.

Hadden, Jeffrey E. *The Gathering Storm in the Churches: The Widening Gap Between Clergy and Laymen*. Garden City, N.Y.: Doubleday, 1969.

Hoge, Dean R. *Division in the Protestant House: The Basic Reasons Behind Intra-Church Conflicts*. Philadelphia: The Westminster Press, 1976.

Lincoln, C. Eric and Lawrence H. Mamiya. "The Black Church and Social Ministry in Politics and Economics: Historical and Contemporary Perspectives." In *Carriers of Faith: Lessons from Congregational Studies*, ed. Carl S. Dudley, Jackson W. Carroll and James P. Wind. Louisville, KY: Westminster/John Knox Press, 1991.

Mock, Alan K. "Congregational Religious Styles and Orientations to Society: Exploring our Linear Assumptions." *Review of Religious Research*. (forthcoming)

Roozen, David A., William McKinney and Jackson W. Carroll. *Varieties of Religious Presence: Mission in Public Life*. New York: The Pilgrim Press, 1984.

Wood, James R. *Leadership in Voluntary Organizations: The Controversy Over Social Action in Protestant Churches*. New Brunswick, NJ: Rutgers University Press, 1981.

SIX BASIC SPIRITUAL NEEDS OF AMERICANS

George H. Gallup Jr.
Chairman, The George H. Gallup International Institute

The vitality of churches, synagogues, and faith communities in the immediate years ahead will depend in considerable measure on how effectively they respond to six basic spiritual needs of Americans.

Following are these needs (apart from natural needs for such things as food, clothing, and shelter); and finally, a discussion of possible steps to help these institutions to better meet these needs.

1. The need to believe that life is meaningful and has a purpose.

During a time when sociologists observe an obsession with self in America, 70 percent of Americans interviewed nevertheless believe that "most churches and synagogues today are not effective in helping people find meaning in life." Here is a basic need apparently being only partially met. The fact is, significant numbers of people find churches irrelevant, unfulfilling, and boring.

2. The need for a sense of community and deeper relationships.

Many factors conspire to cause separateness in our society. At a personal level there is high mobility, divorce, and the breakup of families. In the aggregate, the world is becoming increasingly impersonal with the growth of megacities, multinational corporations, and bureaucracies. "Radical individualism" continues to have a hold on the religious lives of Americans. The large majority of Americans, for example, believe that one can be a good Christian or Jew without attending church or synagogue.

One of the poignant consequences to this separateness is loneliness. As we have discovered from surveys, as many as three persons in 10 say they have been lonely "for a long period of time" in their lives, with half of these people saying this experience has affected their thoughts "a great deal."

Our churches, synagogues, and other faith communities need to deal frontally with the separateness and acute loneliness in our society by encouraging corporate worship, as well as participation in small groups. Small groups, rooted in prayer and Bible study, may be the best hope for revitalizing the church in the 1990s.

3. The need to be appreciated and respected.

This is certainly a basic and fundamental need, yet as many as one-third of the American people have a low sense of self-worth or self-esteem, as a direct consequence of not being loved or appreciated. Low self-esteem brings with it a host of social problems, including alcohol and drug abuse, child and spouse abuse, lawlessness, and crime.

Significantly, surveys suggest that the closer people feel to God, the better they feel about themselves. They are also more satisfied with their lives than are others, more altruistic, enjoy better health, and have a happier outlook. Furthermore, it has been found that experiencing the closeness of God is a key factor in the ability of people to forgive themselves and others.

4. The need to be listened to — to be heard.

The main theme of a book written by Jim Castelli and me, *The People's Religion,* is that religion in the future is more likely to be shaped from the bottom up than by the top down: from the people in the pews rather than by the hierarchy. In a special survey conducted for this book, we discovered that Americans overwhelmingly think the future of the church will be shaped to a greater extent by the laity than by the clergy. Not only do they think it will happen, but they also believe that it *should* happen.

In specific terms, this means that the laity should play a greater role in the church, freeing up clergy to perform what the laity expects of them: to listen to people's religious needs and to provide spiritual counseling and inspiration. When the unchurched in one survey were asked what would most likely draw them back into the community of active worshippers, the lead reason given was "if I could find a pastor or rabbi with whom I could share my religious needs and doubts."

If churches do not heed the voice of the laity for a greater say in the way churches are run, they will continue to lose vitality and will not be able to maintain current levels of membership.

The clergy need to listen more carefully to what the laity are saying, both in one-on-one discussions, as well as in group sessions. One way to enhance the listening process is to undertake carefully designed surveys of church members, as well as surveys of those who are currently unchurched.

5. The need to feel that one is growing in the faith.

People like to feel that they are maturing spiritually, and the fact is we go through passages in our faith lives, just as we do in our secular lives.

It would appear that, basically, people aspire to lead good lives. Significant numbers of people have given thought to living a worthwhile life, to their relationship to God, to the basic meaning and value of their lives, and to developing their faith.

Churches need to pay close attention to the passages people experience in their faith lives, and to religious experiences which often change the course of one's life. People need help in understanding the significance of these experiences and in building upon them.

6. The need for practical help in developing a mature faith.

The clergy tend to make assumptions about the depth of religious commitment in the lives of members of their churches — to assume that their prayer life is more developed, and that people have a higher level of knowledge about their faith and the traditions of their denomination — than actually is the case. Clergy therefore can often find themselves in the unfortunate situation of trying to win support for programs and causes from a laity that is spiritually listless and uninformed.

A close look at where people are in their spiritual lives, and level of their knowledge, would shock most clergy: We read the Bible, but we are a nation of biblical illiterates. We pray and believe the Ten Commandments to be valid rules of life, but are unable to name many of them. We would be hard pressed to defend our faith, because we are uncertain about what we believe, let alone why we believe.

Ungrounded in biblical faith, many are vulnerable and are drawn to a wide variety of bizarre spiritual movements. For example, a large percentage of teen-agers today believe in such superstitions as astrology. Through inattention on the part of religious institutions, and lethargy on the part of the laity, a spiritual vacuum has developed — one which is drawing millions of unwitting and unsuspecting Americans.

There is an urgent need to work to close the gap between belief and practice — to turn professed faith into lived-out faith.

Two major challenges face all religious institutions: to reach as many people as possible, and to reach them as deeply as possible — to broaden the church and to deepen it. Perhaps the deepening process should come first, because parishioners need to be prepared and equipped before they can be effective in evangelistic and outreach efforts.

Thanks to the unprecedented level of freedom in the United States, Americans are able to make choices about their future. These choices, many believe, apply most deeply at the religious level: Will we choose the living God, or will we choose the substitute gods of the modern age — money, possessions, fame, drugs, a self-indulgent lifestyle? Will our religion be God-given or man-made? To quote the Rev. Peter Moore, an Episcopal priest, in *Disarming the Secular Gods,* "We have no significance, health or happiness save that which comes when we surrender the illusion of being the center of the universe and joyfully celebrate God at the center."

(From a speech given by George H. Gallup Jr., at a meeting of the Theological Students Fellowship, Princeton Theological Seminary, on Dec. 10, 1990)

II
DIRECTORIES

1. UNITED STATES COOPERATIVE ORGANIZATIONS, NATIONAL

The organizations listed in this section are cooperative religious organizations that are national in scope. Those cooperative religious organizations which have international memberships are listed with International Cooperative Organizations. Some other cooperating organizations are listed as Social Service Agencies.

All organizations are listed alphabetically including the National Council of the Churches of Christ in the USA.

American Bible Society

In 1816, pastors and laymen representing a variety of Christian denominations gathered in New York City to establish a truly interconfessional effort "to disseminate the Gospel of Christ throughout the habitable world." Since that time the American Bible Society (ABS) has continued to provide God's Word, without doctrinal note or comment, wherever it is needed and in the language and format the reader can most easily use and understand. The ABS is the servant of the denominations and local churches. It provides Scriptures at exceptionally low costs in various attractive formats for their use in outreach ministries here in the United States and all across the world.

Today the ABS has the endorsement of more than 100 denominations and agencies, and its board of managers is composed of distinguished clergy and laity drawn from these Christian groups.

Forty-six years ago the American Bible Society played a leading role in the founding of the United Bible Societies, that is involved in Scripture translation, publication, and distribution in more than 200 countries and territories around the world. The ABS contributes 40.3 percent of the support provided by the UBS to those national Bible Societies financially unable to meet the total Scripture needs of people in their own countries.

The work of the ABS is supported through gifts from individuals, local churches, denominations and cooperating agencies. Their generosity made possible the distribution of 259,930,278 copies of the Scriptures during 1990, out of a total of 639,249,849 copies of the Scriptures distributed by all member societies of the UBS.

HEADQUARTERS

1865 Broadway, New York, NY 10023 Tel. (212)408-1200

OFFICERS

Chpsn., James Wood
Vice-Chpsn., Mrs. Norman Vincent Peale
Pres. & CEO, Dr. Eugene B. Habecker
Vice-Pres., Maria I. Martinez
Treas., Daniel K. Scarberry
Departmental Heads: Dir., Church Relations/Volunteer Activities, Rev. Fred A. Allen; Dir., Translations, Rev. David G. Burke; Dir., Public Relations, William P. Cedfeldt; Dir., Human Resources, Robert P. Fichtel; Exec. Sec., Fund Raising, Lorraine A. Kupper; Dir., Production & Supply, Gary R. Ruth; Dir., Systems, Susan J.

Schaefer; Dir., Library & Archival Services, Dr. Peter Wosh

American Council of Christian Churches

Founded in 1941, The American Council of Christian Churches (ACCC) is comprised of major denominations—Bible Presbyterian Church, Evangelical Methodist Church, Fellowship of Fundamental Bible Churches (formerly Bible Protestant), Fellowship of Independent Methodists, Free Presbyterian Church of North America, Fundamental Methodist Church, General Association of Regular Baptist Churches, Tioga River Christian Conference, Independent Baptist Fellowship and Independent Churches Affiliated, along with hundreds of independent churches. The total membership nears 2 million. Each denomination retains its identity and full autonomy, but cannot be associated with the World Council of Churches, National Council of Churches, or National Association of Evangelicals.

The ACCC stands as an agency for fellowship and cooperation on the part of Bible-believing churches, for the maintenance of a pure testimony to the great fundamental truths of the Word of God: the inspiration and inerrancy of Scripture; the triune God—Father, Son, and Holy Spirit; the virgin birth; substitutionary death and resurrection of Christ, and His second coming; total depravity of man; salvation by grace through faith; and the necessity of maintaining the purity of the church in doctrine and life.

HEADQUARTERS

P.O. Box 816, Valley Forge, PA 19482 Tel. (215)566-8154 Fax (215)566-8942

OFFICERS

Pres., Dr. E. Allen Griffith
Vice-Pres., Rev. Mark Franklin
Exec. Sec., Dr. Donald McKnight
Sec., Rev. David Natale
Treas., Mr. William H. Worrilow, Jr.
Commissions: Chaplaincy; Education; Laymen; Literature; Missions; Radio & Audio Visual; Relief; Youth

American Tract Society

The American Tract Society is a nonprofit, nonsectarian, interdenominational organization, instituted in 1825 through the merger of most of the then-existing tract societies. As one of the earliest religious publishing bodies in the United States, ATS has pioneered in the publishing of Christian books, booklets, and leaflets. The volume of distribution has risen to more than 25 million pieces of literature annually.

HEADQUARTERS

P.O. Box 462008, Garland, TX 75046 Tel. (214)276-9408 Fax (214)272-9642

OFFICERS

Chpsn., Stephen E. Slocum, Jr.
Vice-Chpsns.: Arthur J. Widman; Philip E. Worth
Sec., Edgar L. Bensen
Treas., Kent Bicknell

The Associated Church Press

The Associated Church Press was organized in 1916. Its member publications include major Protestant, Anglican, and Orthodox groups in the U.S. and Canada. Some Roman Catholic publications and major ecumenical journals are also members. It is a professional religious journalistic association seeking to promote better understanding among editors, raise standards, and represent the interests of the religious press. It sponsors seminars, conventions, awards programs, and workshops for editors, staff people, and business managers.

HEADQUARTERS

502 Edgeworthe S.E., Grand Rapids, MI 49546

OFFICERS

Pres., Tom McGrath, 205 W. Monroe, Chicago, IL 60606
Exec. Dir., Rev. John Stapert, P.O. Box 162, Ada, MI 49301 Tel. (616)676-1190
Treas., Chris Woehr, P.O. Box 28001, Santa Ana, CA 92799

The Associated Gospel Churches

Organized in 1939, The Associated Gospel Churches (AGC) endorses chaplains primarily for Fundamental Independent Baptist Churches to the U.S. Armed Forces. The AGC has been recognized by the U.S. Department of Defense for more than 50 years as an Endorsing Agency, and it supports a strong national defense. The AGC also endorses Veterans Administration chaplains, police and prison chaplains.

The AGC provides fellowship and missionary support for Fundamental Independent Churches and represents their seminaries, colleges, and Bible institutes.

The AGC believes in the sovereignty of the local church; the historic doctrines of the Christian faith and the infallibility of the Bible; and practices separation from apostasy.

HEADQUARTERS

7824 Briarcreek Rd. N., Tallahassee, FL 32312 Tel. (904)668-3059

OFFICERS

Pres. & Chpsn., Comm. on Chaplains, Dr. H. P. Kissinger, CH (COL) USA Ret.
Vice-Pres. & Vice-Chpsn., Comm. on Chaplains, Dr. George W. Baugham, AGC Admn. Ofc., P.O. Box 40, Killeen, TX 76540 Tel. (817)539-4242 Fax (817)539-4242
Sec.-Treas., Mrs. Eva Baugham
Natl. Field Rep., Dr. Ev Thomas, CH (COL) USA Ret.

Association of Regional Religious Communicators (ARRC)

ARRC is a professional association of regional, ecumenical and interfaith communicators who work with local, state and regional religious agencies to fulfill their needs by providing occasional syndicated television and radio programs to members. ARRC also publishes the quarterly "ARRC Newsletter." ARRC provides local representation on the Communication Commission of the National Council of Churches, before the Federal Communications Commission, and with the denominations. ARRC offers fellowship by participation at the annual convention of the North American Broadcast Section of the World Association for Christian Communication, by updating names and addresses of national and local communicators.

OFFICERS

Pres., Westy Egmont, WBZ-TV, 11270 Soldiers Field Rd., Boston, MA 02134 Tel. (617)787-7152
Religious Broadcasting Comm., Exec. Sec. & Exec. Dir., J. Graley Taylor, 500 Wall St., Ste. 415, Seattle, WA 98121 Tel. (206)441-6110

Association of Statisticians of American Religious Bodies

This Association was organized in 1934 and grew out of personal consultations held by representatives from The Yearbook of American Churches, The National (now Official) Catholic Directory, the Jewish Statistical Bureau, The Methodist (now The United Methodist), the Lutheran, and the Presbyterian churches.

ASARB has a variety of purposes: to bring together those officially and professionally responsible for gathering, compiling, and publishing denominational statistics; to provide a forum for the exchange of ideas and sharing of problems in statistical methods and procedure; and to seek such standardization as may be possible in religious statistical data.

OFFICERS

Pres., Mac Lynn, David Lipscomb Univ., Granny White Pk., Nashville, TN 37204-3951 Tel. (615)269-1000 Fax (615)269-1796
1st Vice-Pres., Dale E. Jones, Church of the Nazarene, 6401 The Paseo, Kansas City, MO 64131 Tel. (816)333-7000 Fax (816)333-1683
2nd Vice-Pres., Lou McNeil, Glenmary Research Center, 750 Piedmont Ave. N.E., Atlanta, GA 30308 Tel. (404)876-6518 Fax (404)876-0604
Sec.-Treas., Dr. Norman M. Green, Jr., American Baptist Churches, U.S.A., P.O. Box 851, Valley Forge, PA 19082-0851 Tel. (215)768-2480 Fax (215)768-2470

Christian Holiness Association

The Association is a coordinating agency of those religious bodies that hold the Wesleyan-Arminian theological view. It was organized in 1867.

HEADQUARTERS

CHA Center, S. Walnut St., P.O. Box 100, Wilmore, KY 40390

OFFICERS

Pres., Dr. Thomas Hermiz, World Gospel Mission, Box WGM, Marion, IN 46952

Exec. Dir., Burnis H. Bushong, World Gospel Mission, Box WGM, Marion, IN 46952

AFFILIATED ORGANIZATIONS

Bible Holiness Movement
Brethren in Christ Church
Churches of Christ in Christian Union
Evangelical Christian Church
Evangelical Church of North America
Evangelical Friends Alliance
Evangelical Methodist Church
Free Methodist Church in North America
The Church of the Nazarene
The Salvation Army
The Salvation Army in Canada
United Brethren in Christ Church (Sandusky Conference)
The Wesleyan Church
Japan Immanuel Church

A Christian Ministry in the National Parks

The Ministry is an independent ecumenical movement providing interdenominational religious services in 65 National Parks, Monuments, and Recreation Areas. For 20 years it was administered in the National Council of Churches. On Jan. 1, 1972, it became an independent movement representing more than 40 denominations, 60 local park committees, more than 300 theological seminaries, and 16 separate religious organizations. The program recruits and staffs 300 positions, winter and summer, in 65 areas.

HEADQUARTERS

222 1/2 E. 49th St., New York, NY 10017 Tel. (212) 758-3450

OFFICER

Dir., Dr. Warren W. Ost

Church Women United in the U.S.A.

Church Women United in the U.S.A. is an ecumenical lay movement providing Protestant, Orthodox, and Roman Catholic and other Christian women with programs and channels of involvement in church, civic, and national affairs. CWU has some 1,750 units formally organized in communities in all 50 states, greater Washington, D.C., and Puerto Rico.

HEADQUARTERS

475 Riverside Dr., Rm. 812, New York, NY 10115 Tel. (212)870-2347 Fax (212)870-2338

Other Offices: 777 United Nations Plz., New York, NY 10017 Tel. (212)661-3856

Other Offices: CWU Washington Ofc., 110 Maryland Ave. NE, Rm. 108, Washington, DC 20002 Tel. (202)544-8747

OFFICERS

Pres., Claire Randall, New York, NY
1st Vice-Pres., Fran Craddock, Indianapolis, IN
2nd Vice-Pres., Jo Walton, Tuskegee, AL
Sec./Treas., Helen Quirino, Portland, OR

Regional Coordinators: Kathleen Clark, Greenfield, IA, (Central); Helen Hokenson, Huntington Woods, MI, (East Central); Hatti Hamilton, Philadelphia, PA, (Mid-Atlantic); Roberta Grimm, Buffalo, NY, (Northeast); Nadine Riley, Portland, OR, (Northwest); Marjorie Troeh, Independence, MO, (South Central); Catharine Vick, Cary, NC, (Southeast); Beverley Wolford, Phoenix, AZ, (Southwest)

STAFF

Gen. Dir., Patricia J. Rumer, Tel. (212)870-2343
Comptroller, Anne Martin, Tel. (212)870-2345
Consultant for Imperative/Jubilee Coord., Frances Kennedy, Tel. (212)870-3238
Dir. of Admn. Services, Beverly Oates, Tel. (212)870-3035
Dir. of Ecumenical Action, Carol Barton, Tel. (212)870-3046
Dir. of Ecumenical Celebrations, Mary Cline Detrick, (212)870-2348-New York, (703)432-5568-Virginia
Dir. of Fin. Dev./Comp. Services, Marcia Parker, Tel. (212)870-3047
Dir. of Media & Interpretation, Jane Burton, (212)870-2364
Ed./Art Dir., Margaret Schiffert, Tel. (212)870-2344
Prog. Coord. (United Nations Ofc.), Winnie Arceo, Tel. (212)661-3856
Dir., Washington, D.C. Ofc., Sally Timmel, 110 Maryland Ave. N.E., Rm. 108, Washington, DC 20002 Tel. (202)544-8747

CODEL—Coordination in Development

CODEL is a consortium of Protestant and Roman Catholic mission-sending agencies, communions and Christian organizations working together in international development. Founded in 1969, CODEL is committed to an ecumenical approach in the development process. The 40 U.S.-based member organizations combine expertise, funds, planning, project implementation and evaluation in a spirit of Christian unity working toward self-sufficiency of the poorest peoples and communities of the world.

There are more than 90 projects in 38 countries in health, agriculture, community development, and informal education. Other CODEL programs include seminars on current issues, development education activities, environment and development projects and workshops.

CODEL's budget for 1990/91 was $2,100,000.

HEADQUARTERS

475 Riverside Dr., Rm. 1842, New York, NY 10015 Tel. (212)870-3000 Fax (212)870-3545

OFFICERS

Pres., Ms. Betty Jo Swayze
1st Vice-Pres., Sr. Sheila McGinnis
Sec., Sr. Clarita Hanson
Treas., Mr. Thomas Hemphill

STAFF

Exec. Dir., Rev. Boyd Lowry
Coord. for Africa, Dr. Caroline W. Njuki
Coord. for Asia & the Pacific, Mr. Ellis Shenk
Coord. for Latin America & Caribbean, Mr. Kenneth E. Brown, Jr.
Environment & Development, Sr. Mary Ann Smith
Seminar Program, ———-

Ecumenical Relations/Development Educ., Rev. Nathan VanderWerf

Accountant, Robert Lopulisa

Consultation on Church Union

Officially constituted in 1962, the Consultation on Church Union is a venture in reconciliation of nine American communions. It has been authorized to explore the formation of a united church, truly catholic, truly evangelical, and truly reformed. In 1992 the participating churches are African Methodist Episcopal Church, African Methodist Episcopal Zion Church, Christian Church (Disciples of Christ), Christian Methodist Episcopal Church, The Episcopal Church, International Council of Community Churches, Presbyterian Church (U.S.A.), United Church of Christ, and The United Methodist Church.

The Plenary Assembly, which normally meets every four or five years, is composed of 10 delegates and 10 associate delegates from each of the participating churches. Included also are observer-consultants from more than 20 other churches, other union negotiations, and conciliar bodies. The most recent Plenaries have been held in 1984 (Baltimore) and 1988 (New Orleans.)

The Executive Committee is composed of the president, two representatives from each of the participating churches, and the secretariat. The Secretariat consists of the full-time executive staff of the Consultation, all of whom are based at the national office in Princeton, NJ. Various task groups are convened to fulfill certain assignments. In 1990 there were four task groups: Communications, Unity & Justice, Theology, and Special Gifts. In addition there was an Editorial Board for the annual Lenten Booklet of devotional meditations.

HEADQUARTERS

151 Wall St., Princeton, NJ 08540 Tel. (609)921-7866 Fax (609)921-0471

OFFICERS

Gen. Sec., Dr. David W. A. Taylor

Treas./Bus. Mgr., Christine V. Bilarczyk

Conf. Proj. Mgr., Dr. Robert L. Polk

Pres., Dr. Vivian U. Robinson, 125 Hernlen St., Augusta, GA 30901

Vice-Pres.: Bishop Vinton R. Anderson, P.O. Box 6416, St. Louis, MO 63107; Rev. Alice C. Cowen, 3001 Grand, Kansas City, MO 64108

Sec., Rev. Clyde H. Miller, Jr., 7000 Broadway, A.B.S. Bldg., Denver, CO 80221

REP. FROM PARTICIPATING CHURCHES

African Methodist Episcopal Church: Bishop Vinton R. Anderson, 4144 Lindell Blvd., Ste. 222, St. Louis, MO 63108; Bishop Frederick H. Talbot, P.O. Box 684, Frederikstead, St. Croix, VI 00841

African Methodist Episcopal Zion Church: Bishop J. Clinton Hoggard, 1511 K. St. N.W., Ste. 1100, Washington, DC 20005; Bishop Cecil Bishop, 5401 Broadwater St., Temple Hill, MD 20748

Christian Church (Disciples of Christ): Rev. Dr. Paul A. Crow, Jr., P.O. Box 1986, Indianapolis, IN 46206; Rev. Dr. Albert M. Pennybacker, 120 E. Main St., Apt. 2101, Lexington, KY 40507

Christian Methodist Episcopal Church: Bishop Marshall Gilmore, 109 Holcomb Dr., Shreveport, LA 71103; Dr. Vivian U. Robinson, 1256 Hernlen St., Augusta, GA 30901

The Episcopal Church: Rt. Rev. William G. Burrill, 935 East Ave., Rochester, NY 14607; Rev. Alice C. Cowan, 3001 Grand, Kansas City, MO 64108

Intl. Council of Community Churches: Rev. Dr. Jeffrey R. Newhall, 7808 College Dr., Ste. 2-SE, Palos Hts., IL 60463; Mr. Abraham Wright, 1909 East-West Hwy., Silver Springs, MD 20910

Presbyterian Church (U.S.A.): Rev. Michael E. Livingston, CN-821, Princeton, NJ 08542; Rev. Lewis H. Lancaster, Jr., 100 Witherspoon St., Rm. 3418, Louisville, KY 40202

United Church of Christ: Rev. Clyde H. Miller, Jr., 7000 Broadway, A.B.S. Bldg., Ste. 420, Denver, CO 80221; Rev. Dr. Thomas E. Dipko, 4041 N. High St., Ste. 301, Columbus, OH 43214

The United Methodist Church: Bishop William B. Grove, 900 Washington St., E., Charleston, WV 25301; Rev. Dr. Larry D. Pickens, 5600 S. Indiana Ave., Chicago, IL 60649

The Evangelical Church Alliance

The Evangelical Church Alliance was incorporated in 1928 in Missouri as The World's Faith Missionary Association and was later known as The Fundamental Ministerial Association. The title Evangelical Church Alliance was adopted in 1958.

ECA (1) licenses and ordains ministers who are qualified and provides them with credentials from a recognized ecclesiastical body; (2) provides through the Bible Extension Institute courses of study to those who have not had seminary or Bible school training; (3) provides an organization for autonomous churches so they may have communion and association with one another; (4) provides an organization where members can find companionship through correspondence, Regional Conventions, and General Conventions; (5) cooperates with churches in finding new pastors when vacancies occur in their pulpits.

ECA is an interdenominational, nonsectarian, Evangelical organization. Total ordained and licensed clergy members—1,723.

HEADQUARTERS

205 W. Broadway St., P.O. Box 9, Bradley, IL 60915 Tel. (815)937-0720

OFFICERS

Exec. Dir., Rev. George L. Miller

Pres., Dr. Charles Wesley Ewing, 321 W. Harrison St., Royal Oak, MI 48067

1st Vice-Pres., Dr. Sterling L. Cauble, Sunman Bible Church, P.O. Box 216, Sunman, IN 47041

2nd Vice-Pres., Rev. Richard J. Sydnes, P.O. Box 355, Des Moines, IA 50302

Evangelical Press Association

The Evangelical Press Association is an organization of editors and publishers of Christian periodicals which seeks to promote the cause of Evangelical Christianity and enhance the influence of Christian journalism.

OFFICERS

Pres., Roger Palms, Decision Magazine, 1300 Harmon Pl., Minneapolis, MN 55403

Pres.-Elect, Robert Ingram, Tabletalk Magazine, P.O. Box 7500, Orlando, FL 32854

Sec., Doug Trouten, Twin Cities Christian, 1619 Portland Ave., S., Minneapolis, MN 55404

Treas., Ben Johnston, The Associate Reformed Presbyterian, One Cleveland St., Greenville, SC 29601

Exec. Dir., Gary Warner, P.O. Box 4550, Overland Park, KS 66204 Tel. (913)381-2017

Higher Education Ministries Team

The Higher Education Ministries Team has emerged out of United Ministries in Education. It embodies the covenant-based ministry coalition created more than thirty years ago and carries forward the work of United Campus Christian Fellowship, United Ministries in Education and Ministries in Public Education (K-12). HEMT works with churches and educational institutions as they seek to express their concern about the ways in which educating forces affect quality of life. HEMT focuses on the goal to design, manage, facilitate, nurture, and participate in partnerships with regional and denominational organizations in support of ministry in higher education. Current programs include mission and resource partnerships, campus ministry training for fundraising, AIDS prevention education, strategic conversations for developing models and planning strategies at the state and regional levels, training for new campus ministers and chaplains, personnel services, support and network for Christian student organizations including the World Student Christian Federation and the Council for Ecumenical Student Christian Ministry and promoting the informal networking of people, resources and experiences of people in the field.

OFFICERS

Admn. Coord., Clyde O. Robinson, Jr., 7407 Steele Creek Rd., Charlotte, NC 28217 Tel. (704)588-2182 Fax (704)588-3652

Treas., Gary Harke, P. O. Box 386, Sun Prairie, WI 53590 Tel. (608)837-0537 Fax (608)825-6610

Personnel Service, Lawrence S. Steinmetz, 11780 Borman Dr., Ste. 100, St. Louis, MO 63146 Tel. (314)991-3000 Fax (314)993-9018

Resource Center, Linda Freeman, 7407 Steele Creek Rd., Charlotte, NC 28217 Tel. (704)588-2182 Fax (704)588-3652

PARTICIPATING DENOMINATIONS

Christian Church (Disciples of Christ)
Church of the Brethren
Moravian Church (Northern Province)
Presbyterian Church (U.S.A.)
United Church of Christ

Interfaith Impact for Justice and Peace

Interfaith Impact for Justice and Peace is the religious community's united voice in Washington. It helps Protestant, Jewish, Muslim and Catholic national organizations have clout on Capitol Hill and brings grassroots groups and individual and congregational members to Washington and shows them how to turn their values into votes for justice and peace. Interfaith Impact for Justice and Peace is the recently merged organization of Interfaith Action for Economic Justice and National Impact.

Interfaith Impact for Justice and Peace has established the following Issue Networks to advance the cause of justice and peace: domestic poverty and human needs; international peace; civil, human and voting rights; economic policy and sustainable development; energy, environment and agriculture; and justice for women and families.

Members receive the quarterly magazine, periodic Action alerts on initiatives, voting records, etc., and a free subscription to the Issue Network of their choice.

HEADQUARTERS

110 Maryland Ave. N.E., Ste. 509, Washington, DC 20002 Tel. (202)543-2800 Fax (202)547-8107

OFFICERS

Exec. Dir., Rev. James M. Bell
Chair of Bd., Elenora Giddings Ivory, Presbyterian Church (U.S.A.)

MEMBERS

African Methodist Episcopal Zion Church, Home Missions Dept.
American Baptist Churches, USA
American Ethical Union
American Muslim Council
Center of Concern
Columban Fathers
Commission on Religion in Appalachia
Christian Church (Disciples of Christ)
Church of the Brethren
Church Women United
Episcopal Church
Episcopal Urban Caucus
Evangelical Lutheran Church in America
Federation of Southern Cooperatives/LAF
Friends Committee on National Legislation
Jesuit Social Ministries
Maryknoll Fathers and Brothers
Moravian Church in America
National Council of Churches of Christ: Church World Service; Washington Office
National Council of Jewish Women
NETWORK
Peoria Citizens Committee
Presbyterian Church (USA)
Progressive National Baptist Convention
Reformed Church in America
Rural Advancement Fund
Society of African Missions
Southern Baptist Convention: Christian Life Comm.
Southwest Organizing Project
Southwest Voter Registration/Education Project
Toledo Metropolitan Ministries
Union of American Hebrew Congregations
Unitarian Universalist Association
Unitarian Universalist Service Committee
United Church of Christ: Bd. for Homeland Ministries; Bd. for World Ministries; Hunger Action Ofc.; Ofc. of Church in Society
United Methodist Church: Gen. Bd. of Church & Society; Gen. Bd. of Global Ministries Natl. Div.; Gen. Bd. of Global Ministries Women's Div.; Gen. Bd. of Global Ministries World Div.
Virginia Council of Churches

International Christian Youth Exchange (ICYE)

ICYE sponsors the exchange of young people between nations as a means of international and ecumenical education in order to further commitment to and responsibility for reconciliation, justice, and peace. Exchangees 16-30 years of age spend one year in another country and participate in family, school, church, voluntary service projects and community life. Short-term, ecumenical, international work camp experiences are also available for those 18-35 years of age.

The U.S. Committee works in cooperation with national committees in 28 other countries and the Federation of National Committees for ICYE, which has headquarters in Berlin, Germany. ICYE is one of the only two U.S. youth exchange programs operating in Africa.

Exchanges for American youth going abroad and for overseas youth coming to the United States are frequently sponsored by local churches and/or community groups. Participation is open to all regardless of religious affiliation. Denominational agencies are sponsors of ICYE, including: American Baptist Churches in the U.S.A.; Christian Church (Disciples of Christ); Church of the Brethren; Episcopal Church; Evangelical Lutheran Church in America; Presbyterian Church (U.S.A.); Reformed Church in America; United Church of Christ; and The United Methodist Church. Collaborating organizations include the National Federation of Catholic Youth Ministry and the National Catholic Education Association. Scholarships covering part of the cost are provided by most sponsoring denominations.

HEADQUARTERS

134 W. 26th St., New York, NY 10001 Tel. (212)206-7307 Fax (212)633-9085

OFFICERS

Exec. Dir., Rev. James J. Reid
Dir. of Prog., Donna Bollinger-Garcia

International Society of Christian Endeavor

Christian Endeavor is an international, interracial, and interdenominational youth movement in evangelical Protestant churches. It unites its members for greater Christian growth and service under the motto "For Christ and the Church." The first society was formed by Francis E. Clark in Portland, Maine, Feb. 2, 1881.

The movement spread rapidly and, in 1885, the United Society of Christian Endeavor was organized. In 1927, the name was changed to the International Society of Christian Endeavor, to include Canada and Mexico. The World's Union was organized in 1895; in 1981 provision was made to include the territories of the United States. The movement has thousands of groups in local churches, for all age groups. Worldwide there are groups and unions in approximately 78 nations and island groups, with more than 2 million members.

HEADQUARTERS

1221 E. Broad St., P.O. Box 1110, Columbus, OH 43216 Tel. (614)258-9545

OFFICERS

Pres., Rev. Richard Cattermole
Exec. Sec./Treas., Rev. David G. Jackson

Interreligious Foundation for Community Organization (IFCO)

IFCO is a national ecumenical agency created in 1966 by several Protestant, Roman Catholic, and Jewish organizations, to be an interreligious, interracial agency for support of community organization and education in pursuit of social justice. Through IFCO, national and regional religious bodies collaborate in development of social justice strategies and provide financial support and technical assistance to local, national, and international social-justice projects.

IFCO serves as a bridge between the churches and communities, and acts as a resource for ministers and congregations wishing to better understand and do more to advance the struggles of the poor and oppressed. IFCO conducts training workshops for community organizers and uses its vast national and international network of organizers, clergy, and other professionals to crystallize, publicize, and act in the interest of justice.

HEADQUARTERS

402 W. 145th St., New York, NY 10031 Tel. (212)926-5757 Fax (212)926-5842

OFFICERS

Pres., Dr. Ernest Newborn, Christian Church (Disciples of Christ), Dir, Reconciliation Committee
Vice-Pres., Dr. Benjamin Greene, Jr., American Baptist Churches in the U.S.A., Dir., Comm. Dev., Natl. Ministries

Inter-Varsity Christian Fellowship of the U.S.A.

Inter-Varsity Christian Fellowship is a nonprofit, interdenominational student movement that ministers to college and university students in the United States. Inter-Varsity began in the United States when students at the University of Michigan invited C. Stacey Woods, then General Secretary of the Canadian movement, to help establish an Inter-Varsity chapter on their campus. Inter-Varsity Christian Fellowship-USA was incorporated two years later, in 1941. Inter-Varsity's uniqueness as a campus ministry lies in the fact that it is student-initiated and student-led. Inter-Varsity strives to build collegiate fellowships that engage their campus with the gospel of Jesus Christ and develop disciples who live out biblical values. Inter-Varsity students are encouraged in evangelism, spiritual discipleship, serving the church, human relationships, righteousness, vocational stewardship and world evangelization. A triennial missions conference held in Urbana, Ill., jointly sponsored with Inter-Varsity-Canada, has long been a launching point for missionary service.

HEADQUARTERS

6400 Schroeder Road, P.O. Box 7895, Madison, WI 53707 Tel. (608)274-9001 Fax (608)274-7882

OFFICERS

Pres. & CEO, Stephen A. Hayner
Vice-Pres.: C. Barney Ford; Robert A. Fryling; Robert Peitscher; Samuel Barkat; Dan Harrison
Sec., H. Yvonne Vinkemulder
Treas., Thomas H. Witte
Bd. Chpsn., Thomas Dunkerton
Bd. Vice-Chpsn., Gary Ginter

The Liturgical Conference

Founded in 1940 by a group of Benedictines, the Liturgical Conference is an independent, ecumenical, international association of persons concerned about liturgical renewal and meaningful worship. The Liturgical Conference is known chiefly for its periodicals, books, materials, and sponsorship of regional and local workshops on worship-related concerns in cooperation with various church groups.

HEADQUARTERS

1017 12th St., NW, Washington, DC 20005 Tel. (202)898-0885

OFFICERS

Pres., Shawn Madigan, CSJ
Vice-Pres., John B. Foley, SJ
Sec., Eleanor Bernstein, CSJ
Treas., Frank Senn
Exec. Dir., Ralph R. Van Loon

The Lord's Day Alliance of the United States

The Lord's Day Alliance of the United States, founded in 1888 in Washington, D.C., is the only national organization whose sole purpose is the preservation and cultivation of Sunday, the Lord's Day, as a day of rest and worship. The Alliance also seeks to safeguard a Day of Common Rest for all people regardless of their faith. Its Board of Managers is composed of representatives from 25 denominations.

It serves as an information bureau, publishes a magazine "Sunday," furnishes speakers and a variety of materials such as pamphlets, a book, "The Lord's Day," videos, posters, radio spot announcements, decals, cassettes, news releases, articles for magazines and television programs, and a new 15-minute motion picture.

HEADQUARTERS

2930 Flowers Road South, Ste. 107, Atlanta, GA 30341 Tel. (404)451-7315

OFFICERS

Exec. Dir. & Ed., Dr. James P. Wesberry
Pres., Dr. Paul Craven, Jr.
Vice-Pres.: Donald R. Pepper; Roger A. Kvam; Timothy E. Bird; John H. Schall
Vice-Pres: Faith Willard
Vice-Pres.: W. David Sepp
Sec., Rev. Ernest A. Bergeson
Treas., Mr. E. Larry Eidson

The Mennonite Central Committee

The Mennonite Central Committee is the relief and service agency of North American Mennonite and Brethren in Christ Churches. Representatives from Mennonite and Brethren in Christ groups make up the MCC, which meets annually in February to review its program and to approve policies and budget. Founded in 1920, MCC administers and participates in programs of agricultural and economic development, education, health, self-help, relief, peace, and disaster service. MCC has about 950 workers serving in 50 countries in Africa, Asia, Europe, Middle East, and South, Central, and North America.

MCC has service programs in North America that focus on both urban and rural poverty areas. Additionally there are North American programs focusing on such diverse matters as handicap concerns, community conciliation, employment creation and criminal justice issues. These programs are administered by two national bodies—MCC U.S. and MCC Canada.

Contributions from North American Mennonite and Brethren in Christ churches provide the largest part of MCC's support. Other sources of financial support include the contributed earnings of volunteers, grants from private and government agencies, and contributions from Mennonite churches abroad. The total income in 1990, including material aid contributions, amounted to $35,955,704.

MCC tries to strengthen local communities by working in cooperation with local churches or other community groups. Many personnel are placed with other agencies, including missions. Programs are planned with sensitivity to locally felt needs.

HEADQUARTERS

Canadian Office, 134 Plaza Dr., Winnipeg, MB R3T 5K9 Tel. (204)261-6381 Fax (204)269-9875
Box 500, 21 S. 12th St., Akron, PA 17501 Tel. (717)859-1151 Fax (717)859-2171

OFFICERS

Exec. Secs.: International, John A. Lapp; Canada, Daniel Zehr; U.S.A., Lynette Meck

National Association of Ecumenical Staff

This is the successor organization to the Association of Council Secretaries which was founded in 1940. The name change was made in 1971.

NAES is an association of professional staff in ecumenical and interreligious services. It was established to provide creative relationships among them and to encourage mutual support and personal and professional growth. This is accomplished through training programs, through exchange and discussion of common concerns at conferences, and through the publication of the journal.

HEADQUARTERS

475 Riverside Dr., Rm. 870, New York, NY 10115 Tel. (212)870-2156 Fax (212)870-2158

OFFICERS

Pres., Rev. Debra L. Moody, PA Council of Churches, 900 S. Arlington Ave., Ste. 100, Harrisburg, PA 17109 Tel. (717)545-4761
Vice-Pres., Rev. Dr. Mel Luetchens, Interchurch Ministries of Nebraska, 215 Centennial Mall, #411, Lincoln, NE 68508 Tel. (402)464-8116
1992 Program Chair, Rev. Peg Chamberlin, Greater Minneapolis Council of Churches, 122 W. Franklin, Rm. 218, Minneapolis, MN 55404 Tel. (612)870-3660
Sec., Ms. Janet Leng, Associated Min. of Tacoma/Pierce Co., 1224 South I St., Tacoma, WA 98405 Tel. (206)383-3056

The National Association of Evangelicals

The National Association of Evangelicals is a voluntary fellowship of evangelical denominations, churches, schools, organizations and individuals. Its purpose is not to eliminate denominations, but to protect them; not to force individual churches into a mold of liberal or radical sameness, but to provide a means of cooperation in evangelical witness; not to do the work of the churches, but to stand for the right of churches to do their work as they feel called by God.

Based upon the affirmation of a common faith resting squarely in God's Word, the Bible, NAE provides evangelical identification for 50,000 churches from more than 77 denominations; with a service constituency of more than 15 million through its commissions, affiliates and subsidiary.

HEADQUARTERS

Office of Public Affairs, 1023 15th St. N.W., Ste. 500, Washington, DC 20005 Tel. (202)789-1011 Fax (202)842-0392
450 Gundersen Dr., Carol Stream, IL 60188 Tel. (708)665-0500 Fax (708)665-8575

OFFICERS

Pres., Dr. B. Edgar Johnson, 3524 Skyline Dr., Nampa, ID 83686

1st Vice-Pres., Dr. Don Argue, 910 Elliott Ave. S., Minneapolis, MN 55404

2nd Vice-Pres., Dr. David Rambo, P.O. Box 35000, Colorado Springs, CO 80935

Sec., Dr. Jack Estep, P. O. Box 828, Wheaton, IL 60189

Treas., Mr. Paul Steiner, 1825 Florida Dr., Ft. Wayne, IN 46805

STAFF

Exec. Dir., Dr. Billy A. Melvin

Assoc. to the Exec. Dir., Rev. Robert W. Patterson

Dir. of Field Services, Rev. Darrel L. Anderson

Dir. of Information, Rev. Donald R. Brown

Dir. of Business Admn., Mr. Darrell L. Fulton

Natl. Field Rep., Rev. David L. Melvin

Dir. of Public Affairs, Dr. Robert P. Dugan, Jr.

Public Policy Analyst, Richard Cizik

Counsel, Forest Montgomery, 1023 15th St., NW, Ste. 500, Washington, DC 20005 Tel. (202)789-1011

COMMISSIONS, AFFILIATES, SERVICE AGENCIES

Commissions: Chaplains; Christian Higher Educ.; Churchmen; Evangelism & Home Mission; Hispanic; Natl. Christian Educ.; Social Action; Women's

Affiliates: Christian Stewardship Assoc.; Evangelical Child & Family; Evangelical Fellowship of Mission Agencies; National Religious Broadcasters

Subsidiary: World Relief Corp.

Service Agency: Evangelical Adoption & Family Services, Inc.

MEMBER DENOMINATIONS

Advent Christian General Conference
Assemblies of God
Baptist General Conference
Brethren Church (Ashland, OH)
Brethren in Christ Church
Christian Catholic Church (Evang. Prot.)
Christian Church of North America
Christian and Missionary Alliance
Christian Reformed Church in N.A.
Christian Union
Church of God (Cleveland, TN)
Church of God of the Mountain Assembly
Church of the Nazarene
Church of the United Brethren in Christ
Churches of Christ in Christian Union
Congregational Holiness Church
Conservative Congregational Christian Conf.
Conservative Baptist Assoc. of America
Elim Fellowship
Evangelical Christian Church
Evangelical Church of North America
Evangelical Congregational Church
Evangelical Free Church of America
Evangelical Friends Intl./North America
Evangelical Mennonite Church
Evangelical Methodist Church
Evangelical Presbyterian Church
Evangelistic Missionary Fellowship
Fellowship of Evangelical Bible Churches
Fire-Baptized Holiness Church of God of the Am.
Free Methodist Church of North America
General Association of General Baptists
Intl. Church of the Foursquare Gospel
Intl. Pentecostal Church of Christ
Intl. Pentecostal Holiness Church

Mennonite Brethren Churches, USA
Midwest Congregational Christian Fellowship
Missionary Church
Oklahoma State Assoc. of Free Will Baptists
Open Bible Standard Churches
Pentecostal Church of God
Pentecostal Free Will Baptist Church
Presbyterian Church in America
Primitive Methodist Church, USA
Reformed Church in America, Classis Cascades
Reformed Church in America, Particular Synod of Mid-America
Reformed Episcopal Church
Reformed Presbyterian Church of N.A.
Salvation Army
Wesleyan Church
World Confessional Lutheran Association

National Conference of Christians and Jews

The National Conference of Christians and Jews (NCCJ) is a non-profit human relations organization engaged in a nationwide program of intergroup education so that people of different religious, racial, and ethnic backgrounds learn to live together without bigotry and discrimination and without compromising distinctive faiths or identities. Founded in 1928, the NCCJ promotes education for citizenship in a pluralistic democracy and attempts to help diverse groups discover their mutual self-interest. Primary program areas include interfaith and interracial dialogue, youth intercultural communications, training for the administration of justice, and the building of community coalitions. The NCCJ has 70 offices nationally, staffed by approximately 240 people. Nearly 200 members comprise the National Board of Trustees and members from that group form the 22-member Executive Board. Each regional office has its own local board of trustees with a total of about 2,800. The National Board of Trustees meets once annually; the Executive Board at least three times annually.

HEADQUARTERS

71 Fifth Ave., New York, NY 10003 Tel. (212)206-0006

OFFICER

Pres., Gillian Martin Sorensen

National Conference on Ministry to the Armed Forces

The Conference is an incorporated civilian agency. Representation in the Conference with all privileges of the same is open to all endorsing or certifying agencies or groups authorized to provide chaplains for any branch of the Armed Forces.

The purpose of this organization is to provide a means of dialogue to discuss concerns and objectives and, when agreed upon, to take action with the appropriate authority to support the spiritual ministry to and the moral welfare of Armed Forces personnel.

HEADQUARTERS

4141 N. Henderson Rd., Ste. 13, Arlington, VA 22203 Tel. (703)276-7905 Fax (703)276-7906

STAFF

Coord., Clifford T. Weathers

Admn. Asst., Maureen Francis

OFFICERS

Chpsn., Rev. Harold Bode
Chair-elect, Lloyd Lyngdal
Treas., Robert Crick
Sec., Lewis Burnett
Committee Members: Catholic Rep., Msgr. John Glynn; Protestant Rep., Rev. Vincent McMenamy; Jewish Rep., Rabbi David Lapp; Orthodox Rep., Gregory Havrilak; Member-at-Large, Rev. Dr. Calvin French

National Council of the Churches of Christ in the United States of America

The National Council of the Churches of Christ in the United States of America is a community of Christian communions which, in response to the gospel revealed in the Scriptures, confess Jesus Christ, the incarnate Word of God, as Savior and Lord. These communions covenant with one another to manifest ever more fully the unity of the Church. Relying upon the transforming power of the Holy Spirit, the Council brings these communions into common mission, serving in all creation to the glory of God.

HEADQUARTERS

475 Riverside Dr., New York, NY 10115. Tel. (212)870-2511

GENERAL OFFICERS

Pres., Rev. Dr. Syngman Rhee
Gen. Sec., Rev. Joan B. Campbell
Pres.-Elect, Rev. Dr. Gordon L. Sommers
Immediate Past Pres., V. Rev. Leonid Kishkovsky
Sec., Mary A. Love
Treas., Dr. Shirley M. Jones
Vice-Pres./Unit Chpsns.: Dr. William Watley (Unity & Relationships); Dr. Mary D. Matz (Educ., Communication & Discipleship); Rev. Benjamin F. Chavis, Jr. (Prophetic Justice); Dr. Belle Miller McMaster (Church World Service & Witness)

ELECTED STAFF
OFFICE OF THE GENERAL SECRETARY

Tel. (212)870-2141 Fax (212)870-2817
Gen. Sec., Rev. Dr. Joan B. Campbell
Assoc. for Ecumenical Relations, Rev. Eileen W. Lindner
Assoc. for Inclusiveness & Justice, Lois M. Dauway
Assoc. for Public Witness, James A. Hamilton
Coord. for Governance Services, MelRose B. Corley
Washington, D.C.: Mailing Address, NCC, 110 Maryland Ave., NE, Washington, DC 20002. Tel. (202)544-2350; Fax (202)543-1297.
Dir. of the Washington Ofc., James A. Hamilton
Assoc. Dir., Mary Anderson Cooper
Dir. of the CWS/LWR Ofc. on Development Policy, Carol Capps

EDUCATION, COMMUNICATION AND DISCIPLESHIP

Tel. (212)870-2049 Fax (212)870-2030
Unit Dir./Assoc. Gen. Sec., Rev. J. Martin Bailey
Dir., Finance, Robert Temmler
Communication, Department of
Dir., Rev. J. Martin Bailey
Dir., News Services, Carol Fouke
Dir., Electronic Media, Rev. David W. Pomeroy
Dir., Interpretation Resources, Sarah Vilankulu
Assoc. Dir., Electronic Media, Rev. Roy T. Lloyd

Ministries in Christian Education
Dir., Dorothy Savage
Education for Mission
Dir., Educ. for Mission/Friendship Press, Dr. Audrey A. Miller
Editor, Friendship Press, Margaret S. Larom
Audio-Visual Coord., Rev. David W. Pomeroy
Business & Operations Mgr., Claire Isaac
Professional Church Leadership
Staff Assoc., Peggy L. Shriver
Women in Ministry, Elizabeth Verdesi
Bible Translation and Utilization
Dir., Rev. Arthur O. Van Eck
Evangelization
Staff Assoc., Patricia Brown
Worship
Staff Assoc., Herman E. Luben

CHURCH WORLD SERVICE AND WITNESS

Tel. (212)870-2257 Fax (212)870-2055
Unit Dir./Assoc. Gen. Sec., Lani J. Havens
Dir., Financial Management, Howard Jost
Dir., Constituency Information & Development, Melvin Lehman
Global Issues and Programs
Acting Dir., Global Issues & Programs Subunit, David W. Briddell
Dir., Agricultural Missions, Sinforonso Atienza
Dir., Human Rights, Frederick Bronkema
Dir., Intermedia, David W. Briddell
Dir., Global Educ., Loretta Whalen, 2115 N. Charles St., Baltimore, MD 21218. Tel. (301)727-6106
Dir., CWS/LWR Ofc. on Development Policy, Carol Capps, 110 Maryland Ave., NE, Suite 108, Washington, DC 20002. Tel. (202)543-6336
Partner Relations and Programs
Acting Dir., Partner Relations & Programs Subunit, Lowell Brown
Dir., Disaster Response, Kenlynn Schroeder
Dir., Immigration & Refugee Program, Dale S. DeHaan
Dir., Material Resources, Soon-Young Hahn
Dir., Leadership Development, John W. Backer
Dir., Overseas Personnel, Paul W. Yount, Jr.
Dir., Intl. Congregations & Lay Ministry, Arthur O. Bauer
Dir., Africa, Willis H. Logan
Dir., Caribbean & Latin America, Oscar Bolioli; Fax: (212)870-3220
Dir., East Asia & the Pacific, Victor W. C. Hsu
Assoc. Dir./Dir. China Program, Franklin J. Woo
Dir., Japan North America Commission (JNAC), Patricia Patterson
Acting Dir., Europe/USSR, L. Newton Thorber
Dir., Middle East, Dale Bishop
Dir., Southern Asia, R. Lawrence Turnipseed
Community Education and Fund Raising
Tel. (219)264-3102 Fax (219)262-0966
Dir., Community Educ. & Fund Raising Subunit, The Rev. Melvin H. Luetchens, P.O. Box 968, Elkhart, IN 46515
Dir. of Community Outreach, Douglas R. Beane
Dir. of Creative Services, Linda Robbins

PROPHETIC JUSTICE

Tel (212)870-2419
Unit Dir./Assoc. Gen. Sec., Dr. Kenyon C. Burke
Dir., Finance, Mr. Robert Temmler
Program Dir., Racial Justice/Ecumenical Minority Bail Bond Fund, Rev. Joseph E. Agne
Program Dir., Justice for Women, ———
Program Dir., Health Justice, Ms. Karen Collins
Program Dir., Economic & Environmental Justice/Hunger Concerns, Dr. N. Jean Sindab

Child & Family Justice, Ms. Margery Freeman
Religious & Civil Liberty, Rev. Dean M. Kelley
Related Movements of Church and Society
Tel. (212)870-2293 Fax (212)870-2023
Dir., Interfaith Center for Corporate Responsibility, Mr. Timothy Smith
Dir., Natl. Farm Worker Ministry, Sr. Patricia Drydyk, O.S.F., 1337 W. Ohio, Chicago, IL 60622. Tel. (312)829-6436
Dr. Jon A. Lacey, Natl. Farm Worker Ministry, P. O. Box 4897, East Lansing, MI 48826. Tel. (517)351-4780

UNITY AND RELATIONSHIPS
Tel. (212)870-2157 Fax (212)870-2158
Unit Dir./Assoc. Gen. Sec., Dr. Constance Tarasar
Ecumenical Networks
Dir., Dr. Kathleen S. Hurty
Inter-Faith Relations
Christian-Jewish Concerns: Dir., Dr. Jay T. Rock
Christian-Muslim Concerns: Dir., Dr. R. Marston Speight, 77 Sherman St., Hartford, CT 06105. Tel. (203)232-4451
Faith and Order
Interim Dir., Rev. Norman A. Hjelm

FINANCE AND ADMINISTRATION
Tel. (212)870-2094 Fax (212)870-3112
Dir., Robert K. Soong
Financial Management
Controller, Leo Lamb
Deputy Controller, Marian Perdiz
Asst. Controller, William B. Price
Business Services
Dir., Phyllis Sharpe
Publication Services
Dir., Terrence S. Taylor
Management Information Systems
Dir., Rev. Nelson Murphy
Office of Personnel
Dir., Emilio F. Carrillo, Jr.
Dir. of Compensation & Benefits, Michael W. Mazoki

CONSTITUENT BODIES OF THE NATIONAL COUNCIL (with membership dates)
African Methodist Episcopal Church (1950)
African Methodist Episcopal Zion Church (1950)
American Baptist Churches in the U.S.A. (1950)
The Antiochian Orthodox Christian Archdiocese of North America (1966)
Armenian Church of America, Diocese of the (1957)
Christian Church (Disciples of Christ) (1950)
Christian Methodist Episcopal Church (1950)
Church of the Brethren (1950)
The Coptic Orthodox Church (1978)
The Episcopal Church (1950)
Evangelical Lutheran Church in America (1950)
Friends United Meeting (1950)
Greek Orthodox Archdiocese of North & South America (1952)
Hungarian Reformed Church in America (1957)
Intl. Council of Community Churches (1977)
Korean Presbyterian Church in America, Gen. Assembly of the (1986)
Moravian Church in America (1950)
Natl. Baptist Convention of America (1950)
Natl. Baptist Convention, U.S.A., Inc. (1950)
Orthodox Church in America (1950)
Philadelphia Yearly Meeting of the Religious Society of Friends (1950)
Polish Natl. Catholic Church of America (1957)
Presbyterian Church (U.S.A.) (1950)
Progressive Natl. Baptist Convention, Inc. (1966)

Reformed Church in America (1950)
Russian Orthodox Church in the U.S.A., Patriarchal Parishes of the (1966)
Serbian Orthodox Church in the U.S.A. & Canada (1957)
Swedenborgian Church (1966)
Syrian Orthodox Church of Antioch (1960)
Ukrainian Orthodox Church in America (1950)
United Church of Christ (1950)
The United Methodist Church (1950)

National Interfaith Coalition on Aging

The National Interfaith Coalition on Aging (NICA), an affiliate of the National Council on Aging, is composed of Protestant, Roman Catholic, Jewish, and Orthodox organizations and individuals concerned about the needs of older people and the religious community's response to problems facing the aging population in the United States. NICA was organized in 1972 to address spiritual concerns of older adults through religious sector action.

Primary objectives of NICA are: to enable religious organizations to serve older adults; to encourage religious communities to promote ministry by and with older adults; to support religious workers in aging in their many roles; to be a forum for religious dialogue about aging; and to be an advocate for older adults' concerns.

NICA supports development of programs and services for older people by religious organizations, agencies, judicatories and congregations; develops and distributes resources that help churches and synagogues develop ministries that respond to the needs and improve the quality of life of older people; convenes national and regional conferences for those who work with older adults; sponsors training and continuing education programs concerned with quality of life and religious programming for older people.

HEADQUARTERS
c/o NCOA, 409 Third St., SW,, Second Floor, Washington, DC 20024 Tel. (202)479-6689 Fax (202)479-0735

OFFICERS
Chair, Dr. Carol S. Pierskalla
Vice-Chair, Rev. Harry J. Ekstam
Sec., Lt. Col. Beatrice Combs
Prog. Mgr., Rev. John F. Evans

National Interreligious Service Board for Conscientious Objectors

NISBCO, formed in 1940, is a nonprofit service organization sponsored by a broad coalition of national religious bodies. NISBCO responds to the needs of conscientious objectors by: providing information on how to register and document one's convictions as a conscientious objector; providing professional counseling for those who are working through convictions of conscientious objection and training religious conscientious objector counselors; alerting citizens to the latest developments in the drive to bring back the draft and the efforts to institute compulsory national service; aiding conscientious objectors in the armed forces who seek noncombatant transfer or discharge; maintaining an extensive referral service to local counseling agencies in all areas of the country and to attorneys who can aid those in need of legal counsel; acting as a national resource center for those interested in conscientious objector/peace witness of all religious bodies in the United States: encouraging citizens through articles, speaking engagements, and NISBCO publications to decide for themselves what they believe about participation in war based upon the dictates of their own consciences.

HEADQUARTERS
Ste. 750, 1601 Connecticut Ave., NW, Washington, DC 20009 Tel. (202)483-4510 Fax (202)265-8022

National Religious Broadcasters

National Religious Broadcasters is an association of more than 800 organizations which produce religious programs for radio and television or operate stations carrying predominately religious programs. NRB member organizations are responsible for more than 75 percent of all religious radio and television in the United States, reaching an average weekly audience of millions by radio and television.

Dedicated to the communication of the Gospel, NRB was founded in 1944 to safeguard free and complete access to the broadcast media. By encouraging the development of Christian programs and stations, NRB helps make it possible for millions to hear the good news of Jesus Christ through the electronic media.

HEADQUARTERS
299 Webro Rd., Parsippany, NJ 07054 Tel. (201)428-5400 Fax (201)428-1814

OFFICERS
Exec. Dir., Brandt Gustavson
Pres., David Clark, CBN, Virginia Beach, VA
1st Vice-Pres., Robert Straton, Walter Bennett Communications, Ft. Washington, PA
2nd Vice-Pres., Richard Mason, Radio Bible Class, Grand Rapids, MI
Sec., Sue Bahner, WWWG Radio, Rochester, NY
Treas., Brian Erickson, Back to the Bible, Lincoln, NE

North American Academy of Ecumenists

Organized in 1967, the stated purpose of the NAAE is "to inform, relate, and encourage men and women professionally engaged in the study, teaching, and other practice of ecumenism."

HEADQUARTERS
Mailing Address, c/o Prof. Eugene Zoeller, 2001 Newburg Rd., Louisville, KY 40205

OFFICERS
Pres., Rev. Ernest R. Falardeau, S.S.S., Natl. Assoc. of Diocesan Ecum. Officers, Albuquerque, NM
Vice-Pres & Pres.-Elect, Dr. George Vandervelde, Institute for Christian Studies, Toronto, ON
Rec. Sec., Dr. Thomas Prinz, 1300 Collingwood Dr., Alexandria, VA 22308
Membership Sec. & Treas., Prof. Eugene Zoeller, 2001 Newburg Rd., Louisville, KY 40205

North American Baptist Fellowship

Organized in 1964, the North American Baptist Fellowship is a voluntary organization of Baptist Conventions in Canada and the United States,

functioning as a regional body within the Baptist World Alliance. Its objectives are: (a) to promote fellowship and cooperation among Baptists in North America, and (b) to further the aims and objectives of the Baptist World Alliance so far as these affect the life of the Baptist churches in North America. Its membership, however, is not identical with the North American membership of the Baptist World Alliance.

Church membership of the Fellowship bodies is more than 28 million.

The NABF assembles representatives of the member bodies once a year for exchange of information and views in such fields as evangelism and education, missions, stewardship promotion, laymen's activities, and theological education. It conducts occasional consultations for denominational leaders on such subjects as church extension. It encourages cooperation at the city and county level where churches of more than one member group are located.

HEADQUARTERS
5501 Donjoy Drive, Cincinnati, OH 45242

OFFICERS
Pres., Dr. Richard Coffin, Canadian Baptist Federation, 7185 Millcreek Drive, Mississauga, ON L5N 5R4
Vice-Pres., Dr. Arthur Walker, 901 N. Commerce St., Ste. 600, Nashville, TN 37203
Exec. Dir./Treas., Dr. Carolyn Crumpler

MEMBER BODIES
American Baptist Churches in the USA
Canadian Baptist Federation
General Association of General Baptists
National Baptist Convention of America
National Baptist Convention, USA, Inc.
Progressive National Baptist Convention, Inc.
Seventh Day Baptist General Conference
North American Baptist Conference
Southern Baptist Convention

North American Broadcast Section, World Association for Christian Communicators

This group was created in 1970 to bring together those persons in Canada and the United States who have an interest in broadcasting from a Christian perspective.

An annual conference is held during the week after Thanksgiving in the United States that draws more than 200 persons from at least 25 communions.

HEADQUARTERS
1300 Mutual Building, Detroit, MI 48226 Tel. (313)962-0340

OFFICERS
Bus. Mgr., Rev. Edward Willingham

Pentecostal Fellowship of North America

The fellowship was organized at Des Moines, Iowa, in October 1948 shortly after the first World Conference of Pentecostal Believers was held in Zurich, Switzerland, in May, 1947. The PFNA has the following objectives: 1) to provide a vehicle of expression and coordination of efforts in matters common to all member bodies including missionary and evangelistic effort; 2) to demonstrate to the world the essential unity of Spirit-baptized believers; 3) to provide services to its constituents to facilitate world evangelism; 4) to encourage the principles of community for the nurture of the body of Christ, endeavoring to keep the unity of the Spirit until we all come to the unity of the faith.

The PFNA has local chapters in communities where churches of the member groups are located, and fellowship rallies are held. On the national level, representatives of the member bodies are assembled for studies and exchange of views in the fields of home missions, foreign missions, and youth.

OFFICERS

Chpsn., Rev. James M. MacKnight, 10 Overlea Blvd., Toronto, ON M4H 1A5
1st Vice-Chpsn., B. E. Underwood, P.O.Box 12609, Oklahoma City, OK 73157
2nd Vice-Chpsn., Ray E. Smith, 2020 Bell Ave., Des Moines, IA 50315
Sec., Don Sauls, P.O. Box 1568, Dunn, NC 28335
Treas., J. Eugene Kurtz, 1910 W. Sunset Blvd., Los Angeles, CA 90026
Custodial Sec., Wayne E. Warner, 2020 Bell Ave., Des Moines, IA 50315

MEMBER GROUPS

Anchor Bay Evangelistic Association
Apostolic Church of Canada
Assemblies of God
Christian Church of North America
Church of God
Church of God of Apostolic Faith
Church of God, Mountain Assembly
Congregational Holiness Church
Elim Fellowship
Free Gospel Church, Inc.
Garr Memorial Ch., Carolina Evangelistic Assn.
International Church of the Foursquare Gospel
International Pentecostal Holiness Church
International Pentecostal Church of Christ
Italian Pentecostal Church of Canada
Open Bible Standard Churches, Inc.
Pentecostal Assemblies of Canada
Pentecostal Assemblies of Newfoundland
Pentecostal Church of God
Pentecostal Free-Will Baptist Church
Pentecostal Holiness Church of Canada

Project Equality, Inc.

Project Equality is a non-profit national inter-faith program for affirmative action and equal employment opportunity.

Project Equality serves as a central agency to receive and validate the equal employment commitment of suppliers of goods and services to sponsoring organizations and participating institutions, congregations, and individuals. Employers filing an accepted Annual Participation Report are included in the Project Equality "Buyer's Guide."

Workshops, training events, and consultant services in affirmative action and equal employment practices in recruitment, selection, placement, transfer, promotion, discipline and discharge are also available to sponsors and participants.

HEADQUARTERS

1020 E. 63rd St., Ste. 102, Kansas City, MO 64110
Tel. (816)361-9222 Fax (816)361-8997

OFFICERS

Chpsn., Ms. Barbara Thompson, Gen. Sec., Comm. on Religion & Race, United Methodist Church

Vice-Chpsn., Emilio Carrillo, Asst. Gen. Sec. for Personnel, Natl. Council of Churches
Sec., Kenneth Martin, Assoc. Exec. Sec., American Friends Service Cmte.
Treas., Dr. Ernest J. Newborn, Admn. Dir., Reconciliation, Christian Church (Disciples of Christ)
Pres., Rev. Maurice E. Culver

SPONSORS/ENDORSING ORGANIZATIONS

American Baptist Churches in the U.S.A.
American Friends Service Committee
American Jewish Committee
Central Conference of American Rabbis
Christian Church (Disciples of Christ)
Church of the Brethren
Church Women United
Consultation on Church Union
The Episcopal Church
Evangelical Lutheran Church in America
Intl. Council of Community Churches
National Association of Ecumenical Staff
National Catholic Conf. for Interracial Justice
National Council of Churches of Christ in the U.S.A.
National Education Association
National Federation of Priests Council
Presbyterian Church (USA)
Reformed Church in America
Roman Catholic Dioceses & Religious Orders
Unitarian Universalist Association
Union of American Hebrew Congregations
United Church of Christ
United Methodist Church
YWCA of the USA

Religion In American Life, Inc.

Religion In American Life (RIAL) is a unique cooperative program of some 50 major national religious groups (Catholic, Eastern Orthodox, Jewish, Protestant, etc.). It provides services for denominationally-supported, congregation-based outreach and growth projects such as the current Invite a Friend program. These projects are promoted through national advertising campaigns reaching the American public by the use of all media. The ad campaigns are produced by a volunteer agency with production/distribution and administration costs funded by denominations and business groups, as well as by individuals. Since 1949, RIAL ad campaign projects have been among the much coveted major campaigns of The Advertising Council. This results in as much as $20 million worth of time and space in a single year, contributed by media as a public service. Through RIAL, religious groups demonstrate respect for other traditions and the value of religious freedom. The RIAL program also includes seminars and symposia, research, leadership awards programs, and Worship Directories in hotels, motels, and public places throughout the nation.

HEADQUARTERS

2 Queenston Pl., Rm. 200, Princeton, NJ 08540
Tel. (609)921-3639 Fax (609)921-0551

EXECUTIVE COMMITTEE

Natl. Chpsn., O. Milton Gossett, (SSAW)
Chpsn. of Bd., Rabbi Joseph B. Glasser, (CCAR)
Vice-Chpsns.: Bishop Khajag Barsamian, Primate (Armen. Ch. of Am.); Rev. Bryant Kirkland, (ABS); John Cardinal O'Connor, (Archbishop of New York); Rabbi Ronald B. Sobel, (Cong. Emmanu-El of the City of N.Y.)

Sec., Beverly Campbell, (Church of Jesus Christ of LDS)
Treas., Francis J. Palamara, (ARA Service)

STAFF
Pres., Dr. Nicholas B. van Dyck
Exec. Asst., Sharon E. Lloyd
Worship Directory Mgr., Ms. Jane Kelly

Religion Newswriters Association

Founded in 1949, the RNA is a professional association of religion news editors and reporters on secular daily and weekly newspapers, news services, and news magazines. It sponsors four annual contests for excellence in religion news coverage in the secular press. Annual meetings are held during a major religious convocation.

OFFICERS
Pres., John Dart, 20000 Prairie, Chatsworth, CA 91311
1st Vice-Pres., Jim Jones, Ft. Worth Star-Telegram, Ft. Worth, TX 76102
2nd Vice-Pres., Richard Dujardin, Providence Journal-Bulletin, Providence, RI 02902
Sec., Judith Weidman, Religious News Servcie, New York, NY 10101
Treas., Cecile Holmes White, Houston Chronicle, Houston, TX 77210

Religious Conference Management Association, Inc.

The Religious Conference Management Association, Inc. (RCMA) is an interfaith nonprofit professional organization of men and women who have responsibility for planning and/or managing meetings, seminars, conferences, conventions, assemblies, or other gatherings for religious organizations.

Founded in 1972, RCMA is dedicated to promoting the highest professional performance by its members and associate members through the mutual exchange of ideas, techniques, and methods.

Today RCMA has more than 1,500 members and associate members.

The association conducts an annual conference and exposition which provide a forum for its membership to gain increased knowledge in the arts and sciences of religious meeting planning and management.

HEADQUARTERS
One Hoosier Dome, Ste. 120, Indianapolis, IN 46225 Tel. (317)632-1888

OFFICERS
Pres., Melvin L. Worthington, Natl. Assoc. of Free Will Baptists, P.O. Box 1088, Nashville, TN 37202
Vice-Pres., Rainer B. Wilson, Sr., Church of Christ, Holiness, U.S.A., 819 Hampton Ave., Newport News, VA 23607
Sec.-Treas., Rudy Becton, United Pentecostal Church Intl., 8855 Dunn Rd., Hazelwood, MO 63042
Exec. Dir., DeWayne S. Woodring, Religious Conf. Mgt. Assoc., One Hoosier Dome, Ste. 120, Indianapolis, IN 46225

The Religious Public Relations Council, Inc.

RPRC is an international, interfaith, interdisciplinary association of professional communicators who work for religious groups and causes. It was founded in 1929 and is the oldest non-profit professional public relations organization in the world. RPRC's 500 members include those who work in public relations and related fields for church-related colleges, seminaries, denominational agencies, non-and interdenominational organizations, and communications firms who primarily serve religious organizations.

Members represent a wide range of faiths, including Presbyterian, Baptist, Methodist, Lutheran, Episcopalian, Mennonite, Roman Catholic, Seventh-Day Adventist, Jewish, Salvation Army, Brethren, Baha'i, Disciples, Latter-Day Saints, and others.

On the national level, RPRC sponsors an annual three-day convention, and has published four editions of a *Religious Public Relations Handbook* for churches and church organizations, and a filmstrip, *The Church at Jackrabbit Junction*. Members receive a quarterly newsletter (*Counselor*), and a quarterly digest of professional articles (*MediaKit*). From time to time, RPRC sponsors national teleconferences and a summer institute in religious communications. There are 13 regional chapters.

RPRC administers the annual Wilbur Awards competition to recognize high quality coverage of religious values and activities in the public media. Wilbur winners include producers, reporters, editors and broadcasters nationwide. To recognize communications excellence within church communities, RPRC also sponsors the annual DeRose-Hinkhouse Awards for its own members.

In 1970, 1980 and 1990, RPRC initiated a global Religious Communications Congress bringing together thousands of persons from western, eastern and third-world nations who are involved in communicating religious faith. Another Congress is planned for 2000.

HEADQUARTERS
357 Righters Mill Rd., P.O. Box 315, Gladwyne, PA 19035 Tel. (215)642-8895

OFFICERS
Pres., Wesley M. Pattillo, Vice-Pres., University Rel., Samford U., 800 Lakeshore Dr., Birmingham, AL 35229
Vice-Pres., Steve Shenk, Man. Ed., Gospel Herald Mennonite Publ., 616 Walnut Ave., Scottdale, PA 15683
Exec. Dir., J. Ron Byler

Standing Conference of Canonical Orthodox Bishops in the Americas

This body was established in 1960 to achieve cooperation among the various Eastern Orthodox Churches in the United States. The Conference is "a voluntary association of the Bishops in the Americas established to serve as an agency to centralize and coordinate the mission of the Church. It acts as a clearing house to focus the efforts of the Church on common concerns and to avoid duplication and overlapping of services and agencies. Special departments are devoted to campus work, Christian education, military and other chaplaincies, regional clergy fellowships, and ecumenical relations."

HEADQUARTERS

8-10 East 79th St., New York, NY 10021 Tel. (212)570-3500 Fax (212)570-4050

OFFICERS

Chpsn., Most Rev. Archbishop Iakovos
Vice Chpsn., Most Rev. Metropolitan Philip
Treas., Bishop Nicholas of Amissos
Sec., Most Rev. Metropolitan Joseph
Rec. Sec., V. Rev. Paul Schneirla

MEMBER CHURCHES

Albanian Orthodox Diocese of America
American Carpatho-Russian Orthodox Greek Catholic Ch.
Antiochian Orthodox Christian Archdiocese of All N.A.
Bulgarian Eastern Orthodox Church
Greek Orthodox Archdiocese of North & South America
Orthodox Church in America
Romanian Orthodox Church in America
Serbian Orthodox Church for the U.S.A. & Canada
Ukrainian Orthodox Church of America
Ukrainian Orthodox Church of Canada

YMCA of the USA

The YMCA is one of the largest private voluntary organizations in the world, serving about 30 million people in more than 100 countries. In the Untied States, about 2,000 local branches, units, camps, and centers annually serve almost 13 million people of all ages, races, and abilities. About half of those served are female. No one is turned away because of an inability to pay.

The YMCA is best known for health and fitness. The Y teaches kids to swim, organizes youth basketball games, and offers adult aerobics. But the Y represents more than fitness—it works to strengthen families and help people develop values and behavior that are consistent with Christian principles.

The Y offers hundreds of programs including day camp for kids, child care, exercise for people with disabilities, teen clubs, environmental programs, substance abuse prevention, family nights, job training, and many more programs from infant mortality prevention to overnight camping for seniors.

The kind of programs offered at a YMCA will vary; each is controlled by volunteer board members who make their own program, policy, and financial decisions based on the special needs of their community. In its own way, every Y promotes good health, strong families, confident kids, solid communities, and a better world.

The YMCA was founded in London, England, in 1844 by George Williams and friends who lived and worked together as clerks. Their goal was to save other live-in clerks from the wicked life of the London streets. The first members were evangelical Protestants who prayed and studied the Bible as an alternative to vice. The Y has always been nonsectarian and today accepts those of all faiths at all levels of the organization.

HEADQUARTERS

101 N. Wacker Dr., Chicago, IL 60606 Tel. (312)977-0031

OFFICERS

Board Chpsn., Barbara Roper
Exec. Dir., David R. Mercer

Young Women's Christian Association of the United States

The YWCA of the U.S.A. is comprised of some 425 affiliates in communities and on college campuses across the United States and serving some 2 million members and program participants. It seeks to empower women and girls and to enable them, coming together across lines of age, race, religious belief, economic and occupational status to make a significant contribution to the elimination of racism and the achievement of peace, justice, freedom and dignity for all people. Its leadership is vested in a National Board, whose functions are to unite into an effective continuing organization the autonomous member Associations for furthering the purposes of the National Association and to participate in the work of the World YWCA.

HEADQUARTERS

726 Broadway, New York, NY 10003 Tel. (212)614-2700 Fax (212)677-9716

OFFICERS

Pres., Ann Stallard
Sec., Anne H. Perkins
Exec. Dir., Gwendolyn Calvert Baker

Youth for Christ/USA

Founded in 1945, the mission of YFC is to communicate the life-changing message of Jesus Christ to every young person.

Locally controlled YFC programs serve in 220 cities and metropolitan areas of the U.S.

YFC's Campus Life Club program involves teens who attend approximately 1,365 high schools in the United States. YFC's staff now numbers more than 1,000. In addition, approximately 8,800 part-time and volunteer staff supplement the full-time staff. Youth Guidance, a ministry for nonschool-oriented youth includes group homes, court referrals, institutional services, and neighborhood ministries. The year-round conference and camping program involves approximately 35,000 young people each year. A family-oriented ministry designed to enrich individuals and church family education programs is carried on through Family Forum, a daily five minute radio program on more than 300 stations. Independent, indigenous YFC organizations also work in 65 countries overseas.

HEADQUARTERS

U.S. Headquarters, P.O. Box 228822, Denver, CO 80222 Tel. (303)843-9000 Fax (303)843-9002
Canadian Organization, 220 Attwell Dr., Unit #1, Rexdale, ON M9W 5B2

OFFICERS

United States, CEO, Roger Cross
Canada, Pres., Robert Simpson
Intl. Organization: Singapore, Pres., Rev. Jim Groen; Gen. Dir., James Wilson

2. CANADIAN COOPERATIVE ORGANIZATIONS, NATIONAL

This directory of Canadian Cooperative Organizations attempts to list major organizations working interdenominationally on a national basis. Organizations with international membership and focus are listed in the International Agencies section. Organizations that are not cooperatives of religious bodies can be found in the Canadian Service Agencies section.

Canadian Bible Society

As early as 1805, the British and Foreign Bible Society was at work in Canada. The Bible Society branch at Truro, Nova Scotia, has been functioning continually since 1810. In 1904, the various auxiliaries of the British and Foreign Bible Society joined to form the Canadian Bible Society.

The Canadian Bible Society has 17 district offices across Canada, each managed by a District Secretary. The Society holds annual meetings consisting of one representative of each district, plus members appointed by the General Board of the CBS. Each year contributions and bequests in excess of $9 million come from Canadian supporters. Through the Canadian Bible Society's membership in the United Bible Societies' fellowship, more than 71 million Bibles, Testaments and portions, in more than 900 languages, were distributed globally in 1990.

The Canadian Bible Society is nondenominational. Its mandate is to translate, publish, and distribute the Scriptures, without note or comment, in languages that can be easily read and understood.

HEADQUARTERS
10 Carnforth Road, Toronto, ON M4A 2S4 Tel. (416)757-4171 Fax (416)757-3376

OFFICER
Gen. Sec., Rev. Floyd C. Babcock

Canadian Council of Christians and Jews

The Canadian Council of Christians and Jews is an organization which builds bridges of understanding between Canadians. Its techniques of effecting social change are dialogue and education. The CCCJ believes that there exist in any community in Canada the reservoirs of good will, the mediating skills, and the enlightened self-interest which make accommodation to change and the creation of social justice possible.

The CCCJ was established in Toronto in 1947 by a group of prominent business, civic and religious leaders.

Its mandate is: "to promote justice, friendship, cooperation and understanding among people differing in race, religion, or nationality."

HEADQUARTERS
49 Front St., E., Toronto, ON M5E 1B3 Tel. (416)364-3101.

STAFF
Natl. Exec. Dir., Ms. Elyse Graff

The Canadian Council of Churches

The Canadian Council of Churches was organized in 1944. Its basic purpose is to provide the churches with an agency for conference and consultation and for such common planning and common action as they desire to undertake. It encourages ecumenical understanding and action throughout Canada through local councils of churches. It also relates to the World Council of Churches and other agencies serving the worldwide ecumenical movement.

The Council has a Triennial Assembly, a General Board which meets semiannually, and an Executive Committee. Program is administered through three commissions--Faith and Witness, Justice and Peace, and Ecumenical Education and Communication.

HEADQUARTERS
40 St. Clair Ave. E., Toronto, ON M4T 1M9 Tel. (416)921-4152

OFFICERS AND STAFF
Pres., The V. Rev. Bruce McLeod
Vice-Pres.: Anne Thomas; Rev. Joe Williams; Rev. Dr. Ronald Watts
Treas., Mr. John Hart
Assoc. Sec.: Dr. Nancy Cocks; Mr. James Hodgson; Mr. John Siebert
Gen. Sec., Dr. Stuart E. Brown

AFFILIATED INSTITUTION
The Canadian Churches' Forum for Global Ministries, Rev. Tim Ryan, S.F.M., 11 Madison Ave., Toronto, ON M5R 2S2 Tel. (416)924-9351

MEMBERS
The Anglican Church of Canada
The Armenian Church of America--Diocese of Canada
Baptist Convention of Ontario and Quebec
Canadian Conference of Catholic Bishops*
Christian Church (Disciples of Christ)
Coptic Orthodox Church of Canada
Ethiopian Orthodox Church in Canada
Evangelical Lutheran Church in Canada
Greek Orthodox Diocese of Toronto (Canada)
Orthodox Church in America, Diocese of Canada
Polish National Catholic Church
Presbyterian Church in Canada
Ethiopian Orthodox Church in Canada
Reformed Church in Ameraica--Classis of Ontario
Religious Society of Friends--Canada Yearly Meeting
Salvation Army--Canada and Bermuda
The Ukrainian Orthodox Church
The United Church of Canada
*Associate Member

Canadian Tract Society

The Canadian Tract Society was organized in 1970 as an independent distributor of Gospel leaflets to provide Canadian churches and individual Christians with quality materials proclaiming the Gospel through the printed page. It is affiliated with the American Tract Society, which encouraged its formation and assisted in its founding, and for whom it serves as an exclusive Canadian distributor. The CTS is a nonprofit international service ministry.

HEADQUARTERS

Box 203, Port Credit P.O., Mississauga, ON L5G 4L7

OFFICERS

Pres., Stanley D. Mackey
Sec., Robert J. Burns

Evangelical Fellowship of Canada

The Fellowship was formed in 1964. There are 29 denominations, 88 organizations, and 756 local churches, and thousands of individual members.

Its purposes are threefold: "Fellowship in the gospel" (Phil. 1:5). "the defence and confirmation of the gospel" (Phil. 1:7), and "the furtherance of the gospel" (Phil. 1:12).

The Fellowship believes the Holy Scriptures, as originally given, are infallible and that salvation through the Lord Jesus Christ is by faith apart from works.

In national and regional conventions the Fellowship urges Christians to live exemplary lives and to openly challenge the evils and injustices of society. It encourages cooperation with various agencies in Canada and overseas that are sensitive to social and spiritual needs.

HEADQUARTERS

Office: 175 Riviera Dr., Markham, ON L3R 5J6 Tel. (416)479-5885 Fax (416)479-4742
Mailing Address: PO Box 8800, Stn. B, Willowdale, ON M2K 2R6

OFFICERS

Exec. Dir., Dr. Brian C. Stiller
Pres., Dr. John Redekop
Vice-Pres., Dr. Donald Jost
Treas., Rev. Grover Crosby
Sec., Major John Wilder
Past Pres., Bishop Donald Bastian
Committee Members-at-Large: Mrs. Moira Hunt; Rev. David Collins; Dr. W. Harold Fuller; Mr. Donald Simmonds; Rev. Ron Swanson; Mrs. Linda Tripp; Dr. John Vissers; Rev. Andrew Wong
Co-Chpsn., Social Action Commission: Dr. Paul Marshall; Mrs. Aileen VanGinkel
Chpsn., Task Force on Evangelism: Dr. William McRae
Chpsn., Task Force on the Family: Dr. Mavis Olesen
Chpsn., Task Force on Future of Canada: Dr. Paul Marshall

Inter-Varsity Christian Fellowship of Canada

Inter-Varsity Christian Fellowship is a non-profit, interdenominational Canadian student movement centering on the witness to Jesus Christ in campus communities: universities, colleges, high schools, and through a Canada-wide Pioneer camping programme. IVCF was officially formed in 1928-29 through the enthusiastic efforts of the late Dr. Howard Guinness, whose arrival from Britain challenged students to follow the example of the Inter-Varsity Fellowship from which he came, in organizing themselves in prayer and Bible Study fellowship groups. Inter-Varsity has always been a student-initiated movement, emphasizing and developing leadership on the campus to call Christians to outreach, challenging other students to a personal faith in Jesus Christ, and study of the Bible as God's revealed truth within a fellowship of believers. A strong stress has been placed on missionary activity, and the triennial conference held at Urbana, Il (jointly sponsored by U.S. and Canadian IVCF) has been a means of challenging many young people to service in Christian vocation. Inter-Varsity works closely with, and is a strong believer in, the work of local and national churches.

HEADQUARTERS

Unit 17, 40 Vogell Rd., Richmond Hill, ON L4B 3N6 Tel. (416)884-6880 Fax (416)884-6550

OFFICERS

Gen. Dir., James E. Berney

Lutheran Council in Canada

The Lutheran Council in Canada was organized in 1967 and is a cooperative agency of the Evangelical Lutheran Church in Canada and the Lutheran Church-Canada.

The Council's activities include communications, coordinative service, and national liaison in social ministry, chaplaincy, and scout activity.

HEADQUARTERS

1512 S. James St., Winnipeg, MB R3H 0L2 Tel. (204)786-6707 Fax (204)783-7548

OFFICERS

Pres., Rev. Edwin Lehman

Mennonite Central Committee Canada (MCCC)

Mennonite Central Committee Canada was organized in 1964 to continue the work which several regional Canadian inter-Mennonite agencies had been doing in relief, service, immigration, and peace. All but a few of the smaller Mennonite groups in Canada belong to MCC Canada.

MCCC is part of the binational Mennonite Central Committee (MCC) which has its headquarters in Akron, Pennsylvania, from where the overseas development and relief projects are administered. In 1990 MCCC's budget was $20,725,000, representing about 40 percent of the total MCC budget. There were 429 Canadians of a total of 953 MCC workers serving one to three year terms in North America and abroad during the same time period.

The MCC office in Winnipeg administers projects located in Canada. Domestic programs of Voluntary Service, Native Concerns, Peace and Social Concerns, Food Program, Employment Concerns, Ottawa Office, Victim/Offender Ministries, Mental Health and immigration are all part of MCC's Canadian ministry. Whenever it undertakes a project, MCCC attempts to relate to the church or churches in the area, thus supporting the local church.

HEADQUARTERS

134 Plaza Dr., Winnipeg, MB R3T 5K9 Tel. (204)261-6381

OFFICER

Exec. Dir., Daniel Zehr

People for Sunday Association of Canada

A secular organization devoted to achieving for Canada Sunday as a national common day of rest and leisure.

The Association produces its publications *Sound About Sunday* and *Update*, and furnishes speakers when requested.

HEADQUARTERS

P. O. Box 457, Islington, ON M9A 4X4 Tel. (416)625-8759

OFFICERS

Pres., Canon Thomas Rooke
Exec. Dir., Les Kingdon

Student Christian Movement of Canada

The Student Christian Movement of Canada was formed in 1921 from the student arm of the YMCA. It has its roots in the Social Gospel movements of the late 19th and early 20th centuries. Throughout its intellectual history, the SCM in Canada has sought to relate the Christian faith to the living realities of the social and political context of each student generation.

The present priorities are built around the need to form more and stronger critical Christian communities on Canadian campuses within which individuals may develop their social and political analyses, experience spiritual growth and fellowship, and bring Christian ecumenical witness to the university.

The Student Christian Movement of Canada is affiliated with the World Student Christian Federation.

HEADQUARTERS

310 Danforth Ave., Ste. C3, Toronto, ON M4K 1N6 Tel. (416)463-4312

OFFICER

Gen. Sec., Bruce Gilbert

Women's Interchurch Council of Canada

The council is an ecumenical movement through which Christians may express their unity by prayer, fellowship, study, action. The purpose is: to enable Christian women across Canada to live in love and fellowship so that all people may find fullness of life in Christ. WICC sponsors the World Day of Prayer and the Fellowship of the Least Coin in Canada. Human rights projects are supported and ecumenical study kits produced. A newsletter is issued four times a year. Membership is composed of one appointment by each participating national denomination which confesses the Lord Jesus Christ as God and Saviour and members elected through the nominating process set out in the by-laws.

HEADQUARTERS

77 Charles St., W., Toronto, ON M5S 1K5 Tel. (416)922-6177

OFFICERS

Pres., Beryl Reid
Exec. Dir., Vivian Harrower

Young Men's Christian Association in Canada

The first YMCA in Canada was established in Montreal, Nov. 25, 1851, the declared purpose being "the improvement of the spiritual and mental condition of young men." Toronto and Halifax followed in 1853. At the 125th anniversary of the Canadian movement (1976), YMCAs were found in 75 cities from St. John's, Newfoundland to Victoria, B.C., with programs for intellectual, spiritual, and physical development of all Canadians.

Originally forming a single movement with the YMCAs in the United States, the Canadian Associations formed their own National Council in 1912. However, the international outreach (assisting in the establishment of YMCA movements in Latin America, Asia, and Africa) was administered jointly with the YMCA in the United States through an International Committee until 1970, when an agreement recognized the Canadian YMCA's independent service abroad. Today many "partnership Programs" exist between the Canadian Associations and YMCAs in developing countries.

HEADQUARTERS

2160 Yonge St., Toronto, ON M4S 2A9 Tel. (416)485-9447 Fax (416)485-8228

OFFICERS

Dir., Intl. Programs, Alan Hatton
CEO, Sol Kasimer
Chpsn., Donald S. McCreesh

Young Women's Christian Association of/du Canada

The YWCA of/du Canada is a national voluntary organization serving 44 YWCAs and YM-YWCAs across Canada. Dedicated to the development and improved status of women and their families, the YWCA is committed to service delivery, to being a source of public education on women's issues, and an advocate of social change. Services provided by YWCAs and YM-YWCAs include adult education programs, residences and shelters, child care, fitness activities, wellness programs and international development education. As a member of the World YWCA, the YWCA of/du Canada is part of the largest women's organization in the world.

HEADQUARTERS

80 Gerrard St.E., Toronto, ON M5B 1G6 Tel. (416)593-9886 Fax (416)971-8084

OFFICERS

CEO, Rita S. Karakas

CANADIAN COOPERATIVE ORGANIZATIONS

3. RELIGIOUS BODIES IN THE UNITED STATES

The following directories have been supplied by the listed denominations. They are printed in alphabetical order by the official name of the organization. A list of organizations by family group is found at the end of this section. This may help you find a particular group.

To conserve space, information found in other places in this yearbook is not repeated. The denominational listing points you to additional information. Specifically, addresses and editor's names for periodicals are found in the listing of United States Periodicals. Also, statistical information for each organization is found in the statistical section.

When an organization supplied a headquarter's address it is listed immediately following the description of the organization. This address, telephone number, and fax number is not reprinted for entries that have exactly the same address and numbers. An address or telephone number is only printed when it is known to be different from the headquarter's. Individuals listed without an address should be contacted at the headquarters.

This year, for the first time, denominations were asked to provide the name of a media contact. Many responded with a specific person that newspaper or other reporters can contact to obtain official information. These people are listed with the headquarter's address.

The organizations listed here represent the denominations to which the vast majority of church members in the United States belong. It does not include all religious bodies functioning in the United States. *The Encyclopedia of American Religions* (Gale Research Inc., P.O. Box 33477, Detroit MI 48232-5477) contains names and addresses of additional religious bodies.

Advent Christian Church

The Advent Christian Church is a conservative, evangelical denomination, which grew out of the Millerite movement of the 1830s and 1840s. The members stress the authority of Scripture, justification by faith in Jesus Christ alone, the importance of evangelism and world missions, and the soon visible return of Jesus Christ.

Organized in 1860, the Advent Christian Church maintains headquarters in Charlotte, N.C., with regional offices in Rochester, N. H.; Augusta, Ga.; Fort Worth, Texas; Lewiston, Idaho; and Lenoir, N.C. Missions are maintained in India, Nigeria, Japan, Malaysia, the Philippines, Mexico, and Memphis, Tenn.

The Advent Christian Church maintains doctrinal distinctives in three areas: conditional immortality, the sleep of the dead until the return of Christ, and belief that the kingdom of God will be established on earth made new by Jesus Christ.

HEADQUARTERS

P.O. Box 23152, Charlotte, NC 28212 Tel. (704)545-6161 Fax (704)545-2558

OFFICERS

Pres., Rev. Glennon Balser, 6315 Studley Rd., Mechanicsville, VA 23111
Exec. Vice-Pres., David E. Ross
Sec., Rev. John Gallagher, 3601 Sikes Mill Rd., Monroe, NC 28110
Appalachian Vice-Pres., Rev. Orville Harvey, Rt. 9, Box 734, Princeton, WV 24740
Central Vice-Pres., Rev. Dwight Carpenter, 7919 Kandy Lane, N. Richland Hills, TX 76180
Eastern Vice-Pres., Rev. Irvin Verrill, 20 Highland Cliff Rd., Windham, ME 04062
Southern Vice-Pres., Rev. Larry Withrow, 318 Crescent Dr., Clayton, NC 27520
Western Vice-Pres., Mr. Larry McIntyre, 1629 Jamie Cr., West Linn, OR 97068
The Woman's Home & Foreign Mission Soc., Pres., Mrs. Bea Moore, Rt. 8, Box 274, Loudon, NH 03301

PERIODICALS

Advent Christian Witness, The; Advent Christian News; Maranatha; Insight

African Methodist Episcopal Church

This church began in 1787 in Philadelphia when persons in St. George's Methodist Episcopal Church withdrew as a protest against color segregation. In 1816 the denomination was started, led by Rev. Richard Allen, who had been ordained deacon by Bishop Francis Asbury, and who was ordained elder and elected and consecrated bishop.

OFFICERS

Senior Bishop, Bishop John H. Adams, 208 Auburn Ave., N.E., Atlanta, GA 30303 Tel. (404)524-8279
Gen. Sec., Dr. O. Urcille Ifill, Sr., P.O. Box 19039, East Germantown Sta., Philadelphia, PA 19138 Tel. (215)877-8330
Council of Bishops: Pres., Bishop Harold B. Senatle, 18 Cor. Phillips & Anderson St., P.O. Box 261306 Excom. 2023, Johannesburg, Rep. of South Africa; Sec., Bishop Henry A. Belin, Jr., 604 Locust St., N. Little Rock, AR 42114
Genl. Bd.: Pres., Bishop Frederick C. James, Landmark East, 3700 Forest Dr., Ste. 402, Columbia, SC 29204; Sec., Dr. O. Urcille Ifill, Sr., P.O. Box 19039, East Germantown Sta., Philadelphia, PA 19138 Tel. (215)877-8330
Treas., Dr. Joseph C. McKinney, 2311 M St., N.W., Washington, DC 20037 Tel. (202)337-3930
Historiographer, Dr. Dennis Dickerson, P.O. Box 301, Williamstown, MA 02167
Judical Council, Pres., Atty. P. A. Townsend, 1010 Macvicar St., Topeka, KS 66604

DEPARTMENTS

Missions, Dr. Frederick C. Harrison, 475 Riverside Dr., Rm. 1926, New York, NY 10115 Tel. (212)870-2258
Church Extension, Sec.-Treas., Dr. Hercules Miles, 3526 Dodier, St. Louis, MO 63107 Tel. (314)534-4272
Christian Education, Sec., Dr. Edgar Mack, 500 8th Ave., S., Nashville, TN 37203 Tel. (615)242-1420

Sunday School Union, Sec-Treas., Dr. Lee Henderson, 500 Eighth Ave., S., Nashville, TN 37203 Tel. (615)256-5882

Evangelism, Dir., Yale B. Bruce, 5728 Major Blvd., Orlando, FL 82819 Tel. (305)352-6515

Publications, Sec.-Treas., Dr. A. Lee Henderson, 500 8th Ave., S., Nashville, TN 37203 Tel. (615)256-5882

Pension, Sec.-Treas., Dr. J. Anderson Todd, 500 8th Ave., S., Nashville, TN 37203 Tel. (615)256-7725

Fin. Dept., Dr. Joseph C. McKinney, 2311 M St., N.W., Washington, DC 20037 Tel. (202)337-3930

Statistical Dept., Dr. O. Urcille Ifill, Sr., P.O. Box 19039, East Germantown Sta., Philadelphia, PA 19138 Tel. (215)877-8330

Minimum Salary, Dr. Alonzo W. Holman, 280 Hernando St., Memphis, TN 38126 Tel. (901)526-4281

Religious Lit. Dept., Ed.-in-Chief, Dr. Cyrus S. Keller, Sr., P.O. Box 5327, St. Louis, MO 63115 Tel. (314)535-8822

Women's Missionary Soc., Pres., Mrs. Delores L. K. Williams, 2311 M St., N.W., Washington, DC 20037 Tel. (212)337-1335

Lay Organization, Connectional Pres., Dr. Kathryn M. Brown, 171 Ashby St., Atlanta, GA 30314

BISHOPS IN THE U.S.A.

First District, Frank C. Cummings, 5070 Parkside, Ste. 1410, Philadelphia, PA 19131 Tel. (215)877-3771

Second District, H. Hartford Brookins, 6209 Stoneham Ln., McLean, VA Tel. (703)442-0261

Third District, Richard Allen Hildebrand, 700 Bryden Rd., Ste. 135, Columbus, OH 43215 Tel. (614)461-6496

Fourth District, J. Haskell Mayo, Jr., P.O. Box 53539, 400 E. 41st St., Ste. 114, Chicago, IL 60653 Tel. (312)373-6587

Fifth District, Vinton R. Anderson, P.O. Box 6416, St. Louis, MO 63107 Tel. (314)534-4274

Sixth District, John H. Adams, 208 Auburn Ave. N.E., Atlanta, GA 30303 Tel. (404)524-8279

Seventh District, Frederick C. James, 370 Forest Dr., Ste. 402, Columbia, SC 29204

Eighth District, Donald G. Ming, 2138 St. Bernard Ave., New Orleans, LA 70119 Tel. (504)948-4251

Ninth District, Cornelius E. Thomas, 2101 Magnolia, Birmingham, AL 35205 Tel. (205)252-2612

10th District, J. Robert L. Pruitt, Republic Bank Tower, Oak Cliff, Ste. 813, Dallas, TX 75208 Tel. (214)941-9323

11th District, Philip R. Cousin, P.O. Box 2970, Jacksonville, FL 32203 Tel. (904)355-8262

12th District, Henry A. Belin, Jr., 604 Locust St., North, Little Rock, AR 72114 Tel. (501)375-4310

13th District, Vernon R. Byrd, 500 8th Ave., So., Nashville, TN 37203 Tel. (615)242-6814

14th District, John R. Bryant, P.O. Box 4191, Monrovia, Liberia, W. Africa

15th District, Robert Thomas, Jr., 28 Walmer Rd., Woodstock 7925, Capetown, Rep. of S. Africa

16th District, Henry A. Belin, Jr., 131 Ashford Rd., Cherry Hill, NJ 08003 Tel. (609)751-7288

17th District, Richard A. Chapelle, P.O. Box 183, St. Louis, MO 63166 Tel. (314)355-7371

18th District, Richard A. Chappelle, P.O. Box MS 223, Maseru, 100, Lesotho

19th District, Harold Ben Senatle, P.O. Box 12, Residensia 1980, Rep. of S. Africa

Ecumenical Officer, Frederick H. Talbot, P.O. Box 684, Frederiksted, St. Croix, U. S. Virgin Islands, 00840 Tel. (809)772-0723

Located, Rembert E. Stokes, 783 Hidden Circle, Dayton, OH 45459 Tel. (513)436-7347

RETIRED BISHOPS:

Henry W. Murph, 5940 Holt Ave., Los Angeles, CA 90056 Tel. (213)410-0266

D. Ward Nichols, 2295 Seventh Ave., New York, NY 10030 Tel. (516)427-0225

Ernest L. Hickman, 1320 Oakcrest Dr., S.W., Atlanta, GA 30311 Tel. (404)349-1336

Harrison J. Bryant, 4000 Bedford Rd., Baltimore, MD 21207 Tel. (301)484-7508

H. Thomas Primm, 2820 Monaco Parkway, Denver, CO 80207 Tel. (303)335-9545

Hubert N. Robinson, 357 Arden Park, Detroit, MI 48202 Tel. (313)875-4967

PERIODICALS

A.M.E. Christian Recorder; A.M.E. Review; Journal of Christian Education; Secret Chamber; Women's Missionary Magazine; Voice of Missions

African Methodist Episcopal Zion Church

The A.M.E. Zion Church is an independent body, having withdrawn from the John Street Methodist Church of New York City in 1796. The first bishop was James Varick.

OFFICERS

Senior Bishop, Bishop William Milton Smith, 3753 Springhill Ave., Mobile, AL 36608

Sec., Bd. of Bishops, Bishop John Henry Miller, Sr., 8605 Caswell Ct., Raleigh, NC 27612

Asst. Sec., Bishop Clinton R. Coleman, 3513 Ellamont Rd., Baltimore, MD 21215

OTHER AGENCIES

Gen. Sec.-Aud., Rev. W. Robert Johnson, P.O. Box 32843, Charlotte, NC 28232 Tel. (704)332-3851 Fax (704)333-1769

Fin. Sec., Ms. Madie L. Simpson, P.O. Box 31005, Charlotte, NC 28230 Tel. (704)333-4847

A.M.E. Zion Publishing House: Gen. Mgr., Dr. Lem Long, Jr., P.O. Box 30714, Charlotte, NC 28230 Tel. (704)334-9596

Dept. of Overseas Missions: Sec.-Treas, Rev. Dr. Kermit J. DeGraffenreidt, 475 Riverside Dr., Rm. 1935, New York, NY 10115 Tel. (212)870-2952

Dept. of Home Miss., Pensions, & Relief: Sec.-Treas., Rev. Dr. Jewett Walker, P.O. Box 30846, Charlotte, NC 28231 Tel. (704)333-3779

Dept. of Christian Education: Sec., Rev. G. L. Blackwell, 128 E. 58th St., Chicago, IL 60637 Tel. (312)667-0183

Dept. of Church School Literature: Ed., Ms. Mary A. Love, P.O. Box 31005, Charlotte, NC 28230 Tel. (704)332-1034

Dept. of Church Extension: Sec.-Treas., Dr. Lem Long, Jr., P.O. Box 31005, Charlotte, NC 28230 Tel. (704)334-2519

Dept. of Evangelism: Dir., Dr. Norman H. Hicklin, P.O. Box 4, Asheville, NC 28802 Tel. (704)353-5108

Dept. of Public Relations: Dir., Dr. Thaddeus Garrett, Jr., 1730 M St., NW, Ste. 808, Washington, DC 20036 Tel. (202)332-0200

Women's Home & Overseas Missionary Soc.: Gen. Pres., Mrs. Grace L. Holmes, 2565 Linden Ave., Knoxville, TN Tel. (615)525-1523; Exec. Sec., Ms. Barbara Shaw, 4002 Maine Ave., Baltimore, MD 21207 Tel. (301)578-8239; Treas., Mrs. Gwendolyn Brumfield, 2011 Sterns Dr., Los Angeles, CA 90034 Tel. (213)939-9417

Connectional Lay Council: Pres., Mr. James E. Hewitt, Jr., 5718 Victoria Ave., Los Angeles, CA 90043

BISHOPS

First Episcopal District: Bishop William Milton Smith, 3753 Springhill Ave., Mobile, AL 36608 Tel. (205)344-7769

Second Episcopal District: Bishop Alfred G. Dunston, Jr., Executive House, #1117, 6100 City Line Ave., Philadelphia, PA 19131 Tel. (215)877-2659

Third Episcopal District: Bishop J. Clinton Hoggard, 1511 K St. NW, Ste. 1100, Washington, DC 20005 Tel. (202)347-1419

Fourth Episcopal District: Bishop Clinton R. Coleman, 3513 Ellamont Rd., Baltimore, MD 21215 Tel. (301)466-2220

Fifth Episcopal District: Bishop John H. Miller, Springdale Estates, 8605 Caswell Ct., Raleigh, NC 27612 Tel. (919)848-6915

Sixth Episcopal District: Bishop Ruben L. Speaks, 1238 Maxwell St., P.O. Box 986, Salisbury, NC 28144 Tel. (704)637-1471

Seventh Episcopal District: Bishop Herman L. Anderson, 7013 Toby Ct., Charlotte, NC 28213 Tel. (704)598-7419

Eighth Episcopal District: Bishop Cecil Bishop, 5401 Broadwater St., Temple Hill, MD 20748 Tel. (301)894-2165

Ninth Episcopal District: ———-, 607 N. Grand Ave., Ste. 701, St. Louis, MO 63103 Tel. (314)531-1112

Tenth Episcopal District: Bishop Alfred E. White, 10 Hardin Lane, Glastonbury, CT 06033 Tel. (203)633-3089

Eleventh Episcopal District: Bishop George W. Walker, Sr., 3654 Poplar Road, Flossmoor, IL 60422 Tel. (708)799-5599

Twelfth Episcopal District: Bishop Milton A. Williams, 1015 Pineburr Rd., Jamestown, MC 27282 Tel. (919)454-4875

Thirteenth Episcopal District: Bishop S. Chuka Ekemam, Sr., 98 Okigwe Rd., P.O. Box 1149, Owerri, W. Africa, Tel. (083)232-271

PERIODICALS

Star of Zion; Quarterly Review; Missionary Seer; Church School Herald

Albanian Orthodox Archdiocese in America

The Albanian Orthodox Church in America traces its origins to the groups of Albanian immigrants which first arrived in the United States in 1886, seeking religious, cultural, and economic freedoms denied them in the homeland.

In 1908 in Boston, the Rev. Fan Stylian Noli (later Archbishop) served the first liturgy in the Albanian language in 500 years, to which Orthodox Albanians rallied, forming their own diocese in 1919. Parishes began to spring up through New England and the Mid-Atlantic and Great Lakes states. In 1922, clergy from the United States traveled to Albania to proclaim the self-governance of the Orthodox Church in the homeland at the Congress of Berat.

In 1971 the Albanian Archdiocese sought and gained union with the Orthodox Church in America, expressing the desire to expand the Orthodox witness to America at large, giving it an indigenous character. The Albanian Archdiocese remains vigilant for its brothers and sisters in the homeland and serves as an important resource for human rights issues and Albanian affairs, in addition to its programs for youth, theological education, vocational interest programs, and retreats for young adults and women.

HEADQUARTERS

523 E. Broadway, S. Boston, MA 02127
Media Contact, Sec., Ms. Dorothy Adams, Tel. (617)268-1275 Fax (617)268-3184

OFFICERS

Metropolitan Theodosius, 529 E. Broadway, Boston, MA 02127 Tel. (617)268-1275

Chancellor, V. Rev. Arthur E. Liolin, 60 Antwerp St., East Milton, MA 02186 Tel. (617)698-3366

Lay Chpsn., Thomas Sotir, 145 Highland St., Newton, MA 02102 Tel. (617)244-5670

Treas., Ronald Nasson, 26 Enfield St., Jamaica Plains, MA 02130 Tel. (617)522-7715

PERIODICAL

Vineyard (Vreshta), The

Albanian Orthodox Diocese of America

This Diocese was organized in 1950 as a canonical body administering to the Albanian faithful. It is under the ecclesiastical jurisdiction of the Ecumenical Patriarchate of Constantinople (Istanbul).

HEADQUARTERS

2100 S. Stockton Ave., Las Vegas, NV 89104 Tel. (702)457-6443

OFFICER

Vicar General, The Rev. Ik. Ilia Katre

Allegheny Wesleyan Methodist Connection (Original Allegheny Conference)

This body was formed in 1968 by members of the Allegheny Conference (located in eastern Ohio and western Pennsylvania) of the Wesleyan Methodist Church, which merged in 1966 with the Pilgrim Holiness Church to form The Wesleyan Church.

The Allegheny Wesleyan Methodist Connection is composed of persons "having the form and seeking the power of godliness, united in order to pray together, to receive the word of exhortation, and to watch over one another in love, that they may help each other to work out their salvation." There is a strong commitment to congregational government and to holiness of heart and life. There is a strong thrust in church extension within the United States and in missions worldwide.

HEADQUARTERS

1827 Allen Dr., Salem, OH 44460 Tel. (216)337-9376
Media Contact, Pres., Rev. John B. Durfee

OFFICERS

Pres., Rev. John B. Durfee
Vice-Pres., Rev. William Cope, 1231 Conser Dr., Salem, OH 44460
Sec., Rev. W. H. Cornell, Box 266, Sagamore, PA 16250

Treas., Mr. Clair Taylor, 858 E. Philadelphia Ave., Youngstown, OH 44502

PERIODICAL

Allegheny Wesleyan Methodist, The

Amana Church Society

The Amana Church Society was founded by a God-fearing, God-loving, and pioneering group not associated with any other church or organization. It had its beginning as the Community of True Inspiration in 1714 in the province of Hesse, Germany. The members were much persecuted in Germany because of their belief in the "power of divine inspiration," because they would not send their children to the 10 established schools, and because they were pacifistic.

The Community of True Inspiration had its humble beginning under the inspired leadership of Eberhard Ludwig Gruber and Johann Friedrich Rock. Beginning in 1842, Christian Metz, while divinely inspired, led the community to the West and the New World, where they established the Ebenezer Community near Buffalo, N.Y. Because of deterring and worldly influences, the Ebenezer lands were abandoned in 1854. The Amana Colonies were founded in Iowa in 1855.

The Amana Church Society does no proselyting or missionary work. It believes in a peaceful, quiet, "brotherly" way of life. Although many of the stricter church rules have been relaxed over the years, the Amana Church Society maintains its simple, unostentatious churches and rituals. There have been no divinely inspired leaders since the demise of Barbara Landman Heinemann in 1883, but the faith is still paramount in divine revelation of the Word of God through God's chosen representatives, and the testimonies of the aforementioned religious leaders are read in all the regular services. This small group over the years attests to a faith in God that makes the term *Amana* meaningful—"as a rock" or "to remain faithful."

OFFICERS

Pres., Kirk Setzer, Amana, IA 52203 Tel. (319)622-3799
Vice-Pres., Steward Geiger, Cedar Rapids, IA 52203
Sec., Martin Roemig, Amana, IA 52203 Tel. (319)622-3262
Treas., Henry Schiff, Amana, IA 52203

The American Baptist Association

The American Baptist Association (ABA) is an international fellowship of independent Baptist churches voluntarily cooperating in missionary, evangelistic, benevolent, and Christian education activities throughout the world. Its beginnings can be traced to the landmark movement of the 1850s. Led by James R. Graves and J. M. Pendleton, a significant number of Baptist churches in the South, claiming a New Testament heritage, rejected as extrascriptural the policies of the newly formed Southern Baptist Convention (SBC). Because they strongly advocated church equality, many of these churches continued doing mission and benevolent work apart from the SBC, electing to work through local associations. Meeting in Texarkana, Texas, in 1924, messengers from the various churches effectively merged two of these major associations—the Baptist Missionary Association of Texas and the General Association—forming the American Baptist Association.

Since 1924, mission efforts have been supported in Canada, Mexico, Central and South America, Australia, Africa, Europe, Asia, India, New Zealand, Korea, and Japan. An even more successful domestic mission effort has changed the ABA from a predominantly rural southern organization to one with churches in 45 states.

Through its publishing arm in Texarkana, the ABA publishes literature and books numbering into the thousands. Major seminaries include the Missionary Baptist Seminary, founded by Dr. Ben M. Bogard in Little Rock, Arkansas; Texas Baptist Seminary, Henderson, Texas; Oklahoma Missionary Baptist College in Marlow, Oklahoma; and Florida Baptist Schools in Lakeland, Florida.

While no person may speak for the churches of the ABA, all accept the Bible as the inerrant Word of God. They believe Christ was the virgin-born Son of God, that God is a triune God, that the only church is the local congregation of scripturally baptized believers, and that the work of the church is to spread the gospel.

HEADQUARTERS

4605 N. State Line Ave., Texarkana, TX 75503 Tel. (903)792-2783

OFFICERS

Pres., James A. Kirkland, 117 White Oak Rd., White Oak, TX 75693
Vice-Pres.: J. O. Phillips, 107 Woodcliff Ct., Simpsonville, SC 29681; Dr. Don Price, 5300 Stagecoach Rd., Little Rock, AR 72204; Marlin Gipson, 1526 N. Mulberry Ave., Panama City, FL 32405
Rec. Clks.: Larry Clements, P.O. Box 234, Monticello, AR 71655; Gene Smith, 1208 W. 35th St., Pine Bluff, AR 71601
Publications: Ed.-in-Chief, Dr. Bill Johnson, P.O. Box 502, Texarkana, AR 75504; Bus. Mgr., Tom Sannes, Box 1828, Texarkana, AR 75501
Meeting Arrangements, Dir., Edgar N. Sutton, P.O. Box 240, Alexandria, AR 72002
Sec.-Treas., D. S. Madden, P.O. Box 1050, Texarkana, TX 75504

American Baptist Churches in the U.S.A.

Originally known as the Northern Baptist Convention, this body of Baptist churches changed the name to American Baptist Convention in 1950 with a commitment to "hold the name in trust for all Christians of like faith and mind who desire to bear witness to the historical Baptist convictions in a framework of cooperative Protestantism."

In 1972 American Baptist Churches in the U.S.A. was adopted as the new name. Although national missionary organizational developments began in 1814 with the establishment of the American Baptist Foreign Mission Society and continued with the organization of the American Baptist Publication Society in 1824 and the American Baptist Home Mission Society in 1832, the general denominational body was not formed until 1907. American Baptist work at the local level dates back to the organization by Roger Williams of the First Baptist Church in Providence, R. I. in 1638.

OFFICES

P.O. Box 851, Valley Forge, PA 19482 Tel. (215)768-2000 Fax (215)768-2275
Media Contact, Dep. Gen. Sec. for Communication, Philip E. Jenks, Tel. (215)768-2216

US RELIGIOUS BODIES

Pres., James A. Scott
Vice-Pres., Hector M. Gonzales
Budget Review Officer, Dorothy J. Herrin
Gen. Sec., Daniel E. Weiss
Assoc. Gen. Sec.-Treas., Robert J. Allen
National Secs.: Jean B. Kim; Gordon E. Smith; John A. Sundquist; Aidsand F. Wright-Riggins
Office of the General Secretary: Gen. Sec., Daniel E. Weiss; Assoc. Gen. Sec.-Treas., Robert J. Allen; Assoc. Gen. Sec. for Admn. Services, Barbara A. Williams; Dep. Gen. Sec. for Communication, Phillip E. Jenks; Dep. Gen. Sec. for Coop. Christianity, Moley G. Familiaran; Assoc. Gen. Sec. for Regional Ministries, J. Ralph Beaty; Dep. Gen. Sec. for Research & Planning, Richard K. Gladden; Assoc. Gen. Sec. for World Mission Support, Robert H. Roberts

REGIONAL ORGANIZATIONS

Central Region, Am. Bapt. Churches of, Fred W. Thompson, Box 4105, Topeka, KS 66614-4105
Chicago, ABC of Metro, William K. Cober, 28 E. Jackson Blvd., Ste. 210, Chicago, IL 60604-2207
Cleveland Baptist Assoc., Dennis E. Norris, 1737 Euclid Ave., Ste. 603, Cleveland, OH 44115-2141
Connecticut, Am. Bapt. Churches of, Lowell H. Fewster, 100 Bloomfield Ave., Hartford, CT 06105-1097
Dakotas, Am. Bapt. Churches of, Ronald E. Cowles, 1524 S. Summit Ave., Sioux Falls, SD 57105-1697
District of Columbia, Bapt. Conv., W. Jere Allen, 1628 16th St., NW, Washington, DC 20009-3099
Great Rivers Region, ABC of the, Malcolm G. Shotwell, P.O. Box 3786, Springfield, IL 62708-3786
Indiana, Am. Bapt. Churches of, L. Eugene Ton, 1650 N. Delaware St., Indianapolis, IN 46202-2493
Indianapolis, ABC of Greater, Larry D. Sayre, 1350 N. Delaware St., Indianapolis, IN 46202-2493
Los Angeles Bapt. City Mission Soc., Emory C. Campbell, 1212 Wilshire Blvd., Ste. 201, Los Angeles, CA 90017-1902
Maine, Am. Bapt. Churches of, Calvin L. Moon, P.O. Box 667, Augusta, ME 04332-0667
Massachusetts, Am. Bapt. Churches of, Linda C. Spoolstra, 20 Milton St., Dedham, MA 02026-2967
Metropolitan New York, ABC of, Carl E. Flemister, 475 Riverside Dr., Rm. 432, New York, NY 10115-0001
Michigan, Am. Bapt. Churches of, Robert E. Shaw, 4578 S. Hagadorn Rd., East Lansing, MI 48823-5335
Mid-America Bapt. Churches, Telfer L. Epp, Ste. 15, 2400 86th St., Des Moines, IA 50322-4380
Nebraska, Am. Bapt. Churches of, Dennis D. Hatfield, 6404 Maple St., Omaha, NE 68104-4079
New Jersey, Am. Bapt. Churches of, George D. Younger, 161 Freeway Dr. E., East Orange, NJ 07018-4099
New York State, Am. Bapt. Churches of, Sumner M. Grant, 3049 E. Genesee St., Syracuse, NY 13224-1699
Niagara Frontier, ABC of the, Kathryn W. Baker, 1272 Delaware Ave., Buffalo, NY 14209-2496

Northwest, Am. Bapt. Churches of, Gaylord L. Hasselblad, 321 First Ave. W., Seattle, WA 98119-4103
Ohio, Am. Bapt. Churches of, Robert A. Fisher, P.O. Box 376, Granville, OH 43023-0376
Oregon, Am. Bapt. Churches of, James T. Ledbetter, 0245 SW Bancroft St., Ste. G, Portland, OR 97201-4270
Pacific Southwest, ABC of the, W. Lowell Fairley, 970 Village Oaks Dr., Covina, CA 91724-3679
Pennsylvania & Delaware, ABC of, Richard E. Rusbuldt
Philadelphia Baptist Assoc., Larry K. Waltz, 100 N. 17th St., Philadelphia, PA 19103-2736
Pittsburgh Baptist Assoc., Clayton R. Woodbury, 1620 Allegheny Bldg., 429 Forbes Ave., Pittsburgh, PA 15219-1604
Puerto Rico, Bapt. Churches of, E. Yamina Apolinaris, Mayaguez #21, Hato Rey, PR 00917
Rhode Island, Am. Bapt. Churches of, Donald H. Crosby, 734 Hope St., Providence, RI 02906-3535
Rochester/Genessee Region, ABC of, Carrol A. Turner, 151 Brooks Ave., Rochester, NY 14619
Rocky Mountains, Am. Bapt. Churches of, O. Dean Nelson, 1344 Pennsylvania St., Denver, CO 80203-2499
South, Am. Bapt. Churches of the, Walter L. Parrish, II, 525 Main St., Ste. 105, Laurel, MD 20707-4995
Vermont/New Hampshire ABC of, Robert W. Williams, P.O. Box 796, Concord, NH 03302-0796
West, Am. Bapt. Churches of, Robert D. Rasmussen, P.O. Box 23204, Oakland, CA 94623-0204
West Virginia Baptist Convention, Douglas W. Hill, P.O. Box 1019, Parkersburg, WV 26101-1019
Wisconsin, Am. Bapt. Churches of, George E. Daniels, 15330 W. Watertown Plank Rd., Elm Grove, WI 53122-2391

BOARDS

Board of Educational Ministries
Exec. Dir., Jean B. Kim; Treas., Robert J. Allen; Dep. Exec. Dir. for Regional Relations, John L. Carroll; Dir. of Interpretation, Virginia R. Holstrom; Dir. of Planning for Cong. Educ., Linda R. Isham; Educ. for Discipleship, Donald T-M Ng; Fin. & Bus., Robert J. Allen; Judson Press, Kristy Arnesen Pullen; Marketing, Edward Hunter
Officers of the Bd., Pres., Margaret C. Susman; Vice-Pres., Harry F. S. Ng; Rec. Sec., Arthur J. Munson, Jr.
American Baptist Assembly: Green Lake, WI 54941; Pres., Paul W. LaDue; Vice-Pres. for Program, Arlo R. Reichter; Vice-Pres. for Fin., L. B. Standifer, III; Vice-Pres. for Operations, Bradley J. Carroll; Vice-Pres. of Development/Promotion, Ronald W. Newsome
Officers of the Bd., Chpsn., Thomas O. Jones; Vice-Chpsn., J. Ralph Beaty; Treas., William E. Jarvis; Sec., Gloria A. Marshall
American Baptist Historical Society: 1106 S. Goodman St., Rochester, NY 14620;; Admn./Archivist, Beverly C. Carlson; Dir. of Library, James R. Lynch; Pres., John F. Mandt
American Baptist Men: Exec. Dir., Richard S. McPhee; Pres., Harold W. Wolgast
American Baptist Women's Ministries: Exec. Dir., Donna M. Anderson; Pres., Ruth Housam
Commission on the Ministry: Exec. Dir., Craig A. Collemer

Board of International Ministries

Pres., Reid S. Trulson; Vice-Pres., Beverly C. Benton; Exec. Dir., John A. Sundquist; Spec. Asst., Hugh W. Smith; Amer. Bapt. World Relief Officer, Charles W. Sydnor; Budget Dir., Charles H. Stuart

Overseas Division: Dir., Gladys M. Peterson

Area Secs., Africa, Ivan E. George; East Asia & India, Benjamin Shun-Lai; Middle East & Europe, Gladys M. Peterson; Latin America & Caribbean, Victor M. Mercado; Southeast Asia, Keith E. Tennis

Sec. Intl. Issues, Charles W. Sydnor; Sec. for Recruitment & Scholarship, Betty L. Beaman; Public Relations Dir., Corenne Garrison; Sr. Ed. & Dir. of Research, Charlotte Gillespie

Bus. & Fin., Treas. & Dir., Cornelius C. Jones; Assoc. Treas. & Assoc. Dir., Austin B. Windle; Fund Accountant, William F. Bartlett

Board of National Ministries

Pres., Thomas C. Ross, Jr.; Vice-Pres., Bonnie J. Stevens; Exec. Dir., Aidsand F. Wright-Riggins; Sec. to Bd., Susan E. Gillies; Treas., Harold B. Cooper; Mgr., Div. of Congregational Min., Richard D. Sutton; Mgr., Div. of Evangelistic Min., Duncan McIntosh; Mgr., Div. of Corporate Services, Harold B. Cooper; Mgr., Div. of Social Min., Thelma C. Mitchell; Mgr., Div. of Program Services, Susan E. Gillies

Ministers & Missionaries Benefit Board

475 Riverside Dr., New York, NY 10115-0083; Pres., John W. Reed; Vice-Pres., Hella Mears Hueg; Actuary, Hay/Huggins, 229 S. 18th St., Rittenhouse Sq., Philadelphia, PA 19103; Exec. Dir., Gordon E. Smith; Treas., Cheryl H. Wade; Sec., Sara E. Hopkins; Dep. Exec. Dir., Margaret Ann Cowden; Assoc. Exec. Dir., Richard Arnesman; Assoc. Exec. Dir., Terry L. Burch

Minister Council

Dir., Harley D. Hunt

Pres., Wendell A. Johnson

PERIODICALS

American Baptist Quarterly; American Baptist, The

The American Carpatho-Russian Orthodox Greek Catholic Church

The American Carpatho-Russian Orthodox Greek Catholic Church is a self-governing diocese that is in communion with the Ecumenical Partriarchate of Constantinople. The late Patriarch Benjamin I, in an official Patriarchal Document dated Sept. 19, 1938, canonized the Diocese in the name of the Orthodox Church of Christ.

HEADQUARTERS

Johnstown, PA 15906 Tel. (814)536-4207

Media Contact, Chancellor, V. Rev. Msgr. Frank Miloro, 312 Garfield St., Johnstown, PA 15906 Tel. (814)539-8086 Fax (814)536-4699

OFFICERS

Bishop, Rt. Bishop Nicholas (Smisko), 312 Garfield St., Johnstown, PA 15906

Vicar General, V. Rev. Msgr. John Yurcisin, 249 Butler Ave., Johnstown, PA 15906

Chancellor, V. Rev. Msgr. Frank P. Miloro, 312 Garfield St., Johnstown, PA 15906

Treas., V. Rev. Msgr. Ronald A. Hazuda, 115 East Ave., Erie, PA 16503

PERIODICAL

Cerkovnyj Vistnik—Church Messenger

American Evangelical Christian Churches

Founded in 1944, the AECC functions as a denominational body with interdoctrinal views incorporating into its ecclesiastical position both the Calvinistic and Arminian doctrines. The purpose of the organization is the propagation of the gospel through the establishment of churches, missions, and places of worship.

It is not affiliated with any other religious body or organization but seeks fellowship with all who hold to the concepts set forth in the teachings of Jesus the Christ. Ministerial credentials are issued to those approved by the Credentials Committee and who subscribe to the following Articles of faith: the Bible as the written word of God; the Virgin birth; the Deity of Jesus the Christ; salvation through the atonement; the guidance of life through prayer. Its churches operate under the name Community Churches, American Bible Churches, and Evangelical Christian Churches. Each group is an independent sovereign body. An affiliated body operates in the British Isles under the name Ministers of Evangelism.

HEADQUARTERS

P.O. Box 331, Pineland, FL 33945

Media Contact: Natl. Mod., Dr. G. W. Hyatt, Tel. (813)283-6519

OFFICERS

Mod., Dr. G. W. Hyatt

Sec., Dr. Ben Morgan, 64 South St., Southport, IN 46227 Tel. (317)784-9726

American Rescue Workers

Founded in 1884 as a national religious and charitable movement which operates on a quasimilitary basis. Membership includes officers (clergy); soldiers/adherents (laity); members of various activity groups; and volunteers who serve as advisors, associates, and committed participants in ARW service functions.

The American Rescue Workers are a branch of the Christian Church. They are motivated by the love of God and a practical concern for the needs of humanity. The purpose is to preach the gospel, disseminate Christian truths, supply basic personal necessities, provide personal counseling and undertake the spiritual and moral regeneration and physical rehabilitation of all persons in need who come within its sphere of influence regardless of race, color, creed, sex or age.

HEADQUARTERS

2827 Frankford Ave., P.O. Box 4766, Philadelphia, PA 19134 Tel. (215)739-6524

Washington DC Capital Area Office, 716 Ritchie Rd., Capitol Heights, MD 20743 Tel. (301)336-6200

National Field Office, 1209 Hamilton Blvd., Hagerstown, MD 21742 Tel. (301)797-0061

Media Contact, Natl. Info. Dir., Col. Robert N. Coles, Natl. Field Ofc., Fax (301)797-1480

OFFICERS

Commander-In-Chief & Pres. of Corp., General Paul E. Martin

Chief of Staff, Col. Claude S. Astin, Jr.

Natl. Bd. Pres., Col. George B Gossett

39

Special Services/Aide-de-Camp, Col. Robert N. Coles, Natl. Field Ofc.
Natl. Chief Sec., Col. Joyce Gossett

PERIODICAL
Rescue Herald, The

The Anglican Orthodox Church

This body was founded on Nov. 16, 1963, in Statesville, N.C., by the Most Rev. James P. Dees, who was the Presiding Bishop and Metropolitan. The church holds to the Thirty-Nine Articles of Religion, the 1928 Book of Common Prayer, the King James Version of the Bible, and basic Anglican traditions and church government. It upholds biblical morality and emphasizes the fundamental doctrines of the virgin birth, the incarnation, the atoning sacrifice of the cross, the Trinity, the resurrection, the second coming, salvation by faith alone, and the divinity of Christ.

Branches of the worldwide Orthodox Anglican Communion are located in South India, Madagascar, Pakistan, Liberia, Nigeria, the Philippines, the Fiji Islands, South Africa, Kenya, Colombia, and England. The entire membership totals over 300,000.

An active program of Christian education is promoted both in the United States and on a worldwide basis. This includes but is not limited to weekly Sunday School Bible study classes and weekday youth clubs.

The Anglican Orthodox Church operates Cranmer Seminary in Statesville, N.C., to train men for holy orders.

HEADQUARTERS
P.O. Box 128, Statesville, NC 28677 Tel. (704)873-8365
Media Contact, Admn. Asst., Mrs. Betty Hoffman

OFFICER
Presiding Bishop, The Most Rev. George C. Schneller, 323 Walnut St., P.O. Box 128, Statesville, NC 28677 Tel. (704)873-8365

PERIODICAL
News, The

The Antiochian Orthodox Christian Archdiocese of North America

The spiritual needs of Antiochian faithful in North America were first served through the Syro-Arabian Mission of the Russian Orthodox Church in 1892. In 1895, the Syrian Orthodox Benevolent Society was organized by Antiochian immigrants in New York City. Raphael Hawaweeny, a young Damascene clergyman serving as professor of Arabic language at the Orthodox theological academy in Kazan, Russia, came to New York to organize the first Arabic-language parish in North America in 1896, after being canonically received under the omophorion of the head of the Russian Church in North America. Saint Nicholas Cathedral, now located at 355 State St. in Brooklyn, is considered the "mother parish" of the Archdiocese.

On March 12, 1904, Hawaweeny became the first Orthodox bishop to be consecrated in North America. He traveled throughout the continent and established new parishes. The unity of Orthodoxy in the New World, including the Syrian Greek Orthodox community, was ruptured after the death of Bishop Raphael in 1915 and by the Bolshevik revolution in Russia and the First World War.

Unity returned in 1975 when Metropolitan Philip Saliba, of the Antiochian Archdiocese of New York, and Metropolitan Michael Shaheen of the Antiochian archdiocese of Toledo, Ohio, signed the Articles of Reunification, ratified by the Holy Synod of the Patriarchate. Saliba was recognized as the Metropolitan Primate and Shaheen as Auxiliary Archbishop. A second auxiliary to the Metropolitan, Bishop Antoun Khouri, was consecrated at Brooklyn's Saint Nicholas Cathedral, in 1983. A third auxiliary, Bishop Basil Essey, was consecrated at Wichita's St. George Cathedral, in 1992.

The Archdiocesan Board of Trustees (consisting of 50 elected and appointed clergy and lay members) and the Metropolitan's Advisory Council (consisting of clergy and lay representatives from each parish and mission) meet regularly to assist the Primate in the administration of the Archdiocese.

HEADQUARTERS
358 Mountain Rd., Englewood, NJ 07631 Tel. (201)871-1355 Fax (201)871-7954
Media Contact, Vicar, The V. Rev. George S. Corey, 52 78th St., Brooklyn, NY 11209 Tel. (718)748-7940 Fax (718)852-7363

OFFICERS
Primate, Metropolitan Philip Saliba
Auxiliary, Archbishop Michael Shaheen
Auxiliary, Bishop Antoun Khouri
Auxiliary, Bishop Basil Essey

PERIODICAL
Word, The

Apostolic Catholic Assyrian Church of the East, North American Dioceses

The Holy Apostolic Catholic Assyrian Church of the East is the Ancient Christian Church that developed within the Persian Empire from the day of Pentecost. The Apostolic traditions testify that the Church of the East was established by Sts. Perter, Thomas, Thaddaeus and Bartholomew from among the Twelve and by the labors of Mar Mari and Aggai of the Seventy. The Church grew and developed carrying the Christian Gospel into the whole of Asia and Islands of the Pacific. Prior to the Great Persecution at the hands of Tamer'leng the Mongol, it is said to have been the largest Christian church in the world.

The doctrinal identity of the church is that of the Apostles. The church stresses two natures and two Qnume in the One Person, Perfect God-Perfect man. The church gives witness to the original Nicene Creed, the Ecumenical Councils of Nicea and Constantinople, and the church fathers of that era. Since God is revealed as Trinity, the appellation "Mother of God" is rejected for the Ever Virgin Blessed Mary Mother of Christ, rather, she is regarded as "Mother of Emmanuel, God with us."

The church has maintained a line of Catholicos Patriarchs from the time of the Holy Apostles until this present time. Today the present occupant of the Apostolic Throne is His Holiness Mar Dinkha IV, 120th successor to the See of Selucia Ctestiphon.

HEADQUARTERS
Catholicos Patriarch, His Holiness Mar Dinkha, IV, Metropolitanate Residence, The Assyrian Church of the East, Baghdad, Iraq

Media Contact, Chancellor to the Bishop, The Rev. Chancellor C, H. Klutz, 7201 N. Ashland, Chicago, IL 60626 Tel. (312)465-4777 Fax (312)465-0776

BISHOPS
Diocese Eastern USA: His Grace Bishop Mar Aprim Khamis, 8908 Birch Ave., Morton Grove, IL 60053 Tel. (312)465-4777 Fax (708)966-0012

Diocese Western USA: His Grace Bishop Mar Bawai Soro, St. Joseph Cathedral, 680 Minnesota Ave., San Jose, CA 95125 Tel. (408)286-7377 Fax (408)286-1236

Diocese of Canada: His Grace Bishop Mar Emmanuel Joseph, St. Mary Cathedral, 57 Apted Ave., Weston, ON M9L 2P2 Tel. (416)744-9311

PERIODICAL
Qala min M'Dinkha (Voice from the East)

Apostolic Christian Church (Nazarene)

This body was formed in America by an immigration from various European nations, from a movement begun by Rev. S. H. Froehlich, a Swiss pastor, whose followers are still found in Switzerland and Central Europe.

HEADQUARTERS
Apostolic Christian Church Foundation, P.O. Box 151, Tremont, IL 61568

Media Contact, Sec.-Treas., Eugene R. Galat, Tel. (309)925-5162 Fax (309)925-5162

OFFICER
Gen. Sec., Eugene R. Galat

Apostolic Christian Churches of America

The Apostolic Christian Church of America was founded in the early 1830s in Switzerland by Samuel Froehlich, a young divinity student who had experienced a religious conversion based on the pattern found in the New Testament. The church, known then as Evangelical Baptist, spread to surrounding countries. A Froehlich associate, Elder Benedict Weyeneth, established the church's first American congregation in 1847, in upstate New York. In America, where the highest concentration today is in the Midwest farm belt, the church became known as Apostolic Christian.

Church doctrine is based on a literal interpretation of the Bible, the infallible Word of God. The church believes that a true faith in Christ's redemptive work at Calvary is manifested by a sincere repentance and conversion. Members strive for sanctification and separation from worldliness, as a consequence of salvation, not a means to obtain it. Security in Christ is believed to be conditional based on faithfulness. Uniform observance of scriptural standards of holiness are stressed. Holy Communion is confined to members of the church. Male members are willing to serve in the military, but do not bear arms. The holy kiss is practiced and women wear head coverings during prayer and worship.

Doctrinal authority rests with a council of elders, each of whom serves as a local elder (bishop). Both elders and ministers are chosen from local congregations, do not attend seminary, and serve without compensation. Sermons are delivered extemporaneously as led by the Holy Spirit, using the Bible as a text.

HEADQUARTERS
3420 N. Sheridan Rd., Peoria, IL 61604

Media Contact, Sec., Dale R. Eisenmann, 6913 Wilmette, Darien, IL 60559 Tel. (708)969-7021

SECRETARY
Elder (Bishop) Dale Eisenmann, 6913 Wilmette, Darien, IL 60559 Tel. (708)969-7021

Apostolic Faith Mission Church of God

The Apostolic Faith Mission Church of God was founded and organized July 10, 1906, by Bishop F. W. Williams in Mobile, Ala.

Bishop Williams was saved and filled with the Holy Ghost at a revival in Los Angeles under Elder W. J. Seymour of The Divine Apostolic Faith Movement. After being called into the ministry, Bishop Williams went out to preach the gospel in Mississippi, then moved on to Mobile.

On Oct. 9, 1915, the Apostolic Faith Mission Church of God was incorporated in Mobile under Bishop Williams, who was also the general overseer of this church.

HEADQUARTERS
Ward's Temple, 806 Muscogee Rd., Cantonment, FL 32533

Media Contact, Natl. Sunday School Supt., Elder Thomas Brooks, 3298 Toney Dr., Decatur, GA 30032 Tel. (404)284-7596

OFFICERS
Board of Bishops: Presiding Bishop, Houston Ward, P.O. Box 551, Cantonment, FL 39533 Tel. (904)587-2339; Billy Carter; J. L. Smiley; T. L. Frye; D. Brown; T. C. Tolbert

NATIONAL DEPARTMENTS
Missionary Dept., Pres., Sr. Sarah Ward, Cantonment, FL

Youth Dept., Pres., W. J. Wills, Lincoln, AL

Sunday School Dept., Supt., Thomas Brooks, Decatur, GA

Mother Dept., Pres., Mother Juanita Phillips, Birmingham, AL

Apostolic Faith Mission of Portland, Oregon

The Apostolic Faith Mission of Portland, Oregon, was founded in 1907. It had its beginning in the Latter Rain outpouring on Azusa Street in Los Angeles in 1906.

Some of the main doctrines are justification by faith; spiritual new birth, as Jesus told Nicodemus and as Martin Luther proclaimed in the Great Reformation; sanctification, a second definite work of grace, the Wesleyan teaching of holiness, which Jesus prayed for people to have in John 17; the baptism of the Holy Ghost as experienced on the Day of Pentecost, and again poured out at the beginning of the Latter Rain revival in Los Angeles.

Mrs. Florence L. Crawford, who had received the baptism of the Holy Ghost in Los Angeles, brought this Latter Rain message to Portland on Christmas Day, 1906. It has spread to the world by means of literature which is still published and mailed everywhere without a subscription price. Collections are never taken in the meetings and the public is not asked for money.

Camp meetings have been held annually in Portland, Ore., since 1907, with delegations coming from around the world.

US RELIGIOUS BODIES

Missionaries from the Portland headquarters have established churches in Korea, Japan, the Philippines and many countries in Africa.

HEADQUARTERS
6615 SE 52nd Ave., Portland, OR 97206 Tel. (503)777-1741 Fax (503)777-1743
Media Contact, Gen. Overseer, Loyce C. Carver

OFFICER
Gen. Overseer, Rev. Loyce C. Carver

PERIODICAL
Light of Hope, The

Apostolic Lutheran Church of America

Organized in 1872 as the Solomon Korteniemi Lutheran Society, this Finnish body was incorporated in 1929 as the Finnish Apostolic Lutheran Church in America and changed its name to Apostolic Lutheran Church of America in 1962.

This body stresses preaching the Word of God and there is an absence of liturgy and formalism in worship. A seminary education is not required of pastors. Being called by God to preach the Word is the chief requirement for clergy and laity. The church stresses personal absolution and forgiveness of sins, as practiced by Martin Luther, and the importance of bringing converts into God's kingdom.

HEADQUARTERS
Rt 1 Box 462, Houghton, MI 49931 Tel. (906)482-8269
Media Contact, Sec., James Johnson

OFFICERS
Pres., Rev. Ralph Davidson, Rt. 1, 66 Keinanen Rd., Moose Lake, MN 03452
Sec., James Johnson, Rt. 1, Box 462, Houghton, MI 49931
Treas., Rev. Richard Barney, 3952 10th Ln., Anoka, MN 55303

PERIODICAL
Christian Monthly

Apostolic Overcoming Holy Church of God, Inc.

The Right Rev. William Thomas Phillips (1893-1973) was thoroughly convinced in 1912 that Holiness was a system through which God wanted him to serve. In 1916 he was led to Mobile, Ala., where he organized the Ethiopian Overcoming Holy Church of God. On April 1, 1941, the church was incorporated in Alabama under its present title.

Each congregation manages its own affairs, united under districts governed by overseers and diocesan bishops, and assisted by an executive board comprised of bishops, ministers, laymen, and the National Secretary. The General Assembly convenes annually (June 1-10).

The church's chief objective is to enlighten people of God's holy Word and to be a blessing to every nation. The main purpose of this church is to ordain elders, appoint pastors, and send out divinely called missionaries and teachers. This church enforces all ordinances enacted by Jesus Christ. The church believes in water baptism (Acts 2:38, 8:12, and 10:47); administers the Lord's Supper; observes the washing of feet (John 13:4-7); believes that Jesus Christ shed his blood to sanctify the people and cleanse them from all sin; and believes in the resurrection of the dead and the second coming of Christ.

HEADQUARTERS
1120 N. 24th St., Birmingham, AL 35234
Media Contact, Natl. Exec. Sec., Juanita R. Arrington, Tel. (205)324-2202

OFFICERS
Senior Bishop & Exec. Head, Rt. Rev. Jasper Roby
Associate Bishops: G. W. Ayers, 2257 St. Stephens Rd., Mobile, AL 36617; L. M. Bell, 2000 Pio Nono Ave., Macon, GA 31206; Gabriel Crutcher, 526 E. Bethune St., Detroit, MI 48202; John Mathews, 12 College St., Dayton, OH 45407; Bishop Joe Bennett, 15718 Drexel Ave., Dalton, IL 60419
Exec. Sec., Mrs. Juanita R. Arrington

Armenian Apostolic Church of America

Widespread movement of the Armenian people over the centuries caused the development of two seats of religious jurisdiction of the Armenian Apostolic Church in the World: the See of Etchmiadzin, now in Soviet Armenia, and the See of Cilicia, in Lebanon.

In America, the Armenian Church functioned under the jurisdiction of the Etchmiadzin See from 1887 to 1933, when a division occurred within the American diocese over the condition of the church in Soviet Armenia. One group chose to remain independent until 1957, when the Holy See of Cilicia agreed to accept them under its jurisdiction.

Despite the existence of two dioceses in North America, the Armenian Church has always functioned as one church in dogma and liturgy.

HEADQUARTERS
138 E. 39th St., New York, NY 10016 Tel. (212)689-7810 Fax (212)689-7168
Media Contact, Exec. Dir., Vasken Ghougassian

OFFICERS
Eastern Prelacy, Prelate, Archbishop Mesrob Ashjian
Western Prelacy, Prelate, Archbishop Datev Sarkissian, 4401 Russell Ave., Los Angeles, CA 90026 Fax (213)663-0438
Eastern Prelacy, Chpsn., Nerses Chitjian
Western Prelacy, Chpsn., Vatché Madenlian
Exec. Dir, Vasken Ghougassian

DEPARTMENTS
AREC, Armenian Religious Educ. Council, Exec. Coord., Deacon Shant Kazanjian
ANEC, Armenian National Educ. Council, Exec. Coord., Hourig Sahagian-Papazian

PERIODICAL
Outreach

Armenian Church of America, Diocese of the

The Armenian Apostolic Church was founded at the foot of the biblical mountain of Ararat in the ancient land of Armenia, where Saints Thaddeus and Bartholomew preached Christianity. In A.D. 301 the historic Mother Church of Etchmiadzin was built by Saint Gregory the Illuminator, the first Catholicos of All Armenians. This cathedral still stands and serves as the center of the Armenian Church. A branch of this Church was established in North America in 1889 and the first Armenian Diocese was set up in 1898 by the then-Catholicos of All Armenians, Khrimian Hairig. Armenian immigrants built the first Armenian church in the new world in Worcester, Mass., under the jurisdiction of Holy Etchmiadzin.

In 1927, the churches and the parishes in California were formed into a Western Diocese and the parishes in Canada formed their own diocese in 1984. The Armenian Apostolic Church also includes the Catholicate of Cilicia, now located in Lebanon, the Armenian Patriarchate of Jerusalem and the Armenian Patriarchate of Constantinople.

HEADQUARTERS

Eastern Diocese: 630 Second Ave., New York, NY 10016 Tel. (212)686-0710 Fax (212)779-3558
Western Diocese: 1201 N. Vine St., Hollywood, CA 90038 Tel. (213)466-5265
Canadian Diocese: 615 Stuart Ave., Outremont, QU H2V 3H2 Tel. (514)276-9479 Fax (514)276-9960
Media Contact, Dir., Zohiab Information Ctr., V. Rev. Fr. Krikor Maksoudian, Eastern Diocese Ofc.

OFFICERS

Eastern Diocese
Primate, His Eminence Bishop Khajag Barsamian, Eastern Diocese Ofc.
Vicar Gen., V. Rev. Fr. Haigazoun Najarian, Eastern Diocese Ofc.
Diocesan Council, Chpsn., Vincent Gurahian, Macauley Rd., RFD 2, Katonah, NY 10536
Diocesan Council, Sec., Edward Onanian, 13010 Hathaway Dr., Wheaton, MD 20906
Western Diocese
Primate, His Em. Archbishop Vatche Hovsepian, Western Diocese Ofc.
Diocesan Council, Chpsn., The Rev. Fr. Vartan Kasparian, St. Mary Armenian Church, P.O. Box 367, Yettem, CA 93670
Diocesan Council, Sec., Armen Hampar, 6134 Pat Ave., Woodland Hills, CA 91367
Canadian Diocese
Primate, HIs Eminence Bishop Hovanan Derderian, Canadian Diocese Ofc.

PERIODICALS

Mother Church, The

Assemblies of God

From a few hundred delegates at its founding convention in 1914 at Hot Springs, Ark., the Assemblies of God has become one of the largest church groups in the modern Pentecostal movement worldwide. Throughout its existence it has emphasized the power of the Holy Spirit to change lives and the participation of all members in the work of the church.

The revival that led to the formation of the Assemblies of God and numerous other church groups early in the 20th century began during times of intense prayer and Bible study. Believers in the United States and around the world received spiritual experiences like those described in the Book of Acts. Accompanied by baptism in the Holy Spirit and its initial physical evidence of "speaking in tongues," or a language unknown to the person, their experiences were associated with the coming of the Holy Spirit at Pentecost (Acts 2), so participants were called Pentecostals.

Along with the baptism in the Holy Spirit, the church also believes that the Bible is God's infallible Word to man, that salvation is available only through Jesus Christ, that divine healing is made possible through Christ's suffering, and that Christ will return again for those who love him. In recent years, this Pentecostal revival has spilled over into almost every denomination in a new wave of revival sometimes called the charismatic renewal.

Assemblies of God leaders credit their church's rapid and continuing growth to its acceptance of the New Testament as a model for the present-day church. Aggressive evangelism and missionary zeal at home and abroad characterize the denomination.

Assemblies of God believers observe two ordinances—water baptism by immersion and the Lord's Supper, or Holy Communion. The church is trinitarian, holding that God exists in three persons, Father, Son, and Holy Spirit.

HEADQUARTERS

1445 Boonville Ave., Springfield, MO 65802 Tel. (417)862-2781 Fax (417)862-8558
Media Contact, Sec. of Information, Juleen Turnage

EXECUTIVE PRESBYTERY

Gen. Supt., G. Raymond Carlson
Asst. Supt., Everett R. Stenhouse
Gen. Sec., Joseph R. Flower
Gen. Treas., Thomas E. Trask
Foreign Missions, Exec. Dir., Loren O. Triplett
Great Lakes, Robert K. Schmidgall, P.O. Box 296-1155, Aurora Ave., Naperville, IL 60540
Gulf, Phillip Wannenmacher, 1301 N. Boonville, Springfield, MO 65802
North Central, Herman H. Rohde, 1351 Portland Ave. S, Minneapolis, MN 55404
Northeast, Almon Bartholomew, P.O. Box 39, Liverpool, NY 13088
Northwest, R. L. Brandt, 1702 Colton Blvd., Billings, MT 59102
South Central, Paul Lowenberg, 6015 E. Ninth St., Wichita, KS 67208
Southeast, J. Foy Johnson, P.O. Box 24687, Lakeland, FL 33801
Southwest, Glen D. Cole, 9470 Micron Rd., Sacramento, CA 95827

INTERNATIONAL HEADQUARTERS

General Supt.'s Office Administration
Gen. Supt., G. Raymond Carlson
Spiritual Life-Evangelism: Promotions Coord., Helen Braxton; Evangelists Rep., Charles T. Crabtree; Conference & Convention Coord., John V. Ohlin
Decade of Harvest, U.S. Dir., Charles T. Crabtree
Personnel Mgr., Arlyn Pember
Gen. Services Admn., Clyde Hawkins
Buildings & Properties Admn., Melvin Sachs
Legal Counselor, Richard R. Hammar
Research Sec., Norma Thomas
Gen. Secretary's Office Adminstration
Gen. Sec., Joseph R. Flower
Secretariat Supervisor, Linda Reece
Statistician, Sherri Doty
A/G Archives: Dir. of Archives, Wayne Warner; Achives Asst., Joyce Lee
Division of the Treasury: Gen. Treas., Thomas E. Trask; Admn., Clyde L. Hawkins
Stewardship Dept.: Deferred Giving & Trusts, Sec., Mel DeVries; Regional Consultants, David Bowman; Sam Hamilton; Troy Lyon; Promotion Coord., Freda Jackson
Finance Dept.: Admn. of Accounting Services, Kenneth Tripp
Benevolences Dept.: Sec., Stanley V. Michael; Field Rep. & Church Relations Coord., Robert Bornert; Promotions Coord./Ed., Owen Wilkie

Church Loan Dept.: Sec., Glenn A. Renick, Jr.; Field Rep., Phil Illum
Division of Christian Education
Natl. Dir., ——-
Sun. School Curr. & Lit. Dept.: Ed., Gary Legget; Adult Ed., Paul Smith; Youth Ed., Tammy Bicket; Elementary Ed., Sinda Zinn; Early Childhood Ed., Dawn Hartman; Children's Church Ed., Deanna Harris; Special Proj. Ed., Lorraine Mastrorio; Spanish Ed., Camilo Hernandez
Sun. School Promotion & Training Dept.: Sec., George Edgerly; Adult Min. Consultant, William Campbell
Nontraditional Ed. Dept., Promotion Coord./Ed., Melinda Booze
Post Secondary Ed. Dept., Sec., Dayton Kingsriter
Division of Christian Higher Education
Natl. Dir., David Bundrick
Sunday School Lit. Sales Dept.: Sec., David L. Houghton
Sun. School Promotion & Training Dept.: Admn. & Dist. Liaison Consultant, Efraim Espinoza; Publ. Ed. & Training Coord., Sulvia Lee; Growth & Admn. Consultant, Steven R. Mills; BGMC Coord., Sandra K. Askew; Early Childhood Consultant, Sharon Ellard
Division of Church Ministries
Natl. Dir., Terry Raburn
Men's Ministries Dept. Sec., Ken Riemenschneider
Light-for-the-Lost Sec., Billy J. Strickland
Royal Ranger Natl. Deputy Commander, Ken Hunt
Deputy Commander, Paul Stanek
Editor of Publications, Jim Erdman
Music Dept.: Sec., Dan Crace; Music Ed./Promotions Coord., Carmen Wassam; Senior Ed./Comp./Arranger/Prod., Randy Wright
Women's Ministries Dept.: Sec., Sandra Clopine; Publ. Coord., Aleda Swartzendruber; Missionettes Coord., Linda Upton; Training Coord., Joanne Ohlin; Ofc. of Fin./Field Serv. Coord., Karlene Gannon
Youth Dept.: Sec., Dick VanHuss; AIM/High School Ministries Rep., James Wellborn; Disciplineship/Fine Arts Fest./Bible Quiz Rep., Jeff Swaim; Speed-the-Light Field Rep., Brenton Osgood; Ed. of Youth Publications, Thomas Young
Division of Communications
Natl. Dir., ——-
Advance Magazine, Ed., Harris Jansen
Cardone Media Center, Mgr., Vincent Crunk
Office of Information: Sec., Juleen Turnage; Coord. of District/Church Relations, Richard Knoth; Promotions/Prod. Coord., Rick Griepp
Radio & Television Dept.: Broadcast Speaker, Dan Betzer; Sec., Don Upton; Publicity Dir., Stephen J. Vaudrey; Revivaltime Choir Dir., Cyril A. McLellan
Pentecostal Evangel Magazine: Ed., Richard G. Champion; Man. Ed., John Maempa; Tech. & News Ed., Ann Floyd; News Ed., Gary Spear
Division of Foreign Missions
Exec. Dir., Loren O. Triplett
Admn. Asst., Norman L. Correll
Foreign Field Dirs.: Africa, Donald R. Corbin; Eurasia, Jerry L. Parsley; Asia/Pacific, Robert W. Houlihan; Latin American & Caribbean, John Bueno
Foreign Miss. Communication, Sec., Ron Barefield
Foreign Miss. Fin., Sec., Jerry L. Burgess
Publications, Sec., Joyce Wells Booze

Foreign Miss. Personnel, Sec., Cary Tidwell
Foreign Miss. Relations in U.S., Sec., H. H. De-Ment
Missionary Research, Sec., Ronald Iwasko
Life Publishers, Pres., Bob D. Hoskins
Intl. Correspondence Inst., Pres., George M. Flattery
Intl. Media Ministries, Coord., David Lee
Center for Muslim Ministries, Coord., Delmar Kingsriter
HealthCare Ministries, Dr. Paul Williams
Division of Home Missions
Natl. Dir., Charles Hackett
Admn. Coord., Faith Hamilton
College Ministries Dept., Sec., Dennis Gaylor
Chaplaincy Dept.: Comm. of Chaplains, Chpsn., G. Raymond Carlson; Sec., Lemuel McElyea
New Church Evangelism Dept., Sec., Harvey Meppelink
Intercultural Min. Dept.: Sec., James Kessler
Blind & Handicapped Ministries, Rep., Richard Marchand
Deaf Ministries, Rep., Albert Linderman
Native American Min., Rep., William Lee
Black Min., Rep., Robert Harrison
Teen Challenge Dept., Sec., Herb Meppelink
Divison of Publication (Gospel Publishing House)
Natl. Dir., Joseph Kilpatrick
Production Dept., Mgr., Merrell Cooper
Marketing Services, Mgr., Thomas F. Sanders
Marketing Sales, Mgr., Joseph Kilpatrick

PERIODICALS

Fellowscript; High Adventure; Missionettes Memos; Mountain Movers; Paraclete; Pentecostal Evangel; Sunday School Counselor; Woman's Touch

Assemblies of God International Fellowship (Independent/Not affiliated)

April 9, 1906 is the date commonly accepted by Pentecostals as the 20th-century outpouring of God's spirit in America, which began in a humble gospel mission at 312 Azusa Street in Los Angeles.

This spirit movement spread across the United States and gave birth to the Independent Assemblies of God (Scandinavian). Early pioneers instrumental in guiding and shaping the fellowship of ministers and churches into a nucleus of independent churches included Pastor B. M. Johnson, founder of Lakeview Gospel Church in 1911; Rev. A. A. Holmgren, a Baptist minister who received his baptism of the Holy Spirit in the early Chicago outpourings and was publisher of Sanningens Vittne, a voice of the Scandinavian Independent Assemblies of God, and also served as secretary of the fellowship for many years; Gunnar Wingren, missionary pioneer in Brazil; and Arthur F. Johnson, who served for many years as chairman of the Scandinavian Assemblies.

In 1935, the Scandinavian group dissolved its incorporation and united with the Independent Assemblies of God of the U.S. and Canada which by majority vote of members formed a new corporation, Assemblies of God International Fellowship (Independent/Not Affiliated).

HEADQUARTERS
8504 Commerce Ave., San Diego, CA 92121 Tel. (619)530-1727 Fax (619)530-1543
Media Contact, Exec. Dir. & Ed., Rev. T. A. Lanes

Exec. Dir., Rev. T. A. Lanes
Vice-Pres., Rev. Winston Mattsson-Boze
Sec., Rev. Clair Hutchins
Treas., Dr. Joseph Bohac
Canada, Sec., Harry Nunn, Sr., 15 White Crest Ct.,
St. Catherines, ON 62N 6Y1

PERIODICAL

Fellowship Magazine, The

Associate Reformed Presbyterian Church (General Synod)

The Associate Reformed Presbyterian Church (General Synod) stems from the 1782 merger of Associate Presbyterians and Reformed Presbyterians. In 1822, the Synod of the Carolinas broke with the Associate Reformed Church (which eventually became part of the United Presbyterian Church of North America).

The story of the Synod of the Carolinas began with the Seceder Church, formed in Scotland in 1733 and representing a break from the established Church of Scotland. Seceders, in America called Associate Presbyterians, settled in South Carolina following the Revolutionary War. They were joined by a few Covenanter congregations, which, along with the Seceders, had protested Scotland's established church. The Covenanters took their name from the Solemn League and Covenant of 1643, the guiding document of Scotch Presbyterians. In 1790, some Seceders and Covenanters formed the Presbytery of the Carolinas and Georgia at Long Cane, South Carolina. Thomas Clark and John Boyse led in the formation of this presbytery, a unit within the Associate Reformed Presbyterian Church. The presbytery represented the southern segment of that church.

In 1822 the southern church became independent of the northern Associate Reformed Presbyterian Church and formed the Associate Reformed Presbyterian Church of the South. "Of the South" was dropped in 1858 when the northern group joined the United Presbyterian Church and "General Synod" was added in 1935. The General Synod is the denomination's highest court; it is composed of all the teaching elders and at least one ruling elder from each congregation.

Doctrinally, the church holds to the Westminster Confession of Faith. Liturgically, the synod has been distinguished by its exclusive use of psalmody; in 1946 this practice became optional.

HEADQUARTERS

Associate Reformed Presbyterian Center, One Cleveland St., Greenville, SC 29601 Tel. (803)232-8297
Media Contact, Prin. Clk., Rev. C. Ronald Beard, D.D., 3132 Grace Hill Rd., Columbia, SC 29204 Tel. (803)787-6370

OFFICERS

Mod., Rev. James T. Corbitt, 215 Chateau Dr., Greenville, SC 29615
Principal Clk., Rev. C. Ronald Beard, D.D., 3132 Grace Hill Rd., Columbia, SC 29204

AGENCIES AND INSTITUTIONS

Ofc. of Admn. Services, Dir., Mr. Ed Hogan
Assoc. Reformed Presb. Foundation, Inc.
Assoc. Reformed Presb. Retirement Plan
Ofc. Of Christian Education, Dir., Rev. J. B. Hendrick

Ofc. of Church Extension, Dir., Rev. W. C. Lauderdale
Ofc. of Synod's Treasurer, Mr. W. Herman Lesslie
Ofc. of Secretary of World Witness, Exec. Sec., John E. Mariner, Tel. (803)233-5226
Bonclarken Assembly, Dir., Mr. James T. Brice, 500 Pine St., Flat Rock, NC 28731 Tel. (704)692-2223

PERIODICALS

Associate Reformed Presbyterian, The; Adult Quarterly, The

Bahá'í Faith

The Bahá'í Faith is an independent world religion with adherents in virtually every country. Bahá'ís are followers of Bahá'u'lláh (1817-1892). The religion upholds the basic principles of the oneness of God, the oneness of religion, and the oneness of humankind. The central aim of the Bahá'í Faith is the unification of mankind.

The Bahá'í administrative order consists of elected local Spiritual Assemblies, National Spiritual Assemblies and the Universal House of Justice. The Local and National Spiritual Assemblies are elected annually. The Universal House of Justice is elected every five years. There are 165 National Assemblies and approximately 20,000 local Spiritual Assemblies worldwide. Literature of the Bahá'í Faith has been published in 802 languages.

The period from April 21, 1992 to April 20, 1993 has been designated a Holy Year by the Bahá'í Faith. The Holy Year commemorates the centenary of the passing of Bahá'u'lláh, the Prophet-Founder of the religion.

HEADQUARTERS

National Spiritual Assembly, 536 Sheridan Rd., Wilmette, IL 60091 Tel. (708)869-9039 Fax (708)869-0247
Media Contact, Dir., Ofc. of Information, Ronald B. Precht

OFFICERS

Chpsn., Judge James Nelson
Sec. Gen., Robert Henderson
Sec. for External Affairs, Firuz Kazemzadeh

Baptist Bible Fellowship International

Organized on May 24, 1950 in Fort Worth, Texas, the Baptist Bible Fellowship was founded by about 100 pastors and lay people who had grown disenchanted with the policies and leadership of the World Fundamental Baptist Missionary Fellowship, an outgrowth of the Baptist Bible Union formed in Kansas City in 1923 by fundamentalist leaders from the Southern Baptist, Northern Baptist, and Canadian Baptist Conventions. The BBF elected W. E. Dowell as its first president and established offices and a three-year (now four-year with a graduate school) Baptist Bible College.

The BBF statement of faith was essentially that of the Baptist Bible Union, adopted in 1923, a variation of the New Hampshire Confession of Faith. It presents an infallible Bible, belief in the substitutionary death of Christ, his physical resurrection, and his premillennial return to earth. It advocates local church autonomy and strong pastoral leadership and maintains that the fundamental basis of fellowship is a missionary outreach. The BBF vigorously stresses evangelism and the international missions office reports 782 adult missionaries working on 83 fields throughout the world in 1991.

There are BBF-related churches in every state of the United States, with special strength in the upper South, the Great Lakes region, southern states west of the Mississippi, Kansas, and California. There are six related colleges and one graduate school or seminary.

A Committee of Forty-Five, elected by pastors and churches within the states, sits as a representative body, meeting in three subcommittees, each chaired by one of the principal officers: an administration committee chaired by the president; a missions committee chaired by a vice-president; an education committee chaired by a vice-president.

HEADQUARTERS

Baptist Bible Fellowship Missions Bldg., 720 E. Kearney St., Springfield, MO 65803 Tel. (417)862-5001 Fax (417)865-0794

Mailing Address, P.O. Box 191, Springfield, MO 65801

OFFICERS

Pres., Parker Dailey, Blue Ridge

First Vice-Pres., Jack Baskin, Western Hills Baptist Church, 700 Mars Hill Rd., NW, Kennesaw, GA 30144

Second Vice-Pres., Don Elmore, Temple Baptist Church, P.O. Box 292, Springdale, AR 72764

Sec., K. B. Murray, Millington Street Baptist Church, Box 524, Winfield, KS 67156

Treas., Billy Hamm, Mtn. States Baptist Temple, 8333 Acoma Way, Denver, CO 80221

Mission Dir., Dr. Bob Baird, P.O. Box 191, Springfield, MO 65801

PERIODICALS

Baptist Bible Tribune, The; Preacher, The

Baptist General Conference

The Baptist General Conference, rooted in the pietistic movement of Sweden during the 19th century, traces its history to Aug. 13, 1852. On that day a small group of believers at Rock Island, Ill., under the leadership of Gustaf Palmquist, organized the first Swedish Baptist Church in America. Swedish Baptist churches flourished in the upper Midwest and Northeast, and by 1879, when the first annual meeting was held in Village Creek, Iowa, 65 churches had been organized, stretching from Maine to the Dakotas and south to Kansas and Missouri.

By 1871, John Alexis Edgren, an immigrant sea captain and pastor in Chicago, had begun the first publication and a theological seminary. The Conference grew to 324 churches and nearly 26,000 members by 1902, to 40,000 in 1945, and 135,000 in 1982.

Many churches began as Sunday schools. The seminary evolved into Bethel, a four-year liberal arts college with 1,800 students, and the theological seminary in Arden Hills, Minn.

Missions and the planting of churches have been main objectives both in America and overseas. Today churches have been established in the United States, Canada and Mexico, as well as a dozen countries overseas. In 1985 the churches of Canada founded an autonomous denomination, The Baptist General Conference of Canada.

The Baptist General Conference is a member of the Baptist World Alliance, the Baptist Joint Committee on Public Affairs, and the National Association of Evangelicals. It is characterized by the balancing of a conservative doctrine with an irenic and cooperative spirit. Its basic objective is to seek the fulfillment of the Great Commission and the Great Commandment.

HEADQUARTERS

2002 S. Arlington Heights Rd., Arlington Heights, IL 60005 Tel. (708)228-0200 Fax (708)228-5376

Media Contact, Exec. Vice-Pres., C. Herbert Hage

OFFICERS

Pres. & Chief Exec. Officer, Dr. Robert S. Ricker

OTHER ORGANIZATIONS

Business & Planning, Vice-Pres., Rev. C. Herbert Hage

Bd. of Home Missions, Exec. Dir., Dr. John C. Dickau

Bd. of World Missions, Exec. Dir., Rev. Herbert Skoglund

Bd. of Regents: Bethel College & Seminary, Pres., Dr. George Brushaber, 3900 Bethel Dr., St. Paul, MN 55112

PERIODICAL

Standard, The

Baptist Missionary Association of America

A group of regular Baptist churches organized in associational capacity in May, 1950, in Little Rock, Ark., as the North American Baptist Association. The name changed in 1969 to Baptist Missionary Association of America. There are several state and numerous local associations of cooperating churches. In theology, these churches are evangelical, missionary, fundamental, and, in the main, premillennial.

OFFICERS

Pres., Rev. Vernon R. Lee, 4621 Hillsboro St., El Dorado, AR 71730

Vice-Pres.: Rev. Jerry L. Burnaman, 220 S. Market St., Carthage, TX 75633; Charles R. Curtman, 6299 Miller Rd., Swartz Creek, MI 48473

Rec. Sec.: Rev. Ralph Cottrell, P.O. Box 1203, Van, TX 75790; Rev. O. D. Christian, Rt. 1, Box 267, Streetman, TX 75859; G. H. Gordon, 3202 W. 7th St., Hattiesburg, MS 39401

DEPARTMENTS

Missions: Gen. Sec., Rev. F. Donald Collins, 721 Main St., Little Rock, AR 72201

Publications: Ed.-in-Chief, Rev. James L. Silvey, 1319 Magnolia, Texarkana, TX 75501

Christian Education: Bapt. Missionary Assoc. Theological Sem., Pres., Dr. Phillip R. Bryan, Seminary Heights, 1410 E. Pine St., Jacksonville, TX 75766; Dean, Wilbur Benningfield

Baptist News Service: Dir., Rev. James C. Blaylock, P.O. Box 97, Jacksonville, TX 75766; Asst., Rev. Douglas A. Wilson, P.O. Box 97, Jacksonville, TX 75766

LifeWord Broadcast Ministries: Dir., Rev. George Reddin, P.O. Box 6, Conway, AR 72032

Armed Forces Chaplaincy: Exec. Dir., William Charles Pruitt, Jr., P.O. Box 912, Jacksonville, TX 75766

National Youth Department: Bobby Tucker, P.O. Box 3376, Texarkana, TX 75504

Daniel Springs Encampment: James Speer, P.O. Box 310, Gary, TX 75643

Ministers Benefit Dept.: James A. Henry, 4001 Jefferson St., Texarkana, AR 75501

Baptist Missionary Assoc. Brotherhood: Pres., Randy Boyd, Rt. 2, Box 520, Warren, AR 71671

National Women's Missionary Auxiliary: Pres., Barbara White, P.O. Box 1583, Nashville, AR 71852

PERIODICALS

Advancer, The; Gleaner, The; Baptist Progress; Baptist Trumpet; Baptist Herald; Advocate, The; Midwest Missionary Baptist; Northwest Profile

Beachy Amish Mennonite Churches

This group originates mostly from the Old Order Amish Mennonite Church.

Two congregations had been formed as early as 1927, but the others have all been organized since 1938.

Worship is held in meeting houses. Nearly all have Sunday schools, many have prayer meetings, and most of them either sponsor or have access to Christian day schools. They sponsor evangelical missions at home and abroad; a monthly magazine, *Calvary Messenger,* as an evangelical and doctrinal witness; and Calvary Bible School, nine weeks each winter, for an in-depth study of the Word of God to better equip their youth for Christian service.

Churches: 99; Inclusive Membership: 6,872; Sunday or Sabbath Schools: 99; Total Enrollment: N.R.; Ordained Clergy: 376

INFORMATION

Ervin N. Hershberger, R. D. 1, Meyersdale, PA 15552. Tel. (814)662-2483

Berean Fundamental Church

Founded 1932 in North Platte, Neb., this body emphasizes conservative Protestant doctrines.

HEADQUARTERS

Lincoln, NE 68506 Tel. (402)483-6512

OFFICERS

Pres., Rev. Curt Lehman, 6400 South 70th St., Lincoln, NE 68516 Tel. (402)483-4840

Vice-Pres., Rev. Richard Cocker, 419 Lafayette Blvd., Cheyenne, WY 82009 Tel. (307)635-5914

Sec., Rev. Frank Van Campen, P.O. Box 1136, Chadron, NE 69337 Tel. (308)432-4272

Tres., Virgil Wiebe, P.O. Box 6103, Lincoln, NE 68506

Founder Advisor to the Council, Dr. Ivan E. Olsen

Exec. Advisor, Rev. Carl M. Goltz, P.O. Box 397, North Platte, NE 69103 Tel. (308)532-6723

The Bible Church of Christ, Inc.

The Bible Church of Christ was founded on March 1, 1961 by Bishop Roy Bryant, Sr. Since that time, the Church has grown to include congregations in the United States, Africa, and India. The church is trinitarian and accepts the Bible as the divinely inspired Word of God. Its doctrine includes miracles of healing and the baptism of the Holy Ghost.

HEADQUARTERS

1358 Morris Ave., Bronx, NY 10456 Tel. (212)588-2284

Media Contact, Pres., Bishop Roy Bryant, Sr.

OFFICERS

Pres., Bishop Roy Bryant, Sr., 3033 Gunther Ave., Bronx, NY 10469 Tel. (212)379-8080

Vice-Pres., Bishop Roy Bryant, Jr., 34 Tuxedo Rd., Montclair, NJ 07042 Tel. (201)746-0063

Sec., Sissieretta Bryant

Treas., Elder Artie Burney

EXECUTIVE TRUSTEE BOARD

Chpsn., Leon T. Mims

Vice-Chpsn., Evangelist Peggy Rawls, 100 W. 2nd St., Mount Vernon, NY 10550 Tel. (914)664-4602

OTHER ORGANIZATIONS

Foreign Missions: Pres., Elder Diane Cooper

Home Missions: Pres., Evangelist Eleanor Samuel

Sunday Schools: Gen. Supt., Elder Diane Cooper

Evangelism: Natl. Pres., Evangelist Gloria Gray

Youth: Pres., Deacon Tommy Robinson

Minister of Music: Leon T. Mims; Asst., Ray Brown

Prison Ministry Team: Pres., Evangelist Marvin Lowe

Presiding Elders: Delaware, Elder Roland Miflin, Diamond Acre, Dagsboro, DE 19939; North Carolina, Elder Larry Bryant, West Johnson Rd., Clinton, NC 28328; Monticello, Elder Jesse Alston, 104 Waverly Ave., Monticello, NY 12701; Mount Vernon, Elder Artie Burney, Sr., 100 W. 2nd St., Mount Vernon, NY 10550; Bronx, Elder Anita Robinson; Annex, Elder Betty Gilliard, 1069 Morris Ave., Bronx, NY 10456

Bible School: Pres., Dr. Roy Bryant, Sr.

Bookstore: Mgr., Elder Elizabeth Johnson, Tel. (212)293-1928

PERIODICAL

Voice, The

Bible Way Church of Our Lord Jesus Christ World Wide, Inc.

This body was organized in 1957 in the Pentecostal tradition for the purpose of accelerating evangelistic and foreign missionary commitment and to effect a greater degree of collective leadership than leaders found in the body in which they had previously participated.

The doctrine is the same as that of the Church of Our Lord Jesus Christ of the Apostolic Faith, Inc., of which some of the churches and clergy were formerly members.

This organization has churches and missions in Africa, England, Guyana, Trinidad, and Jamaica, and churches in 25 states in the United States. The Bible Way Church WW is involved in humanitarian, as well as evangelical outreach, with concerns for urban housing and education and economic development.

HEADQUARTERS

1100 New Jersey Ave., N.W., Washington, DC 20001 Tel. (202)789-0700

Media Contact, Presiding Bishop, Lawrence G. Campbell, Apostle, 141 Andes Dr., Danville, VA 24541 Tel. (804)793-9493

OFFICERS

Presiding Bishop, Bishop Lawrence G. Campbell
Gen. Sec., Bishop Edward Williams, 5118 Clarendon Rd., Brooklyn, NY 11226 Tel. (718)451-1238

Brethren Church (Ashland, Ohio)

It was organized by progressive-minded German Baptist Brethren in 1883. They reaffirmed the teaching of the original founder of the Brethren movement, Alexander Mack, and returned to congregational government.

HEADQUARTERS

524 College Ave., Ashland, OH 44805 Tel. (419)289-1708 Fax (419)281-0450
Media Contact, Dir. of Brethren Church Ministries, Ronald W. Waters

GENERAL ORGANIZATION

Dir. of Pastoral Ministries, Rev. Dale Cooksey
Dir. of Brethren Church Ministries, Rev. Ronald W. Waters
Ed. of Publications, Rev. Richard C. Winfield
Conf. Mod. (1991-1992), Rev. Marlin McCann

BOARD

The Missionary Bd., Exec. Dir., Rev. James R. Black
Dir. of Home Missions, Rev. Russell Gordon

PERIODICALS

Brethren Evangelist, The

Brethren in Christ Church

The Brethren in Christ Church was founded in Lancaster County, Pa. in about the year 1778 and was an outgrowth of the religious awakening which occurred in that area during the latter part of the 18th century. This group became known as "River Brethren" because of their original location near the Susquehanna River. The name "Brethren in Christ" was officially adopted in 1863. In theology they have accents of the Pietist, Anabaptist, Wesleyan, and Evangelical movements.

HEADQUARTERS

General Church Office, P.O. Box 290, Grantham, PA 17027
Media Contact, Mod., Harvey R. Sider, Tel. (717)697-2634 Fax (717)697-7714

OFFICERS

Mod., Rev. Harvey R. Sider, 1301 Niagara Pkwy, Ft. Erie, ON L2A 5M4
Dir. of Bishops, Dr. John A. Byers, P.O. Box 547, Elizabethtown, PA 17022
Gen. Sec., Dr. R. Donald Shafer, P.O. Box 245, Upland, CA 91785 Fax (714)982-4353
Dir. of Finance, Harold D. Chubb, P.O. Box 450, Mechanicsburg, PA 17055 Fax (717)697-7714

OTHER ORGANIZATIONS

Board of Administration: Rev. Harvey R. Sider, 1301 Niagara Pkwy., Fort Erie, ON L2A 5M4; Dir. of Bishops, Dr. John A. Byers, P.O. Box 547, Elizabethtown, PA 17022; Gen. Sec., Dr. R. Donald Shafer, P.O. Box 245, Upland, CA 91785; Dir. of Fin., Harold D. Chubb, P.O. Box 450, Mechanicsburg, PA 17055

Board of Brotherhood Concerns: Rev. Ross E. Nigh, RR #1, Stevensville, ON L0S 1S0; Rodney White, 152 Fairview Ave., Waynesboro, PA 17268; Treas., Glenn Dalton, Jr., 201 S. 20th St., Harrisburg, PA 17104; Dir., Dr. R. Donald Shafer, P.O. Box 245, Upland, CA 91785

Board for Congregational Life: Chpsn., John G. Reitz, 7717 Hillcrest Ave., Harrisburg, PA 17027; Sec., Mary J. Davis, 2703 Mill Rd., Grantham, PA 17207; Treas., Ronald L. Miller, Messiah College, Grantham, OA 17207; Exec. Dir., Dr. John A. Byers, P.O. Box 547, Elizabethtown, PA 17022

Board of Directors: Chpsn., M. Lloyd Hogg, RR 3, Stouffville, ON L4A 7X4; Asst. Chpsn., Doug P. Sider, 142 Streb Cresc., Saskatoon, SK S7M 4T8; Gen. Sec., Dr. R. Shafer, P.O. Box 245, Upland, CA 91785; Treas., Harold D. Chubb, P.O. Box 450, Mechanicsburg, PA 17055

Board for Evangelism & Church Planting: Chpsn., Douglas P. Sider, 142 Streb Cresc., Saskatoon, SK S7M 4T8; Sec., Dale H. Engle, RD 1, Box 464, Mt. Joy, PA 17552; Canadian Treas., Walter J. Kelly, 32 Canora Ct., Welland, ON L3C 6H7; Dir. of Bishops, John A. Byers, P.O. Box 547, Elizabeth, PA 17022

Board for Media Ministries: Chpsn., Emerson C. Frey, Box 317, Owl Bridge Rd., Millersville, PA 17551; Sec., J. Wilmer Helsey, 1533 Harrisburg Ave., Mt. Joy, PA 17552; Treas., Marlin E. Benedict, 5 Valley View Ct., Lititz, PA 17543; Exec. Dir., Roger Williams, 2000 Evangel Way, P.O. Box 189, Nappanee, IN 46550

Board for Ministry and Doctrine: Chpsn., Gerald E. Tyrrell, 6033 Featherhead Cresc., Mississiauga, ON L5N 2B5; James Ernst, 1865 Fruitville Pk., Lancaster, PA 17601; Treas., Roy J. Peterman, 33 N. Grant St., Manheim, PA 17545; Mod., Harvey S. Sider, 1301 Niagara Pkwy., Fort Erie, ON L2A 5M4

Board for World Missions: Chpsn., Lowell D. Mann, 6 W. Bainbridge St., Elizabethtown, PA 17022 Fax (717)653-6911; Sec., Harold H. Engle, 925 Messiah Village, P.O. Box 2015, Mechanicsburg, PA 17055; Canadian Treas., Harold Albrecht, RR 2, Petersburg, ON N0B 2H0; U.S. Treas., ———; Dir., Rev. Jack McClane, P.O. Box 390, Mt. Joy, PA 17552-0390

Commission on Christian Education Lit.: Chpsn., Dale W. Engle, 1067 Foxhaven Dr., Ashland, OH 44805; Sec., Glen A. Pierce, P.O. Box 166, Nappanee, IN 46550

Jacob Engle Foundation Bd. of Directors: Chpsn., Charles F. Frey, 529 Willow Valley Dr., Lancaster, PA 17602 Fax (717)697-7714; Sec., Ivan Beachy, 648 Belvedere St., Carlisle, PA 17013; Canadian Treas., Craig, 2246 Munn's Ave., Oakville, ON L6H 3M8; Exec. Dir., Donald R. Zook, P.O. Box 450, Mechanicsburg, PA 17055

Pension Fund Trustees: Chpsn., Donald R. Zook, P.O. Box 390, Mt. Joy, PA 17552; Sec., Elbert N. Smith, 309 Woodlawn Ln., Carlisle, PA 17013; Robert A. Leadley, RR 1, Stevensville, ON L0S 1S0; U.S. Treas., Keith Heise, 2904 Dallas NE, Albuquerque, NM 87110

Board for Stewardship: Chpsn., Charles F. Frey, 259 Willow Valley Dr., Lancaster, PA 17602; Sec., Ivan Beachy, 648 Belvedere St., Carlisle, PA 17013; Dir. of Fin., Canada, Robert A. Leadley, RR 1, Stevensville, ON L0S 1S0; Dir. of Stewardship, Rev. W. Edward Rickman, P.O. Box 450, Mechanicsburg, PA 17055-0450

Publishing House: Exec. Dir., Roger Williams, Evangel Press, P.O. Box 189, Nappannee, IN 46550

PERIODICAL

Evangelical Visitor

Buddhist Churches of America

Founded in 1899, organized in 1914 as the Buddhist Mission of North America, this body was incorporated in 1944 under the present name and represents the Jodo Shinshu Sect of Buddhism affiliated with the Hongwanji-ha Hongwanji denomination in the continental United States. It is a school of Buddhism which believes in becoming aware of the ignorant self and relying upon the infinite wisdom and compassion of Amida Buddha, which is expressed in sincere gratitude through the recitation of the Nembutsu, Namu Amida Butsu.

HEADQUARTERS

1710 Octavia St., San Francisco, CA 94109 Tel. (415)776-5600 Fax (415)771-6293

OFFICERS

Bishop Seigen H. Yamaoka
Exec. Asst. to the Bishop, Rev. Seikan Fukuma
Admn. Officer, Henry Shibata
Dir. of Buddhist Education, Rev. Carol Himaka

OTHER ORGANIZATIONS

Fed. of Buddhist Women's Assoc.
Fed. of Dharma School Teachers' League
Institute of Buddhist Studies
Young Adult Buddhist Association
Western Young Buddhist League
Affiliated U.S. Organizational Juris., Honpa Hongwanji Mission of Hawaii, 1727 Pali Hwy., Honolulu, HI 96813
Affiliated Can. Organizational Juris., Buddhist Churches of Canada, 220 Jackson Ave., Vancouver, BC V6A 3B3

Bulgarian Eastern Orthodox Church

Bulgarian immigration to the United States and Canada started around the turn of the century, and the first Bulgarian Orthodox church was built in 1907 in Madison, Ill. In 1938, the Holy Synod of the Bulgarian Eastern Orthodox Church established the diocese in New York as an Episcopate, and Bishop Andrey was sent as diocesan Bishop. In 1947, the diocese was officially incorporated in New York and Bishop Andrey became the first elected Metropolitan.

By a decision of the Holy Synod in 1969, the Bulgarian Eastern Orthodox Church was divided into the Diocese of New York (incorporated Bulgarian Eastern Orthodox Church—Diocese of America, North and South, and Australia) and the Diocese of Akron (incorporated American Bulgarian Eastern Orthodox Diocese of Akron, Ohio). In 1989 both Dioceses were united into one Bulgarian Eastern-Orthodox Diocese in the USA, Canada and Australia.

HEADQUARTERS

Holy Metropolia, 550 A West 50th St., New York, NY 10019 Tel. (212)246-4608

OFFICER

His Eminence Metropolitan Joseph

Christ Catholic Church

The church is a catholic communion established in 1968 to minister to the growing number of people seeking an experiential relationship with God, and who desire to make a total commitment of their lives to God. The church is catholic in faith and tradition and its orders are recognized as valid by catholics of every tradition.

HEADQUARTERS

1062 Woodbine Ave., Toronto, ON M4C 4C5
Media Contact, Suffragen Bishop, Most Rev. Karl Pruter, P.O. Box 98, Highlandville, MO 65669 Tel. (417)587-3951

OFFICERS

Archbishop, The Most Rev. Frederick Dunleavy, 1062 Eoodvine Ave., Toronto, ON M4C 4C5 Tel. (616)422-2782

PERIODICAL

St. Willibrord Journal

Christadelphians

The Christadelphians are a body of people who believe the Bible to be the divinely inspired word of God, written by "Holy men who spoke as they were moved by the Holy Spirit" (II Peter 1:21); in the return of Christ to earth to establish the Kingdom of God; the resurrection of those dead, at the return of Christ, who come into relation to Christ in conformity with his instructions, to be judged as to worthiness for eternal life; in opposition to war; spiritual rebirth requiring belief and immersion in the name of Jesus; and in a godly walk in this life.

The denomination was organized in 1844 by a medical doctor, John Thomas, who came to the United States from England in 1832, having survived a near shipwreck in a violent storm. This experience affected him profoundly, and he vowed to devote his life to a search for the truth of God and a future hope from the Bible.

MEDIA CONTACT

Media Contact, Trustee, Norman D. Zilmer, Christadelphian Action Society, 1000 Mohawk Dr., Elgin, IL 60120 Tel. (708)741-5253

LEADERS

Co-Ministers: Norman Fadelle, 815 Chippewa Dr., Elgin, IL 60120; Norman D. Zilmer, 1000 Mohawk Dr., Elgin, IL 60120

PERIODICALS

Christadelphian Tidings; Christadelphian Watchman; Christadelphian Advocate

Christian Brethren (also known as Plymouth Brethren)

An orthodox and evangelical movement which began in the British Isles in the 1820s and is now worldwide. Congregations are usually called "assemblies." The name Plymouth Brethren was given by others because the group in Plymouth, England, was a large congregation. In recent years the term Christian Brethren has replaced Plymouth Brethren for the "open" branch of the movement in Canada and British Commonwealth countries, and to some extent in the United States.

The unwillingness to establish a denominational structure makes the autonomy of local congregations an important feature of the movement. Other features are weekly observance of the Lord's Supper and adherence to the doctrinal position of conservative, evangelical Christianity.

In the 1840s the movement divided. The "exclusive" branch, led by John Darby, stressed the interdependency of congregations. Since disciplinary decisions were held to be binding on all assemblies, exclusives had sub-divided into seven or eight main groups by the end of the century. Since 1925 a trend toward reunification has reduced that number to three or four. United States congregations number approximately 300, with an estimated 19,000 members.

The "open" branch of the movement, stressing evangelism and foreign missions, now has about 850 U.S. congregations, with an estimated 79,000 members. Following the leadership of George Muller in rejecting the "exclusive" principle of binding discipline, this branch has escaped large-scale division.

CORRESPONDENT

Interest Ministries, Pres., Bruce R. McNicol, 218 W. Willow, Wheaton, IL 60187 Tel. (708)653-6573 Fax (708)653-6573

OTHER ORGANIZATIONS

Christian Missions in Many Lands, Box 13, Spring Lake, NJ 07762

Stewards Foundation, 218 W. Willow, Wheaton, IL 60187

International Teams, Box 203, Prospect Heights, IL 60070

Emmaus Bible College, 2570 Asbury Rd., Dubuque, IA 52001

PERIODICAL

Interest

Christian Catholic Church (Evangelical-Protestant)

This church was founded by the Rev. John Alexander Dowie on Feb. 22, 1896 at Chicago, Ill. In 1901 the church opened the city of Zion, Ill., as its home and headquarters. Theologically, the church is rooted in evangelical orthodoxy. The Scriptures are accepted as the rule of faith and practice. Other doctrines call for belief in the necessity of repentance for sin and personal trust in Christ for salvation, baptism by triune immersion, and tithing as a practical method of Christian stewardship. The church teaches the Second Coming of Christ.

The Christian Catholic Church is a denominational member of The National Association of Evangelicals. It has work in 10 other nations in addition to the United States. Branch ministries are found in Michigan City, Ind.; Phoenix, Ariz.; Tonalea, Ariz.; Russell, Ill., and Lindenhurst, Ill.

HEADQUARTERS

2500 Dowie Memorial Dr., Zion, IL 60099 Tel. (708)746-1411 Fax (708)746-1452

OFFICER

Gen. Overseer, Roger W. Ottersen

PERIODICAL

Leaves of Healing

Christian Church (Disciples of Christ)

Born on the American frontier in the early 1800s as a movement to unify Christians, this body drew its major inspiration from Thomas and Alexander Campbell in western Pennsylvania and Barton W. Stone in Kentucky. Developing separately, the "Disciples," under Alexander Campbell, and the "Christians," led by Stone, united in 1832 in Lexington, Ky.

The Christian Church (Disciples of Christ) is marked by informality, openness, individualism and diversity. The Disciples claim no official doctrine or dogma. Membership is granted after a simple statement of belief in Jesus Christ and baptism by immersion—although most congregations accept transfers baptized by other forms in other denominations. The Lord's Supper—generally called Communion—is open to Christians of all persuasions. The practice is weekly Communion, although no church law insists upon it.

Thoroughly ecumenical, the Disciples helped organize the National and World Councils of Churches. The church is a member of the Consultation on Church Union. The Disciples and the United Church of Christ have declared themselves to be in "full communion" through the General Assembly and General Synod of the two churches. Official theological conversations have been going on since 1967 directly with the Roman Catholic Church, and since 1987 with the Russian Orthodox Church.

Disciples have vigorously supported world and national programs of education, agricultural assistance, urban reconciliation, care of mentally retarded, family planning, and aid to victims of war and calamity. Operating ecumenically, Disciples personnel or funds work in more than 100 countries outside North America.

Three levels of church polity (general, regional, and congregational) operate as equals, managing their own finances, property, and program, with strong but voluntary ties to one another. Local congregations own their property and control their budgets and program. A General Assembly meets every two years and has voting representation from each congregation.

HEADQUARTERS

222 S. Downey Ave., P.O. Box 1986, Indianapolis, IN 46206-1986 Tel. (317)353-1491 Fax (800)458-3318

Media Contact, Dir. of News & Information, Cliff Willis

OFFICERS

Gen. Minister & Pres., C. William Nichols

Mod., Marilyn J. Moffett, RR 1, Box 252, Waynetown, IN 47990

1st Vice-Mod., Mary E. Jacobs, 1651 Oakhaven Pl., Tucson, AZ 85746

2nd Vice-Mod., Michael Saenz, 4427 Tamworth Rd., Fort Worth, TX 76116

GENERAL OFFICERS

Gen. Minister & Pres., C. William Nichols

Dep. Gen. Min./Vice-Pres. for Communication, Claudia E. Grant

Dep. Gen. Min./Vice-Pres. for Admn., Donald B. Manworren

Dep. Gen. Min./Vice-Pres. for Inclusive Ministries, John R. Foulkes

ADMINISTRATIVE UNITS

Board of Church Extension: Pres., Harold R. Watkins, 110 S. Downey Ave., Box 7030, Indianapolis, IN 46207-7030 Tel. (317)356-6333

Christian Bd. of Pub. (Chalice Press): Pres., James C. Suggs, Box 179, 1316 Convention Plaza Dr., St. Louis, MO 63166-0179 Tel. (314)231-8500 Fax (314)231-8524

Christian Church Foundation: Pres., James P. Johnson

Church Finance Council, Inc.: Pres., Robert K. Welsh

Council on Christian Unity: Pres., Paul A. Crow, Jr.

Disciples of Christ Historical Society: Pres., James M. Seale, 1101 19th Ave. S., Nashville, TN 37212-2196 Tel. (615)327-1444

Division of Higher Education: Pres., James I. Spainhower, 11780 Borman Dr., Ste. 100, St. Louis, MO 63146-4159 Tel. (314)991-3000 Fax (314)993-9018

Division of Homeland Ministries: Pres., Ann Updegraff Spleth

Division of Overseas Ministries: Pres., William J. Nottingham

National Benevolent Association: Pres., Richard R. Lance, 11780 Borman Dr., Ste. 200, St. Louis, MO 63146-4157 Tel. (314)993-9000 Fax (314)993-9018

Pension Fund: Pres., Lester D. Palmer, 200 Barrister Bldg., 155 E. Market St., Indianapolis, IN 46204-3215 Tel. (317)634-4504 Fax (317)634-4071

REGIONAL UNITS OF THE CHURCH

Alabama-Northwest Florida: Regional Minister, Carl R. Flock, 1336 Montgomery Hwy. S., Birmingham, AL 35216-2799 Tel. (205)823-5647

Arizona: Regional Minister, M. Jane Nesby, 4423 N. 24th St., Ste 700, Phoenix, AZ 85016-5544 Tel. (602)468-3815

Arkansas: Exec. Minister, W. Chris Hobgood, 6100 Queensboro Dr., P.O. Box 191057, Little Rock, AR 72219-1057 Tel. (501)562-6053

California North-Nevada: Regional Minister/Pres., Richard Lauer, 111-A Fairmount Ave., Oakland, CA 94611-5918 Tel. (510)839-3550

Canada: Exec. Regional Minister, Robert W. Steffer, 128 Woolwich St., Ste. 202, P.O. Box 64, Guelph, ON N1H 6J6 Tel. (519)823-5190

Capital Area: Regional Minister, Richard L. Taylor, 8901 Connecticut Ave., Chevy Chase, MD 20815-6700 Tel. (301)654-7794

Central Rocky Mountain Region: Exec. Regional Minister, William E. Crowl, ABS Building, 7000 N. Broadway, Ste. 400, Denver, CO 80221-2994 Tel. (303)427-1403

Florida: Regional Minister, Jimmie L. Gentle, 924 N. Magnolia, Ste. 248, Orlando, FL 32803 Tel. (407)843-4652

Georgia: Regional Minister, David L. Alexander, 2370 Vineville Ave., Macon, GA 31204-3163 Tel. (912)743-8649

Idaho-South: Regional Minister, Larry Crist, 4900 No. Five Mile Rd., Boise, ID 83704-1826 Tel. (208)322-0538

Illinois-Wisconsin: Regional Minister/Pres., Nathan S. Smith, 1011 N. Main St., Bloomington, IL 61701-1797 Tel. (309)828-6293

Indiana: Regional Minister, C. Edward Weisheimer, 1100 W. 42nd St., Indianapolis, IN 46208-3375 Tel. (317)926-6051

Kansas: Regional Minister/Pres., Ralph L. Smith, 2914 S.W. MacVicar Ave., Topeka, KS 66611-1787 Tel. (913)266-2914

Kansas City (Greater): Regional Minister/Pres., David C. Downing, 5700 Broadmoor, Ste 408, Mission, KS 66202-2405 Tel. (913)432-1414

Kentucky: Gen. Minister, A. Guy Waldrop, 1125 Red Mile Rd., Lexington, KY 40504-2640 Tel. (606)233-1391

Louisiana: Regional Minister, Bill R. Boswell, 3524 Holloway Prairie Rd., Pineville, LA 71360-9998 Tel. (318)443-0304

Michigan: Regional Minister, Morris Finch, Jr., 2820 Covington Ct., Lansing, MI 48912-4830 Tel. (517)372-3220

Mid-America Region: Regional Minister, Stephen V. Cranford, Hwy. 54 W., Box 104298, Jefferson City, MO 65110-4298 Tel. (314)636-8149

Mississippi: Regional Minister, William E. McKnight, 1619 N. West St., Jackson, MS 39202 Tel. (601)352-6774

Montana: Regional Minister, James E. Kimsey, Jr., 1019 Central Ave., Great Falls, MT 59401-3784 Tel. (406)452-7404

Nebraska: Regional Minister, N. Dwain Acker, 1268 S. 20th St., Lincoln, NE 68502-1699 Tel. (402)476-0359

North Carolina: Regional Minister, Bernard C. Meece, 509 NE Lee St., Box 1568, Wilson, NC 27894 Tel. (919)291-4047

Northeastern Region: Regional Minister, Charles F. Lamb, 1272 Delaware Ave., Buffalo, NY 14209-1531 Tel. (716)882-4793

Northwest Region: Regional Minister/Pres., Robert Clarke Brock, 6558-35th Ave. SW, Seattle, WA 98126-2899 Tel. (206)938-1008

Ohio: Regional Pastor/Pres., Howard M. Ratcliff, 38007 Butternut Ridge Rd., P.O. Box 299, Elyria, OH 44036-0299 Tel. (216)458-5112

Oklahoma: Exec. Regional Minister, Eugene N. Frazier, 301 N.W. 36th St., Oklahoma City, OK 73118-8699 Tel. (405)528-3577

Oregon: Regional Minister, Mark K. Reid, 0245 S.W. Bancroft St., Suite F, Portland, OR 97201-4267 Tel. (503)226-7648

Pacific Southwest Region: Acting Regional Minister, John D. Wolfersberger, 3126 Los Feliz Blvd., Los Angeles, CA 90039-1599 Tel. (213)665-5126

Pennsylvania: Regional Minister, Dwight L. French, 670 Rodi Rd., Pittsburgh, PA 15235-4524 Tel. (412)731-7000

South Carolina: Regional Minister, ——-, 1098 E. Montague Ave., North Charleston, SC 29406 Tel. (803)554-6886

Southwest Region: Regional Minister, M. Margaret Harrison, 3209 S. University Dr., Fort Worth, TX 76109-2239 Tel. (817)926-4687

Tennessee: Regional Minister/Pres., Richard L. Hamm, 3700 Richland Ave., Nashville, TN 37205-2499 Tel. (615)269-3409

Upper Midwest Region: Regional Minister, William L. Miller, Jr., 3300 University Ave., Box 1024, Des Moines, IA 50311 Tel. (515)255-3168

Utah: Exec. Regional Minister, William E. Crowl, ABS Building, 7000 N. Broadway, Ste. 400, Denver, CO 80221-2994 Tel. (303)427-1403

Virginia: Regional Minister, ——-, 518 Brevard St., Lynchburg, VA 24501 Tel. (804)846-3400

West Virginia: Regional Minister, William B. Allen, Rt. 5, Box 167, Parkersburg, WV 26101-9576 Tel. (304)428-1681

PERIODICALS

Disciple, The; Vanguard; Mid-Stream: An Ecumenical Journal

Christian Church of North America, General Council

Originally known as the Italian Christian Church, its first General Council was held in 1927 at Niagara Falls, N. Y. This body was incorporated in 1948 at Pittsburgh, Pa., and is described as Pentecostal but does not engage in the "the excesses tolerated or practiced among some churches using the same name."

The movement recognizes two ordinances—baptism and the Lord's Supper. Its moral code is conservative and its teaching is orthodox. Members are exhorted to pursue a life of personal holiness, setting an example to others. A conservative position is held in regard to marriage and divorce. The governmental form is, by and large, congregational. District and National officiaries, however, are referred to as Presbyteries led by Overseers.

The group functions in cooperative fellowship with the Italian Pentecostal Church of Canada and the Evangelical Christian Churches—Assemblies of God in Italy. It is an affiliate member of the Pentecostal Fellowship of North America and of the National Association of Evangelicals.

HEADQUARTERS

Rt. 18 & Rutledge Rd., Box 141-A, RD 1, Transfer, PA 16154 Tel. (412)962-3501 Fax (412)962-1766
Media Contact, Gen. Sec., Rev. R. Allen Noyd

OFFICERS

Executive Bd., Gen. Overseer, Rev. David Farina, 41 Sherbrooke Rd., Trenton, NJ 08638
Asst. Gen. Overseers: Exec. Vice-Pres., Rev. Andrew Farina, 3 Alhambra Pl., Greenville, PA 16125; Rev. James Demola, P.O. Box 159, Mullica Hill, NJ 08072; Rev. Charles Gay, 26 Delafield Dr., Albany, NY 12205; Rev. Anthony Freni, 10 Elkway Ave., Norwood, MA 02062; Rev. Raymond Patronelli, 6203 Kelly Rd., Plant City, FL 33565
Gen. Sec.-Treas., Rev. R. Allen Noyd

DEPARTMENTS

Publications & Promotion, Rev. John Tedesco, 1188 Heron Rd., Cherry Hill, NJ 08003
Faith/Order/Credentials/Unity & Standard, Rev. Andrew Farina, 3 Alhambra Pl., Greenville, PA 16125
Church Growth & Media Ministries, Rev. Carmine Reigle, P.O. Box 644, Niles, OH 44446
Youth, Sunday School & Education, Rev. Lou Fortunato, Jr., 248 Curry Pl., Youngstown, OH 44504
Foreign Missions, Rev. John Del Turco
Institutions, Benevolences & Fellowships, Rev. Eugene DeMarco, 155 Scott St., New Brighton, PA 15066
Finance, Rev. R. Allen Noyd, 16 Rosedale Ave., Greenville, PA 16125

HONORARY PERSONNEL

Gen. Overseer, Rev. Frank P. Fortunato, 3167 Welsh Rd., Philadelphia, PA 19136
Carmine Saginario, 526 S. Queen Ann Dr., Fairless Hills, PA 19030
Rev. Carmelo Paglia, 314 Madison Ave., Pitman, NJ 08071
Missions, Rev. Richard L. Corsini, 921 6th Ave., Apt. #3, New Brighton, PA 15066

PERIODICAL

Vista

Christian Churches and Churches of Christ

The fellowship, whose churches were always strictly congregational in polity, has its origin in the American movement to "restore the New Testament church in doctrine, ordinances and life" initiated by Thomas and Alexander Campbell, Walter Scott and Barton W. Stone in the early 19th century.

CONVENTIONS

North American Christian Convention: Dir., Rod Huron, 3533 Epley Rd., Cincinnati, OH 45239; NACC Mailing Address, Box 39456, Cincinatti, OH 45239 Tel. (513)385-2470
National Missionary Convention, Coord., Walter Birney, Box 11, Copeland, KS 67837 Tel. (513)668-5250
Eastern Christian Convention, 5300 Norbeck Rd., Rockville, MD 10853

PERIODICAL

Lookout, The

The Christian Congregation, Inc.

The Christian Congregation is a denominational evangelistic association that originated in 1798 and was active on the frontier in areas adjacent to the Ohio River. The church was an unincorporated organization until 1887. At that time a group of ministers who desired closer cooperation formally constituted the church. The charter was revised in 1898 and again in 1970.

Governmental polity basically is congregational. Local units are semi-autonomous. Doctrinal positions, strongly biblical, are essentially universalist in the sense that ethical principles, which motivate us to creative activism, transcend national boundaries and racial barriers. A central tenet, John 13:34-35, translates to such respect for sanctity of life that abortions on demand, capital punishment, and all warfare are vigorously opposed. All wars are considered unjust and obsolete as a means of resolving disputes.

Early leaders were John Chapman, John L. Puckett, and Isaac V. Smith. Bishop O. J. Read was chief administrative and ecclesiastic officer for 40 years until 1961. Rev. Dr. Ora Wilbert Eads has been general superintendent since 1961. Ministerial affiliation for independent clergymen is provided.

HEADQUARTERS

804 W. Hemlock St., LaFollette, TN 37766
Media Contact, Gen. Supt., Rev. Ora W. Eads, D.D., Tel. (615)562-8511

OFFICER

Gen. Supt., Rev. Ora Wilbert Eads, D.D.

Christian Methodist Episcopal Church

In 1870 the General Conference of the Methodist Episcopal Church, South, approved the request of its colored membership for the formation of their conferences into a separate ecclesiastical body, which became the Colored Methodist Episcopal Church.

At its General Conference in Memphis, Tenn., May 1954, it was overwhelmingly voted to change the name of the Colored Methodist Episcopal Church to the Christian Methodist Episcopal Church. This became the official name on Jan. 3, 1956.

HEADQUARTERS

First Memphis Plaza, 4466 Elvis Presley Blvd., Memphis, TN 38116
Media Contact, Exec. Sec., Dr. W. Clyde Williams, 201 Ashby St., N.W., Ste. 312, Atlanta, GA 30314 Tel. (404)522-2736 Fax (901)345-0541

Exec. Sec., Dr. W. Clyde Williams, 201 Ashby St., NW, Suite 312, Atlanta, GA 30314 Tel. (404)522-2736

Sec. Gen. Conf., Rev. Edgar L. Wade, P.O. Box 3403, Memphis, TN 38103

OTHER ORGANIZATIONS

Christian Education: Gen. Sec., Dr. Ronald M. Cunningham, 1474 Humber St., Memphis, TN 38106 Tel. (901)345-0580

Lay Ministry: Gen. Sec., Dr. I. Carlton Faulk, 1222 Rose St., Berkeley, CA 94702 Tel. (415)655-4106

Evangelism, Missions & Human Concerns: Gen. Sec., Rev. Raymond F. Williams, 909 Shanon Bradley Rd., Gastonia, NC 28052 Tel. (704)867-8119

Finance: Sec., Mr. Joseph C. Neal, Jr., P.O. Box 75085, Los Angeles, CA 90075 Tel. (213)233-5050

Publications: Gen. Sec., Rev. Lonnie L. Napier, P.O. Box 2018, Memphis, TN 38101 Tel. (901)345-0580

Personnel Services: Gen. Sec., Dr. N. Charles Thomas, P.O. Box 74, Memphis, TN 39101 Tel. (901)345-0580

Women's Missionary Council: Pres., Dr. Sylvia M. Faulk, 623 San Fernando Ave., Berkeley, CA 94707 Tel. (415)526-5536

BISHOPS

First District: Bishop William H. Graves, 564 Frank Ave., Memphis, TN 38101 Tel. (901)947-6180

Second District: Bishop Othal H. Lakey, 6322 Elwynne Dr., Cincinnati, OH 45236 Tel. (513)984-6825

Third District: Bishop Dotcy I. Isom, Jr., 11470 Northway Dr., St. Louis, MO 63136 Tel. (314)381-3111

Fourth District: Bishop Marshall Gilmore, 109 Holcomb Dr., Shreveport, LA 71103 Tel. (318)222-6284

Fifth District: Bishop Richard O. Bass, 308 10th Ave. W., Birmingham, AL 35204 Tel. (205)252-3541

Sixth District: Bishop Joseph C. Coles, Jr., 2780 Collier Dr., Atlanta, GA 30018 Tel. (404)794-0096

Seventh District: Bishop Oree Broomfield, Sr., 6524 16th St., N.W., Washington, DC 20012 Tel. (202)723-2660

Eighth District: Bishop C. D. Coleman, Sr., 2330 Sutter St., Dallas, TX 75216 Tel. (214)942-5781

Ninth District: Bishop E. Lynn Brown, P.O. Box 11276, Los Angeles, CA 90011 Tel. (213)216-9278

Tenth District: Bishop Nathaniel L. Linsey, P.O. Box 170127, Atlanta, GA 30317

Retired: Bishop E. P. Murchison, 4094 Windsor Castle Way, Decatur, GA 30034; Bishop Henry C. Bunton, 853 East Dempster Ave., Memphis, TN 38106; Bishop Chester A. Kirkendoll, 10 Hurtland, Jackson, TN 38305; Bishop P. Randolph Shy, 894 Falcon Dr. S.W., Atlanta, GA 30311

PERIODICAL

Missionary Messenger, The

The Christian and Missionary Alliance

An evangelical and evangelistic church begun in 1887 when Dr. Albert B. Simpson founded two organizations, The Christian Alliance (a fellowship of Christians dedicated to the experiencing of the deeper Christian life) and the Evangelical Missionary Alliance (a missionary sending organization). The two groups were merged in 1897 and became The Christian and Missionary Alliance. The denomination stresses the sufficiency of Jesus—Savior, Sanctifier, Healer, and Coming King—and has earned a worldwide reputation for its missionary accomplishments. The Canadian districts became autonomous in 1981 and formed The Christian and Missionary Alliance in Canada.

HEADQUARTERS

P.O. Box 35000, Colorado Springs, CO 80935 Tel. (719)599-5999 Fax (719)593-8692

OFFICERS

Pres., Rev. D. L. Rambo

Vice-Pres., Rev. P. F. Bubna

Sec., R. H. Mangham

Vice-Pres. for Fin./Treas., Mr. D. A. Wheeland

Vice-Pres. for Church Ministries, Rev. R. W. Bailey

Vice-Pres. for Overseas Ministries, P. N. Nanfelt

Vice-Pres. for Gen. Services, Rev. J. A. Davey

BOARD OF MANAGERS

Chpsn., Rev. P. F. Bubna

Vice-Chpsn., Rev. G. M. Cathey

EXECUTIVE ADMINISTRATION

Admn. Staff: Pres., D. L. Rambo; Asst. to Pres. for Publications, R. L. Niklaus; Asst. to Pres. for Development, R. M. Shellrude; Admn. Asst., Pearl Swope

Division of Finance: Vice-Pres./Treas., D. A. Wheeland; Asst. Vice-Pres./Asst. Treas., L. L. McCooey; Dir. of Alliance Development Fund, H. M. Maynard; Asst. Dir. of Alliance Development Fund, J. C. Brown; Coord., Employee Benefit, P. R. Christie; Senior Accountant, D. W. Graf; Payroll Mgr., L. L. Keeports; Dir of Accounting, W. E. Stedman; Trust Accountant, A. N. Steele; Trust Accounting Analyst, D. A. Young

Division of Church Ministries: Vice-Pres., R. W. Bailey; Asst. Vice-Pres., J. L. Ng; Dir. of Youth, D. L. Bergstrom; Dir. of Intercultural Ministries, E. A. Cline; Dir. of Christian Ed., D. D. Dale; Assoc. Dir. of Intercultural Ministries, A. E. Hall; Dir. of Church Growth, F. G. King; Dir. of Missionary Deputation, R. H. Pease; Dir. of Church Devel., D. A. Wiggins; Dir. of Alternative Ed., M. L. Winters; Admn. Asst., Darlene Chamberlain

Division of Overseas Ministries: Vice-Pres., P. N. Nanfelt; Asst. Vice-Pres., D. L. Kennedy; Dir. for Africa, R. L. Fetherlin; Dir. for East Asia & Pacific Islands, M. A. Sohm; Dir. for SE Asia/Middle East/Eur./Aust./ New Zealand, R. W. Reed; Dir. for Latin America North, F. H. Smith; Dir. for Latin America South, D. K. Volstad; Dir. for CAMA Services & IFAP, C. M. Westergren; Dir. for Missionary Candidates, C. McGarvey; Admn. Asst., Juanita Fowler

Division of General Services: Vice-Pres., J. A. Davey; Dir. of Stewardship, S. L. Bjornson; Asst. Dir. of Stewardship, J. J. Loscheider; Mgr. of Computer Operations, D. G. Inghram; Dir. of Personnel, D. M. Johnson; Dir. of Data Processing, R. N. Mapstone; Dir. of Communications, J. G. McAlister; Dir. of Business Services, M. J. Reese; Asst. Dir. of Business Services, K. E. Olson; Dir. of Education, D. E. Schroeder; Admn. Asst., Janet Burford

Alliance Life: Ed., M. R. Irvin; Mkt. Mgr., R. J. Sanford; Assoc. Ed., M. L. Saunier; Mgr. Ed., D. B. Wicks

DISTRICT SUPERINTENDENTS

Central: Rev. Howard D. Bowers, 1218 High St., Wadsworth, OH 44281 Tel. (216)336-2911

Central Pacific: Rev. D. Duane Adamson, 3824 Buell St., Suite A, Oakland, CA 94619 Tel. (510)530-5410

Eastern: Rev. Leon W. Young, 1 Sherwood Dr., Mechanicsburg, PA 17055 Tel. (717)766-0261 Fax (717)766-0486

Great Lakes: Rev. Dahl B. Seckinger, 315 W. Huron St., Ste. 380-B, Ann Arbor, MI 48103 Tel. (313)662-6702

Metropolitan: Rev. Paul B. Hazlett, 349 Watchung Ave., N. Plainfield, NJ 07060 Tel. (908)668-8421 Fax (908)757-6299

Mid-Atlantic: Rev. C. E. Mock, 7100 Roslyn Ave., Rockville, MD 20855 Tel. (301)258-0035 Fax (301)258-1021

Midwest: Rev. Gerald R. Mapstone, 260 Glen Ellyn Rd., Bloomingdale, IL 60108 Tel. (708)893-1355

New England: Rev. Cornelius W. Clarke, 34 Central St., S. Easton, MA 02375 Tel. (508)238-3820

Northeastern: Rev. Woodford C. Stemple, Jr., 6275 Pillmore Dr., Rome, NY 13440 Tel. (315)336-4720

Northwestern: Rev. Gary M. Benedict, 1813 N. Lexington Ave., St. Paul, MN 55113 Tel. (612)489-1391

Ohio Valley: Rev. Keith M. Bailey, LLD, 4050 Executive Park Dr., Ste. 402, Cincinnati, OH 45241 Tel. (513)733-4833

Pacific Northwest: Rev. R. Harold Mangham, DD, P.O. Box 1030, Canby, OR 97013 Tel. (503)226-2238

Puerto Rico: Rev. Jorge Cuevas, P.O. Box 51394, Levittown, PR 00950 Tel. (809)261-0101 Fax (809)261-0107

Rocky Mountain: Rev. Harvey A. Town, LLD, 1215 24th W., Ste. 210, Billings, MT 59102 Tel. (406)656-4233

South Atlantic: Rev. Gordon G. Copeland, 3421-B St. Vardell Ln., Charlotte, NC 28217 Tel. (704)523-9456

South Pacific: Rev. Bill J. Vaughn, 9055 Haven Ave., Ste. 107, Rancho Cucamonga, CA 91730 Tel. (714)945-9244 Fax (714)948-0794

Southeastern: Rev. Harry J. Arnold, P.O. Box 720430, Orlando, FL 32872 Tel. (407)823-9662 Fax (407)823-9668

Southern: Rev. Garfield G. Powell, 8420 Division Ave., Birmingham, AL 35206 Tel. (205)836-7048

Southwestern: Rev. Loren G. Calkins, D.Min., P.O. Box 120756, Arlington, TX 76012 Tel. (817)261-9631

Western: Rev. Anthony G. Bollback, 1301 S. 119th St., Omaha, NE 68144 Tel. (402)330-1888

Western Great Lakes: Rev. John W. Fogal, W6107 Aerotech Dr., Appleton, WI 54915 Tel. (414)734-1123

Western Pennsylvania: Rev. D. Paul McGarvey, P.O. Box 429, Punxsutawney, PA 15767 Tel. (814)938-6920 Fax (814)938-7528

INTERCULTURAL MINISTRIES DISTRICTS

Cambodian: Supt., Rev. Joseph S. Kong, 1616 S. Palmetto Ave., Ontario, CA 91762 Tel. (714)988-9434

Dega: c/o Rev. A. E. Hall

Haitian: c/o Rev. A. E. Hall

Hmong: Supt., Rev. Timothy Teng Vang, P.O. Box 219, Brighton, CO 80601 Tel. (303)659-1538

Jewish: Missionary, Rev. Abraham Sandler, 9820 Woodfern Rd., Philadelphia, PA 19115 Tel. (215)676-5122

Native American: Dir., Rev. Stephen Wood, 5664 Corinth Dr., Colorado Springs, CO 80918 Tel. (719)531-7823

Korean: Supt., Rev. Gil Kim, P.O. Box 399, Tenafly, NJ 07670 Tel. (201)567-5233

Lao: Dir., Mr. Sisouphanh Ratthahao, 459 Addison St., Elgin, IL 60120 Tel. (708)741-3871

Spanish Central: Supt., Rev. Kenneth N. Brisco, 515 Ogden Ave., 3rd Fl., Downers Grove, IL 60515 Tel. (708)964-5592 Fax (708)916-8681

Spanish Eastern: Supt., ——

Spanish Western: Dir., Rev. Angel V. Ortiz, 334 Springtree Pl., Escondido, CA 92026-1417 Tel. (619)489-4835

Vietnamese: Supt., Rev. Tai Anh Nguyen, 1681 W. Broadway, Anaheim, CA 92802 Tel. (714)491-8007

NATIONAL ASSOCIATIONS

Black Ministries Consultation: c/o Div. of Church Ministries, P.O. Box 35000, Colorado Springs, CO 80935

Chinese Association of the C&MA: c/o Rev. Peter Chu, 14209 Secluded La., Gaithersburg, MD 20878 Tel. (301)294-8067

Filipino Association of the C&MA: c/o Rev. Hernan C. Pada, 5662 Cathy La., Cypress, CA 90630 Tel. (714)761-9287

PERIODICAL

Alliance Life

Christian Nation Church U.S.A.

Organized in 1895, at Marion, Ohio, as a group of "equality evangelists," who later formed the Christian Nation Church. This church is Wesleyan and Arminian in doctrine, emphasizes the premillenial coming of Christ, semi-congregational in government; and emphasizes evangelism. Reincorporated as Christian Nation Church U.S.A., 1961.

MEDIA CONTACT

Media Contact, Gen. Overseer, Rev. Harvey Monjar, Box 513, Lebanon, OH 43036 Tel. (513)932-0360

OFFICERS

Gen. Overseer, Rev. Harvey Monjar

Asst. Overseer, Rev. Ronald Justice, 11245 State Rt. 669 NE, Rosedale, OH 43777 Tel. (614)982-7827

Gen. Sec., Rev. Randy Lusk, P.O. Box 113, Fanrock, WV 24834 Tel. (304)732-7792

Exec. Sec., Rev. Carl M. Eisenhart, 10303 Murdock-Cozaddale Rd., Goshen, OH 45122

Christian Reformed Church in North America

The Christian Reformed Church represents the historic faith of Protestantism. Founded in the United States in 1857, it asserts its belief in the Bible as the inspired Word of God, and is creedally united in the Belgic Confession (1561), the Heidelberg Catechism (1563), and the Canons of Dort (1618-19). (For total statistics for this body see also those listed under the Christian Reformed Church in North America under the Religious Bodies in Canada.)

HEADQUARTERS

2850 Kalamazoo Ave., SE, Grand Rapids, MI 49560
Media Contact, Gen. Sec., Leonard J. Hofman, Tel. (616)246-0744 Fax (616)246-0834

OFFICERS

Gen. Sec., Rev. Leonard J. Hofman
Financial Coord., Harry Vander Meer

OTHER ORGANIZATIONS

The Back to God Hour: Dir. of Ministries, Dr. Joel H. Nederhood; Exec. Dir., Mr. David Vander Ploeg, International Headquarters, 6555 W. College Dr., Palos Heights, IL 60463
Christian Ref. Bd. World Ministries: Exec. Dir., Dr. Peter Borgdorff
Christian Reformed Bd. of Home Missions: Exec. Dir., Rev. John A. Rozeboom
CRC Publications: Exec. Dir., Gary Mulder
Ministers' Pension Fund: Admn., Dr. Ray Vander Weele

PERIODICAL

Banner, The

Christian Union

Organized in 1864 in Columbus, Ohio. It stresses the oneness of the Church with Christ as its only head. The Bible is the only rule of faith and practice and good fruits the only condition of fellowship. Each local church governs itself.

HEADQUARTERS

P.O. Box 27, Greenfield, OH 45123 Tel. (513)981-2897

OFFICERS

Pres., Dr. Joseph Harr, Rt. 1 Box 132, Grover Hill, OH 45849 Tel. (419)587-3226
Vice-Pres., Rev. Dan Williams, 2-4964-B, Delta, OH 43515 Tel. (419)822-4261
Sec., Rev. Joseph Cunninham, 1005 N. 5th St., Greenfield, OH 45123 Tel. (513)981-3476
Asst. Sec., Rev. Earl Mitchell, 17500 Hidden Valley Rd., Independence, MO 64057 Tel. (816)373-3416
Treas., Rev. Lawrence Rhoads, 902 N.E. Main St., West Union, OH 45693 Tel. (513)544-2950

Church of the Brethren

German pietists-anabaptists founded in 1708 under Alexander Mack, Schwarzenau, Germany, entered the colonies in 1719 and settled at Germantown, Pa. They have no other creed than the New Testament, hold to principles of nonviolence, temperance, and voluntarism, and emphasize religion in life.

HEADQUARTERS

Church of the Brethren General Offices, 1451 Dundee Ave., Elgin, IL 60120 Tel. (708)742-5100 Fax (708)742-6103
New Windsor Service Center, P.O. Box 188, New Windsor, MD 21776 Tel. (301)635-6464 Fax (301)635-8789
Washington Office, 110 Maryland Ave. NE, Box 50, Washington, DC 20002 Tel. (202)546-3202 Fax (202)544-5852
Media Contact, Dir. of Interpretation, Howard Royer, Elgin Ofc.

OFFICERS

Mod., Phyllis N. Carter
Mod.-Elect, Charles L. Boyer
Sec., Anne M. Myers

GENERAL BOARD STAFF

Office of General Secretary: Gen. Sec., Donald E. Miller; Dir. of District Ministries, NW, Donald Rowe; Asst. to Gen. Sec., Sue E. Snyder
Treasurer's Office: Treas., Darryl K. Deardorff; Corp. Controller, Elgin, Judy Keyser; Controller, NW, Kent Shisler; Sr. Acct., Elgin, Brenda Reish; Sr. Acct., NW, Roberta Lee; Dir. of Computer Operations, Perry Hudkins; Dir. of Buildings & Grounds, Elgin, David Ingold; Special Projects/Marketing Assoc., William Christiansen
General Services Commission: Assoc. Gen. Sec./Exec. of Comm., Dale E. Minnich; Admn. Asst., Elsie Holderread; Dir. of Brethren Historical Library & Archives, Kenneth Shaffer; Congregational Support, Donald Michaelsen; Dir. of Interpretation, Howard Royer; MESSENGER Editor, Kermon Thomasson; MESSENGER Man. Ed./Dir. News Services; Personnel Assoc., Barbara Greenwald; Dir. of Human Resources, David Leatherman; Dir. of Human Resources, NW, Eleanor Rowe; Dirs. of Volunteer Services, Mary & Ned Stowe; Coord. of Planned Giving, James Replogle; Planned Giving Officer, SE, Ronald Wyrick; Planned Giving Officer, NE, Roy Johnson; Planned Giving Officer, W, Herbert Fisher; Stewardship Education, Wayne Eberly
Parish Ministries Commission: Assoc. Gen. Sec./Exec. of Commission, ———; Admn. Asst., Joan Pelletier; Congregational Nurture, June Gibble; Hispanic Ministries, Rudolpho Jimenez; Consultant for Ministry, Robert Faus; Dir. of Ministry Training, Rick Gardner; Training in Ministry, East, Wayne Eberly; Training in Ministry, West, Jean Hendricks; Dir. Brethren Press, Wendy McFadden; Editor/Brethren Press Production Mgr., Julie Garber; Evangelism, Paul Mundey; Health & Welfare, Jay Gibble; Church Development, Merle Crouse; Urban Ministries, ———; Korean Ministries (Domestic), David Radcliff; Family Ministries, Anna Mary & Curtis Dubble; Outdoor Ministries, Nancy Knepper; Program for Women, Judith Kipp; Youth & Young Adult Program, Christine Michael

World Ministries Commission: Assoc. Gen. Sec./Exec. of Commission, Joan G. Deeter; Admn. Asst., Barbara Ober; Africa & Middle East Rep., Mervin Keeney; Dir. of Brethren Volunteer Service, Janet Schrock; BVS Recruitment & Orientation, Debra Eisenbise; Economic Justice/Rural Concerns, Shantilal Bhagat; Latin America & Caribbean Rep., Yvonne Dilling; Peace Consultant/Korean Ministries, David Radcliff; Peace & International Affairs/Eur. & Asia Rep., Lamar Gibble; Dir. of Center Operations, NW, Miller Davis; Dir., On Earth Peace, NW, Thomas Hurst; Dir. of Refugee/Disaster Services, NW, Donna Derr; Dir. SERRV, NW, Robert Chase; Washington, DC Rep., Timothy McElwee

Annual Conference: Mgr., Doris I. Lasley; Treas., Darryl Deardorff

Brethren Benefit Trust: Exec. Sec., Wilfred E. Nolen; Admn. Asst., Sandra Pryde; Treas./Dir. of Brethren Foundation, Inc., Jerry Rodeffer; Mgr. of Information Systems, James Skelnik; Dir. of Benefits, Joel Thompson; Dir. of Interpretation, Marilyn Nelson

PERIODICAL
Messenger

Church of Christ
Organized April 6, 1830 at Fayette, New York, by Joseph Smith and five others. In 1864 this body was directed by revelation through Granville Hedrick to return in 1867 to Independence, Missouri to the "consecrated land" dedicated by Joseph Smith. They did so and purchased the temple lot dedicated in 1831.

HEADQUARTERS
Temple Lot, P.O. Box 472, Independence, MO 64051
Media Contact, Gen. Church Rep., William A. Sheldon, Tel. (816)833-3995

OFFICERS
Gen. Church Rep., Apostle William A. Sheldon, Tel. (816)833-3995
Gen. Bus. Mgr., Bishop Alvin Harris
Gen. Recorder, Isaac Brockman

PERIODICAL
Zion's Advocate

Church of Christ, Scientist
The Christian Science Church was founded by New England religious leader Mary Baker Eddy in 1879 "to commemorate the word and works of our Master (Christ Jesus), which should reinstate primitive Christianity and its lost element of healing." In 1892 the church was reorganized and established as The First Church of Christ, Scientist, in Boston, also called The Mother Church, with local branch churches around the world, of which there are nearly 2,700 in 68 countries today.

The church is administered by a five-member board of directors in Boston. Local churches govern themselves democratically. Since the church has no clergy, services are conducted by laypersons elected to serve as Readers. There are also about 3,000 Christian Science practitioners who devote their full time to healing through prayer.

Organizations within the church include the Board of Education, the Board of Lectureship, the Committee on Publication and the Publishing Society.

HEADQUARTERS
The First Church of Christ, Scientist, 175 Huntington Ave., Boston, MA 02115
Media Contact, Mgr., Comm. on Publication, M. Victor Westberg, Tel. (617)450-3301 Fax (617)450-3325

OFFICERS
Bd. of Dirs.: Chpsn., Virginia S. Harris; Richard C. Bergenheim; Olga M. Chaffee; Al M. Carnesciali; John Lewis Selover
Pres., Jill Gooding
Treas., John Lewis Selover
Clk., Olga M. Chaffee
First Reader, Howard E. Johnson
Second Reader, Margaret Rogers

PERIODICALS
Herald of Christian Science, The; World Monitor Mazagine; Christian Science Quarterly

Church of Daniel's Band
A body Methodistic in form and evangelistic in spirit, organized in Michigan in 1893.

OFFICERS
Pres., Rev. Jim Seaman, Adams St., Coleman, MI 48618 Tel. (517)465-6059
Vice-Pres., Rev. Wesley Hoggard, 213 S. Five Mile Rd., Midland, MI 48640
Sec.-Treas., Rev. Marie Berry, Roehrs St., Beaverton, MI 48612

The Church of God
Inaugurated by Bishop A. J. Tomlinson, who served as General Overseer, 1903 to 1943, and from which many groups of the Pentecostal and Holiness Movement stemmed. Bishop Homer A. Tomlinson served as General Overseer, 1943 to 1968. Episcopal in administration, evangelical in doctrines of justification by faith, sanctification as a second work of grace, and of the baptism of the Holy Ghost, speaking with other tongues, miracles of healing. Bishop Voy M. Bullen has been the General Overseer since 1968.

HEADQUARTERS
Box 13036, 1207 Willow Brook, Apt. #2, Huntsville, AL 35802 Tel. (205)881-9629
Media Contact, Gen. Overseer, Voy M. Bullen

OFFICERS
Gen. Overseer & Bishop, Voy M. Bullen
Gen. Sec.-Treas., Marie Powell
Bus. Mgr., ——-

CHURCH AUXILIARIES
Assembly Band Movement, Gen. Sec., Bishop Bill Kinslaw
Women's Missionary Band, Gen. Sec., Maxine McKenzie
Theocratic Bands, Gen. Sec., Rev. Ted Carr
Victory Leader's Band, Youth, Gen. Sec., Rev. Linda Russell
Admn. for Highway & Hedge Campaign, Earnest Hoover
Sunday School, Gen. Sec., Judy Foskey

PERIODICAL
Church of God Quarterly, The

Church of God (Anderson, Ind.)
The Church of God (Anderson, Ind.) began in 1881 when Daniel S. Warner and several associates in northern Indiana felt constrained to forsake

all denominational hierarchies and formal creeds, trusting solely in the Holy Spirit as their overseer and the Bible as their statement of belief. Warner and those of similar persuasion saw themselves at the forefront of a movement to restore unity and holiness to the church, not to establish another denomination, but to promote primary allegiance to Jesus Christ so as to transcend (and even obliterate) denominational loyalties.

Deeply influenced by Wesleyan theology and Pietism, the Church of God has emphasized conversion, holiness, and attention to the Bible. Worship services tend to be informal, accentuating expository preaching and robust singing.

There is no formal membership. Persons are assumed to be members on the basis of witness to a conversion experience and evidence that supports such witness. The absence of formal membership is also consistent with the church's understanding of how Christian unity is to be achieved—that is, by preferring the label Christian before all others.

The Church of God is congregational in its government. Each local congregation is autonomous and may call any recognized Church of God minister to be its pastor and may retain him or her as long as it is mutually pleasing. Ministers are ordained and disciplined by state or provincial assemblies made up predominantly (but not usually exclusively) of ministers. National program boards serve the church through coordination and resource materials.

There are Church of God congregations in 81 foreign countries, most of which are resourced by one or more missionaries. There are slightly more Church of God adherents overseas than in North America. The heaviest concentration is in the nation of Kenya.

HEADQUARTERS
Box 2420, Anderson, IN 46018 Tel. (317)642-0256
Media Contact, Exec. Dir., Div. of Church Service, Keith Huttenlocker, Tel. (317)642-0260

EXECUTIVE COUNCIL
Exec. Sec., Edward L. Foggs
Assoc. Sec., David L. Lawson
Church Service, Exec. Dir., Keith Huttenlocker
World Service, Exec. Dir., James Williams

OTHER ORGANIZATIONS
Bd. of Christian Education, Exec. Dir., Sherrill D. Hayes, Box 2458, Anderson, IN 46018
Bd. of Church Extension & Home Missions, Pres., J. Perry Grubbs, Box 2069, Anderson, IN 46018
Foreign Missionary Bd., Pres., Norman S. Patton, Box 2498, Anderson, IN 46018
Women of the Church of God, Exec. Sec.-Treas., Doris Dale, Box 2328, Anderson, IN 46018
Bd. of Pensions, Exec. Sec.-Treas., Harold A. Conrad, Box 2299, Anderson, IN 46018
Mass Communications Bd., Sec.-Treas., Dwight L. Dye, Box 2007, Anderson, IN 46018
Warner Press, Inc., Pres., Robert G. Rist, Box 2499, Anderson, IN 46018

PERIODICALS
Vital Christianity; Church of God Missions

Church of God by Faith, Inc.
Founded 1914, in Jacksonville Heights, Fla., by Elder John Bright. This body believes the word of God as interpreted by Jesus Christ to be the only hope of salvation, and Jesus Christ the only media-

tor for people.

HEADQUARTERS
3220 Haines St., P.O. Box 3746, Jacksonville, FL 32206 Tel. (904)353-5111 Fax (904)355-8582
Media Contact, Ofc. Mgr., Sarah E. Lundy

OFFICERS
Bishop Emeritus, W. W. Matthews, P.O. Box 907, Ozark, AL 36360
Bishop James E. McKnight, P.O. Box 121, Gainesville, FL 32601
Treas., Elder Theodore Brown, 93 Girard Pl., Newark, NJ 07108
Ruling Elders: Elder John Robinson, 300 Essex Dr., Ft. Pierce, FL 33450; Elder D. C. Rourk, 107 Chestnut Hill Dr., Rochester, NY 14617
Exec. Sec., Elder George Matthews, 8834 Camphor Dr., Jacksonville, FL 32208

Church of God (Cleveland, Tenn.)
America's oldest Pentecostal Church began in 1886 as an outgrowth of the holiness revival under the name Christian Union. Reorganized in 1902 as the Holiness Church, in 1907 the church adopted the name Church of God. Its doctrine is fundamental and Pentecostal; it maintains a centralized form of government and an evangelistic and missionary program.

HEADQUARTERS
P.O. Box 2430, Cleveland, TN 37320 Tel. (615)472-3361 Fax (615)478-7052
Media Contact, Dir. of Publ. Relations, Lewis J. Willis, Tel. (615)478-7112 Fax (615)478-7066

EXECUTIVES
Gen. Overseer, R. Lamar Vest
Asst. Gen. Overseers: Robert White; John D. Nichols; Robert E. Fisher
Gen. Sec.-Treas., Gene D. Rice

DEPARTMENTS
Black Evangelism, Dir., C. C. Pratt
Business & Records, Dir., Julian B. Robinson
Evangelism & Home Missions, Dir., Bill F. Sheeks
Ladies Ministries, Pres., Mrs. Iris Vest
Lay Ministries, Dir., Leonard Albert
Media Ministries, Dir., Robert E. Fisher
Ministerial Dev., Exec. Dir., Robert E. Fisher
Pension & Legal Services, Dir., O. Wayne Chambers
Publications, Dir., Donald T. Pemberton
Public Relations, Dir., Lewis J. Willis
Stewardship, Dir., Al Taylor
World Missions, Dir., Lovell R. Cary
Youth & C. E., Dir., Junus C. Fulbright
Benevolence, Dir., B. J. Moffett
Computer Info. Serv., Dir., Timothy D. O'Neal
Cross-Cultural Min., Dir., Billy J. Rayburn
Hispanic Min., Dir., Esdras Betancourt
Insurance, Dir., Josh Thomas
Ministerial Care, Dir., Sam Crisp
Ministry to the Military, Dir., John D. Nichols
Music Min., Dir., Delton Alford

Church of God General Conference (Oregon, IL)
This church is the outgrowth of several independent local groups of similar faith. Some were in existence as early as 1800, and others date their beginnings to the arrival of British immigrants in this country around 1847. Many local churches

carried the name Church of God of the Abrahamic Faith. The corporate name is Church of God General Conference, Oregon, Illinois and Morrow, Ga.

State and district conferences of these groups were formed as an expression of mutual cooperation. A national organization was instituted at Philadelphia in 1888. Because of strong convictions on the questions of congregational rights and authority, however, it ceased to function until 1921, when the present General Conference was formed at Waterloo, Iowa.

The Bible is accepted as the supreme standard of faith. Adventist in viewpoint, the second (premillenial) coming of Christ is strongly emphasized. The church teaches that the kingdom of God will be literal, beginning in Jerusalem at the time of the return of Christ and extending to all nations. Emphasis is placed on the oneness of God and the Sonship of Christ, that Jesus did not pre-exist prior to his birth in Bethlehem, and that the Holy Spirit is the power and influence of God. It believes in the restoration of Israel, the times of restitution, the mortality of people, the literal resurrection of the dead, the reward of the righteous on earth, and the complete destruction of the wicked in the second death. Membership is dependent on faith, repentance, and baptism (for the remission of sins) by immersion.

The work of the General Conference is carried on under the direction of the board of directors. The executive officer is a president who administers the work. Because of the congregational nature of the church's government, the General Conference exists primarily as a means of mutual cooperation and for the development of yearly projects and enterprises.

Delegates to the 1990 Annual Conference voted to relocate the headquarters and Bible College to 5823 Trammell Road, Morrow, Ga. The relocation occurred in the summer of 1991. Publishing offices will continue to be located in Oregon, Ill.

HEADQUARTERS

P.O. Box 100, Oregon, IL 61601 Tel. (815)732-7991

P.O. Box 100,000, Morrow, GA 30260 Tel. (404)362-0052 Fax (404)362-9307

Media Contact, Pres., David Krogh, Georgia Ofc.

OFFICERS

Chpsn., Pastor Scott Ross, 7606 Jaynes St., Omaha, NE 68134

Vice-Chpsn., Dr. William D. Lawrence, 32 E. Marshall, Phoenix, AZ 85012

Pres., David Krogh, Georgia Ofc.

Sec., Dr. Donna Deane, 5185 Upper Valley Pk., Springfield, OH 45502

Treas., Pastor Vivian Kirkpatrick, II, Box 636, Hector, MN 55342

OTHER ORGANIZATIONS

Bus. Adm., Controller, Harry McMinn, Georgia Ofc.

Publishing Dept., Ed., Hollis Partlowe, Illinois Ofc.

Atlanta Bible College, Pres., David Krogh, Georgia Ofc.

PERIODICALS

Restitution Herald, The; Church of God Progress Journal

The Church Of God In Christ

The Church of God in Christ was founded in 1907 in Memphis, Tenn., and was organized by Bishop Charles Harrison Mason, a former Baptist minister who pioneered the embryonic stages of the Holiness movement beginning in 1895 in Mississippi.

Its founder organized four major departments between 1910-1916: the Women's Department, the Sunday School, Young Peoples Willing Workers, and Home and Foreign Mission.

The Church is trinitarian, and teaches the infallibility of scripture, the need for regeneration and subsequent baptism of the Holy Ghost. It emphasizes holiness as God's standard for Christian conduct. It recognizes as ordinances Holy Communion, Water Baptism, and Feet Washing. Its governmental structure is basically episcopal with the General Assembly being the legislative body.

HEADQUARTERS

National Headquarters, Mason Temple, 939 Mason St., Memphis, TN 38126

World Headquarters, 272 S. Main St., Memphis, TN 38103 Tel. (901)578-3800

Mailing Address, P.O. Box 320, Memphis, TN 38101

The Mother Church, Pentecostal Institutional, 229 S. Danny Thomas Blvd., Memphis, TN 38126 Tel. (901)527-9202

GENERAL OFFICES

Office of the Presiding Bishop: Presiding Bishop, Rt. Rev. L. H. Ford, Tel. (901)578-3838; Exec. Sec., Elder A. Z. Hall, Jr.; Sec., Mrs. Linda K. Wilkins

The General Board: Presiding Bishop, Rt. Rev. L. H. Ford, 9401 M.L. King Dr., Chicago, IL 60619; Bishop Ithiel Clemmons, 190-08 104th Ave., Hollis, NY 11412; First Asst. Presiding Bishop, C. D. Owens, 14 Van Velsor Pl., Newark, NJ 07112; Second Asst. Presiding Bishop, C. L. Anderson, Jr., 20485 Mendota, Detroit, MI 48221; Bishop L. R. Anderson, 265 Ranch Trail West, Amherst, NY 14221; Bishop O. T. Jones, Jr., 363 N. 60th St., Philadelphia, PA 19139; Bishop Jacob Cohen, 3120 N.W. 48th Terr., Miami, FL 33142; Bishop P. A. Brooks, 30945 Wendbrook La., Birmingham, MI 48010; Bishop S. L. Green, 2416 Orcutt Ave., Newport News, VA 23607; Bishop J. N. Haynes, 6743 Talbot, Dallas, TX 75216; Bishop C. E. Blake, 3045 S. Crenshaw, Los Angeles, CA 90016; Bishop Levi Willis, 645 Church St., Ste. 400, Norfolk, VA 23510; Bishop R. L. H. Winbush, 317 12th St., Lafayette, LA 70501

Office of the General Secretary: Gen. Sec., Bishop W. W. Hamilton, (901)521-1163; Asst. Gen. Sec. for Registration, Bishop E. Harris Moore; Asst. Gen. Sec. for Records, Bishop Herbert J. Williams; Coord., Bishop A. LaDell Thomas; Dir. of Research & Survey, Elder Ronald A. Blumenburg

Office of the Financial Secretary: Sec., Dr. S. Y. Burnett, Tel. (901)744-0710; Gen. Treas., Bishop Theodore Davis; Chmn. of Finance, Bishop Benjamin Crouch

Office of the Board of Trustees: Chmn., Dr. Roger L. Jones; Sec., Elder Warren Miler

Office of the Clergy Bureau: Dir., Elder Samuel Smith, Tel. (901)523-7045; Sec., Mrs. Dorothy Motley

Office of Supt. of National Properties: Supt., Bishop W. L. Porter, Tel. (901)774-0710; Sec., Ms. Sandra Allen

Board of Publications: Chmn., Bishop Norman Quick, Tel. (901)578-3841; Sec.-Treas., Bishop Nathaniel Jones; Headquarters Rep., Dr. David Hall

Publishing House: Mgr., Mr. Hughea Terry, Tel. (901)578-3842

Dept. of Missions: Pres., Bishop Carlis L. Moody, Tel. (901)578-3876; Exec. Sec., Elder Jesse W. Denny

Dept. of Women: Pres.-Gen. Supervisor, Dr. Mattie McGlothen, Tel. (901)578-3834; Asst. Supervisor, Mrs. Emma Crouch; Exec. Sec., Mrs. Elizabeth C. Moore; Sec. of the Women's Convention, Mrs. Freddie J. Bell; Treas., Mrs. Mary L. Belvin; Fin. Sec., Mrs. Olive Brown

Dept. of Evangelism: Pres., Dr. Edward L. Battles, 4310 Steeplechase Trail, Arlington, TX 76016 Tel. (817)429-7166

Dept. of Music: Pres., Mrs. Mattie Moss Clark, 18203 Sorrento, Detroit, MI 48235; Vice-Pres., Mrs. Mattie Wigley, 1726 S. Wellington, Memphis, TN 38106

Dept. of Youth (Youth Congress): Pres., Bishop C. H. Brewer, 260 Roydon Rd., New Haven, CT 06511

Dept. of Sunday Schools: Gen. Supt., Bishop Cleveland W. Williams, 270 Division St., Derby, CT 06418

United National Auxiliaries Convention: UNAC-5, Chmn., Bishop F. E. Perry, Jr.; Sec. of Exec. Comm., Bishop G. R. Ross

Church of God in Christ Book Store: Mgr., Mrs. Geraldine Miller, 272 S. Main St., Memphis, TN 38103 Tel. (901)578-3803

Charles Harrison Mason Foundation: Exec. Dir., Elder O. T. Massey, 272 S. Main St., Memphis, TN 38103 Tel. (901)578-3803; Bd. of Dir., Chmn., Bishop P. A. Brooks

Dept. of Finance: Chief Financial Officer, Mrs. Sylvia H. Law; Asst. to C.F.O., Elder A. Z. Hall, Jr.; Acntg. Clk., Gloria Hall; Acntg. Clk., Carol Robinson

Fine Arts Dept.: Dir., Mrs. Sara J. Powell; Natl. Orchestra Dir., Mrs. Luvonia Whittley; Natl. Drama Dept. Dir., Mrs. Brenda Rivette

BISHOPS IN THE U.S.A.

Alabama: First, Chester A. Ashworth, 2901 Snavely Ave., Birmingham, AL 35211; Second, W. S. Harris, 3005 Melrose Pl., N.W., Huntsville, AL 35810

Alaska: Charles D. Williams, 2212 Vanderbilt Cir., Anchorage, AK 99504

Arizona: Felton King, P.O. Box 3791, Phoenix, AZ 84030

Arkansas: First, L. T. Walker, 2315 Chester St., Little Rock, AR 72206; Second, D. L. Lindsey, 401 W. 23rd St., North Little Rock, AR 72114

California: North-Central, G. R. Ross, 815 Calmar Ave., Oakland, CA 94610; Northern, B. R. Stewart, 734 12th Ave., San Francisco, CA 94118; Northeast, L. B. Johnson, 3121 Patridge Ave., Oakland, CA 94605; Evangel, E. E. Cleveland, 31313 Braeburn Ct., Haywood, CA 96045; Northwest, Bishop W. W. Hamilton, 14145 Mountain Quail Rd., Salinas, CA 93906; Southern #1, C. E. Blake, 1731 Wellington Rd., Los Angeles, CA 90019; Southern #2, George McKinney, 5848 Arboles, San Diego, CA 92120; Southern Metropolitan, Bishop B. J. Crouch, 12418 Gain St., Pacoima, CA 91331; Southwest, B. R. Benbow, 504 Rexford Dr., Beverly Hills, CA 90210; Valley, Warren S. Wilson, 1435 Modoc St., Fresno, CA 93706

Colorado: Colorado, Frank Johnson, 12231 E. Arkansas Pl., Aurora, CO 80014

Connecticut: First, Charles H. Brewer, Jr., 180 Osborne St., New Haven, CT 06515; Second, H. Bordeaux, 135 Westwood Rd., New Haven, CT 06511

Delaware: Lieutenant T. Blackshear, Sr., 17 S. Booth Dr., Penn Acres, New Castle, DE 19720

District of Columbia: Bishop W. Crudup, 5101 Martin Dr., Oxon Hill, MD 20745

Florida: Central, Calvin D. Kensey, 9462 August Dr., Jacksonville, FL 32208; Eastern, Jacob Cohen, 3120 N.W. 48th Terr., Miami, FL 33142; Southwestern, W. E. Davis, 2008 33rd Ave., Tampa, FL 33610; Western, M. L. Sconiers, P.O. Box 5472, Orlando, FL 32805

Georgia: Central & Southeast, J. D. Husband, P.O. Box 824, Atlanta, GA 30301; Southeast, Andrew Hunter, Rt. 4, Box 328, St. Simons Island, GA 31502; Northern, J. Howard Dell, 1717 Havilon Dr., S.W., Atlanta, GA 30311; Southern, C. J. Hicks, 1894 Madden Ave., Macon, GA 31204

Hawaii: First, ———; Second, W. H. Reed, 1223 W. 80th St., Los Angeles, CA 90044

Idaho: Nathaniel Jones, 630 Chateau, Barstow, CA 92311

Illinois: First, L. H. Ford, 9401 M. L. King Dr., Chicago, IL 60619; Fifth, B. E. Goodwin, 286 E. 16th St., Chicago Heights, IL 60411; Sixth, W. Haven Bonner, 1039 Bonner Ave., Aurora, IL 60505; Central, T. T. Rose, 1000 Dr. Taylor Rose Sq., Springfield, IL 62703; Northern, Cody Marshall, 8836 Blackstone, Chicago, IL 60637; Southeast, L. E. Moore, 7840 Contour Dr., St. Louis, MO 63121; Southern, J. Cobb, 323-30th St., Cairo, IL 62914

Indiana: First, Milton L. Hall, 1404 Delphos, Kokomo, IN 46901; Second, Oscar Freeman, 1760 Taft St., Gary, IN 46404; Indiana Northern, J. T. Dupree, 1231 Hayden St., Fort Wayne, IN 40806

Iowa: Hurley Bassett, 1730 4th Ave., S.E., Cedar Rapids, IA 52403

Kansas: Central, I. B. Brown, 1635 Hudson Blvd., Topeka, KS 66607; East, William H. McDonald, 1627 N. 78th St., Kansas City, KS 66112; Southwest, J. L. Gilkey, 2403 Shadybrook, Wichita, KS 67214

Kentucky: First, Bishop M. Sykes, P.O. Box 682, Union City, TN 38621

Louisiana: Eastern, #1, Bishop J. E. Gordon, 6610 Chenault Dr., Marrero, LA 70072; Eastern #2, Bishop J. A. Thompson, 2180 Holiday, New Orleans, LA 70114; Eastern #3, Bishop H. E. Quillen, 1913 Lasley St., Bogalusa, LA 70427; Western, Roy L. H. Winbush, 235 Diamond Dr., Lafayette, LA 70501

Maine: Bishop B. W. Grayson, 1237 Eastern Pkwy., Brooklyn, NY 11213

Maryland: Central, S. L. Butts, P.O. Box 4504, Upper Marboro, MD 20775; Eastern Shore, James L. Eure, 635 West Main St., Salisbury, MD 21801; Greater, David Spann, 5023 Gwynn Oak Ave., Baltimore, MD 21207

Massachusetts: First, L. C. Young, 19 Almont St., Mattanpan, MA 02126; Second & New Hampshire, C. W. Williams, 270 Division St., Derby, CT 06418; West, Bryant Robinson, Sr., 1424 Plumtree Rd., Springfield, MA 01119

Michigan: Great Lakes, C. L. Anderson, 20485 Mendota, Detroit, MI 48221; North Central, Herbert J. Williams, 1600 Cedar St., Saginaw, MI 48601; Northeast, P. A. Brooks, II, 30945 Wendbrook Lane, Birmingham, MI 48010; Southwest, First, W. L. Harris, 1834 Outer Dr., Detroit, MI 48234; Second, Earl J. Wright, 18655 Autumn La., Southfield, MI 48076; Third, Rodger L. Jones, 1118 River Forest, Flint, MI 48594; Fourth, N. W. Wells, 530 Sue Lane, Muskegon, MI 49442

Minnesota: Bishop S. N. Frazier, 4309 Park Ave. So., Minneapolis, MN 55409

Mississippi: Northern, T. T. Scott, 1066 Barnes Ave., Clarksdale, MS 38614; Southern #1, Theodore Roosevelt Davis, 1704 Topp Ave., Jackson, MS 39204; Southern #2, Bishop R. Nance, 803 Fayard St., Biloxi, MS 39503

Missouri: Eastern #1, R. J. Ward, 4724 Palm Ave., St. Louis, MO 63115; Eastern #2, W. W. Sanders, 8167 Garner La., Berkeley, MO 63134; Western, E. Harris Moore, 405 E. 64th Terr., Kansas City, MO 64131

Montana: Bishop C. L. Moody, 2413 Lee St., Evanston, IL 60202

Nebraska: Eastern, Monte J. Bradford, 3901 Ramelle Dr., Council Bluff, IA 51501; Northeastern, B. T. McDaniels, 1106 N. 31st St., Omaha, NE 68103

Nevada: E. N. Webb, 1941 Goldhill, Las Vegas, NV 89106

New Jersey: First, Esau Courtney, 12 Clover Hill Cir., Trenton, NJ 08538; Third, Chandler David Owens, 14 Van Velsor Pl., Newark, NJ 07112

New Mexico: W. C. Griffin, 3322 Montclaire, Albuquerque, NM 87110

New York: Eastern #1, Bishop Ithiel Clemmons, 190-08 104th Ave., Hollis, NY 11412; Eastern #2, Bishop Frank White, 67 The Boulevard, Amityville, NY 11701; Eastern #3, Bishop D. W. Grayson, 1233 Eastern Pkwy., Brooklyn, NY 11213; Eastern #4, Bishop C. L. Sexton, 153 McDougal St., Brooklyn, NY 11233; Western #1, LeRoy R. Anderson, 265 Ranch Trail, W., Amherst, NY 14221; Western #2, Charles H. McCoy, 168 Brunswick Blvd., Buffalo, NY 14208

North Carolina: Greater, L. B. Davenport, P.O. Box 156, Plymouth, NC 28803; Second, J. Howard Sherman, Sr., P.O. Box 329, Charlotte, NC 28201

North Dakota: Mission Dept., Carlis L. Moody, 272 S. Main St., Memphis, TN 38103

Ohio: Northern, Bishop William James, 3758 Chippendale Ct., Toledo, OH 44320; Robert S. Fields, 419 Crandell Ave., Youngstown, OH 44504; Northwest, Robert L. Chapman, 3194 E. 18th St., Cleveland, OH 44120; Northern, Bishop Warren Miller, 3618 Beacon Dr., Cleveland, OH 44122; Southern, Floyde E. Perry, Jr., 3716 Rolliston Rd., Shaker Hts., OH 44120

Oklahoma: Northwest, J. A. Young, P.O. Box 844, Lawton, OK 73501; Southeast, Bishop F. D. Lawson, P.O. Box 581, Stillwater, OK 74076

Oregon: First, Bishop A. R. Hopkins, 1705 N.E. Dekum, Portland, OR 97211; Second, J. C. Foster, 2716 N.E. 9th Ave., Portland, OR 97212

Pennsylvania: Commonwealth, O. T. Jones, Jr., 363 N. 60th St., Philadelphia, PA 19139; Eastern, DeWitt A. Burton, 1400 Wistar Dr., Wyncote, PA 19095; Western, Gordon E. Vaughn, 6437 Stanton Ave., Pittsburgh, PA 15206

Rhode Island: Norman Quick, 1031 E. 215th St., Brooklyn, NY 11221

South Carolina: Johnnie Johnson, 679 Liberty Hall Rd., Goose Creek, SC 29445

South Dakota: Carlis L. Moody, 2413 Lee St., Evanston, IL 60202

Tennessee: Headquarters, F. Douglas Macklin, 1230 Tipton, Memphis, TN 38071; Second, H. J. Bell, P.O. Box 6118, Knoxville, TN 37914; Central, W. L. Porter, 1235 East Parkway, S., Memphis, TN 38114

Texas: Eastern, J. E. Lee, 742 Calcutta Dr., Dallas, TX 75241; Northeast, J. Neauell Haynes, 6743 Talbot, Dallas, TX 75216; Northwest, W. H. Watson, 1301 47th St., Lubbock, TX 79412; South Central, Nathan H. Henderson, 15622 Rockhouse Rd., Houston, TX 77060; Southeast #1, Robert E. Woodard, 2614 Wichita, Houston, TX 77004; Southeast #2, A. LaDell Thomas, 4401 McArthur Dr., Waco, TX 76708; Southeast, R. E. Ranger, 6604 Sabrosa Ct., W., Fort Worth, TX 76110; Southwest, T. D. Iglehart, 325 Terrell Rd., San Antonio, TX 78209

Utah: Nathaniel Jones, c/o Mission Dept., 630 Chateau Rd., Barstow, CA 92311

Vermont: Frank Clemons, Sr., 1323 Carroll St., Brooklyn, NY 11216

Virginia: First, Ted Thomas, Sr., 4145 Sunkist Rd., Chesapeake, VA 23321; Second, Samuel L. Green, Jr., 2416 Orcutt Ave., Newport News, VA 23607; Third, Levi E. Willis, 5110 Nichal Ct., Norfolk, VA 23508

Washington: T. L. Westbrook, 1256 176th St., Spanaway, WA 98402

West Virginia: Northern, Bishop G. F. Walker, P.O. Box 1467, Princeton, VA 24740; Southern, St. Claire Y. Burnett, P.O. Box 245, Altamonte Springs, FL 32715

Wisconsin: First, Dennis Flakes, 3420 N. 1st St., Milwaukee, WI 53212; Northwest, P. J. Henderson, 1312 W. Burleigh, Milwaukee, WI 53206; Third, J. C. Williams, 4232 N. 24th Pl., Milwaukee, WI 53209

Wyoming: A. W. Martin, 2453 N. Fountain St., Wichita, KS 67220

PERIODICAL

Voice of Missions, The

Church of God in Christ, International

Organized in 1969 in Kansas City, Mo., by 14 bishops of the Church of God in Christ of Memphis, Tenn. The doctrine is the same, but the separation came because of disagreement over polity and governmental authority. The Church is Wesleyan in theology (two works of grace) but stresses the experience of full baptism of the Holy Ghost with the initial evidence of speaking with other tongues as the spirit gives utterance.

HEADQUARTERS

170 Adelphi St., Brooklyn, NY 11205 Tel. (718) 625-9175

Media Contact, Natl. Sec., Rev. Sis. Sharon R. Dunn

OFFICERS

Presiding Bishop, The Most Rev. Carl E. Williams, Sr.

Vice-Presiding Bishop, Rt. Rev. J. P. Lucas, 90 Holland St., Newark, NJ 07103

Sec.-Gen., Rev. William Hines

Women's Dept., Natl. Supervisor, Dr. Louise Norris, 360 Colorado Ave., Bridgeport, CT 06605

Youth Dept., Pres., Evangelist Joyce Taylor, 137-17 135th Ave., S., Ozone Park, NY 11420

Music Dept., Pres., Beatrice Summerville, 210 Elmwood Ave., Bridgeport, CT 06605

Bd. of Bishops, Chpsn., Bishop J. C. White, 360 Colorado Ave., Bridgeport, CT 06605

Natl. Dir. of Public Relations, Rev. Eric Dunn

Church of God in Christ (Mennonite)

A section of the Mennonite body organized in 1859, in Ohio, for the re-establishment of the order and discipline of the Church.

HEADQUARTERS

420 N. Wedel St., Moundridge, KS 67107 Tel. (316)345-2532

PERIODICAL

Messenger of Truth

Church of God, Mountain Assembly, Inc.

The church was formed in 1895 and organized in 1906 by J. H. Parks, S. N. Bryant, Tom Moses, and Andrew Silcox.

HEADQUARTERS

110 S. Florence Ave., Jellico, TN 37762 Tel. (615)784-8260

Media Contact, Gen. Sec.-Treas., Rev. James Kilgore, P.O. Box 157, Jellico, TN 37762 Tel. (615)784-8260

OFFICERS

Gen. Overseer, Rev. Jasper Walden, Box 157, Jellico, TN 37762

Asst. Gen. Overseer/World Missions Dir., Rev. Cecil Johnson, Box 157, Jellico, TN 37762

Gen. Sec.-Treas., Rev. James Kilgore, Box 157, Jellico, TN 37762

PERIODICAL

Gospel Herald, The

Church of God of Prophecy

The Church of God of Prophecy is one of the churches that grew out of the work of A.J. Tomlinson in the first half of this century. It was named in 1952, but historically shares the traditions of the holiness classical pentecostal church, the Church of God (Cleveland, TN).

At the death of A.J. Tomlinson in 1943, M. A. Tomlinson was named overseer and served until 1990. He emphasized unity and fellowship that is not limited socially, racially, or nationally. The present general overseer, Billy D. Murray, Sr. is committed to promoting Christian unity and moving forward with world-wide evangelism.

The official teachings include special emphasis on sanctification, the doctrine of Spirit-baptism, and belief that tongues-speech is an initial evidence. The church teaches an imminence-oriented escatology that involves a premillennial return of the risen Jesus which itself will be preceded by a series of events; a call for the sanctity of the home which includes denial of a multiple marriage; practice of water baptism by immersion, the Lord's Supper and washing of the saints' feet; total abstinence from intoxicating beverages and tobacco; a concern for moderation in all dimensions of life; an appreciation for various gifts of the Holy Spirit, with special attention given to divine healing.

The Church is racially integrated on all levels and various leadership positions are occupied by women. The Church's history includes a strong emphasis on youth ministries, national and international missions and various parochial educational ministries.

HEADQUARTERS

P.O. Box 2910, Cleveland, TN 37320-2910

Media Contact, Dir., Public Relations, Perry Gillum, Tel. (615)476-3271 Fax (615)339-1945

OFFICERS

Gen. Overseer, Bishop Billy D. Murray, Sr.

Gen. Overseer Emeritus, Bishop Milton A. Tomlinson

Admn. Comm.: Gen. Overseer, Billy D. Murray, Sr.; Fin. Dir., Ms. Jerlena Riley; Bus. Mgr. of White Wing Publ. House, Henry O'Neal; Admn. Assts. to Gen. Overseer, Hugh R. Edwards; Jose A. Reyes, Sr.; E. L. Jones; Tomlinson College Pres., Perry Gillum; World Mission Sec., Adrian L. Varlack

GENERAL STAFF

Bible Training Inst.: Supt., Ray C. Wynn; Rep., Felix Santiago; Benjamin Lawrence

Church of Prophecy Marker Assoc., J. Wendell Lowe

Communications Business Mgr., Thomas Duncan

Communications Minister (English), Elwood Matthews

Communications Minister (Spanish), Jose A. Reyes, Sr.

Dept. of Pastoral Care, E. L. Jones

Evangelism & Church Planting, Dir., Hugh R. Edwards

Fin. Dir. & Personnel Mgr., Jerlena Riley

Gen. Ofc. Mgr., J. Wendell Lowe

Ministerial Aid, Dir., Jerlena Riley

Music Dept., Dir., Ronald Scotton

Public Relations, Dir., Perry Gillum

Sun. School & Personal Evangelism, Randy Howard

Tomlinson College President, Perry Gillum

Victory Leaders (Youth), William M. Wilson

Women's Miss. Aux., Elva Howard

World Language Sec., Henry O'Neal

World Missions: Adrian Varlack; Rep., Daniel J. Corbett; Sherman O. Allen; Felix Santiago; Chris Stathis; Arthur C. Moss

The Church of God (Seventh Day), Denver, Colo.

The Church of God (Seventh Day) began in southwestern Michigan in 1858, when a group of Sabbath-Keepers led by Gilbert Cranmer refused to give endorsement to the visions and writings of Ellen G. White, a principal in the formation of the Seventh-Day Adventist Church. Another branch of Sabbath-keepers, which developed near Cedar Rapids, Iowa, in 1860, joined the Michigan church in 1863 to publish a paper called The Hope of Israel, the predecessor to the Bible Advocate, the church's present publication. As membership grew and spread into Missouri and Nebraska, it organized the General Conference of the Church of God in 1884. The words (Seventh Day) were added to its name in 1923. The headquarters of the church was in Stanberry, Mo., from 1888 until 1950, when it moved to Denver.

The church observes the seventh day as the Sabbath; believes in the imminent, personal, and visible return of Jesus; that the dead are in an unconscious state awaiting to be resurrected, the righteous to immortality and the wicked to extinction by fire; and that the earth will be the eternal abode of the righteous. It observes two ordinances: baptism by immersion and an annual Communion service accompanied by foot washing.

HEADQUARTERS
330 W. 152nd Ave., P.O. Box 33677, Denver, CO 80233 Tel. (303)452-7973 Fax (303)452-0657
Media Contact, Pres., Calvin Burrell

OFFICERS
Chpsn., Calvin Burrell
Sec.-Treas., Jayne Kuryluk
Spring Vale Academy, Principal, Clark Caswell
Youth Agency, Dir., John & Ruth Tivald
Bible Advocate Press, Dir., LeRoy Dais
Women's Assoc., Pres., Mrs. Emogene Coulter
Summit School of Theology, Dir., Jerry Griffin
Missions Abroad, Dir., Victor Burford

PERIODICAL
Harvest Field Messenger

Church of God (Which He Purchased with His Own Blood)

This body was organized in 1953 in Oklahoma City, Okla. by William Jordan Fizer after his excommunication from the Church of the Living God (C.W.F.F.) over doctrinal disagreements relating to the Lord's Supper. The first annual convention was held in Oklahoma City, Nov. 19-21, 1954.

The church believes that water is not the element to be used in the Lord's Supper, observed every Sunday, but rather grape juice or wine and unleavened bread.

Its doctrine holds that the Holy Ghost is given to those who obey the Lord. Feet washing is observed as an act of humility and not the condition of salvation. Baptism must be administered in the name of the Father, Son, and Holy Ghost. The Church of God believes it is the Body of Christ, and because of scriptural doctrine and practice, that it is the church organized by Jesus Christ. The members are urged to lead consecrated lives unspotted from the world. Tobacco and strong drinks are condemned. Divine healing is an article of faith, but not to the exclusion of doctors.

HEADQUARTERS
1628 N.E. 50th, Oklahoma City, OK 73111 Tel. (405)427-8264
Media Contact, Chief Bishop, William J. Fizer, 1907 N.E. Grand Blvd., Oklahoma City, OK 73111 Tel. (405)427-2166

OFFICERS
Chief Bishop, William J. Fizer
Gen. Sec.-Treas., Alsie Mae Fizer
Overseers: J. W. Johnson, Rt. 1, Box 214, Choctaw, OK 73020; M. Roberson, Rt. 2, Box 214, Mounds, OK 74047; Supt. of Sunday Schools, Rueben Tyson, 1628 N.E. 50, Oklahoma City, OK Tel. (405)427-8264; Vice-Chief Bishop, George Hill, 1109 N.W. 74, Lawton, OK 73505 Tel. (405)536-4941; Thomas R. Smith, P.O. Box 27431, Tucson, AZ 85726 Tel. (602)624-0138

The Church of Illumination

Organized in 1908 for the express purpose of establishing congregations at large, offering a spiritual, esoteric, philosophical interpretation of the vital biblical teachings, thereby satisfying the inner spiritual needs of those seeking spiritual truth, yet permitting them to remain in, or return to, their former church membership.

HEADQUARTERS
Beverly Hall, Clymer Rd., Quakertown, PA 18951

OFFICERS
Dir., Gerald E. Poesnecker, P.O. Box 220, Quakertown, PA 18951

The Church of Jesus Christ (Bickertonites)

Organized 1862 at Green Oak, Pennsylvania, by William Bickerton, who obeyed the Restored Gospel under Sidney Rigdon's following in 1845.

HEADQUARTERS
Sixth & Lincoln Sts., Monongahela, PA 15063 Tel. (412)258-3066

OFFICERS
Pres., Dominic Thomas, 6010 Barrie, Dearborn, MI 48126
First Counselor, Nicholas Pietrangelo, 24106 Meadow Bridge Dr., Mt. Clemens, MI 48043
Second Counselor, V. James Lovalvo, 5769 Pleasant Ave., Fresno, CA 93711
Exec. Sec., Paul Palmieri, 319 Pine Dr., Aliquippa, PA 15001 Tel. (412)378-4264

PERIODICAL
Gospel News, The

The Church of Jesus Christ of Latter-day Saints

Organized April 6, 1830, at Fayette, N.Y., by Joseph Smith. Members believe Joseph Smith was divinely directed to restore the gospel to the earth, and that through him the keys to the Aaronic and Melchizedek priesthoods and temple work also were restored. In addition to the Bible, members believe the Book of Mormon (a record of the Lord's dealings with His people on the American continent 600 B.C. - 421 A.D.) to be scripture. Membership is worldwide, approaching nine million in 1992.

In addition to the First Presidency, the governing bodies of the church include the Quorum of the Twelve, the Presidency of the Seventy, the First Quorum of the Seventy, the Second Quorum of the Seventy and the Presiding Bishopric.

HEADQUARTERS
50 East North Temple St., Salt Lake City, UT 84150 Tel. (801)240-1000 Fax (801)240-1167
Media Contact, Dir., Media Relations, Don Le-Fevre, Tel. (801)240-4377

OFFICERS
Pres., Ezra Taft Benson
1st Counselor, Gordon B. Hinckley
2nd Counselor, Thomas S. Monson
Council of the Twelve Apostles: Pres., Howard W. Hunter; Boyd K. Packer; Marvin J. Ashton; L. Tom Perry; David B. Haight; James E. Faust; Neal A. Maxwell; Russell M. Nelson; Dallin H. Oaks; M. Russell Ballard; Joseph B. Wirthlin; Richard G. Scott

AUXILIARY ORGANIZATIONS
Sunday Schools, Gen. Pres., Hugh W. Pinnock
Relief Society, Gen. Pres., Elaine Jack
Young Men, Pres., Jack H. Goaslind

Young Women, Gen. Pres., Janette C. Hales
Primary, Gen. Pres., Michaelene P. Grassli

Church of the Living God (Motto: Christian Workers for Fellowship)

William Christian was born a slave in Mississippi on Nov. 10, 1856 and grew up uneducated. In 1875, he united with the Missionary Baptist Church and began to preach. In 1888, he left the Baptist Church and began what was known as Christian Friendship Work. Believing himself to have been inspired by the Spirit of God, through divine revelation and close study of the Scriptures, he was led to the truth that the Bible refers to the church as The Church of the Living God (I Tim. 3:15).

At Caine Creek, near Wrightsville, Ark., in April 1889, Christian became founder and organizer of The Church of the Living God, the first black church in America without Anglo-Saxon roots or not begun by white missionaries.

The church believes in the infallibility of the Scriptures, is Trinitarian, and believes there are three sacraments ordained by Christ: baptism (by immersion), the Lord's Supper (unleavened bread and water), and foot washing.

The Church of the Living God, C.W.F.F., believes in holiness as a gift of God subsequent to the New Birth and manifested only by a changed life acceptable to the Lord.

HEADQUARTERS

434 Forest Ave., Cincinnatti, OH 45229 Tel. (513)569-5661
Media Contact, Chief Bishop, W. E. Crumes, Tel. (513)221-1487

OFFICERS

Executive Board: Chief Bishop, W. E. Crumes, Tel. (513)221-1487; Vice-Chief Bishop, Alonza Ponder, 5609 N. Terry, Oklahoma City, OK 73111; Exec. Sec., Bishop C. A. Lewis, 1360 N. Boston, Tulsa, OK 73111; Gen. Sec., Elder Milton S. Herring, Los Angeles, CA; Gen. Treas., Elder Harry Hendricks, Milwaukee, WI; Bishop E. L. Bowie, 2037 N.E. 18th St., Oklahoma City, OK 73111; Chaplain, Bishop E. A. Morgan, 735 S. Oakland Dr., Decatur, IL 62525; Bishop L. A. Crawford, 3711 Biglow, Dallas, TX 74216; Bishop A. R. Powell, 8557 S. Wabash, Chicago, IL 60619; Bishop Jeff Ruffin, Phoenix, AZ; Aux. Bishop, R. S. Morgan, 4508 N. Indiana, Oklahoma City, OK 73118; Overseer, S. E. Shannon, 1034 S. King Hwy., St. Louis, MO 63110

NATIONAL DEPARTMENTS

Convention Planning Committee
Young People's Progressive Union
Christian Education Dept.
Sunday School Dept.
Natl. Evangelist Bd.
Natl. Nurses Guild
Natl. Women's Work Dept.
Natl. Music Dept.
Gen. Sec.'s Ofc.

Church of the Lutheran Brethren of America

The Church of the Lutheran Brethren of America was organized in December 1900. Five independent Lutheran congregations met together in Milwaukee, Wisc., and adopted a constitution patterned very closely to that of the Lutheran Free Church of Norway.

The spiritual awakening in the Midwest during the 1890s crystallized into convictions that led to the formation of a new church body. Chief among the concerns were church membership practices, observance of Holy Communion, confirmation practices and local church government.

The Church of the Lutheran Brethren practices a simple order of worship with the sermon as the primary part of the worship service. It believes that personal profession of faith is the primary criterion for membership in the congregation. The Communion service is reserved for those who profess faith in Christ as savior. Each congregation is autonomous and the synod serves the congregations in advisory and cooperative capacities.

The synod supports a world mission program in Cameroon, Chad, Japan and Taiwan. Approximately 40 percent of the synodical budget is earmarked for world missions. A growing home mission ministry is planting new congregations in the United States and Canada. Affiliate organizations operate several retirement/nursing homes, conference and retreat centers.

HEADQUARTERS

1007 Westside Dr., Box 655, Fergus Falls, MN 56538 Tel. (218)739-3336 Fax (218)739-5514

OFFICERS

Pres., Rev. Robert M. Overgard, Sr.
Vice-Pres., Rev. David Rinden
Sec., Rev. Richard Vettrus, 707 Crestview Dr., West Union, IA 52175
Dir. of Finance, Mr. Brad Mattinson
Lutheran Brethren Schools, Pres., Rev. Joel Egge, Lutheran Brethren Schools, Box 317, Fergus Falls, MN 56538
World Missions, Exec. Dir., Rev. Jarle Olson
Home Missions, Exec. Dir., Rev. John Westby
Church Services, Exec. Dir., Rev. David Rinden

Church of the Lutheran Confession

The Church of the Lutheran Confession held its constituting convention in Watertown, S.D., in August of 1960. The Church of the Lutheran Confession was born as a result of the people and congregations who came to their own individual convictions, based on Scripture, and were moved to withdraw from church bodies that made up what was then known as the Synodical Conference, over the issue of unionism. Following such passages as I Corinthians 1:10 and Romans 16:17-18, the Church of the Lutheran Confession holds the conviction that agreement with the doctrines of Scripture is essential and necessary before exercise of church fellowship is appropriate.

Members of the Church of the Lutheran Confession uncompromisingly believe the Holy Scriptures to be verbally inspired and therefore inerrant. They subscribe to the historic Lutheran Confessions as found in the Book of Concord of 1580 because they are a correct exposition of Scripture.

The Church of the Lutheran Confession exists to proclaim, preserve, and spread the saving truth of the gospel of Jesus Christ, so that the redeemed of God may learn to know Jesus Christ as their Lord and Savior, and to follow him through this life to the life to come.

460 75th Ave., NE, Minneapolis, MN 55432 Tel. (612)784-8784

Media Contact, Pres., Daniel Fleischer

OFFICERS

Pres., Rev. Daniel Fleischer
Vice-Pres., Rev. Elton Hallauer, 608 1st St., Hancock, MN 56244
Mod., Prof. Ronald Roehl, 515 Ingram Dr. W., Eau Claire, WI 54701
Sec., Rev. Paul Nolting, 626 N. Indian Landing Rd., Rochester, NY 14625
Treas., Lowell Moen, 3455 Jill Ave., Eau Claire, WI 54701
Archivist-Historian, John Lau
Statistician, Harvey Callies

PERIODICALS

C.L.C. Directory; Journal of Theology

Church of the Nazarene

The origins of the Church of the Nazarene are in the broader holiness movement which arose soon after the American Civil War. It is the result of the merging of three independent holiness groups already in existence in the United States. The Association of Pentecostal Churches in America, located principally in New York and New England, joined at Chicago in 1907 with a California body called the Church of the Nazarene. This united body was called the Pentecostal Church of the Nazarene. The southern group, known as the Holiness Church of Christ, united with this Pentecostal Church of the Nazarene at Pilot Point, Texas, in 1908. In 1919, the word Pentecostal was dropped from the name. Principal leaders in the organization were Phineas Bresee, founder of the church in the West; William Howard Hoople and H. F. Reynolds from the East; and C. B. Jernigan in the southern group. The first Church of the Nazarene in Canada was organized in November 1902 by Dr. H. F. Reynolds, in Oxford, Nova Scotia.

The Church of the Nazarene is distinctive in its emphasis on the doctrine of entire sanctification on the proclamation of Christian Holiness. It stresses the importance of a devout and holy life and a positive witness before the world by the power of the Holy Spirit. The church feels that caring is a way of life.

Nazarene government is representative, a studied compromise between episcopacy and congregationalism. Quadrennially, the various districts elect delegates to a general assembly, at which six general superintendents are elected.

The international denomination has 10 liberal arts colleges, two graduate seminaries, 16 seminaries, and 24 Bible colleges. The church maintains missionaries in 95 countries. World services include medical, education, and religious ministries. Books, periodicals, and other Christian literature are published at the Nazarene Publishing House.

The church is a member of the Christian Holiness Association and the National Association of Evangelicals.

HEADQUARTERS

6401 The Paseo, Kansas City, MO 64131 Tel. (816)333-7000 Fax (816)333-1748

Media Contact, Gen. Sec., Dr. Jack Stone

OFFICERS

Gen. Supts.: Eugene L. Stowe; Jerald Johnson; John A. Knight; Raymond Hurn; William J. Prince; Donald D. Owens

Gen. Sec., Jack Stone
Gen. Treas., Norman O. Miller

OTHER ORGANIZATIONS

General Bd.: Sec., Jack Stone; Treas., Norman O. Miller
Church Growth Div., Dir., Bill Sullivan
Chaplaincy Min., Dir., Curt Bowers
Church Ext. Min., Dir., Mike Estep
Evangelism Min., Dir., M. V. Scutt
Pastoral Min., Dir., Wilbur Brannon
Communications Div., Dir., Paul Skiles
Editor, "Herald of Holiness", Wesley Tracy
Media Services, Dir., David Anderson
Publications Intl., Dir., Ray Hendrix
Fin. Div., Dir., D. Moody Gunter
Planned Giving, Dir., Martin Butler
Pensions & Benefits Services, Dir., Dean Wessels
Stewardship Services, Dir., D. Moody Gunter
Sunday School Min. Div., Dir., Phil Riley
Adult Min., Dir., Randy Cloud
Children's Min., Dir., Miriam Hall
NYI Min., Dir., Fred Fullerton
World Mission Div., Dir., Robert H. Scott
Missionary Min., Dir., John Smee
Fin. Services, Dir., Dennis Berard
Nazarene World Missionary Soc., Dir., Nina Gunter
Intl. Bd. of Educ., Ed. Commissioner, Stephen Nease

PERIODICALS

Preacher's Magazine; Bread

Church of Our Lord Jesus Christ of the Apostolic Faith, Inc.

This Church as an organized body was founded by Bishop R. C. Lawson in Columbus, Ohio, and moved to New York City in 1919. It is founded upon the teachings of the Apostles and Prophets, Jesus Christ being its chief cornerstone.

HEADQUARTERS

2081 Adam Clayton Powell Jr. Blvd., New York, NY 10027 Tel. (212)866-1700

Media Contact, Exec. Sec., Bishop T. E. Woolfolk, P.O. Box 119, Oxford, NC 27565 Tel. (919)693-9449 Fax (919)693-6115

OFFICERS

Board of Apostles: Pres., Bishop William L. Bonner; Chief Apostle, Bishop J. P. Steadman; Bishop Frank S. Solomon; Bishop Henry A. Ross, Sr.; Bishop Matthew A. Norwood; Bishop Gentle L. Groover; Bishop Wilbur L. Jones
Bd. of Bishops, Chmn., Bishop James I. Clark
Bd. of Presbyters, Pres., District Elder Kenneth Bligen
Exec. Secretariat, Sec., Bishop T. E. Woolfolk
Natl. Rec. Sec., Bishop Fred Rubin, Sr. (J.B.)
Natl. Fin. Sec., Bishop Clarence Groover
Natl. Corr. Sec., Bishop Raymond J. Keith, Jr. (J.B.)
Natl Treas., Bishop Thomas J. Richardson

Churches of Christ

Churches of Christ are autonomous congregations, whose members appeal to the Bible alone to determine matters of faith and practice. There are no central offices or officers. Publications and institutions related to the churches are either under local congregational control or independent of any one congregation.

Churches of Christ shared a common fellowship in the 19th century with the Christian Churches/Churches of Christ and the Christian Church (Disciples of Christ). Fellowship was gradually estranged following the Civil War due to theistic evolution, higher critical theories, and centralization of church-wide activities through a missionary society.

Members of Churches of Christ believe in the inspiration of the Scriptures, the divinity of Jesus Christ, and immersion into Christ for the remission of sins. The New Testament pattern is followed in worship and church organization.

MEDIA CONTACT

Media Contact, Ed., Gospel Advocate, Dr. F. Furman Kearley, P.O. Box 167, Monahans, TX 79756-0167

PERIODICALS

Gospel Advocate; Guardian of Truth; Image; Power for Today; Restoration Quarterly; 21st Century Christian; Upreach; Rocky Mountain Christian

Churches of Christ in Christian Union

Organized in 1909 at Washington Court House, Ohio, as the Churches of Christ in Christian Union, this body believes in the new birth and the baptism of the Holy Spirit for believers. It is Wesleyan, with an evangelistic and missionary emphasis.

The Reformed Methodist Church merged in September, 1952, with Churches of Christ in Christian Union.

HEADQUARTERS

1426 Lancaster Pike, Box 30, Circleville, OH 43113 Tel. (614)474-8856 Fax (614)477-7766
Media Contact, Gen. Supt., Daniel L. Tipton

OFFICERS

Gen. Supt., Dr. Daniel Tipton
Asst. Gen. Supt., Rev. David Dean
Gen. Sec., Rev. Robert Barth, 4205 Cedar St., New Boston, OH 45662
Gen. Treas., Bevery R. Salley
Gen. Bd. of Trustees: Chpsn., Dr. Daniel Tipton; Vice-Chpsn., Rev. David Dean; Sec., Rev. Robert Barth
District Superintendents: West Central District, Dr. Robert L. Sayre; South Central District, Rev. Jack Norman; Northeast District, Rev. Art Penird, Rt. 2, P.O. Box 790, Port Crane, NY 13833

Churches of God, General Conference

The Churches of God, General Conference had its beginnings in Harrisburg, Pa., in 1825.

John Winebrenner, recognized founder of the Church of God movement, was an ordained minister of the German Reformed Church. His experience-centered form of Christianity, particularly the "new measures" he used to promote it, his close connection with the local Methodists, his "experience and conference meetings" in the church, and his "social prayer meetings" in parishioners' homes resulted in differences of opinion and the establishment of new congregations. Extensive revivals, camp meetings, and mission endeavors led to the organization of additional congregations across central Pennsylvania and westward through Ohio, Indiana, Illinois, and Iowa.

In 1830 the first system of cooperation between local churches was initiated as an "eldership" in eastern Pennsylvania. The organization of other elderships followed. General Eldership was organized in 1845, and in 1974 the official name of the denomination was changed from General Eldership of the Churches of God in North America to its present name.

The Churches of God, General Conference, is composed of 16 conferences in the United States. The polity of the church is presbyterial in form. The church has mission ministries in the southwest among native Americans and is extensively involved in church planting and whole life ministries in Bangladesh, Haiti, and India.

The General Conference convenes in business session triennially. An Administrative Council composed of 38 regional representatives serving on seven commissions is responsible for the administration and ministries of the church between sessions of the General Conference.

HEADQUARTERS

Legal Headquarters, United Church Center, Rm. 200, 900 S. Arlington Ave., Harrisburg, PA 17109 Tel. (717)652-0255
Administrative Offices, General Conf. Adm., Pastor William H. Reist, 700 E. Melrose Ave., P.O. Box 926, Findlay, OH 45839 Tel. (419)424-1961

OFFICERS

Pres., Pastor George Reser, 506 N. Main St., Columbia City, IN 46725 Tel. (219)248-2482
Journalizing Sec., Pastor David L. Meador, 5665 New Design Rd., Frederick, MD 21701 Tel. (301)663-0741
Treas., Mr. Robert E. Stephenson, 700 E. Melrose Ave., P.O. Box 926, Findlay, OH 45839 Tel. (419)424-1961

DEPARTMENTS

Assoc. in Ministry: Church Publications, Mrs. Linda M. Draper; Cross-Cultural Ministries, Mr. Travis C. Perry; Pensions, Dr. Royal P. Kear; Curriculum, Rev. Marilyn Rayle Kern; Campus Ministries, Rev. Douglas E. Nolt; Development, Rev. Frederick C. Quade; Education & Family Life, Rev. R. Joe Roach; Dir. of Youth Ministry, Mr. Philip J. Scott; Fin., Mr. Robert E. Stephenson

COMMISSIONS

Church Development: Chpsn., Pastor Alvin D. Rockey, Box 221, Idaville, IN 47950; Sec., Pastor James L. Monticue, RR 1, Box 51, Markleton, PA 15551
Church Vocations: Chpsn., Pastor Dale R. Brougher, 1015 S. West St., Findlay, OH 45840; Sec., Mrs. Rosamond E. Kear, 1718 Cherry La., Findlay, OH 45840
Education: Chpsn., Pastor Ronald E. Dull, 12 Dogwood Ct., Shippensburg, PA 17257; Sec., Mrs. Marilyn J. Dunn, 2211 Market St., Harrisburg, PA 17103
Evangelism: Chpsn., Pastor Glenn E. Beatty, 1114 Circle Dr., Latrobe, PA 15650; Sec., Dr. John A. Parthemore, Jr., 235 W. High St., Middletown, PA 17057
National Ministries: Chpsn., Howard L. Ruley, 100 W. Franklin, P.O. Box 247, Wharton, OH 43359; Sec., Pastor G. Gordon Jenkins, 3827 N. East Ct. Dr., Decatur, IL 62526

Stewardship: Chpsn., Pastor Larry G. White, 936 W. Main St., Mt. Pleasant, PA 15666; Sec., Dr. A. Gail Dunn, 900 S. Arlington Ave., Rm. 200, Harrisburg, PA 17109

World Missions: Chpsn., Pastor Lester L. Swope, 248 Newburg Rd., Newburg, PA 17240; Sec., Pastor Paul E. Tobias, 16924 Raven Rock Rd., Cascade, MD 21719

PERIODICALS
Church Advocate, The; Workman, The; Gem, The

Community Churches, International Council of
This body is a fellowship of locally autonomous, ecumenically minded, congregationally governed, non-creedal Churches. The Council came into being in 1950 as the union of two former councils of community churches, one formed of black churches known as the Biennial Council of Community Churches, and the other of white churches known as the National Council of Community Churches.

HEADQUARTERS
7808 College Dr., 2 SE, Palos Heights, IL 60463 Tel. (708)361-2600

OFFICERS
Pres., Larry McClellan
Vice-Pres.: Orsey Malone; Ronald Miller
Sec., Abraham Wright, .
Treas., Martha Nolan
Exec. Dir., Jeffrey R. Newhall

OTHER ORGANIZATIONS
Commission on Church Relations
Commission on Ecumenical Relations
Commission on Clergy Relations
Commission on Laity Relations
Commission on Faith & Order
Commission on Social Concerns
Commission on Missions
Commission on Informational Services
Women's Christian Fellowship, Pres., Mozella Weston
Samaritans (Men's Fellowship), Pres., Louis Oatis
Young Adult Fellowship, Pres., Michelle Kiah
Youth Fellowship, Pres., Dara Wilson

PERIODICALS
Christian Community, The; Pastor's Journal, The

Congregational Christian Churches, National Association of
Organized 1955 in Detroit, Mich., by delegates from Congregational Christian Churches committed to continuing the Congregational way of faith and order in church life. Participation by member churches is voluntary.

HEADQUARTERS
P.O. Box 1620, Oak Creek, WI 53154 Tel. (414)764-1620 Fax (414)764-0319
Media Contact, Exec. Sec., Michael S. Robertson, 8473 So. Howell Ave., Oak Creek, WI 53154 Tel. (414)764-1620 Fax (414)764-0319

OFFICERS
Mod., Steven S. Hoth
Exec. Sec., Michael S. Robertson, 8473 South Howell Ave., Oak Creek, WI 53154
Assoc. Exec. Secs.: Rev. Dr. Michael Halcomb; Rev. Dr. Harry W. Clark

PERIODICAL
Congregationalist, The

Congregational Holiness Church
A body which was organized in 1921 and which embraces the doctrine of Holiness and Pentecost. It carries on mission work in Mexico, Honduras, Costa Rica, Cuba, Brazil, Guatemala, India, Nicaragua and El Salvador.

HEADQUARTERS
3888 Fayetteville Hwy., Griffin, GA 30223 Tel. (404)228-4833
Media Contact, Gen. Supt., Bishop L. G. Howard, Fax (404)228-1177

EXECUTIVE BOARD
Gen. Supt., Bishop L. G. Howard
1st Asst. Gen. Supt., Rev. William L. Lewis
2nd Asst. Gen. Supt., Rev. Wayne Hicks
Gen. Sec., Rev. Kenneth Law
Gen. Treas., Rev. Dennis Phillips

PERIODICAL
Gospel Messenger, The

Conservative Baptist Association of America
Organized May 17, 1947, at Atlantic City, N.J. The Old and New Testaments are regarded as the divinely inspired Word of God and are therefore infallible and of supreme authority. Each local church is independent and autonomous, and free from ecclesiastical or political authority.

HEADQUARTERS
25W560 Geneva Rd., P.O. Box 66, Wheaton, IL 60189 Tel. (708)653-5350 Fax (708)653-5387
Media Contact, Dir. of Comm., Rev. Walter Fricke

OTHER ORGANIZATIONS
Conservative Baptist For. Mission Soc., Gen. Dir., Dr. Warren W. Webster, Box 5, Wheaton, IL 60189
Conservative Baptist Home Mission Soc., Gen. Dir., Dr. Jack Estep, Box 828, Wheaton, IL 60189
Conservative Baptist Higher Ed. Council, Dr. Paul Bordem, Denver Conservative Baptist Seminary, P.O. Box 10,000, Denver, CO 80210

Conservative Congregational Christian Conference
In the 1930s, evangelicals within the Congregational Christian Churches felt a definite need for fellowship and service. By 1945, this loose association crystallized in the Conservative Congregational Christian Fellowship, concerned to maintain a faithful, biblical witness.

In 1948 in Chicago, the Conservative Congregational Christian Conference was established to provide a continuing fellowship for evangelical churches and ministers on the national level. In recent years, many churches have joined the Conference from backgrounds other than Congregational. These Community or Bible Churches are truly congregational in polity and thoroughly evangelical in conviction. The CCCC welcomes all evangelical churches that are, in fact, congregational. The CCCC believes in the necessity of a regenerate membership, the authority of the Holy Scriptures, the Lordship of Jesus Christ, the autonomy of the local church, and the universal fellowship of all Christians.

The Conservative Congregational Christian Conference is a member of the World Evangelical Congregational Fellowship (formed in 1986 in London, England) and the National Association of Evangelicals.

HEADQUARTERS

7582 Currell Blvd., Ste. #108, St. Paul, MN 55125
Media Contact, Conf. Min., Rev. Clifford R. Christensen, Tel. (612)739-1474

OFFICERS

Pres., Mr. William V. Nygren, 583 Sterling, Maplewood, MN 55119
Vice-Pres., Rev. Don Ehler, 620 High Ave., Hillsboro, WI 54634
Conf. Min., Rev. Clifford R. Christensen, 57 Kipling St., St. Paul, MN 55519
Controller, Mr. Leslie Pierce, 5220 E. 105th St. S., Tulsa, OK 74137
Treas., Mr. John D. Nygren, 579 Sterling St., Maplewood, MN 55119
Rec. Sec., Rev. Larry E. Scovil, 317 W. 40th St., Scottsbluff, NE 69361
Editor, Mrs. Wanda Evans, 4072 Clifton Ridge, Highland, MI 48357
Historian, Rev. Rodney Wetzig, 605 Bethel St., Parkerburg, IA 50665

PERIODICALS

Foresee

Coptic Orthodox Church

This body is part of the ancient Coptic Orthodox Church of Egypt which is currently headed by His Holiness Pope Shenouda III. In the United States many parishes have been organized, consisting of Egyptian immigrants to the United States. Copts exist outside of Egypt in Ethiopia, Europe, Asia, Australia, Canada and the United States. The world Coptic community is estimated at 14 million, the vast majority being located in Egypt.

CORRESPONDENT

Archpriest Gabriel Abdelsayed, 427 West Side Ave., Jersey City, NJ 07304 Tel. (201)333-0004 Fax (201)333-0502

Cumberland Presbyterian Church

The Cumberland Presbyterian Church was organized in Dickson County, Tenn., on Feb. 4, 1810. It was an outgrowth of the Great Revival of 1800 on the Kentucky and Tennessee frontier. The founders were Finis Ewing, Samuel King, and Samuel McAdow, ministers in the Presbyterian Church who rejected the doctrine of election and reprobation as taught in the Westminster Confession of Faith.

By 1813, the Cumberland Presbytery had grown to encompass three presbyteries, which constituted a synod. This synod met at the Beech Church in Sumner County, Tenn., and formulated a "Brief Statement," which set forth the points in which Cumberland Presbyterians dissented from the Westminster Confession.

1. That there are no eternal reprobates;
2. That Christ died not for a part only, but for all mankind;
3. That all those dying in infancy are saved through Christ and the sanctification of the Spirit;
4. That the Spirit of God operates on the world, or as coextensively as Christ has made atonement, in such a manner as to leave all men inexcusable.

From its birth in 1810, the Cumberland Presbyterian Church grew to a membership of 200,000 at the turn of the century. In 1906 the church voted to merge with the then-Presbyterian Church. Those who dissented from the merger became the nucleus of the continuing Cumberland Presbyterian Church.

OFFICERS

Mod., Mr. Floyd T. Hensley, 2096 Old Lebanon Rd., Campbellsville, KY 42718
Stated Clk., Rev. Robert Prosser, 1978 Union Ave., Memphis, TN 38104
General Assembly Exec. Comm., Chpsn., Rev. Robert E. Shelton, 8525 Audelia, Dallas, TX 75238

INSTITUTIONS

Cumberland Presbyterian Children's Home, Exec. Dir., Dr. Marvin E. Leslie, Drawer G, Denton, TX 76202 Tel. (817)382-5112
Cumberland Presbyterian Center, 1978 Union Ave., Memphis, TN 38104 Tel. (901)276-4572 Fax (901)276-4578

BOARDS

Bd. of Christian Education, Exec. Dir., Mrs. Claudette Pickle, 1978 Union Ave., Memphis, TN 38104
Bd. of Missions, Exec. Dir., Rev. Joe E. Matlock, 1978 Union Ave., Memphis, TN 38104
Bd. of Finance, Exec. Sec., Rev. Richard Magrill, 1978 Union Ave., Memphis, TN 38104

PERIODICALS

Cumberland Presbyterian, The; Missionary Messenger, The

Duck River (and Kindred) Associations of Baptists

This group of Baptist associations is found in Tennessee, Alabama, Georgia, and Kentucky.

OFFICERS

Duck River Assoc., Mod., Elder Wayne L. Smith, Rt. 1, Box 429, Lynchburg, TN 37352
Clk., Elder Marvin Davenport, Rt. 1, Auburntown, TN 37016
General Assoc., Mod., Elder Charles Bell, Rt. 1, Box 385A, Valley Head, TN 35989 Tel. (205)635-6539
Clk., Br. Timothy Pellen, Morrison, TN 37357 Tel. (615)635-2946

Elim Fellowship

The Elim Fellowship, a Pentecostal Body, established in 1947, is an outgrowth of the Elim Missionary Assemblies, which was formed in 1933.

It is an association of churches, ministers and missionaries seeking to serve the whole Body of Christ. It is of Pentecostal conviction and charismatic orientation, providing ministerial credentials and counsel and encouraging fellowship among local churches. Elim Fellowship sponsors leadership seminars at home and abroad, and serves as a transdenominational agency sending long-term, short-term, and tent-making missionaries to work with national movements.

OFFICERS

Gen. Overseer, L. Dayton Reynolds, Elim Fellowship, Lima, NY 14485 Tel. (716)582-2790
Asst. Gen. Overseer, Bernard J. Evans, 3727 Snowden Hill Rd., New Hartford, NY 13413 Tel. (315)736-0966

Gen. Sec., Chester Gretz, Elim Fellowship, Lima, NY 14485 Tel. (716)582-2790

Acting Gen. Treas., Kenneth Beukema, 7284 McDonald Dr., Lima, NY 14485 Tel. (716)624-1059

The Episcopal Church

The Episcopal Church entered the colonies with the earliest settlers (Jamestown, Virginia., 1607) as the Church of England. After the American Revolution, it became autonomous in 1789 as The Protestant Episcopal Church in the United States of America. (The Episcopal Church became the official alternate name in 1967.) Samuel Seabury of Connecticut was elected the first bishop and consecrated in Aberdeen by bishops of the Scottish Episcopal Church in 1784.

In organizing as an independent body The Episcopal Church created a bicameral legislature, the General Convention, modeled after the new U.S. Congress. It comprises a House of Bishops and a House of Clerical and Lay Deputies and meets every three years. A 40-member Executive Council, which meets three times a year, is the interim governing body. An elected presiding bishop serves as Primate and Chief Pastor.

After severe setbacks in the years immediately following the Revolution because of its association with the British Crown and the fact that a number of its clergy and members were Loyalists, the church soon established its own identity and sense of mission. It sent missionaries into the newly settled territories of the United States, establishing dioceses from coast to coast, and also undertook substantial missionary work in Africa, Latin America and the Far East. Today, the overseas dioceses are developing into independent provinces of the Anglican Communion, the worldwide fellowship of churches in communion with the Church of England and the Archbishop of Canterbury.

The beliefs and practices of The Episcopal Church, like those of other Anglican churches, are both Catholic and Reformed, with bishops in the apostolic succession and the historic creeds of Christendom regarded as essential elements of faith and order, along with the primary authority of Holy Scripture and the two chief sacraments of Baptism and Eucharist.

HEADQUARTERS

815 Second Ave., New York, NY 10017 Tel. (212)867-8400

OFFICERS

Presiding Bishop & Primate, Most Rev. Edmond L. Browning

House of Bishops, Sec., Rt. Rev. Herbert A. Donovan, Jr., Box 164668, Little Rock, AR 72216

House of Deputies: Pres., V. Rev. David B. Collins; Vice-Pres., Mrs. Pamela P. Chinnis; Sec., Rev. Canon Donald A. Nickerson, Jr.

Gen. Conv.: Sec. & Exec. Officer, Rev. Donald A. Nickerson, Jr.; Treas., Mrs. Ellen F. Cooke

EXECUTIVE COUNCIL

Pres. & Chpsn., Most Rev. Edmond L. Browning
Vice-Chpsn., V. Rev. David B. Collins
Vice-Pres., Rt. Rev. Furman C. Stough
Treas., Mrs. Ellen F. Cooke
Sec., Rev. Donald A. Nickerson, Jr.

EPISCOPAL CHURCH CENTER

OFFICE OF THE PRESIDING BISHOP: Presiding Bishop & Primate, Most Rev. Edmond L. Browning; Sr. Exec. for Mission Operations, D. Barry Menuez; Exec. for Mission Support/Treas., Mrs. Ellen F. Cooke; Exec. for Mission Planning, Rt. Rev. Furman C. Stough; Dep. for Admn., Rev. Richard Chang; Dep. for Anglican Relationships, Rev. Patrick Mauney; Suf. Bishop for Chaplaincies to Military/Prisons/Hosp., Rt. Rev. Charles L. Keyser; Asst., Rev. Donald W. Beers; Suf. Bishop for Europe & the Diaspora, Rt. Rev. Matthew P. Bigliardi; Exec. for Pastoral Dev., Rt. Rev. Harold A. Hopkins, Jr.; Exec. Officer, Gen. Conv., Rev. Canon Donald A. Nickerson, Jr.

STEWARDSHIP DEVELOPMENT: Dir., Rev. Ronald Reed; Staff Officer for Planned Giving, Frederick H. Osborn, III; Staff Officer for Cong. Dev., Rev. Robert H. Bonner; Staff Officer for Stewardship Educ., Mrs. Laura E. Wright

COMMUNICATION: Exec., Ms. Sonia J. Francis; News Dir., James Soldheim; Asst. News Dir., Jeffrey Penn; Dir. Publications, Frank Tedeschi; Dir. of Electronic Publishing, Br. Tobias Haller; Video Producer, Andy Stauffer; Electronic Media Dir., Clement W. K. Lee; Printing Production Dir., Robert Nangle; Art Dir., Ms. Rochelle Arthur; Publ. Specialists, Susan Reul; Bruce Campbell

EDUCATION FOR MISSION & MINISTRY: Exec., Rev. David Perry; Admn. Asst., Mrs. Ruby Miller; Field Officer for Educ. & Training, Dr. John D. Vogelsang; Coord for Inst. of Higher Educ., Dr. E. Nathaniel Porter; Youth Min. Coord., Rev. Sheryl Kujawa; Min. Dev. Officer, Rev. John T. Docker; Evang. Officer, Rev. A. Wayne Schwab; Cong. Dev., Rev. Arlin Rothauge; Prog. Resource Dev., Dr. Irene V. Jackson-Brown; Coord. for Children's Min., Harold Williams; Exec. Dir., Bd. for Theol. Educ., Rev. Preston T. Kelsey; Exec. Dir. Church Deployment Ofc., Mr. William A. Thompson; Exec. Dir., Ofc. of Pastoral Development, Rt. Rev. Harold Hopkins; Suf. Bishop for Chaplaincies to Military & Prisons, Rt. Rev. Charles L. Keyser; Exec. Asst. Chaplain, Rev. Donald Beers

NATL. MISSION IN CHURCH & SOCIETY: Exec., Rev. Earl A. Neil; Staff Ofc. for Housing & Training, Howard Quander; Staff Ofc. for Coalition for Human Needs Comm., Ms. Gloria Brown; Staff Officer for Social & Specialized Min., Marcia L. Newcombe; Staff Ofc. for Black Min., Rev. Canon Harold T. Lewis; Staff Ofc. for Indian Min., Ms. Owanah B. Anderson; Staff Ofc. for Hispanic Min., Rev. Dr. Herbert Arrunategui; Staff Ofc. for Asiamerica Min., Rev. Winston W. Ching; Staff Ofc. for Natl. Mission Dev., Rev. Richard E. Gary; Women in Mission & Min., Ms. Ann Smith; Assoc. Ecumenical Ofc. for Washington Affairs, Rev. Robert Brooks; Staff Ofc. for Jubilee Min., Ms. Iniski Langford; Public Issues Ofc., Rev. Brian Grieves

WORLD MISSION IN CHURCH & SOCIETY: Exec., Ms. Judith M. Gillespie; Dep. & Partnership Ofc. for Asia/Pacific/Middle East, Rev. Dr. William L. Wipfler; Partnership Ofc. for Latin America & Caribbean, Rev. Richardo T. Potter; Partnership Ofc. for Africa, ———; Admn. Asst. to Exec., Br. James E. Teets, BSG; Automation Supervisor, Mrs. Rita G. Maroney

MISSION INFORMATION & EDUCATION: Staff Ofc., Ms. Margaret S. Larom
OVERSEAS PERSONNEL: Coord., Rev. Mark Harris; Assoc. for Partnership & Training, Ms. Anne Connors; Assoc. for Volunteers for Mission & Overseas Service, Mrs. Dorothy Gist; Interim Assoc. for Logistics, Ms. Linda C. Nash; Asst. for Volunteers for Mission, Ms. Virginia K. Hummel
OVERSEAS DEVELOPMENT PLANNING: Coord., Mrs. Carolyn Rose-Avila; Assoc. Coord., Rev. Linda L. Grenz; Program Staff Ofc., Ms. Soledad M. Longid
ECUMENICAL RELATIONS: Staff Ofc., Rev. William A. Norgren; Assoc., Dr. Christopher M. Agnew
UNITED THANK OFFERING: Coord., Ms. Willeen V. Smith; Grant Admn., Rev. Daniel D. Darko
PRESIDING BISHOPS FUND FOR WORLD RELIEF: Interim Exec. Dir., Ms. Bobbie Bevill; Asst. Dir. for Migration Affairs, Mrs. Marion M. Dawson; Asst. for Admn., Mrs. Nancy Marvel; Asst. for Interpretation & Network Dev., Dr. David Crean; Communications/Info. Ofc. Refugee/Migration, Rev. Gene T. White; Sponsorship Dev. Ofc. Refugee/Migration, Ms. Sarah Dresser
MISSION SUPPORT: Exec. & Treas., Mrs. Ellen F. Cooke; Asst. Treas., J. Thompson Hiller; Philippe Labbe; Dir. Mission Operation Support/Controller, Robert E. Brown; Internal Auditor, Dr. Christopher Cabrera; Dir. MIS, Barbara Keliher-Bunten; Data Processing Supervisor, Ms. Barbara Price
ADMINISTRATION: Exec. Dir. Admn. Services, Terence Adair; Asst., Dick Rene; Human Resources Ofc., Ms. Mary De Paolo; Asst. Human Resources Ofc., Mr. John Colon
GENL. CONVENTION EXECUTIVE OFFICE: Exec. Ofc./Sec./Registrar, Rev. Donald A. Nickerson, Jr.; Dep. Registrar, Canon Richard T. Biernacki, BSG; Treas., Mrs. Ellen F. Cooke; Asst., Ms. Cheryl J. Dawkins; Convention Mgr., Ms. Lori M. Arnold; Asst. Meeting Coord., Ms. Carolyn Zimei; Ed., Rev. Charles Scott; Info. Systems Mgr., Mrs. Diana Morris

OFFICIAL AGENCIES

Church Pension Fund & Affiliates: Pres., Robert A. Robinson, 800 Second Ave., New York, NY 10017
Episcopal Church Building Fund: Exec., Rev. Sherrill Scales, Jr., Tel. (212)697-6066
The Episcopal Church Foundation: Exec., Mr. Jeffrey H. Kittros, Tel. (212)698-2858
Archives of the Episcopal Church: Archivist, Dr. V. Nelle Bellamy

BISHOPS IN THE U.S.A.

(C, Coadjutor; S, Suffragan; A Assistant)
(Address: Right Reverend)
Headquarters Staff: Presiding Bishop & Primate, The Most Rev. Edmond L. Browning; Field Ofc., Right Rev. Harold Hopkins; Suf. Bishop for Chaplaincies to Military\Prisons\Hosp., Rev. Charles L. Keyser
Alabama: Robert O. Miller, 521 N. 20th St., Birmingham, AL 35203
Alaska: Steve Charlston, Box 441, Fairbanks, AK 99707
Albany: David S. Ball, 62 S. Swan St., Albany, NY 12210
Arizona: Joseph T. Heistand, P.O. Box 13647, Phoenix, AZ 85002

Arkansas: Herbert Donovan, Jr., 300 W. 17th St., P.O. Box 6120, Little Rock, AR 72206
Atlanta: Frank Kellog Allan, 2744 Peachtree Rd. N.W., Atlanta, GA 30305
Bethlehem: J. Mark Dyer, 333 Wyandotte St., Bethelehem, PA 18015
California: William E. Swing, 1055 Taylor St., San Francisco, CA 94108
Central Florida: John H. Howe, 324 N. Interlachen Ave., Box 790, Winter Park, FL 32789
Central Gulf Coast: Charles F. Duvall, P.O. Box 8547, Mobile, AL 36608
Central New York: O'Kelley Whittaker, 310 Montgomery St., Syracuse, NY 13203
Central Pennsylvania: Charlie F. McNutt, P.O. Box W, Harrisburg, PA 17108
Chicago: Frank T. Griswold, III, 65 E. Huron St., Chicago, IL 60611
Colorado: William J. Winterrond; William Harvey Wolfrum, (S), P.O. Box M, Capitol Hill Sta., Denver, CO 80218
Connecticut: Arthur E. Walmsley; Clarence N. Coleridge, (S); Jeffrey William Rowthorn, (S), 1335 Asylum Ave., Hartford, CT 06105
Dallas: Donis D. Patterson, 1630 Garrett St., Dallas, TX 75206
Delaware: Calvin C. Tennis, 2020 Tatnall St., Wilmington, DE 19802
East Carolina: B. Sidney Sanders, P.O. Bpx 1336, Kinston, NC 28501
East Tennessee: William E. Sanders, Box 3807, Knoxville, TN 37917
Eastern Oregon: Rustin R. Kimsey, P.O. Box 620, The Dalles, OR 97058
Easton: Elliot L. Sorge, P.O. Box 1027, Easton, MD 21601
Eau Clair: William C. Wantland, 510 S. Farwell St., Eau Claire, WI 54701
El Camino Real: Richard Shimpfky, P.O. Box 1093, Monterey, CA 93940
Florida: Frank S. Cerveny, 325 Market St., Jacksonville, FL 32202
Fond du Lac: William L. Stevens, P.O. Box 149, Fond du Lac, WI 54935
Fort Worth: Clarence Cullam Pope, Jr., 3572 Southwest Loop 820, Fort Worth, TX 76133
Georgia: Harry W. Shipps, 611 East Bay St., Savannah, GA 31401
Hawaii: Donald P. Hart, Queen Emma Square, Honolulu, HI 93813
Idaho: John S. Thornton, IV, Box 936, Boise, ID
Indianapolis: Edward W. Jones, 1100 W. 42nd St., Indianapolis, IN 46208
Iowa: C. Christopher Epting, 225 37th St., Des Moines, IA 50312
Kansas: William E. Smalley, Bethany Place, Topeka, KS 66612
Kentucky: David B. Reed 421 S. 2nd St., Louisville, KY 40202
Lexington: Don A. Wimberly, 530 Sayre Ave., Lexington, KY 40508
Long Island: Robert Campbell Witcher; Henry B. Hucles, III, (S), 36 Cathedral Ave., Garden City, NY 11530
Los Angeles: Federick H. Borsch; Oliver B. Garver, Jr., (S), 1220 W. 4th St., Los Angeles, CA 90017
Louisiana: James Barrow Brown, P.O. Box 15719, New Orleans, LA 70175
Maine: Edward C. Chalfant, 143 State St., Portland, ME 04101
Maryland: A. Theodore Eastman; Barry Valentine, (A), 105 W. Monument St., Baltimore, MD 21230

Massachusetts: David Elliott Johnson; Morris F. Arnold, (S); Barbara Harris, (S); Asst. Bishop, David B. Birney, 1 Joy St., Boston, MA 02108

Michigan: H. Coleman McGehee, Jr; Harry Irving Mayson, (S); William J. Gordon, (A), 4800 Woodward Ave., Detroit, MI 48201

Milwaukee: Roger J. White, 804 E. Juneau Ave., Milwaukee, WI 53202

Minnesota: Robert M. Anderson, 309 Clinton Ave., Minneapolis, MN 55403

Mississippi: Duncan M. Gray, Jr., P.O. Box 1636, Jackson, MS 39205

Missouri: William Augustus Jones, Jr, 1210 Locust St., St. Louis, MO 63103

Montana: Charles I. Jones, 515 North Park Ave., Helena, MT 59601

Nebraska: James E. Krotz, 200 N. 62nd St., Omaha, NE 68132

Nevada: Stewart C. Zabriski, 2930 W. 7th St., Reno, NV 89503

New Hampshire: Douglas E. Theuner, 63 Green St., Concord, NH 03301

New Jersey: G. P. Mellick Belshaw; Vincent K. Pettit, (S), 808 W. State St., Trenton, NJ 08618

New York: Richard F. Grein; Walter D. Dennis, (S), 1047 Amsterdam Ave., New York, NY 10025

Newark: John Shelby Spong, 24 Rector St., Newark, NJ 07102

North Carolina: Robert W. Estill; Frank Harris Vest, Jr., (S), 201 St. Alban's, P.O. Box 17025, Raleigh, NC 27609

North Dakota: Andrew H. Fairfield, 809 8th Ave. S., Fargo, ND 58102

Northern California: John L. Thompson, III, 1322 27th St., P.O. Box 131268, Sacramento, CA 95816

Northern Indiana: Frank C. Gray, 117 N. Lafayette Blvd., South Bend, IN 46601

Northern Michigan: Thomas K. Ray, 131 E. Ridge St., Marquette, MI 49855

Northwest Texas: Sam Byron Hulsey, Texas Commerce Bldg., Ste. 506, 1314 Ave. K, P.O. Box 1067, Lubbock, TX 79408

Northwestern Pennsylvania: Robert D. Rowley, 145 W. 6th St., Erie, PA 16501

Ohio: James R. Moodey; Arthur B. Williams, (S), 2230 Euclid Ave., Cleveland, OH 44115

Oklahoma: Robert M. Moody, P.O. Box 1098; William J. Cox, (A)

Olympia: Robert H. Cochrane, 1551 Tenth Ave. East, Seattle, WA 98102

Oregon: Robert Louis Ladehoff, P.O. Box 467, Portland, OR 97034

Pennsylvania: Allan C. Bartlett; Franklin D. Turner, (S), 1700 Market St., Ste. 1600, Philadelphia, PA 19103

Pittsburgh: Alden M. Hathaway, 325 Oliver Ave., Pittsburgh, PA 15222

Quincy: Edward H. MacBurney, 3601 N. North St., Peoria, IL 61604

Rhode Island: George Hunt, 275 N. Main St., Providence, RI 02903

Rio Grande: Terence Kellshaw, 4304 Carlisle NE, Albuquerque, NM 87107

Rochester: William G. Burrill, Jr., 935 East Ave., Rochester, NY 14607

San Diego: C. Brinkley Morton, St. Paul's Church, 2728 6th Ave., San Diego, CA 92103

San Joaquin: David Schofield, 4159 East Dakota, Fresno, CA 93726

South Carolina: Edward L. Salmon; G. Edward Haynesworth, (A), 1020 King St., Drawer 2127, Charleston, SC 29403

South Dakota: Craig B. Anderson, 200 W. 18th St., P.O. Box 517, Sioux Falls, SD 57101

Southeast Florida: Calvin O. Schofield, Jr., 525 NE 15 St., Miami, FL 33132

Southern Ohio: William G. Black; Herbert Thompson, Jr., (C), 412 Sycamore St., Cincinnati, OH 45202

Southern Virginia: Claude Charles Vaché, 600 Talbot Hill Rd., Norfolk, VA 23505

Southwest Florida: Roger S. Harris, Box 20899, St. Petersburg, FL 33742

Southwestern Virginia: A. Heath Light, P.O. Box 2068, Roanoke, VA 24009

Spokane: Leigh Allen Wallace, Jr., 245 E. 13th Ave., Spokane, WA 99202

Springfield: Donald M. Hultstrand, 821 S. 2nd St., Springfield, IL 62704

Tennessee: George Lazenby Reynolds, Box 3807, Knoxville, TN 37917

Texas: Maurice M. Benitez, (S); Anselmo Carroll, (A), 520 San Jacinto St., Houston, TX 77002

Upper South Carolina: William A. Beckman, (S), P.O. Box 1789, Columbia, SC 29202

Utah: George E. Bates, 231 E. First St. South, Salt Lake City, UT 84111

Vermont: Daniel L. Swenson, Rock Point, Burlington, VT 05401

Virginia: Peter J. Lee; David H. Lewis, Jr. (S), 110 W. Franklin St., Richmond, VA 23220

Washington: Ronald Haines, Mt. St. Alban, Washington, DC 20016

West Missouri: Arthur Vogel, 415 W. 13th St., P.O. Box 23216, Kansas City, MO 64141

West Tennessee: Alex D. Dickson, 692 Poplar Ave., Memphis, TN 38105

West Texas: John H. McNaughton; Earl N. MacArthur, (S), P.O. Box 6885, San Antonio, TX 78209

West Virginia: Robert P. Atkinson; William Franklin Carr, (S), 1608 Virginia St. E., Charleston, WV 25311

Western Kansas: John F. Ashby, 142 S. 8th St., P.O. Box 1383, Salina, KS 67401

Western Louisiana: Robert J. Hargrove, P.O. Box 4046, Alexandria, LA 71301

Western Massachusetts: Andrew F. Wissemann, 37 Chestnut St., Springfield, MA 01103

Western Michigan: Edward L. Lee, Jr., 2600 Vincent Ave., Kalamazoo, MI 49001

Western New York: David C. Bowman, 1114 Delaware Ave., Buffalo, NY 14209

Western North Carolina: William G. Weinhauer, P.O. Box 368, Black Mountain, NC 28711

Wyoming: Bob Gordon Jones, 104 W. 4th St., Box 1007, Laramie, WY 82070

Am. Churches in Europe—Jurisdiction: Matthew P. Bigliardi, The American Cathedral, 23 Avenue Georges V, 75008, Paris, France

Navajoland Area Mission: Steven Plummer, P.O. Box 720, Farmington, NM 47401

PERIODICAL

Episcopal Life

The Estonian Evangelical Lutheran Church

For information on the Estonian Evangelical Lutheran Church (EELC), please see the listing in Chapter 4, "Religious Bodies in Canada."

Ethical Culture Movement

The American Ethical Union is a federation of Ethical Culture/Ethical Humanist Societies. Ethical Culture, founded in 1876 in New York by Felix Adler, is a humanistic religious and educational movement, based on the primacy of ethics, the belief in intrinsic worth of every human being and the faith in the capacity of human beings to act in their personal relationships and in the larger community to help create a better world.

HEADQUARTERS
2 West 64th St., New York, NY 10023 Tel. (212)873-6500

OFFICERS
Pres., Annabelle Glasser
Vice-Pres., Hank Gassner
Treas., Sophie Meyer
Sec., Stephanie Dohner
Admn., Margaretha E. Jones
Dir. Religious Educ./Growth & Development, Joy McConnell
Washington Ethical Action Ofc., Herb Blinder

ORGANIZATIONS
Natl. Leaders' Council, Chpsn., Joseph Chuman
Natl. Service Conference: Co-Pres., Jean S. Kotkin; Rose Walker
Intl. Humanist & Ethical Union: Reps., Dr. Matthew Ies Spetter; Joseph Chuman
Youth of Ethical Societies (YES), Youth Rep., Daniella Ballou

The Evangelical Church

The Evangelical Church was born June 4, 1968 in Portland, Ore. when 46 congregations and about 80 ministers, under the leadership of V.A. Ballantyne and George Millen, met in an organizing session. Within two weeks a group of about 20 churches and 30 ministers from the Evangelical United Brethren and Methodist churches in Montana and North Dakota became a part of the new church. Richard Kienitz and Robert Strutz were the superintendents.

Under the leadership of Superintendent Robert Trosen, the former Holiness Methodist Church became a part of the Evangelical Church in 1969, bringing its membership and a flourishing mission field in Bolivia. The Wesleyan Covenant Church joined in 1977, with its missionary work in Mexico, Brownsville, Texas, and among the Navahos in New Mexico.

The Evangelical Church in Canada, where T. J. Jesske was superintendent, became an autonomous organization on June 5, 1970. In 1982, after years of discussions with the Evangelical Church of North America, a founding General Convention was held at Billings, Montana, where the two churches united. Currently there are just under 200 congregations, with the denominational office located in Salem, Oregon.

The following guide the life, program and devotion of this church: faithful, biblical, and sensible preaching and teaching of those truths proclaimed by scholars of the Wesleyan-Arminian viewpoint; an itinerant system which reckons with the rights of individuals and the desires of the congregation; local ownership of all church properties and assets.

The church is affiliated with the Christian Holiness Association, the National Association of Evangelicals, Wycliffe Bible Translators, World Gospel Mission and OMS International. Through the two latter agencies and the mission in Bolivia, over 55 of the denomination's more than 200 missionaries have been appointed.

MEDIA CONTACT
Media Contact, Gen. Supt., John F. Sills, 3000 Market St., NE, Ste. 528, Salem, OR 97301 Tel. (503)371-4818 Fax (503)375-9646

OFFICER
Gen. Supt., Rev. John F. Sills

The Evangelical Congregational Church

This denomination had its beginning in the movement known as the Evangelical Association, organized by Jacob Albright in the early nineteenth century. In 1891 a division occurred in the Evangelical Association, which resulted in the organization of the United Evangelical Church in 1894. An attempt to heal this division was made in 1922, but a portion of the United Evangelical Church was not satisfied with the plan of merger and remained apart, taking the above name in 1928. This denomination is Arminian in doctrine, evangelistic in spirit, and Methodistic in church government, with congregational ownership of local church property.

Congregations are located from New Jersey to Illinois. A denominational center is located in Myerstown, Pa., as well as a retirement village and a seminary. Three summer youth camps and three camp meetings continue evangelistic outreach. A worldwide missions movement includes conferences in North East India, Liberia, Mexico and Japan. The denomination is a member of National Association of Evangelicals.

HEADQUARTERS
Evangelical Congregational Church Center, 100 W. Park Ave., P.O. Box 186, Myerstown, PA 17067 Fax (717)866-7581
Media Contact, Bishop, Rev. Richard W. Kohl, Tel. (717)-866-7581

OFFICERS
Presiding Bishop, Rev. Richard W. Kohl, Myerstown, PA 17067
1st Vice-Chpsn., Rev. Robert W. Zetterberg, 242 E. Ralston, Akron, OH 44301
2nd Vice-Chpsn., Rev. Robert M. Daneker, Sr., 122 S. Emerson St., Allentown, PA 18104
Sec., Rev. Robert J. Stahl, RD 2, Box 1468, Schuylkill Haven, PA 17972
Asst. Sec.: Rev. Gregory Dimick, Hatfield, PA; Rev. Richard Reigle, Dixon, IL
Treas., Martha Metz, P.O. Box 186, Myerstown, PA 17067
E.C.C. Retirement Village, Supt., Rev. Franklin H. Schock, Myerstown, PA 17067 Fax (717)866-6448
Evangelical School of Theology, Pres., Dr. Ray A. Seilhamer, Myerstown, PA 17067 Fax (717)866-4667

OTHER ORGANIZATIONS
Administrative Council: Chpsn., Bishop Richard W. Kohl; Vice-Chpsn., Rev. Robert W. Zetterberg; Treas., Martha Metz
Div. of Evangelism & Spiritual Care, Chpsn., Bishop Richard W. Kohl, Myerstown, PA 17067
Div. of Church Ministries, Chpsn., Rev. Keith R. Miller, Myerstown, PA 17067
Div. of Church Services, Chpsn., Rev. Keith R. Miller, Myerstown, PA 17067
Div. of Missions, Chpsn., Rev. David G. Hornberger, P.O. Box 186, Myerstown, PA 17067

Div. of Christian Ed., Chpsn., Dr. Donald Metz, Myerstown, PA 17067
Bd. of Pensions: Pres., Mr. Homer Luckenbill, Jr., Pine Grove, PA; Sec., Dr. James D. Yoder, Myerstown, PA 17067

PERIODICAL

Doors and Windows

The Evangelical Covenant Church

The Evangelical Covenant Church has its roots in historical Christianity as it emerged in the Protestant Reformation, in the biblical instruction of the Lutheran State Church of Sweden, and in the great spiritual awakenings of the 19th century.

The Covenant Church adheres to the affirmations of the Protestant Reformation regarding the Holy Scriptures, the Old and the New Testament as the Word of God and the only perfect rule for faith, doctrine, and conduct. It has traditionally valued the historic confessions of the Christian church, particularly the Apostles' Creed, while at the same time it has emphasized the sovereignty of the Word over all creedal interpretations. It has especially cherished the pietistic restatement of the doctrine of justification by faith as basic to its dual task of evangelism and Christian nurture, the New Testament emphasis upon personal faith in Jesus Christ as Savior and Lord, the reality of a fellowship of believers which recognizes but transcends theological differences, and the belief in baptism and the Lord's Supper as divinely ordained sacraments of the church.

While the denomination has traditionally practiced the baptism of infants, in conformity with its principle of freedom it has given room to divergent views. The principle of personal freedom, so highly esteemed by the Covenant, is to be distinguished from the individualism that disregards the centrality of the Word of God and the mutual responsibilities and disciplines of the spiritual community.

HEADQUARTERS

5101 N. Francisco Ave., Chicago, IL 60625 Tel. (312)784-3000 Fax (312)784-4366
Media Contact, Pres., Paul E. Larsen

OFFICERS

Pres., Dr. Paul E. Larsen, Chicago, IL
Vice-Pres., Rev. Timothy C. Ek, Chicago, IL
Sec., John R. Hunt, Chicago, IL
Treas., Dean A. Lundgren, W. Hartford, CT

ADMINISTRATIVE BOARDS

Bd. of Christian Educ. & Discipleship: Chpsn., Rev. Stanley Olsen; Sec., Eugene S. Gibbs; Exec. Sec., Rev. Evelyn M. R. Johnson
Bd. of Church Growth & Evangelism: Chpsn., Rev. Phillip K. Brockett; Sec., Rev. Richard D. Holmlund; Exec. Sec., Dr. James E. Persson
Bd. of Covenant Women Ministries: Chpsn., Mrs. Ruth West; Sec., Mrs. Gwen Bagaas; Exec. Sec., Rev. Deirdre M. Banks
Bd. of Human Resources: Chpsn., Sheldon Peterson; Sec., Frances Gunberg
Bd. of the Ministry: Chpsn., Rev. Wendell E. Danielson; Sec., Rev. Curtis D. Peterson; Exec. Sec., Rev. Donald A. Njaa
Bd. of Pensions: Chpsn., Charles G. Beckstrom; Sec., John R. Hunt; Dir. of Pensions, John R. Hunt

Bd. of Publication: Chpsn., Rev. Donn W. Anderson; Sec., Mrs. Marguerite A. Johnson; Exec. Sec., Rev. John R. Hawkinson
Bd. of World Mission: Chpsn., Robert H. Jones; Sec., Mrs. Joan G. Spjut; Exec. Sec., Rev. Raymond L. Dahlberg
Bd. of Benevolence: Chpsn., Lawrence P. Anderson; Sec., William R. Ahlem; Pres. of Covenant Benevolent Institutions, Nils G. Axelson, 5145 N. California Ave., Chicago, IL 60625
North Park College & Theological Sem.: Bd. of Dir., Chpsn., Rev. Robert C. Dvorak; Sec., Peter A. Fellowes; Pres., Dr. David G. Horner, 3225 W. Foster Ave., Chicago, IL 60625

PERIODICALS

Covenant Companion; Covenant Quarterly; Covenant Home Altar

The Evangelical Free Church of America

In October 1884, 27 representatives from Swedish churches met in Boone, Iowa, to establish the Swedish Evangelical Free Church. In the fall of that same year, two Norwegian-Danish groups began worship and fellowship (in Boston and in Tacoma) and by 1912 had established the Norwegian-Danish Evangelical Free Church Association. These two denominations, representing 275 congregations, came together at a merger conference in 1950.

The Evangelical Free Church is an association of local, autonomous churches across the United States and Canada, blended together around common principles, policies, and practices. A 12-point statement addresses the major doctrines, but also provides for differences of understanding on minor issues of faith and practice.

Overseas outreach includes 450 missionaries serving in 15 countries.

HEADQUARTERS

901 East 78th St., Bloomington, MN 55420-1300 Tel. (612)854-1300 Fax (612)853-8488

OFFICERS

Pres., Dr. Paul Cedar
Exec. Vice-Pres., Rev. William Hamel
Mod., Mr. Kenneth Larson, 3060 Centerville Rd., Little Canada, MN 55117
Vice-Mod., Rev. Joseph Bubar, Jr., RR 4, 3936 CTH "B", LaCrosse, WI 54601
Sec., Mrs. Betty Stattine, 2713 Abbott Ave. N., Minneapolis, MN 55422
Vice-Sec., Mr. Gerald Childs, Rte. 3, Box 821, Gaylord, MI 49735
Treas., Mr. Gordon Engdahl, 110 Wildwood Bay Dr., Mahtomedi, MN 55115
Fin. Sec., Mr. James Hagman, 1895 Hampshire La., Golden Valley, MN 55427
Exec. Dir. of Overseas Missions, Rev. Robert Dillon
Exec. Dir. of Church Ministries, Rev. Bill Hull

PERIODICAL

Evangelical Beacon

Evangelical Friends International—North America Region

The organization restructured from Evangelical Friends Alliance in 1990 to become internationalized for the benefit of its world-wide contacts. The North America Region continues to function within the United States as EFA formerly did. The organization represents one corporate step of denominational unity, brought about as a result of several movements of spiritual renewal within the Society of Friends. These movements are: (1) the general evangelical renewal within Christianity, (2) the new scholarly recognition of the evangelical nature of 17th-century Quakerism, and (3) EFA, which was formed in 1965.

The EFA is conservative in theology and makes use of local pastors. Sunday morning worship includes singing, Scripture reading, a period of open worship—usually—and a sermon by the pastor.

HEADQUARTERS

393 S. Vaughn Way, Aurora, CO 80012 Tel. (303)363-0116 Fax (303)363-0116
Media Contact, Regional Dir., Stanley Perisho

YEARLY MEETINGS

Evangelical Friends Church, Eastern Region, Ron Johnson, 1201-30th St. N.W., Canton, OH 44709 Tel. (216)493-1660 Fax (216)493-0852
Rocky Mountain YM, John Brawner, 3350 Reed St., Wheat Ridge, CO 80033 Tel. (303)238-5200 Fax (303)766-9609
Mid-America YM, Roscoe Townsend, 2018 Maple, Wichita, KS 67213 Tel. (316)267-0391 Fax (316)263-1092
Northwest YM, Mark Ankeny, 600 E. Third St., Newberg, OR 97132 Tel. (503)538-9419 Fax (503)538-7033
Alaska YM, P.O. Box 687, Kotebue, AK 99752 Tel. (907)442-3906

Evangelical Lutheran Church in America

The Evangelical Lutheran Church in America (ELCA) was organized April 20-May 3, 1987, in Columbus, Ohio, bringing together the 2.3 million-member American Lutheran Church, the 2.9 million-member Lutheran Church in America, and the 100,000-member Association of Evangelical Lutheran Churches.

The ELCA is both the youngest and at the same time, through its predecessors, the oldest of the major U.S. Lutheran churches. In the mid-17th century, a Dutch Lutheran congregation was formed in New Amsterdam (now New York). Most of the oldest congregations were the result of early 18th-century German and Scandinavian immigration to Delaware, Pennsylvania, the Hudson and Mohawk River Valleys in New York, and the Piedmont region of the Carolinas.

The first Lutheran association of congregations, the Pennsylvania Ministerium, was organized in 1748 under Henry Melchior Muhlenberg, known as the patriarch of American Lutheranism.

In 1820, a national federation of synods, the General Synod, was formed. A split in 1867 resulted in a second major body, the General Council. Earlier, as a result of the Civil War, southern synods had broken away to form the United Synod in the South. These three bodies were reunited in 1918 as the United Lutheran Church in America.

In 1960, the American Lutheran Church (ALC) was created through a merger of an earlier American Lutheran Church, which was formed in 1930 by four synods that traced their roots primarily to German immigration; the Evangelical Lutheran Church, which dated from 1917 through churches chiefly of Norwegian ethnic heritage; and the United Evangelical Lutheran Church in America,

which arose from Danish immigration. On Feb. 1, 1963, the Lutheran Free Church merged with the ALC.

In 1962, the Lutheran Church in America (LCA) was formed by a merger of the United Lutheran Church with the Augustana Lutheran Church, founded in 1860 by Swedish immigrants; the American Evangelical Lutheran Church, founded in 1872 by Danish immigrants; and the Finnish Lutheran Church or Suomi Synod, founded in 1891 by Finnish immigrants.

The Association of Evangelical Lutheran Churches arose in 1976 from a doctrinal split with the Lutheran Church—Missouri Synod.

The ELCA, through its predecessor church bodies, was a founding member of the Lutheran World Federation, the World Council of Churches, and the National Council of the Churches of Christ in the USA.

The church is divided into 65 geographical areas, or synods. These 65 synods, in turn, are grouped into nine regions for mission, joint programs, and service.

HEADQUARTERS

8765 W. Higgins Rd., Chicago, IL 60631 Tel. (312)380-2700
Media Contact, Dir. for News, Carolyn J. Lewis, Tel. (312)380-2957 Fax (312)380-1465

OFFICERS

Bishop, The Rev. Dr. Herbert W. Chilstrom
Sec., The Rev. Dr. Lowell G. Almen
Treas., Richard L. McAuliffe
Vice-Pres., Kathy J. Magnus
Office of the Bishop: Exec. for Admn., Rev. Dr. Robert N. Bacher; Exec. Asst. for Federal Chaplaincies, Rev. Lloyd W. Lyngdal; Exec. Assts., Lita B. Johnson; Rev. Dr. Craig Lewis; Rev. Lee S. Thoni

DIVISIONS

Div. for Congregational Min.: Exec. Dir., Revs. Mark R. & Mary Ann Moller-Gunderson; Bd. Chpsn., Jim Myers; Lutheran Youth Organization, Pres., Tim Seitz
Div. for Higher Educ. & Schools: Exec. Dir., Rev. Dr. W. Robert Sorensen; Bd. Chpsn., Rev. Stephen P. Bauman
Div. for Global Mission: Exec. Dir., Rev. Dr. Mark W. Thomsen; Bd. Chpsn., Rev. Dr. Marjorie J. Carlson
Div. for Ministry: Exec. Dir., Rev. Dr. Joseph M. Wagner; Bd. Chpsn., Marybeth A. Peterson
Div. for Outreach: Exec. Dir., Rev. Dr. Malcolm L. Minnick, Jr.; Bd. Chpsn., Susan C. Barnard
Div. for Church in Society: Exec. Dir., Rev. Charles S. Miller; Chpsn., Ingrid Christiansen

COMMISSIONS

Comm. for Multicultural Ministries: Exec. Dir., Rev. Fred E.N. Rajan; Chpsn., Rev. Dr. Edmond Yee
Comm. for Women: Exec. Dir., Joanne Chadwick; Chpsn., Audrey R. Mortensen

CHURCHWIDE UNITS

Conference of Bishops: Dir., Rev. Dr. Thomas L. Blevins; Chpsn., Rev. Dr. Kenneth H. Sauer
ELCA Foundation: Exec. Dir., Rev. Dr. Harvey A. Stegemoeller; ELCA Publishing House, Exec. Dir., Albert E. Anderson; Bd. Chpsn., Rev. Dr. George Anderson; Bd. of Pensions, Exec. Dir., John G. Kapanke; Bd. Chpsn, Mildred M. Berg; Women of the ELCA, Exec. Dir., Charlotte E. Fiechter; Bd. Chpsn., Gwenn Carr

DEPARTMENTS

Dept. for Communication, Dir., Carol E. Becker
Dept. for Ecumenical Affairs, Dir., Rev. Dr. William G. Rusch
Dept. for Human Resources, Dr., Rev. A. C. Stein
Dept. for Research & Evaluation, Dir., Kenneth W. Inskeep
Dept. for Synodical Relations, Dir., Rev. Dr. Thomas L. Blevins

SYNODICAL BISHOPS

Region 1

Alaska, Rev. Donald D. Parsons, 1836 W. Northern Lights Blvd., Anchorage, AK 99517-3342 Tel. (907)272-8899

Northwest Washington, Rev. Dr. Lowell E. Knutson, 5519 Pinney Ave., N. Seattle, WA 98103-5899 Tel. (206)783-9292

Southwestern Washington, Rev. David C. Wold, 420 121st St., S., Tacoma, WA 98444-5218 Tel. (206)535-8300

Eastern Washington-Idaho, Rev. Robert M. Keller, S. 314-A Spruce, Spokane, WA 99204-1098 Tel. (509)838-9871

Oregon, Rev. Paul R. Swanson, 2801 N. Gantebein Ave., Portland, OR 97227-1674 Tel. (503)280-4191

Montana, Rev. Dr. Mark P. Ramseth, 2415 13th Ave. S., Great Falls, MT 59405 Tel. (406)453-1461

Regional Coord., Ronald Coen, Region 1, 766-B John St., Seattle, WA 98109-5186 Tel. (206)624-0093

Region 2

Sierra Pacific, Rev. Lyle G. Miller, 401 Roland Way, #215, Oakland, CA 94621-2011 Tel. (510)430-0500

Southern California (West), Rev. J. Roger Anderson, 1340 S. Bonnie Brae St., Los Angeles, CA 90006-5416 Tel. (213)387-8183

Pacifica, Rev. Robert L. Miller, 23655 Via Del Rio, Ste. B, Yorba Linda, CA 92687-2718 Tel. (714)692-2791

Grand Canyon, Rev. Dr. Howard E. Wennes, 4423 N. 24th St., Ste. 400, Phoenix, AZ 85016-5544 Tel. (602)957-3223

Rocky Mountain, Rev. Dr. Wayne Weissenbuehler, ABS Bldg., #101, 7000 Broadway, Denver, CO 80211 Tel. (303)427-7553

Regional Coord., Rev. James E. Miley, Region 2, 2700 Chandler, Ste. A6, Las Vegas, NV 89120 Tel. (702)798-3980

Region 3

Western North Dakota, Rev. Robert D. Lynne, 721 Memorial Way, P.O. Box 370, Bismarck, ND 58502-3070 Tel. (701)223-5312

Eastern North Dakota, Rev. Dr. Wesley N. Haugen, 1703 32nd Ave., S., Fargo, ND 58103-5936 Tel. (701)232-3381

South Dakota, Rev. Norman D. Eitrheim, Augustana College, Sioux Falls, SD 57197 Tel. (605)336-4011

Northwestern Minnesota, Rev. Dr. Arthur V. Rimmereid, P.O. Box 678, Moorhead, MN 56561-0678 Tel. (218)299-3019

Northeastern Minnesota, Rev. Roger L. Munson, 3900 London Rd., Duluth, MN 55804 Tel. (218)525-1947

Southwestern Minnesota, Rev. Charles D. Anderson, 175 E. Bridge St., P.O. Box 277, Redwood Falls, MN 56283 Tel. (507)637-3904

Minneapolis Area, Rev. David W. Olson, 122 W. Franklin Ave., Rm. 600, Minneapolis, MN 55404-2474 Tel. (612)870-3610

Saint Paul Area, Rev. Lowell O. Erdahl, 105 W. University Ave., St. Paul, MN 55103-2094 Tel. (612)224-4313

Southeastern Minnesota, Rev. Glenn W. Nycklemoe, Assisi Heights, 1001-14 St. NW, P.O. Box 4900, Rochester, MN 55903-4900 Tel. (507)280-9457

Regional Coord., Ms. Shirley A. Teig, Region 3, Brockman Hall, 2481 Como Ave., W. St. Paul, MN 55108 Tel. (612)649-0454

Region 4

Nebraska, Rev. Dr. Richard N. Jessen, 4980 S. 118th St., Ste. D, Omaha, NE 68137-2220 Tel. (402)836-5311

Central States, Rev. Dr. Charles H. Maahs, 6400 Glenwood, Ste. 210, Shawnee Mission, KS 66202 Tel. (913)362-0733

Arkansas-Oklahoma, Rev. Dr. Robert H. Studtmann, 4803 S. Lewis Ave., Tulsa, OK 74105-5199 Tel. (918)747-8517

Northern Texas-Northern Louisiana, Rev. Mark B. Hebener, 1230 Riverbend Dr., Ste. 105, P.O. Box 560587, Dallas, TX 75356-0587 Tel. (214)637-6865

Southwestern Texas, Rev. Henry Schulte, Jr., 1800 Northeast Loop 410, Ste. 202, P.O. Box 171270, San Antonio, TX 78217-8270 Tel. (512)824-0068

Southeastern Texas-Southern Louisiana, Rev. Paul J. Blom, 350 Glenborough Dr., Ste. 310, Houston, TX 77067-3609 Tel. (713)873-5665

Regional Coord., Rev. Roger J. Gieschen, Region 4, 6901 W. 63rd St., Rm. 205, Overland Park, KS 66202 Tel. (913)831-3727

Region 5

Metropolitan Chicago, Rev. Sherman G. Hicks, 18 S. Michigan Ave., Rm. 605, Chicago, IL 60603-3283 Tel. (312)346-3150

Northern Illinois, Rev. Ronald K. Hasley, 103 W. State St., Rockford, IL 61101-1105 Tel. (815)964-9934

Central/Southern Illinois, Rev. Dr. John P. Kaitschuk, 1201 Veterans Pkwy., Ste. D, Springfield, IL 62704-6321 Tel. (217)546-7915

Southeastern Iowa, Rev. Dr. Paul M. Werger, 2635 Northgate Dr., P.O. Box 3167, Iowa City, IA 52244-3167 Tel. (319)388-1273

Western Iowa, Rev. Curtis H. Miller, 318 E. Fifth St., P.O. Box 1145, Storm Lake, IA 50588-2312 Tel. (712)732-4968

Northeastern Iowa, Rev. Dr. L. David Brown, 201-20th St. SW, P.O. Box 804, Waverly, IA 50677-0804 Tel. (319)352-1414

Northern Great Lakes, Rev. Dale R. Skogman, 1029 N. Third St., Marquette, MI 49855 Tel. (906)228-2300

Northwest Synod of Wisconsin, Rev. Gerhard I. Knutson, 12 W. Marshall St., P.O. Box 730, Rice Lake, WI 54868-0730 Tel. (715)234-3373

East-Central Synod of Wisconsin, Rev. Dr. Robert H. Herder, 3003B N. Richmond St., Appleton, WI 54911 Tel. (414)734-5381

Greater Milwaukee, Rev. Peter Rogness, 1212 S. Layton Blvd., Milwaukee, WI 53215-1653 Tel. (414)671-1212

South-Central Synod of Wisconsin, Rev. Dr. Jon S. Enslin, 2705 Packers Ave., Madison, WI 53704 Tel. (608)249-4848

LaCrosse Area, Rev. Stefan T. Guttormsson, 2350 S. Ave., LaCrosse, WI 54601 Tel. (608)788-5000

Regional Coord., Rev. Edward F. Weiskotten, Region 5, 333 Wartburg Pl., Dubuque, IA 52003-7797 Tel. (319)589-0312

Region 6

Southeast Michigan, Rev. J. Philip Wahl, 19711 Greenfield Rd., Detroit, MI 48235 Tel. (313)837-3522

North/West Lower Michigan, Rev. Dr. Reginald H. Holle, 801 S. Waverly Rd., Ste. 201, Lansing, MI 48917 Tel. (517)321-5066

Indiana-Kentucky, Rev. Dr. Ralph A. Kempski, 9102 N. Meridian St., Ste. 405, Indianapolis, IN 46260-1809 Tel. (317)846-4026

Northwestern Ohio, Rev. James A. Rave, 241 Stanford Pkwy., Ste. A, Findlay, OH 45840 Tel. (419)423-3664

Northeastern Ohio, Rev. Dr. Robert W. Kelley, 282 W. Bowery, 3rd Fl., Akron, OH 44307-2598 Tel. (216)253-1500

Southern Ohio, Rev. Dr. Kenneth H. Sauer, 57 E. Main St., Columbus, OH 43215-7102 Tel. (614)464-3532

Regional Coord., Rev. Hermann J. Kuhllmann, Region 6, 6100 Channing Way Blvd., Ste. 503, Columbus, OH 43232 Tel. (614)759-9090

Region 7

New Jersey, Rev. E. Leroy Riley, Jr., 1930 State Hwy. 33, Trenton, NJ 08690-1714 Tel. (609)586-6800

New England, Rev. Robert L. Isaksen, 90 Madison St., Ste. 303, Worcester, MA 01608-2030 Tel. (508)791-1530

Metropolitan New York, Rev. Dr. William H. Lazareth, 360 Park Ave., S., 7th Floor, New York, NY 10016-8803 Tel. (212)532-6350

Upstate New York, Rev. Dr. Edward K. Perry, 3049 E. Genesee St., Syracuse, NY 13224 Tel. (315)446-2502

Northeastern Pennsylvania, Rev. Dr. Harold S. Weiss, 4865 Hamilton Blvd., Wescosville, PA 18106-9705 Tel. (215)395-6891

Southeastern Pennsylvania, Rev. Michael G. Merkel, 4700 Wissahickon Ave., Philadelphia, PA 19144 Tel. (215)438-0600

Slovak Zion, Rev. Dr. Kenneth E. Zindle, 6605 MacArthur Dr., Woodridge, IL 60517 Tel. (708)810-9786

Regional Coord., Rev. George E. Handley, Region 7, Hagan Hall, 7301 Germantown Ave., Philadelphia, PA 19119 Tel. (215)248-4616

Region 8

Northwestern Pennsylvania, Rev. Paull E. Spring, 308 Seneca St., Oil City, PA 16301-1378 Tel. (814)677-5706

Southwestern Pennsylvania, Rev. Donald J. McCoid, 9625 Perry Hwy., Pittsburgh, PA 15237 Tel. (412)367-8222

Allegheny, Rev. Gerald E. Miller, 701 Quail Ave., Altoona, PA 16602-3010 Tel. (814)942-1042

Lower Susquehanna, Rev. Dr. Guy S. Edmiston, Jr., 900 S. Arlington Ave., Rm. 208, Harrisburg, PA 17109-5031 Tel. (717)652-1852

Upper Susquehanna, Rev. Dr. A. Donald Main, P.O. Box 36, Lewisburg, PA 17837-0036 Tel. (717)524-9778

Delaware-Maryland, Rev. Dr. George P. Mocko, 7604 York Rd., Baltimore, MD 21204-7570 Tel. (410)825-9520

Metropolitan Washington, D.C., Rev. Dr. E. Harold Jansen, 224 E. Capitol St., Washington, DC 20003-1036 Tel. (202)543-8610

West Virginia-Western Maryland, Rev. L. Alexander Black, The Atrium, Ste. 100, 503 Morgantown Avenue, Fairmont, WV 26554-4374 Tel. (304)363-4030

Regional Coord., Rev. Eugene W. Beutel, Region 8, United Ch. Ctr., 900 S. Arlington Ave., Rm. 210, Harrisburg, PA 17109 Tel. (717)652-6001

Region 9

Virginia, Rev. Richard F. Bansemer, P.O. Drawer 70, Salem, VA 24153 Tel. (703)389-1000

North Carolina, Rev. Dr. Mark W. Menees, 1988 Lutheran Synod Dr., Salisbury, NC 28144 Tel. (704)633-4861

South Carolina, Rev. Dr. James S. Aull, P.O. Box 43, Columbia, SC 29202-0043 Tel. (803)765-0590

Southeastern, Rev. Dr. Harold C. Skillrud, 756 Peachtree St. NW, Atlanta, GA 30308-1188 Tel. (404)873-1977

Florida-Bahamas, Rev. Lavern G. Franzen, 3838 W. Cyprus St., Tampa, FL 33607-4897 Tel. (813)876-7660

Caribbean, Rev. Rafael Malpica-Padilla, P.O. Box 14426, Barrio-Obrero Station, Santurce, PR 00916 Tel. (809)727-6015

Regional Coord., Ms. Dorothy L. Jeffcoat, Region 9, 4201 N. Main St., Columbia, SC 29203 Tel. (803)754-2879

PERIODICAL

Lutheran, The

Evangelical Lutheran Synod

The Evangelical Lutheran Synod had its beginning among the Norwegian settlers who brought with them their Lutheran heritage and established it in this country. It was organized in 1853. It was reorganized in 1917 by those who desired to adhere to these principles not only in word, but also in deed.

To carry out the above-mentioned objectives, the Synod owns and operates Bethany Lutheran College and Bethany Lutheran Theological Seminary. It has congregations located in 20 states and maintains foreign missions in Peru, Chile, Czechoslovakia, and Ukraine. It operates seminaries in Lima, Peru and Plzen, Czechoslovakia.

HEADQUARTERS

The Evangelical Lutheran Synod, 447 N. Division St., Mankato, MN 56001

Media Contact, Pres., Rev. George Orvick, Tel. (507)388-4868 Fax (507)625-1849

OFFICERS

Pres., Rev. George Orvick, 447 Division St., Mankato, MN 56001 Tel. (507)388-4868 Fax (507)625-1849

Sec., Rev. Alf Merseth, 106 13th St. S., Northwood, IA 50459

Treas., Mr. LeRoy W. Meyer, 1038 S. Lewis Ave., Lombard, IL 60148

OTHER ORGANIZATIONS

Lutheran Synod Book Co., Bethany Lutheran College, Mankato, MN 56001

PERIODICAL

Lutheran Synod Quarterly

Evangelical Mennonite Church

The Evangelical Mennonite Church is an American denomination in the European free church tradition. It traces its heritage directly to the early Reformation period of the 16th century, to a group known as Swiss Brethren, who believed that salvation could come only by repentance for sins and faith in Jesus Christ; that baptism was only for believers; and that the church should be separate

US RELIGIOUS BODIES

from controls of the state. Their enemies called them Anabaptists, since they insisted on rebaptizing believers who had been baptized as infants. As the Anabaptist movement spread to other countries, Menno Simons, formerly a Dutch Roman Catholic priest, became its principal leader. In time his followers were called Mennonites.

In 1693 a Mennonite minister, Jacob Amman, insisted that the church should adopt a more conservative position on dress and style of living, and should more rigidly enforce the "ban"—the church's method of disciplining disobedient members. Amman's insistence finally resulted in a division within the South German Mennonite groups; his followers became known as the Amish.

Migrations to America, involving both Mennonites and Amish, took place in the 1700s and 1800s, for both religious and economic reasons.

The Evangelical Mennonite Church was formed in 1866, out of a spiritual awakening among the Amish in Indiana, and was first known as the Egly Amish, after its founder Bishop Henry Egly. A preacher in an Amish congregation in Berne, Ind., Egly underwent a spiritual experience in 1864 and began to emphasize regeneration, separation, and nonconformity to the world. His willingness to rebaptize anyone who had been baptized without repentance created a split in his church, prompting him to gather a new congregation in 1866. The conference, which has met annually since 1895, united a number of other congregations of like mind. This group became The Defenseless Mennonite Church in 1898, and has been known as the Evangelical Mennonite Church since 1948.

HEADQUARTERS

1420 Kerrway Ct., Fort Wayne, IN 46805 Tel. (219)423-3649
Media Contact, Pres., Rev. Donald W. Roth

OFFICERS

Pres., Rev. Donald W. Roth
Chpsn., Rev. Douglas R. Habegger, 1033 Lee, Morton, IL 61550
Vice-Chpsn., Rev. Charles L. Rupp, Box 1, Lawton, MI 49065
Sec., Gene L. Rupp, Taylor Univ., Upland, IN 46989
Treas., Alan L. Rupp, 5724 Spring Oak Ct., Ft. Wayne, IN 46845

PERIODICAL

EMC Today

Evangelical Methodist Church

Organized 1946 at Memphis, Tenn., largely as a movement of people who opposed modern liberalism and wished for a return to the historic Wesleyan position. In 1960 merged with the Evangel Church (formerly Evangelistic Tabernacles) and with the People's Methodist Church in 1962.

HEADQUARTERS

3000 West Kellogg, Wichita, KS 67213 Tel. (316)943-3278
Media Contact, Gen. Conf. Sec.-Treas., Vernon W. Perkins

OFFICERS

Gen. Supt., Rev. Clyde Zehr
Gen. Conf. Sec.-Treas., Rev. Vernon W. Perkins

Evangelical Presbyterian Church

The Evangelical Presbyterian Church (EPC), established in March 1981, is a conservative denomination of 11 geographic presbyteries—10 in the United States, and one in Argentina. From its inception, with 12 churches, the EPC has grown to 160 churches with a membership of over 54,000. In 1991, the General Assembly approved the formation of the newest presbytery, in the heartland of the nation, to begin operations in late 1991.

Planted firmly within the historic Reformed tradition, evangelical in spirit, the EPC places high priority on church planting and development along with world missions. Eleven missionary families serve in the church's mission.

The sixth annual meeting of the Joint Committee on Missions between the EPC and the Presbyterian Church of Brazil (IPB) was held in the fall of 1991 in Sao Paulo, Brazil.

Based on the truth of Scripture and adhering to the Westminster Confession of Faith plus its Book of Order, the denomination is committed to the "essentials of the faith." The historic motto "In essentials, unity; In nonessentials, liberty; In all things charity" catches the spirit of the EPC, along with the Ephesians theme of "truth in love."

The Evangelical Presbyterian Church is a member of the World Alliance of Reformed Churches, National Association of Evangelicals, World Evangelical Fellowship, and the Evangelical Council for Financial Accountability. Though not members, observers annually attend the North American Presbyterian and Reformed Churches (NAPARC).

HEADQUARTERS

Office of the General Assembly, 26049 Five Mile Rd., Detroit, MI 48239 Tel. (313)532-9555. Fax (313)532-8447

OFFICERS

Mod., Dr. William M. Flannagan, Westminster Presbyterian Church, Box 6435, Laurel, MS 39441
Stated Clk., Dr. L. Edward Davis

PERMANENT COMMITTEES

Committee on Admn., Chmn., Mr. James E. Rimmel, The Cardinal Towers, 565 E. Main, Ste. 210, Canfield, OH 44406
Committee on Church Development, Chmn., Rev. Douglas Klein, Grace Chapel, 23233 Drake Rd., Farmington Hills, MI 48024
Committee on World Outreach, Chmn., Dr. Donald Giesmann, First Presbyterian Church, 2799 West Rd., Trenton, MI 48187
Committee on Fraternal Relations, Chmn., Dr. Robert Norris, Fourth Presbyterian Church, 5500 River Rd., Bethesda, MD 20816
Committee on Ministerial Vocation, Chmn., Rev. Malcolm Brown, Covenant Presbyterian Ch., P.O. Box 7269, Ann Arbor, MI 48107
Comm. on Christian Educ. & Publ., Chmn., Dr. Robert Bayley, Central Presbyterian Ch., 7700 Davis Dr., St. Louis, MO 63105
Committee on Women's Ministries, Chpsn., Mrs. Sara Mathers, 14336 Ramblewood, Livonia, MI 48154
Committee on Theology, Chmn., Mr. Philip Tiews, Covenant Presbyterian Church, P.O. Box 7087, Ann Arbor, MI 48107
Committee on Youth Ministries, Chmn., Rev. Steve Wilkinson, First Presbyterian Church, 107 E. Jefferson, Anna, IL 62906

Allegheny, Stated Clk., Rev. Kenneth Burbidge, Calvary Presbyterian Church, 123 E. Diamond St., Butler, PA 16001

Central South, Stated Clk., Rev. Michael Swain, First Presbyterian Church, P.O. Box 366, West Point, MS 39773

East, Stated Clk., Mr. Richard Bingham, 95 Prospect Ave., Maybrook, NY 12543

Far West, Stated Clk., Dr. Charles Wickman, Christ Community Church, 123 E. Palm Ave., Monrovia, CA 91016

Florida, Stated Clk., Rev. Robert Garment, Trinity EPC, 5150 Oleander, Ft. Pierce, FL 34982

Heartland, Stated Clk., Rev. Austin McCaskill, Central Presbyterian Church, 7700 Davis Dr., St. Louis, MO 63105

Mid-Atlantic, Stated Clk., Mr. Llew Fischer, 3164 Golf Colony Dr., Salem, VA 24153

Midwest, Stated Clk., Mr. Robert Sanborn, 26049 Five Mile Road, Detroit, MI 48239

Southeast, Stated Clk., Rev. Ronald Ragon, Brainerd Presbyterian Church, 7 N. Tuxedo, Chattanooga, TN 37411

West, Stated Clk., Mr. Claude Russell, Faith Presbyterian Church, 11373 E. Alameda Ave., Aurora, CO 80012

St. Andrews, Stated Clk., Mr. Freddie Berk, Iglesia Presbiteriana San Andres, Peru 352, 1067 Buenos Aires, Argentina

Fellowship of Evangelical Bible Churches

Formerly known as Evangelical Mennonite Brethren, this body emanates from the Russian immigration of Mennonites into the United States, 1873-74. Established with the emphasis on true repentance, conversion, and a committed life to Jesus as Savior and Lord, the conference was founded in 1889 under the leadership of Isaac Peters and Aaron Wall. The founding churches were located in Mountain Lake, Minn., and in Henderson and Janzen, Neb. The conference has since grown to a fellowship of 36 churches with approximately 4,400 members in Argentina, Canada, Paraguay, and the United States.

Foreign missions have been a vital ingredient of the total ministry. Today missions constitute about 75 percent of the total annual budget, with one missionary for every 30 members in the home churches. The conference does not develop and administer foreign mission fields of its own, but actively participates with existing evangelical "faith" mission societies. The conference has representation on several mission boards and has missionaries serving under approximately 32 different agencies around the world.

The church is holding fast to the inerrancy of Scripture, the Deity of Christ, the need for spiritual regeneration of man from his sinful natural state, by faith in the death, burial, and resurrection of Jesus Christ as payment for sin. They look forward to the imminent return of Jesus Christ and retain a sense of urgency to share the gospel with those who have never heard of God's redeeming love.

HEADQUARTERS

5800 S. 14th St., Omaha, NE 68107 Tel. (402)731-4780

OFFICERS

Pres., Rev. Melvin Epp, RR 1, Wymark, SK S0N 2Y0

Vice-Pres., Mr. Stan Seifert, 2732 Springhill St., Clearbrook, BC V2T 3V9

Rec. Sec., Mr. Ruben Dyck, 7324 Jefferson St., Omaha, NE 68127

Admn. Sec., Robert L. Frey, 5800 S. 14th, Omaha, NE 68107

Commission on Churches, Chpsn., Dr. J. Paul Nyquist, 7820 Fort St., Omaha, NE 68134

Commission on Missions, Chpsn., Rev. Allan Wiebe, 1104 Day Dr., Omaha, NE 68005

Commission of Trustees, Chpsn., Mr. Neil C. J. DeRuiter, 298 Regal Ave., Winnipeg, MB R2M 0P5

Commission on Educ. & Publ., Chpsn., Mr. Joel Penner, Rte. 1, Box 55, Butterfield, MN 56120

Commission on Church Planting, Chpsn., Rev. Randy Smart, Box 1446, Winkler, MB R0G 2X0

PERIODICAL

Gospel Tidings

Fellowship of Fundamental Bible Churches

This body, until 1985, was called the Bible Protestant Church. The FFBC is a fellowship of fundamental Bible-believing local autonomous churches which believe in an inerrant and infallible Bible, is dispensational as related to the study of the Scriptures, espouses the pre-Tribulation Rapture, and is premillenial. The FFBC is evangelistic and missions-oriented. It regards itself as separatistic in areas of personal life and ecclesiastical association and believes that Baptism by immersion of believers most adequately reflects the symbolic truth of death and resurrection with Christ.

The Fellowship of Fundamental Bible Churches relates historically to the Eastern Conference of the Methodist Protestant Church, which changed its name to Bible Protestant Church at the 2nd Annual Session, held in Westville, N.J., Sept. 26-30, 1940.

HEADQUARTERS

P.O. Box 43, Glassboro, NJ 08028

Media Contact, Natl. Rep., Rev. Harold E. Haines, Tel. (609)881-5516

OFFICERS

Pres., Mr. Ronald Schaffer, RD 2 Box 196, Waymart, PA 18472 Tel. (717)937-4032

Vice-Pres., Rev. Mark Franklin, RD 1 Box 300, Monroeville, NJ 08343 Tel. (609)881-0057

Sec., Rev. A. Glenn Doughty, 134 Delsea Dr., Westville, NJ 08093 Tel. (609)456-3791

Asst. Sec., Rev. Albert Martin, 195 East Front St., Atco, NJ 08004 Tel. (609)767-9376

Treas., Mr. William Rainey, RD 1 Box 302, Monroeville, NJ 08343 Tel. (609)881-4790

Stat. Sec., Rev. James Korth, 237 W. Main St., Moorestown, NJ 08057 Tel. (609)235-8077

Natl. Rep., Rev. Howard E. Haines, Tel. (609)881-5516

PERIODICAL

Skopeo

The Fire Baptized Holiness Church (Wesleyan)

This church came into being about 1890 as the result of definite preaching on the doctrine of holiness in some Methodist churches in southeastern Kansas. It became known as The Southeast Kansas Fire Baptized Holiness Association, which name was changed in 1945 to The Fire Baptized

Holiness Church. It is entirely Wesleyan in doctrine, episcopal in church organization, and intensive in evangelistic zeal.

HEADQUARTERS
600 College Ave., Independence, KS 67301 Tel. (316)331-3049
Media Contact, Gen. Supt., Gerald Broadaway

OFFICERS
Gen. Supt., Gerald Broadaway
Gen. Sec., Wayne Knipmeyer, Box 457, South Pekin, IL 61564
Gen. Treas., Victor White, 709 N. 13th, Independence, KS 67301

PERIODICALS
Flaming Sword, The; John Three Sixteen

Free Christian Zion Church of Christ
Organized 1905, at Redemption, Ark., by a company of Negro ministers associated with various denominations, with polity in general accord with that of Methodist bodies.

HEADQUARTERS
1315 Hutchinson St., Nashville, AR 71852 Tel. (501)845-4933
Media Contact, Gen. Sec., Shirlie Cheatham

OFFICER
Chief Pastor, Willie Benson, Jr.

Free Lutheran Congregations, The Association of
The Association of Free Lutheran Congregations, rooted in the Scandinavian revival movements, was organized in 1962 by a Lutheran Free Church remnant which rejected merger with The American Lutheran Church. The original 42 congregations were joined by other like-minded conservative Lutherans, especially from the former Evangelical Lutheran Church and the Suomi Synod. There has been a fourfold increase in the number of congregations. Congregations subscribe to the Apostles', Nicene, and Athanasian creeds; Luther's Small Catechism; and the Unaltered Augsburg Confession. The Fundamental Principles and Rules for Work (1897), declare that the local congregation is the right form of the kingdom of God on earth, subject to no authority but the Word and the Spirit of God.

Distinctive emphases are: (1) the infallibility and inerrancy of Holy Scriptures as the Word of God; (2) congregational polity; (3) the spiritual unity of all believers, resulting in fellowship and cooperation transcending denominational lines; (4) evangelical outreach, calling all to enter a personal relationship with Jesus Christ; (5) a wholesome Lutheran pietism that proclaims the Lordship of Jesus Christ in all areas of life and results in believers becoming the salt and light in their communities; (6) a conservative stance on current social issues.

A two-year Bible school and a theological seminary are in suburban Minneapolis. Support is channeled to churches in Brazil, Mexico, and Canada.

HEADQUARTERS
3110 E. Medicine Lake Blvd., Minneapolis, MN 55441 Tel. (612)545-5631 Fax (612)545-0079
Media Contact, Pres., Rev. Robert L. Lee

OFFICERS
Pres., Rev. Robert L. Lee
Sec., Rev. Richard Anderson, 16070 Highview Ave., Lakeville, MN 55044

PERIODICAL
Lutheran Ambassador, The

Free Methodist Church of North America
The Free Methodist Church was organized in 1860 in Western New York by ministers and laymen who had called the Methodist Episcopal Church to return to what they considered the original doctrines and lifestyle of Methodism. The issues included human freedom (anti-slavery), freedom and simplicity in worship, free seats so that the poor would not be discriminated against, and freedom from secret oaths (societies) so the truth might be spoken freely at all times. They emphasized the teaching of the entire sanctification of life by means of grace through faith.

The denomination continues to be true to its founding principles. It communicates the gospel and its power to all people without discrimination through strong missionary, evangelistic, and educational programs. Six colleges, a Bible college, and numerous overseas schools train the youth of the church to serve in lay and ministerial roles.

Its members covenant to maintain simplicity in life and worship, daily devotion to Christ, and responsible stewardship of time, talent, and finance.

HEADQUARTERS
World Ministries Center: 770 N. High School Rd., Indianapolis, IN 46214 Tel. (317)244-3660 Fax (317)244-1247
Mailing Address, P.O. Box 535002, Indianapolis, IN 46253 Tel. (800)342-5531
Media Contact, Yearbook Ed., P.O. Box 535002, Indianapolis, IN 46253

OFFICERS
Bishops: Gerald E. Bates; David M. Foster; Bya'ene Akulu Ilangyi; Noah Nzeyimana; Daniel Ward; Richard D. Snyder
Gen. Conf. Sec., Melvin J. Spencer
Finance & Admn., Gen. Dir., Gary M. Kilgore
Christian Educ., Gen. Dir., Daniel L. Riemenschneider
Evangelism & Church Growth, Gen. Dir., Raymond W. Ellis
Free Methodist Publishing House, Gen. Dir., John E. Van Valin
Higher Educ. & Ministry, Gen. Dir., Bruce L. Kline
Light & Life Magazine, Ed., Robert B. Haslam
Light & Life Men Intl., Exec. Dir., Lucien E. Behar
Free Methodist Foundation, Stanley B. Thompson
Women's Ministries Intl., Pres., Mrs. Carollyn Ellis
World Missions, Gen. Dir., M. Doane Bonney

Free Will Baptists, National Association of
This evangelical group of Arminian Baptists was organized by Paul Palmer in 1727 at Chowan, N.C. Another movement (teaching the same doctrines of free grace, free salvation, and free will) was organized June 30, 1780, in New Durham, N.H., but there was no connection with the southern organization except for a fraternal relationship.

The northern line expanded more rapidly and

extended into the West and Southwest. This body merged with the Northern Baptist Convention Oct. 5, 1911, but a remnant of churches reorganized into the Cooperative General Association of Free Will Baptists Dec. 28, 1916, at Pattonsburg, Mo.

Churches in the southern line were organized into various conferences from the beginning and finally united in one General Conference in 1921.

Representatives of the Cooperative General Association and the General Conference joined Nov. 5, 1935 to form the National Association of Free Will Baptists.

HEADQUARTERS

5233 Mt. View Rd., Antioch, TN 37013-2306 Tel. (615)731-6812 Fax (615)731-0049

Mailing Address, P.O. Box 5002, Antioch, TN 37011-5002

Media Contact, Exec. Sec., Melvin Worthington

OFFICERS

Exec. Sec., Dr. Melvin Worthington
Mod., Rev. Ralph Hampton, P.O. Box 50117, Nashville, TN 37205

DENOMINATIONAL AGENCIES

Free Will Baptist Foundation, Exec. Sec., Herman Hersey

Free Will Baptist Bible College, Pres., Dr. Tom Malone

Foreign Missions Dept., Dir., Rev. R. Eugene Waddell

Home Missions Dept., Dir., Rev. Roy Thomas
Bd. of Retirement, Dir., Rev. Herman Hersey
Historical Commission, Chpsn., Mary Wisehart
Commission for Theological Integrity, Chpsn., Rev. Leroy Forlines, P.O. Box 50117, Nashville, TN 37205

Music Commission, Chpsn., Vernon Whaley, 104 S. Ramblin Oake Dr., Moore, OK 73160

Radio & Television Commission, Chpsn., Bob Shockey, P.O. Box 50117, Nashville, TN 37205

Sunday School & Church Training Dept., Dir., Dr. Roger Reeds

Woman's National Auxiliary Convention, Exec. Sec., Dr. Mary R. Wisehart

Master's Men Dept., Dir., Mr. James Vallance

PERIODICALS

Contact; Free Will Baptist Gem; Bible College Bulletin; Heartbeat; Mission Grams; Happenings; Co-Laborer

Friends General Conference

Friends General Conference is an association of yearly meetings open to all Friends meetings which wish to be actively associated with its programs and services. It was organized in 1900, bringing together four associations, including the First-day School Conference (1868) and the Friends Union for Philanthropic Labor (1882).

Friends General Conference is primarily a service organization and has no authority over constituent meetings. A Central Committee, to which constituent yearly meetings name appointees approximately in proportion to membership, or its Executive Committee, is responsible for the direction of the FGC's year-round services.

There are seven standing program committees: Advancement & Outreach, Christian & Interfaith Relations, Long Range Conference Planning, Ministry & Nurture, Publications & Distribution, Religious Education, and Friends Meeting House Fund.

HEADQUARTERS

1216 Arch St., 2B, Philadelphia, PA 19107 Tel. (215)561-1700

Media Contact, Gen. Sec., Meredith Walton

OFFICERS

Gen. Sec., Meredith Walton
Clk., Tyla Ann Burger-Arroyo
Treas., David Miller

YEARLY MEETINGS

Philadelphia YM, Edwin Staudt, 1515 Cherry St., Philadelphia, PA 19102

Lake Erie YM, Marty Grundy, 2602 Exeter Rd., Cleveland Heights, OH 44118 Tel. (216)932-2144

*New England YM, Elizabeth Cazden, 118 Walnut St., Manchester, NH 03014 Tel. (603)622-9835

*New York YM, George Rubin, 545 Rockland St., Westbury, NY 11590 Tel. (516)977-9665

*Baltimore YM, Katherine Smith, P.O. Box 503, Buena Vista, VA 24416 Tel. (703)261-2562

*Canadian YM, Elaine Bishop, 1A Nugent St., Thunder Bay, ON K7P 4S8 Tel. (715)892-9015

Illinois YM, Jerry Nurenberg, 60255 Myrtle Rd., South Bend, IN 46614 Tel. (219)232-5729

Ohio Valley YM, Ellen Armontine Hodge, 4240 Cornelius Ave., Indianapolis, IN 46208 Tel. (612)879-2835

South Central YM, Dan O'Brien, 1007 NW 32nd St., Oklahoma City, OK 73118 Tel. (405)521-8720

*Southeastern YM, Ken Leibman, 4545 Highway 346, Archer, FL 32618 Tel. (904)495-9482

Northern YM, Laura Fraser, 3078 Lake Elmo Ave. N., Lake Elmo, MN 55042 Tel. (612)879-2835

Piedmont FF, Ralph McCracken, 913 Ridgecrest Dr., Greensboro, NC 27410-3237 Tel. (919)292-8631

Southern Appalachian YM & Assoc., Peggy Bonnington, 408 West Coy Cir., Clarksville, TN 37043 Tel. (615)647-9284

Central Alaska, Kim McGee, 2428 Tulik, Anchorage, AK 99517

* also affiliated with Friends United Meeting

PERIODICAL

Focus

Friends United Meeting

Friends United Meeting was organized in 1902 (originally Five Years Meeting of Friends, the name was changed in 1963) as a loose confederation of North American yearly meetings to facilitate a united Quaker witness in missions, peace work, and Christian education.

Today Friends United Meeting is comprised of 18 member yearly meetings (12 North American plus Cuba, East Africa, East Africa Yearly Meeting (South), Elgon Religious Society of Friends, Nairobi and Jamaica Yearly Meetings) representing about half the Friends in the world. FUM's current work includes programs of mission and service, peace education, leadership and stewardship development, and the publication of Christian education curriculum, books of Quaker history and religious thought, and a magazine, Quaker Life.

HEADQUARTERS

101 Quaker Hill Dr., Richmond, IN 47374 Tel. (317)962-7573 Fax (317)966-1293

Media Contact, Interim Gen. Sec., Harold Smuck

OFFICERS

Presiding Clk., Sarah Wilson

Treas., John Norris
Interim Gen. Sec., Harold Smuck

DEPARTMENTS

World Ministries Commission, Assoc. Sec., Bill Wagoner
Meeting Ministries Commission, Assoc. Sec., Mary Glenn Hadley
Quaker Hill Bookstore, Mgr., Dick Talbot
Friends United Press, Ed., Ardith Talbot

YEARLY MEETINGS

Nebraska YM, Don Reeves, RR 1 Box 66, Central City, NV 68826
*New England YM, Elizabeth Cazden, 118 Walnut St., Manchester, NH Tel. (603)622-9835
*New York YM, George Rubin, 545 Rockland St., Westbury, NY 11590 Tel. (516)997-9665
*Baltimore YM, Katherine Smith, P.O. Box 503, Buena Vista, VA 24416 Tel. (703)261-2562
Iowa YM, Louise Davis, 1644 140th St., Clemons, IA 50051
Western YM, Lester Paulsen, P.O. Box 235, Plainfield, IN 46168
North Carolina YM, Carter Pike, 903 New Garden Rd., Greensboro, NC 27410
Indiana YM, Horace Smith, Rt. 2 Box 291, Hagerstown, IN 47346
Wilmington YM, Rudy Haag, P.O. Box 19, Cuba, OH 45114
Cuba YM, Maulio Ajo Berencen, Libertad 114, c/o Argamente & Garayalde, Holguin 80100, Holguin, Cuba
*Canadian YM, Edward Bell, 2339 Briar Hill Dr., Ottawa, ON K2H 7A7 Tel. (613)733-3255
Jamaica YM, Angela Johnson, 4 Worthington Ave., Kingston 5, Jamaica, W.I.
*Southeastern YM, Ken Leibman, 4545 Highway 346, Archer, FL 32618 Tel. (904)495-9482
Southwest YM, Lind Coop, 15915 E. Russell St., Whittier, CA 90603
East Africa YM, James Ashihunde, P.O. Box 1510, Kakamega, Kenya
East Africa YM (South), Joseph Kisia, P.O. Box 160, Vihiga, Kenya
Nairobi YM, Stanley Ndezwa, P.O. Box 377, Nakuru, Kenya
Elgon Religious Society of Friends, Elisha Wakube, P.O. Box 98, Kimilili, Kenya, East Africa

* also affiliated with Friends Gen. Conference

PERIODICAL

Quaker Life

Full Gospel Assemblies International

This Pentecostal body had its beginning in 1972 as an adjunct to an established school of biblical studies known as Full Gospel Bible Institute under the leadership of Dr. Charles E. Strauser.

HEADQUARTERS

RD 2, Box 520, Parkesburg, PA 19365 Tel. (215)857-2357

OFFICERS

Pres., Dr. Charles E. Strauser
Asst., Dr. Annamae Strauser
Executive Board: Dr. C. E. Strauser; Dr. Annamae Strauser; Rev. Simeon Strauser; Carol Ann Strauser
Sec., Betty B. Stewart

Board of Directors: Rev. Harold Oswold, 340 R and St., Rochester, NY 14611; Rev. Simeon Strauser, Box 26, Sadsburyville, PA 19369; Dr. Samuel Strauser, Box 450, Delaware Water Gap, PA 18327; Rev. Richard Hartman, 4001 Elmerton Ave., Harrisburg, PA 17109; Rev. David Alessi, P.O. Box 168, Dunkirk, NY 14048; Rev. James Scott, P.O. Box 93, Mad River, CA 95552; Rev. Marilyn Allen, 5204 A5 Kissing Camels Dr., Colorado Springs, CO 80904; Rev. Victor Fisk 398 Gill Rd., Apollo, PA 15613

PERIODICALS

Charisma Courier, The; Pentecost Today

Full Gospel Fellowship of Churches and Ministers International

In the early 1960s, a conviction grew in the hearts of many ministers that there ought to be closer fellowship between the people of God who believed in the apostolic ministry. Also, a great number of independent churches were experiencing serious difficulties in receiving authority from the IRS to give governmentally accepted tax-exempt receipts for donations.

In September 1962, a group of ministers met in Dallas, Texas, to form a Fellowship to give expression to the essential unity of the Body of Christ under the leadership of the Holy Spirit—a unity that goes beyond individuals, churches, or organizations. This was not a movement to build another denomination, but rather an effort to join ministers and churches of like feeling across denominational lines.

To provide opportunities for fellowship and to support the objectives and goals of local and national ministries, regional conventions and an annual international convention are held.

HEADQUARTERS

4325 W. Ledbetter Dr., Dallas, TX 75233 Tel. (241)339-1200

OFFICERS

Pres., Dr. Don Arnold, P.O. Box 324, Gadsden, AL 35901
1st Vice-Pres., Dr. Ray Chamberlain, P.O. Box 986, Salisbury, MD 21801
Sec., Dr. Chester P. Jenkins
Treas., Rev. S. K. Biffle, 3833 Westerville Rd., Columbus, OH 43224
Ofc. Sec., Mrs. Anne Rasmussen, 4325 Ledbetter Dr., Dallas, TX 75233 Tel. (241)339-1200
Vice-Pres. at Large: Rev. Maurice Hart, P.O. Box 4316, Omaha, NE 68104; Rev. Don Westbrook, 3518 Rose of Sharon Rd., Durham, NC 27705
Regional Vice-Pres.: Southeast, Rev. R. Richard Edgar, 5937 Franconia Rd., Alexandria, VA 22310; South Central, Rev. David Ellis, 4301 N.E. 28th St., Ft. Worth, TX 76117; Southwest, Rev. Don Shepherd, 631 Southgate Rd., Sacramento, CA 95815; Northeast, Rev. Roy C. Smith, P.O. Box 193, Shrewsbury, PA 17361; North Central, Rev. Raymond Rothwell, P.O. Box 367, Eaton, OH 45320; Northwest, Rev. Ralph Trask, 3212 Hyacinth NE, Salem, OR 97303
Exec. Sec., Dr. Chester P. Jenkins
Chmn. of Evangelism, Dr. Marty Tharp
Past Pres., Dr. James Helton

PERIODICAL

Tidings

Fundamental Methodist Church, Inc.

This group traces its origin through the Methodist Protestant Church. It withdrew from The Methodist Church and organized on Aug. 27, 1942.

HEADQUARTERS

1034 N. Broadway, Springfield, MO 65802
Media Contact, Dist. Supt., Pastor Ronnie Fieker, 804 13th, Monett, MO 65708 Tel. (417)235-3168

OFFICERS

Treas., Mr. Everett Etheridge, 3844 W. Dover, Springfield, MO 65802 Tel. (417)865-4438
Sec., Mrs. Betty Nicholson, Rt. 2, Box 397, Ash Grove, MO 65604 Tel. (417)672-2268
Dist. Supt., Rev. Ronnie Fieker, 804 13th, Monett, MO 65708 Tel. (417)235-3168

General Association of Regular Baptist Churches

Founded in May, 1932, in Chicago, by a group of churches which had withdrawn from the Northern Baptist Convention (now the American Baptist Churches in the U.S.A.) because of doctrinal differences. Its Confession of Faith, which it requires all churches to subscribe to, is essentially the old, historic New Hampshire Confession of Faith with a premillennial ending applied to the last article.

HEADQUARTERS

1300 N. Meacham Rd., Schaumburg, IL 60173 Tel. (708)843-1600 Fax (708)843-3757

OFFICERS

Chpsn., Dr. David Nettleton
Vice-Chpsn., Dr. John Polson
Treas., Vernon Miller
Sec., Dr. John Greening
Natl. Rep., Dr. Paul Tassell

PERIODICAL

Baptist Bulletin

General Baptists (General Association of)

Similar in doctrine to those General Baptists organized in England in the early 17th century, the first General Baptist churches were organized on the Midwest frontier following the Second Great Awakening. The first church was established by the Rev. Benoni Stinson, in 1823 at Evansville, Ind.

Stinson's major theological emphasis was general atonement—"Christ tasted death for every man." The group also allows for the possibility of apostasy. It practices open Communion and believer's baptism by immersion.

Called "liberal" Baptists because of their emphasis on the freedom of man, General Baptists organized a General Association in 1870 and invited other "liberal" Baptists (e.g., "free will" and Separate Baptists) to participate.

The policy-setting body is composed of delegates from local General Baptist churches and associations. Each local church is autonomous but belongs to an association. The group currently consists of more than 60 associations in 16 states, as well as several associations in the Philippines, Guam, Saipan, Jamaica, and India. Ministers and deacons are ordained by a presbytery.

A number of boards continue a variety of missions, schools, and other support ministries. General Baptists belong to the Baptist World Alliance and the North American Baptist Fellowship, and the National Association of Evangelicals.

HEADQUARTERS

100 Stinson Dr., Poplar Bluff, MO 63901 Tel. (314)785-7746 Fax (314)785-0564
Media Contact, Ed., Gen. Bapt. Messenger, Wayne Foust, Fax (314)686-5198

OFFICERS

Mod., Rev. Ray Phelps, 1214 W. Hemphill Rd., Flint, MI 48507
Clk., Rev. Franklin Dumond, 1717 N. Main, Mt. Vernon, IN 47620
Exec. Dir., Dr. Glen O. Spence

OTHER ORGANIZATIONS

Gen. Bd., Sec., Rev. Franklin Dumond, 1717 N. Main, Mt. Vernon, IN 47620
Foreign Missions Bd., Exec. Dir., Rev. Charles Carr
Bd. of Christian Educ. & Publication, Exec. Dir., Rev. Sam Ramdial
Home Mission Bd., Exec. Dir., Dr. Leland Duncan
Ministerial Services Bd., Exec. Dir., Rev. Gary Watson
Brotherhood Bd., Pres., Mr. Phil Simmons, 553 Walton Ferry Rd., Hendersonville, TN 37075
Women's Mission Bd., Exec. Dir., Mrs. Sandra Trivitt
Stewardship Dir., Rev. Ron D. Black
Nursing Home Admn., Ms. Wanda Britt, Rt. #2, Box 230, Campbell, MO 63933
College Bd., Pres., Dr. James Murray, Oakland City College, P.O. Box 235, Oakland City, IN 47660
Publishing House, Stinson Press, Rev. Wayne Foust, 400 Stinson Dr., Poplar Bluff, MO 63901

PERIODICALS

General Baptist Messenger; Capsule; Voice; WAVE

General Church of the New Jerusalem

The General Church of the New Jerusalem is the result of a reorganization in 1897 of the General Church of The Advent of the Lord. It stresses the full acceptance of the doctrines contained in the theological writings of Emanuel Swedenborg.

HEADQUARTERS

Bryn Athyn, PA 19009 Tel. (215)947-4200
Media Contact, Ed., Church Journal, Donald L. Rose, Box 277, Bryn Athyn, PA 19009 Tel. (215)947-6225 Fax (215)938-2616

OFFICERS

Presiding Bishop, Rt. Rev. P. M. Buss
Sec., Mr. Boyd Asplundh
Treas., Neil M. Buss

PERIODICAL

New Church Life

General Conference of the Evangelical Baptist Church, Inc.

This denomination is an Arminian, Wesleyan, premillennial group whose form of government is congregational.

It was organized in 1935, and was formerly known as the Church of the Full Gospel, Inc.

1601 E. Rose St., Goldsboro, NC 27530 Tel.
(919)734-2482

OFFICERS

Pres., Rev. David J. Crawford, 101 William Dr.,
Goldsboro, NC 27530 Tel. (919)734-2482
1st Vice-Pres., Dr. Harry E. Jones, 3741 Sunset
Ave., Westridge Village, Apt. B-1, Rocky
Mount, NC 27801 Tel. (919)443-1239
2nd Vice-Pres., Rev. George C. Wallace, 909 W.
Walnut St., Chanute, KS 66720 Tel. (316)431-
0706
Sec.-Treas., Mrs. Evelyn Crawford, 101 William
Dr., Goldsboro, NC 27530 Tel. (919)734-2482
Dir. of Evangelism, Rev. B. L. Proctor, Rt. 3, Box
442, Nashville, NC 27856 Tel. (919)459-2063
Dir. of Women's Work, ——
Dir. of Youth Work, Rev. Ralph Jarrell, P.O. Box
1112, Burgaw, NC 28425 Tel. (919)259-9329

General Convention of The Swedenborgian Church

Founded in North America in 1792 as the Church
of the New Jerusalem, the General Convention was
organized as a national body in 1817 and incorporated in the state of Illinois in 1861.

Its biblically-based theology is derived from the
spiritual, or mystical, experiences and exhaustive
biblical studies of the Swedish scientist and phi-
losopher Emanuel Swedenborg (1688-1772).

The church centers its worship and teachings on
the historical life and the risen and glorified present
reality of the Lord Jesus Christ. It looks with an
ecumenical vision toward the establishment of the
kingdom of God in the form of a universal Church,
active in the lives of all people of good will who
desire and strive for freedom, peace, and justice for
all. It is a member of the National Council of
Churches and is active in many local councils of
churches.

With churches and groups throughout the United
States and Canada, the Convention's central administrative offices and its seminary—Swedenborg School of Religion—are located in Newton,
Mass. Affiliated churches are found in Africa,
Asia, Australia, Canada, Europe, the United Kingdom, Japan, and South America. Many interna-
tionally prominent philosphers and writers, past
and present, have acknowledged their appreciation
of the teachings of Emanuel Swedenborg, which
form the basis of this global church.

HEADQUARTERS

48 Sargent St., Newton, MA 02158 Tel. (617)969-
4240 Fax (617)964-3258
Media Contact, Central Ofc. Mgr., Martha Bauer

OFFICERS

Pres., Rev. Richard H. Tafel, Jr.
Vice-Pres., Mrs. Elizabeth S. Young, 3715 Via
Palomino, Palos Verdes Estates, CA 90274
Rec. Sec., Mrs. Gloria L. Toot, 10280 Gentlewind
Dr., Montgomery, OH 45242
Treas., John C. Perry, RFD 2, Box 2341A, Bruns-
wick, ME 04011
Ofc. Mgr., Mrs. Martha Bauer

PERIODICALS

Messenger, The; Our Daily Bread

General Six Principle Baptists

A Baptist Group, organized in Rhode Island in
1653, drawing its name from Heb. 6:1-2.

OFFICERS

Rhode Island Conference: Pres., Rev. Edgar S.
Kirk, 350 Davisville Rd., North Kingstown, RI
02852 Tel. (401)884-2750; Clk., Miss Sylvia
Stoner, RR 1, Box 170, Wyoming, RI 02898
Pennsylvania Association: Pres., Elder Daniel E.
Carpenetti, RR 1, Box 1750, Nicholson, PA
18446-9470 Tel. (717)942-6578; Clk., Mrs.
Eleanor Warner, RR 1, Box 1778, Nicholson, PA
18446-9275

Grace Brethren Churches, Fellowship of

A division occurred in the Church of the Brethren
in 1882 on the question of the legislative authority
of the annual meeting. It resulted in the establishment of this body under a legal charter requiring congregational government.

MEDIA CONTACT

Media Contact, Fellowship Coord., Rev. Charles
Ashman, P.O. Box 386, Winona Lake, IN 46590
Tel. (219)269-1269

OFFICERS

Mod., David Plaster, RR 8, Box 232, Warsaw, IN
46580
Mod.-Elect, William Shell, 1210 W. 100 South,
Warsaw, IN 46580
Fellowship Coord., Charles Ashman, P.O. Box
386, Winona Lake, IN 46590 Tel. (219)267-
5566
Sec., John Snow, P.O. Box 6, Portis, KS 67474
Treas., Steve Poppenfoose, R. 1, Box 425A, War-
saw, IN 46580

OTHER BOARDS

Grace Brethren Foreign Missions, Exec. Dir., Rev.
Tom Julien, P.O. Box 588, Winona Lake, IN
46590
Grace Brethren Home Missions, Exec. Dir., Larry
Chamberlain, P.O. Box 587, Winona Lake, IN
46590
Grace Schools, Pres., Dr. John Davis, 200 Semi-
nary Dr., Winona Lake, IN 46590 Tel. (210)372-
5100
Brethren Missionary Herald Co., Pub. & Gen.
Mgr., Charles Turner, P.O. Box 544, Winona
Lake, IN 46590
Women's Missionary Council, Pres., Mrs. Betty
Ogden, 8400 Good Luck Rd., Lanham, MD
20706
CE National, Exec. Dir., Rev. Ed Lewis, P.O. Box
365, Winona Lake, IN 46590
Grace Brethren Men & Boys, Exec. Dir., Rev. Ed
Jackson, c/o Grace Brethren Church of Colum-
bus, 6675 Worthington-Galena Rd.,
Worthington, OH 43085
Brethren Evangelistic Ministries, Dir., Ron
Thompson, 3580 Robin Hood Cir., Roanoke, VA
24019
Brethren Navajo Ministries, Dir., Steve Galegor,
Counselor, NM 87018
Grace Village Retirement Community, P.O. Box
337, Winona Lake, IN 46590

PERIODICAL

Brethren Missionary Herald

Grace Gospel Fellowship

The Grace Gospel Fellowship was organized in
1944 by a group of pastors who held to a dispensational interpretation of Scripture. Most of these
men had ministries in Illinois, Indiana, Wisconsin,

US RELIGIOUS BODIES

Ohio, and Missouri. Two prominent leaders were J. C. O'Hair of Chicago and Charles Baker of Milwaukee.

Subsequent to 1945, a Bible Institute was founded (now Grace Bible College of Grand Rapids, Mich.), and a previously organized foreign mission (now Grace Ministries International of Grand Rapids) was affiliated with the group. Churches have now been established in most sections of the country.

The body has remained a fellowship, each church being autonomous in polity. All support for its college, mission, and headquarters is on a contributary basis.

The binding force of the Fellowship has been the members' doctrinal position. They believe in the Deity and Saviorship of Jesus Christ and subscribe to the inerrant authority of Scripture. Their method of biblical interpretation is dispensational, with emphasis on the distinctive revelation to and the ministry of the apostle Paul.

MEDIA CONTACT

Media Contact, Pres., Roger G. Anderson, 2125 Martindale SW, P.O. Box 9432, Grand Rapids, MI 49509 Tel. (616)245-0100 Fax (616)241-2542

OFFICER

Pres., Roger Anderson

OTHER ORGANIZATIONS

Grace Bible College, Pres., Rev. Bruce Kemper, 1011 Aldon St. SW, Grand Rapids, MI 49509

Grace Ministries Intl., Exec. Dir., Dr. Samuel Vinton, 2125 Martindale Ave. SW, Grand Rapids, MI 49509

Missionary Literature Distributors, Dir., Mrs. Betty Strelow, 7514 Humbert Rd., Godfrey, IL 62305

Prison Mission Association, Gen. Dir., Mr. Vern Bigelow, P.O. Box 1587, Port Orchard, WA 98366-0140

Grace Publications Inc., Exec. Dir., Roger Anderson, 2125 Martindale Ave. SW, Grand Rapids, MI 49509

Bible Doctrines to Live By, Exec. Dir., Lee Homoki, P.O. Box 2351, Grand Rapids, MI 49501

PERIODICAL

Truth

Greek Orthodox Archdiocese of North and South America

The Greek Orthodox Archdiocese of North and South America is under the jurisdiction of the Ecumenical Patriarchate of Constantinople, in Istanbul. It was chartered in 1922 by the State of New York and has parishes in the United States, Canada, Central and South America. The first Greek Orthodox Church in the United States was founded in New Orleans, in 1864.

HEADQUARTERS

8-10 E. 79th St., New York, NY 10021 Tel. (212)570-3500 Fax (212)861-2183

Media Contact, News Media Liaison, Jim Golding, Tel. (212)628-2590 Fax (212)570-4005

ARCHDIOCESAN COUNCIL

Chpsn., Archbishop Iakovos
Vice-Chpsn., Metropolitan Silas of New Jersey
Pres., Andrew A. Athens, Chicago, IL
1st Vice-Pres., George Chimples, Cleveland, OH
2nd Vice-Pres., Elenie K. Huszagh

Sec., Basil C. Foussianes, Detroit, MI
Treas., Peter Dion, New York, NY
Theodore Prounis, New York, NY

SYNOD OF BISHOPS

Chpsn., His Eminence Archbishop Iakovos
His Excellency Metropolitan Silas of New Jersey, 8 East 79th St., New York, NY 10021
His Grace Bishop Iakovos of Chicago, Forty East Burton Pl., Chicago, IL 60610
His Grace Bishop Timothy of Detroit, 19504 Renfrew, Detroit, MI 48211
His Grace Bishop Sotirios of Toronto, 40 Donlands Ave., Toronto, ON M4J 3N6
His Grace Bishop Anthony of San Francisco, 372 Santa Clara Ave., San Francisco, CA 94117
His Grace Bishop Maximos of Pittsburgh, 5201 Ellsworth Ave., Pittsburgh, PA 15232
His Grace Bishop Gennadios of Buenos Aires, Avenida Figueroa Alcorta 3187, Buenos Aires, Argentina
His Grace Bishop Methodios of Boston, 162 Goddard Ave., Brookline, MA 02146
Assistant Bishops to Archbishop Iakovos: His Grace Bishop Philotheos of Meloa; His Grace Bishop Philip of Daphnousia, 2801 Buford St., Ste. 365, Atlanta, GA; His Grace Bishop Isaiah of Aspendos, Chancellor; His Grace Bishop Alexios of Troas, Chorepiscopos of Astoria, 27-09 Crescent St., Astoria, NY 11102

ARCHDIOCESAN DEPARTMENTS

Rel. Educ., 50 Goddard Ave., Brookline, MA 02146
Go Telecom, 27-09 Crescent St., Astoria, NY 11102
Archives Logos, Mission Center, P.O. Box 4319, St. Augustine, FL 32085
Youth Ministry & Camping
Economic Development
Church & Society
Ecumenical Ofc.
Stewardship
Registry
Ionian Village
Communications

ORGANIZATIONS

Ladies Philoptochos Society, 345 E. 74th St., New York, NY 10021
Greek Orthodox Young Adult League (GOYAL)
Order of St. Andrew the Apostle
Archdiocesan Presbyters' Council
National Sisterhood of Presbyteres
Natl. Forum of Greek Orthodox Church Musicians, 1700 N. Walnut St., Bloomington, IN 47401

PERIODICAL

Orthodox Observer, The

The Holiness Church of God, Inc.

This church was established at Madison, N.C., in 1920; and was incorporated in 1928 at Winston-Salem, N.C.

HEADQUARTERS

Winston-Salem, NC

OFFICERS

Pres., Bishop B. McKinney, 602 E. Elm St., Graham, NC 27253
Vice-Bishop, Melvin Charley, 140-39 172nd St., Springfield Gardens, NY 11434

Gen. Sec., Mrs. Nina B. Hash, Box 541, Galax, VA 24333

Northern Area of N.E. Dist., Overseer, Melvin Charley, 140-39 172nd St., Springfield Gardens, NY 11434

So. Dist., Overseer, Bishop T. R. Rice, 1439 Sedgefield Dr., Winston-Salem, NC 27105 Tel. (919)227-4755

Va. & W. Va. Area of N.W. Dist., Overseer, Elder Arnie Joyce, Thorpe, WV 24888

North Carolina Area of N.W. Dist., Overseer, James Himes, 3661 Barkwood Dr., Winston-Salem, NC 27105

Holy Ukrainian Autocephalic Orthodox Church in Exile

The laymen and clergy who organized this church, in 1951, came from among the Ukrainians who settled in the Western Hemisphere after World War II. In 1954 two bishops, immigrants from Europe, met with clergy and laymen and formally organized the religious body.

HEADQUARTERS

103 Evergreen St., W. Babylon, NY 11704

OFFICERS

Admn., Rt. Rev. Serhij K. Pastukhiv, Tel. (516)669-7402

House of God, Which is the Church of the Living God, the Pillar and Ground of the Truth, Inc.

This body, founded by Mary L. Tate in 1919, is episcopally organized.

OFFICER

Bishop, Raymond W. White, 6107 Cobbs Creek Pkwy., Philadelphia, PA 19143 Tel. (215)748-6338

PERIODICAL

Spirit of Truth Magazine

Hungarian Reformed Church in America

A Hungarian Reformed Church was organized in New York in 1904 in connection with the Reformed Church of Hungary. In 1922 the Church in Hungary transferred most of her congregations in the United States to the Reformed Church in the U.S. Some, however, preferred to continue as an autonomous, self-supporting American denomination, and these formed the Free Magyar Reformed Church in America. This group changed its name in 1958 to Hungarian Reformed Church in America.

This Church is a member of the World Alliance of Reformed Churches, Presbyterian and Congregational, the World Council of Churches and the National Council of Churches. It is deeply involved in the Roman Catholic, Presbyterian Reformed Consultation, of which for over 12 years Dr. Andrew Harsanyi was co-chairman.

HEADQUARTERS

Bishop's Office, P.O. Box D, Hopatcong, NJ 07843 Tel. (201)398-2764

Media Contact, Bishop, Dr. Andrew Harsanyi, Tel. (210)398-2764

OFFICERS

Bishop, Rt. Rev. Dr. Andrew Harsanyi

Chief Lay-Curator, Prof. Stephen Szabo, 464 Forest Ave., Paramus, NJ 07652

Gen. Sec. (Clergy), Rt. Rev. Paul A. Mezö, 8 Dunthorne Ct., Scarborough, ON M1B 2S9

Gen Sec. (Lay), Zolt Lan Ambrus, 3358 Maple Dr., Melvindale, MI 48122

Eastern Classis, Dean (Senior of the Deans, Chair in Bishop's absence), The V. Rev. Stefan M. Torok, 331 Kirkland Pl., Perth Amboy, NJ 08861

New York Classis, Dean, The V. Rev. Alex Forro, 13 Grove St., Poughkeepsie, NY 12601

Western Classis, Dean, The V. Rev. Andor Demeter, 3921 W. Christy Dr., Phoenix, AZ 85029

PERIODICAL

Magyar Egyhaz

Hutterian Brethren

Small groups of Hutterites derive their names from Jacob Hutter, a 16th-century Anabaptist who advocated communal ownership of property and was burned as a heretic in Austria in 1536.

Many believers are of German descent and still use their native tongue at home and in church. Much of the denominational literature is produced in German and English. "Colonies" share property, practice non-resistance, dress differently, refuse to participate in politics, and operate their own schools. There are 375 colonies with 40,000 members in North America.

Each congregation conducts its own youth work through Sunday school. Until age 15, children attend German school after attending public school. All youth, ages 15 to 20 must attend Sunday school. They are baptized upon confession of faith, around age 20.

MEDIA CONTACT

Media Contact, Correspondent, Rev. Paul S. Gross, Rt. 1, Box 6E, Reardon, WA 99029 Tel. (509)299-5400

OFFICERS

Vice-Pres., Rev. Joseph Hofer, P.O. Box 159, Sunburst, MT 59482 Tel. (406)937-3045

Hutterite Bishop, Rev. John Wipf, P.O. Box 1509, Rosetown, SK S0L 2V0 Tel. (306)882-3112

Independent Fundamental Churches of America

Organized 1930 at Cicero, Ill., by representatives of the American Council of Undenominational Churches and representatives of various independent churches. The founding churches and members had separated themselves from various denominational affiliations.

The IFCA provides an advance movement among independent churches and ministers to unite in a close fellowship and cooperation, in defense of the fundamental teachings of Scripture and in the proclamation of the gospel of God's grace.

HEADQUARTERS

3520 Fairlanes, Grandville, MI 49468 Tel. (616)531-1840

Mailing Address, P.O. Box 810, Grandville, MI 49418

Natl. Exec. Dir., Dr. Richard Gregory, 2684 Meadow Ridge Dr., Byron Center, MI 49315 Tel. (616)878-1285

Pres., Dr. Elwood Chipchase, 3645 South 57th Ct., Cicero, IL 60650 Tel. (708)656-6857

1st Vice-Pres., Rev. David Meschke, 6763 South High St., Littleton, CO 80122 Tel. (803)794-0095

2nd Vice-Pres., Leslie Madison, 10101 East 147th St., Kansas City, MO 64149 Tel. (816)331-3342

PERIODICAL

Voice, The

International Church of the Foursquare Gospel

Founded by Aimee Semple McPherson in 1927, the International Church of the Foursquare Gospel proclaims the message of Jesus Christ the Savior, Healer, Baptizer with the Holy Spirit, and Soon-coming King. Headquartered in Los Angeles, this evangelistic missionary body of believers consists of nearly 1,568 churches in the United States and Canada.

The International Church of the Foursquare Gospel is incorporated in the State of California and governed by a Board of Directors who direct its corporate affairs. A Foursquare Cabinet, consisting of the Corporate Officers, Board of Directors, District Supervisors of the various districts of the Foursquare Church in the United States and other elected or appointed members, serves in an advisory capacity to the President and the Board of Directors.

Each local Foursquare Church is a subordinate unit of the International Church of the Foursquare Gospel. The pastor of the church is appointed by the Board of Directors and is responsible for the spiritual and physical welfare of the church. To assist and advise the pastor, a church council is elected by the local church members.

Foursquare Churches seek to build strong believers through Christian education, Christian day schools, youth camping and ministry, United Foursquare Women who support and encourage Foursquare missionaries abroad, radio and television ministries, the Foursquare World Advance Magazine, and 149 Bible Colleges worldwide.

Worldwide missions remains the focus of the Foursquare Gospel Church with nearly 25,577 churches, 17,773 national Foursquare pastors/leaders and 1,683,267 members and adherents in 72 countries around the globe. The Church is affiliated with the Pentecostal Fellowship of North America, National Association of Evangelicals, and the World Pentecostal Fellowship.

HEADQUARTERS

1910 W. Sunset Blvd., Ste. 200, Los Angeles, CA 90026 Tel. (213)484-2400 Fax (213)413-3824
Media Contact, Editor, Rev. Ron Williams

OFFICERS

Pres., Dr. John R. Holland
Pres. Emeritus, Dr. Rolf K. McPherson
Vice-Pres., Dr. Roy Hicks, Jr.
Gen. Sup., Dr. J. Eugene Kurtz
Dir. of Missions Intl., Dr. Roy Hicks, Jr.
Sec., Dr. John W. Bowers
Treas., Rev. Virginia Cravens
Exec. Sec., Rev. James Rogers

Bd. of Directors: Dr. John R. Holland; Dr. Rolf K. McPherson; Dr. Roy Hicks, Jr.; Dr. John W. Bowers; Dr. Harold Helms; Dr. Howard P. Courtney, Sr.; Mr. Douglas L. Slaybaugh; Dr. J. Eugene Kurtz; Rev. Ron Williams; Rev. Loren Edwards

District Supervisors: Eastern, Rev. Dewey Morrow; Great Lakes, Rev. Fred Parker; Midwest, Dr. Glenn Metzler; Northwest, Dr. Cliff Hanes; South Central, Dr. Sidney Westbrook; Southeast, Dr. Glenn Burris, Sr.; Southern California, Rev. Don Long; Southwest, Rev. John Watson; Western, Dr. Fred Wymore

Foursquare Cabinet: Composed of Bd. of Directors; District Supervisors; Rev. James Rogers; Dr. Jack Hamilton; Rev. Charles Aldridge; Rev. Tom Ferguson; Rev. Ken Wold, Jr.; Dr. Daniel Brown; Rev. David Holland

SUPPORT MINISTRIES

Natl. Dept. of Youth, Natl. Youth Minister, Rev. Gregg Johnson

Natl. Dept. of Chr. Educ. & Publications, Dir., Rev. Rick Wulfestieg

United Foursquare Women, Pres., Rev. Beverly Brafford

PERIODICALS

Foursquare World Advance; United Foursquare Women's Magazine

The International Pentecostal Church of Christ

At a General Conference held at London, Ohio, Aug. 10, 1976, the International Pentecostal Assemblies and the Pentecostal Church of Christ, after a two-year trial period, by overwhelming majority votes from each group, consolidated into one body, taking the name International Pentecostal Church of Christ.

The International Pentecostal Assemblies was the successor of the Association of Pentecostal Assemblies and the International Pentecostal Missionary Union. The other body involved in the merger, the Pentecostal Church of Christ, was founded by John Stroup of Flatwoods, Kentucky, on May 10, 1917, and was incorporated at Portsmouth, Ohio, in 1927.

The International Pentecostal Church of Christ is an active member of the Pentecostal Fellowship of North America, as well as a member of the National Association of Evangelicals.

The priorities of the International Pentecostal Church of Christ are to be an agency of God for evangelizing the world, to be a corporate body in which man may worship God, and to be a channel of God's purpose to build a body of saints being perfected in the image of his Son.

The Annual Conference is held each year during the first full week of August on Route 42 in London, Ohio, which houses the Conference Center offices and national campgrounds.

HEADQUARTERS

2245 St. Rt. 42 SW, P.O. Box 439, London, OH 43140 Tel. (614)852-0348
Media Contact, Gen. Overseer, Clyde Hughes

EXECUTIVE COMMITTEE

Gen. Overseer, Clyde M. Hughes, P.O. Box 439, London, OH 43140 Tel. (614)852-0348
Asst. Gen. Overseer, Wells T. Bloomfield, P.O. Box 439, London, OH 43140 Tel. (614)852-0448

Gen. Sec., Rev. Thomas Dooley, 3200 Dueber Ave. S.W., Canton, OH 44706 Tel. (216)484-6053

Gen. Treas., Rev. Clifford A. Edwards, P.O. Box 18145, Atlanta, GA 30316 Tel. (404)627-2681

Dir. of Global Missions, Dr. James B. Keiller, P.O. Box 18145, Atlanta, GA 30316 Tel. (404)627-2681

DISTRICT OVERSEERS

Blue Ridge District, Robert Culler, Rt. 2, Box 12, Pinnacle, NC 27043 Tel. (919)368-2540

Central District, Ervin Hargrave, 3208 Tackett St., Springfield, OH 45505 Tel. (513)399-0668

Mid-Eastern District, Phil Russell, 300 Pearl St., Elizabeth City, NC 27909 Tel. (919)338-8353

Mountain District: Wells T. Bloomfield, P.O. Box 439, London, OH 43140 Tel. (614)852-0448; Member-at-Large, Jerry L. Castle, Rt. 276, Box 377, Paintsville, KY 41240 Tel. (606)789-5598

New River District, Calvin Weikel, Rt. 2, Box 300, Ronceverte, WV 24970 Tel. (304)647-4301

North Central District, Larry Austin, 8495 Smith Rd., Perrinton, MI 48871 Tel. (517)236-0587

North Eastern District, Thomas Dillow, P.O. Box 7, Millville, WV 25432 Tel. (304)725-0587

South Eastern District: Clifford Edwards, 892 Berne St. SE, Atlanta, GA Tel. (404)627-2681; Member-at-Large, Samuel Chand, P.O. Box 18145, Atlanta, GA 30316 Tel. (404)627-2681

Tri-State, J. W. Ferguson, 9724 US Rt. 60, Ashland, KY 41102 Tel. (606)928-6651

Gen. Pres. of Pentecostal Ambassadors, Asa Lowe, 3153 Old Carolina Rd., Virginia Beach, VA 23457 Tel. (404)421-3773

IPCC Loan Committee, Chmn., Cecil McCarty, 3113 Penrose Ave., Springfield, OH 45505 Tel. (513)324-2748

Locust Grove Rest Home, Dir., Frank Myers, Rt. 3, Box 175, Harpers Ferry, WV 25425 Tel. (304)535-6355

Ladies Auxiliary, Gen. Pres., Janice Boyce, 121 W. Hunters Trail, Elizabeth City, NC 27909 Tel. (919)338-3003

Men's Fellowship, Gen. Pres., Maynard Bingamon, 4369 Wolford Rd., Xenia, OH 45385 Tel. (513)675-2325

PERIODICAL

Bridegroom's Messenger, The

Israelite House of David

The Israelite House of David, commonly called House of David, was established in 1903 in Benton Harbor, Mich., by Brother Benjamin, the founder and leader, after he had preached the Life of the Body without going to the grave, while traveling for seven years throughout a number of mid-American states.

This denomination is a Christian Association following Jesus' teachings (I Tim. 1:16) and the firstborn among many brethren (Rom. 8:29). They believe Brother Benjamin to have been the voice of the seventh angel referred to in Revelation 10:7; Malachi 3:1; Job 33:23-25. In his writings he points out the way for the elect to receive the Life of the Body (Hosea 13:14; Isa. 38:18; I Thess. 5:23; Matt. 7:14; Titus 1:2; II Tim. 1:10; John 10:10, 27, 28).

House of David leaders say three classes are mainly referred to in the Bible--Jew, Gentile, and Israel. They believe the Jew and the Gentile will receive the Soul Salvation, a free Gift (Eph. 2:8). They believe the Elect of Israel--a few (Matt. 5:5),

numbered in the seventh and fourteenth chapters of Revelation as 144,000 of all the tribes of the children of Israel--will receive the Life of the Body. Zechariah 13:8 reads, "Two parts shall be cut off and die, but the third part shall be left therein." According to Isaiah 19:24, Israel will be the third.

Brother Benjamin's writings try to bring harmony to many apparent contradictions sealed until the time of the end (Dan. 12:9; I Cor. 10:11). They expect to gather the 12 tribes of Israel (Jer. 31:1; Ezek. 20:34, 34:13, 14; Hosea 1:11), to be carried over into the millennium day of rest, 1,000 years (Rev. 20:1, 2 and 21:2, 4; Isa. 11:6-9, 35:1, 55:13, 54:13). Israel will be gathered from both Jew and Gentile.

The Church uses the King James version of the Bible and the Apocrypha.

HEADQUARTERS

P.O. Box 1067, Benton Harbor, MI 49023 Tel. (616)926-6695

Media Contact, Pillar & Sec., H. Thomas Dewhirst, Fax (616)429-5594

OFFICERS

Chpsn. of Bd., Lloyd H. Dalager

Pillar & Sec., H. Thomas Dewhirst

PERIODICAL

Shiloh's Messenger of Wisdom

Jehovah's Witnesses

The modern history of Jehovah's Witnesses began a little more than 100 years ago. In the early 1870s, a Bible study began in Allegheny City, Pa., now a part of Pittsburgh. Charles Taze Russell was the prime mover of the group. In July 1879, the first issue of Zion's Watch Tower and Herald of Christ's Presence appeared. (Now called *The Watchtower* with a circulation of 15,570,000 in 111 languages.) By 1880 scores of congregations had spread into nearby states. In 1881 Zion's Watch Tower Tract Society was formed, and in 1884 was incorporated with Russell as president. The Society's name was later changed to Watch Tower Bible and Tract Society. Many witnessed from house to house, offering biblical literature.

By 1909, the work had become international, and the Society's headquarters was moved to its present location in Brooklyn, N.Y. Printed sermons were syndicated in newspapers, and by 1913 were in four languages in 3,000 newspapers in the United States, Canada, and Europe. Books, booklets, and tracts had been distributed by the hundreds of millions.

Russell died in 1916 and was succeeded the following year by Joseph F. Rutherford. Under his direction the magazine *Golden Age* was introduced (now called *Awake!* with a circulation of 13,110,000 in 67 languages). In 1931 the name Jehovah's Witnesses, based on Isaiah 43:10-12, was adopted.

During the 1930s and 1940s Jehovah's Witnesses fought many court cases in the interest of preserving freedom of speech, press, assembly, and worship. In the United States, appeals from lower courts resulted in the Witnesses winning 43 cases before the Supreme Court. Professor C. S. Braden stated, "In their struggle they have done much to secure those rights for every minority group in America."

When Rutherford died in 1942, he was succeeded by N. H. Knorr, who immediately instituted a concerted program of training for all Jehovah's Witnesses. The Watchtower Bible School of

Gilead was established in 1943 for training missionaries. It has been primarily through the efforts of these missionaries that the word has expanded today to include 211 countries.

The Witnesses number more than 4.2 million. The present president F. W. Franz and a small group of fellow administrators serve as a governing body, overseeing the work, organized under 93 branches.

From the beginning, Jehovah's Witnesses have believed in one almighty God, Jehovah, creator of heaven and earth. They believe that Christ is God's Son, the first of God's creations and subject to Jehovah. They believe Christ's human life was paid as a ransom for obedient humans; that Jehovah has assigned him a Kingdom, a government for which all Christians pray and through which Christ will cleanse the earth of wickedness and rule it in righteousness and peace. They believe the book of Revelation assigns 144,000 individuals "who have been bought from the earth," to rule with him; that this Kingdom government will rule over the "meek who will inherit the earth" mentioned in the Sermon on the Mount; and that these people from all nations, along with the resurrected dead, will work to transform the earth into a global Edenic paradise. This is the "good news" Jehovah's Witnesses are commissioned to preach from house to house during these last days of the present system. They believe that when this has been accomplished Jesus says "the end will come" and will be followed by the righteous rule of his kingdom (Matt. 24:14).

HEADQUARTERS

25 Columbia Heights, Brooklyn, NY 11201 Tel. (718)625-3600

OFFICER

Pres., Frederick W. Franz

Jewish Organizations

Jews arrived in the colonies before 1650. The first Congregation is recorded in 1654, in New York City, the Shearith Israel (Remnant of Israel).

CONGREGATIONAL AND RABBINICAL

Fed. of Reconst. Congs. & Havurot: Pres., Roger Price, Church Road & Greenwood Ave., Wyncote, PA 19095 Tel. (215)887-1988

*Union of Am. Hebrew Congs. (Reform), Pres., Rabbi Alexander M. Schindler; Bd., Chpsn., 838 Fifth Ave., New York, NY 10021 Tel. (212)249-0100

*United Synagogue of Am. (Conservative), Pres., Alan Tichnor, 155 Fifth Ave., New York, NY 10010 Tel. (212)533-7800

*Union of Orthodox Jewish Congs. of Am., Pres., Sheldon Rudoff, 333 - 7th Ave., New York, NY 10001 Tel. (212)563-4000

*Central Conf. of Am. Rabbis (Reform), Pres., Rabbi Samuel E. Kariff, 192 Lexington Ave., New York, NY 10016 Tel. (212)684-4990

Rabbinical Alliance of Am. (Orthodox), Pres., Rabbi Abraham B. Hecht, 3 W. 16th St., 4th Fl., New York, NY 10011 Tel. (212)242-6420

*The Rabbinical Assembly (Conservative), Pres., Rabbi Irwin Groner, 3080 Broadway, New York, NY 10027 Tel. (212)678-8060

*Rabbinical Cncl. of Am. Inc. (Ortho.), Pres., Rabbi Max N. Schreier, 275 Seventh Ave., New York, NY 10001 Tel. (212)807-7888

Reconstructionist Rabbinical Assn., Pres., Rabbi Sandy Sasso, Church Rd. & Greenwood Ave., Wyncote, PA 19095 Tel. (215)576-0800

Union of Orthodox Rabbis of US & Canada, Dir., Rabbi Hersh M. Ginsberg, 235 E. Broadway, New York, NY 10002 Tel. (212)964-6337

*Synagogue Council of America, Pres., Rabbi Joel H. Zaiman, 327 Lexington Ave., New York, NY 10016 Tel. (212)686-8670

*Star indicates Synagogue Council of Am. coordinates

EDUCATIONAL AND SOCIAL SERVICE

The American Council for Judaism, Dir., Allan C. Brownfield, P.O. Box 9009, Alexandria, VA 22304 Tel. (703)836-2546

American Jewish Committee, Pres., Sholom D. Comay, 165 E. 56th St., New York, NY 10022 Tel. (212)751-4000 Fax (212)319-0975

American Jewish Congress, Pres., Robert L. Lifton, 15 E. 84th St., New York, NY 10028 Tel. (212)879-4500

American Jewish Historical Society, Pres., Phil David Fine, 2 Thornton Rd., Waltham, MA 02154 Tel. (617)891-8110 Fax (617) 899-9208

Am. Jewish Joint Distribution Comm., Pres., Sylvia Hassenfeld, 711 Third Ave., New York, NY 10017 Tel. (212)687-6200

Anti-Defamation League of B'nai B'rith, Chpsn., Burton S. Levinson, 823 United Nations Plaza, New York, NY 10017 Tel. (212)490-2525

B'nai B'rith Hillel Foundations Inc., Chpsn. B'nai B'rith Hillel Committee, David Bittker, 1640 Rhode Island Ave. NW, Washington, DC 20036 Tel. (202)857-6560

Conf. of Presidents of Major American Jewish Organizations, Chpsn., Seymour D. Reich, 515 Park Ave, New York, NY 10022 Tel. (212)752-1616

Council for Jewish Education, Pres., Reuven Yalon, 426 W. 58th St., New York, NY 10019 Tel. (212)713-0290

Council of Jewish Federations, Pres., Mandell Berman, 730 Broadway, New York, NY 10003 Tel. (212)475-5000

Hadassah: Women's Zionist Org. of America, Natl. Pres., Carmela E. Kalmanson, 50 W. 58th St., New York, NY 10019 Tel. (212)355-7900

HIAS Inc. (Hebrew Immigrant Aid Society), Pres., Ben Zion Leuchter, 200 Park Ave. S., New York, NY 10003 Tel. (212)674-6800

Jewish Publication Society, Pres., Edward E. Elson, 1930 Chestnut St., Philadelphia, PA 19103 Tel. (215)564-5925

Jewish Reconstructionist Foundation, Pres., Rabbi Elliot Skiddell, Church Rd. & Greenwood Ave., Wycote, PA 19095 Tel. (215)887-1988

JWB (National Jewish Welfare Bd.), Pres., Donald R. Mintz, 15 E 26th St., New York, NY 10010 Tel. (212)532-4949

Jewish War Veterans of the U S of A Inc., Natl. Exec. Dir., Steven Shaw, 1811 R St., Washington, DC 20009 Tel. (202)265-6280

Natl. Fed. of Temple Brotherhoods, Pres., Richard D. Karfunkle, 838 Fifth Ave., New York, NY 10021 Tel. (212)570-0707

Natl. Federation of Temple Sisterhoods, Pres., Judith Hertz, 838 Fifth Ave., New York, NY 10021 Tel. (212)249-0100

Natl. Jewish Comm. Rel. Adv. Council, Chpsn., Arden E. Shenker, 443 Park Ave. S., 11th Fl., New York, NY 10016 Tel. (212)684-6950

United Jewish Appeal, Natl. Chmn., Morton A. Kornreich, 99 Park Ave. Ste. 300, New York, NY 10016 Tel. (212)818-9100

Women's Branch, Pres., 156 Fifth Ave., New York, NY 10010 Tel. (212)929-8857

Women's League for Conservative Judaism, Pres., Evelyn Auerbach, 48 E. 74th St., New York, NY 10021 Tel. (212)628-1600

Zionist Organization of America, Pres., Sidney Silverman, 4 E. 34th St., New York, NY 10016 Tel. (212)481-1500

PERIODICALS

Jewish Action; United Synagogue Review; Journal of Reform Judaism; Reconstructionist, The; Jewish Education; Reform Judaism

Kodesh Church of Immanuel

Founded 1929 and incorporated in April 1930 by Rev. Frank Russell Killingsworth and 120 laymen, some of whom were former members of the African Methodist Episcopal Zion Church. On Jan. 22, 1934, the Christian Tabernacle Union, a body of fundamental believers with headquarters in Pittsburgh, merged with the Kodesh Church of Immanuel. The Hebrew word "Kodesh" means sanctified, holy; and Immanuel is one of the distinctive titles of the Messiah which means God with us. Therefore, the name Kodesh Church of Immanuel means Sanctified or Holy Church of Jesus Christ, i.e., a church composed of a sanctified, Spirit-filled constituency. This body is an interracial body of believers whose teachings are Wesleyan and Arminian.

HEADQUARTERS

2601 Centre Ave., Pittsburgh, PA 15219

Media Contact, Sup. Elder, Dr. Kenneth O. Barbour, 932 Logan Rd., Bethel Park, PA 15102 Tel. (412)833-1351

OFFICERS

Supervising Elder, Dr. Kenneth O. Barbour

OTHER ORGANIZATIONS

Church Extension Bd., Chmn., Mrs. Thelma P. Holmes, 2516 Graham Blvd., Pittsburgh, PA 15235

Foreign Mission Bd., Pres., Mrs. E. Lucille Lockhart, Roosevelt Arms Apts. #603, 6th Penn Ave., Pittsburgh, PA 15222

Young People's Societies, Gen. Pres., Mrs. Catherine B. Harris, 1428 Forrester Ave., Greenhill Park, Sharon Hill, PA 19079

Harty Bible School, Dr. Kenneth O. Barbour, 932 Logan Rd., Bethel Park, PA 15102

Sunday Schools, Gen. Supt., Miss Dolores Laremore, 6220 Carpenter St., Philadelphia, PA 19143

Korean Presbyterian Church in America, General Assembly of

This body came into official existence in the United States in 1976 and is currently an ethnic church, using the Korean language.

HEADQUARTERS

1251 Crenshaw Blvd., Los Angeles, CA 90019 Tel. (213)857-0361.

OFFICERS

Mod., Rev. Moo Yeoul Rah, 2207 W. Woodley Ave., Anaheim, CA 92801 Tel. (714)772-7909

Vice-Mod., Rev. Yong Ju Kim, 344 Hoffman Ave., New Milford, NJ 07646 Tel. (201)967-1497

Stated Clk., Rev. Do Seuk Kim, 523 N. Harvard Bl. #2, Los Angeles, CA 90004 Tel. (213)662-1838

Intl. Mission Commitee, Chpsn., Rev. Chung Kuk Kim, 39-29 57th St., Woodside, NY 11377

The Latvian Evangelical Lutheran Church in America

This body was organized into a denomination on Aug. 22, 1975, after having existed as the Federation of Latvian Evangelical Lutheran Churches in America since 1955. This church is a regional constituent part of the Lutheran Church of Latvia in Exile, a member of the Lutheran World Federation and the World Council of Churches.

The Latvian Evangelical Lutheran Church in America works to foster religious life, traditions and customs in its congregations in harmony with the Holy Scriptures, the Apostles', Nicean and Athanasian Creeds, the unaltered Augsburg Confession, Martin Luther's Small and Large Catechisms and other documents of the Book of Concord.

The LELCA is ordered by its Synod (General Assembly), executive board, auditing committee, and district conferences.

HEADQUARTERS

6551 West Montrose Ave., Chicago, IL 60634 Tel. (312)725-3820 Fax (312)725-3835

Media Contact, Pres., Rev. Vilis Varsbergs

OFFICERS

Pres., Dean Vilis Varsbergs

Vice-Pres., Rev. Maris Kirsons, 171 Erskin Ave. #1101, Toronto, ON M4P 1Y8 Tel. (416)486-3910

2nd Vice-Pres., Aivrs Ronis, 449 S. 40th St., Lincoln, NE 68510 Tel. (402)489-2776

Sec., Ansis Abele, 25182 Northrup Dr., Laguna Beach, CA 92653 Tel. (714)830-9712

Treas., Mr. Alfreds Trautmanis, 103 Rose St., Freeport, NY 11520 Tel. (516)623-2646

PERIODICAL

Cela Biedrs

The Liberal Catholic Church--Province of the United States of America

Founded Feb. 13, 1916 as a reorganization of the Old Catholic Church in Great Britain, the Rt. Rev. James I. Wedgwood being the first Presiding Bishop. The first ordination of a Priest in the United States was Fr. Charles Hampton, later a Bishop. The first Regionary Bishop for the American Province was the Rt. Rev. Irving S. Cooper (1919-1935).

HEADQUARTERS

1620 San Gabriel Rd., Ojai, CA 93023 Tel. (805)646-2960

Media Contact, Pres., Rt. Rev. Lawrence J. Smith, 9740 S. Avers Ave., Evergreen Park, IL 60642 Tel. (708)424-8329

OFFICERS

Pres. & Regionary Bishop, The Rt. Rev. Lawrence J. Smith

Vice-Pres., Rev. Alfred Strauss, 10606 Parrot Ave., Apt. A, Downey, CA 90241 Tel. (310)861-7569

Sec. (Provincial), Rev. Lloyd Worley, 1232 24th Avenue Ct., Greeley, CO 80631 Tel. (303)356-3002

Provost, The V. Rev. Wm. Holme, P.O. Box 7042, Rochester, MN 55903

Treas., Rev. Lloyd Worley

Chancellor, The Rt. Rev. Dr. Gerrit Munnik, 16 Krotona, Ojai, CA 93023 Tel. (805)646-2960

Regionary Bishop for the American Province, The Rt. Rev. Lawrence J. Smith

Ep. Vicar Gen. for the Americas & Regionary Emeritus, The Rt. Rev. Dr. Gerrit Munnik, 16 Krotona, Ojai, CA 93023

Aux. Bishops of the American Province: Rt. Rev. Dr. Robert S. McGinnis, Jr., 2204 Armond Blvd., Destrehan, LA 70065; Rt. Rev. Joseph L. Tisch, P.O. Box 1117, Melbourne, FL 32901; Rt. Rev. Dr. Hein VanBeusekom, 12 Krotona Hill, Ojai, CA 93023

PERIODICAL

Ubique: American Province

Liberty Baptist Fellowship

The Liberty Baptist Fellowship consists of independent Baptist churches and pastors organized for the purpose of planting indigenous local New Testament churches in North America. The Fellowship is in general accord with the doctrines and philosophy of the Independent Baptist movement.

HEADQUARTERS

Candler's Mountain Rd., Lynchburg, VA 24506 Tel. (804)582-2061

Media Contact, Exec. Dir., Dr. Elmer Towns, Tel. (804)582-2569

OFFICERS

Exec. Comm.: Chmn., Jerry Falwell; A. Pierre Guillermin; Exec. Dir., Elmer L. Towns; Exec. Sec., Kenneth Chapman

Natl. Comm.: Pres., Lamarr Mooneyham; Johnny Basham; John Cartwright; Herb Fitzpatrick; Bob Gass; Eddie Guy; Lindsay Howan; Frank Lacey; Danny Lovett; Allen McFarland; Steve Reynolds; David Rhodenhizer; Daren Ritchey; Gary Roy; George Sweet

The Lutheran Church--Missouri Synod

The Lutheran Church--Missouri Synod, which began in the state of Missouri in 1847, has more than 6,000 congregations in the United States and works in various capacities in 42 other countries. Its 2.6 million North American membership forms the second-largest Lutheran denomination.

Christian education for all ages offers an array of weekday, Sunday school and Bible-class opportunities. The 6,000-plus North American congregations operate the largest elementary and secondary school systems of any Protestant denomination in the nation, and eight colleges, two universities and two seminaries in the United States enroll 10,546 students.

Traditional beliefs concerning the authority and interpretation of Scripture are important. In the late 1960s, a controversy developed, but following a decade of soul-searching that resulted in the walk-out of most faculty members and students from one seminary and the eventual departure of slightly more than 100,000 members, little evidence of the controversy remains.

The synod is known for mass-media outreach through "The Lutheran Hour" on radio, "This Is The Life" dramas on television, and the products of Concordia Publishing House, the third-largest Protestant publisher, whose Arch Books children's series has sold more than 55 million copies.

An extensive Braille volunteer network of more than 1,000 volunteers in 40 work centers makes devotional materials for the blind; 54 of the 85 deaf congregations affiliated with U.S. denominations are LCMS; and many denominations use the Bible lessons prepared for developmentally disabled persons.

The involvement of women is high, though they do not occupy clergy positions. Serving as teachers, deaconesses, and social workers, women comprise approximately 48 percent of total professional workers.

The members' responsibility for congregational leadership is a distinctive characteristic of the synod, a word that means walking together. Practice holds that the pastor is the equipper of the saints, but a pastor might find it difficult to locate the proper slot in a modern-day organizational chart. Power is vested in voters' assemblies, generally comprised of adults of voting age. Synod decision making is given to the delegates at national and regional conventions, where the franchise is equally divided between lay and pastoral representatives.

HEADQUARTERS

The Lutheran Church--Missouri Synod, International Center, 1333 S. Kirkwood Rd., St. Louis, MO 63122

Media Contact, Dir., News & Information, Rev. David Mahsman, Tel. (314)965-9000 Fax (314)822-8307

OFFICERS

Pres., Dr. Ralph A. Bohlmann

1st Vice-Pres., Dr. August T. Mennicke

2nd Vice-Pres., Dr. Robert King

3rd Vice-Pres., Dr. Robert C. Sauer

4th Vice-Pres., Dr. Eugene Bunkowske

5th Vice-Pres., Dr. Walter A. Maier

Sec., Dr. Walter L. Rosin

Treas., Dr. Norman Sell

Admn. Officer of Bd. of Dir., Dr. John P. Schuelke

Dir. of Personnel, Mr. Gary Mittendorf

Bd. of Directors: Dr. Henry L. Koepchen, Setauket, NY; Rev. Arnold G. Kuntz, Cypress, CA; Rev. Victor H. Marxhausen, White Bear Lake, MN; Rev. Richard L. Thompson, Billings, MT; Mr. Clifford Dietrich, Ft. Wayne, IN; Mr. Donald J. Brosz, Laramie, WY; Mr. John L. Daniel, Emmaus, PA; Mr. Robert W. Hirsch, Yankton, SC; Dr. Florence Montz, Bismarck, ND; Dr. Harold M. Olsen, Springfield, IL; Mr. Lester W. Schultz, Russellville, AR; Mr. Gilbert E. LaHaine, Lansing, MI; Dr. Donald Snyder, Henrietta, NY

BOARDS AND COMMISSIONS

Bd. for Communication Services, Exec. Dir., Rev. Paul Devantier

Bd. for Evangelism Services, Exec. Dir., Rev. Lyle Muller

Bd. for Mission Services, Exec. Dir., Dr. Glenn O'Shoney

Bd. for Parish Services, Exec. Dir., Dr. H. James Boldt

Bd. for Higher Education Services, Exec. Dir., Dr. William F. Meyer

Bd. for Youth Services, Exec. Dir., Mr. LeRoy Wilke

Bd. for Social Ministry Services, Exec. Dir., Rev. Richard L. Krenzke

Bd., Worker Benefit Plans, Admn., Mr. Earl E. Haake

Lutheran Church Ext. Fund-Missouri Synod, Pres., Mr. Arthur C. Haake

Min. to the Armed Forces Standing Comm., Exec. Dir., Rev. James Shaw

Dept. of Stewardship, Acting Dir., Rev. David Schmidt

Concordia Publishing House, Pres./CEO, John Gerber, 3558 S. Jefferson Ave., St. Louis, MO 63118

Concordia Historical Institute, Dir., Dr. August R. Suelflow, Concordia Seminary, 801 De Mun Ave., St. Louis, MO 63105

Intl. Lutheran Laymen's League, Exec. Dir., Mr. Laurence E. Lumpe, 2185 Hampton Ave., St. Louis, MO 63110

KFUO Radio, Exec. Dir., Rev. Paul Devantier, 85 Founders Ln., St. Louis, MO 73105

Intl. Lutheran Women's Missionary League, Pres., Mrs. Ida Mall, 3558 S. Jefferson Ave., St. Louis, MO 63118

PERIODICALS

Lutheran Witness, The; Reporter

Lutheran Churches, The American Association of

This church body was constituted on Nov. 7, 1987. The AALC was formed by laity and pastors of the former American Lutheran Church in America who held to a high view of Scripture (inerrancy and infallibility). This church body also emphasizes the primacy of evangelism and world missions and the authority and autonomy of the local congregation.

Congregations of the AALC are distributed throughout the continental United States from Long Island, N.Y., to Los Angeles. The primary decision-making body is the General Convention to which each congregation has proportionate representation.

HEADQUARTERS

The AALC National Office, 10800 Lyndale Ave. S., Ste. 124, Minneapolis, MN 55420

Mailing Address, P.O. Box 17097, Minneapolis, MN 55417

The AALC Regional Office, 214 South St., Waterloo, IA 50701

OFFICERS

Presiding Pastor, Dr. Daune R. Lindberg, P.O. Box 416, Waterloo, IA 50701 Tel. (319)232-3971

Asst. Presiding Pastor, Rev. Donald C. Thorson, P.O. Box 775, Chippewa Falls, WI 54729

Sec., Rev. Thomas V. Aadland, 2415 Ensign St., Duluth, MN 55811 Tel. (218)722-7931

Treas., Rev. James E. Minor, 341 S. Hamline Ave., St. Paul, MN 55105

Admn. Coord., Mr. Gene Quist, 11 Norman Ridge Dr., Bloomington, MN 55437

PERIODICAL

Evangel, The

Mennonite Brethren Churches, The United States Conference of

A small group, which had been requesting that closer attention be paid to prayer and Bible study, withdrew in 1860 from the Mennonite Church in the Ukraine. Pietistic in organization, the group adopted a Baptistic policy. In 1874, small bodies of German-speaking Mennonites left Russia, reached Kansas in 1876, then spread to the Pacific Coast and into Canada. In 1960, the Krimmer Mennonite Brethren Conference merged with this body. Today the General Conference of Mennonite Brethren Churches conducts services in many European languages as well as in Vietnamese, Mandarin, and Hindi. It works with other denominations in missionary and development projects in 25 countries outside North America.

OFFICERS

Mod., Edmund Janzen, 4935 E. Heaton, Fresno, CA 93727

Asst. Mod., Harry Heidebrecht, 2285 Clearbrook Rd., Clearbrook, BC V2T 2X4

Sec., Roland Reimer, 1631 N. Callahan, Wichita, KS 67212

Exec. Sec., Marvin Hein, 4812 E. Butler, Fresno, CA 93727

PERIODICALS

Mennonite Brethren Herald

Mennonite Church

The Mennonite Church in North America traces its beginnings back to 16th century Europe and the Protestant Reformation. Conrad Grebel, Georg Blaurock, and a small band of radical believers who felt that reformers Martin Luther and Ulrich Zwingli had not gone far enough in their break with Roman Catholic tradition and a return to New Testament discipleship Christianity, baptized one another in Zurich, Switzerland, on Jan. 21, 1525. First nicknamed Anabaptists (Rebaptizers) by their opponents (they themselves preferred to use the term Brothers and Sisters in Christ), the Mennonites later took their name from the Dutch priest Menno Simons who joined the movement in 1536, and emerged as their leader.

The Mennonites' refusal to conform to magisterial decrees including bearing of arms and the swearing of oaths, attracted fierce animosity. Thousands were martyred for their beliefs in nearly a century of persecution. Eager to find freedom to live out their faith elsewhere, they moved to many places, including the United States and Canada where some arrived as early as 1683. Between four and five thousand Mennonites settled in southeastern Pennsylvania between 1717 and 1756 in the first major migration from Europe. Caught between the warring factions of America's struggle for independence, many moved west to Ohio, Indiana, Iowa, and especially north to upper Canada (now Ontario).

North American Mennonites began their first home mission program in Chicago, Ill., in 1893 and their first overseas mission program in India in 1899. Since the 1920s the church has established extensive emergency relief and development services in conjunction with its mission program.

Mennonites hold that the Word of God is central and that new life in Christ is available to all who believe. Adult "Believer's" baptism is practiced, symbolizing a conscious decision to follow Christ. Mennonites take seriously Christ's command to witness in word and deed. Concerned for both physical and spiritual aspects of life, they regard faith and works as two sides of the same coin. They stress that Christians need the support of a faith community for encouragement and growth. In times of crisis their "mutual aid" network makes time, money, and goods available to those in need. They view Jesus' teachings as directly applicable to their lives. Following the Prince of Peace, Mennonites generally refuse to serve in the military or to use violent resistance.

Currently the largest body of Mennonites in

North America, the denomination has approximately 93,000 members in 42 states and the District of Columbia, and 9,500 members in six Canadian provinces (1991 statistics). The Mennonite Church is a member of the Mennonite and Brethren in Christ World Conference--a fellowship of 171 bodies in 60 countries around the world with a membership of 850,000. The denomination is also a member of Mennonite Central Committee with offices in Akron, Pa., and Winnipeg, Man., a world-wide relief and service agency representing 12 North American churches and bodies. While the denomination does not hold membership in any major ecumenical organizations in the United States and Canada, individuals and program agencies do participate in a variety of ecumenical activities at various levels of church life.

HEADQUARTERS

421 S. Second St., Ste. 600, Elkhart, IN 46516 Tel. (219)294-7131
Media Contact, Churchwide Communications Dir., John Bender, Fax (219)294-8669

OFFICER

Mod., David W. Mann

OTHER ORGANIZATIONS

Gen. Bd., Gen. Sec., James M. Lapp
Historical Cmte., Dir., Levi Miller, 1700 S. Main, Goshen, IN 46526 Tel. (219)535-7477
Council on Faith, Life & Strategy, Staff, Miriam Book
Bd. of Congregational Min., Exec. Sec., Everett Thomas, Box 1245, Elkhart, IN 46515 Tel. (219)294-7523
Bd. of Educ., Exec. Sec., Albert Meyer, Box 1142, Elkhart, IN 46515 Tel. (219)294-7523
Bd. of Missions, Pres., Paul M. Gingrich, Box 370, Elkhart, IN 46515 Tel. (219)294-7523
Mutual Aid Bd., Pres., Howard Brenneman, 1110 North Main, P.O. Box 483, Goshen, IN 46526 Tel. (219)533-9511
Mennonite Publication Bd., Publisher, J. Robert Ramer, 616 Walnut Ave., Scottdale, PA 15683 Tel. (412)887-8500

PERIODICALS

Gospel Herald; Christian Living; Builder; Rejoice!; Mennonite Historical Bulletin; Mennonite Yearbook; Mennonite Quarterly Review; With; Purpose; On the Line; Sharing; Story Friends; Voice

Mennonite Church, The General Conference

The General Conference Mennonite Church was formed in 1860, uniting Mennonites throughout the U.S. who were interested in doing missionary work together. Today 65,000 Christians in 368 congregations try to follow the way of Jesus in their daily lives.

The conference consists of people of many ethnic backgrounds--Swiss and German, Russian and Dutch, Black, Hispanic, Chinese, Vietnamese, Laotian. Some native Americans in both Canada and the U.S. also relate to the conference.

The basic belief and practice of the conference come from the life and teachings of Jesus Christ, the early church of the New Testament, and the Anabaptists of the 16th-century Reformation. Thus the conference seeks to be evangelical, guided by the Bible, led by the Holy Spirit, and supported by a praying, discerning community of believers in congregations and fellowships. Peace, or shalom, is at the very heart of members, who seek to be peacemakers in everyday life.

The goals of the conference for the next three to six years are to evangelize, teach and practice biblical principles, train and develop leaders, and work for Christian unity.

HEADQUARTERS

722 Main, Newton, KS 67114 Tel. (316)283-5100 Fax (316)283-0454

OFFICERS

Mod., Florence Driedger, 3833 Montague St., Regina, SK S4S 3J6
Asst. Mod., Ronald Krehbiel, RR 2, Box 161, Freeman, SD 57029
Sec., Myron Schultz, Bloomfield, MT 59315
Gen. Sec., Vern Preheim

OTHER ORGANIZATIONS

Commission on Home Ministries, Exec., Hubert Brown
Commission on Overseas Mission, Exec. Sec., Erwin Rempel
Women in Mission, Coord., Susan Jantzen
Commission on Education, Exec. Sec., Norma Johnson
Div. of General Services: Bus. Mgr., Ted Stuckey; Stewardship Dir., Ray Frey; Planned Giving Dir., Gary Franz; Communications Dir., David Linscheid
Mennonite Men, Coord., Heinz Janzen
Faith & Life Press, Mgr., Dietrich Rempel
Committee on Ministry, Dir. of Ministerial Leadership, John A. Esau

PERIODICAL

Mennonite, The; Window to Mission; Being In Touch

The Metropolitan Church Association, Inc.

Organized after a revival movement in Chicago in 1894 as the Metropolitan Holiness Church. In 1899 it as chartered as the Metropolitan Church Association. It has Wesleyan theology.

HEADQUARTERS

323 Broad St., Lake Geneva, WI 53147 Tel. (414)248-6786

OFFICERS

Pres., Rev. Warren W. Bitzer
Vice-Pres. & Sec., Elbert L. Ison
Treas., Gertrude J. Puckhaber

PERIODICAL

Burning Bush, The

Metropolitan Community Churches, Universal Fellowship

Founded Oct. 6, 1968 by the Rev. Troy D. Perry in Los Angeles, California, with a particular but not exclusive outreach to the gay community. Since that time, the Fellowship has grown to include congregations throughout the world.

The group is trinitarian and accepts the Bible as the divinely inspired Word of God. The Fellowship has two sacraments, baptism and holy communion, as well as a number of traditionally recognized rites such as ordination.

"This Fellowship acknowledges the Holy Scriptures interpreted by the Holy Spirit in conscience and faith, as its guide in faith, discipline, and government. The government of this Fellowship is vested in its General Council (consisting of Elders and District Coordinators), Clergy and church delegates, who exert the right of control in all of its affairs, subject to the provisions of its Articles of Incorporation and By-Laws."

HEADQUARTERS

5300 Santa Monica Blvd. #304, Los Angeles, CA 90029 Tel. (213)464-5100 Fax (213)464-2123
Media Contact, Asst. to the Mod., Frank Zerilli

OFFICERS

Mod., Rev. Elder Troy D. Perry
Vice-Mod., Rev. Elder Freda Smith, P.O. Box 20125, Sacramento, CA 95820
Treas., Rev. Elder Donald Eastman
Clk., Elder Larry Rodriguez
Rev. Elder Nancy L. Wilson
Rev. Elder Willem Hein, P.O. Box 392, Elsternwick, VIC 3185, Australia
Rev. Elder Jean A. White, 2A Sistova Rd., Balham, London SW12 9QT England
Dir. of Admn., Mr. Ravi Verma

DISTRICT COORDINATORS

Australian District, Rev. Greg Smith, 109 Maiala Rd., Cooks Gap, Mudgee, NSW 2850, Australia
Eastern Canadian District, Ms. Lydia Segal, 50 Cosburn Ave. #802, Toronto, ON M4K 2G5
European North Sea District, Rev. Hong Tan, 72 Fleet Rd., Hampstead, London NW3 2QT England
Great Lakes District, Judy Dale, 1300 Ambridge Dr., Louisville, KY 40207 Tel. (502)897-3821
Gulf Lower Atlantic District, Mr. Jay Neely, P.O. Box 8356, Atlanta, GA 30306
Mid-Central District, Rev. Bonnie Daniel, 1364 Collins Ave., Topeka, KS 66604
Mid-Atlantic District, R. Adam DeBaugh, P.O. Box 7864, Gaithersburg, MD 20898
Northeast District, Rev. Jeff Pulling, P.O. Box 340529, Hartford, CT 06134
Northwest District, Rev. Edward Sherriff, P.O. Box 5795, Sacramentao, CA 95817
South Central District, Clarke Friesen, P.O. Box 262822, Houston, TX 77207
Southeast District, Rev. Thomas Bigelow, 625 Jefferson Ave. N., Sarasota, FL 34237
Southwest District, Rev. Don Pederson, 10913 Fruitland Dr., #117, Studio City, CA 91604
Western Canadian District, Rev. Bev Baptiste, 3531-33rd Ave., Edmonton, AB T6L 4N6

OTHER COMMISSIONS & COMMITTEES

Excel International, Exec. Dir., Brenda Blizzard, P.O. Box 20054, Ferndale, MI 48220
World Church Extension, Exec. Sec., Rev. Elder Jean White, 2A Sistova Rd., Balham, London SW12 9QT England
Faith Fellowship & Order, Chpsn., Rev. Steven Torrence, 1215 Petronia St., Key West, FL 33040
Dept. of People of Color, Dir., Rev. LaPaula Turner, c/o UFMCC
Commission on the Laity, Chpsn., JoNee Shelton, 917 Elysian Fields, New Orleans, LA 70117
Clergy Credentials & Concerns, Chpsn., Rev. Candace Shultis, 415 M St. N.W., Washington, DC 20001
Bd. of Pensions: Pres., Rev. Arthur R. Green, 13655 NE 10th Ave., Unit 112, N. Miami, FL 33161; Admn., Lois Luneburg, P.O. Box 107, Arnold, CA 95223

Ecumenical Witness & Ministry: Chief Officer, Rev. Elder Nancy Wilson, 5879 Washington Blvd., Culver City, CA 90232; Dir., Rev. Sandi Robinson, c/o UFMCC, Los Angeles, CA 90034
UFMCC AIDS Ministry: Exec Dir., Rev. Elder Don Eastman, c/o UFMCC; Field Dir., Rev. Steve Pieters, c/o UFMCC

PERIODICALS

Keeping in Touch; Alert

The Missionary Church

The Missionary Church was formed in 1969 through a merger of the United Missionary Church (organized in 1883) and the Missionary Church Association (founded in 1898). It is evangelical and conservative with a strong emphasis on missionary work and church planting.

There are three levels of church government with local, district, and general conferences. There are ten church districts in the United States. The general conference meets every two years. The denomination operates one college in the United States.

HEADQUARTERS

3901 S. Wayne Ave., Ft. Wayne, IN 46807 Tel. (219)456-4502 Fax (219)456-4903
Publishing Headquarters, Bethel Publishing Co., 1819 S. Main St., Elkhart, IN 46516 Tel. (219)293-8585
Media Contact, Pres., Dr. John P. Moran

OFFICERS

Pres., Dr. John Moran
Vice-Pres., Rev. William Hossler
Sec., Rev. Dave Engbrecht
Treas., Mr. Edwin W. Crewson
Asst. to the Pres., Rev. Bob Ransom
Overseas Ministries (World Partners): Dir., Rev. Charles Carpenter; Assoc. Dir., Rev. Paul Fretz; Dir. of Mission Ministries, Rev. David Mann
Services Dir., Mr. David von Gunten
Bethel Publishing Co., Exec. Dir., Mr. Richard Oltz
Stewardship, Dir., Rev. Ken Stucky
Youth Dir., Mr. Eric Liechty
Children's Dir., Dr. Neil McFarlane
Adult Dir., Dr. Duane Beals
Missionary Men Intl., Pres., Mr. Carl White
Missionary Women Intl., Pres., Mrs. Opal Speicher
Investment Foundation, Mr. Bob Henschen

PERIODICALS

Emphasis on Faith and Living; Ministry Today; World Partners; Priority

Moravian Church in America (Unitas Fratrum)

In 1735 German Moravian missionaries of the pre-Reformation faith of Jan Hus came to Georgia, in 1740 to Pennsylvania, and in 1753 to North Carolina. They established the American Moravian Church, which is broadly evangelical, ecumenical, liturgical, with an episcopacy as a spiritual office and in form of government "conferential."

HEADQUARTERS

See Provincial addresses
Media Contact, Editor, THE MORAVIAN, The Rev. Hermann I. Weinlick, P.O. Box 1245, Bethlehem, PA 18016-1245 Tel. (215)867-7566 Fax (215)866-9223

92

NORTHERN PROVINCE

1021 Center St., P.O. Box 1245, Bethlehem, PA 18016-1245 Tel. (215)867-7566 Fax (215)866-9223

OFFICERS

Provincial Elders' Conference: Pres., Dr. Gordon L. Sommers; Vice-Pres./Sec. (Eastern Dist.), -----; Vice-Pres. (Western Dist.), Rev. R. Burke Johnson, P.O. Box 386, Sun Prairie, WI 53590; Treas., John F. Ziegler, 1021 Center St., P.O. Box 1245, Bethlehem, PA 18016

SOUTHERN PROVINCE

459 S. Church St., Winston-Salem, NC 27108 Tel. (919)725-5811

OFFICERS

Provincial Elders' Conference: Pres., Rev. Graham H. Rights; Vice-Pres., Mrs. Becky K. Cook; Sec., Rev. Carl S. Southerland; Treas., Ronald R. Hendrix, Drawer O, Salem Station, Winston-Salem, NC 27108

ALASKA PROVINCE

P.O. Box 545, Bethel, AK 99559

OFFICERS

Pres., The Rev. John P. Andrew
Vice-Pres., The Rev. David Paul
Sec., Ferdinand Sharp
Treas., Rebecca J. Nelson
Dir. of Theological Education, Rev. Dr. Kurt H. Vitt

PERIODICALS

Moravian, The

Muslims

Islam now claims approximately 6 million adherents in the United States. Some of them are immigrants, who represent almost every part of the world, or children of such immigrants. Others are Americans who converted to Islam or children of such converts. These are apart from those who come to America temporarily, such as Muslim diplomats, students, and those who work in international institutions such as the World Bank, the International Monetary Fund, and the United Nations.

Muslims are found in nearly every American town, and are engaged in all professions, including teaching, medicine, accounting, engineering, and business. Their number increases in large industrial and commercial cities in the East and Midwest, but there are also large numbers of Muslims in some areas on the West Coast, such as Los Angeles and San Francisco.

Many Islamic organizations exist in the United States, under such titles as Islamic Society, Islamic Center, or Muslim Mosque. The aim is to provide a group in a locality with a place of worship and of meeting for other religious, social, and educational purposes. These societies and organizations are not regarded as religious sects or divisions. Their multiplication arises from the needs of each group in a given area, long distances separating the groups, and the absence in Islam of organized hierarchy, a factor which gives liberty to ambitious personalities to start their own group. All the groups hold the same beliefs, aspire to practice the same rituals: namely, prayers, fasting, almsgiving, and pilgrimage to Makkah. The only difference that may exist between black organizations and other Muslim institutions is that the former may mix civil rights aspirations with Islamic objectives and may, therefore, follow a rigid discipline for their members.

The main Islamic organizations are the Islamic centers which are found in all 300 large cities. Their objectives are cultural, religious, and educational; and each one has a mosque or a prayer hall.

The regional and national groups listed below were started with the objective of helping local groups coordinate their work, and promote closer unity among them. Prominent among these is: The Islamic Center of Washington, 2551 Massachusetts Ave. NW, Washington, DC 20008. Tel. (202)332-8343.

REGIONAL AND NATIONAL GROUPS

American Muslim Council, Exec. Dir., Abdurahman Alamoudi, 1212 New York Ave., NW, Ste. 525, Washington, DC 20005 Tel. (202)789-2262 Fax (202)789-2550
Council of Masajid (Mosques) in the USA, Pres., Dawud Assad, 99 Woodview Dr., Old Bridge, NJ 08857 Tel. (908)679-8617 Fax (908)679-1216
Fed. of Islamic Assoc. in US & Canada, Sec. Gen., Nihad Hamid, 25351 Five Mile Rd., Redford Township, MI 48239 Tel. (313)535-0014
Islamic Society of North America, Pres., Dr. Syed Imtiaz Ahmad, P.O. Box 38, Plainfield, IN 46168 Tel. (317)839-8157
Council of Muslim Communities of Canada, Dir., Dr. Mir Iqbal Ali, 1250 Ramsey View Ct., Ste. 504, Sudbury, ON P3E 2E7 Tel. (705)522-2948
Muslim World League: Dir., Dr. Gutbi M. Ahmed, 1655 N. Fort Myer Dr., Ste. 700, Arlington, VA 22209 Tel. (703)351-5296 Fax (703)351-5241; Assoc. Dir., Dawad Assad

PERIODICAL

Majallat Al-Masjid

National Baptist Convention of America

The National Baptist Convention of America, Incorporated, was organized in 1880 following a dispute over control of the publishing board in which another Convention was organized. Membership of the churches is largely African-American.

MEDIA CONTACT

Media Contact, Liaison Officer, Dr. Richard A. Rollins, 777 S. R.L. Thornton Fwy., Ste. 205, Dallas, TX 75203 Tel. (214)946-8913 Fax (214)946-9619

OFFICERS

Pres., Dr. E. Edward Jones, 1540 Pierre Ave., Shreveport, LA 71103 Tel. (318)221-3701 Fax (318)222-7512
1st Vice-Pres., Dr. Albert E. Chew, 2823 N. Houston St., Ft. Worth, TX 76106
2nd Vice-Pres., Dr. Wallace Hartsfield, 3100 E. 31 St., Ft. Worth, TX 76106
3rd Vice-Pres., Rev. Stephen J. Thurston, 740 E. 77 St., Chicago, IL 60619
Gen. Recording Sec., Dr. Clarence C. Pennywell, 2016 Russell Rd., Shreveport, LA 71107
1st Asst. Sec., Dr. Louis W. Smith, 1455 Granada St., New Orleans, LA 70122
2nd Asst. Sec., Rev. T. E. Gainous, 2020 W. Gore St., Orlando, FL 32805
3rd Asst. Sec., Dr. W. A. Johnson, 225 Wood St., Georgetown, SC 29440
4th Asst. Sec., Dr. L. Z. Blankenship, Rt. 3, Box 280, Foxworth, MS 39483

Corresponding Sec., Dr. E. E. Stafford, 6614 South Western Ave., Los Angeles, CA 90047

Treas., Rev. Floyd N. Williams, 5902 Beall St., Houston, TX 77091

Hist., Dr. Marvin C. Griffin, 1010 E. Tenth St., Austin, TX 78702 Tel. (512)478-1875 Fax (512)478-1892

Statistician, Rev. Clyde Kelly, P.O. Box 6354, N. Little Rock, AR 72116

Auditor, Rev. J. Carlton Allen, 1639 Hays St., San Antonio, TX 78202 Tel. (512)225-7907

Liaison Officer, Dr. Richard A. Rollins, 777 So. R.L. Thornton Frwy., Ste. 205, Dallas, TX 75203 Tel. (214)946-8913 Fax (214)946-9619

Public Relations Dir., Rev. Joe R. Gant, 5823 Ledbetter St., Shreveport, LA 77108

Dir. of Music, Mrs. Jessie M. Berry, 3530 Fillmore St., Houston, TX 77729

Youth Dir., Dr. Benjamin J. Maxon, Jr., 2926 Jackson Ave., New Orleans, LA 70126

Social Justice Commission, Rev. Mac Charles Jones, 1414 Truman Rd., Kansas City, MO 64106

Commission on Orthodoxy, Rev. F. D. Sampson, 4812 Bennington, Houston, TX 77016

Commission on Chaplaincy, Rev. J. William Dailey, P.O. Box 37324, San Antonio, TX 78237

Lantern Editor, Rev. L. A. Williams, P.O. Box 200763, San Antonio, TX 78220

BOARDS AND AUXILIARIES

Education Bd.: Chpsn., Dr. J. B. Adams, 609 S.W. Ninth St., Belle Glade, FL 33480; Sec., Rev. William Brent, 3639 Mt. Vernon Dr., Los Angeles, CA 90008

Christian Education Bd.: Chpsn., Rev. Gusta Booker, 7701 Jutland, Houston, TX 77033; Sec., Rev. Timothy Winters, 6126 Benson Ave., San Diego, CA 92114; Rev. George Brooks, 600 28th Ave., N., Nashville, TN 37209

Evangelical Bd.: Chpsn., Rev. Earl A. Pleasant, 601 E. 99 St., Inglewood, CA 90301; Sec., Rev. Hayward Wiggins, 1621 Pleasantville Dr., Houston, TX 77087

Foreign Mission Bd.: Chpsn., Rev. Asa W. Sampson, 149 Winkler, Houston, TX 77087; Sec., Rev. Isadore Edwards, P.O. Drawer 223665, Dallas, TX 75222

Home Mission Bd.: Chpsn., Rev. Luke W. Mingo, 3993 S. King Dr., Chicago, IL 60653; Sec., Rev. J. D. Williams, 715 W. 26 St., Marion, IN 46953

Benevolent Bd.: Chpsn., Dr. C. B. T. Smith, 1101 E. Sabine St., Dallas, TX 75203; Sec., Rev. N. S. Sanders, 1131 N. Webster Ave., Lakeland, FL 33805

Publishing Bd.: Chpsn., Rev. H. T. Rhim, 485 W. First St., Jacksonville, FL 32202; Dr. Frank Pinkard, 408 W. MacArthur Blvd., Oakland, CA 94609

Congress of Christian Workers: Pres., Dr. Robert H. Wilson, 2811 W. Camp Wisdom Rd., Dallas, TX 75237

Senior Women's Auxiliary: Pres., Mrs. Evelyn Reed, 4233 College Ave., Kansas City, MO 64130

Junior Women's Auxiliary: Pres., Ms. Deborah Johnson, 2750 W. Jackson, Chicago, IL 60612

Matrons: Pres., Mrs. Susan Turner, P.O. Box 325, Biloxi, MI 38533

Nurses: Pres., Mrs. Della H. Bryson, 3040 Kings La., Nashville, TN 37216

Ushers: Pres., Mrs. Frankie A. Carter, 3013 E. 14th St., Austin, TX 78702

Brotherhood: Pres., Mr. Cornelius Lee, 2715 Park Row, Dallas, TX 75215

Men of Christian Action—Young Men: Pres., Mr. Al Curtis Green, 2310 S. Pace St., Marion, IN 76953

Youth Convention: Pres., Mr. Darwan Lazard, 2926 Jackson Ave., New Orleans, LA 70125

National Baptist Convention, U.S.A., Inc.

The older and parent convention of black Baptists. This body is to be distinguished from the National Baptist Convention of America.

HEADQUARTERS

1620 Whites Creek Pike, Nashville, TN 37207 Tel. (615)228-6292 Fax (615)226-5935

OFFICERS

Pres., Dr. T. J. Jemison, 356 East Blvd., Baton Rouge, LA 70802 Tel. (504) 383-5401

Gen. Sec., Dr. W. Franklyn Richardson, 52 South 6th Ave., Mt. Vernon, NY 10550 Tel. (914) 664-2676

Vice-Pres.-at-large, Dr. C. A. W. Clark, 3110 Bonnie View Rd., Dallas, TX 75216 Tel. (214)375-6982

Treas., Dr. Isaac Green, 3068 Iowa St., Pittsburgh, PA 15219 Tel. (412)556-1437

Vice-Pres.: Dr. David Matthews, P.O. Box 627, Indianola, MS; Dr. P. J. James, 1104 E. Cherry St., Blytheville, AZ 72315; Dr. Henry L. Lyons; Dr. E. Victor Hill; Dr. Allen Stanley

Asst. Sec.: Dr. B. J. Whipper, Sr., 15 Ninth St., Charleston, SC 29403; Rev. Otis B. Smith, P.O. Box 544, Tuscaloosa, AL 35404; Dr. Roger P. Derricotte, 539 Roseville Ave., Newark, NJ 07107; Dr. McKinley Dukes, 4223 S. Benton, Kansas City, MO 64130

Stat., Rev. H. L. Harvey, Jr., 3212 Reading Rd., Cincinnati, OH 45229

Hist., Dr. Clarence Wagner, 500 Myrtle St., Gainesville, GA 30501 Tel. (404)536-8474

OFFICERS OF BOARDS

Foreign Mission Bd., Sec., Dr. William J. Harvey, 701 S. 19th St. Philadelphia, PA 19146

Home Mission Bd., Exec. Sec., Dr. Jerry Moore, 1612 Buchanan St. N.W., Washington, DC 20011

Sunday School Publishing Bd., Exec. Dir., Mrs. C. N. Adkins, 330 Charlotte Ave., Nashville, TN 37201

Education Bd., Chpsn., Dr. J. Parrish Wilson, 114 S. 22nd St., Saginaw, MI 48601

Evangelism Bd., Dr. Manuel Scott, 2600 S. Marsalis Ave., Dallas, TX 75216

Laymen's Movement, Pres., Mr. Walter Cade, 537 N. 82nd St., Kansas City, KS 66112

Woman's Auxiliary Convention, Pres., Mrs. Mary O. Ross, 584 Arden Pk., Detroit, MI 48202

Congress of Christian Education, Dr. A. Lincoln James, Sr., 5302 S. Michigan Ave., Chicago, IL 60615 Tel. (312)723-3488

PERIODICALS

National Baptist Voice

National Primitive Baptist Convention, Inc.

Throughout the years of slavery and the Civil War, the Negro population of the South worshipped with the white population in their various churches. At the time of emancipation, their white brethren helped them to establish their own churches, granting them letters of fellowship, ordaining their deacons and ministers, and helping them in other ways.

The doctrine and polity of this body are quite similar to that of white Primitive Baptists, except that they are "opposed to all forms of church organization"; yet there are local associations and a national convention, organized in 1907.

Each church is independent and receives and controls its own membership. This body was formerly known as Colored Primitive Baptists.

HEADQUARTERS
P.O. Box 2355, Tallahassee, FL

OFFICERS
Natl. Convention, Pres., Elder F. L. Livingston, 1334 Carson St., Dallas, TX 75216 Tel. (214) 949-4650

Natl. Convention, Sec. Bd. of Dirs., Elder M. G. Miles, 1525 S. Bronough St., Tallahassee, FL 32301

Natl. Church School Training Union, Pres., Elder W.D. Judge, 1718 West Grand Ave., Orlando, FL 32805

Natl. Ushers Congress, Pres. & Sec., Bro. Carl Batts, 21213 Garden View Dr., Maples Heights, OH 44137

Publishing Bd., Chpsn., Elder T. W. Samuels, 6433 Hidden Forest Dr., Charlotte, NC 28206

Women's Congress, Pres., Mrs. Lillian J. Brantley, 1795 N.W. 58th St., Miami, FL 33142

Natl. Laymen's Council, Pres., George W. Brown, 405 E. 26th St., Patterson, NJ 07514

Natl. Youth Congress, Pres., Levy Freeman, 3920 Gardenside Dr. NW, Huntsville, AL 35810

National Spiritualist Association of Churches

This organization is made up of believers that Spiritualism is a science, philosophy, and religion based upon the demonstrated facts of communication between this world and the next.

MEDIA CONTACT
Media Contact, Sec., Rev. Sharon L. Snowman, 13 Cottage Row, Lily Dale, NY 14752 Tel. (716)595-2000 Fax (716)595-2020

OFFICERS
Pres., Rev. Joseph H. Merrill, 13 Cleveland Ave., Lily Dale, NY 14752

Vice-Pres., Rev. Evelyn Muse, 1104 Susan Dr., Edinburg, TX 78539

Sec., Rev. Sharon L. Lynch, P.O. Box 217, Lily Dale, NY 14752 Tel. (716)595-2000 Fax (716)595-2020

Treas., Rev. Alfred A. Conner, 293 Jersey St., San Francisco, CA 94114

OTHER ORGANIZATIONS
Bureau of Educ., Supt., Rev. Joseph Sax, Morris Pratt Institute, 11811 Watertown Plank Rd., Milwaukee, WI 53226

Bureau of Public Relations, Rev. Brenda Wittich, 3903 Connecticut St., St. Louis, MO 63116

The Stow Memorial Foundation, Sec., Rev. Sharon L. Lynch, P.O. Box 217, Lily Dale, NY 14752 Tel. (716)595-2000 Fax (716)595-2020

Spiritualist Benevolent Society, Inc., P.O. Box 128, Cassadaga, FL 32706

PERIODICAL
National Spiritualist Summit, The

Netherlands Reformed Congregations

The Netherlands Reformed Congregations organized denominationally in 1907. In the Netherlands, the so-called Churches Under the Cross (established in 1839, after breaking away from the 1834 Secession congregations) and the so-called Ledeboerian churches (established in 1841 under the leadership of the Rev. Ledeboer, who seceded from the Reformed State Church), united in 1907 under the leadership of the then 25-year-old Rev. G. H. Kersten, to form the Netherlands Reformed Congregations. Many of the North American congregations left the Christian Reformed Church to join the Netherlands Reformed Congregations after the Kuyperian presupposed regeneration doctrine began making inroads into that denomination.

All Netherlands Reformed Congregations, office-bearers, and members subscribe to three Reformed Forms of Unity: The Belgic Confession of Faith (by DeBres), the Heidelberg Catechism (by Ursinus and Olevianus), and the Canons of Dort. Both the Belgic Confession and the Canons of Dort are read regularly at worship services, and the Heidelberg Catechism is preached weekly, except on church feast days.

MEDIA CONTACT
Media Contact, Synodical Clk., Dr. Joel R. Beeke, 2115 Romence Ave., N.E., Grand Rapids, MI 49503 Tel. (616)459-6565 Fax (616)459-7709

OFFICERS
Clk. of Synod, Dr. Joel R. Beeke, 2115 Romence Ave. N.E., Grand Rapids, MI 49503

OTHER ORGANIZATION
Netherlands Reformed Book and Publishing, 1020 N. Main Ave., Sioux Center, IA 51250

PERIODICALS
Banner of Truth, The; Paul; Insight Into

New Apostolic Church of North America

This body is a variant of the Catholic Apostolic Church, which movement began in England in 1830. The New Apostolic Church distinguished itself from the parent body in 1863 by recognizing a succession of Apostles.

HEADQUARTERS
3753 N. Troy St., Chicago, IL 60618

Media Contact, Sec. & Treas., Ellen E. Eckhardt, Tel. (312)539-3652 Fax (312)478-6691

OFFICERS
Pres., Rev. Michael Kraus, 267 Lincoln Rd., Waterloo, ON

First Vice-Pres., Rev. John W. Fendt, 36 Colony La., Manhasset, NY 11030

Second Vice-Pres., Rev. Erwin Wagner, 330 Arlene Pl., Waterloo, ON

Treas. & Asst. Sec., Ellen E. Eckhardt, 6380 N. Indian Rd., Chicago, IL 60646

Asst. Sec., Rev. William K. Schmeerbauch, 5516 Pine Wood Forest, St. Louis, MO 63128

PERIODICAL
Our Family

North American Baptist Conference

The North American Baptist Conference had its

beginning through immigrants from Germany in the middle of the 19th Century. The first church was organized by the Rev. Konrad Fleischmann in Philadelphia, in 1843. Actual organization of the North American Baptist Conference took place in 1865 when delegates of the churches met in Wilmot, Ont. Today only a few churches still use the German language, mostly in a bilingual setting.

The Conference meets in general session once every three years for fellowship, inspiration and to conduct the business of the Conference through elected delegates from the local churches. The General Council, composed of representatives of the various Associations and Conference organizations and departments, meets annually to determine the annual budget and programs for the Conference and its departments and agencies. The General Council also makes recommendations to the Triennial Conference on policies, long-range plans and election of certain personnel, boards and committees. Conference departments and agencies make their recommendations for program and finances to the General Council.

Approximately 80 missionaries serve in Cameroon, Nigeria, West Africa, Japan, Brazil, Eastern Europe, Mexico and the Philippines, as well as among various ethnic groups throughout the United States and Canada. They are supported through the Conference Established and Expansion Ministries Budget.

Nine homes for the aged are affiliated with the Conference and 10 camps are operated on the association level.

HEADQUARTERS

1 S. 210 Summit Ave., Oakbrook Terrace, IL 60181 Tel. (708)495-2000 Fax (708)495-3301
Media Contact, Development Dir., Rev. Lewis Petrie

OFFICERS

Mod., Mr. Richard Russell
Vice-Mod., Rev. Ron Norman
Exec. Dir., Dr. John Binder
Treas., Mr. Jackie Loewer

OTHER ORGANIZATIONS

Missions Dept., Dir., Rev. Herman Effa
Church Growth Min. Dept., Acting Dir., Dr. Ronald Mayforth
Management Services Dept., Dir., Mr. Ron Salzman
Development Dept., Dir., Rev. Lewis Petrie
Area Ministries, Dir., Dr. Ronald Mayforth
Church Extension Investors Fund, Dir., Mr. Robert Mayforth

PERIODICAL

Baptist Herald, The

North American Old Roman Catholic Church

The North American Old Roman Catholic Church can be traced back to the early 1700s to the Ultrajectine Tradition when the Church in Holland experienced a truly catholic reform. The Church came to the United States and Mexico in its present form in the early part of this century.

English and Latin pre-Vatican II masses are celebrated. The Baltimore Cathechism is used in all CCD and adult classes. The Pontificale Romanum is used for consecration and other episcopal and liturgical functions. This Church recognizes the authority of the See of St. Peter.

Records of Succession may be found in the Vatican Library, as recorded by the Ecclesiastical Committee.

The sacraments and holy orders of the Old Roman Catholic Church are universally accepted as valid

HEADQUARTERS

4200 N. Kedvale Ave., Chicago, IL 60641 Tel. (312)685-0461
Media Contact, Presiding Archbishop, Most Rev. Theodore J. Rematt, SGS

OFFICERS

Archbishop, Most Rev. Theodore J. Rematt

PERIODICAL

North American Catholic, The

North American Old Roman Catholic Church (Archdiocese of New York)

This body is identical with the Roman Catholic Church in faith, but differs from it in discipline and worship. The Mass is offered with the appropriate rite either in Latin or in the vernacular. All other sacraments are taken from the Roman Pontifical. This jurisdiction allows for married clergy.

HEADQUARTERS

Box 021647 GPO, Brooklyn, NY 11202 Tel. (718)855-0600 Fax (718)858-0690

OFFICERS

Ordinary, The Most Rev. Archbishop James H. Rogers, 118-09 Farmers Blvd., St. Albans, NY 11412
Vicar-Gen., Most Rev. Joseph M. Nevilloyd
Chancellor, Rev. Albert J. Berube

Old German Baptist Brethren

A group which separated from the Church of the Brethren (formerly German Baptist Brethren) in 1881 as a protest against a liberalizing tendency.

MEDIA CONTACT

Media Contact, Vindicator Ofc. Ed., Elder Keith Skiles, 1876 Beamsville-Union City Rd., Union City, OH Tel. (513)968-3877

OFFICERS

Foreman, Elder Clement Skiles, Rt. 1, Box 140, Bringhurst, IN 46913 Tel. (219)967-3367
Reading Clk., Elder Herman Shuman, Rt. 4, Box 301, Pendleton, IN 46064
Writing Clk., Elder Carl Bowman, 4065 State Rt. 48, Covington, OH 45318 Tel. (513)473-2729

PERIODICAL

Vindicator, The

Old Order Amish Church

The congregations of this Old Order Amish group have no annual conference. They worship in private homes. They adhere to the older forms of worship and attire. This body has bishops, ministers, and deacons.

MEDIA CONTACT

Media Contact, LeRoy Beachy, Beachy Amish Menn. Church, 4324 SR 39, Millersburg, OH 44654 Tel. (216)893-2883

INFORMATION

Der Neue Amerikanische Calendar, c/o Raber's Book Store, 2467 C R 600, Baltic, OH 43804

Old Order (Wisler) Mennonite Church

This body arose from a separation of Mennonites dated 1870, under Jacob Wisler, in opposition to what were thought to be innovations.

At present, this group is located in the Eastern United States and Canada. There are approximately 9,850 members and 46 congregations, with 10 bishops, 100 ministers, and deacons.

Each state, or district, has its own organization or government and holds a yearly conference.

MEDIA CONTACT

Media Contact, Arthur Van Pelt, 13550 Germantown Rd., Columbiana, OH 44408 Tel. (216)482-3691

Open Bible Standard Churches, Inc.

Open Bible Standard Churches originated from two revival movements: Bible Standard Conference, founded in Eugene, Ore., under the leadership of Fred L. Hornshuh, in 1919, and Open Bible Evangelistic Association, founded in Des Moines, Iowa, under the leadership of John R. Richey, in 1932.

Basically similar in doctrine and government, the two groups amalgamated on July 26, 1935, taking the combined name, "Open Bible Standard Churches, Inc.," with headquarters in Des Moines, Iowa.

Two hundred ten ministers formed the original group which has enlarged to incorporate over 1,865 ministers and 850 churches in 30 countries.

Historical roots of the parent groups reach back to the outpouring of the Holy Spirit in 1906 at Azusa Street Mission in Los Angeles, and to the great full gospel movement in the Midwest. Both groups were organized under the impetus of pentecostal revival. Simple faith, freedom from fanaticism, emphasis on evangelism and missions, and free fellowship with other groups were characteristics of the growing organizations.

Open Bible Standard churches have emphasized world evangelism. The first missionary left Lodi, Cal., for India in 1926. Since that time, the program has grown to minister in China, Japan, Philippines, Papua New Guinea, Canada, Puerto Rico, Dominican Republic, Canary Islands, Cayman Islands, Cuba, Jamaica, St. Vincent, Grenada, Trinidad, Mexico, Guatemala, El Salvador, Argentina, Chile, Brazil, Spain, Uruguay, Paraguay, Peru, Guinea, Liberia, Ghana, Kenya, Uganda, and Nigeria.

The highest governing body of Open Bible Standard Churches meets biennially and is composed of all ministers and one voting delegate per 100 members, or fraction thereof, from each church. A National Board of Directors, elected by the national and regional conferences, conducts the business of the organization. The U.S. church serves through 14 national departments, five geographical regions and 25 districts.

The official Bible College is Eugene Bible College, Eugene, Ore.

Open Bible Standard Churches, Inc., is a charter member of the National Association of Evangelicals and of the Pentecostal Fellowship of North America. It is also a member of the Pentecostal World Conference. Officers serve on the governing bodies of these organizations.

HEADQUARTERS

2020 Bell Ave., Des Moines, IA 50315 Tel. (515)288-6761 Fax (515)288-2510
Media Contact, Pres., Ray E. Smith

OFFICERS

Pres., Ray E. Smith
Sec.-Treas., Patrick L. Bowlin
Dir. of Intl. Min., Paul V. Canfield
Dir. of Christian Education, Randall A. Bach

PERIODICALS

World Vision; Outreach Magazine

The (Original) Church of God, Inc.

This body was organized in 1886 as the first church in the United States, to take the name "The Church of God." In 1917 a difference of opinion led this particular group to include the word (Original) in its name. It is a holiness body and believes in the whole Bible, rightly divided, using the New Testament as its rule and government.

HEADQUARTERS

P.O. Box 3086, Chattanooga, TN 37404 Tel. (615)629-4505

OFFICERS

Gen. Overseer, Rev. Johnny Albertson
Asst. Gen. Overseer, Rev. Alton Evans
Sec.-Treas., Michael B. Mitchell

PERIODICAL

Messenger, The

The Orthodox Church in America

The Russian Orthodox Greek Catholic Church of America entered Alaska in 1794 before its purchase by the United States in 1867. Its canonical status of independence (autocephaly) was granted by its Mother Church, the Russian Orthodox Church, on April 10, 1970, and it is now known as The Orthodox Church in America.

HEADQUARTERS

P.O. Box 675, Syosset, NY 11791 Tel. (516)922-0550 Fax (516) 922-0954

OFFICERS

Primate: The Most Blessed Theodosius,, Archbishop of Washington, Metropolitan of All America & Canada
Chancellor, V. Rev. Robert S. Kondratick, Fax (516)922-0954

SYNOD

Chpsn., His Beatitude Theodosius
Archbishop of New York, The Most Rev. Peter, 33 Hewitt Ave., Bronxville, NY 10708
Bishop of Pittsburgh, The Rt. Rev. Kyrill, P.O. Box R, Wexford, PA 15090
Bishop of Dallas, The Rt. Rev. Dmitri, 4112 Throckmorton, Dallas, TX 75219
Bishop of Philadelphia, The Rt. Rev. Herman, St. Tikhon's Monastery, South Canaan, PA 18459
Bishop of Sitka, The Rt. Rev. Gregory, St. Michael's Cathedral, Box 697, Sitka, AK 99835
Bishop of Detroit, The Rt. Rev. Nathaniel, 2522 Grey Tower Rd., Jackson, MI 49201
Bishop of Hartford, The Rt. Rev. Job, 6 Clark Rd., Cumberland, RI 02864
Bishop of San Francisco, The Rt. Rev. Tikhon, 649 North Robinson St., Los Angeles, CA 90026

Bishop of Ottawa, The Rt. Rev. Seraphim, RR 5, Box 179, Spencerville, ON K0E 1X0
Auxiliary Bishop, Titular Bishop of Bethesda, The Rt. Rev. Mark, 9511 Sun Pointe Dr., Boynton Beach, FL 33437

The Orthodox Presbyterian Church

On June 11, 1936, certain ministers, elders, and lay members of the Presbyterian Church in the U.S.A. withdrew from that body to form a new denomination. Under the leadership of the late Rev. J. Gresham Machen, noted conservative New Testament scholar, the new church determined to continue to uphold the Westminster Confession of Faith as traditionally understood by Presbyterians, and to engage in proclamation of the gospel at home and abroad.

The church has grown modestly over the years and suffered early defections, most notably one in 1937 that resulted in the formation of the Bible Presbyterian Church under the leadership of Dr. Carl McIntire. It now has congregations throughout the states of the continental United States.

The denomination is a member of the North American Presbyterian and Reformed Council.

HEADQUARTERS
303 Horsham Rd., Ste. G, Horsham, PA 19044 Tel. (215)956-0123

OFFICERS
Mod., Rev. William E. Warren, 9826 Luders Ave., Garden Grove, CA 92644 Tel. (714)539-7385
Stated Clk., Rev. Donald J. Duff

Pentecostal Assemblies of the World, Inc.

An interracial Pentecostal holiness of the Apostolic Faith, believing in repentance, baptism in Jesus' Name, and being filled with the Holy Ghost, with the evidence of speaking in tongues. This organization, originating in the early part of the century in the Middle West has now spread throughout the country.

HEADQUARTERS
3939 Meadows Dr., Indianapolis, IN 46205 Tel. (317)547-9541

OFFICERS
Presiding Bishop, James A. Johnson, 12643 Conway Downs Dr., St. Louis, MO 63141
Asst. Presiding Bishop, Paul A. Bowers, 1201 Egan Hills, Cincinnati, OH 45225
Bishops: Arthus Brazier; George Brooks; Ramsey Butler; Morris Golder; Francis L. Smith; Brooker T. Jones; C. R. Lee; Robert McMurray; Philip L. Scott; William L. Smith; Samuel A. Layne; Freeman M. Thomas; James E. Tyson; Charles Davis; Willie Burrell; Harry Herman; Jermiah Reed; Jeron Johnson; Clifton Jones; Robert Wauls; Ronald L. Young; Henry L. Johnson; Leodis Warren; Thomas J. Weeks; Eugene Redd; Thomas W. Weeks, Sr.; Willard Saunders; Davis L. Ellis; Earl Parchia; Vanuel C. Little; Norman Wagner; George Austin; Benjamin A. Pitt; Markose Thopil; John K. Cole; Peter Warkie; Norman Walters; Alphonso Scott; David Dawkins
Gen. Sec, Elder Richard Young
Dist. Treas., Elder James Loving
Asst. Treas., Elder Willie Ellis

PERIODICAL
Christian Outlook

Pentecostal Church of God

Growing out of the pentecostal revivals at the turn of the century, the Pentecostal Church of God was organized in Chicago, on Dec. 30, 1919, as the Pentecostal Assemblies of the U.S.A. The name was changed to Pentecostal Church of God on Feb. 15, 1922, in 1934 was changed again to The Pentecostal Church of God of America, Inc., and finally to Pentecostal Church of God (Incorporated) in 1979.

The International Headquarters was moved from Chicago to Ottumwa, Iowa, in 1927, then to Kansas City, Mo., in 1933, and finally to Joplin, Mo., in 1951.

The denomination is evangelical and pentecostal in doctrine and practice. Active membership in the National Association of Evangelicals and the Pentecostal Fellowship of North America is maintained.

Doctrinally, the church is Trinitarian and teaches the absolute inerrancy of the Scripture from Genesis to Revelation. Among its cardinal beliefs are the doctrines of salvation, which includes regeneration; divine healing, as provided for in the atonement; the baptism in the Holy Ghost, with the initial physical evidence of speaking in tongues; and the premillennial second coming of Christ.

HEADQUARTERS
4901 Pennsylvania, P.O. Box 850, Joplin, MO 64802 Tel. (417)624-7050 Fax (417)624-7102
Media Contact, Gen. Sec., Dr. Ronald R. Minor

OFFICERS
Gen. Supt., Dr. James D. Gee
Gen. Sec., Dr. Ronald R. Minor

OTHER GENERAL EXECUTIVES
Dir. of World Missions, Rev. Charles R. Mosier
Dir. of Indian Missions, Dr. C. Don Burke
Gen. PYPA Pres., Dr. Phil L. Redding
Dir. of Christian Ed., Dr. Aaron M. Wilson
Dir. of Home Missions/Evangelism, Dr. H. O. (Pat) Wilson

ASSISTANT GENERAL SUPERINTENDENTS
Northwestern Division, Rev. Robert L. McGee
Southwestern Division, Dr. Norman D. Fortenberry
North Central Division, Rev. Billy G. Jennings
South Central Division, Rev. E. L. Redding
Northeastern Division, Rev. Thomas E. Branham
Southeastern Division, Rev. James F. Richter

OTHER DEPARTMENTAL OFFICERS
Bus. Mgr., Rev. George Gilmore
Gen. PLA Dir., Mrs. Diana L. Gee
Sunday School Curriculum Ed., Ms. Billie Blevins, Messenger Publishing House, 4901 Pennsylvania, Joplin, MO 64802

PERIODICAL
Pentecostal Messenger, The

Pentecostal Fire-Baptized Holiness Church

Organized in 1918, and consolidated with Pentecostal Free Will Baptists in 1919, the church maintains rigid discipline over members.

HEADQUARTERS
Dry Fork, VA 24549 Tel. (804)724-4879

Media Contact, Gen. Mod., Steve E. Johnson, Rt. 2, Box 203, Dry Fork, VA 24549 Tel. (804)724-4879

OFFICERS

Gen. Treas., Kenwin N. Johnson, P.O. Box 1528, Laurinburg, NC 28352 Tel. (919)276-1295
Gen. Sec., W. H. Preskitt, Sr., Rt. 1, Box 169, Wetumpka, AL 36092 Tel. (205)567-6565
Gen. Mod., Steve E. Johnson, Rt. 1, Box 203, Dry Fork, VA 24549 Tel. (804)724-4879
Gen. Supt. Mission Bd., Jerry Powell, Rt. 1, Box 384, Chadourn, NC 28431

PERIODICAL

Faith and Truth

The Pentecostal Free Will Baptist Church, Inc.

Organized in 1855, as the Cape Fear Conference of Free Will Baptists, the church merged in 1959 with The Wilmington Conference and The New River Conference of Free Will Baptists and was renamed the Pentecostal Free Will Baptist Church, Inc. The doctrines include regeneration, sanctification, the Pentecostal baptism of the Holy Ghost, the Second Coming of Christ, and divine healing.

HEADQUARTERS

P.O. Box 1568, Dunn, NC 28335 Tel. (919)892-4161
Media Contact, Genl. Supt., Don Sauls

OFFICERS

Gen. Supt., Rev. Don Sauls
Asst. Gen. Supt., Dr. W. L. Ellis
Gen. Sec., Rev. J. T. Hammond
Gen. Treas., Dr. W. L. Ellis
World Witness Dir., Rev. David Taylor
Christian Ed. Dir., Rev. J. T. Hammond
Gen. Services Dir., Rev. Tim Crowder
Ministerial Council Dir., Rev. Preston Heath
Ladies' Auxiliary Dir., Mrs. Dolly Davis
Heritage Bible College, Pres., Dr. W. L. Ellis
Crusader Youth Camp, Dir., Rev. J. T. Hammond

OTHER ORGANIZATIONS

Heritage Bible College, P.O. Box 1628, Dunn, NC 28335 Tel. (919)892-4268
Crusader Youth Camp
Mutual Benefit Assoc.
Blessings Bookstore, 1006 W. Cumberland St., Dunn, NC 28334 Tel. (919)892-2401

PERIODICAL

Messenger, The

Pentecostal Holiness Church, International

This body grew out of the National Holiness Association movement of the last century and has direct roots in Methodism. Beginning in the South and Midwest, the present church represents the merger of three different holiness bodies: the Fire-Baptized Holiness Church founded by B.H. Irwin in Iowa in 1895; the Pentecostal Holiness Church founded by A. B. Crumpler in Goldsboro, N.C., in 1898; and the Tabernacle Pentecostal Church founded by N. J. Holmes in 1898.

All three bodies joined the ranks of the pentecostal movement as a result of the Azusa Street revival in Los Angeles in 1906 and a 1907 pentecostal revival in Dunn, North Carolina, conducted by G. B. Cashwell, who had visited Azusa Street. In 1911 the Fire-Baptized and Pentecostal Holiness bodies

merged in Falcon, N.C., to form the present church; the Tabernacle Pentecostal Church was added in 1915 in Canon, Ga.

The church stresses the new birth, the Wesleyan experience of entire sanctification, the pentecostal baptism in the Holy Spirit, evidenced by speaking in tongues, divine healing and the premillennial second coming of Christ.

HEADQUARTERS

P.O. Box 12609, Oklahoma City, OK 73157 Tel. (405)787-7110 Fax (405)789-3957
Media Contact, Admn. Asst., Rick Hurst

OFFICERS

Gen. Supt., Bishop B. E. Underwood
Vice Chpsn./Asst. Gen. Supt., Rev. Jesse Simmons
Asst. Gen. Supt., Rev. James Leggett
Gen. Sec.-Treas., Rev. Jack Goodson

OTHER ORGANIZATIONS

The Publishing House (Advocate Press), Gen. Admn., Greg Hearn, Franklin Springs, GA 30639
Christian Education Dept., Gen. Dir., Rev. Doyle Marley
Gen. Woman's Ministries, Pres., Mrs. Doris Moore

PERIODICALS

Pentecostal Holiness Advocate, The; Helping Hand; Sunday School Literature; Witness; Worldorama

Pillar of Fire

The Pillar of Fire was founded by Alma Bridwell White in Denver, Colo., Dec. 29, 1901 as the Pentecostal Union. In 1917, the name was changed to Pillar of Fire. Alma White was born in Kentucky in 1862 and taught school in Montana where she met her husband, Kent White, a Methodist minister, who was a University student in Denver.

Because of Alma White's evangelistic endeavors, she was frowned upon by her superiors, which eventually necessitated withdrawing from Methodist Church supervision. She was ordained as Bishop and her work spread to many states, to England, and since her decease to Liberia, West Africa, Malawi, East Africa, Yugoslavia, Spain, India, and the Philippines.

The Pillar of Fire organization emphasizes Christian education, with a college and two seminaries stressing Biblical studies. The church continues to keep in mind the founder's goals and purposes.

HEADQUARTERS

Zarephath, NJ 08890 Tel. (201)356-0102
Western Headquarters, 1302 Sherman St., Denver, CO 80203

OFFICERS

Pres. & Gen. Supt., Bishop Donald J. Wolfram
1st Vice-Pres. & Asst. Supt., Bishop Robert B. Dallenbach
2nd Vice-Pres./Sec.-Treas., Lois R. Stewart
Trustees: Kenneth Cope; Elsworth N. Bradford; S. Rea Crawford; June Blue

PERIODICAL

Pillar of Fire

Polish National Catholic Church of America

After a number of attempts to resolve differences

regarding the role of the laity in parish administration in the Roman Catholic Church in Scranton, Pa., this Church was organized in 1897. With the consecration to the episcopacy of the Most Rev. F. Hodur, this Church became a member of the Old Catholic Union of Utrecht in 1907.

HEADQUARTERS

Office of the Prime Bishop, 1002 Pittston Ave., Scranton, PA 18505 Tel. (717)346-9131

Media Contact, Prime Bishop, Most Rev. John F. Swantek, Fax (717)346-2188

OFFICERS

Prime Bishop, Most Rev. John F. Swantek, 115 Lake Scranton Rd., Scranton, PA 18505

Bishop of the Central Diocese, Rt. Rev. Anthony M. Rysz, 529 E. Locust St., Scranton, PA 18505

Bishop of the Eastern Diocese, Rt. Rev. Thomas J. Gnat, 166 Pearl St., Manchester, NH 03104

Bishop of the Buffalo-Pittsburgh Diocese, Rt. Rev. Thaddeus S. Peplowski, 182 Sobieski St., Buffalo, NY 14212

Bishop of Western Diocese, Rt. Rev. Joseph K. Zawistowski, 2019 W. Charleston St., Chicago, IL 60647

Bishop of the Canadian Diocese, Rt. Rev. Joseph I. Nieminski, 186 Cowan Ave., Toronto, ON

Ecumenical Officer, V. Rev. Stanley Skrzypek, 206 Main Street, New York Mills, NY 13416 Tel. (315)736-9757

PERIODICALS

God's Field; Polka

Presbyterian Church in America

The Presbyterian Church in America has a strong commitment to evangelism, missionary work at home and abroad and to Christian education.

Organized at a constitutional assembly in December 1973, this church was first known as the National Presbyterian Church but changed its name in 1974 to Presbyterian Church in America (PCA).

The PCA made a firm commitment on the doctrinal standards which had been significant in presbyterianism since 1645, namely the Westminster Confession of Faith and Catechisms. These doctrinal standards express the distinctives of the Calvinistic or Reformed tradition.

The PCA maintains the historic polity of Presbyterian governance, namely rule by presbyters (or elders) and the graded courts which are the session governing the local church, the presbytery for regional matters and the general assembly at the national level. It has taken seriously the position of the parity of elders, making a distinction between the two classes of elders, teaching and ruling.

In 1982, the Reformed Presbyterian Church, Evangelical Synod (RPCES) joined the PCA. It brought with it a tradition that had antecedents in Colonial America. It also included Covenant College in Lookout Mountain, Ga., and Covenant Theological Seminary in St. Louis, both of which are national denominational institutions of the PCA.

HEADQUARTERS

1852 Century Pl., Atlanta, GA 30345 Tel. (404)320-3366 Fax (404)320-7219

Media Contact, Ed., Rev. Robert G. Sweet, Tel. (404)320-3388 Fax (404)320-7964

OFFICERS

Mod., Mr. Mark Belz, St. Louis, MO
Stated Clk., Dr. Paul R. Gilchrist

PErmANENT COMMITTEES

Admn., Dr. Paul R. Gilchrist

Christian Educ. & Publ., Dr. Charles Dunahoo, Tel. (404)320-3388

Mission to North America, Rev. Terry Gyger
Mission to the World, Rev. John E. Kyle

PERIODICALS

Messenger, The

Presbyterian Church (U.S.A.)

The Presbyterian Church (U.S.A.) was organized June 10, 1983, when the Presbyterian Church in the United States and the United Presbyterian Church in the United States of America united in Atlanta. The union healed a major division which began with the Civil War when Presbyterians in the South withdrew from the Presbyterian Church in the United States of America to form the Presbyterian Church in the Confederate States.

The United Presbyterian Church in the United States of America had been created by the 1958 union of the Presbyterian Church in the United States of America and the United Presbyterian Church of North America. Of those two uniting bodies, the Presbyterian Church in the U.S.A. dated from the first Presbytery organized in Philadelphia, about 1706. The United Presbyterian Church of North America was formed in 1858, when the Associate Reformed Presbyterian Church and the Associate Presbyterian Church united.

Strongly ecumenical in outlook, the Presbyterian Church (U.S.A.) is the result of at least 10 different denominational mergers over the last 250 years. A Structural Design for Mission, adopted by the General Assembly meeting in June 1986, has been implemented, and on Oct. 29, 1988, the Presbyterian Church (U.S.A.) celebrated the dedication of its new headquarters in Louisville, Ky.

HEADQUARTERS

100 Witherspoon St., Louisville, KY 40202 Tel. (502)569-5000 Fax (502)569-5018

Media Contact, Mgr., Ofc. of News Service, Marj Carpenter, Tel. (502)569-5418 Fax (502)569-8073

OFFICERS

Mod., Herbert D. Valentine
Vice-Mod., Sang Whang
Stated Clk., James E. Andrews
Assoc. Stated Clk., Catherine M. Phillippe

THE OFFICE OF THE GENERAL ASSEMBLY

Tel. (502)569-5360 Fax (502)569-8005

Stated Clk., James E. Andrews

Dept. of the Stated Clerk, Dir., Juanita H. Granady

Dept. of Administration: Dir., J. Scott Schaefer; Mgr., Publishing, Maggie Houston; Statistical Reports, Deloris Moore

Dept. of Constitutional Services: Dir., C. Fred Jenkins; Mgr., Judicial Process, Gene Witherspoon; Mgr., Comm. on Rep. Staff Services, Marjorie Ward

Dept. of Governing Body, Ecumenical & Agency Rel., Dir., ——

Dept. of Assembly Services, Dir., Catherine M. Phillippe

Mgr. for Assembly Arrangements, Kerry Clements

Dept. of Hist., Philadelphia: 425 Lombard St., Philadelphia, PA 19147 Tel. (215)627-1852 Fax (215)627-0509; Dir., Frederick J. Heuser, Jr; Mgr. of Research & Library Services, Dep. Dir. Gerald Gillette; Mgr. of Technical Services, Barbara Schnur; Mgr. of Archives & Records Mgmt., Kristin L. Gleeson; Mgr. of Information Services, Boyd T. Reese; Reference Librarian, Kenneth Ross; Mgr. of Operations, John G. Peters

Dept. of Hist., Montreat: Montreat, P.O. Box 847, Montreat, NC 28757 Tel. (704)669-7061; Deputy Dir. of Prog., Michelle Francis; Research Historian, William Bynum; Admn. Local Church History, Diana Sanderson; Technical Service Librarian, John Walker

GENERAL ASSEMBLY COUNCIL

Office: Exec. Dir., ———, Fax (502)569-8080; Assoc. Dir., Wayne W. Allen; Coord., HR/Fin./Ofc. Mgmt., Marion L. Liebert; Coord., Fin. & Budgets, Robb Gwaltney; Coord., Governing Body Relationship, Evelyn W. Fulton; Coord., Internal Audits, Sharon Adams; Coord., Policies & Spec. Proj., Frank Diaz; Coord., Resources & Planning, Ruth McCreath

New York Liaison Ofc.: Coord., John B. Lindner, Interchurch Center, Rm. 420, 475 Riverside Dr., New York, NY 10115 Tel. (212)870-2101 Fax (212)870-3229

UNITS

CHURCH VOCATIONS MINISTRY UNIT:
Office of Director

Dir., ———; Assoc. for Admn., Jewel McRae; Assoc. Dir., Program Services, Mary V. Atkinson; Assoc., Equal Employment/Affirmative Action, Lillian Anthony; Assoc. Dir., Personnel Services, Ernest G. Clark

Section on Program Services

Ofc., Enlistment & Preparation for Min., Assoc., Charles Marks; Assoc., Enlistment Services, Judy Atwell

Ofc. of Examinations, Certif., & Accred., Assoc., Examination Services, Jerry W. Houchens; Assoc. Cert. & Accred., Donna Cook

Ofc. for Services to Committees on Min., Assoc., R. Howard McCuen

Ofc. of Human Resources Dev., Coord., Carlos Santin; Assoc., Support & Dev. of Governing Body Staff, Francis Perrin

Ofc. of Financial Aid for Studies, Assoc., Margaret Brown; Assoc. for Program Admn./Budget & Computer, Tim McCallister

Section on Personnel Services

Ofc. of Human Resource Mgmt., Group Dir., Frances A. White; Assoc. Salary Admn., Norman Folsom; Assoc. for Benefits/Payroll Admn., Amine Issa

Ofc. for Personnel Referral Services, Coord., Evelyn Hwang; Assoc. Operations, Agnes Holswade; Assoc., Matching, Margaret Willis; Assoc., Specialized Referrel & Matching, JoRene Willis; Assoc., Specialized Personnel Services, Mary Serovy

Ofc. of *Monday Morning*, Ed., Theodore A. Gill, Jr.; Asst. Ed., Susan Ellison; Ed. Asst., Rosetta Holland

EDUCATION AND CONGREGATIONAL NURTURE MINISTRY UNIT:
Director's Office

Dir., Donald Brown; Asoc. Dir., Coord. & Communication, Ed Craxton; Assoc., Conferencing (Dir. Ghost Ranch), Joe Keesecker, Abiquiu, NM 87510 Tel. (505)685-4333; Co-Dirs. Plaza Resolana en Santa Fe Study & Conf. Ctr., Kathleen M. Jimenez; Michael A. Chamberlain, 417 Paseo de Peralta, Santa Fe, NM 87501 Tel. (505)982-8539; Assoc. Conferencing (Dir. Montreat), William Peterson, P.O. Box 969, Montreat, NC 28757 Tel. (704)669-2911; Assoc. Conferencing (Dir. Stony Point), Jim Palm, Crickettown Rd., Stony Point, NY 10980 Tel. (914)786-5674; Assoc. for Budget & Personnel Admn., Mabel M. Wimer, Tel. (502)569-5446

Leadership Development Division

Assoc. Dir., Marvin L. Simmers; Assoc. Asian Leader Dev., C. W. Choi; Assoc. Leader Dev. Educ./Governing Bodies, Margaret Haney; Assoc. Leader Dev. Among Prof. Educators/Pastors, Dottie Hedgepeth; Assoc. Leader Dev., Ministry with Men, Art Kamitsuka; Assoc. Leader Dev., Youth, Rodger Nishioka; Assoc. Leader Dev., Youth in Global Ministry, Janice Nessibou; Intern, Youth Ministry, Dorcas Miller; Assoc. Leader Dev. Older Adult/Family Ministry, S. Miriam Dunson; Assoc. Leader Dev., Single Adults/Family Min., Ray Trout; Contract Staff Leader Dev., Youth/Singles Ministry, Lynn Turnage

Resourcing Division

Assoc. Dir., Donna Blackstock; Assoc. Hispanic Res. Dev., Ernestina Gutierrez; Assoc. Korean Res. Dev., Grace (Choon) Kim; Assoc. Curriculum Dev./Preschool Res., Martha Pillow; Assoc. Curriculum Dev./Children's Res., Kent Chrisman; Assoc. Curric. Dev./Older Youth Res., faye Burdick; Assoc. Curriculum Dev./Youth & Family Res., Beth Basham; Assoc. Curriculum Dev./Youth Res. Bible Discovery Older Youth & Middle Youth Celebrate, James Clinefelter; Assoc. Curriculum Res./Adult Res., Janice Weaver; Assoc. Curriculum Res./Adult Res., Frank Hainer; Assoc. for Curriculum Dev., Children & Family Res. Dev., Tom Malone; Assoc. Men's Res., David Lewis; Assoc. Public/Social Ed./Disability Concerns, Lew Merrick; Assoc., Resource Ctr. Dev., Jo Bales Gallagher; Intern, Men's Ministry, Jon Walthour

Publications Service

Publisher/Director, Robert McIntyre; Publishing Assoc., Wanda Fuller; Ed. Denom. Res., Maureen O'Connor; Copy Ed., Susan Jackson; Dir. Trade Books, Davis Perkins; Assoc. Dir. Church/Gen., Walt Sutton; Assoc. Dir. Reference/Academic, Cynthis Thompson; Ed. Church/Gen., Alexa Smith; Ed. Reference/Academic, Jeffries Hamilton; Ed. Assoc./Intl. Rights, Shirley Marshall; Dir. Copy Ed./Trade, Danielle Alexander; Copy Ed./Trade, Katy Monk; Copy Ed./Trade, Carl Helmich; Dir. Production, Joan Crawford; Assoc. Dir./ Trade, ———; Assoc. Dir./Curriculum, Jane James; Art Dir./Trade, Peter Gall; Art Dir./Curriculum, Russ Jackson; Dir. Copy Editing/Curriculum, Nancy Roseberry; Copy Ed./Curriculum, Carrie McCollough; Copy Ed./Curriculum, Shirley Murphey; Dir. Marketing, Robert Stratton; Marketing Associate, Vicki Miller; Marketing Dir., Curriculum/Retail Sales, Joe Paul Pruett; Assoc. Marketing Dir./Gen. Materials, Paul Tuttle; Assoc. Marketing Dir./Curriculum, Susan Spalding; Marketing Assoc./Curriculum, Brenda Hooks; Marketing Asst./Curriculum Res., Tracey Crockett; Marketing Asst./Curriculum Interpretation, Vicki Rucker; Bookstore Mgr., Pen Bogert; Dir. Sales Dept., Mina Grier; Sales Promotions Mgr., Ann McCannon; Dir. Publicity/Public Relations, Sally Telford; Dir. Subsidiary Rights & Permissions, Janine Bogert; Dir. Advertising, Bill Hendrick; Assoc. Advertising Dir., Curriculum, Tommy Larson; Copywriting/Curriculum, Debbie McCallister; Assoc. Advertising Dir./Trade, David Miller; Copywriting/Trade, Lina Bryant

SURVEY: Ed./Publisher, Ken Little; Managing Ed., Catherine Cottingham; Assoc. Ed., Eva Stimson; Art Dir., Meg Goodson; Dir. Advertising/Promotion, ——-

EVANGELISM AND CHURCH DEVELOPMENT MINISTRY UNIT: Dir., Andrea Pfaff; Assoc. for Budget & Communication, Julianne Jens-Horton; Coord. for Personnel & Ofc. Admn., Jacqueline Nelson Peden; Assoc. Dir. Presbyterian Evangelism, Gary Demarest; Assoc. Dir. Rural & Urban Church Dev., James Cushman; Assoc. Dir. Mission Financial Res., Diana Stephen; Assoc. for Mission Program Grants, Clarisa Piecuch; Assoc. for Church Loan Services, Dan Park; Assoc. for Small Church Dev., Carol Seaton; Assoc. for Racial/Ethnic Res. Dev. & Training, Mildred Brown; Assoc. for Redevelopment, Thomas Dietrich; Assoc. for Resource Dev. & Training, Mary B. Love; Assoc. for Church Growth & New Church Dev., H. Stanley Wood; Assoc. for Intl. Ch. Development & Evangelism, Morton Taylor; Informark Technician, Bonnie Jenkins

GLOBAL MISSION MINISTRY UNIT: Dir., Clifton Kirkpatrick; Assoc. Dir., Unit Coord., Syngman Rhee; Assoc., Mgmt. & Budget, Mehdi Abhari

Ecumenical/Interfaith Office

Assoc. Ecumenical Coord., Lewis Lancaster; Assoc. Ecumenical Educ. & Facilitation, ——; Assoc. Interfaith Relations, Margaret Thomas; Coord., New York Liaison Ofc., John B. Lindner

Health Ministries Office

Assoc. Dir. Health Ministries, Gwen Crawley; Assoc. for Program Dev. & Resourcing, Bob Ellis

Mutual Mission Office

Assoc. Dir. Internationalization of Mission, Elizabeth McAliley; Assoc., Mission to USA Personnel, Patricia Lloyd-Sidle; Assoc., Ecumenical Exchange, Nancy Miller; Assoc. Synod/Presbytery Partnerships, Homer Rickabaugh

Partnership in Mission Office

Assoc. Dir. Partnership Coordination, Bruce Gannaway; Assoc. Southern Africa, Jon Chapman; Assoc. East/West Africa, B. Hunter Farrell; Assoc. East Asia/Pacific, Insik Kim; Assoc. Middle East/South Asia, Victor E. Makari; Assoc. South America/Mexico, Benjamin Gutierrez; Assoc. Central America/Caribbean, Julia Ann Junkin; Assoc. Europe, Robert Lodwick; Assoc. Intl. Evangelism, Morton Taylor

People in Mission Offices

Assoc. Dir., Mission Personnel, William Hopper; Assoc., Mission Volunteers (USA), Linda Crawford; Assoc., Mission Volunteers (Intl.), Mike Stuart; Assoc., Missionary Recruitment, Morrisine Smith; Assoc., Missionary-Fraternal Worker Concerns, Marcia Borgeson; Assoc., Missionary Services/Pastoral Care, Harry Phillips

RACIAL ETHNIC MINISTRY UNIT: Dir., James Foster Reese; Assoc. Dir. Racial Justice Ministries, Jovelino Ramos; Coord. Asian Congregational Enhancement, Shun Chi Wang; Coord. Black Congregational Enhancement, Rita Dixon; Coord. Hispanic Congregational Enhancement, Jose Rodriguez; Coord. Korean Congregational Enhancement, Sun Bai Kim; Coord. Native American Congregational Enhancement, Gene Wilson; Coord. Racial Justice Ministries, ——-; Coord. Racial Justice Policy Development, Otis Turner; Coord. Racial Justice Leadership Development, Helen Locklear

SOCIAL JUSTICE AND PEACEMAKING MINISTRY UNIT:; Dir., Belle Miller McMaster; Assoc. Dir., Donald J. Wilson; Assoc. Dir. for Communication & Interpretation, Kathy Copas; Group Dir. Human Dev./Coord. Presby. Hunger Prog., Colleen Shannon; Assoc. Coord. PHP/Assoc. for Intl. Relief & Dev., Lionel Derenoncourt; Assoc. for Hunger Educ., Lifestyle, & Public Policy, Rose C. Tau; Prog. Asst. for Resourcing, Hunger Prog., Diane Hockenberry; Assoc. for Natl. Relief & Development, Gary R. Cook; Assoc. for Community Development, Philip Newell; Coord., Jinishian Memorial Program, Margaret Thomas; Assoc. for Jinishian Field Service (Lebanon), Haig Tilbian; Assoc. for Disaster Response, Daniel O. Rift; Assoc. for Refugee Services, Susan E. Ryan; Dir., Self-Development of People Program (SDOP), Fredric T. Wall; Assoc. for Program Admn. (SDOP), Cynthia White; Group Dir. for Human Services, Donald J. Wilson; Assoc. for Health Ministries, David Zuverink; Assoc. for Social Welfare Orgs. (PHEWA), Mark W. Wendorf; Group Dir., Church & Public Issues, Vernon S. Broyles, III; Assoc. for Criminal Justice, Kathy Lancaster; Assoc. For Mission Responsibility Thru Investments, William Somplatsky-Jarman; Assoc. for International Justice, ——; Group Dir., Peacemaking, Richard L. Killmer; Assoc. for Peacemaking Program, Ollie Gannaway; Presbyterian Ofc., United Nations, Church Center for the UN, Tel. (212)697-4568 Fax (212)986-3002; Assoc. for United Nations, Robert F. Smylie, 777 United Nations Plaza, New York, NY 10017; Washington Ofc., 110 Maryland Ave. NE, Washington, DC 20002 Tel. (202)543-1126 Fax (202)543-7755; Group Dir., Elenora Giddings Ivory; Assoc., Washington Ofc., Walter L. Owensby; Assoc., Washington Ofc., Barbara G. Green; Int. Assoc., Washington Ofc., Bernadine McRipley; Jarvie Commonweal Service, 475 Riverside Dr., 4th Fl., New York, NY 10115 Tel. (212)870-2965; Coord., Ellsworth G. Stanton, III; Assoc. Coord., Ann Brownhill Gubernick; Social Caseworkers, Ann Bonnell; Adele Malhotra; Hazel Schuller; Patricia Charles; Helene Walker; Ofc./Financial Mgr., Sarah Roberts

STEWARDSHIP AND COMMUNICATION DEV. MINISTRY UNIT: Dir., John Coffin; Assoc. Dir., Plan/Budget & Program, Vivian Johnson; Assoc. Dir. for Comm. Dev., Lois Stover; Assoc. for Comm./Inf. Services, Nancy Heinze; Assoc. for Communication Educ., Suzanne Iida; Assoc. for Mktg., Teresa Metzger; Assoc. for Computer Communications, Merrill Cook; Asst. for Computer Systems, Stanley Williams; Assoc. Dir. for Media Services, Ann Gillies; Assoc. for Media Services, Bill Gee; Assoc. for Media Services, Arnold Johnston; Assoc. for Media Coord. & Marketing, Betsy Kandle; Operations Manager, Greg Kapfhammer; Media Specialist, Dee Howard White; Assoc. Dir. for

Mission Funding, Claude Godwin; Assoc. for Extra Commitment, Bill Amey; Assoc. for Selected Giving, Margaret Anderson; Assoc. for Unified Mission Support, ——; Assoc. for Relationships with Foundations, Bruce Berry; Assoc. for CFCS Coord., Donald S. Myer, 11466 Ashley Woods Dr., Westchester, IL 60154 Tel. (708)409-0164; Asst. for CFCS, Ruth Anne Boklage, (Louisville Ofc.)

Assoc. Dir. Mission Inter. & Prom., James T. Magruder; Assoc. for Interpretation/Publications & Audiovisuals, Ted Yaple; Assoc. for Interpretation/Resources, David Eddy; Assoc. for Interpretation Resources/Coordinator, Sandra Woodcock; Assoc. for Interpretation/Speakers & Correspondence, Anne Howland; Assoc. for Interpretaion/Special Offerings, Alan Krome; Asst. for Resource Admn., Donna Jones; Asst. Ed., Frances Furlow; Assoc. for Interp./Mission Support, Kevin Piecuch; Asst. Ed., Christopher Miller; Assoc. Dir. Research Services, Arthur Benjamin; Assoc. for Research Coord., Keith Wulff; Assoc. for Research/Information, Ida Smith; Assoc. for Survey Research, John Marcum; Asst. for Research/Admn., Betty Partenheimer; Assoc. Dir. for Stewardship Educ., David McCreath; Assoc. for Stewardship Prom., Saundy Templeton; Assoc. for Stewardship Resources, Yvette Dalton; Assoc. for Stewardship Training, Phil Williams; Asst. for Resource Admn., Debra Oates

THE BICENTENNIAL FUND: Dir., Richard M. Ferguson; Co-Dir., George N. Pike; Assoc. Dir., Rev. Earl Underwood; Assoc. Dir. for Public Rel., Dale M. Williams; Counselor at Large, Judy Shideler

THEOLOGY AND WORSHIP MINISTRY UNIT: Dir., George Telford, Jr.; Assoc. Dir., Joseph D. Small, III; Assoc. Admn., Valerie Hofmann; Assoc., Worship, Deborah A. McKinley; Assoc., Faith & Order, Aurelia T. Fule; Assoc., Liturgical Resources, Harold M. Daniels; Assoc., Worship & the Arts, Nalini (Marcia) Jayasuriya; Assoc., Discipleship & Spirituality, E. Dixon Junkin; Assoc., Theol. Studies, John Burgess

WOMEN'S MINISTRY UNIT: Dir., Mary Ann Lundy; Assoc. Dir., Annie Wu King; Assoc. Presbyterian Women, Gladys Strachan; Assoc., Women Employed by the Church, Rebecca Tollefson; Assoc., Comte. of Women of Color, Patricia Gill Turner; Assoc., Justice for Women, Mary Kuhns; Assoc., Mission Participation, Jean Cutler; UN Prog. Asst., Katie Jacobs

National Staff in the Regions; Eastern Area Ofc., Yolanda Hernandez, 475 Riverside Dr., New York, NY 10115; Frances Unsell; East Central Ofc., Margaret Hall, Glendora Paul, 300 Sixth Ave., Ste. 1110, Pittsburgh, PA 15222; Western Area Ofc., Joan Richardson, Lucille Rieben, 330 Ellis St., Rm. 414, San Francisco, CA 94102; South Eastern Area Ofc., Elisabeth Lunz, Vera Swann, 159 Ralph McGill Blvd., Rm. 411, Atlanta, GA 30365; Synod of Rocky Mountains, Judith Wrought, 7000 N. Broadway, Denver, CO 80221

Women's Ministry Unit Program Assistants, Synod of Lakes & Prairies, Karen Dimon, 8012 Cedar Ave. South, Bloomington, MN 55425-1210; Synod of Mid-America, Debbie Vial, 324 South Crawford, Fort Scott, KS 66701

SUPPORT SERVICES: Dir., Robert T. Mehrhoff; Mgr., Ofc. of News Services, Marj Carpenter; Mgr., Ofc. of Gen. Services, Susan D. Johns; Mgr., Ofc. of Inf. Services, John M. Mayberry; Mgr. Ofc., of Distribution Management Services, Gregg Talarovich; Gen. Counsel, Carolyn F. Shain

CENTRAL TREASURY CORPORATION: Pres./Treas., G. A. Goff; Vice-Pres./Assoc. Treas., Arthur Clark, Sr.; Vice-Pres., Controller, Nagy Tawfik; Vice-Pres./Financial Planning, Carmen L. Lopez; Mgr. Central Receiving, William Partenheimer; Mgr. Accounts Payable, Thomas Abraham; Vice-Pres. Property & Risk Mgmt., William Gatewood

COMMITTEES

COMMITTEE ON SOCIAL WITNESS POLICY: Dir., Kenneth G. Y. Grant; Assoc. Dir. Policy Devel. & Interpretation, Ruth Duba; Interim Assoc. for Resources & Admn., Michael W. Purinton

COMMITTEE ON HIGHER EDUCATION: Dir., Duncan S. Ferguson; Assoc. Colleges & Universities, Jean Jones; Budget Mgr., Beneva Thomas; Assoc., Global Education & Leadership Devel., Haydn O. White; Missionary-in-Residence, Richard Rodman; Assoc., Racial-Ethnic Schools & Colleges, George M. Conn, Jr; Assoc., Higher Education Ministries, Clyde O. Robinson, Jr; Assoc., Financial Aid for Studies, Margaret Brown; Assoc. Budget, Computer & Prog. Mgmt., Tim McCallister

COMMITTEE ON THEOLOGICAL EDUCATION: Dir., Joyce Tucker; Assoc. Dir., Daniel L. Force; Assoc. for Institutional Support, Patsy Godwin

PRESBYTERIAN CHURCH (U.S.A.) FOUNDATION

Ofices, 200 E. Twelfth St., Jeffersonville, IN 47130 Tel. (812)288-8841 Fax (502)569-5980

Chair of the Bd., Helen R. Walton

Vice-Chair, Frank S. Deming

Pres., Geoffrey R. Cross

Sr. Vice-Pres. for Fin., Dennis J. Murphy

Vice-Pres. for Development, Robert F. Langwig

Vice-Pres. for Mktg., W. Scott Harrah

Vice-Pres. for Gift Admn., Julianne B. Singh

SYNOD EXECUTIVES

Alaska-Northwest, David C. Meekhof, 233 6th Ave. N., Ste. 100, Seattle, WA 98109-5000 Tel. (206)448-6403

Covenant, H. Davis Yeuell, 6172 Bush Blvd., Ste. 3000, Columbus, OH 43229-2564 Tel. (614)436-3310

Lakes & Prairies, Rev. Robert T. Cuthill, 8012 Cedar Ave. S., Bloomington, MN 55425-1204 Tel. (612)854-0144

Lincoln Trails, Rev. Verne E. Sindlinger, 1100 W. 42nd St., Indianapolis, IN 46208-3381 Tel. (317)923-3681

Living Waters, Rev. J. Harold Jackson, P.O. Box 290275, Nashville, TN 37229-0275 Tel. (615)370-4008

Mid-America, Rev. John L. Williams, 6400 Glenwood, Ste. 111, Overland Park, KS 66202-4072 Tel. (913)384-3020

Mid-Atlantic, Carroll D. Jenkins, P.O. Box 27026, Richmond, VA 23261-7026 Tel. (804)342-0016

Northeast, Rev. Eugene G. Turner, 3049 E. Genesee St., Syracuse, NY 13224-1644 Tel. (315)446-5990

Pacific, Rev. Philip H. Young, P.O. Box 1810, San Anselmo, CA 94960-7091 Tel. (415)258-0333

Puerto Rico, Rev. Harry Fred Del Valle, Medical Center Plaza, Oficina 216, Mayaguez, PR 00708 Tel. (809)832-8375

Rocky Mountains, Ramona McKee, 7000 N. Broadway, Suite 410, Denver, CO 80221-2475 Tel. (303)428-0523

South Atlantic, Rev. John Niles Bartholomew, Interstate North Office Center, 435 Clark Rd., Ste. 404, Jacksonville, FL 32218-5574 Tel. (904)764-5644

Southern California, Hawaii, Rev. Rafael J. Aragon, 1501 Wilshire Blvd., Los Angeles, CA 90017-2293 Tel. (213)483-3840

Southwest, Rev. Gary Skinner, 4423 N. 24th St., Ste. 800, Phoenix, AZ 85016-5544 Tel. (602)468-3800

Sun, Rev. William J. Fogelman, 920 S. 135 E, Denton, TX 76205-7898 Tel. (817)382-9656

Trinity, Rev. Thomas M. Johnston, Jr., 3040 Market St., Camp Hill, PA 17011-4599 Tel. (717)737-0421

PERIODICALS

American Presbyterians: Journal of Presbyterian History; Monday Morning; Church & Society Magazine; Horizons; These Days

Primitive Advent Christian Church

This body split from the Advent Christian Church. All its churches are located in West Virginia. The Primitive Advent Christian Church believes that the Bible is the only rule of faith and practice and that Christian character is the only test of fellowship and communion. The church agrees with Christian fidelity and meekness; exercises mutual watch and care; counsels, admonishes, or reproves as duty may require; and receives the same from each other as becomes the household of faith. Primitive Advent Christians do not believe in taking up arms against our fellow man in case of war.

The church believes that three ordinances are set forth by the Bible to be observed by the Christian church: (1) baptism by immersion; (2) the Lord's Supper, by partaking of unleavened bread and wine; (3) feet washing, to be observed by the saints' washing of one another's feet.

OFFICERS

Pres., Roger Hammons, 273 Frame Rd., Elkview, WV 25071 Tel. (304)965-6247

Vice-Pres., Herbert Newhouse, 7632 Hughart Dr., Sissionville, WV 25320 Tel. (304)984-9277

Sec. & Treas., Hugh W. Good, 395 Frame Rd., Elkview, WV 25071 Tel. (304)965-1550

Primitive Baptists

A large group of Baptists, located throughout the United States, who are opposed to all centralization and to modern missionary societies. This body believes and preaches Salvation by Grace alone.

HEADQUARTERS

Cayce Publ. Co., S. Second St., P.O. Box 38, Thornton, AR 71766 Tel. (501)352-3694

CORRESPONDENT

Elder W. H. Cayce

PERIODICALS

Baptist Witness; Christian Baptist; Christian Pathway; Primitive Baptist; For the Poor

Primitive Methodist Church in the U.S.A.

Hugh Bourne and William Clowes, local preachers in the Wesleyan Church in England in the early 1800s, became interested in seeing their fellow workers converted and brought to Christ. Lorenzo Dow, a Methodist preacher from America, recounted with enthusiasm the story of the American camp meeting to Bourne and Clowes, and a whole day's meeting at Mow Cop in Staffordshire, England, on May 31, 1807, was arranged. Thousands were present and many were converted but, strange as it may seem, the church founded by that great open air preacher John Wesley refused to accept these converts and reprimanded the preachers for their evangelistic effort.

After waiting for a period of two years for a favorable action by the Wesleyan Society, Bourne and Clowes established The Society of the Primitive Methodists. The words of Bourne provide the evidence that this was not a schism, for "we did not take one from them...it now appeared to be the will of God that we, as a Camp Meeting Community, should form classes and take upon us the care of churches in the fear of God." The first Primitive Methodist missionaries were sent to New York in 1829, and a distinct conference in America was established on Sept. 16, 1840.

Missionary efforts reach into Guatemala, Spain, and numerous other countries, with both Spanish and English work in the U.S.A. The denomination joins in federation with the Evangelical Congregational Church and the United Brethren in Christ Church, and is a member of the National Association of Evangelicals.

The Primitive Methodist Church believes the Bible to be the only true rule of faith and practice, the inspired Word of God, and holds its declarations final. It believes in the existence of one Triune God, the Deity of Jesus Christ, the Deity and personality of the Holy Spirit, the innocence of Adam and Eve, the Fall and corruption of the human race, the necessity of repentance, justification by faith of all who believe and regeneration witnessed by the Holy Spirit, sanctification by the Holy Spirit producing holiness of heart and life, the second coming of the Lord Jesus Christ, the resurrection of the dead and conscious future existence of all people, and future judgments and eternal rewards and punishments.

MEDIA CONTACT

Media Contact, Exec. Dir., Rev. William H. Fudge, 1045 Laurel Run Rd., Wilkes-Barre, PA 18702 Tel. (717)472-3436 Fax (717)472-9283

OFFICERS

Pres., Dr. K. Gene Carroll, 223 Austin Ave., Wilkes-Barre, PA 18702

Vice-Pres., Rev. John D. Sargent, 750 Madison St., Platteville, WI 53818

Exec. Dir., Rev. William H. Fudge, 1045 Laurel Run Rd., Wilkes-Barre, PA 18702 Fax (717)472-9283

Treas., Mr. Raymond Baldwin, 11012 Langton Arms Ct., Oakton, VA 22124

Gen. Sec., Rev. Reginald H. Thomas, 110 Pittston Blvd., Wilkes-Barre, PA 18702 Tel. (717)823-3425

Progressive National Baptist Convention, Inc.

A body which held its organizational meeting in Cincinnati, November, 1961. Subsequent regional sessions were followed by the first annual session in Philadelphia in 1962.

OFFICERS

Pres., Dr. Charles G. Adams, Hartford Memorial Baptist Church, 18700 James Couzens Hwy., Detroit, MI 48235

Gen. Sec., Rev. Tyrone S. Pitts, 601 50th St., NE, Washington, DC 20019 Tel. (202)396-0558 Fax (202)398-4998

OTHER ORGANIZATIONS

Bd. of Christian Education, Sec., Rev. C. B. Lucas, 3815 W. Broadway, Louisville, KY 40211

Women's Dept., Mrs. Earl C. Bryant, 537 Woolfolk St., Macon, GA 31201

Home Mission Bd., Exec. Dir., Rev. Archie LeMone, 601 50th St., NE, Washington, DC 20019

Congress of Christian Education, Pres., Dr. Thomas H. Peoples, Jr., Pleasant Green Missionary Baptist Church, 540 W. Maxwell St., Lexington, KY 40508

Baptist F. M. Bureau, Dr. Ronald K. Hill, 161-163 60th St., Philadelphia, PA 19139

The Protestant Conference (Lutheran), Inc.

The Conference came into being in 1927 as the result of expulsions of pastors and teachers from the Wisconsin Evangelical Lutheran Synod (WELS). The underlying cause which ignited the suspensions was a rebellion against what was labeled The Wauwatosa Theology, so named after the location of the Wisconsin Synod seminary at that time and the fresh approach to Scripture study there by the faculty. This approach sought to overcome the habits of dogmatism. Chiefly responsible for this renewal was Professor John Philipp Koehler.

The Conference was formed as the result of these suspensions, which were to be followed by other suspensions. To give testimony to the issues at operation in this controversy and in particular to bear witness to the grace of the Wauwatosa Theology, the Conference has published *Faith-Life* since 1928. The congregations are chiefly in Wisconsin. The Conference has no official officers. Chief in influence have been Professor J. P. Koehler (1859-1951); his son Karl Koehler (1885-1948), who was the chief architect of *Faith-Life* with its Policy and Purpose; and Paul Hensel (1888-1977) who displayed the Wauwatosa Theology in his writings and commentary.

OFFICERS

Recording Sec., Pastor Gerald Hinz, P.O. Box 86, Shiocton, WI 54170 Tel. (414)986-3918

Fin. Sec.-Treas., Michael Meler, 1023 Colan Blvd., Rice Lake, WI 54868

PERIODICAL

Faith-Life

Protestant Reformed Churches in America

The Protestant Reformed Churches in America were organized in 1926 as a result of doctrinal disagreement relating to such matters as world conformity, problems of higher criticism and God's grace that pervaded the Christian Reformed Church in the early 1920s.

After the passage of the formula on Three Points of Common Grace by the Synod of the Christian Reformed Church in 1924, and during the resulting storm of controversy, three clergy, and those in their congregations who agreed with them, were expelled from the Christian Reformed Church. These clergy were Herman Hoeksema of the Eastern Ave. Christian Reformed Church in Grand Rapids, Mich., George Ophoff, pastor of the Hope congregation in Riverbend, Mich., and Henry Danhof in Kalamazoo, Mich.

In March 1925, the consistories of these congregations signed an Act of Agreement and adopted the temporary name of "Protesting Christian Reformed Churches." Following the Synod of the Christian Reformed Church of 1926, when the break was made final, the three consistories participating in the Act of Agreement met, and in November, 1926, organized the Protestant Reformed Churches in America.

The Protestant Reformed Churches in America hold to the doctrinal tenets of Calvinism, the Belgic Confession, the Heidelberg Catechism and the Canons of Dordrecht.

HEADQUARTERS

16515 South Park Ave., South Holland, IL 60473 Tel. (708)333-1314

Media Contact, Stat. Clk., Rev. M. Joostens, 2016 Tekonsha, S.E., Grand Rapids, MI 49506 Tel. (616)247-0638

OFFICER

Stat. Clk., Rev. M. Joostens

Reformed Church in America

The Reformed Church in America was established in 1628 by the earliest settlers of New York. It is the oldest Protestant denomination with a continuous ministry in North America. Until 1867 it was known as the Reformed Protestant Dutch Church.

The first ordained minister, Domine Jonas Michaelius, arrived in New Amsterdam from The Netherlands in 1628. Throughout the colonial period, the Reformed Church lived under the authority of the Classis of Amsterdam. Its churches were clustered in New York and New Jersey. Under the leadership of Rev. John Livingston, it became a denomination independent of the authority of the Classis of Amsterdam in 1776. Its geographical base was broadened in the nineteenth century by the immigration of Reformed Dutch and German settlers in the midwestern United States. In the twentieth century, the Reformed Church spans the United States and Canada.

The Reformed Church accepts as its standards of faith the Heidelberg Catechism, Belgic Confession, and Canons of Dort. It has a rich heritage of world mission activity. It claims to be loyal to reformed tradition which emphasizes obedience to God in all aspects of life.

Although the Reformed Church in America has worked in close cooperation with other churches, it has never entered into merger with any other denomination. It is a member of the World Alliance of Reformed Churches, the World Council of Churches, and the National Council of the Churches of Christ in the United States of America.

475 Riverside Dr., New York, NY 10115 Tel. (212)870-2841 Fax (212)870-2499
Media Contact, Dir., Promotion, Communication, Development, E. Wayne Antworth, Tel. (212)870-2954

OFFICERS AND STAFF OF GENERAL SYNOD
Pres., Louis E. Lotz
Gen. Sec., Edwin G. Mulder

OTHER ORGANIZATIONS
Bd. of Direction, Pres., Gerald Verbridge
Bd. of Pensions: Pres., John E. Hiemstra; Sec., Edwin G. Mulder
General Program Council: Mod., Vern Boss; Sec. for Program, Eugene P. Heideman
Ofc. of Human Resources, Coord., Alvin J. Poppen
Ofc. of Finance, Treas., Wayne D. Kramer
Ofc. of Promotion, Comm., & Dev., Dir., E. Wayne Antworth
Reformed Church Women, Exec. Dir., Diana Paulsen
The African-American Council, Exec. Dir., -----
The Council for Hispanic Ministries, Natl. Sec., Johnny Alicea-Baez
The American Indian Council, Interim Sec., Kenneth W. Mallory
Council for Pacific/Asian-American Min., Natl. Sec., Ella White

PERIODICAL
Church Herald, The

Reformed Church in the United States

Lacking pastors, early German Reformed immigrants to the American colonies were led in worship by "readers." One reader, schoolmaster John Philip Boehm, organized the first congregations near Philadelphia in 1725. A Swiss pastor, Michael Schlatter, was sent by the Dutch Reformed Church in 1746. Strong ties with the Netherlands existed until the formation of the Synod of the Reformed High German Church in 1793.

The "Mercersburg Theology" of the 1840s was a precursor to twentieth century liberalism and to the merger of the Reformed Church with the Evangelical Synod of North America in 1934. Conservatives vigorously opposed the union, holding that it sacrificed the Reformed heritage. (The merged Evangelical and Reformed Church became part of the United Church of Christ in 1957.)

The Eureka Classis was organized in North and South Dakota in 1910 as one of fifty-eight classes (districts) in the church. These congregations were strongly influenced by the writings of H. Kohlbruegge, P. Geyser and J. Stark, who emphasized salvation by grace through faith, not by works. Under the leadership of pastors W. Grossmann and W. J. Krieger, the Eureka Classis refused to become part of the merger of 1934, and in 1942 incorporated as the continuing Reformed Church in the United States.

The growing Eureka Classis dissolved in 1986 to form a Synod with four regional classes. An heir to the Reformation theology of Zwingli and Calvin, the Heidelberg Catechism of 1563 is used as the confessional standard of the church. The Bible is strictly held to be the inerrant, infallible Word of God.

The RCUS has close relationships with other conservative Reformed and Presbyterian bodies. It supports Westminster Theological Seminary in Philadelphia and Escondido, Cal.; Dordt College and Mid-America Reformed Seminary in Iowa. The RCUS is the official sponsor to the Reformed Confessing Church of Zaire.

OFFICERS
Pres., Rev. Vernon Pollema, 235 James Street, Shafter, CA 93263
Vice-Pres., Rev. Paul Treick, 1515 Carlton Ave., Modesto, CA 95350 Tel. (209)526-0637
Stated Clk., Rev. Frank Walker, 927 E. Graceway Dr., Napoleon, OH 43545 Tel. (419)599-2266
Treas., Mr. Clayton Greimon, RR 3, Garner, IA 50438

PERIODICAL
Reformed Herald, The

Reformed Episcopal Church

The Reformed Episcopal Church was founded in 1873, in New York City by Bishop George D. Cummins. Cummins was a major evangelical figure in the Protestant Episcopal Church and from 1866 until 1873 was the assistant bishop of the diocese of Kentucky. However, Cummins and other evangelical Episcopalians viewed with alarm the influence of the Oxford Movement in the Protestant Episcopal Church, not only for the interest it stimulated in Roman Catholic ritual and doctrine but also for the intolerance it bred toward evangelical Protestant doctrine, both within and outside the Episcopal Church.

Throughout the late 1860s, evangelicals and ritualists clashed over ceremonies and vestments, exchanges of pulpits with clergy of other denominations, and the proper meaning of critical passages in the Book of Common Prayer as well as the interpretation of the sacraments and validity of the so-called Apostolic Succession.

These clashes culminated in October, 1873, when other bishops publicly attacked Cummins in the church newspapers for participating in an ecumenical Communion service sponsored by the Evangelical Alliance. On Nov. 10, 1873, Cummins resigned his office and, on Nov. 13, drafted a call to Episcopalians to organize a new Episcopal Church for the "purpose of restoring the old paths of their fathers." At the organization of the new church on Dec. 2 (known as the First General Council), a *Declaration of Principles* was adopted and Dr. Charles E. Cheney was elected bishop to serve with Cummins. The Second General Council, meeting in May 1874 in New York City, approved a *Constitution and Canons* and a slightly amended version of the *Book of Common Prayer*. In 1875, the Third General Council adopted a set of *Thirty-Five Articles* as a recast substitute to the Church of England's *Thirty-Nine Articles of Religion*.

By the time Cummins died in 1876, the church had grown to nine jurisdictions in the United States and Canada. Although substantial growth ceased after 1900, the church now comprises three synods (New York-Philadelphia, Chicago, Charleston-Atlanta-Charlotte) and a missionary jurisdiction of the West. It maintains in its doctrine the founding principles of episcopacy (as an ancient and desirable form of church polity), a Biblical liturgy, Reformed doctrine, and evangelical zeal, and in its practice it continues to recognize the validity of nonepiscopal orders of evangelical ministry. The Reformed Episcopal Church is a member of the National Association of Evangelicals; it was a long-time member of the National Council of

Churches but withdrew, and in 1938 it rejected remerger efforts with the Protestant Episcopal Church.

OFFICERS

Pres. & Presiding Bishop, Rev. Franklin H. Sellers, Sr., 1629 W. 99th St., Chicago, IL 60643
Vice-Pres., Bishop Sanco K. Rembert, P.O. Box 20068, Charleston, SC 29413
Sec., Rev. Willie J. Hill, Jr., 271 W. Tulpehocken St., Philadelphia, PA 19144
Treas., Mr. William B. Schimpf, 67 Westaway Lane, Warrington, PA 18976

OTHER ORGANIZATIONS

Bd. of Foreign Missions: Pres., Dr. William J. Hollman, Jr., 319 E. 50th St., New York, NY 10022; Sec., Mrs. Lyla Wildermuth, 22 Forest Ave., Willow Grove, PA 19090; Treas., Rev. Daniel Olsen, III, 3403 Winchester Ave., Atlantic City, NJ 08401
Bd. of Natl. Church Extension: Pres., Rev. George B. Fincke, 901 Church Rd., Oreland, PA 19075; Sec., Rev. Dale H. Crouthamel, 14 Culberson Rd., Basking Ridge, NJ 07920; Treas., Mrs. Joan Workowski, 1162 Beverly Rd., Jenkintown, PA 19046
Trustees Sustentation Fund: Pres., Mr. E. Earl Shisler, Jr., RD #2, Perkasie, PA 18944; Treas., Mr. William B. Schimpf, 67 Westaway La., Warrington, PA 18976
Publication Society: Pres., Rev. Richard K. Barnard, 8027 Inwood Rd., Dallas, TX 75209
The Reapers: Pres., Mrs. Nancy Fleischer, RR #1, Box 500, Pipersville, PA 18947; Treas., Mrs. Loralee Holiman, 319 E. 50th St., New York, NY 10022

BISHOPS

William H.S. Jerdan, Jr., 414 W. 2nd South St., Summerville, SC 29483
Sanco K. Rembert, P.O. Box 20068, Charleston, SC 29413
Franklin H. Sellers, Sr., 1629 W. 99th St., Chicago, IL 60643
Leonard W. Riches, Sr., RD 1, Box 501, Smithown Rd., Pipersville, PA 18947
Daniel G. Cox, 9 Hilltop Pl., Catonsville, MD 21228
Royal U. Grote, Jr., 19 Heather Ct., New Providence, NJ 07974
James C. West, Sr., 91 Anson St., Charleston, SC 29401
Robert H. Booth, 1222 Haworth St., Philadelphia, PA 19124

PERIODICAL

Episcopal Recorder

Reformed Mennonite Church

This group was reorganized in 1812 under John Herr because they did not know of any other organization that fully carried out New Testament teachings. They believe there can only be one church, consisting of regenerated persons who are united in love and doctrine.

HEADQUARTERS

Lancaster County only, Reformed Mennonite Church, 602 Strasburg Pike, Lancaster, PA 17602

OFFICER

Bishop Earl Basinger, 1036 Lincoln Heights Ave., Ephrata, PA 17522

Reformed Methodist Union Episcopal Church

The Reformed Methodist Union Episcopal Church was formed after a group of ministers withdrew from the African Methodist Episcopal Church following a dispute over the election of ministerial delegates to the General Conference.

These ministers held a meeting on Jan. 22, 1885 at Hills Chapel (now known as Mt. Hermon RmUE church), on Fishburn Street, in Charleston, S.C. This four-day meeting resulted in the organization of the Reformed Methodist Union Church.

In this meeting the Rev. William E. Johnson was unanimously elected president of the new church. Following the death of Rev. Johnson in 1896 an extra session of the General Conference was called to elect a new leader for the church.

It was decided in this conference that the church would conform to regular American Methodism (the Episcopacy); the first Bishop, Edward Russell Middleton, was elected, and "Episcopal" was added to the name of the church.

Bishop Middleton was consecrated on Dec. 5, 1896, by Bishop P. F. Stephens of the Reformed Episcopal Church.

HEADQUARTERS

Charleston, SC 29407

OFFICERS

Bishop, Rt. Rev. Leroy Gethers, 1136 Brody Ave., Charleston, SC 29407 Tel. (803) 766-3534
Asst. Bishop:, Rt. Rev. Eugene Davies, Jr
Gen. Sec., Rev. Fred H. Moore, 115 St. Margaret St., Charleston, SC 29403. (803)723, 3-8857
Treas., Rev. Rufus German
Sec. of Education, Rev. William Polite
Sec. of Books Concerns, Rev. Thomas Watson, Jr
Sec. of Pension Fund, Rev. Joseph Powell
Sec. of Church Extension, ----------
Sec. of Sunday School Union, Rev. Hercules Champaigne
Sec. of Mission, Rev. Jerry M. DeBoer

Reformed Presbyterian Church of North America

Also known as the Church of the Covenanters. Origin dates back to the Reformation days of Scotland when the Covenanters signed their "Covenants" in resistance to the king and the Roman Church in the enforcement of state church practices. The Church in America has signed two "Covenants" in particular, those of 1871 and 1954.

MEDIA CONTACT

Media Contact, Dir. of Publ. & Youth Min., James C. Pennington, 7408 Penn Ave., Pittsburgh, PA 15208 Tel. (412)241-0436 Fax (412)731-8861

OFFICERS

Mod., Dr. Roy Blackwood, Jr., 1175 Princeton Pl., Zionsville, IN 46077 Tel. (317)873-4775
Clk., J. Bruce Martin, 1328 Goodin Dr., Clay Center, KS 67432 Tel. (913)632-5861
Asst. Clk., Ronald L. Graham, P.O. Box 197, Minneola, KS 67865 Tel. (316)885-4538
Stated Clk., Louis D. Hutmire, 7408 Penn Ave., Pittsburgh, PA 15208 Tel. (412)731-1177

PERIODICAL

Covenanter Witness, The

Reformed Zion Union Apostolic Church

Organized in 1869, at Boydton, Va., by Elder James R. Howell of New York, a minister of the A.M.E. Zion Church; with doctrines of the Methodist Episcopal Church.

OFFICER

Sec., Deacon James C. Feggins, 416 South Hill Ave., South Hill, VA 23970 Tel. (804)447-3374

Religious Society of Friends (Conservative)

These Friends mark their present identity from separations occurring by regions at different times from 1845 to 1904. They hold to a minimum of organizational structure. Their meetings for worship, which are unprogrammed and based on silent, expectant waiting upon the Lord, demonstrate the belief that all individuals may commune directly with God and may share equally in vocal ministry.

They continue to stress the importance of the Living Christ and the experience of the Holy Spirit working with power in the lives of individuals who obey it.

YEARLY MEETINGS

North Carolina YM, Lloyd Lee Wilson, 536 Carnaby Ct., Virginia Beach, VA 23459

Iowa YM, Martha Davis and Bill Deutsch, 678 38th St., Des Moines, IA 50312

Ohio YM, Susan S. Smith, RD #4 Box 288, Harrisonburg, VA 22801

Religious Society of Friends (Unaffiliated Meetings)

Though all groups of Friends acknowledge the same historical roots, 19th-century divisions in theology and experience led to some of the current organizational groupings. Many newer yearly meetings, often marked by spontaneity, variety, and experimentation and hoping for renewed Quaker unity, have chosen not to identify with past divisions by affiliating in traditional ways with the larger organizations within the Society. Some of these unaffiliated groups have begun within the past 25 years.

UNAFFILIATED YEARLY MEETINGS

Amigos Central de Bolivia, Casilla 11070, La Paz, Bolivia

Amigos de Santidad de Bolivia, Casilla 992, La Paz, Bolivia

Central Yearly Meeting, 109 West Berry St., Alexandria, IN 46001

Iglesia Evangelica Amigos, Apartado 235, Santa Rosa de Capan, Honduras

Iglesia Nacional Evangelica de Los Amigos-Bolivia, Casilla 8385, La Paz, Bolivia

Iglesia Nacional Evangelica de Los Amigos-Peru, Apartado 369, Puno, Peru

Intermountain Yearly Meeting, 1720 Linden Ave., Boulder, CO 80304

North Pacific Yearly Meeting, 3311 N.W. Polk, Corvallis, OR 97330

Pacific Yearly Meeting, 808 Melba Rd., Encinitas, CA 92024

Reunion Gen. de Mexico, 5y6 Matamoros, Ciudad Victoria, Tamaulipas, Mexico

El Salvador Yearly Meeting, Calle Roosevelt, Km. 4.5, #60, Soyapango, San Salvador, El Salvador

Guatemala Yearly Meeting, Apartado 8, Chiquimula, Guatemala

Reorganized Church of Jesus Christ of Latter Day Saints

Founded April 6, 1830, by Joseph Smith, Jr., and reorganized under the leadership of the founder's son, Joseph Smith III, in 1860. The Church, with headquarters in Independence, Missouri, is established in 36 countries in addition to the United States and Canada. A biennial world conference is held in Independence, Missouri. The current president is Wallace B. Smith, great-grandson of the original founder.

The Church is currently engaged in a $50 million Temple project, involving the construction of an administrative, educational and worship center in Independence, Missouri dedicated to peace and reconciliation. The church has a world-wide membership of approximately 245,000.

HEADQUARTERS

The Auditorium, P.O. Box 1059, Independence, MO 64051 Tel. (816)833-1000 Fax (816)833-1000

Media Contact, Publ. Rel. Commissioner, Stephanie Kelley

OFFICERS

First Presidency: Wallace B. Smith; Counselor, Howard S. Sheehy, Jr.; Counselor, W. Grant McMurray

Council of 12 Apostles, Pres., Geoffrey F. Spencer

Presiding Bishopric: Presiding Bishop, Norman E. Swails; Counselor, Larry R. Norris; Counselor, Dennis D. Piepergerdes

Presiding Evangelist, Paul W. Booth

World Church Sec., A. Bruce Lindgren

Public Relations, Stephanie Kelley

PERIODICALS

Saints Herald; Restoration Witness

The Roman Catholic Church

The largest single body of Christians in the United States, the Roman Catholic Church, is under the spiritual leadership of His Holiness the Pope. Its establishment in America dates back to the priests who accompanied Columbus on his second voyage to the New World. A settlement, later discontinued, was made at St. Augustine, Fla. The continuous history of this Church in the Colonies began at St. Mary's in Maryland, in 1634.

(The following information has been furnished by the editor of The Official Catholic Directory, published by P. J. Kenedy & Sons, 3004 Glenview Rd., Wilmette, IL 60091. Reference to this complete volume will provide additional information.)

INTERNATIONAL ORGANIZATION

His Holiness the Pope, Bishop of Rome, Vicar of Jesus Christ, Supreme Pontiff of the Catholic Church.

Pope John Paul II, Karol Wojtyla (born May 18, 1920; installed Oct. 22, 1978)

APOSTOLIC PRO NUNCIO TO THE UNITED STATES

Archbishop Agostino Cacciavillan, 3339 Massachusetts Ave., N.W., Washington, DC 20008. Tel. (202)333-7121

U.S. ORGANIZATION

National Conference of Catholic Bishops, 3211 Fourth St., Washington, DC 20017. Tel. (202)541-3000; Fax (202)541-3088

The National Conference of Catholic Bishops (NCCB) is a canonical entity operating in accord-

ance with the Vatican II Decree, **Christus Dominus.** Its purpose is to foster the Church's mission to mankind by providing the Bishops of this country with an opportunity to exchange views and insights of prudence and experience and to exercise in a joint manner their pastoral office.
Pres., Archbishop Daniel Pilarczyk
Vice-Pres., Archbishop William H. Keeler
Treas., Archbishop Daniel Kucera
Sec., Bishop Raymond W. Lessard

GENERAL SECRETARIAT
Gen. Sec., Rev. Msgr. Robert N. Lynch
Assoc. Gen. Sec., Francis X. Doyle, Sr. Sharon A. Euart, R.S.M.
Sec. for Communication, Richard Daw

COMMITTEES
Ecumenical and Interreligious Affairs (Ecumenism): Chmn., Archbishop J. Francis Stafford
Secretariat: Exec. Dir., Rev. John Hotchkin
Assoc. Dir., Bro. Jeffrey Gros
Liturgy:
Chmn., Bishop Joseph Delaney
Secretariat: Dir., Rev. Ronald Krisman, Assoc. Dir., Rev. Msgr. Alan Detscher; Rev. Kenneth F. Jenkins
Priestly Formation: Chpsn., Bishop James P. Kelcher
Staff: Exec. Dir., Rev. Howard Bleichner, S.S.
Permanent Diaconate:
Chmn., Archbishop Patrick F. Flores
Secretariat: Exec. Dir., Deacon Constantino J. Ferriola, Jr.
Priestly Life and Ministry:
Chmn., Bishop Doanld W. Wuerl
Secretariat: Exec. Dir., Rev. David E. Brinkmoeller
Pro-Life Activities:
Chmn., John Cardinal O'Connor
Secretariat: Dir., Rev. John W. Gouldrick, C.M.
United States Catholic Conference,«MDNM» 3211 Fourth St., Washington, DC 20017, Tel. (202)541-3000
The United States Catholic Conference (USCC) is a civil entity of the American Catholic Bishops assisting them in their service to the Church in this country by uniting the people of God where voluntary, collective action on a broad diocesan level is needed. The USCC provides an organization structure and the resources needed to insure coordination, cooperation, and assistance in the public, educational, and social concerns of the church at the national, regional, state, interdiocesan and, as appropriate, diocesan levels.

OFFICERS
Pres., Archbishop Daniel E. Pilarczyk
Vice-Pres., Archbishop William H. Keeler
Treas., Archbishop Daniel Kucera
Sec., Bishop Raymond W. Lessard

GENERAL SECRETARIAT
Gen. Sec., Rev. Robert Lynch
Assoc. Gen. Sec., Rev. Donald Heintschel, Francis X. Doyle, Jr., Sr. Sharon Euart, R.S.M.
Sec. for Communications, Richard W. Daw

STAFF OFFICES
Finance, Dir., Sister Frances A. Mlocek, I.H.M.
Accounting, Kenneth Korotky
Human Resources, Dir., Thomas Meehan
Office of Publishing and Promotion Services, Dir., Dan Juday
General Counsel, Mark E. Chopko
Government Liaison, Dir., Frank Monahan

Research, Dir., Rev. Eugene Hemrick

COMMITTEES AND DEPARTMENTS
Communication: Chmn., Edward J. O'Donnell; Sec., Richard W. Daw; National Catholic News Services Thomas N. Lorsung, Dir. & Ed.-in-Chief; Film and Broadcasting, Henry Herx, Dir.
Education: Chpsn., Archbishop Francis Shulte
Social Development and World Peace: Chmn., Bishop Joseph M. Sullivan; Sec., John Carr; Domestic Social Development, Sharon Daly; Health and Welfare Issues, Rev. Fred Kammer; Rural Energy and Food Issues, Walter Grazer; Urban and Economic Issues, Thomas Schellabarger; International Justice and Peace, Robert Hennemeyer; Latin American Affairs, Thomas Quigley; African and Western European Affairs, Robert A. Dumas, Sr.; Political and Military Affairs and Human Rights, Dr. Gerard F. Powers

RELATED ORGANIZATIONS
Campaign for Human Development: Nat'l. Chmn., Bishop Joseph A. Fiorenza; Exec. Dir., Catholic Relief Services, 209 W. Fayette St., Baltimore, MD 21201 Tel. (301)625-2220. Exec. Dir., Lawrence Pezzulo

U.S.CATHOLIC BISHOPS' NATIONAL ADVISORY COUNCIL
Chmn., Elizabeth Habergerger

NATIONAL ORGANIZATIONS
Catholic Charities,-USA Exec. Dir., Rev. Thomas J. Harvey, 1319 F St., N.W., Washington, DC 20004
Conference of Major Religious Superiors of Men, Men's Institutes of the United States, Inc., Exec. Dir., Rev. Roland Faley, T.O.R., 8808 Cameron St., Silver Spring, MD 20910. Tel. (301)588-4030
Leadership Conference of Women Religious, Exec. Dir., Sr. Janet Roesener, C.S.J., 8808 Cameron St., Silver Spring, MD 20910. Tel. (301)588-4955
National Catholic Educational Association, Pres., Sr. Catherine McNamee, 1077 30th St., N.W., Suite 100, Washington, DC 20007. Tel. (202)337-6232
National Council of Catholic Laity, Pres., Thomas Simmons, 5664 Midforest Ln., Cincinnati, OH 45233. Tel. (513)922-2495
National Council of Catholic Women, Pres., Beverly Medved; Exec. Adm., Annette Kane, 1275 K. St., NW, Washington, DC 20005. Tel. (202)682-0334
National Office for Black Catholics, The Paulist Center, 3025 4th St., N.E., Washington, D.C. 20017. Tel. (202)635-1778

CATHOLIC ORGANIZATIONS WITH INDIVIDUAL I.R.S. RULINGS
Canon Law Society of America, Exec. Coord., Rev. Edward Pfnausch, Catholic University, Washington, DC 20064. Tel. (202)269-3491
National Institute for the Word of God, Exec. Dir., Rev. John Burke, O. P., 487 Michigan Ave., NE, Washington, DC 20017. Tel. (202)529-0001

ARCHDIOCESES AND DIOCESES
There follows an alphabetical listing of Archdioceses and Dioceses of The Roman Catholic Church. Each Archdiocese or Diocese contains the following informa- tion in sequence: Name of incumbent Bishop; name of Auxiliary Bishop or Bishops, and the Chancellor or Vicar General of the

Archdiocese or Diocese, or just the address and telephone number of the chancery office.

Cardinals are addressed as "His Eminence" and Archbishops and Bishops as "Most Reverend."

Albany, Bishop Howard J. Hubbard; Chancellor, Rev. Rev. Randall P. Patterson. Chancery Office, Pastoral Center, 40 N. Main Ave., Albany, NY 12203; Tel. (518) 453-6611. Fax (518)453-6793

Diocese of Alexandria, Bishop Sam G. Jacobs; Chancellor, Rev. Msgr. Joseph M. Susi. Office, 4400 Coliseum Blvd., P.O. Box 7417, Alexandria, LA 71306. Tel. (318) 445-2401

Allentown, Bishop Thomas J. Welsh; Chancellor, Rev. Joseph M. Whalen. Chancery Office, 202 N. 17th St., P.O. Box F, Allentown, PA 18105. Tel. (215)437-0755

Altoona-Johnstown, Bishop Joseph V. Adamec; Chancellor, Rev. Msgr. George B. Flinn. Chancery Office, Box 126, Logan Blvd., Hollidaysburg, PA 16648. Tel. (814)695-5579. Fax (814)695-8894

Amarillo, Bishop Leroy T. Matthiesen; Chancellor, Rev. Allen F. Bruening, OSF. Chancery Office, 1800 N. Spring St., P.O. Box 5644, Amarillo, TX 79117. Tel.(806)383-2243

Archdiocese of Anchorage, Archbishop Francis T. Hurley; Chancery Office, 225 Cordova St., P.O. Box 102239, Anchorage, AK 99510. Tel. (907)258-7898. Fax (905)279-3885

Arlington, Bishop John Richard Keating; Chancellor, Rev. Msgr. William T. Reinecke. Chancery, Ste. 704, 200 N. Glebe Rd., Arlington, VA 22203. Tel. (703) 841-2500. (703)524-5028

Archdiocese of Atlanta, Archbishop James P. Lyke, OFM; Vicar General, Edward J. Dillon. Chancery Office, 680 West Peachtree St., N.W., Atlanta, GA 30308. Tel. (404)888-7802. Fax (404)885-7494

Austin, Bishop John E. McCarthy; Vicar General, Rev. Msgr. Edward C. Matocha. Chancery Office, N. Congress and 16th, P.O. Box 13327 Capital Sta. Austin, TX 78711. Tel. (512)476-4888. (512)489-9537

Baker, Bishop Thomas J. Connolly; Chancellor, Rev. Charles T. Grant. Chancery Office, 411 S.E. Armour, Bend, OR 97702; P.O. Box 5999 Bend, OR 97708. Tel. (503)388-4004.

Archdiocese of Baltimore, Archbishop William H. Keeler; Auxiliary Bishops of Baltimore: Bishop William C. Newman, Bishop P. Francis Murphy, Bishop John H. Ricard, Chancellor, W. Francis Malooly. Chancery Office, 320 Cathedral St., Baltimore, MD 21201. Tel. (301)547-5446.

Baton Rouge, Bishop Stanley J. Ott; Chancellor, Rev. Msgr. Robert Berggreen. Chancery Office, 1800 S. Acadian Thruway, P.O. Box 2028, Baton Rouge, LA 70821. Tel. (504)387-0561. Fax (504)336-8789

Beaumont, Bishop Bernard J. Ganter; Chancellor Rev. Bennie J. Patillo. Chancery Office, 703 Archie St., P.O. Box 3948, Beaumont, TX 77704, Tel. (409)838-0451

Belleville, Bishop James P. Keleher; Chancellor, Rev. Msgr. Bernard O. Sullivan. Chancery Office, 222 S. Third St., Belleville IL 62220. Tel. (618)277-8181. Fax (618)277-0387

Biloxi, Bishop Joseph L. Howze; Chancellor, Rev. Msgr. Andrew Murray. Chancery Office, 120 Reynoir St., P.O. Box 1189, Biloxi, MS 39533. Tel. (601)374-0222. Fax (601)435-7949

Birmingham, Bishop Raymond J. Boland; Chancellor, Rev. Paul L. Rohling. Chancery Office, 8131 Fourth Ave. South, P.O. Box 12047, Birmingham, AL 35202. Tel. (205)833-0175. Fax (205)836-1910

Bismarck, Bishop John F. Kinney, Chancellor, Sr. Joanne Graham, OSB. Chancery Office, 420 Raymond St., Box 1575, Bismarck, ND 58502. Tel. (701)223-1347

Boise, Bishop Tod D. Brown; Chancellor, Deacon James Bowen; Chancery Office, Box 769, 303 Federal Way, Boise, ID 83701. Tel. (208)342-1311. Fax (208)342-0224

Archdiocese of Boston, Archbishop Bernard Cardinal Law; Auxiliary Bishops of Boston: Bishop Daniel A. Hart, Bishop Alfred C. Hughes, Bishop John J. Mulcahy, Bishop Lawrence J. Riley, Bishop Roberto O. Gonzales, OFM. Chancellor, Gerald T. Reilly. Chancery Office, 2121 Commonwealth Ave., Brighton, MA 02135. Tel. (617)254-0100. Fax (617)787-8144, 783-5642

Bridgeport, Bishop Edward M. Egan; Chancellor, Rev. Msgr. Thomas J. Driscoll. Chancery Office, 238 Jewett Ave., Bridgeport CT 06606. Tel. (203)372-4301. Fax (203)371-8698

Brooklyn, Bishop Thomas V. Daily; Auxiliary Bishops of Brooklyn: Bishop Joseph M. Sullivan, Bishop Rene A. Valero, Chancellor, Rev. Msgr. Otto L. Garcia. Chancery Office, 75 Greene Ave., Box C, Brooklyn, NY 11202. Tel. (718)638-5500. Fax (718)399-5934

Brownsville, Bishop Enrique San Pedro; Chancellor, Sr. Esther Dunegan. Chancery Office, P.O. Box 2279, Brownsville, TX 78522. Tel. (512)542-2501. (512)542-6751

Buffalo, Bishop Edward D. Head; Auxiliary Bishop of Buffalo: Bishop Edward M. Grosz; Chancellor, Rev. Msgr. Robert J. Cunningham. Chancery Office, 795 Main St., Buffalo, NY 14203. Tel. (716)847-5500. Fax (716)847-5557

Burlington, (Vacant See); Chancellor, Rev. Jay C. Haskin. Chancery Office, 351 North Ave., Burlington, VT 05401. Tel. (802)658-6110. Fax (802)658-0436

Camden, Bishop James T. McHugh; Auxiliary Bishop of Camden, Bishop James L. Schad; Chancellor, Rev. Msgr. Joseph W. Pokusa. Chancery Office, 1845 Haddon Ave., P.O. Box 709, Camden, NJ 08101. Tel. (609)756-7900. Fax (609)963-2655

Charleston, Bishop David B. Thompson; Vicar General, Rev. Msgr. Thomas R. Duffy; Chancellor for Administration, Miss Cleo C. Cantey. Chancery Office, 119 Broad St., P.O. Box 818, Charleston, SC 29402. Tel. (803)723-3488. Fax (803)724-6387

Charlotte, Bishop John F. Donoghue; Chancellor, Rev. John T. McSweeney. Chancery Office P.O. Box 36776, Charlotte, NC 28236. Tel. (704)377-6871

Cheyenne, Bishop Joseph H. Hart; Chancellor, Rev. Carl Beavers. Chancery Office, 2121 Capitol Ave., Box 426, Cheyenne, WY 82003. Tel. (307)638-1530. Fax (307)637-7936

Archdiocese of Chicago, Archbishop Joseph Cardinal Bernardin; Auxiliary Bishops of Chicago: Bishop Alfred L. Abramowicz, Bishop Wilton D. Gregory; Bishop Timothy J. Lyne, Bishop Placido Rodriquez, C.M.F.; Bishop Thad J. Jakubowski; Bishop John R. Gorman; Chancellor, Rev. Robert L. Kealy. Chancery Office, P.O. Box 1979, Chicago, IL 60690. Chancery Office, 155 E. Superior Ave., P.O. Box 1979, Chicago, IL 60611. Tel. (312)751-7999

Archdiocese of Cincinnati, Archbishop Daniel E. Pilarczyk; Auxiliary Bishop of Cincinnati: Bishop James H. Garland. Chancellor, Rev. R. Daniel Conlon. Chancery Office, 100 E. 8th St., Cincinnati, OH 45202. Tel. (513)421-3131. Fax (513)381-2242

Cleveland, Bishop Anthony M. Pilla; Auxiliary Bishops of Cleveland: Bishop A. Edward Pevec, Bishop Gilbert I. Sheldon, Bishop A. James Quinn; Chancellor, Rev. Ralph E. Wiatrowski. Chancery Office, 350 Chancery Bldg., Cathedral Square, 1027 Superior Ave., Cleveland, OH 44114. Tel. (216)696-6525. Fax (216)696-3226

Colorado Springs, Bishop Richard C. Hanifen; Chancel- lor, Rev. George V. Fagan, Chancery Office, 29 West Kiowa St., Colorado Springs, CO 80903. Tel. (719)636-2345

Columbus, Bishop James A. Griffin; Chancellor, Rev. Joseph M. Hendricks. Chancery Office, 198 E. Broad St., Columbus, OH 43215. Tel. (614)224-2251. Fax (614)224-6306

Corpus Christi, Bishop Rene H. Gracida; Chancellor, Deacon Roy M. Grassedonio. Chancery Office, 620 Lipan St., Corpus Christi, TX 78401. Tel. (512)882-6191. Fax (512)882-1018

Covington, Bishop William A. Hughes; Chancellor, Rev. Roger L. Kriege. Chancery Office, The Catholic Center, P. O. Box 18548 Erlanger, KY 41018. Tel. (606)283-6210. Fax (606)283-6334

Crookston, Bishop Victor Balke; Chancellor, Very Rev. Michael Patnode. Chancery Office, 1200 Memorial Dr., P.O. Box 610, Crookston, MN 56716. Tel. (218) 281-4533. Fax (218)281-3328

Dallas, Bishop Charles V. Grahmann; Chancellor, Rev. Msgr. Raphael Kamel. Chancery Office, 3915 Lemmon Ave., P.O. Box 190507, Dallas, TX 75219. Tel. (214) 528-2240. Fax (214)526-1743

Davenport, Bishop Gerald Francis O'Keefe; Chancellor, Rev. Msgr. Leo Feeney. Chancery Office, 2706 N. Gaines St., Davenport, IA 52804. Tel. (319)324-1911. Fax (319)324-5842

Archdiocese of Denver. Archbishop J. Francis Stafford; Chancellor, Sr. Rosemary Wilcox. Chancery Office, 200 Josephine St., Denver, CO 80206. Tel. (303) 388-4411. Fax (303)388-0517

Des Moines, Bishop William H. Bullock; Chancellor, Lawrence Breheny. Chancery Office, 818 5th Ave., P.O. Box 1816, Des Moines, IA 50306. Tel. (515) 243-7653. Fax (515)283-1982

Archdiocese of Detroit, Archbishop Adam J. Maida; Auxiliary Bishops of Detroit: Bishop Moses B. Anderson, S.S.E., Bishop Thomas J. Gumbleton, Bishop Dale J. Melczek, Bishop Walter J. Schoenherr; Chancellor, Rev. John P. Zenz. Chancery Office, 1234 Washington Blvd., Detroit, MI 48226. Tel. (313) 237-5816. Fax (313)965-3989

Dodge City, Bishop Stanley G. Schlarman; Chancellor, Rev. David H., Kraus. Chancery Office, 910 Central Ave., P.O. Box 849, Dodge City, KS 67801. Tel. (316) 227-3131. Fax (316)227-1570

Archdiocese of Dubuque, Archbishop Daniel W. Kucera; Auxiliary Bishop of Dubuque: Bishop William E. Franklin; Chancellor, Sr. Mary Kevin Gallagher, BVM. P.O. Box 479, Dubuque IA 52001. Tel. (319) 556-2580. Fax (319)588-0557

Duluth, Bishop Roger L. Schwietz; Chancellor, Edward N. Peters. Chancery Office, 2803 E. 4th St., Duluth, MN 55812. Tel. (218)727-6861. Fax (218)724-1056

El Paso, Bishop Raymundo J. Pena; Chancellor, Very Rev. John Telles. Chancery Office, 499 St. Matthews, El Paso, TX 79907. Tel. (915)595-5038. Fax (915)595-5095

Erie, Bishop Donald W. Trautman; Chancellor, Rev. Msgr. Lawrence E. Brandt. Chancery Office, P.O. Box 10397, Erie, PA 16514. Tel. (814)825-3333. Fax (814)825-4363

Evansville, Bishop Gerald A. Gettelfinger; Chancellor, Sr. Louise Bond. Chancery Office, 4200 N. Kentucky Ave., Evansville, IN 47711. Tel. (812) 424-5536. Fax (812)421-1334

Fairbanks, Bishop Michael Kaniecki, S.J.; Chancellor, Sr. Eileen Brown. Tel. (907)456-6753. Chancery Office, 1316 Peger Rd., Fairbanks, AK 99709. Tel. (907) 474-0753.

Fall River, (Vacant See); Chancellor, Rev. Msgr. John J. Oliveira. Chancery Office, 47 Underwood St., Box 2577, Fall River, MA 02722. Tel. (508) 675-1311. Fax (508)679-9220

Fargo, Bishop James S. Sullivan; Chancellor, Rev. James A. Leith. Chancery Office, 1310 Broadway, P.O. Box 1750, Fargo, ND 58107. Tel. (701)235-6429. (701)235-6429

Fort Wayne-South Bend, Bishop John M. D'Arcy; Auxiliary Bishop of Fort Wayne-South Bend: Bishop John R. Sheets. Vicar General-Chancellor, James J. Wolf, Rev. Msgr. J. William Lester. Chancery Office, 1103 S. Calhoun St., P.O. Box 390. Fort Wayne, IN 46801. Tel. (219)422-4611. Fax (219)423-3382

Fort Worth, Bishop Joseph D. Delaney; Chancellor, Rev. Robert W. Wilson. Chancery Office, 800 W. Loop 820 South, Fort Worth TX 76108. Tel. (817)560-3300

Fresno, Bishop John T. Steinbock; Chancellor, Rev. Raymond C. Dreiling. Chancery Office, P.O. Box 1668, 1550 N. Fresno St., Fresno, CA 93717. Tel. (209) 237-5125

Gallup, Bishop Donald Pelotte, SSS; Chancellor, Br. Duane Torisky. Chancery Office, 711 S. Puerco Dr., P.O. Box 1338, Gallup, NM 87301. Tel. (505)863-4406

Galveston-Houston, Bishop Joseph A. Fiorenza; Auxil- liary Bishops of Galveston-Houston: Bishop Curtis J. Guillory, SVD; Chancellor, Rev. Msgr. Daniel Scheel. Chancery Office, 1700 San Jacinto St., Houston, TX 77002. Tel. (713)659-5461. Fax (713)759-9151

Gary, Bishop Norbert F. Gaughan; Chancellor, Rev. Richard A. Emerson. Chancery Office, 9292 Broadway, Merrill- ville, IN 46410 Tel. (219)769-9292. Fax (219)738-9034

Gaylord, Bishop Patrick R. Cooney; Vicar Gen., Raymond C. Mulka. Chancery Office, 1665 West M-32, Seton Bldg., Gaylord, MI 49735. Tel. (517)732-5147. Fax (517)732-1706

Grand Island, Bishop Lawrence J. McNamara; Chancel- lor, Rev. Richard L. Piontkowski. Chancery Office, 311 W. 17th St., P.O. Box 996, Grand Island, NE 68802. Tel. (308)382-6565

Grand Rapids, Bishop Robert J. Rose; Auxiliary Bishop of Grand Rapids: Bishop Joseph McKinney; Chancellor, Sr. Patrice Konwinski. Chancery Office, 660 Burton St. S.E., Grand Rapids, MI 49507. Tel. (616)243-0491. Fax (616)243-4910

Great Falls-Billings, Bishop Anthony M. Milone; Chan- cellor, Rev. Martin J. Burke. Chancery Office, 121 23rd St. So., P.O. Box 1399, Great Falls, MT 59403. Tel. (406)727-6683. Fax (406)454-3480

Green Bay, Bishop Robert J. Banks; Auxiliary Bishop of Green Bay: Bishop Robert F. Morneau; Chancellor, Sr. Ann F. Rehrauer, OSF. Chancery Office, Box 20366, Green Bay, WI 54305. Tel. (414)435-4406. Fax (414)435-1330

Greensburg, Bishop Anthony G. Bosco; Chancellor, Rev. Lawrence T. Persico. Chancery Office, 723 E. Pitts- burgh St., Greensburg, PA 15601. Tel. (412)837-0901

Harrisburg, Bishop Nicholas C. Dattilo; Chancellor, Carol Houghton. Chancery Office, P.O. Box 2153, 4800 Union Deposit Rd., Harrisburg, PA 17105. Tel. (717) 657-4804

Archdiocese of Hartford, Archbishop Daniel A. Cronin; Auxiliary Bishops of Hartford: Bishop Peter A. Rosazza, Bishop Paul S. Loverde. Chancellor, Sr. Marie Margaret Feeney, C.S.J. Chancery Office, 134 Farmington Ave., Hartford, CT 06105. Tel. (203) 527-4201. Fax (203)525-2037

Helena, Bishop Elden F. Curtiss; Chancellor, Rev. John W. Robertson. Chancery Office, 515 N. Ewing, P.O. Box 1729, Helena, MT 59624. Tel. (406)442-5820. Fax (406)442-5191

Honolulu, Bishop Joseph A. Ferrario; Chancellor, Sr. Grace Dorothy Lim, MM. Chancery Office, 1184 Bishop St., Honolulu, HI 96813. Tel. (808)533-1791. Fax (808)521-8428

Houma-Thibodaux, Bishop Warren L. Boudreaux; Chan- cellor, Rev. Msgr. James B. Songy. Chancery Office, P.O. Box 9077, Houma, LA 70361. Tel. (504)868-7720. Fax (504)868-7727

Archdiocese of Indianapolis, Archbishop Edward T. O'Meara; Chancellor, Susan L. Magnant. Chancery Office, 1400 N. Meridian St., P.O. Box 1410, Indianap- olis, IN 46206. Tel. (317)236-1405. Fax (317)236-1406

Jackson, Bishop William R. Houck; Vicar General-Chancellor, Rev. Francis J. Cosgrove. Chancery Office, 237 E. Amite St., P.O. Box 2248, Jackson, MS 39225. Tel. (601)969-1880. Fax (601)960-8455

Jefferson City, Bishop Michael F. McAuliffe; Chancellor, Sr. Mary Margaret Johanning. Chancery Office, 605 Clark Ave., P.O. Box 417, Jefferson City, MO 65102. Tel. (314)635-9127. Fax (314)635-2286

Joliet, Bishop Joseph L. Imesch; Auxiliary Bishop of Joliet: Bishop Roger L. Kaffer; Chancellor, Sr. Judith Davies. Chancery Office, 425 Summit St., Joliet, IL 60435. Tel. (815) 722-6606. Fax (815)722-6602

Juneau, Bishop Michael H. Kenny; Vicar General, Rev. Msgr. James F. Miller. Chancery Office, 419 6th St. Juneau, AK 99801. Tel. (907)586-2227

Kalamazoo, Bishop Paul V. Donovan; Chancellor, Rev. Msgr. Dell F. Stewart. Chancery Office, P.O. Box 949, 215 N. Westnedge Ave., Kalamazoo, MI 49005. Tel. (616)349-8714. Fax (616)349-6440

Archdiocese of Kansas City in Kansas, Archbishop Ignatius J. Strecker; Auxiliary Bishop of Kansas City in Kansas: Bishop Marion F. Forst; Chancellor, Rev. Msgr. William T. Curtin. Chancery Office, 12615 Parallel, KS 66109, Tel. (913) 721-1570

Kansas City-St. Joseph, Bishop John J. Sullivan; Chan- cellor, Rev. Richard F. Carney. Chancery Office, P.O. Box 419037, Kansas City, MO 64141. Tel. (816) 756-1850. (816)756-0878

Knoxville, Bishop Anthony J. O'Connell; Vicar General/ Chancellor, Rev. Xavier Mankel. Chancery Office, 417 Erin Drive, Knoxville, TN 37919. Tel. (615)584-3307.

La Crosse, Bishop John J. Paul; Chancellor, Rev. Michael J. Gorman, Chancery Office. 3710 East Ave., La Crosse, WI 54602. Tel. (608)788-7700. Fax (608)788-8413

Lafayette in Indiana, Bishop William L. Higi; Chancellor, Rev. Robert L. Sell. Chancery Office, P. O. Box 260, 610 Lingle Ave., Lafayette, IN 47902. Tel. (317) 742-0275

Lafayette (Louisiana), Bishop Harry J. Flynn; Chancellor, Sr. Joanna Valoni, SSND. Chancery Office, Diocesan Office Bldg., 1408 Carmel Ave., Lafayette, LA 70501. Tel. (318)261-5500

Lake Charles, Bishop Jude Speyrer; Chancellor Deacon George Stearns. Chancery Office, 414 Iris St., P.O. Box 3223, Lake Charles, LA 70602. Tel. (318) 439-7404. (318)439-7413

Lansing, Bishop Kenneth J. Povish; Chancellor, Rev. James Murray. Chancery Office, 300 W. Ottawa, Lansing, MI 48933. Tel. (517)342-2440. Fax (517)342-2515

Las Cruces, Bishop Ricardo Ramirez; CSB; Chancellor, Sr. Mary Ellen Quinn. Chancery Office, P.O. Box 16318, Las Cruces, NM 88004. Tel. (505)523-7577. Fax (505)524-3874

Lexington, Bishop James K. Williams; Chancellor, Sr. Mary Kevan Seibert, SND. Chancery Office, P. O. Box 12350. Erlanger, KY 41018. Tel. (606)283-6200. Fax (606)254-6284

Lincoln, Bishop Glennon P. Flavin; Chancellor, Rev. Msgr. Thomas M. Kealy. Chancery Office, 3400 Sheridan Blvd., P.O. Box 80328, Lincoln, NE 68501. Tel. (402)488-0921

Little Rock, Bishop Andrew J. McDonald; Chancellor, Francis I. Malone. Chancery Office, 2415 N. Tyler St., P.O. Box 7239, Little Rock, AR 72217. Tel. (501) 664-0340

Archdiocese of Los Angeles, Archbishop Roger M. Mahony; Auxiliary Bishops of Los Angeles: Bishop Juan Arzube, Bishop John J. Ward, Bishop Carl Fisher, S.S.J., Bishop Armando Ochoa, Bishop Patrick Zie- mann, Bishop Stephen E. Blaire; Chancellor, Bishop Stephen E. Blaire. Chancery Office, 1531 W. Ninth St., Los Angeles, CA 90015. Tel. (213) 251-3200. Fax (213)251-2607

Archdiocese of Louisville, Archbishop Thomas C. Kelly, OP; Chancellor, Very Rev. Bernard J. Breen. P.O. Box 1073, Louisville, KY 40201. Chancery Office, 212 E. College St., Louisville, KY 40201. Tel. (502) 585-3291

Lubbock, Bishop Michael Sheehan; Chancellor, Sr. Elena Gonzalez, RSM. Chancery Office. 4620 4th St., P.O. Box 98700, Lubbock, TX 79499-8700. Tel. (806)792-3943

Madison, Bishop Cletus F. O'Donnell; Auxiliary Bishop of Madison: Bishop George O. Wirz; Chancellor, Rev. Joseph P. Higgins. Chancery Office, 15 E. Wilson St., Box 111, Madison, WI 53701. Tel. (608)256-2677

Manchester, Bishop Leo Edward O'Neil; Chancellor Rev. Msgr. Francis J. Christian. Chancery Office, 153 Ash St., P.O. Box 310, Manchester, NH 03105. Tel. (603)669-3100 Fax (603)669-0377

Marquette, Bishop Mark F. Schmitt; Chancellor, Rev. Peter Oberto. Chancery Office, 444 S. Fourth St., P.O. Box 550, Marquette, MI 49855. Tel. (906) 225-1141. Fax (906)225-0437

Memphis, Bishop Daniel Mark Buechlein, OSB.; Chancellor, Rev. J. Peter Sartain. Chancery Office, 1325 Jefferson Ave., P.O. Box 41679, Memphis, TN 38174. Tel. (901)722-4737. Fax (901)722-4769

Metuchen, Bishop Edward Hughes; Chancellor, Sr. M. Michaelita Wiechetek, CSSF. Chancery Office, P.O. Box 191, Metuchen, NJ 08840. Tel. (201)283-3800. Fax (908)283-2012

Archdiocese of Miami, Archbishop Edward A. McCarthy; Auxiliary Bishop of Miami: Bishop Agustin A. Roman; Chancellor, Very Rev. Gerard T. LaCerra. Chancery Office, 9401 Biscayne Blvd., Miami Shores, FL 33138. Tel. (305)757-6241. Fax (305) 754-1797.

Archdiocese for the Military Services, Bishop Joseph T. Dimino; Auxiliary Bishops: Bishop Francis X. Roque, Bishop John G. Nolan, Bishop Joseph J. Madera, Bishop John J. Glynn; Chancellor, Bishop John Glynn. Chancery Office, 962 Wayne Ave., Silver Spring, MD 20910. Tel. (301)495-4100. Fax (301)589-3774

Archdiocese of Milwaukee, Archbishop Rembert G. Weakland, OSB; Auxiliary Bishop of Milwaukee: Bishop Richard J. Sklba; Chancellor, Rev. Ralph C. Gross. Chancery Office, 3501 S. Lake Dr., P.O. Box 07912, Milwaukee, WI 53207. Tel. (414)769-3340. Fax (414)769-3408

Archdiocese of Mobile, Archbishop Oscar H. Lipscomb; Chancellor, Very Rev. G. Warren Wall. Chancery Office, 400 Government St., P.O. Box 1966, Mobile, AL 36633. Tel. (205)433-2241. Fax (205) 434-1588

Monterey, (Vacant See); Chancellor, Rev. Msgr. D. Declan Murphy. Chancery Office, 580 Fremont St., P.O. Box 2048, Monterey, CA 93940. Tel. (408) 373-4345. Fax (408)373-1175

Nashville, Bishop James D. Niedergeses; Chancellor, Rev. J. Patrick Connor. Chancery Office, 2400 21st Ave., S., Nashville, TN 37212. Tel. (615)383-6393. Fax (615)292-8411

Archdiocese of Newark, Archbishop Theodore E. McCarrick; Auxiliary Bishops of Newark: Bishop David Arias, OAR, Bishop Joseph Francis, SVD, Bishop Robert F. Garner, Bishop Dominic A. Marconi, Bishop Michael A. Salterelli; Chancellor, Sr. Thomas Mary Salerno, SC. Chancery Office, 31 Mulberry St., Newark, NJ 07102. Tel. (201)596-4000. Fax (201)596-3763

Archdiocese of New Orleans, Archbishop Francis B. Schulte; Auxiliary Bishops of New Orleans: Bishop Nicholas D'Antonio, OFM, SVD; Bishop Robert W. Muench; Chancellor, Rev. Msgr. Earl C. Woods. Chancery Office, 7887 Walmsley Ave., New Orleans, LA 70125. Tel. (504) 861-9521. Fax (504)866-2906

Melkite Diocese of Newton, Bishop Ignatius Ghattas; Auxiliary Bishops of Newton: Bishop John A. Elya, Bishop Nicholas J. Samra. Chancellor, Very Rev. James E. King. Chancery Office, 19 Dartmouth St., West Newton, MA 02165. Tel. (617)969-8957. Fax (617)969-4115

New Ulm, Bishop Raymond A. Lucker; Chancellor, Rev. Dennis C. Labat. Chancery Office, 1400 Sixth North St., New Ulm, MN 56073. Tel. (507)359-2966

Archdiocese of New York, Archbishop John Cardinal O'Connor; Auxiliary Bishops of New York: Bishop Patrick V. Ahern, Bishop Francis Garmendia, Bishop James P. Mahoney, Bishop Emerson J. Moore, Bishop Austin B. Vaughan, Bishop Anthony F. Mestice, Bishop William J. McCormack, Bishop Patrick J. Sheridan. Chancellor, Rev. Msgr. Henry Mansell. Chancery Office, 1011 First Ave., New York, NY 10022. Tel. (212)371-1000. Fax (212)319-8265

Norwich, Bishop Daniel P. Reilly; Chancellor, Rev. Robert L. Brown. Chancery Office, 201 Broadway, P.O. Box 587, Norwich, CT 06360. Tel. (203)887-9294. Fax (203)886-1670

Oakland, Bishop John S. Cummins; Chancellor, Rev. Raymond Breton. Chancery Office, 2900 Lakeshore Ave., Oakland, CA 94610. Tel. (415)893-4711. Fax (415)893-0945

Ogdensburg, Bishop Stanislaus J. Brzana; Chancellor, Rev. Robert H. Aucoin. Chancery Office, Box 369, 622 Washington St., Ogdensburg, NY 13669. Tel. (315) 393-2920

Archdiocese of Oklahoma City, Archbishop Charles A. Salatka; Chancellor, Rev. John A. Steichen. Chancery Office, 7501 Northwest Expressway, P.O. Box 32180, Oklahoma City, OK 73123. Tel. (405)721-5651. Fax (405)721-5210

Archdiocese of Omaha, Archbishop Daniel E. Sheehan; Chancellor, Rev. Eldon J. McKamy. Chancery Office, 100 N. 62nd St., Omaha, NE 68132. Tel. (402)558-3100

Orange, Bishop Norman F. McFarland; Auxiliary Bishop: Michael P. Driscoll; Chancellor, Rev. John Urell. Chancery Office, 2811 Villa Real Dr., Orange, CA 92667. Tel. (714)974-7120

Orlando, Bishop Norbert M. Dorsey; Chancellor, Sr. Lucy Vazquez. Chancery Office, 421 E. Robinson, P.O. Box 1800, Orlando, FL 32802. Tel. (305)425-3556. Fax (407)649-7846

Owensboro, Bishop John J. McRaith; Chancellor, Sr. Joseph Angela Boone. Chancery Office, 600 Locust St., Owensboro, KY 42301. Tel. (502)683-1545. Fax (502)683-6883

Palm Beach, Bishop J. Keith Symons; Chancellor, Rev. Charles Hawkins. Chancery Office, 9995 N. Military Trail, Bldg. C #201, Palm Beach Gardens, FL 33410. Tel. (407)775-9500. Fax (407)775-9556

Byzantine Eparchy of Parma, Bishop Andrew Pataki; Chancellor, Rev. Emil Masich. Chancery Office, 1900 Carlton Rd., Parma, OH 44134. Tel. (216)741-8773. Fax (216)741-9356

Byzantine Diocese of Passaic, Bishop Michael J. Dudick; Chancellor, Rev. Msgr. Raymond Misulich. Chancery Office, 445 Lackawanna Ave., West Paterson, NJ 07424. Tel. (201)890-7777. Fax (201)890-7175

Paterson, Bishop Frank J. Rodimer; Chancellor, Rev. Msgr. Herbert K. Tillyer. Chancery Office, 777 Valley Rd., Clifton, NJ 07013. Tel. (201)777-8818. Fax (201)777-8976

Pensacola-Tallahassee, Bishop John M. Smith; Chancellor, Rev. Msgr. James Amos. Chancery Office, 11 N. "B" St., Pensacola, FL 32501. Tel. (904)432-1515. Fax (904)469-8176

Peoria, Bishop John J. Myers; Chancellor, Rev. James F. Campbell. Chancery Office, P.O. Box 1406, 607 NE Madison Ave., Peoria, IL 61655. Tel. (309)671-1550. Fax (309)671-5079

Archdiocese of Philadelphia, Archbishop Anthony Cardinal Bevilacqua; Auxiliary Bishops of Philadelphia: Bishop Louis A. DeSimone, Bishop Martin N. Lohmuller; Chancellor, Rev. Msgr. Joseph A. Pepe. Chancery Office, 222 N. 17th St. Philadelphia, PA 19103. Tel. (215)587-4538. Fax (215)587-4545

Archdiocese of Philadelphia, Ukrainian, Archbishop Stephen Sulyk; Chancellor, Sr. Thomas Hrynewich, SSMI. Chancery Office, 827 N. Franklin St., Philadelphia, PA 19123. Tel. (215)627-0143. Fax (215)627-0377

Phoenix, Bishop Thomas J. O'Brien; Chancellor, Rev. Timothy R. Davern. Chancery Office, 400 E. Monroe St., Phoenix, AZ 85004. Tel. (602)257-0030. Fax (602)258-3425

Pittsburgh, Bishop Donald W. Wuerl; Auxiliary Bishop of Pittsburgh: Bishop John B. McDowell, Bishop William J. Winter. Chancellor, Rev. Lawrence A. DiNardo. Chancery Office, 111 Blvd. of Allies, Pittsburgh, PA 15222. Tel. (412)456-3000

Archdiocese of Pittsburgh, Byzantine Rite, Archbishop Thomas V. Dolinay; Auxiliary Bishop of Pittsburgh, Byzantine: Bishop John M. Bilock; Chancellor. Rev. Msgr. Raymond Balta. Chancery Office, 54 Riverview Ave., Pittsburgh, PA 15214. Tel. (412)322-7300. Fax (412)322-9935

Portland, Bishop Joseph J. Gerry; Auxiliary Bishop of Portland: Bishop Amedee Proulx; Co-Chancellors, Rev.Michael J. Henchal, Sr. Rita-Mae Bissonnette. Chancery Office, 510 Ocean Ave., P.O. Box 6750, Portland, ME 04101-6750. Tel.(207)773-6471. Fax (207)773-0182

Archdiocese of Portland in Oregon, Archbishop William J. Levada; Auxiliary Bishops of Portland in Oregon: Bishop Kenneth Steiner, Bishop Paul Waldschmidt, CSC; Chancellor, Mary Jo Tully. Chancery Office, 2838 E. Burnside St., Portland, OR 97214-1895. Tel. (503)234-5334. Fax 503-234-2545

Providence, Bishop Louis E. Gelineau; Auxiliary Bishop of Providence: Bishop Kenneth A. Angell; Chancellor, Rev. Msgr. William I. Varsanyi. Chancery Office, 1 Cathedral Square, Providence, RI 02903-3695. Tel. (401) 278-4500. Fax (401)278-4548

Pueblo, Bishop Arthur N. Tafoya; Chancellor, Rev. Edward H. Nunez. Chancery Office, 1001 N. Grand Ave., Pueblo, CO 81003. Tel. (303)544-9861

Raleigh, Bishop F. Joseph Gossman; Chancellor, Rev. Joseph G. Vetter. Chancery Office, 300 Cardinal Gibbons Dr., Raleigh, NC 27606. Tel. (919)821-9700. Fax (919)821-9705

Rapid City, Bishop Charles J. Chaput, OFM Cap.; Chancellor, Sr. M. Celine Erk. Chancery Office, 606 Cathedral Dr., P.O. Box 678, Rapid City, SD 57709. Tel. (605)343-3541. Fax (605)345-7985

Reno-Las Vegas, Bishop Daniel F. Walsh; Chancellor, Rev. Anthony Vercellone, Jr. Chancery Office, 515 Court St., Reno, NV 89501. Tel. (702)329-9274. Fax (702)873-4946

Richmond, Bishop Walter F. Sullivan; Auxiliary Bishop of Richmond: Bishop David E. Foley; Chancellor, Bishop David E. Foley. Chancery Office, 811 Cathedral Pl., Suite C, Richmond, VA 23220-4898. Tel. (804)359-5661. Fax 358-9159

Rochester, Bishop Matthew H. Clark; Chancellor, (Vacant). Chancery Office, 1150 Buffalo Rd., Rochester, NY 14624-1890. Tel. (716)328-3210. Fax (716)328-3149

Rockford, Bishop Arthur J. O'Neill; Chancellor, Very Rev. Charles W. McNamee. Chancery Office, 1245 N. Court St., Rockford, IL 61103 Tel. (815)962-3709. Fax (815)968-2824

Rockville Centre, Bishop John R. McGann; Auxiliary Bishops of Rockville Centre: Bishop James J. Daly, Bishop Alfred J. Markiewicz, Bishop Emil A. Wcela, Bishop John C. Dunne; Chancellor, Rev. Msgr. John A. Alesandro. Chancery Office, 50 N. Park Ave. Rockville Centre, NY 11570. Tel. (516)678-5800. Fax (516)678-1786

Sacramento, Bishop Francis A. Quinn; Chancellor, Sr. Bridget Mary Flynn, SM. Chancery Office, 1119 K St., P.O. Box 1706, Sacramento, CA 95812-1706. Tel. (916)443-1996 Fax (916)4436-4990

Saginaw, Bishop Kenneth E. Untener; Chancellor, Rev. Msgr. Thomas P. Schroeder. Chancery Office, 5800 Weiss St., Saginaw, MI 48603. Tel. (517)799-7910

St. Augustine, Bishop John J. Snyder; Chancellor, Rev. Msgr. Eugene C. Kohls. Chancery Office, 11625 Old St. Augustine Road, P.O. Box 24000, Jacksonville, FL 32241. Tel. (904)262-3200. Fax (904)262-0698

St. Cloud, Bishop Jerome Hanus, OSB; Chancellor, Rev. Severin Schwieters. Chancery Office, P.O. Box 1248, 214 Third Ave. S., St. Cloud, MN 56302. Tel. (612)251-2340

St. Josaphat in Parma, Ukrainian Bishop Robert M. Moskal; Chancellor, Rev. Msgr. Thomas A. Sayuk. Chancery Office 5720 State Rd., P.O. Box 347180, Parma, OH 44134. Tel. (216)888-1522. Fax (216)888-3477

Archdiocese of St. Louis, Archbishop John L. May; Auxiliary Bishops of St. Louis: Bishop Charles R. Koester, Bishop Edward J. O'Donnell, Bishop J. Terry Steib, Bishop Paul A. Zipfel; Chancellor, Rev. George J. Lucas. Chancery Office, 4445 Lindell Blvd., St. Louis, MO 63108. Tel. (314)533-1887. Fax (314)533-1887 (Station 212)

St. Maron of Brooklyn, Bishop Francis M. Zayek: Auxiliary Bishop of St. Maron: Bishop John G. Chedid; Chancellor, Rev. John D. Faris. Chancery Office, 8120 15th Ave., Brooklyn, NY 11228. Tel. (718)259-9200. Fax (718)259-8968

St. Nicholas in Chicago for Ukrainians, Bishop Innocent Lotocky, OSBM; Chancellor, Sonia Ann Peczeniuk. Chancery Office, 2245 W. Rice St., Chicago, IL 60622. Tel. (312)276-5080. Fax (312)276-6799

Archdiocese of St. Paul and Minneapolis, Archbishop John R. Roach; Auxiliary Bishops of St. Paul-Minneapolis: Bishop Robert J. Carlson, Bishop Joseph J. Charron, Bishop Lwarence H. Welsh; Chancellor, Rev. Thomas V. Vowell. Chancery Office, 226 Summit Ave., St. Paul, MN 55102. Tel. (612)291-4400. Fax (612)290-1629

St. Petersburg, Bishop John C. Favalora; Chancellor, Very Rev. Robert Sherman. Chancery Office, 6363 9th Ave. N., P.O. Box 40200. St. Petersburg, FL 33743. Tel. (813)344-1611. Fax (813)345-2143

Salina, Bishop George K. Fitzsimons; Chancellor, Rev. Msgr. James E. Hake. Chancery Office, 103 N. 9th, P.O. Box 980, Salina, KS 67402. Tel. (913)827-8746. Fax (913)827-8746

Salt Lake City, Bishop William K. Weigand; Chancellor, Deacon Silvio Mayo. Chancery Office, 27 C. St., Salt Lake City, UT 84103. Tel. (801)328-8641. Fax (801)328-9680

San Angelo, Bishop Michael Pfeifer, OMI; Chancellor, Rev. Msgr. Larry J. Droll. Chancery Office, 804 Ford, Box 1829, San Angelo, TX 76902. Tel. (915)653-2466.

Archdiocese of San Antonio, Archbishop Patrick F. Flores; Auxiliary Bishops of San Antonio: Bishop Bernard F. Popp, Bishop Edmund Carmody. Chancel- lor, Rev. Msgr. Patrick J. Murray, Chancery Office, 2718 W. Woodlawn Ave., P.O. Box 28410, San Antonio, TX 78228. Tel. (512)734-2620. Fax (512)734-2774

San Bernardino, Bishop Phillip F. Straling; Chancellor, Sr. Maura Feeley. Chancery Office, 1450 North D St., San Bernardino, CA 92405 Tel. (714)384-8200. Fax (714)884-4890

San Diego, Bishop Robert Brom; Auxiliary Bishop of San Diego: Bishop Gilbert E. Chavez; Chancellor, Rev. Msgr. Daniel J. Dillabough. Chancery Office, Alcala Park, P.O. Box 85728, San Diego, CA 92186-5728. Tel. (619)574-6300. Fax (619)574-0962

Archdiocese of San Francisco, Archbishop John R. Quinn; Auxiliary Bishops of San Francisco: Bishop Carlos A. Sevilla, Bishop Patrick J. McGrath. Chancel- lor, Sr. Mary B. Flaherty, RSCJ. Chancery Office, 445 Church St., San Francisco, CA 94114. Tel. (415) 565-3600. Fax (415)565-3633

San Jose, Bishop Pierre DuMaine; Chancellor, Sr. Patricia Marie Mulpeters, PBVM. Chancery Office, 841 Lenzen Ave., San Jose, CA 95126-2700. Tel. (408)925-0181

Archdiocese of Santa Fe, Archbishop Robert F. Sanchez; Chancellor, Rev. Richard Olona. Chancery Office, 4000 St. Joseph Place, N.W. Albuquerque, NM 87120. Tel. (505)831-8100

Santa Rosa, (Vacant See); Chancellor, Rev. Msgr. James E. Pulskamp. Chancery Office, 547 "B" St., P.O. Box 1297, Santa Rosa, CA 95402. Tel. (707) 545-7610. Fax (707)542-9702

Savannah, Bishop Raymond W. Lessard; Chancellor, Rev. Jeremiah J. McCarthy. Chancery Office, 601 E. Liberty St., Savannah, GA 31401-5196. Tel. (912)238-2320 (912)238-2335

Scranton, Bishop James C. Timlin; Auxiliary Bishop of Scranton: Bishop Francis X. DiLorenzo; Chancellor, Rev. Neil J. Van Loon. Chancery Office, 300 Wyoming Ave., Scranton, PA 18503. Tel. (717)346-8910

Archdiocese of Seattle, Archbishop Thomas J. Murphy; Chancellor, Very Rev. George L. Thomas. Chancery Office, 910 Marion St., Seattle, WA 98104. Tel. (206)382-4560. Fax (206)382-4840

Shreveport, Bishop William B. Friend; Chancellor, Sr. Margaret Daues, CSJ, 2500 Line Ave., Shreveport, LA 71104. Tel. (318)222-2006. Fax (318)222-2080

Sioux City, Bishop Lawrence D. Soens; Chancellor, Rev. Kevin C. McCoy. Chancery Office, 1821 Jackson St., P.O. Box 3379, Sioux City, IA 51102. Tel. (712)255-7933

Sioux Falls, Bishop Paul V. Dudley; Chancellor, Rev. Gregory Tschakert. Chancery Office, 609 W. 5th St., Box 5033, Sioux Falls, SD 57117. Tel. (605)334-9861. Fax (605)334-2092

Spokane, Bishop William Skylstad; Chancellor, Rev. Mark Pautler. Chancery Office, 1023 W. Riverside Ave., P.O. Box 1453, Spokane, WA 99201. Tel. (509)456-7100

Springfield-Cape Girardeau, Bishop John J. Leibrecht; Chancellor, Rev. Msgr. Thomas E. Reidy. Chancery Office, 601 South Jefferson, Springfield, MO 65806-3107. Tel. (417)866-0841. Fax (417)866-1140

Springfield in Illinois, Bishop Daniel L. Ryan; Vicar Gen., Rev. John Renken. Chancery Office, 1615 W. Washing- ton, P.O. Box 3187, Springfield, IL 62708. Tel. (217)698-8500. Fax (217)698-8620

Springfield in Massachusetts, Bishop John A. Marshall; Auxiliary Bishop of Springfield: Bishop Thomas L. Dupre, Chancellor, Bishop Thomas L. Dupre. Chancery Office, 76 Elliot St., P.O. Box 1730, Springfield, MA 01101. Tel. (413) 732-3175. Fax (413)737-2337

Stamford, Ukrainian Byzantine, Bishop Basil H. Losten; Chancellor, Rt. Rev. Mitred Matthew Berko. Chancery Office, 161 Glenbrook Rd., Stamford, CT 06902-3092. Tel. (203)324-7698. Fax (203)967-9948

Steubenville, Bishop Albert H. Ottenweller; Chancellor, Linda A. Nichols. Chancery Office, 422 Washing- ton St., P.O. Box 969, Steubenville, OH 43952. Tel. (614)282-3631. Fax (614)282-3327

Stockton, Bishop Donald W. Montrose; Chancellor, Rev. Richard J. Ryan. Chancery Office, 1105 N. Lincoln St., P.O. Box 4237, Stockton, CA 95204-0237. Tel. (209)466-0636. Fax (209)941-9722

Superior, Bishop Raphael M. Fliss; Chancellor, Rev. James F. Tobolski. Chancery Office, 1201 Hughitt Ave., Box 969, Superior, WI 54880. Tel. (715)392-2937

Syracuse, Bishop Joseph T. O'Keefe; Auxiliary Bishop of Syracuse: Bishop Thomas J. Costello; Co-Chancellors, Rev. David W. Barry, Rev. Richard M. Kopp. Chancery Office, 240 E. Onandaga St., P.O. Box 511, Syracuse, NY 13201. Tel. (315)422-7203. Fax (315)478-4619

Toledo, Bishop James R. Hoffman; Auxiliary Bishop of Toledo: Bishop Robert W. Donnelly. Chancery Office, 1933 Spielbush, P.O. Box 985, Toledo, OH 43624. Tel. (419)244-6711. Fax (419)244-4791

Trenton, Bishop John C. Reiss; Auxiliary Bishop of Trenton: Bishop Edward U. Kmiec; Chancellor, Rev. Msgr. William F. Fitzgerald. Chancery Office, 701 Lawrenceville Road, P.O. Box 5309, Trenton, NJ 08638. Tel. (609)882-7125. Fax (609)771-6793

Tucson, Bishop Manuel D. Moreno; Chancellor, Rev. John F. Allt. Chancery Office, 192 S. Stone Ave., Box 31, Tucson, AZ 85702. Tel. (602)792-3410

Tulsa, Bishop Eusebius J. Beltran. Chancellor, Rev. Patrick J. Gaalaas. Chancery Office, 820 S. Boulder St., P.O. Box 2009, Tulsa, OK 74101. Tel. (918)587-3115

Tyler, (Vacant See); Vicar General, Rev. Msgr. Milam J. Joseph. Chancery Office, 1920 Sybil Lane, Tyler, TX 75703. Tel. (214)534-1077. Fax (903)534-1370

Van Nuys Eparchy, Byzantine Rite, Bishop George M. Kuzma; Chancellor, Rev. Msgr. Michael Moran. Chancery Office, 18024 Parthenia St., Northridge, CA 91325. Tel. (818)701-6114. Fax (818)701-6116

Venice, Bishop John J. Nevins; Chancellor, Very Rev. Jerome A. Carosella. Chancery Office, 1000 Pinebrook Rd., P.O. Box 2006, Venice, FL 34284. Tel. (813)484-9543. Fax (813)484-1121

Victoria, Bishop David E. Fellhauer; Chancellor, Rev. Msgr. Thomas C. McLaughlin. Chancery Office, 1505 E. Mesquite Lane, P.O. Box 4708, Victoria, TX 77903. Tel. (512)573-0828. Fax (512)573-5725

Archdiocese of Washington, Archbishop James Cardinal Hickey; Auxiliary Bishops of Washington: Bishop Alvaro Corrada, SJ; Bishop Leonard J. Oliver; Bishop William C. Curlin; Chancellor, Rev. William J. Kane. Chancery Office, 5001 Eastern Ave., P.O. Box 29260, NW, Washington, DC 20017. Tel. (301)853-3800. Fax (301)853-3246

Wheeling-Charleston, Bishop Bernard W. Schmitt; Chancellor, Rev. Robert C. Nash. Chancery Office, 1300 Byron St., P.O. Box 230, Wheeling, WV 26003. Tel. (304) 233-0880. Fax (304)233-0890

Wichita, Bishop Eugene J. Gerber; Chancellor, Rev. Robert E. Hemberger. Chancery Office, 424 N. Broadway, Wichita, KS 67202. Tel. (316)269-3900

Wilmington, Bishop Robert E. Mulvee; Auxiliary Bishop of Wilmington: Bishop James C. Burke, OP; Chan-cellor, Rev. Msgr. Joseph F. Rebman. Chancery Office, P.O. Box 2030, 1925 Delaware Ave., Ste 1A, Wilming- ton, DE 19899. Tel. (302)573-3100. Fax (302)573-3128

Winona, Bishop John G. Vlazny; Chancellor, Rev. Edward F. McGrath. Chancery Office, 55 W. Sanborn, P.O. Box 588, Winona, MN 55987. Tel. (507)454-4643. Fax (507)454-8106

Worcester, Bishop Timothy J. Harrington; Auxiliary Bishop of Worcester: Bishop George E. Rueger. Chancery Office, 49 Elm St., Worcester, MA 01609. Tel. (617)791-7171. Fax (508)753-7180

Yakima, Bishop Francis E. George; Vicar General, Very Rev. Perron J. Auve. Chancery Office, 5301-A Tieton Dr., Yakima, WA 98908. Tel. (509)965-7117

Youngstown, Bishop James W. Malone; Auxiliary Bishop of Youngstown: Bishop Benedict C. Franzetta; Chancellor, Rev. Robert J. Siffrin. Chancery Office, 144 W. Wood St., Youngstown, OH 44503. Tel. (216)744-8451

The Romanian Orthodox Church in America

The Romanian Orthodox Church in America is an autonomous Archdiocese chartered under the name of "Romanian Orthodox Missionary Archdiocese in America."

Diocese was founded in 1929 and approved by the Holy Synod of the Romanian Orthodox Church in Romania in 1934. A decision of the Holy Synod of the Romanian Orthodox Church of July 12, 1950, granted it ecclesiastical autonomy in America, continuing to hold only dogmatical and canonical ties with the Holy Synod and the Romanian Orthodox Patriarchate of Romania.

In 1951, a group of approximately 40 parishes with their clergy from USA and Canada separated from this church and eventually joined in 1960 the Russian Orthodox Greek Catholic Metropolia, now called the Orthodox Church in America which reordained for these parishes a bishop with the title "Bishop of Detroit and Michigan."

The Holy Synod of the Romanian Orthodox Church, in its session of June 11, 1973, elevated the Bishop of Romanian Orthodox Missionary Episcopate in America to the rank of Archbishop. Consequently the Annual Congress of the Romanian Orthodox Church in America, held on July 21, 1973, at Edmonton-Boian, Alberta, decided to change the title of the Diocese from "Episcopate" to that of "Archdiocese." This decision was approved by the Holy Synod of the Romanian Orthodox Church of Romania in its session of Dec. 12,

1974, renewing at the same time the status as an Autonomous Archdiocese with the right to elect in addition to the Archbishop an Auxiliary Bishop for the Archdiocese.

HEADQUARTERS

19959 Riopelle, Detroit, MI 48203 Tel. (313)893-8390

OFFICERS

Archbishop, His Eminence the Most Rev. Archbishop Victorin (Ursache)

Vicar, V. Rev. Archim. Dr. Vasile Vasilachi, 45-03 48th Ave., Woodside, Queens, NY 11377 Tel. (718)784-4453

Inter-Church Relations, Dir., Rev. Fr. Nicholas Apostola, 14 Hammond St., Worcester, MA 01610 Tel. (617)799-0040

Sec., V. Archim. Rev. Felix Dubneae, Tel. (313)892-2402

PERIODICALS

Credinta--The Faith; Calendarul Credinta

The Romanian Orthodox Episcopate of America

This body of Eastern Orthodox Christians of Romanian descent was organized in 1929 as an autonomous Diocese under the jurisdiction of the Romanian Patriarchate. In 1951 it severed all relations with the Orthodox Church of Romania. Now under the canonical jurisdiction of the autocephalous Orthodox Church in America, it enjoys full administrative autonomy and is headed by its own Bishop.

HEADQUARTERS

2522 Grey Tower Road, Jackson, MI 49201-9120 Tel. (517)522-4800 Fax (517)522-5907

Media Contact, Ed./Sec., Dept. of Publications, David Oancea, P.O. Box 185, Grass Lake, MI 49240-0185 Tel. (517)522-3656 Fax (517)522-5907

OFFICERS

Ruling Bishop, His Grace Bishop Nathaniel (Popp)

The Council of the Episcopate: Sec., Rev. Fr. Laurence Lazar, 18430 W. Nine Mile Rd., Southfield, MI 48075; Treas., Rev. Fr. Leonte Copacia, 5993 Wilmington Dr., Shelby Twp., MI 48316

OTHER ORGANIZATIONS

The American Romanian Orthodox Youth, Pres., David Maxim, 3633 22nd St., Wyandotte, MI 48192

Assoc. of Romanian Orthodox Ladies' Aux., Pres., Mrs. Pauline Trutza, 1466 Waterbury Ave., Lakewood, OH 44107

Orthodox Brotherhood U.S.A., Pres., George Aldea, 824 Mt. Vernon Blvd., Royal Oak, MI 48073

Orthodox Brotherhood of Canada, Pres., Thrisia Pana, #510 - 2243 Hamilton St., Regina, SK S4P 4B6

Russian Orthodox Church in the U.S.A., Patriarchal Parishes of the

This group of parishes is under the direct jurisdiction of the Patriarch of Moscow and All Russia, His Holiness Aleksy II, in the person of a Vicar Bishop, His Grace Paul, Bishop of Zaraisk.

HEADQUARTERS

St. Nicholas Cathedral, 15 E. 97th St., New York, NY 10029 Tel. (212)831-6294 Fax (212)427-5003

Media Contact, Office of the Bishop

PERIODICAL

One Church

The Russian Orthodox Church Outside of Russia

Organized in 1920 to unite in one body of dioceses the missions and parishes of the Russian Orthodox Church outside of Russia. The governing body, set up in Constantinople, was sponsored by the Ecumenical Patriarchate. In November 1950, it came to the United States. The Russian Orthodox Church Outside of Russia lays emphasis on being true to the old traditions of the Russian Church. It is not in communion with the Moscow Patriarchate.

HEADQUARTERS

75 E. 93rd St., New York, NY 10128 Tel. (212)534-1601 Fax (212)534-1798

Media Contact, Dep. Sec., Bishop Hilarian

COUNCIL OF BISHOPS

Synod, His Eminence Metropolitan Vitaly

Sec., Archbishop Laurus of Syracuse and Trinity

Dep. Sec., Hilarion, Bishop of Manhattan, Tel. (212)722-6577

Dir. of Public & Foreign Relations Dept., Archbishop Laurus of Syracuse and Trinity

The Salvation Army

The Salvation Army, founded in 1865 by William Booth (1829-1912) in London, England, and introduced into America in 1880, is an international religious and charitable movement organized and operated on a paramilitary pattern, and is a branch of the Christian church. To carry out its purposes, The Salvation Army has established a widely diversified program of religious and social welfare services which are designed to meet the needs of children, youth, and adults in all age groups.

HEADQUARTERS

615 Slaters La., Alexandria, VA 22313 Tel. (703)684-5500 Fax (703)684-5538

OFFICERS

Natl. Commander, Commissioner James Osborne

Natl. Chief Sec., Commissioner Kenneth Hood

Natl. Communications Dept., Dir., Colonel Leon Ferraez

TERRITORIAL ORGANIZATIONS

Eastern Territory: 440 W. Nyack Rd., P.O. Box C-635, West Nyack, NY 10994 Tel. (914)623-4700 Fax (914)620-7466; Territorial Commander, Commissioner Robert E. Thomson; Chief Sec., Col. Robert A. Watson

Central Territory: 10 W. Algonquin Rd., Des Plains, IL 60016 Tel. (708)294-2000 Fax (708)294-2299; Territorial Commander, Commissioner Harold E. Shoults; Chief Sec., Col. Edward Johnson

Western Territory: 30840 Hawthorne Blvd., Ranchos Palos Verdes, CA 90274 Tel. (310)541-4721 Fax (310)544-1674; Territorial Commander, Commissioner Paul A. Rader; Chief Sec., Col. Ronald G. Irwin

Southern Territory: 1424 Northeast Expressway, Atlanta, GA 30329 Tel. (404)728-1300 Fax (404)728-1331; Territorial Commander, Commissioner Kenneth L. Hodder; Chief Sec., Col. Harold D. Hinson

PERIODICAL

War Cry, The

The Schwenkfelder Church

The Schwenkfelders are the spiritual descendants of the Silesian nobleman Caspar Schwenkfeld von Ossig (1489-1561), a scholar, reformer, preacher, and prolific writer who endeavored to aid in the cause of the Protestant Reformation. A contemporary of Martin Luther, John Calvin, Ulrich Zwingli, and Phillip Melanchthon, Schwenkfeld sought no following, formulated no creed, and did not attempt to organize a church based on his beliefs. He labored for liberty of religious belief--a fellowship of all believers, for one united Christian church--the ecumenical Church.

He and his cobelievers supported a movement known as the Reformation by the Middle Way. Persecuted by state churches, ultimately 180 Schwenkfelders exiled from Silesia emigrated to Pennsylvania. They landed at Philadelphia Sept. 22, 1734, affirmed their allegiance to the crown of Great Britain on the 23rd and, the following day, held a service of Thanksgiving for their deliverance and safe arrival in the New World.

In 1882, the Society of Schwenkfelders, the forerunner of the present Schwenkfelder Church, was formed. The church was incorporated in 1909.

The General Conference of the Schwenkfelder Church is a voluntary association for the Schwenkfelder Churches at Palm, Worcester, Lansdale, Norristown, and Philadelphia, Pa.

They practice adult baptism and dedication of children, and observe the Lord's Supper regularly with open Communion. In theology, they are Christo-centric; in polity, congregational; in missions, world-minded; in ecclesiastical organization, ecumenical.

The Schwenkfelder Church has no publishing house of its own. The ministry is recruited from graduates of colleges, universities, and accredited theological seminaries. In each community, the churches have been noted for leadership in ecumenical concerns through ministerial associations, community service and action groups, councils of Christian education, and other agencies.

HEADQUARTERS

Pennsburg, PA 18073

OFFICERS

Mod., Kenneth D. Slough, Jr., 197 N. Whitehall Rd., Norristown, PA 19403

Sec., Miss Florence Schultz, P.O. Box 221, Palm, PA 18070

Treas., Ellis W. Kriebel, 523 Meetinghouse Rd., Harleysville, PA 19438

PERIODICAL

Schwenkfeldian, The

Second Cumberland Presbyterian Church in U.S.

This church, originally known as the Colored Cumberland Presbyterian Church, was formed in May 1874. Prior to its founding, a convention was held on October 1868 in Henderson, Ky., at which

US RELIGIOUS BODIES

Black ministers of the Cumberland Presbyterian Church began to speak openly about forming a new denomination.

In May 1869, at the General Assembly meeting in Murfreesboro, Tenn., Moses Weir, the spokesperson for the black delegation, appealed for help in organizing a separate African church. Four reasons were cited: Blacks could learn self-reliance and independence; they could have more financial assistance; they could minister more effectively among Blacks if they existed as a separate denomination; and they wanted to worship close to the altar, not in the balconies, which symbolized restriction. At the 1869 General Assembly, the Black churches of the Cumberland Presbyterian Church were set apart with their own ecclesiastical organization.

In 1874 the first General Assembly of the Colored Cumberland Presbyterian Church met in Nashville. The moderator was Rev. P. Price and the stated clerk was Elder John Humphrey. At that time there were 46 ordained clergy, 20 licentiates, 30 candidates, and 3,000 communicants.

Currently the denomination's General Assembly, the national governing body, is organized around its three program boards and agencies: Finance, Publication and Christian Education, and Missions and Evangelism. Other agencies of the General Assembly are under these three program boards.

The greatest strength of the SCPC is its Alabama synod which comprises nearly one-third of the denomination; East and Middle Tennessee areas also contain large numbers of members. The SCPC extends as far north as Cleveland, Ohio and Chicago; as far west as Marshalltown, Iowa, and Dallas, and as far south as Selma, Ala.

OFFICERS

Mod., Rev. Joel P. Rice, 6951 Clearglenn, Dallas, TX 75232

Stated Clk., Rev. Dr. R. Stanley Wood, 226 Church St., Huntsville, AL 35801 Tel. (205)536-7481

SYNODS

Alabama, Stated Clk., Arthur Hinton, 511 10th Ave. N.W., Aliceville, AL 35442

Kentucky, Stated Clk., Leroy Hunt, 1317 Monroe St., Paducah, KY 42001

Tennessee, Stated Clk., Elder Clarence Norman, 145 Jones St., Huntington, TN 38334

Texas, Stated Clk., Arthur King, 2435 Kristen, Dallas, TX 75216

PERIODICAL

Cumberland Flag, The

Separate Baptists in Christ

This group of Baptists is found in Indiana, Ohio, Kentucky, Tennessee, Virginia, West Virginia, Florida and North Carolina, dating back to an association formed in 1758 in North Carolina and Virginia.

Today this group consists of approximately 100 churches. They believe in the infallibility of the Bible, the divine ordinances of the Lord's Supper, feetwashing, baptism, and that those who endureth to the end shall be saved.

At the 1991 General Association, an additional article of doctrine was adopted, which identifies the belief of the Separate Baptists concerning Christ's return. "We believe that at Christ's return in the clouds of heaven all Christians will meet the Lord in the air, and time shall be no more," thus leaving no time for a literal 1,000-year reign. Two

of the sister associations which were members of the General Association withdrew in protest of the adoption of the new article. There are now seven sister associations comprising the General Association of Separate Baptists.

MEDIA CONTACT

Media Contact, Clk., Rev. Mark Polston, 787 Kitchen Rd., Mooresville, IN 46158 Tel. (317)834-0286

OFFICERS

Mod., Rev. Jim Goff, 1020 Gagel Ave., Louisville, KY 40216

Asst. Mod., Rev. Jimmy Polston, 3127 N. Lesley Ave., Indianapolis, IN 46218

Clk., Rev. Mark Polston

Asst. Clk., Bro. Randy Polston, 3105 N. Elmhurst Dr., Indianapolis, IN 46226 Tel. (317)357-9898

Serbian Orthodox Church in the U.S.A. and Canada

The Serbian Orthodox Church is an organic part of the Eastern Orthodox Church. As a local church it received its autocephaly from Constantinople in 1219 A.D. The Patriarchal seat of the church today is in Belgrade, Yugoslavia. In 1921, a Serbian Orthodox Diocese in the United States of America and Canada was organized. In 1963, it was reorganized into three dioceses, and in 1983 a fourth diocese was created for the Canadian part of the church. The Serbian Orthodox Church in the USA and Canada received its administrative autonomy in 1982. The Serbian Orthodox Church is in absolute doctrinal unity with all other local Orthodox Churches.

HEADQUARTERS

St. Sava Monastery, P.O. Box 519, Libertyville, IL 60048 Tel. (708)362-2440

BISHOPS

Metropolitan of Midwestern America, Most Rev. Metropolitan Christopher, Tel. (708)367-0698

Bishop of Canada, Rt. Rev. Georgije, 5A Stockbridge Ave., Toronto, ON M8Z 4M6 Tel. (416)231-4009

Bishop of Western America, Rt. Rev. Chrysostom, 2541 Crestline Terr., Alhambra, CA 91803 Tel. (818)264-6825

Bishop of Eastern America, Rt. Rev. Bishop Mitrophan, P.O. Box 368, Sewickley, PA 15143 Tel. (412)741-5686

OTHER ORGANIZATIONS

Brotherhood of Serbian Orth. Clergy in U.S.A. & Canada, Pres., V. Rev. Branko Skaljac, Lorain, OH

Federation of Circles of Serbian Sisters

Serbian Singing Federation

PERIODICALS

Path of Orthodoxy (Eng.), The; Path of Orthodoxy (Serbian), The

Seventh-day Adventist Church

The Seventh-day Adventist Church grew out of a worldwide religious revival in the mid-19th century. People of many religious persuasions believed Bible prophecies indicated that the second coming or advent of Christ was imminent.

When Christ did not come in the 1840s, a group of these disappointed Adventists in the United States continued their Bible studies and concluded they had misinterpreted prophetic events and that the second coming of Christ was still in the future. This same group of Adventists later accepted the teaching of the seventh-day Sabbath and became known as Seventh-day Adventists. The denomination organized formally in 1863.

The church was largely confined to North America until 1874, when its first missionary was sent to Europe. Today 31,650 congregations meet in 185 countries. Membership exceeds 6 million and increases between six and seven percent each year.

In addition to a vigorous mission program, the church has the largest worldwide Protestant parochial school system with more than 5,200 schools with close to 750,000 students on elementary through college and university levels.

The Adventist Development and Relief Agency (ADRA) helps victims of war and natural disasters, and many local congregations have community service facilities to help those in need close to home.

The church also has a worldwide publishing ministry with more than 50 printing facilities producing magazines and other publications in over 180 languages and dialects. In the United States and Canada, the church sponsors a variety of radio and television programs, including "Christian Lifestyle Magazine," "It Is Written," "Breath of Life," "Ayer, Hoy, y Mañana," "Voice of Prophecy," and "La Voz de la Esperanza."

The North American Division of Seventh-day Adventist includes 58 Conferences which are grouped together into 9 organized Union Conferences. The various Conferences work under the general direction of these Union Conferences.

HEADQUARTERS

12501 Old Columbia Pike, Silver Spring, MD 20904-6600 Tel. (301)680-6000

WORLD-WIDE OFFICERS

Pres., Robert S. Folkenberg
Sec., G. Ralph Thompson
Treas., Donald F. Gilbert

WORLD-WIDE DEPARTMENTS

Church Ministries, Dir., Israel Leito
Communication, Dir., Shirley Burton
Education, Dir., Humberto M. Rasi
Health & Temperance, Dir., Albert S. Whiting
Ministerial Assoc., Sec., W. Floyd Bresee
Public Affairs & Religious Liberty, Dir., B. B. Beach
Publishing, Dir., Ronald E. Appenzeller

NORTH AMERICAN OFFICERS

Pres., Alfred C. McClure
Admn. Asst. to Pres., Gary B. Patterson
Secs.: Harold W. Baptiste; Rosa T. Banks
Treas.: George H. Crumley; Meade C. VanPuttern

NORTH AMERICAN ORGANIZATIONS

Atlantic Union Conf.: P.O. Box 1189, South Lancaster, MA 01561-1189; Pres., Phillip S. Follett; Sec., Alvin R. Goulbourne; Treas., Juan R. Prestol
Canada: Seventh-day Adventist Church in Canada (see Ch. 4)
Columbia Union Conf.: 5427 Twin Knolls Rd., Columbia, MD 21045; Pres., Ron M. Wisbey; Sec., Henry M. Wright; Treas., D. J. Russell
Lake Union Conf.: P.O. Box C, Berrien Springs, MI 49103; Pres., R. H. Carter; Sec., Herbert S. Larsen; Treas., Herbert Pritchard
Mid-America Union Conf.: P.O. Box 6128, Lincoln, NE 68506; Pres., Joel O. Tompkins; Sec., George W. Timpson; Treas., Duane P. Huey

North Pacific Union Conf.: P.O. Box 16677, Portland, OR 97216; Pres., Bruce Johnston; Sec., Paul Nelson; Treas., Robert L. Rawson
Pacific Union Conf.: P.O. Box 5005, Westlake Village, CA 91359; Pres., Thomas J. Mostert, Jr; Sec., Ernest Castillo; Treas., S. D. Bietz
Southern Union Conf.: P.O. Box 849, Decatur, GA 30031; Pres., M. D. Gordon; Sec., W. D. Sumpter; Treas., Richard P. Center
Southwestern Union Conf.: P.O. Box 4000, Burleson, TX 76028; Pres., Cyril Miller; Sec., Clayton R. Pritchett; Treas., Max A. Trevino

PERIODICALS

Message Magazine, The; Ministry; Mission, Adult and Junior; Our Little Friend; Primary Treasure; Shabat Shalom; Signs of the Times; Vibrant Life; Youth Ministry Accent

Seventh Day Baptist General Conference, USA and Canada

Seventh Day Baptists emerged during the English Reformation, organizing their first churches in England in the mid-1600s. The oldest of them all, the Mill Yard Seventh Day Baptist Church of London, continues to be active over 300 years later.

The first Seventh Day Baptists of record in America were Stephen and Anne Mumford, who emigrated from England in 1664. Beginning in 1665 several members of the First Baptist Church at Newport, R.I., began observing the seventh day Sabbath, or Saturday. In 1671 five members together with the Mumfords covenanted together to form the first Seventh Day Baptist Church in America at Newport. In 1708 a portion of that congregation living in Hopkinton, R.I., established their own church, which is the oldest, living Seventh Day Baptist church in America today.

Beginning about 1700, other Seventh Day Baptist churches were established in New Jersey and Pennsylvania. It was from these three centers that the denomination grew and expanded westward.

A desire to increase their fellowship and to organize for missionary efforts led to the founding of the Seventh Day Baptist General Conference in 1802.

The organization of societies and related agencies of the denomination reflect Seventh Day Baptist interest in home and foreign missions, publications and education. Women have been encouraged to participate actively at local and denominational levels. From the earliest years religious freedom has been championed for all, and the separation of church and state advocated.

In the 20th century Seventh Day Baptists have been characterized by their ecumenical spirit on local, national and international levels. They are members of the Baptist World Alliance and affiliated organizations. In 1965 the Seventh Day Baptist World Federation was organized. The SDB General Conference in the U.S.A. and Canada is one of 17 member conferences located in six continents.

HEADQUARTERS

Seventh Day Baptist Center, 3120 Kennedy Rd., P.O. Box 1678, Janesville, WI 53547-1678 Tel. (608)752-5055 Fax (608)752-7711
Media Contact, Gen. Services Admn., Calvin Babcock

OTHER ORGANIZATIONS

Seventh Day Baptist Missionary Society, Exec. Vice-Pres., Mr. Kirk Looper, 119 Main St., Westerly, RI 02891

Seventh Day Bapt. Bd. of Christian Ed., Exec. Dir., Rev. Ernest K. Bee, Jr., Box 115, Alfred Station, NY 14803

Women's Soc. of the Gen. Conference, Pres., Mrs. Donna Bond, RFD 1, Box 426, Bridgeton, NJ 08302

American Sabbath Tract & Comm. Council, Dir. of Communications, Rev. Kevin Butler, 3120 Kennedy Rd., P.O. Box 1678, Janesville, WI 53547

Seventh Day Baptist Historical Society, Historian, Don A. Sanford, 3120 Kennedy Rd., P.O. Box 1678, Janesville, WI 53547

Seventh Day Baptist Center on Ministry, Dir. of Pastoral Services, Rev. Rodney L. Henry, 3120 Kennedy Rd., P.O. Box 1678, Janesville, WI 53547

PERIODICAL

Sabbath Recorder

Social Brethren

This evangelical body was organized in 1867 among members of various bodies. Its confession of faith has nine articles.

OFFICERS

General Assembly, Mod., Rev. Earl Vaughn, RR #2, Flora, IL 62839 Tel. (618)662-4373

Union Association, Mod., Rev. Herbert Tarleton, 420 S. Mill, Harrisburg, IL 62946 Tel. (618)252-7196

Illinois Association, Mod., Rev. Norman Cozart, Rt. 1, Stonefort, IL 62987

Midwestern Association, Mod., Rev. Edward Darnell, 53 E. Newport, Pontiac, MI 48055 Tel. (313)335-9125

Southern Baptist Convention

The Southern Baptist Convention was organized on May 10, 1845, in Augusta, Ga.

Cooperating Baptist churches are located in all 50 states, the District of Columbia, Puerto Rico, American Samoa, and the Virgin Islands. The members of the churches work together through 1,208 district associations and 39 state conventions and/or fellowships. The Southern Baptist Convention has an Executive Committee and 20 national agencies--four boards, six seminaries, seven commissions, a foundation and two associated organizations.

The purpose of the Southern Baptist Convention is "to provide a general organization for Baptists in the United States and its territories for the promotion of Christian missions at home and abroad and any other objects such as Christian education, benevolent enterprises, and social services which it may deem proper and advisable for the furtherance of the Kingdom of God" (Constitution, Article II).

The Convention exists in order to help the churches lead people to God through Jesus Christ.

From the beginning, there has been a burning mission desire to share the Gospel with the peoples of the world. The Cooperative Program is the basic channel of mission support. In addition, the Lottie Moon Christmas Offering for Foreign Missions and the Annie Armstrong Easter Offering for Home Missions support Southern Baptists' world mission programs.

In 1991, there were 3,887 foreign missionaries serving in 122 foreign countries and 4,922 home missionaries serving within the United States.

In 1987, the Southern Baptist Convention adopted themes and goals for the major denominational emphasis of Bold Mission Thrust for 1990-2000. Bold Mission Thrust is an effort to enable every person in the world to have opportunity to hear and to respond to the Gospel of Christ by the year 2000.

HEADQUARTERS

901 Commerce St., Ste. 750, Nashville, TN 37203 Tel. (615)244-2355

Media Contact, Vice-Pres. for Convention Relations, Mark Coppenger, Fax (615)742-8919

OFFICERS

Pres., Morris M. Chapman, First Baptist Church, 1200 Ninth, Wichita Falls, TX 76301

Recording Sec., David W. Atchison, P.O. Box 1543, Brentwood, TN 37027

Executive Committee: Pres., Harold C. Bennett; Exec. Vice-Pres., Ernest E. Mosley; Vice-Pres., Business & Finance, Richard Rosenbaum; Vice-Pres., Convention Relations, Mark Coppenger; Vice-Pres., Baptist Press, Herb V. Hollinger

GENERAL BOARDS AND COMMISSIONS

Foreign Mission Board: Pres., R. Keith Parks, Box 6767, Richmond, VA 23230

Home Mission Board: Pres., Larry L. Lewis, 1350 Spring St., NW, Atlanta, GA 30367 Tel. (404)898-7700

Annuity Board: Pres., Paul W. Powell, P.O. Box 2190, Dallas, TX 75221 Tel. (214)720-0511

Sunday School Board: Pres., James T. Draper, Jr., 127 Ninth Ave., N., Nashville, TN 37234 Tel. (615)251-2000

Brotherhood Commission: Pres., James D. Williams, 1548 Poplar Ave., Memphis, TN 38104 Tel. (901)272-2461

SB Commis. on the Am. Bapt. Theol. Sem.: Exec. Sec.-Treas., Arthur L. Walker, Jr.; Pres. of the Seminary, Odell McGlothian, Sr.

Christian Life Commission: Exec. Dir., Richard D. Land, 901 Commerce St., Nashville, TN 37203 Tel. (615)244-2495

Education Commission: Exec. Sec.-Treas., Arthur L. Walker, Jr., 901 Commerce St., Nashville, TN 37203 Tel. (615)244-2362

Historical Commission: Exec. Dir., Treas., Lynn E. May, Jr., 901 Commerce Street, Nashville, TN 37203 Tel. (615)244-0344

The Radio & TV Commission: Pres., Jack Johnson, 6350 West Freeway, Ft. Worth, TX 76150 Tel. (817)737-4011

Stewardship Commission: Pres., A. R. Fagan, 901 Commerce St., Nashville, TN 37203 Tel. (615)244-2303

STATE CONVENTIONS

Alabama, Troy L. Morrison, 2001 E. South Blvd., Montgomery, AL 36198 Tel. (205)288-2460

Alaska, Bill G. Duncan, 1750 O'Malley Rd., Anchorage, AK 99516 Tel. (907)344-9627

Arizona, Dan C. Stringer, 4520 N. Central Ave., Ste. 550, Phoenix, AZ 85013 Tel. (602)264-9421

Arkansas, Don Moore, P.O. Box 552, Little Rock, AR 72203 Tel. (501)376-4791

California, C. B. Hogue, 678 E. Shaw Ave., Fresno, CA 93710 Tel. (209)229-9533

Colorado, Charles Sharp, 7393 So. Alton Way, Englewood, CO 80112 Tel. (303)771-2480

District of Columbia, W. Jere Allen, 1628 16th St. NW, Washington, DC 20009 Tel. (202)265-1526

Florida, John Sullivan, 1230 Hendricks Ave., Jacksonville, FL 32207 Tel. (904)396-2351

Georgia, James N. Griffith, 2930 Flowers Rd., S, Atlanta, GA 30341 Tel. (404)455-0404

Hawaii, O. W. Efurd, 2042 Vancouver Dr., Honolulu, HI 96822 Tel. (808)946-9581

Illinois, Maurice Swinford, P.O. Box 19247, Springfield, IL 62794 Tel. (217)786-2600

Indiana, Charles Sullivan, 900 N. High School Rd., Indianapolis, IN 46224 Tel. (317)241-9317

Kansas-Nebraska, R. Rex Lindsay, 5410 W. Seventh St., Topeka, KS 66606 Tel. (913)273-4880

Kentucky, William W. Marshall, P.O. Box 43433, Middletown, KY 40243 Tel. (502)245-4101

Louisiana, Mark Short, Box 311, Alexandria, LA 71301 Tel. (318)448-3402

Maryland-Delaware, Kenneth Lyle, 10255 S. Columbia Rd., Columbia, MD 21064 Tel. (301)290-5290

Michigan, Robert Wilson, 15635 W. 12 Mile Rd., Southfield, MI 48076 Tel. (313)557-4200

Minnesota-Wisconsin, Otha Winningham, 519 16th St. SE, Rochester, MN 55904 Tel. (507)282-3636

Mississippi, William W. Causey, P.O. Box 530, Jackson, MS 39205 Tel. (601)968-3800

Missouri, Donald V. Wideman, 400 E. High, Jefferson City, MO 65101 Tel. (314)635-7931

Nevada, David Meacham, 406 California Ave., Reno, NV 89509 Tel. (702)786-0406

New England, -----, Box 688, 5 Oak Ave., Northboro, MA 01532 Tel. (508)393-6013

New Mexico, Claude Cone, P.O. Box 485, Albuquerque, NM 87103 Tel. (505)247-0586

New York, R. Quinn Pugh, 6538 Collamer Dr., East Syracuse, NY 13057 Tel. (315)475-6173

North Carolina, Roy J. Smith, 205 Convention Dr., Cary, NC 27511 Tel. (919)467-5100

Ohio, Acting Exec. Dir., Orville H. Griffin, 1680 E. Broad St., Columbus, OH 43203 Tel. (614)258-8491

Northwest Baptist Convention, Cecil Sims, 1033 N.E. 6th Ave., Portland, OR 97232 Tel. (503)238-4545

Oklahoma, William G. Tanner, 3800 N. May Ave., Oklahoma City, OK 73112 Tel. (405)942-3800

Pennsylvania-South Jersey, Wallace A. C. Williams, 4620 Fritchey St., Harrisburg, PA 17109 Tel. (717)652-5856

South Carolina, B. Carlisle Driggers, 907 Richland St., Columbia, SC 29201 Tel. (803)765-0030

Tennessee, D. L. Lowrie, P.O. Box 728, Brentwood, TN 37024 Tel. (615)373-2255

Texas, William M. Pinson, Jr., 333 N. Washington, Dallas, TX 75246 Tel. (214)828-5100

Utah-Idaho, Sec., C. Clyde Billingsley, P.O. Box 1039, Sandy, UT 84091 Tel. (801)255-3565

Virginia, Reginald M. McDonough, P.O. Box 8568, Richmond, VA 23226 Tel. (804)672-2100

West Virginia, Don R. Mathis, Number One Mission Way, Scott Depot, WV 25560 Tel. (304)757-0944

Wyoming, John W. Thomason, Box 3074, Casper, WY 82602 Tel. (307)472-4087

FELLOWSHIPS

Dakota Southern Baptist Fellowship, Dewey W. Hickey, P.O. Box 7187, Bismark, ND 58502 Tel. (701)255-3765

Iowa Southern Baptist Fellowship, O. Wyndell Jones, Westview #27, 2400 86th St., Des Moines, IA 50322 Tel. (515)278-1516

Montana Southern Baptist Fellowship, James Nelson, P.O. Box 99, Billings, MT 59103 Tel. (406)252-7537

Canadian Convention of Southern Baptists, Allen Schmidt, Postal Bag 300, Cochrane, AL T0L 0W0 Tel. (403)932-5688

PERIODICALS

Western Recorder; Word and Way; WSBC Horizons; Capital Baptist; Baptist True Union; Commission, The; Baptist Program; Baptist Beacon; Baptist and Reflector; Baptist Courier; Baptist Messenger; Baptist Record; Baptist Standard; Biblical Recorder; Religious Herald; Northwest Baptist Witness; MissionsUSA; Baptist Digest; Contempo; Baptist Message

Southern Methodist Church

Organized in 1939, this body is composed of congregations desirous of continuing in true Biblical Methodism and preserving the fundamental doctrines and beliefs of the Methodist Episcopal Church, South. These congregations declined to be a party to the merger of the Methodist Episcopal Church, The Methodist Episcopal Church, South, and the Methodist Protestant Church into The Methodist Church.

HEADQUARTERS

P.O. Drawer A, 872 Broughton SW, Orangeburg, SC 29116-0039 Tel. (803)536-1378

Media Contact, Pres., Rev. Dr. Richard G. Blank, Fax (803)536-0237

OFFICERS

Pres., Rev. Dr. Richard G. Blank

Admn. Asst. to Pres., Philip A. Rorabaugh

Vice-Presidents:

The Carolinas-Virginia Conf., Rev. E. Legrand Adams, Rt. 2, Box 1050, Laurens, SC 29360

Alabama-Florida-Georgia Conf., Rev. John F. Walker, 3341 Gocio Rd., Sarasota, FL 34235

Mid-South Conf., Rev. Bedford F. Landers, 1307 Walnut St., Waynesboro, MS 39367

South-Western Conf., Rev. Dr. Arthur P. Meacham, 5910 Youree Dr., Ste. C, Shreveport, LA 71105

Gen. Conf., Treas., Rev. Philip A. Rorabaugh

Sovereign Grace Baptists

The Sovereign Grace Baptist movement began stirring in the mid-1950s when some pastors in traditional Baptist churches returned to a Calvinist-theological perspective.

The first "Sovereign Grace" conference was held in Ashland, Ky., in 1954 and since then, conferences of this sort have been sponsored by various local churches on the West Coast, Southern and Northern states, and Canada.

This movement is a spontaneous phenomenon concerning reformation at the local church level. Consequently, there is no interest in establishing a Reformed Baptist "Convention" or "Denomination." Part of the oneness of doctrine of the Sovereign Grace Baptists is the conviction that each local church is to administer the keys to the kingdom. Thus any ecclesiastical structure above the local church is ruled out. Most Sovereign Grace Baptists formally or informally relate to the "First London" (1646), "Second London" (1689), or "Philadelphia" (1742) Confessions.

There is a wide variety of local church government in this movement. Many Calvinist Baptists have or desire a plurality of elders in each assembly. These elders are responsible for the spiritual oversight of the church. Deacons are primarily responsible to take care of the financial and physical needs of the flock. Other Sovereign Grace Baptists, however, prefer to function with one pastor and several deacons.

Membership procedures vary from church to church but all would require a credible profession of faith in Christ, and proper Baptism as a basis for membership.

Calvinistic Baptists financially support gospel efforts (missionaries, pastors of small churches at home and abroad, literature publication and distribution, radio programs, etc.) in various parts of the world. Some local churches have institutional training programs, advanced Bible studies, and Christian schools.

MEDIA CONTACT

Media Contact, Corres., Jon Zens, P.O. Box 548, St. Croix Falls, WI 54024 Tel. (715)755-3560 Fax (612)465-5101

PERIODICAL

Reformation Today

Syrian Orthodox Church of Antioch (Archdiocese of the United States and Canada)

An archdiocese in North America of the Syrian Orthodox Church of Antioch. The Syrian Orthodox Church - composed of several archdioceses, numerous parishes, schools and seminaries - professes the faith of the first three Ecumenical Councils of Nicaea, Constantinople, and Ephesus, and numbers faithful in the Middle East, India, the Americas, Europe and Australia. The Church traces its origin to the Patriarchate established in Antioch by St. Peter the Apostle and is under the supreme ecclesiastical jurisdiction of His Holiness the Syrian Orthodox Patriarch of Antioch and All the East, now residing in Damascus, Syria.

The first Syrian Orthodox faithful came to North America during the late 1800s, and by 1907 the first Syrian Orthodox priest was ordained to tend to the community's spiritual needs. In 1949, His Eminence Archbishop Mar Athanasius Y. Samuel came to America and was soon appointed Patriarchal Vicar.

There are 24 official archdiocesan parishes in the United States, located in California, Maryland, Georgia, Illinois, Massachusetts, Michigan, New Jersey, New York, Oklahoma, Oregon, Pennsylvania, Rhode Island and Texas. In Canada, there are five official parishes: three in the Province of Ontario and two in the Province of Quebec.

HEADQUARTERS

Archdiocese of the U.S. and Canada, 49 Kipp Ave., Lodi, NJ 07644 Tel. (201)778-0638 Fax (201)773-7506
Media Contact, Archdiocesan Gen. Sec., V. Rev. Chorepiscopus John Meno, 45 Fairmount Ave., Hackensack, NJ 07061 Tel. (201)646-9443 Fax (201)773-7506

OFFICERS

Primate, Archbishop Mar Athanasius Y. Samuel
Archdiocesan Gen. Sec., V. Rev. Chorepiscopus John Meno

Triumph the Church and Kingdom of God in Christ Inc. (International)

This church was given through the wisdom and knowledge of God to the Late Apostle Elias Dempsey Smith, on Oct. 20, 1897, at noon in Issaquena County, Miss., while he was pastor of a Methodist church.

The Triumph Church, as this body is more commonly known, was founded in 1902, its doors opened in 1904, and confirmed in Birmingham, Ala., with 225 members in 1915. It was incorporated in Washington, D.C., in 1918 and currently operates in 31 states and overseas. The General Church is divided into 18 districts, including the Africa District.

Triumphant doctrine and philosophy is based on the following concepts and principles: Life, Truth and Knowledge; God in man, and being expressed through man; Manifested Wisdom; Complete and Full Understanding; and Constant New Revelations. Its concepts and methods of teaching "the second coming of Christ" are based on these and all other attributes of goodness.

Triumphians put strong emphasis on the fact that God is the God of the living, and not the God of the dead.

HEADQUARTERS

213 Farrington Ave. S.E., Atlanta, GA 30315

OFFICERS

Chief Bishop, Rt. Rev. A. J. Scott, 1323 N.E. 36th St., Savannah, GA 31404 Tel. (912)236-2877
Asst. Chief Apostle, Bishop C. W. Drummond, 7114 Idlewild, Pittsburgh, PA 15208 Tel. (412)731-2286
Gen. Bd of Trustees, Chmn., Bishop Leon Simon, 1028 59th St., Oakland, CA 94608 Tel. (415)652-9576
Gen. Treas., Bishop Hosea Lewis, 1713 Needlewood Ln., Orlando, FL 32818 Tel. (407)295-5488
Gen. Rec. Sec., Bishop Zephaniah Swindle, Box 1927, Shelbyville, TX 75973 Tel. (409)598-3082

True Orthodox Ch. of Greece (Synod of Metropolitan Cyprian), American Exarchate

The American Exarchate of the True (Old Calendar) Orthodox Church of Greece adheres to the tenets of the Eastern Orthodox Church, which considers itself the legitimate heir of the historical Apostolic Church.

When the Orthodox Church of Greece, the official state Church, adopted the New or Gregorian Calendar in 1924, many felt that this breach with tradition compromised the Church's festal calendar, which is based on the Old or Julian calendar, and its unity with world Orthodoxy. In a resistance movement to the reform, three State Church Bishops in 1935 returned to the Old Calendar and established a Synod in Resistance, The True Orthodox Church of Greece. When the last of these Bishops died, the Russian Orthodox Church Abroad consecrated a new hierarchy for the Greek Old Calendarists and, in 1969, declared them a sister Church.

In the face of persecution by the state Church, some Old Calendarists denied the validity of the Mother Church of Greece and formed into two Synods, now under the direction of Archbishop

Chrysostomos of Athens and Archbishop Andreas of Athens. A moderate faction under Metropolitan Cyprian of Oropos and Fili does not maintain communion with what it considers the ailing Mother Church of Greece, but recognizes its validity and seeks for a restoration of unity between the Old and New Calendarist factions by a return to the Julian Calendar and traditional ecclesiastical polity by the State Church. About 2 million Orthodox Greeks belong to the Old Calendar Church.

The first Old Calendarist communities in the United States were formed in the 1930s. There are about 20,000 Old Calendarist Greeks in America, unevenly distributed among the Exarchates of the three Greek Synods. The Exarchate under Metropolitan Cyprian, headed by a Princeton-educated, former university professor, was established in 1986 and has attracted large numbers of the Faithful. Placing emphasis on clergy education, youth programs, and recognition of the Old Calendarist minority in American Orthodoxy, the Exarchate has encouraged the establishment of monastic communities and missions. Cordial contacts with the New Calendarist and other Orthodox communities are encouraged at the parish and administrative levels. A center for theological training and Patristic studies has been established at the Exarchate headquarters in Etna, Cal.

HEADQUARTERS

St. Gregory Palamas Monastery, P.O. Box 398, Etna, CA 96027 Tel. (916)467-3228 Fax (916)467-3996
Media Contact, His Eminence Bishop Chrysostomos

OFFICERS

Synodal Exarch in America, His Eminence Bishop Chrysostomos
Asst. to the Exarch, His Grace Bishop Auxentios
Dean of Exarchate, The Rev. James P. Thornton, P.O. Box 2833, Garden Grove, CA 92642

PERIODICAL

Orthodox Tradition

Ukrainian Orthodox Church of America (Ecumenical Patriarchate)

This body was organized in America in 1928, when the first convention was held. In 1932 Dr. Joseph Zuk was consecrated as first Bishop. His successor was the Most Rev. Bishop Bohdan, Primate, who was consecrated by the order of the Ecumenical Patriarchate of Constantinople on Feb. 28, 1937, in New York City. He was succeeded by the Most Rev. Metropolitan Andrei Kuschak, consecrated by the blessing of Ecumenical Patriarch by Archbishop Iakovos, Metropolitan Germanos and Bishop Silas of Greek-Orthodox Church, on Jan. 26, 1967. His successor is Bishop Vsevolod, ordained on Sept. 27, 1987, by Archbishop Iakovos, Metropolitan Silas and Bishops Philip and Athenagoras.

HEADQUARTERS

Ukrainian Orthodox Church of America, 90-34 139th St., Jamaica, NY 11435 Tel. (718)297-2407 Fax (718)291-8308
Media Contact, Primate, Bishop Vsevolod

OFFICERS

Primate, Rt. Rev. Bishop Vsevolod
Administrator for Canada, Rev. Michael Pawlyshyn

Chancellor, Rev. W. Czekaluk

PERIODICAL

Ukrainian Orthodox Herald

Ukrainian Orthodox Church of the U.S.A.

This church was formally organized in the United States in 1919. Archbishop John Theodorovich arrived from Ukraine in 1924.

HEADQUARTERS

P.O. Box 495, South Bound Brook, NJ 08880 Tel. (908)356-0090 Fax (908)356-5556

OFFICERS

Patriarch: His Holiness Patriarch Mstyslav I; Archbishop Constantine Buggan, 15157 Waterman Dr., S., Holland, IL 60473; Archbishop Antony, 4 Von Steuben Lane, South Bound Brook, NJ 08880
Consistory: Pres., V. Rev. William Diakiw; Vice-Pres., V. Rev. Nestor Kowal; Sec., Rev. Frank Estocin; Treas., V. Rev. Taras Chubenko

Unitarian Universalist Association

The Unitarian Universalist Association is the consolidated body of the former American Unitarian Association and the Universalist Church of America. The Unitarian movement arose in congregationalism in the 18th century, producing the American Unitarian Association in 1825. In 1865 a national conference was organized. The philosophy of Universalism originated with the doctrine of universal salvation in the first century, and was brought to America in the 18th century. Universalists were first formally organized in 1793. In May, 1961, the Unitarian and Universalist bodies were consolidated to become the Unitarian Universalist Association. The movement is noncreedal. The UUA has observer status with the National Council of Churches.

HEADQUARTERS

25 Beacon St., Boston, MA 02108 Tel. (617)742-2100
Media Contact, Dir. of Publ. Info., Deborah Weiner, Fax (617)367-3237

OFFICERS

Pres., Rev. William F. Schulz
Exec. Vice-Pres., Kathleen C. Montgomery
Mod., Natalie W. Gulbrandsen
Sec., Ralph Robins
Treas., David E. Provost
Financial Advisor, Arnold W. Bradburd

OTHER ORGANIZATIONS

Beacon Press, Dir., Wendy Strothman
Unitarian Universalist Ministers' Assoc., Pres., Rev. Leon Hopper
Unitarian Universalist Women's Fed., Pres., Kay Aler-Maida
Young Religious Unitarian Universalists, Contact, Rev. Jory Agate
Unitarian Universalist Serv. Comm., Inc., Exec. Dir., Dr. Richard Scobie, 78 Beacon St., Boston, MA 02108
Unitarian Universalist Hist. Society, Pres., Rev. Janet Bowering
Church of the Larger Fellowship, Rev. Scott Alexander

US RELIGIOUS BODIES

123

United Brethren in Christ

The Church of the United Brethren in Christ had its beginning with Philip William Otterbein and Martin Boehm, who were leaders in the revivalistic movement in Pennsylvania and Maryland during the late 1760s and which continued into the early 1800s.

On Sept. 25, 1800, they and others associated with them formed a society under the name of United Brethren in Christ. Subsequent conferences adopted a Confession of Faith in 1815 and a constitution in 1841. The Church of the United Brethren in Christ adheres to the original constitution as amended in 1957, 1961 and 1977.

HEADQUARTERS

302 Lake St., Huntington, IN 46750 Tel. (219)356-2312 Fax (219)356-4730
Media Contact, Chmn., Bd. of Bishops, Dr. C. Ray Miller

OFFICERS

Bishops: Chpsn., C. Ray Miller; Clarence A. Kopp, Jr.; Jerry Datema
Pres., Tony Tallas
1st Vice-Pres., W. Baletca
Sec., Dorothy Kocian
Fin. Sec., Roy Vajdak
Treas., Ron Sulak
Gen. Treas./Office Mgr., Marda J. Hoffman
Dept. of Education, Dir., Dr. G. Blair Dowden
Dept. of Church Services, Dir., Rev. Paul Hirschy

ORGANIZATIONS

Bd. of Chrisitian Educ., Chm., Rev. Gary Olsen, 1400 Louise St., Rosenberg, TX 77471

PERIODICAL

United Brethren, The

United Christian Church

The United Christian Church originated during the period of the Civil War or shortly thereafter, about 1864 or 1865. There were some ministers and laymen in the United Brethren in Christ Church who were in disagreement with the position and practice of the church on issues such as infant baptism, voluntary bearing of arms and belonging to oath bound secret combinations. It was this group which formed a nucleus developing into United Christian Church, organized at a conference held in Campbelltown, Pa., on May 9, 1877, and given its name by a conference held Jan. 1, 1878.

The principal founders of the denomination were George Hoffman, John Stamn, and Thomas Lesher. Hoffman appears to have been predominant because before they were organized, they were called Hoffmanites.

The United Christian Church has district conferences, a general conference held yearly, a general board of trustees, a mission board, a board of directors of the United Christian Church Home, a campmeeting board, a young peoples board, and has local organized congregations.

It believes in the Holy Trinity, the inspired Holy Scriptures with the doctrines they teach, and practices the ordinances of Baptism, Holy Communion, and Foot Washing.

It welcomes all into its fold who are born again, believe in Jesus Christ our Savior and Lord, and who have received the Holy Spirit and, therefore, are a part of the Church of Jesus Christ, or His Body.

HEADQUARTERS

c/o John P. Ludwig, Jr., 523 W. Walnut St., Cleona, PA 17042 Tel. (717)273-9629
Media Contact, Presiding Elder, John P. Ludwig, Jr.

OFFICERS

Mod. & Presiding Elder, Elder John P. Ludwig, Jr.
Conf. Sec., Elder David W. Heagy, RD 4, Box 100, Lebanon, PA 17042

OTHER ORGANIZATIONS

Mission Board: Pres., Elder John P. Ludwig, Jr.; Sec., Elder Walter Knight, Jr., Rt. #3, Box 98, Palmyra, PA 17078; Treas., Elder Henry C. Heagy, 2080 S. White Oak St., Lebanon, PA 17042

United Church of Christ

The United Church of Christ was duly constituted on June 25, 1957 by the regularly chosen representatives of the Congregational Christian Churches and of the Evangelical and Reformed Church, in a Uniting General Synod held in Cleveland, Ohio.

The Preamble to the Constitution states the denomination's theological base: "The United Church of Christ acknowledges as its sole head, Jesus Christ, the Son of God and Saviour. It acknowledges as kindred in Christ all who share in this confession. It looks to the Word of God in the Scriptures, and to the presence and power of the Holy Spirit, to prosper its creative and redemptive work in the world. It claims as its own the faith of the historic Church expressed in the ancient creeds and reclaimed in the basic insights of the Protestant Reformers. It affirms the responsibility of the Church in each generation to make this faith its own in reality of worship, in honesty of thought and expression, and in purity of heart before God. In accordance with the teaching of our Lord and the practice prevailing among evangelical Christians, it recognizes two sacraments: Baptism and the Lord's Supper or Holy Communion."

The creation of the United Church of Christ brought together four unique traditions:

(1) The Congregational Way first achieved prominence among English Protestants during the civil war of the 1640s, groundwork for the Congregational form having been laid by Calvinist Puritans and Separatists during the half-century preceding. Opposition to state control of their religious worship promoted followers of the Congregational form to emigrate to America, where an active part in colonizing New England occupied their energies throughout the 17th century. Congregationalists (self-consciously a denomination from the middle of the 19th century) have made strong contributions to the religious, civil, educational, and secular dimensions of American institutions and culture.

(2) The Christian Churches originated as a restorationist movement in several parts of the United States late in the 18th century. Throughout their history the Christians emphasized Christ as the only head of the church, the New Testament as their only rule of faith, and "Christian" as their sole name. Unitive in spirit, this loosely organized denomination in 1931, the united with the Congregational Churches as the Congregational Christian Churches.

(3) The German Reformed Church comprised an irenic aspect of the Protestant Reformation, as a second generation of Reformers drew on the insights of Zwingli, Luther, and Calvin to formulate the Heidelberg Catechism of 1563. This confession of faith proved to be a unifying force, first in the German Palatinate, and then in other German lands. People of the German Reformed Church began immigrating to the New World early in the 18th century. Settlement in the middle Atlantic colonies saw the heaviest concentration locating in Pennsylvania. Independence from European supervision and the formal organization of the American denomination were completed in 1793. The church spread across the country, and in the Mercersburg Movement, developed a strong emphasis on evangelical catholicity and Christian unity.

(4) By the opening of the 19th century in Germany, Enlightenment criticism and Pietist inwardness had worked a marked decrease in long-standing conflicts between religious groups. In Prussia, a royal proclamation merged Lutheran and Reformed people into one United Evangelical Church (1817). Members of this new church way migrated to America just as earlier German migrants were moving west. The Evangelicals settled in large numbers in Missouri and Illinois, there continuing their noncontroversial emphasis on pietistic devotion and unionism; in 1840 they formed the German Evangelical Church Society in the West. Union with other Evangelical church associations further expanded the movement's membership until in 1877 it took the name of the German Evangelical Synod of North America.

On June 25, 1934, this Synod and the Reformed Church in the U.S. (formerly the German Reformed Church) united to form the Evangelical and Reformed Church. The formation of the Evangelical and Reformed Church blended the Reformed tradition's passion for the unity of the church and the Evangelical tradition's commitment to the liberty of conscience inherent in the gospel.

HEADQUARTERS

700 Prospect Ave. E, Cleveland, OH 44115 Tel. (216)736-2100 Fax (216)736-2120
Media Contact, UCC-Sec., Edith A. Guffey, Tel. (216)736-2110

OFFICERS

Pres., Rev. Paul H. Sherry
Sec., Ms. Edith Guffey
Dir. of Finance & Treas., Rev. Doris R. Powell
Exec. Assoc. to the Pres., Ms. Bernice Powell
Asst. to Pres. For Ecumenical Conerns, Rev. John H. Thomas
Asst. to Pres., Ms. Marilyn Dubasek
Affirmative Action Officer, Mr. Hollis Wilson
Chpsn. Exec. Council, Ms. Juanita J. Helphrey
Vice-Chpsn., Mr. Douglas S. Hatfield
Mod., Mr. David Ruhe (NE)
Asst. Mod., Ms. Lilia L. Enriquez (CAL. S)
Asst. Mod., Mr. William A. Malaski, Sr. (ND)

ORGANIZATIONS

UNITED CHURCH BOARD FOR WORLD MIN.:; 475 Riverside Dr., New York, NY 10115 Tel. (212)870-2637; 14 Beacon St., Boston, MA 02018; Exec. Vice-Pres., Rev. Scott S. Libbey Planning, Correlation & Admn. Unit, Gen. Sec., Rev. Scott S. Libbey; Assoc., Ofc. of the Exec. Vice-Pres., Rev. Bertrice Y. Wood; Staff Personnel Mgr., Ms. Rita E. Maslanek

Mission Program Unit, Gen. Sec., Rev. Daniel F. Romero; Assoc. Gen. Sec., Rev. Lloyd Van Vactor; Regional Sec. for Middle East, Mr. Dale Bishop; Sec. for Racial/Ethnic Minority Constituency & Dev., Rev. Arthur L. Cribbs, Jr.; Asst. Treas., Mr. Bruce Foresman; Regional Sec. for Southern Asia, Rev. Eric A. Gass; Regional Sec. for Africa, Rev. Bonganjalo Goba; Regional Sec. for East Asia/Pacific, Rev. Ching-fen Hsiao; Sec. for Mission Educ. & Interpretation, Ms. Sandra Rooney; Exec. Sec. for Common Ministry in Latin Amer./Caribbean, Rev. David A. Vargas; Assoc. to Rev. Vargas, Ms. Carmen A. Nebot; Overseas Personnel Sec. (Int.), Ms. Evelyn Wilson; Assoc. for Foreign Policy Advocacy, Ms. Andrea I. Young; Reg. Sec. Europe, Assoc. Sec. Global Educ. & Advocacy, Rev. Kenneth R. Ziebell; Admn., Refugee Resettlement, Ms. Mary K. Kuenning; Admn., Child Sponsorship, Ms. Murcy Poulard; Sec. for Global Educ. & Advocacy, Susan Peacock; Sec. for World Ministries in the US, Theron Provance

Support Services Unit, Treas. & Gen. Sec., Rev. Myles Walburn; Assoc. Treas., Mr. Bruce C. Foresman; Mgr. Fin. Services, Ms. Dorothy E. Teffeau; Mgr. Computer Services, Mr. James Nash; Mgr. Bus. Services, Ms. Arlene Yellen

UNITED CHURCH BOARD FOR HOMELAND MIN.: Tel. (216)736-3800 Fax (216)736-3803

Office of Exec. Vice-Pres., Exec. Vice-Pres., Rev. Charles Shelby Rooks; Gen. Sec., Rev. Robert P. Noble, Jr.; Clk. of the Bd. of Dir., Ms. Mary Ann Murray; Sec. for Business Affairs, Mr. Bill G. Hendricks; Personnel Mgr., Ms. Angela McCray; Coord. of Computer Services, -----; Coord. Special Mission Emphasis, Rev. Ted Erickson; Sec. for Res. & Eval., Mr. C. Kirk Hadaway; Sec. for Information Services, Ms. Sheila Kelly

Office of the Treasurer, Treas., Rev. Robert P. Noble, Jr.; Corp. Social Responsibility Officer, Rev. Wayne Owens

Div. of Evangelism & Local Church Dev., Secs. for Evang. & Membership Growth, Rev. R. Alan Johnson; Rev. Martha McMane; Sec. for Church Dev., Rev. John W. Mingus; Sec. for Ethnic & Minority Church Dev., Rev. Paul H. Sadler; Secs. for Local Church Finance Advisory Services, Rev. George C. Hawkins; Ms. Beatrice H. Starrett; Rev. P. William VanderWyden; Sec. for Local Church Capital Dev., Rev Robert F. Haskins, Jr.; Telecommunications Assoc., Ms. Karin Stork-Whiteson; Mr. Charles M. Whitson; Sec. for Local Church Building, Mr. Michael Downs

Div. of Education & Publication, Gen. Sec., Rev. Ansley Coe Throckmorton; Sec. for Biblical & Theological Found. for Educ., Rev. Grant Sontag; Sec. for Educ. in the Local Church, Mr. Jose Abraham Dejesus; Sec. for Educ. in the Parish Community, Rev. Thomas M. Carson; Sec. for Educ. in the Family, Ms. Patricia J. Goldberg; Sec. Educ. in Human Identity & Youth/Young Ad. Prog., Rev. Gordon J. Svoboda, III; Sec. for Racial & Ethnic Educ. Ministries, Rev. Vilma M. Machin; Sec. for High Educ. & Ministries Resources., Rev. Verlyn L. Barker; Sec. for Higher Educ. Relationships, Rev. James A. Smith, Jr.; Coord. of Church-College Relations, -----; Sec. for Curriculum Services, Rev. Morris D. Pike; Sec. for Publications & Publisher, Mr. James J. Heaney; Ed., United Church Press, -----; Ed., The Pilgrim Press, Ms. Barbara Withers; Bus. Mgr., Publications Operations, Mr. Bill L. Shaw;

Sales/Dist. Mgr. Pilgrim Press/United Church Press, Ms. Angela M. Fasciana; Marketing Dir., Mr. David Martin Perkins

Div. of American Missionary Association, Co-Gen. Secs., Rev. B. Ann Eichhorn; Rev. L. William Eichhorn; Sec. for AIDS Prog. & Ministries Coord., Rev. William R. Johnson; Sec. for Citizen Empowerment, -----; Sec. for Health Prog., Ms. Loretta M. Richardson; Sec. for Homelessness & Economic Justice Prog., Mr. James A. McDaniel; Sec. for Human Dev. Prog. & Concerns, Ms. Faith A. Johnson; Sec. for Local Churches in Community Mission, Rev. Paul R. Peters; Sec. for Ministries to Special Groups, Rev. Cynthia Ikuta; Sec. for Public Issues in Educ., Ms. Nanette M. Roberts; Sec. for Racial Justice Prog., Ms. Juanita Helphrey; Sec. for Special Prog. & Services, Ms. Susan M. Sanders; Community Organizing, Rev. Phillip Newell; Dir. UCC Hunger Action Office, Rev. Steven Nunn-Miller

COMMISSION FOR RACIAL JUSTICE:; Ofc. for Urban & Natl. Racial Justice, 5113 Georgia Ave. NW, Washington, DC 20011 Tel. (202)291-1593; Ofc. for Constituency Dev./Rural Racial Justice, Frankcinton Center, P.O. Box 187, Enfield, NC 27823 Tel. (919)437-1723; Ofc. for Ecumenical Racial Justice, 475 Riverside Dr., Room 1948, New York, NY 10115 Tel. (212)870-2077; Exec. Dir., Rev. Benjamin F. Chavis, Jr. (OH); Exec. Asst., Ms. Estomarys Tall (OH), Tel. (216)736-2161; Natl. Assoc. for Fiscal & Ofc. Mgmt., Ms. Andrea C. Gibbs; Natl. Assoc. for Mission Interpretation, Rev. Leon White; Dir. Ofc. for Natl. & Urban Racial Justice, Mrs. Toni A. Killings; Assoc. for Fiscal & Ofc. Mgmt., Ms. Della Owens; Dir. Ofc. for Constituency Dev. & Rural Racial Justice, Ms. Vivian L. Wynn; Assoc. for Constituency Dev., Ms. Margaret Ellis; Assoc. for Fiscal & Ofc. Mgmt., Rev. Collins Kornegay; Dir. Ofc. for Ecumenical Racial Justice, Mr. Charles Lee

COUNCIL FOR AMERICAN INDIAN MINISTRY: 122 W. Franklin Ave., Rm. 304, Minneapolis, MN 55405 Tel. (612)870-3679; Exec. Dir., Rev. Armin L. Schmidt; Ofc. Mgr., -----

COUNCIL FOR HEALTH & HUMAN SERVICE MINS.: Tel. (216)736-2250; Exec. Dir., Bryan Sickbert; Admn. Services Coord., Ms. Christine Williams; Sec. for Membership & Fin., Carol Cashmere

COORD. CTR. FOR WOMEN IN CHURCH & SOC.: Tel. (216)736-2150; Exec. Dir., Rev. Mary Sue Gast; Assoc. for Advocacy & Prog. Dev., -----; Assoc. for Admn. & Ofc. Mgmt., Ms. Deborah Bailey; Ed., Common Lot, Ms. Marti Marrison

OFFICE FOR CHURCH IN SOCIETY:; 110 Maryland Ave. NE, Washington, DC 20002; Exec. Dir., ----- (OH); Dir., Washington Ofc., Rev. Jay E. Lintner; Assoc. for Policy Advocacy, Rev. Patrick W. Grace Conover (DC); Assoc., Network Dev., Ms. Rebecca Gallatin (DC); Assoc., Communications, Rev. Rubin Tendal (DC); Assoc., Church Empowerment, Rev. Dale Susan Edmonds (OH); Rev. Charles R. McCullough (OH); Exec. Assoc., Ms. Verna Rapp Uthman (OH)

OFFICE FOR CHURCH LIFE AND LEADERSHIP:; Exec. Dir., Rev. William A. Hulteen, Jr. (OH); Exec. Assoc., Rev. Thomas R. Tupper (OH); Assoc., Great Lakes Region, Rev. Charlotte H. Still (OH); Assoc., Middle Atlantic Region, Rev. Felix Carrion, 505 2nd Ave., Box 400, Collegeville, PA 19426; Assoc., Southern Region, Rev. Ervin Milton, P.O. Box 658, Graham, NC 27253; Assoc., West Central Region, Peter Monkres, 3000 5th St. NW, Brightan, MN 55112; Assoc., Western Region, Rev. Rodney C. Yee, 20 Woodside Ave., San Francisco, CA; Assoc., New England Region, Rev. Ann Suzedell, 210 Herrick Rd., Newton Centre, MA 02159; Assoc. for Media Res., Ms. Dorothy M. Lester (OH)

OFFICE OF COMMUNICATION: Tel. (216)736-2222 Fax (216)736-2223; 475 Riverside Dr., 16th Fl., New York, NY 10115 Tel. (212)870-2137; Dir., Dr. Beverly J. Chain; Adm. Asst., Doris M. Tate; Educ./Mktg. Coord., Rev. Eugene A. Schneider; Ed., United Church News, Rev. W. Evan Golder (OH); Ed. Asst., Ms. Charlene J. Smith (OH); Pub. Rel. Coord., Mr. Hans Holznagel (OH); Pub. Rel. Asst. (Bios, photos), Andrea B. Fields; Writer, Ms. Sharon Jefferson (OH); Copy Ed., Barbara Powell; Video, Mr. William C. Winslow (NY); Writer, Rev. Kathi D. Wolfe (OH); Assoc. for Communication Policy/Advocacy (DC), Mr. Anthony L. Pharr, Tel. (202)331-4236; Writer, Rev. Rubin Tendai (DC); Bus. Mgr., Barbara Fryman; Educ./Marketing Asst., Alice Dinicola

STEWARDSHIP COUNCIL:; 1400 N. Seventh St., St. Louis, MO 63106; 254 College St., Ste. 501, New Haven, CT 06510; 475 Riverside Dr., Rm. 1950, New York, NY 10115; Exec. Dir., Rev. George W. Otto; Exec. Assoc., Rev. Dean O. Warburton; Assoc. for Stewardship Program & Admn., United Church Resources, -----; Consultant for Financial Development, Rev. Paul E. Baumer, 59 E. Mound St., Columbus, OH 43215 Tel. (615)224-8634; Assoc. for Stewardship Educ., David L. Beebe (MO); Assoc. for Steward Program, Rev. M. Douglas Borko (OH); Adm. Assoc., Ms. Ventrice G. Cadette (OH); Consultant for Special Projects, Rev. Charles W. Cooper, Jr. (OH); Consultant, Comp. Oper., Ms. Lucy P. Werner, P.O. Box 462, Hartsdale, NY; Assoc. for Mission & Stewardship Communication, Rev. Christopher P. Stockwell-Goerine (OH); Assoc. for Stewardship Dev., Ms. Veronica Jefferson (NY); Assoc. for Mission Educ., Mr. Alfred H. Jones (NY); Prog. Assoc., Rev. C. David Langerhans, 22 Longcourse Ln., Paoli, PA 19301; Managing Ed., Ms. Christina Brochu (CT); Conference-Affiliated Staff, Dr. Randall Y. Furushima (HI), 15 Craigside Pl., Honolulu, HI 96817; Rev. Stephen C. Gray (MA); Rev. Kenneth W. Taylor (CT); Rev. Raymond W. Hargrove (Southern), P.O. Box 658, Graham, NC 27253

COMMISSION ON DEVELOPMENT: Dir. Planned Giving, Rev. Donald G. Stoner; Assoc., Ms. Stella Schoen; Sec., Audrey Boughman

HISTORICAL COUNCIL:; Office of Archivist, Phillip Schaff Library, Lancaster Theological Seminary, 555 W. James St., Lancaster, PA 17603

PENSION BOARDS: 475 Riverside Dr., New York, NY 10115; Exec. Vice-Pres., Dr. John Ordway; Admn. Vice-Pres., Mrs. Joan F. Brannick; Vice-Pres., Conference Relations, Rev. Lawrence J. Rezash; Treas., Mr. Richard H. Dubie; Asst. Treas., Mr. Osborne D. Nichols; Mr. Raymond J. Healey; Mrs. Norma M. Robinson; Ms. Patricia S. Rossi; Controller, Mr. Donald G. Hart; Sec., Member Relations, Mr. Edmund G. Tortora; Sec., Policies & Procedures, Ms. Maria Lucia; Benefits, Mr. Frank Patti; Sec.,

Ministerial Asst., Rev. Donald E. Stumpf
UNITED CHURCH FOUNDATION, INC.: 475 Riverside Dr., New York, NY 10115; Financial Vice-Pres. & Treas., Richard H. Dubie

CONFERENCES

Western Region
California, Northern, Rev. David J. Jamieson, 20 Woodside Ave., San Francisco, CA 94127
California, Southern, Rev. Davida Foy Crabtree, 466 E. Walnut St., Pasadena, CA 91101
Hawaii, Rev. Norman Jackson, 15 Craigside Pl., Honolulu, HI 96817
Montana-Northern Wyoming, Rev. John M. Schaeffer, 2016 Alderson Ave., Billings, MT 59102
Central Pacific, Rev. Donald J. Sevetson, 0245 SW Bancroft St., Ste. E, Portland, OR 97201
Rocky Mountain, Rev. Clyde H. Miller, Jr., 7000 Broadway, Ste. 420, ABS Bldg., Denver, CO 80221
Southwest, Rev. Carole G. Keim, 4423 N. 24th St., Ste. 600, Phoenix, AZ 85016
Washington-North Idaho, Rev. David J. Brown, 720 14th Ave. E., Seattle, WA 98102

West Central Region
Iowa, Rev. Donald A. Gall, 600 42nd St., Des Moines, IA 50312
Kansas-Oklahoma, Rev. Ronald L. Eslinger, 1248 Fabrique, Wichita, KS 67218
Minnesota, Rev. Jeffrey N. Stinehelfer, 122 W. Franklin Ave., Rm. 323, Minneapolis, MN 55404
Missouri, A. Gayle Engel (Interim), 461 E. Lockwood Ave., St. Louis, MO 63119
Nebraska, Rev. Clarence M. Higgins, Jr., 2055 "E" Street, Lincoln, NE 68510
North Dakota, Rev. Jack J. Seville, Jr., 227 W. Broadway, Bismarck, ND 58501
South Dakota, Rev. Ed Mehlhaff, Ste. B, 801 E. 41st St., Sioux Falls, SD 57105

Great Lakes Region
Illinois, Rev. W. Sterling Cary, 1840 Westchester Blvd., Ste. 200, P.O. Box 7208, Westchester, IL 60154
Illinois South, Rev. Martha Ann Baumer, Box 325 Broadway, Highland, IL 62249
Indiana-Kentucky, Rev. Ralph C. Quellhorst, 1100 W. 42nd St., Indianapolis, IN 46208
Michigan, Rev. Marwood E. Rettig, P.O. Box 1006, East Lansing, MI 48826
Ohio, Rev. Carlton N. Weber, 4041 N. High St., Ste. 301, Columbus, OH 43214
Wisconsin, Rev. Frederick R. Trost, 2719 Marshall Ct., Madison, WI 53705

Southern Region
Florida, Rev. Charles L. Burns, Jr., 222 E. Welbourne Ave., Winter Park, FL 32789
South Central, Rev. James Tomasek, Jr., 2704 Rio Grande #8, Austin, TX 78705
Southeast, Rev. Roger Knight, P.O. Box 29883, Atlanta, GA 30359
Southern, Rev. Rollin O. Russell, 217 N. Main St., Box 658, Graham, NC 27253

Middle Atlantic Region
Central Atlantic, Rev. John R. Deckenback, 916 S. Rolling Rd., Baltimore, MD 21228
New York, Rev. William Briggs, The Church Center, Rm. 260, 3049 E. Genesee St., Syracuse, NY 13224
Penn Central, Rev. Lyle J. Weible, The United Church Center, Rm. 126, 900 S. Arlington Ave., Harrisburg, PA 17109

Penn Northeast, Rev. Donald E. Overlock, 431 Delaware Ave., P.O. Box 177, Palmerton, PA 18071
Penn Southeast, Rev. Ronald G. Kurtz, 505 Second Ave., P.O. Box 400, Collegeville, PA 19426
Penn West, Rev. Paul L. Westcoat, Jr., 320 South Maple Ave., Greensburg, PA 15601
Puerto Rico, Rev. Jaime Rivera-Solero, Box 5427, Hato Rey, PR 00919

New England Region
Connecticut, Rev. David Y. Hirano, 125 Sherman St., Hartford, CT 06105
Maine, Rev. Otto E. Sommer, 68 Main St., P.O. Box 966, Yarmouth, ME 04096
Massachusetts, Rev. Bennie E. Whiten, Jr., P.O. Box 2246, Salem & Badger Rds., Framingham, MA 01701
New Hampshire, Rev. Carole C. Carlson
New Hampshire, Rev. Robert D. Witham, 314 S. Main, P.O. Box 465, Concord, NH 03302
Rhode Island, Rev. H. Dahler Hayes, 56 Walcott St., Pawtucket, RI 02860
Vermont, Rev. D. Curtis Minter, 285 Maple St., Burlington, VT 05401

Nongeographic
Calvin Synod, Rev. Zoltan D. Szucs, 3036 Globe Ave., Lorain, OH 44055

United Holy Church of America, Inc.

The United Holy Church of America, Inc. is an outgrowth of the great revival that began with the early outpouring of the Holy Ghost on the Day of Pentecost when 120 were filled. The church is built upon the foundation of the Apostles and Prophets, Jesus Christ being the chief cornerstone.

It was during this time of revival of repentence, regeneration and holiness of heart and life that swept through the South and West, that the United Holy Church was born. There was no desire on the part of the founding fathers to establish another denomination, but they were pushed out of organized churches because of this experience of holiness and testimony of the Spirit-filled life.

In May 1886, in Method, N.C., a meeting gave birth to what is today known as the United Holy Church of America, Inc. The church was incorporated on Sept. 25, 1918 and its work has steadily grown since that time into a great organization.

Ordinances of baptism by immersion, the Lord's Supper, and feet washing are observed. Members accept the premillennial teaching of the Second Coming of Christ, Divine healing—not to the exclusion of medicine, justification by faith, sanctification as a second work of grace, and Spirit baptism.

HEADQUARTERS

5104 Dunstan Rd., Greensboro, NC 27405 Tel. (919)621-0669
Mailing Address, Bishop J. T. Bowens, 825 Fairoak Ave., Chillum, MD 20783

OFFICERS

Gen. Pres., Bishop Joseth T. Bowens, 825 Fairoak Ave., Chillum, MD 20783 Tel. (301)559-0537
1st Vice-Pres., Bishop Thomas E. Talley, P.O. Box 1035, Portsmouth, VA 23705
2nd Vice-Pres., Bishop Odell McCollum, 3206 BlueRidge Rd., Columbus, OH 43219 Tel. (614)475-4713
Gen. Rec. Sec., Rev. A. Thomas Godfrey, P.O. Box 7940, Chicago, IL Tel. (312)849-2525
Asst. Rec. Sec., Mrs. Beatrice S. Faison, 224 Wenz Rd., Toledo, OH 43615 Tel. (419)531-1859

Gen. Fin. Sec., Rev. Mrs. Clarice L. Chambers, P.O. Box 3327, Harrisburg, PA 17105 Tel. (717)238-1380

Gen. Asst. Fin. Sec., Mrs. Vera Perkins Hughes, 3425 Rosedale Rd., Cleveland Hts., OH 44112 Tel. (216)851-9645

Gen. Corres. Sec., Mrs. Gloria Rainey, 198 Easton South/102, Laurel, MD 20707 Tel. (301)725-6982

Gen. Treas., Mrs. Bertha Williams, 4749 Shaw Dr., Wilmington, NC 28405 Tel. (919)395-4462

Gen Pres. Missionary Dept., Rev. Mrs. Iris C. Fischer, 460 W. 155th St., New York, NY 10032 Tel. (212)926-9283

Gen. Supt. Bible Church School, Mr. C. M. Corbett, 519 Madera Ave., Youngstown, OH 44504 Tel. (216)744-3284

Gen. Pres. Y.P.H.A., Elder Dennis Ball, 409 N. Mountain Trail Ave., Sierra Madre, CA 91024

Gen. Educ. Dept., Dr. Chester Gregory, 1302 Lincoln Woods Dr., Baltimore, MD 21218 Tel. (301)788-5144

Gen. Usher's Dept., Mrs. Sherly Hughes, 1491 E. 191st St., Apt. H-604, Euclid, OH 44117 Tel. (216)383-0038

Gen. Statistician, Mr. Robert L. Rollins, 1628 Avondale Ave., Toledo, OH 43607 Tel. (419)246-4046

Music Dept., Gen. Chair, Mrs. Rosie Johnson, 2009 Forest Dale Dr., Silver Spring, MD 20932

PRESIDENTS OF CONVOCATIONAL DISTRICTS

Barbados, New England & Northern Dist., Bishop Joseph T. Bowens, 825 Fairoak Ave., Chillum, MD 20783

Bermuda Dist., Bishop Norris N. Dickenson, P.O. Box Cr32, 27 Old Road, Crawl CR BX, Bermuda, CR01

Central Western Dist., Bishop Bose Bradford, 6279 Natural Bridge, Pine Lawn, MO 63121 Tel. (314)355-1598

Haiti Dist., Bishop Cannier Guillaume, 108 Bas Fort National, Port-au-Prince, Haiti, West Indies

Florida/Georgia Dist., Bishop Elijah Williams, 901 Briarwood St., Reidsville, NC 27320 Tel. (919)349-7275

Northwestern Dist., Bishop Odell McCollum, 3206 BlueRidge Rd., Columbus, OH 43219

Southern Dist./W. North Carolina Dist., Bishop Jesse Jones, 608 Cecil St., Durham, NC 27707 Tel. (919)682-8249

Virginia Dist., Bishop Thomas E. Talley, 2710 Magnolia St., Portsmouth, VA 23705

West Virginia Dist., Bishop Alvester McConnell, Rte. 3, Box 263, Bluefield, WV 24701 Tel. (304)248-8046

Western Dist., Bishop M. D. Borden, 8655 Melody Land, Macedonia, OH 44056 Tel. (216)468-0270

PERIODICAL

Holiness Union, The

The United Methodist Church

The United Methodist Church was formed April 23, 1968, in Dallas, Texas, by the union of The Methodist Church and The Evangelical United Brethren Church. The two churches shared a common historical and spiritual heritage. The Methodist Church resulted in 1939 from the unification of three branches of Methodism--the Methodist Episcopal Church; the Methodist Episcopal Church, South; and the Methodist Protestant Church.

The Methodist movement began in 18th-century England under the preaching of John Wesley, but the Christmas Conference of 1784 in Baltimore is regarded as the date on which the organized Methodist Church was founded as an ecclesiastical organization. It was there that Francis Asbury was elected the first bishop in this country. The Evangelical United Brethren Church was formed in 1946 with the merger of the Evangelical Church and the Church of the United Brethren in Christ, both of which had their beginnings in Pennsylvania in the evangelistic movement of the 18th and early 19th centuries. Philip William Otterbein and Jacob Albright were early leaders of this movement among the German-speaking settlers of the Middle Colonies.

MEDIA CONTACT

Media Contact, Dir., United Methodist News Service, Thomas S. McAnally, P.O. Box 320, Nashville, TN 37202 Tel. (615)742-5470 Fax (615)742-5469

OFFICERS

Gen. Conference, Sec., Carolyn M. Marshall, 204 N. Newlin St., Veedersburg, IN 47987

Council of Bishops: Pres., Bishop Joseph H. Yeakel, 9226 Colesville Rd., Silver Spring, MD 20910-1658 Tel. (301)587-9226; Sec., Bishop Melvin G. Talbert, P.O. Box 467, San Francisco, CA 94101 Tel. (415)474-3101

BISHOPS AND CONFERENCE COUNCIL DIRECTORS

North Central Jurisdiction

Central Illinois: Bishop Woodie W. White, Tel. (217)544-4604; Donald Jones, P.O. Box 2050, Bloomington, IL 61701 Tel. (309)559-7000

Detroit: Bishop Judith Craig, Tel. (313)559-7000; Theodore E. Doane, 21700 Northwestern Hwy., Southfield, MI 48075 Tel. (313)559-7000

East Ohio: Bishop Edwin C. Bolton, Tel. (216)499-8471; Judith A. Olin, 8800 Cleeveland Ave. NW, North Canton, OH 44720 Tel. (216)499-3972

Iowa: Bishop Reuben P. Job, Tel. (515)283-1991; Bruce Ough, 1019 Chestnut St., Des Moines, IA 50309 Tel. (515)283-1991

Minnesota: Bishop Sharon Brown Christopher, Tel. (612)870-3648; Delton Kraueger, 122 W. Franklin Ave., Room 400, Minneapolis, MN 55404 Tel. (612)870-3647

North Dakota: Bishop William B. Lewis, Tel. (701)232-2241; Ray Wagner, 2410 12th St. N., Fargo, ND 58102 Tel. (701)232-2241

North Indiana: Bishop Leroy C. Hodapp, Tel. (317)924-1321; Louis E. Haskell, P.O. Box 869, Marion, IN 46952 Tel. (317)664-5138

Northern Illinois: Bishop R. Sheldon Duecker, Tel. (312)782-1422; Carolyn H. Oehler, 77 W. Washington St., Ste. 1806, Chicago, IL 60602 Tel. (312)346-8752

South Dakota: Bishop William B. Lewis, Tel. (701)232-2241; Richard Fisher, P.O. Box 460, Mitchell, SD 57301 Tel. (605)996-6552

South Indiana: Bishop Leroy C. Hodapp, Tel. (317)924-1321; Robert Coleman, Box 5008, Bloomington, IN 47402 Tel. (812)336-0186

Southern Illinois: Bishop Woodie W. White, Tel. (217)544-4604; William Frazier, 1919 Broadway, Mt. Vernon, IL 62864 Tel. (618)242-4070

West Michigan: Bishop Judith Craig, Tel. (313)961-8340; David B. Nelson, P.O. Box 6287, Grand Rapids, MI 49506 Tel. (616)459-4503

West Ohio: Bishop Edsel A. Ammons, Tel. (614)228-6784; Vance Summers, 471 E. Broad St., Ste. 1106, Columbus, OH 43215 Tel. (614)228-6784

Wisconsin: Bishop David J. Lawson, Tel. (608)837-8526; Bill Bross, P.O. Box 220, Sun Prairie, WI 53590 Tel. (608)837-7328

Northeastern Jurisdiction

Baltimore: Bishop Joseph H. Yeakel, Tel. (301)587-9226; Marcus Matthews, 5124 Greenwich Ave., Baltimore, MD 21229 Tel. (301)233-7300

Central Pennsylvania: Bishop Felton E. May, Tel. (717)652-6705; Bruce Fisher, 3920 Woodvale Rd., Harrisburg, PA 17109 Tel. (717)652-0460

Eastern Pennsylvania: Bishop Susan M. Morrison, Tel. (215)666-9090; Robert Daughtery, P.O. Box 820, P.O. Box 820, Valley Forge, PA 19482 Tel. (215)666-9090

Maine: Bishop F. Herbert Skeete, Tel. (617)536-7764; Beverly Abbott, P.O. Box 277, Winthrop, ME 04364 Tel. (207)377-2912

New Hampshire: Bishop F. Herbert Skeete, Tel. (617)536-7764; Philip M. Polhemus, 722A, Route 3A, Concord, NH 03301 Tel. (603)225-6312

New York: Bishop C. Dale White, Tel. (914)997-1570; Wilson Boots, 252 Bryant Ave., White Plains, NY 10605 Tel. (914)997-1570

North Central New York: Bishop Forrest C. Stith, Tel. (315)446-6731; James Pollard, P.O. Box 515, Cicero, NY 13039 Tel. (315)699-5506

Northern New Jersey: Bishop Neil L. Irons, Tel. (609)737-3940; Barrie T. Smith, P.O. Box 546, Madison, NJ 07940 Tel. (201)377-3800

Peninsula: Bishop Susan M. Morrison, Tel. (212)666-9090; Harvey Manchester, 139 N. State St., Dover, DE 19901 Tel. (302)674-2626

Puerto Rico: Bishop C. Dale White, Tel. (914)997-1570; Victor Ortiz, Francisco Stein St., #430, Hato Rey, PR 00918 Tel. (809)765-3195

Southern New England: Bishop F. Herbert Skeete, Tel. (617)536-7764; Donald J. Rudalevige, 566 Commonwealth Ave., Boston, MA 02115 Tel. (617)266-3900

Southern New Jersey: Bishop Neil F. Irons, Tel. (609)737-3940; George T. Wang, 1995 E. Marlton Pike, Cherry Hill, NJ 08003 Tel. (609)424-1701

Troy: Bishop James K. Mathews, Tel. (518)425-0386; James M. Perry, P.O. Box 560, Saratoga Springs, NY 12866 Tel. (518)584-8214

West Virginia: Bishop William B. Grove, Tel. ((304)344-8330; Thomas E. Dunlap, Sr., P.O. Box 2313, Charleston, WV 25328 Tel. (304)344-8331

Western New York: Bishop Forrest C. Stith, Tel. (315)446-6731; J. Fay Cleveland, 8499 Main St., Buffalo, NY 14221 Tel. (716)633-8558

Western Pennsylvania: Bishop George W. Bashore, Tel. (412)776-2300; John Ross Thompson, 1204 Freedom Rd., Mars, PA 16046 Tel. (412)776-2300

Wyoming: Bishop James K. Mathews, Tel. (518)425-0386; Kenneth E. Wood, 3 Orchard Rd., Binghamton, NY 13905 Tel. (607)772-8840

South Central Jurisdiction

Exec. Dir.: L. Ray Branton, 6155 Samuel Blvd., Dallas, TX 75228 Tel. (214)321-7077

Central Texas: Bishop John W. Russell, Tel. (817)877-5222; Michael Patison, 464 Bailey, Ft. Worth, TX 76107 Tel. (817)877-5222

Kansas East: Bishop Kenneth W. Hicks, Tel. (913)272-0587; H. Sharon Howell, P.O. Box 4187, Topeka, KS 66604 Tel. (913)272-9111

Kansas West: Bishop Kenneth W. Hicks, Tel. (913)272-0587; Wayne D. Findley, Sr., 151 N. Volutsia, Wichita, KS 67214 Tel. (316)684-0266

Little Rock: Bishop Richard B. Wilke, Tel. (501)374-6679; Jay Lofton, 715 Center St., Ste. 202, Little Rock, AR 72201 Tel. (501)374-5027

Louisiana: Bishop William B. Oden, Tel. (504)346-1646; Donald C. Cottrill, 527 North Blvd., Baton Rouge, LA 70802 Tel. (504)346-1646

Missouri East: Bishop W. T. Handy, Jr., Tel. (314)367-5001; Duane Van Giesen, 4625 Lindell Blvd., #424, St. Louis, MO 63108 Tel. (314)367-7422

Missouri West: Bishop W. T. Handy, Jr., Tel. (314)237-5001; Keith T. Berry, 1512 Van Brunt Blvd., Kansas City, MO 64127 Tel. (816)241-7650

Nebraska: Bishop J. Woodrow Hearn, Tel. (402)464-5994; Richard D. Turner, P.O. Box 4553, Lincoln, NE 68504 Tel. (402)464-5994

New Mexico: Bishop Louis W. Schowengerdt, Tel. (505)883-5418; Mark Dorff, 8100 Mountain Rd. NE, Albuquerque, NM 87110 Tel. (505)255-8786

North Arkansas: Bishop Richard B. Wilke, Tel. (501)374-6679; Jim Beal, 715 Center St., Little Rock, AR 72201 Tel. (501)753-8946

North Texas: Bishop Bruce Blake; Gary E. Mueller, P.O. Box 516069, Dallas, TX 75251 Tel. (214)490-3438

Northwest Texas: Bishop Louis W. Schowengerdt, Tel. (505)883-5418; Louise Schock, 1415 Ave. M, Lubbock, TX 79401 Tel. (806)762-0201

Oklahoma: Bishop Dan E. Solomon, Tel. (405)525-2252; David Severe, 2420 N. Blackwelder, Oklahoma City, OK 73106 Tel. (405)525-2252

Oklahoma Indian Missionary: Bishop Dan E. Solomon, Tel. (405)525-2252; Becky Thompson, 147 Delaware Ave., Tulsa, OK 74110 Tel. (405)632-2006

Rio Grande: Bishop Ernest T. Dixon, Tel. (512)432-0401; Arturo Mariscal, Jr., P.O. Box 28098, San Antonio, TX 78284 Tel. (512)432-2534

Southwest Texas: Bishop Ernest T. Dixon, Tel. (512)432-0401; Harry G. Kahl, P.O. Box 28098, San Antonio, TX 78284 Tel. (512)432-4680

Texas: Bishop Benjamin R. Oliphint, Tel. (713)528-6881; Asbury Lenox, 5215 S. Main St., Houston, TX 77002 Tel. (713)521-9383

Southeastern Jurisdiction

Exec. Sec.: Reginald Ponder, P.O. Box 237, Lake Junaluska, NC 28745 Tel. (704)452-1881

Alabama-West Florida: Bishop C. W. Hancock, Tel. (205)277-1787; William Calhoun, P.O. Box 700, Andalusia, AL 36420 Tel. (205)222-3127

Florida: Bishop H. Hasbrock Hughes, Jr., Tel. (813)688-4427; Robert Bledsoe, P.O. Box 3767, Lakeland, FL 33802 Tel. (813)688-5563

Holston: Bishop Clay F. Lee, Tel. (615)525-1809; Gordon C. Goodgame, P.O. Box 1178, Johnson City, TN 37601 Tel. (615)928-2156

Kentucky: Bishop Robert H. Spain, Tel. (502)893-6715; Larry B. Gardner, P.O. Box 5107, Lexington, KY 40555 Tel. (606)254-7388

Louisville: Bishop Robert H. Spain, Tel. (502)893-6715; Rhoda Peters, 1115 S. Fourth St., Louisville, KY 40203 Tel. (502)584-3838

Memphis: Bishop Ernest W. Newman, Tel. (615)327-3462; James H. Holmes, St., 575 Lambuth Blvd., Jackson, TN 38301 Tel. (901)427-8589

Mississippi: Bishop Robert C. Morgan, Tel. (601)948-4561; W. F. Appleby, P.O. Box 1147, Jackson, MS 39215 Tel. (601)354-0515

North Alabama: Bishop L. Lloyd Knox, Tel. (205)879-8665; George W. Hayes, 898 Arkadelphia Rd., Birmingham, AL 35204 Tel. (205)251-9279

North Carolina: Bishop C. P. Minnick, Jr., Tel. (919)832-9560; G. Robert McKenzie, Jr., P.O. Box 10955, Raleigh, NC 27605 Tel. (919)832-9560

North Georgia: Bishop Ernest A. Fitzgerald, Tel. (404)659-0002; Robert Bridges, 159 Ralph McGill Blvd. NE, Atlanta, GA 30365 Tel. (404)659-0002

Red Bird Missionary: Bishop Robert H. Spain, Tel. (502)893-6715; Ruth Wiertzema, Queendale Ctr., Box 3, Beverly, KY 40913 Tel. (606)598-5915

South Carolina: Bishop Joseph B. Bethea, Tel. (803)786-9486; Lemuel C. Carter, 4908 Colonial Dr., Ste. 101, Columbia, SC 29203 Tel. (803)754-0297

South Georgia: Bishop Richard C. Looney, Tel. (404)659-0002; William E. McTier, Jr., P.O. Box 408, St. Simons Island, GA 31522 Tel. (912)638-8626

Tennessee: Bishop Ernest W. Newman, Tel. (615)327-3462; Thomas C. Cloyd, P.O. Box 120607, Nashville, TN 37212 Tel. (615)329-1177

Virginia: Bishop Thomas B. Stockton, Tel. (804)359-9451; Lee B. Sheaffer, P.O. 11367, Richmond, VA 23230 Tel. (804)359-9451

Western North Carolina: Bishop L. Bevel Jones, Tel. (704)535-2260; Donald W. Maynes, P.O. Box 18005, PO Box 18005, Charlotte, NC 28218 Tel. (704)535-2260

Western Jurisdiction

Alaska Missionary: Bishop William W. Dew, Jr., Tel. (503)226-7931; Dennis Holway, 3402 Wesleyan Dr., Anchorage, AK 99508 Tel. (907)274-1571

California-Nevada: Bishop Melvin G. Talbert, Tel. (415)474-3101; James H. Corson, P.O. Box 467, San Francisco, CA 94101 Tel. (415)474-3101

California-Pacific: Bishop Jack M. Tuell, Tel. (818)796-6607; J. Delton Pickering, 472 E. Colorado Blvd., P.O. Box 6006, Pasadena, CA 91109 Tel. (818)796-6607

Desert Southwest: Bishop Elias Galvin, Tel. (602)496-9446; Lawrence A. Hinshaw, 2933 E. Indian School Rd., #402, Phoenix, AZ 85016 Tel. (602)496-9446

Oregon-Idaho: Bishop William A. Dew, Jr., Tel. (503)226-7931; Arvin Luchs, 1505 SW 18th Ave., Portland, OR 97201 Tel. (503)226-7931

Pacific Northwest: Bishop Calvin D. McConnell, Tel. (206)728-7462; W. F. Summerour, 2112 Third Ave., Ste. 300, Seattle, WA 98121 Tel. (206)728-7462

Rocky Mountain: Bishop Roy I. Sano, Tel. (303)733-3736; John Blinn, 2200 S. University Blvd., Denver, CO 80210 Tel. (303)733-3736

Yellowstone: Bishop Roy I. Sano, Tel. (303)733-3736; Gary Keene, 335 Broadwater Ave., Billings, MT 59101 Tel. (406)256-1385

OTHER ORGANIZATIONS

Judicial Council: Pres., Tom Matheny; Sec., Wayne Coffin, 2420 N. Blackwelder, Oklahoma City, OK 73106

Council on Finance & Administration: Pres., Bishop John W. Russell, 1200 Davis St., Evanston, IL 60201 Tel. (708)869-3345; Vice-Pres., Bishop Forrest C. Stith; Rec. Sec., Ron Gilbert; Gen. Sec.and Treas., Clifford Droke; Dept. of Episcopal Services, Asst. Gen. Sec. Elizabeth Okayama; Section on Legal Services, Gen. Counsel Craig R. Hoskins; Section on Mgnt. Informations Systems, Asst. Gen. Sec. Al Fifhause; Dir. of Council Operations, Mary Simmons; Local Church Insurance Program, Asst. Gen. Sec. Diane O. Pinney; Div. of Financial Services, Assoc. Gen. Sec. Gary K. Bowen; Controller, Beth Taylor; Asst. Controller, Lesslie Keller; Payroll Dept., Dir. Phyllis Anderson; Service Ctr. Dayton, Asst. Gen. Treas. Lola Conrad; Service Ctr. Nashville, Comptroller W. C. Hawkins; Service Ctr. Washington, DC, Asst. Controller Clarence Waldroff; Service Ctr., New York, Asst. Gen. Treas. Stephen F. Brimigion; Section on Investments, Gary K. Bowen; Div. of Admn. Services: Sect. on Records & Statistics, Asst. Gen. Sec. John L. Schreiber; Dept. of Records, Dir. Cynthia Haralson; Dept. of Statistics, Dir. Daniel A. Nielsen

Council on Ministries: Pres., Bishop Felton E. May, 601 W. Riverview Ave., Dayton, OH 45406 Tel. (513)227-9400; Vice-Pres., Jean Dowell; Vice-Pres., Joel N. Martinez; Sec., J. Taylor Phillips; Gen. Sec., C. David Lundquist; Assoc. Gen. Sec., Trudie Kibbe Preciphs; Donald L. Hayashi; Mearle L. Griffith

Comm. on Communication/UM Communications: Pres., Bishop Rueben P. Job, P.O. Box 320, 810 12th Ave. S., Nashville, TN 37202 Tel. (615)742-5400; Vice-Pres., Mary Silva; Sec., James Lane; Gen Sec., Roger L. Burgess; Assoc. Gen Sec., Personnel & Admn., Newtonia Harris Coleman; Treas., Peggy Williamson; Dir., Conf. Serv. & Communication Ed., Shirley Whipple Struchen; Dir. of Public Relations, Roger L. Burgess; Dir., Mgmt. Info. Systems Dept., Susan Peek; Div. of Prog. & Benevolence Interpretation, Assoc. Gen. Sec., Donald E. Collier; Dir., Pulications, Darrell R. Shamblin; Editorial Dir., Barbara Dunlap-Berg; Dir., InfoServ, Woodley McEachern; Div. of Production & Distribution, Assoc. Gen. Sec., Peggy J. West; AV/Media Production, Dir., Stephen Downey; Media Distribution, Dir., Furman York; Tech. Servs. Mgr., Dixie Parman; Div. of Public Media, Assoc. Gen.Sec., Wil Bane, 475 Riverside Dr., Ste. 1901, New York, NY 10115 Tel. (212)663-8900; Public Media Mktg. Dir., Letty LaFontaine, Tel. (615)742-5405; Radio Dir., William R. Richards; United Methodist News Service, P.O. Box 320, Nashville, TN 37202 Tel. (615)742-5470 Fax (615)742-5469;

Board of Church & Society: Pres., Bishop Robert C. Morgan, 100 Maryland Ave. NE, Washington, DC 20002 Tel. (202)488-5600; Vice-Pres., Edward Iwamoto; Rec. Sec., Helen G. Taylor; Treas., Andrea Allen; Gen. Sec., Thom White Wolf Fassett; Assoc. Gen. Sec., Martha Cline; Ministry of God's Human Community, Jane Hull Harvey; Ministry of God's Creation, Dir., Jaydee Hanson; Ministry of Resourcing Congregational Life, Manuel Espartero; Communications & Ed., Christian Social Action, Dir., Lee Ranck; U.N. Office, Coordinator Robert McClean, 777 U.N. Plaza, New York, NY 10017 Tel. (212)682-3633

Board of Discipleship: Pres., Bishop Woodie White, P.O. Box 840, (1908 Grand Ave. & 1001 19th Ave. S.), Nashville, TN 37202 Tel. (615)340-7200; Vice-Pres., Bishop David Lawson; Sec., Evelyn Laycock; Treas., Issac Brown; Gen. Sec., Ezra Earl Jones; Assoc. Gen. Sec., Alan K. Waltz; Victor Perez-Silvestry; James H. Snead, Jr.; Janice T. Grans; Duane A. Ewers; Ofc. of Human Resources & Staff Services, Exec. Sec. Jean Suiter

Ofc. Family Min. & Conf. Relationships: Exec. Sec., Marilyn W. Magee

Office of Financial Services: Exec. Sec., Isaac W. Brown; National Youth Ministry Org., Exec. Dir., Angela Gay Kinkead

Office of Publ. & Interpretation Service: Exec. Sec., David L. Hazlewood; Discipleship Resources Ed., Craig Galloway

Covenant Discplshp & Christian Formation: Exec. Sec., David Lowes Watson

Section on Ethnic Local Church Concerns: Asst. Gen. Sec., David L. White

Section on Ministry of the Laity: Asst. Gen. Sec., David L. White

Section on Stewardship: Asst. Gen. Sec., Herbert Mather

Division on United Methodist Men: Assoc. Gen. Sec., James H. Snead, Jr.

Section on Evangelism: Asst. Gen. Sec., David Brazelton

Section on Worship: Asst. Gen. Sec., Thomas A. Langford, III

Sec.: Christ. Ed. & Age Level Ministries: Asst. Gen. Sec., -----

The Upper Room: World Editor, Janice T. Grana

Division of Church School Publications: Ed., Duane A. Ewers; Managing Ed., John P. Gilbert, Curricuphone: 1-800-251-8591, TN Call collect: (615)749-6482

Board of Global Ministries: Pres., Bishop Woodrow Hearn, 475 Riverside Dr., New York, NY 10115 Tel. (212)870-3600; Vice-Pres., Bishop F. Herbert Skeete; Gen. Sec., Randolph Nugent; Int. Deputy Gen Sec., Marilyn Winters; Deputy Gen. Sec., Robert Harman; Joyce Sohl; Assoc. Gen. Sec., Admn., Lorene F. Wilbur; Assoc. Gen. Sec., Mission Resources, John McCullough; Assoc. Gen. Sec., Health & Welfare, Cathie Lyons; Acting, UM Committee on Relief, Bruce Weaver; Ombudsperson, Cherryetta Williams; Gen. Treas., Stephen F. Brimigion; Assoc. & Div. Treas., Brenda Norwood; Connie Takamine; William Wyman; Gen. Comptroller, Lynette Davis Rice; Public Relations Dir., Betty Thompson; National Division, Pres., Bishop F. Herbert Skeete; Asst. Gen. Sec., Lula Garrett; Eli Rivera; Myong Gul Son; Treas., Brenda Norwood; Women's Division, Pres., Sally Ernst; Deputy Gen. Sec., Joyce Sohl; Asst. Gen. Sec., Barbara E. Campbell; Ellen Kirby; Barbara Weaver; World Division, Pres., Bishop J. Lloyd Knox; Treas., William Wayman; Deputy Gen. Sec., Robert Harman; Asst. Gen. Sec., Wilma Roberts; Doreen Tilghman; Jiro Mizuno; Nora O. Boots; Mission Ed. Cultivation Dept., Chpsn., Carolyn H. Oehler; Assoc. Gen. Sec., Rena Yokum; Health & Welfare Dept., Chpsn., Martha Sanchez; Treas., Brenda Norwood; Assoc. Gen. Sec., Cathie Lyons; UM Committee on Relief, Chpsn., Bishop C. P. Minnick, Jr; Assoc. Gen. Sec., Kenneth R. Lutgen, Jr.; Treas., William Wyman; Mission Resources Dept., Chpsn., Bishop Edsel Ammons; Assoc. Gen. Sec., John McCullough; Treas., Stephen Brimigion

Board of Higher Education & Ministry: Pres., Benjamin R. Oliphint, P.O. Box 871, (1001 Nineteenth Ave. S), Nashville, TN 37202 Tel. (615)340-7000; Gen. Sec., Roger Ireson; Dir., Lisa Jarman; Assoc. Gen. Sec. for Admn., Clarke McClendon; Dir., Jennie Stockard; Office of Interpretation, Assoc. Gen. Sec., Judith E. Smith; Dir., Terri J. Hiers; Sharon J. Hels; Office of Loans & Scholarships, Assoc. Gen. Sec., Angella Current; Div. of Chaplains & Related Ministries, Assoc. Gen. Sec. James Townsend; Dir., Patricia Barrett; Richard Stewart; Janie Stevenson; Division of Diaconal Ministry, Assoc. Gen. Sec., Rosalie Bentzinger; Dirs., Joaquin Garcia; Paul Van Buren; Division of Higher Education, Assoc. Gen. Sec., Ken Yamada; Asst. Gen. Sec., Morris Wray; Donald Shockley; Dir., James Noseworthy; Barbara Issacs; Richard Hicks; Office of the Black College Fund, Exec. Dir. Shirley Lewis; Natl. Methodist Found. for Christian Higher Education, Pres. Raymond Devery; Div. of the Ordained Ministry, Assoc. Gen. Sec. Donald H. Treese; Dirs., Robert Kohler; Richard Yeager; Kil Sang Yoon; Lynn Scott

Board of Pensions: Pres., Bishop Jack M. Tuell, 1200 Davis St., Evanston, IL 60201 Tel. (708)869-4550; Vice-Pres., Robert W. Stevens; Sec., Carrie L. Carter; Gen. Sec., James F. Parker; Treasury Division: Treas., Gale Whitson-Schmidt; Treasury, Dir. Norb Lieblang; Internal Audit., Dir., Gary McWilliams; Special Asst., Joyce Gilman; Gen. Counsel/Legislative Affairs, Carl Mowry; Gen. Counsel/Corporate Affairs, James Walton-Myers; Actuary, Susan Wilson; Corporate Services Div., Sr. Assoc. Gen. Sec. Geneva Dalton; Human Resources, Dir., Michael Biladeau; Communications, Dir., Cheryl Haack; Pension & Benefit Services Div., Sr. Assoc. Gen. Sec. Dale Knapp; Plan Sponsor Services, Dir., Thom Andrews; Participant Services, Dir., Mary Norman; Group Health Care Service Div., Dir., Kathie Martine; Investment Div., Chief Financial Officer, Gayle Whitson-Schmidt; Dir. of Portfolio, Mary Pat Kincaid; Corporate Relations & Social Concerns, Dir., Vidette K. Bullock; Support Services Div., Sr. Assoc. Gen. Sec. Ken Truman; Project Mgmt., Dir., Phil Moulden; Mgmt. Info. Systems, Dir., Bruce Slown; Office Services, Dir., John Lukasik; Bldg. & Grounds, Dir., Bill Hagwood

Board of Publication: Chpsn., Anita J. Burrous; Vice-Chpsn., W. Clark Randall; Sec., Cornelius L. Henderson

The United Methodist Publishing House: Pres. & Publisher, Robert K. Feaster, P.O. Box 801, 201 Eighth Ave. S, Nashville, TN 37202 Tel. (615)749-6000; Treas., Vice-Pres., Financial & Admn., Larry L. Wallace; Operations, Vice-Pres., Gary H. Vincent; Vice-Pres., Editorial Div., Book Editor, H. Claude Young, Jr.; Vice-Pres., Product Mgmt., Marc Lewis; Vice-Pres., Production & Inventory Mgmt., H. Louis Jordan; Vice-Pres., Sales, Donald G. Sherrod; Vice-Pres., Customer & Distribution Services, Patricia G. Correll; Vice-Pres., Public & Church Relations, Walter H. McKelvey; Vice-Pres., Human Resources, Stephen C. Tippens; Ed., Church School Publications, Duane A. Ewers

Commission on Archives & History: Pres., Bishop Neil L. Irons, P.O. Box 127, Madison, NJ 07940 Tel. (201)822-2787; Vice-Pres., Mark Conrad; Rec. Sec., Marilyn Martin; Gen. Sec., Charles Yrigoyen, Jr.; Asst. Gen. Sec., Susan Eltsher; Archivist & Records Admn., William C. Beal, Jr.

Comm. Christian Unity/Interrel. Concerns: Pres., Bishop William Boyd Grove, 475 Riverside Dr., Rm. 1300, New York, NY 10115 Tel. (212)749-3553; Vice-Pres., Dorothy Mae Taylor; Sec., E. Dale Dunlap; Treas., Clifford Droke; Gen. Sec., Bruce Robbins; Assoc. Gen. Secs., Jeanne Audrey Powers; Nehemiah Thompson

Commission on Religion & Race: Pres., Bishop Calvin D. McConnell, 100 Maryland Ave. NE, Washington, DC 20002 Tel. (202)547-4270; Vice-Pres., Bishop Joseph B. Bethea; Rec. Sec., Bradley Watkins; Gen. Sec., Barbara R. Thompson; Assoc. Gen. Secs., Kenneth Deere; Esdras Rodriguez-Dias; Hidetoshi Tanaka

Commission on the Status & Role of Women: Pres., Joetta Rinehart, 1200 Davis St., Evanston, IL 60201 Tel. (312)869-7330; Rec. Sec., Winonah McGee; Sec., Cecilia Long

Worship/Music & Other Arts: Int. Exec. Sec., Bill Weisser, 228 W. Edenton St., Raleigh, NC 27603 Tel. (919)832-0160; Pres., Sara Collins

PERIODICALS

Christian Social Action; Pockets; Response; World Parish; Quarterly Review; El Interprete; The Interpreter; New World Outlook

United Pentecostal Church International

The United Pentecostal Church International came into being through the merger of two oneness Pentecostal organizations--the Pentecostal Church, Inc., and the Pentecostal Assemblies of Jesus Christ. The first of these was known as the Pentecostal Ministerial Alliance from its inception in 1925 until 1932. The second was formed in 1931 by a merger of the Apostolic Church of Jesus Christ with the Pentecostal Assemblies of the World.

The United Pentecostal Church International contends that the Bible does not teach three separate, coequal and coeternal members of the Godhead, but rather one God who manifested himself as the Father in creation, in the Son in redemption, and as the Holy Spirit in regeneration. It is further believed that Jesus is the name of this absolute deity and that water baptism should be administered in his name, not in the titles Father, Son, and Holy Ghost. Scriptural basis for this teaching can be found in Acts 2:38, 8:16, and 19:6. This position should not be confused with the Unitarian view, which denies the deity of Jesus Christ.

The Fundamental Doctrine of the United Pentecostal Church International, as stated in its *Articles of Faith*, is "the Bible standard of full salvation, which is repentance, baptism in water by immersion in the name of the Lord Jesus Christ for the remission of sins, and the baptism of the Holy Ghost with the initial sign of speaking with other tongues as the Spirit gives utterance."

Further doctrinal teachings concern of a life of holiness and separation, the operation of the gifts of the Spirit within the church, the second coming of the Lord, and the church's obligation to take the gospel to the whole world. The traditional slogan of the United Pentecostal Church International is "The Whole Gospel to the Whole World."

HEADQUARTERS

8855 Dunn Rd., Hazelwood, MO 63042 Tel. (314)837-7300 Fax (314)837-4503

Media Contact, Gen. Sec.-Treas., Rev. C. M. Becton

OFFICERS

Gen. Supt., Rev. Nathaniel A. Urshan
Asst. Gen. Supts.: Rev. James Kilgore, Box 15175, Houston, TX 77020; Jesse Williams, P.O. Box 64277, Fayetteville, NC 28306
Gen. Sec.-Treas., Rev. C. M. Becton
Dir. of Foreign Missions, Rev. Harry Scism
Gen. Dir. of Home Missions, Rev. Jack E. Yonts
Editor-in-Chief, Rev. J. L. Hall
Gen. Sunday School Dir., Rev. E. J. McClintock

OTHER ORGANIZATIONS

The Pentecostal Publishing House, Mgr., Rev. Marvin Curry
Youth Division (Pentecostal Conquerors), Pres., Jerry Jones, Hazelwood, MO 63042
Ladies Auxiliary, Pres., Vera Kinzie, 4840 Elm Pl., Toledo, OH 43608
Harvestime Radio Broadcast, Dir., Rev. J. Hugh Rose, 698 Kerr Ave., Cadiz, OH 43907
Stewardship Dept., Contact Church Division, Hazelwood, MO 63042
Education Division, Supt., Rev. Arless Glass, 4502 Aztec, Pasadena, TX 77504
Public Relations Division, Contact Church Division, Hazelwood, MO 63042
Historical Society & Archives

PERIODICALS

Pentecostal Herald, The; Global Witness, The; Outreach, The; Ephphatha, The (Deaf Ministry); Homelife; Conqueror; Reflections; Forward

United Zion Church

This branch of the Brethren in Christ settled in Lancaster County, Pa., and was organized under the leadership of Matthias Brinser in 1855.

HEADQUARTERS

United Zion Home, 722 Furnace Hills Pk, Lititz, PA 17543
Media Contact, Bishop, Luke G. Showalter, 181 Hurst Dr, Ephrata, PA 17522 Tel. (717)733-8392

OFFICERS

Gen. Conf. Mod., Bishop Luke Showalter, 181 Hurst Dr., Ephrata, PA 17522 Tel. (717)733-8392
Asst. Mod., Rev. Leon Eberly, 615 N. Ridge Rd., Reinholds, PA 17569 Tel. (215)484-2614
Gen. Conf. Sec., Rev. Eugene Kreider, RD #2, Manheim, PA 17545 Tel. (717)653-8226
Gen. Conf. Treas., Kenneth Kleinfelter, 919 Sycamore Lane, Lebanon, PA 17042

Zion's Herald

Unity of the Brethren

Czech and Moravian immigrants in Texas (beginning about 1855) established congregations which grew into an Evangelical Union in 1903, and with the accession of other Brethren in Texas, into the Evangelical Unity of the Czech-Moravian Brethren in North America. In 1959, it shortened the name to the original name used in 1457, the Unity of the Brethren (Unitas Fratrum, or Jednota Bratrska).

HEADQUARTERS

3829 Sandstone, San Angelo, TX 76904
Media Contact, Sec. of Exec. Committee, Dorothy E. Kocian, 107 S. Barbara, Waco, TX 76705 Tel. (817)799-5331 Fax (817)799-6277

OFFICERS

Pres., Rev. Tommy Tallas
1st Vice Pres., Rev. W. John Baletka, P.O. Box 614, Caldwell, TX 77836
Sec., Dorothy Kocian, 107 S. Barbara, Waco, TX 76705 Tel. (817)799-5331
Fin. Sec., Roy Vajdak, 6424 Hudson, Littleton, CO 80121
Treas., Ron Sulak, 1217 Christine, Troy, TX 76579

OTHER ORGANIZATIONS

Bd. of Christian Educ., Chmn., Rev. Gary Olsen, 1400 Louise St., Rosenberg, TX 77471
Brethren Youth Fellowship, Pres., Becky Turner, 404 Pintail La., Taylor, TX 76574
Young Adult Fellowship, Pres., Joyce Koslovsky, 921 Erath Dr., Temple, TX 76501
Christian Sisters Union, Pres., Mrs. Janet Pomykal, P.O. Box 560, Brenham, TX 76705
Sunday School Union, Pres., Mrs. Dorothy Kocian, 107 S. Barbara, Waco, TX 76705

PERIODICAL

Brethren Journal

Vedanta Societies

Followers of the Vedas, the scriptures of the Indo-Aryans, doctrines expounded by Swami Vivekananda at the Parliament of Religions, Chicago, 1893. There are altogether 13 such centers in the United States and one in Canada. All are under the spiritual guidance of the Ramakrishna Mission, organized by Swami Vivekananda in India.

HEADQUARTERS

34 W. 71st St., New York, NY 10023 Tel. (212)877-9197

Volunteers of America

Volunteers of America, founded in 1896 by Ballington and Maud Booth, provides spiritual and material aid for those in need in more than 300 communities across the United Statess. As one of the nation's largest multipurpose human-service agencies, VOA offers more than 400 programs for the elderly, families, youth, alcoholics, drug abusers, offenders, and the disabled.

HEADQUARTERS

3813 N. Causeway Blvd., Metairie, LA 70002 Tel. (504)837-2652 Fax (504)837-4200
Media Contact, Dir. of Publ. Relations, Arthur Smith

OFFICERS

Chpsn., Walter Faster
Pres., J. Clint Cheveallier
Vice-Pres.: Alex Brodrick; David Cheveallier; Thomas Clark; Jack Dignum; James Hogie; Robert Nolte; Margaret Ratcliff; John Hood

The Wesleyan Church

The Wesleyan Church was formed on June 26, 1968, through the union of the Wesleyan Methodist Church of America (1843) and the Pilgrim Holiness Church (1897). Headquarters was established at Marion, Ind., and relocated to Indianapolis in 1987.

The Wesleyan movement centers around the beliefs, based on Scripture, that the atonement in Christ provides for the regeneration of sinners and the entire sanctification of believers. John Wesley led a revival of these beliefs in the 18th century.

When a group of New England ministers led by Orange Scott began to crusade for the abolition of slavery, with which many Methodist ministers and members had become involved, the bishops and others sought to silence them. This led to a series of withdrawals from the Methodist Episcopal Church. In 1843, the organization of the Wesleyan Methodist Connection of America was organized. Scott, Jotham Horton, LaRoy Sunderland, Luther Lee, and Lucius C. Matlack were prominent leaders in the new denomination.

As the holiness revival swept across many denominations in the last half of the 19th century, holiness replaced social reform as the major tenet of the Connection. In 1947 the name was changed from Connection to Church and a central supervisory authority was set up.

The Pilgrim Holiness Church was one of many independent holiness churches which came into existence as a result of the holiness revival. Led by Martin Wells Knapp and Seth C. Rees, the International Holiness Union and Prayer League was inaugurated in 1897 in Cincinnati. Its purpose was to promote worldwide holiness evangelism and the Union had a strong missionary emphasis from the beginning. It developed into a church by 1913.

The Wesleyan Church is now spread across most of the United States and Canada and 37 other countries. The Wesleyan World Fellowship was organized in 1972 to unite Wesleyan mission bodies developing into mature churches.

The Wesleyan Church is a member of the Christian Holiness Association, the National Association of Evangelicals, and the World Methodist Council.

HEADQUARTERS

P.O. Box 50434, Indianapolis, IN 46250 Tel. (317)842-0444

OFFICERS

Gen. Supts.: Dr. O. D. Emery; Dr. Earle L. Wilson; Dr. Lee M. Haines; Dr. H. C. Wilson
Gen. Sec., Dr. Ronald R. Brannon
Gen. Treas., Mr. Daniel D. Busby
Gen. Editor, Dr. Wayne E. Caldwell
Gen. Publisher, Rev. Nathan Birky
Evangelism & Church Growth, Gen. Sec., Dr. B. Marlin Mull
World Missions, Gen. Sec., Dr. Wayne W. Wright
Local Church Educ., Gen. Sec., Dr. Keith Drury
Youth, Gen. Sec., Rev. Thomas E. Armiger
Education & the Ministry, Gen. Sec., Dr. Kenneth Heer
Estate Planning, Gen. Dir., Rev. Howard B. Castle

US RELIGIOUS BODIES

Broadcast Ministries, Gen. Dir., Dr. Norman G. Wilson

Wesleyan Pension Fund, Gen. Dir., Mr. Bobby L. Temple

Wesleyan Investment Foundation, Gen. Dir., Dr. John A. Dunn

PERIODICAL

Wesleyan World

Wesleyan Holiness Association of Churches

This body was founded Aug. 4, 1959 near Muncie, Ind., by a group of ministers and laymen who were drawn together for the purpose of spreading and conserving sweet, radical, scriptural holiness. These men came from various church bodies. This group is Wesleyan in doctrine and standards.

HEADQUARTERS

108 Carter Ave., Dayton, OH 45405

OFFICERS

Gen. Supt., Rev. J. Stevan Manley, Tel. (513)278-3770

Asst. Gen. Supt., Rev. Jack W. Dulin, Rt. 2, Box 309, Milton, KY 40045 Tel. (502)268-5826

Gen. Sec.-Treas., Rev. Robert W. Wilson, 10880 State Rt. 170, Negley, OH Tel. (216)385-0416

Gen. Youth Pres., Rev. John Brewer, 504 W. Tyrell St., St. Louis, MI 48880 Tel. (517)681-2591

PERIODICAL

Eleventh Hour Messenger

Wisconsin Evangelical Lutheran Synod

Organized in 1850 at Milwaukee, Wisconsin by three pastors sent to America by a German mission society. The name Wisconsin Evangelical Lutheran Synod still reflects its origins, although it has lost its local character and presently has congregations in 50 states and 3 Canadian provinces.

The Wisconsin Synod federated with the Michigan and Minnesota Synods in 1892 in order to more effectively carry on education and mission enterprises. A merger of these three Synods followed in 1917 to give the Wisconsin Evangelical Lutheran Synod its present form.

Although at its organization in 1850 the Synod turned away from conservative Lutheran theology, today it is ranked as one of the most conservative Lutheran bodies in the United States. The Synod confesses that the Bible is the verbally inspired, infallible Word of God and subscribes without reservation to the confessional writings of the Lutheran Church. Its interchurch relations are determined by a firm commitment to the principle that unity of doctrine and practice are the prerequisites of pulpit and altar fellowship and ecclesial cooperation. Consequently it does not hold membership in ecumenical organizations.

HEADQUARTERS

2929 N. Mayfair Rd., Milwaukee, WI 53222 Tel. (414)771-9357 Fax (414)771-3708

Publ. Rel. Dir., Rev. James P. Schaefer, 2929 N. Mayfair Rd., Milwaukee, WI 53222 Tel. (414)771-9357 Fax (414)771-3708

OFFICERS

Pres., Rev. Carl H. Mischke, 2929 N. Mayfair Rd., Milwaukee, WI 53222

1st Vice-Pres., Rev. Richard E. Lauersdorf, 105 Aztalan Ct., Jefferson, WI 53549

2nd Vice-Pres., Rev. Robert J. Zink, S68 W14329 Gaulke Ct., Muskego, WI 53150

Sec., Rev. David Worgull, 1201 W. Tulsa, Chandler, AZ 85224

OTHER ORGANIZATIONS

Bd. of Trustees, Admn., Rev. Robert C. VanNostrand

Bd. for Worker Trng., Admn., Rev. Wayne Borgwardt

Bd. for Parish Services, Admn., Rev. Wayne Mueller

Bd. for Home Missions, Admn., Rev. Harold J. Hagedorn

Bd. for World Missions, Admn., Rev. Duane K. Tomhave

Public Relations, Dir., Rev. James P. Schaefer

PERIODICALS

Northwestern Lutheran; Lutheran Educator, The

World Confessional Lutheran Association

The World Confessional Lutheran Association (WCLA) was originally named Lutheran's Alert National (LAN) when it was founded in 1965 by a small group of conservative Lutheran pastors and laymen meeting in Cedar Rapids, Iowa. Its purpose was to help preserve from erosion the basic doctrines of Christian theology, including the inerrancy of Holy Scripture. The small group of ten grew to a worldwide constituency, similarly concerned over maintaining the doctrinal integrity of the Bible and the Lutheran Confessions.

The name World Confessional Lutheran Association was adopted by the board in 1984 to reflect the growing global outreach and involvement of our movement.

HEADQUARTERS

3504 N. Pearl St., P.O. Box 7186, Tacoma, WA 98407 Tel. (206)759-0588 Fax (206)759-1790

OFFICERS

Pres., Dr. Rueben H. Redal, 409 N. Tacoma Ave., Tacoma, WA 98403

Vice-Pres., Rev. Pomeroy Moore, 420 Fernhill Lane, Anaheim, CA 92807

Sec., Mr. Forest Knapp, P.O. Box 1505, Gig Harbor, WA 98335

Treas., Mr. Warren Siem, 608 Iowa, Mediapolis, IA 52637

Faith Seminary, Dean, Rev. Michael J. Adams, P.O. Box 7186, Tacoma, WA 98407

PERIODICAL

Lutherans Alert-National

RELIGIOUS BODIES IN THE UNITED STATES ARRANGED BY FAMILIES

The following list of religious bodies appearing in the Directory Section of this yearbook shows the "families," or related clusters into which American religious bodies can be grouped. For example, there are many communions that can be grouped under the heading "Baptist" for historical and theological reasons. It is not to be assumed, however, that all denominations under one family heading are similar in belief or practice. Often, any similarity is purely coincidental. The family clusters tend to represent historical factors more often than theological or practical ones. The family categories provided one of the major pitfalls of church statistics because of the tendency to combine the statistics by "families" for analytical and comparative purposes. Such combined totals are almost meaningless, although often used as variables for sociological analysis.

Religious bodies not grouped under family headings appear alphabetically and are not indented in the following list.

Adventist Bodies
Advent Christian Church
Church of God General Conference (Oregon, IL.)
Primitive Advent Christian Church
Seventh-day Adventists

Amana Church Society
American Evangelical Christian Churches
American Rescue Workers
Apostolic Christian Church (Nazarene)
Apostolic Christian Churches of America
The Anglican Orthodox Church
Bahá'í Faith

Baptist Bodies
American Baptist Association
American Baptist Churches in the U.S.A.
Baptist Bible Fellowship, International
Baptist General Conference
Baptist Missionary Association of America
Conservative Baptist Association of America
Duck River (and Kindred) Associations of Baptists
Free Will Baptists
General Association of Regular Baptist Churches
General Baptists, General Association of
General Conference of the Evangelical Baptist Church, Inc.
General Six-Principle Baptists
Liberty Baptist Fellowship
National Baptist Convention of America
National Baptist Convention, U.S.A., Inc.
National Primitive Baptist Convention, Inc.
North American Baptist General Conference
Primitive Baptists
Progressive National Baptist Convention, Inc.
Separate Baptists in Christ
Seventh Day Baptist General Conference
Southern Baptist Convention
Sovereign Grace Baptists

Berean Fundamental Church

Brethren (German Baptists)
Brethren Church (Ashland, Ohio)
Church of the Brethren
Grace Brethren Churches, Fellowship of
Old German Baptist Brethren

Brethren, River
Brethren in Christ Church
United Zion Church

Buddhist Churches of America
Christadelphians
The Christian and Missionary Alliance
Christian Brethren
Christian Catholic Church
The Christian Congregation
Christian Nation Church U.S.A.
Christian Union
Church of Christ, Scientist
Church of Daniel's Band
The Church of Illumination
Church of the Living God (C.W.F.F.)
Church of the Nazarene
Churches of Christ in Christian Union

Churches of Christ-Christian Churches
Christian Church (Disciples of Christ)
Christian Churches and Churches of Christ
Churches of Christ

Churches Of God
Church of God (Anderson, Ind.)
Church of God by Faith
The Church of God (Seventh Day), Denver, Colo.,
Church of God (Which He Purchased With His Own Blood)
Churches of God, General Conference

Churches of the New Jerusalem
General Church of the New Jerusalem
General Convention, The Swedenborgian Church

Community Churches, International Council of
Congregational Christian Churches, National Association of
Conservative Congregational Christian Conference

Eastern Churches
Albanian Orthodox Archdiocese in America
Albanian Orthodox Diocese of America
The American Carpatho-Russian Orthodox Greek Catholic Church
The Antiochian Orthodox Christian Archdiocese of N.A.
Apostolic Catholic Assyrian Church of the East, North American Diocese
Armenian Apostolic Church of America
Armenian Church of America, Diocese of the

Bulgarian Eastern Orthodox Church
Coptic Orthodox Church
Greek Orthodox Archdiocese of North and South America
Holy Ukrainian Autocephalic Orthodox Church in Exile
The Orthodox Church in America
Romanian Orthodox Church in America
The Romanian Orthodox Episcopate of America
Russian Orthodox Church in the U.S.A., Patriarchal Parishes of the
The Russian Orthodox Church Outside Russia
Serbian Orthodox Church in the U.S.A. and Canada
Syrian Orthodox Church of Antioch (Archdiocese of the U.S.A. and Canada)
True Orthodox Church of Greece (Synod of Metropolitan Cyprian), American Exarchate
Ukrainian Orthodox Church of the U.S.A.
Ukrainian Orthodox Church in America (Ecumenical Patriarchate)

The Episcopal Church
Ethical Culture Movement
Evangelical Church of North America
Evangelical Congregational Church
The Evangelical Covenant Church
The Evangelical Free Church of America
Fellowship of Fundamental Bible Churches
The Fire-Baptized Holiness Church (Wesleyan)
Free Christian Zion Church of Christ

Friends

Evangelical Friends Alliance
Friends General Conference
Friends United Meeting
Religious Society of Friends (Conservative)
Religious Society of Friends (Unaffiliated Meetings)

Grace Gospel Fellowship
The Holiness Church of God, Inc.
House of God, Which is the Church of the Living God, the Pillar and Ground of the Truth, Inc.
Independent Fundamental Churches of America
Israelite House of David
Jehovah's Witnesses
Jews
Kodesh Church of Immanuel

Latter Day Saints

Church of Christ
The Church of Jesus Christ (Bickertonites)
The Church of Jesus Christ of Latter-day Saints
Reorganized Church of Jesus Christ of Latter Day Saints

The Liberal Catholic Church-Province of the United States of America

Lutherans

Apostolic Lutheran Church of America
Church of the Lutheran Brethren of America
Church of the Lutheran Confession
Estonian Evangelical Lutheran Church
Evangelical Lutheran Church in America
Evangelical Lutheran Synod
Free Lutheran Congregations, The Association of
Latvian Evangelical Lutheran Church in America
The Lutheran Church--Missouri Synod
Lutheran Churches, The American Association of
The Protestant Conference (Lutheran)
Wisconsin Evangelical Lutheran Synod
World Confessional Lutheran Association

Mennonite Bodies

Beachy Amish Mennonite Churches
Church of God in Christ (Mennonite)
Evangelical Mennonite Church
Fellowship of Evangelical Bible Churches
General Conference of Mennonite Brethren Churches
Hutterian Brethren
Mennonite Church
Mennonite Church, The General Conference
Old Order Amish Church
Old Order (Wisler) Mennonite Church
Reformed Mennonite Church

Methodist Bodies

African Methodist Episcopal Church
African Methodist Episcopal Zion Church
Allegheny Wesleyan Methodist Connection (Original Allegheny Conference)
Christian Methodist Episcopal Church
Evangelical Methodist Church
Free Methodist Church of North America
Fundamental Methodist Church, Inc.
Primitive Methodist Church in the U.S.A.
Reformed Methodist Union Episcopal Church
Reformed Zion Union Apostolic Church
Southern Methodist Church
The United Methodist Church
The Wesleyan Church

The Metropolitan Church Association
Metropolitan Community Churches, Universal Fellowship of
The Missionary Church

Moravian Bodies

Moravian Church in America (Unitas Fratrum)
Unity of the Brethren

Muslims
National Spiritualist Association of Churches
New Apostolic Church of North America
North American Old Roman Catholic Church (Archdiocese of New York)

Old Catholic Churches

Christ Catholic Church
North American Old Roman Catholic Church

Pentecostal Bodies

The Apostolic Faith
Apostolic Faith Mission Church of God
Apostolic Overcoming Holy Church of God
Assemblies of God
Assemblies of God International Fellowship (Independent/Not Affiliated)
The Bible Church of Christ, Inc.

Bible Way Church of Our Lord Jesus Christ, World Wide, Inc.
Christian Church of North America, General Council
The Church of God
Church of God (Cleveland, Tenn.)
The Church of God in Christ
Church of God in Christ, International
The Church of God of Prophecy
The Church of God of the Mountain Assembly
Church of Our Lord Jesus Chrost of the Apostolic Faith
Congregational Holiness Church
Elim Fellowship
Full Gospel Assemblies, International
Full Gospel Fellowship of Churches and Ministers, International
International Church of the Foursquare Gospel
International Pentecostal Church of Christ
Open Bible Standard Churches
The (Original) Church of God
Pentecostal Assemblies of the World
Pentecostal Church of God
Pentecostal Fire-Baptized Holiness Church
Pentecostal Free-Will Baptist Church, Inc.
Pentecostal Holiness Church, International
United Holy Church of America
United Pentecostal Church, International

Pillar of Fire
Polish National Catholic Church of America

Presbyterian Bodies

Associate Reformed Presbyterian Church (General Synod)
Cumberland Presbyterian Church

Evangelical Presbyterian Church
Korean Presbyterian Church in America, General Assembly of the
The Orthodox Presbyterian Church
Presbyterian Church in America
Presbyterian Church in (U.S.A.)
Reformed Presbyterian Church of North America
Second Cumberland Presbyterian Church in U.S.

Reformed Bodies

Christian Reformed Church in North America
Hungarian Reformed Church in America
Netherlands Reformed Congregations
Protestant Reformed Churches in America
Reformed Church in America
Reformed Church in the U.S.
United Church of Christ

Reformed Episcopal Church
The Roman Catholic Church
The Salvation Army
The Schwenkfelder Church
Social Brethren
Triumph the Church and Kingdom of God in Christ
Unitarian Universalist Association

United Brethren Bodies

United Brethren in Christ
United Christian Church

Vedanta Society
Volunteers of America
Wesleyan Holiness Association of Churches

4. RELIGIOUS BODIES IN CANADA

A large number of Canadian religious bodies were organized by immigrants from Europe and elsewhere, and a smaller number sprang up originally on Canadian soil. In the case of Canada, moreover, many denominations that overlap the U.S.-Canada border have headquarters in the United States.

What follows is, first, an alphabetical directory of religious bodies in Canada that have supplied information. The second section is an alphabetical list, with addresses and other information, of bodies known to exist in Canada that have not yet supplied complete directory information. This second section is titled "Other Religious Bodies in Canada." A final section lists denominations according to denominational families.

Complete statistics for Canadian denominations are found in the table "Canadian Current and Non-current Statistics" in the statistical section of the **Yearbook**. Addresses for periodicals are found in the listing of Canadian Religious Periodicals. Information about finances for some of the denominations is in the Church Finance section.

The Anglican Church of Canada

Anglicanism came to Canada with the early explorers such as Martin Frobisher and Henry Hudson. Continuous services began in Newfoundland about 1700 and in Nova Scotia in 1710. The first Bishop, Charles Inglis, was appointed to Nova Scotia in 1787. The numerical strength of Anglicanism was increased by the coming of American Loyalists and by massive immigration both after the Napoleonic wars and in the later 19th and early 20th centuries.

The Anglican Church of Canada has enjoyed self-government for over a century and is an autonomous member of the worldwide Anglican Communion. The General Synod, which normally meets triennially, consists of the Archbishops, Bishops, and elected clerical and lay representatives of the 30 dioceses. Each of the Ecclesiastical Provinces—Canada, Ontario, Rupert's Land, and British Columbia—is organized under a Metropolitan and has its own Provincial Synod and Executive Council. Each diocese has its own Diocesan Synod.

HEADQUARTERS

Church House, 600 Jarvis St., Toronto, ON M4Y 2J6 Tel. (416)924-9192 Fax (416)968-7983

GENERAL SYNOD OFFICERS

Primate of the Anglican Church of Canada, Most Rev. M. G. Peers, 600 Jarvis St., Toronto, ON M4Y 2J6

Prolocutor, Ven. R. T. Pynn, 903-75th, Calgary, AB T2V 0S7

Gen. Sec., Ven. D. J. Woeller, 600 Jarvis St., Toronto, ON M4Y 2J6

Treas. of Gen. Synod, John R. Ligertwood, 600 Jarvis St., Toronto, ON M4Y 2J6

Exec. Dir. of Program, ——, 600 Jarvis St., Toronto, ON M4Y 2J6

DEPARTMENTS AND DIVISIONS

Anglican Book Centre, Dir. & Publ., Rev. M. J. Lloyd

Missionary Society, Exec. Sec., Rev. J. S. Barton

Dir. of World Mission, Rev. J. S. Barton

Div. of Pensions, Dir., Mrs. J. Mason

Dir. of Admn. & Fin., J. R. Ligertwood

Dir. of Communications, D. Tindal

Dir. of Ministries in Church & Society, Rev. P. Elliott

METROPOLITANS (ARCHBISHOPS)

Ecclesiastical Province of:

Canada, The Most Rev. Stewart Payne, 83 West Street, Corner Brook, NF A2H 2Y6 Tel. (709)639-8712 Fax (709)634-8889

Rupert's Land, The Most Rev. Walter Jones, 935 Nesbitt Bay, Winnipeg, MB R3T 1W6 Tel. (204)453-6130 Fax (204)452-3915

British Columbia, The Most Rev. Douglas Hambidge, 302-814 Richards Street, Vancouver, BC V6B 3A7 Tel. (604)684-6306 Fax (604)386-4013

Ontario, The Most Rev. John Bothwell, 67 Victoria Ave. S., Hamilton, ON L8N 2S8 Tel. (416)527-1117 Fax (416)527-1281

DIOCESAN BISHOPS

Algoma: The Rt. Rev. L. Peterson, 619 Wellington St. E, Box 1168 Sault Ste., Marie, ON P6A 5N7 Tel. (705)256-5061

Arctic: The Rt. Rev. J. C. R. Williams, 1055 Avenue Rd., Toronto, ON M5N 2C8 Tel. (416)481-2263 Fax (416)487-4948

Athabasca: ——, P.O. Box 6868, Peace River, AB T8S 1S6 Tel. (403)624-2767 Fax (403)624-4443

Brandon: The Rt. Rev. J. F. S. Conlin, 341-13th St., Brandon, MB R7A 4P8 Tel. (204)727-7550 Fax (204)727-4135

British Columbia: The Rt. Rev. R. F. Shepherd, 912 Vancouver St., Victoria, BC V8V 3V7 Tel. (604)386-7781 Fax (604)386-4013

Caledonia: The Rt. Rev. J. E. Hannen, Box 278, Prince Rupert, BC V8J 3P6 Tel. (604)624-6013 Fax (604)624-4299

Calgary: The Rt. Rev. J. B. Curtis, 3015 Glencoe Rd. S. W., Calgary, AB T2S 2L9 Tel. (403)243-3673 Fax (403)243-2182

Cariboo: ——, 1-440 Victoria St., Kamloops, BC V2C 2A7 Tel. (604)374-0237 Fax (604)374-6449

Edmonton: The Rt. Rev. K. Genge, 10033 - 84 Ave., Edmonton, AB T6E 2G6 Tel. (403)439-7344 Fax (403)439-6549

Fredericton: The Rt. Rev. G. C. Lemmon, 115 Church St., Fredericton, NB E3B 4C8 Tel. (506)459-1801

Huron: The Rt. Rev. P. R. O'Driscoll, 4-220 Dundas St., London, ON N6A 1H3 Tel. (519)434-6893 Fax (519)673-4151

Keewatin: The Rt. Rev. T. W. R. Collings, Box 118, Kenora, ON P9N 3X1 Tel. (807)468-7011 Fax (807)468-6685

Kootenay: The Rt. Rev. D. P. Crawley, Box 549, Kelowna, BC V1Y 7P2 Tel. (604)762-3306

Montreal: The Rt. Rev. A. S. Hutchison, 1444 Union Ave., Montreal, QC H3A 2B8 Tel. (514)843-6577 Fax (514)843-6344

Moosonee: The Rt. Rev. C. J. Lawrence, Box 841, Schumacher, ON P0N 1G0 Tel. (705)360-1129 Fax (705)360-1120

Eastern Newfoundland and Labrador: The Rt. Rev. M. Mate, 19 King's Bridge Rd., St. John's, NF A1C 3K4 Tel. (709)576-6697 Fax (709)576-7122

Central Newfoundland: The Rt. Rev. E. Marsh, 34 Fraser Rd., Gander, NF A1V 2E8 Tel. (709)256-2372 Fax (709)256-2396

Western Newfoundland: Archbishop, The Most Rev. S. S. Payne, 83 West St., Corner Brook, NF A2H 2Y6 Tel. (709)639-8712 Fax (709)639-1636

New Westminster: Archbishop, The Most Rev. D. W. Hambidge, 302-814 Richards St., Vancouver, BC V6B 3A7 Tel. (604)684-6306 Fax (604)684-7017

Niagara: Archbishop, The Most Rev. J. C. Bothwell, 67 Victoria Ave. S., Hamilton, ON L8N 2S8 Tel. (416)527-1117 Fax (416)527-1281

Nova Scotia: The Rt. Rev. A. G. Peters, 5732 College St., Halifax, NS B3H 1X3 Tel. (902)420-0717 Fax (902)425-0717

Ontario: The Rt. Rev. A. A. Read, 90 Johnson St., Kingston, ON K7L 1X7 Tel. (613)544-4774

Ottawa: The Rt. Rev. E. K. Lackey, 71 Bronson Ave., Ottawa, ON K1R 6G6 Tel. (613)232-7124 Fax (613)232-7088

Qu'Appelle: The Rt. Rev. E. Bays, 1501 College Ave., Regina, SK S4P 1B8 Tel. (306)522-1608 Fax (306)352-6808

Quebec: The Rt. Rev. A. B. Stavert, 36 rue des Jardins, Quebec, QC G1R 4L5 Tel. (418)692-3858 Fax (418)692-3876

Rupert's Land: Archbishop, The Most Rev. W. Jones, 935 Nesbitt Bay, Winnipeg, MB R3T 1W6 Tel. (204)453-6130 Fax (204)452-3915

Saskatchewan: The Rt. Rev. T. O. Morgan, Box 1088, Prince Albert, SK S6V 5S6 Tel. (306)763-2455 Fax (306)764-5172

Saskatoon: The Rt. Rev. R. A. Wood, Box 1965, Saskatoon, SK S7K 3S5 Tel. (306)244-5651

Toronto: The Most Rev. T. Finlay, 135 Adelaide St., E., Toronto, ON M5C 1L8 Tel. (416)363-6021 Fax (416)363-7678

Yukon: The Rt. Rev. R. C. Ferris, Box 4247, 41 Firth Rd., Whitehorse, YT Y1A 3T3 Tel. (403)667-7746

PERIODICALS

Anglican Journal/Journal Anglican; Anglican Magazine: Living Message; Crosstalk; Crusader, The; Journal of the Canadian Church Historical Society; Rupert's Land News; Saskatchewan Anglican; Montreal Churchman; Huron Church News

The Antiochian Orthodox Christian Archdiocese of North America

The approximately 100,000 members of the Antiochian Orthodox community in Canada are under the jurisdiction of the Antiochian Orthodox Christian Archdiocese of North America with headquarters in Englewood, N.J. There are churches in Edmonton, Winnipeg, Halifax, London, Ottawa, Toronto, Windsor, Montreal, and Saskatoon.

HEADQUARTERS

Metropolitan Philip Saliba, 358 Mountain Rd., Englewood, NJ 07631 Tel. (201)871-1355 Fax (201)871-7954

Media Contact, Vicar, The Very Rev. George S. Corey, 52 78th St., Brooklyn, NY 11209 Tel. (718)748-7940 Fax (201)871-7954

PERIODICAL

Word, The

Apostolic Christian Church (Nazarene)

This church was formed in Canada as a result of immigration from various European countries. The body began as a movement originated by the Rev. S. H. Froehlich, a Swiss pastor, whose followers are still found in Switzerland and Central Europe.

HEADQUARTERS

Apostolic Christian Church Foundation, P.O. Box 151, Tremont, IL 61568

OFFICER

Gen. Sec., Eugene R. Galat, Tel. (309)925-5162

The Apostolic Church in Canada

The Apostolic Church in Canada is affiliated with the worldwide organization of the Apostolic Church with headquarters in Great Britain. A product of the Welsh Revival (1904 to 1908), its Canadian beginnings originated in Nova Scotia in 1927. Today its main centers are in Nova Scotia, Ontario, and Québec. This church is evangelical, fundamental, and Pentecostal, with special emphasis on the ministry gifts listed in Ephesians 4:11-12.

HEADQUARTERS

27 Castlefield Ave., Toronto, ON M4R 1G3

Media Contact, Natl. Sec., John Kristensen, 388 Gerald St., La Salle, QC H8P 2A5 Tel. (514)366-8356

OFFICERS

Pres., Rev. D. S. Morris, 685 Park St. S., Peterborough, ON K9J 3S9 Tel. (705)743-3418

Natl. Sec., Rev. J. Kristensen, 388 Gerald St., Ville LaSalle, QC H8P 2A5

Apostolic Church of Pentecost of Canada Inc.

This body was founded in 1921 at Winnipeg, Manitoba, by Pastor Frank Small. Doctrines include belief in eternal salvation by the grace of God, baptism of the Holy Spirit with the evidence of speaking in tongues, water baptism by immersion in the name of the Lord Jesus Christ.

HEADQUARTERS

105-807 Manning Rd. N.E., Calgary, AB T2E 7M8

Media Contact, Clk./Admn., Leonard Larsen, Tel. (403)273-5777 Fax (403)273-8102

OFFICERS

Mod., Rev. G. Killam

Clk., Leonard K. Larsen

Missionary Council Chpsn., E. G. Bradley, Box 322, Maple Ridge, BC V2X 7G2

PERIODICAL

End Times' Messenger

The Armenian Church of North America, Diocese of Canada

The Canadian branch of the ancient Church of Armenia founded in A.D. 301 by St. Gregory the Illuminator. It was established in Canada at St. Catherines, Ontario, in 1930. The diocesan organization is under the jurisdiction of the Holy See of Etchmiadzin, Armenia. The Diocese has churches in St. Catherine, Hamilton, Toronto, Scarborough, Ottawa, Vancouver, Mississauga, and Montréal.

HEADQUARTERS

Diocesan Offices: Primate, Canadian Diocese, Rt. Rev. Hovnan Derderian, 615 Stuart Ave., Outremont, QC H2V 3H2 Tel. (514)276-9479 Fax (514)276-9960

Armenian Evangelical Church

Founded in 1960 by immigrant Armenian evangelical families from the Middle East, this body is conservative doctrinally, with an evangelical, biblical emphasis. The polity of churches within the group differ with congregationalism being dominant, but there are Presbyterian Armenian Evangelical churches as well. Most of the local churches have joined main-line denominations. All of the Armenian Evangelical (Congregational or Presbyterian) local churches in the United States and Canada have joined with the Armenian Evangelical Union of North America.

MEDIA CONTACT

Media Contact, Chief Editor, Y. Sarmazian, 42 Glenforest Rd., Toronto, ON M4N 1Z8 Tel. (416)489-3188 Fax (416)485-4336

AEUNA OFFICERS

Min. to the Union, Rev. Karl Avakian, 1789 E. Frederick Ave., Fresno, CA 93720

OFFICERS

Min., Rev. Yessayi Sarmazian, 42 Glenforest Rd., Toronto, ON M4N 1Z8 Tel. (416)489-3188

PERIODICAL

Canada Armenian Press

Associated Gospel Churches

The Associated Gospel Churches (AGC) body traces its historical roots to the early years of the 20th century, which were marked by the growth of liberal theology in many established denominations. Individuals and whole congregations, seeking to uphold the final authority of the Scriptures in all matters of faith and conduct, withdrew from those denominations and established churches with an evangelical ministry under the inspired Word of God. These churches defended the belief that "all Scripture is given by inspiration of God" and also declared that the Holy Spirit "gave the identical words of sacred writings of holy men of old, chosen by Him to be the channel of His revelation to man."

In 1922, four churches of similar background in Ontario banded together in fellowship for counsel and cooperation. Known as The Christian Workers' Church in Canada, the group consisted of the Gospel Tabernacle, Hamilton; the Winona Gospel Tabernacle; the Missionary Tabernacle, Toronto; and West Hamilton Gospel Mission. The principal organizers were Dr. P. W. Philpott of Hamilton and H. E. Irwin, K. C., of Toronto.

In 1925 the name was changed to Associated Gospel Churches under a new Dominion Charter. Since that time the AGC has grown steadily.

HEADQUARTERS

3430 South Service Rd., Burlington, ON L7N 3T9 Tel. (416)634-8184 Fax (416)634-6283

Media Contact, Pres., D. G. Hamilton

OFFICERS

Pres., Rev. D. G. Hamilton
Vice-Pres., ——-
Mod., Rev. S. R. Sadlier, Box 55, King City, ON L0G 1K0 Tel. (416)833-5104
Sec.-Treas., Ritchie Penhall, 2 Bonaventure Dr., Hamilton, ON L9C 4P3 Tel. (416)388-3672

PERIODICAL

Advance

Association of Regular Baptist Churches (Canada)

Organized in 1957 by a group of churches for the purpose of mutual cooperation in missionary activities. The Association believes the Bible to be God's word, stands for historic Baptist principles, and opposes modern ecumenism.

HEADQUARTERS

130 Gerrard St. E., Toronto, ON M5A 3T4 Tel. (416)925-3261
Media Contact, Sec., Rev. W. P. Bauman, Tel. (416)925-3263 Fax (416)925-8305

OFFICERS

Pres., Rev. Norman Street
Sec., Rev. W. P. Bauman

PERIODICAL

Gospel Witness, The

Bahá'í Faith

Bahá'ís are followers of Bahá'u'lláh (1817-1892) whose religion teaches the essential oneness of all the great religions and promotes the oneness of mankind and racial unity.

The Bahá'í administrative order consists of nine-member elected institutions called spiritual assemblies, which function at the local and national level. The international administrative institution, the Universal House of Justice, is located in Haifa, Israel, at the Bahá'í World Centre, the spiritual headquarters of the Bahá'í community and the burial place of its founders.

In Canada, the Bahá'í Faith is administered by the National Spiritual Assembly. This body was incorporated by Act of Parliament in 1949. There are approximately 1,500 Bahá'í centers in Canada, of which 380 elect local Spiritual Assemblies.

HEADQUARTERS

Bahá'í National Centre of Canada, 7200 Leslie St., Thornhill, ON L3T 6L8 Tel. (416)889-8168 Fax (416)889-8184
Media Contact, Dir., Dept. of Public Affairs, Mrs. Brit-Karina Regan

OFFICER

Sec., Mr. M. E. Muttart

Baptist General Conference of Canada

Founded in Canada by missionaries from the United States. Originally a Swedish body, but no longer an ethnic body. The BGC-Canada includes people of many nationalities and is conservative and evangelical in doctrine and practice.

HEADQUARTERS

4306-97 St., Edmonton, AB T6E 5R9 Tel. (403)438-9127 Fax (403)435-2478
Media Contact, Exec. Dir., Rev. Abe Funk

OFFICERS

Exec. Dir., Rev. Abe Funk, 11635-51st. Ave., Edmonton, AB T6H 0M4 Tel. (403)435-4403
Bd. Chm., John Harapiak, 193 Woodford Close SW, Calgary, AB T2W 6E2

PERIODICAL

BGC Canada News

The Central Canada Baptist Conference

Central Baptist Conference, originally a Scandinavian group, is one of three districts of the Baptist General Conference of Canada. In 1907, churches from Winnipeg—Grant Memorial, Teulon, Kenora, Port Arthur, Sprague, Erickson, and Midale—organized under the leadership of Fred Palmberg. Immigration from Sweden declined, and in 1947 only nine churches remained. In 1948 the group dropped the Swedish language, withdrew from the Baptist Union, city churches were started, and today CCBC has 37 functioning churches.

An evangelical Baptist association holding to the inerrancy of the Bible, CCBC seeks to reach Central Canada for Christ by establishing local gospel-preaching churches.

CCBC offers pastoral aid to new churches, loans for building, recommendations as to pastoral supply, counsel, and fellowship. It encourages contributions to the CCBC and BGC of Canada budgets, the purchase of CCBC Serial Notes, support of the Conference BATT program (contributions to special needs of churches), and other projects to assist needy churches and pastors.

HEADQUARTERS

Box 135, Stonewall, MB R0C 2Z0 Tel. (204)467-2169

OFFICER

Exec. Min., Dr. Dave Selness

Baptist General Conference of Alberta

HEADQUARTERS

10727-114 St., Edmonton, AB T5H 3K1 Tel. (403)424-8440

OFFICER

Exec. Sec., Virgil Olson, 1843-104A St., Edmonton, AB T6J 5C1

PERIODICAL

Alberta Alert, The

British Columbia Baptist Conference

British Columbia Baptist Conference is a district of the Baptist General Conference of Canada, with roots in Sweden, where Christians began to read the Bible in their homes. One convert, F.O. Nilsson, saw the significance of baptism subsequent to a personal commitment to Christ; he went to Hamburg, Germany, where he was baptized in the Elbe River by Rev. John Oncken. When Nilsson returned to Sweden, five of his converts were baptized in the North Sea and, with him, formed the first Swedish Baptist Church. Nilsson was imprisoned by the local government for violation of state church regulations and later, when exiled from Sweden, settled in Germany and Wisconsin and carried on aggressive evangelism among other immigrating Swedes. In 1879 they formed the Swedish Baptist

General Conference of America, later named The Baptist General Conference.

HEADQUARTERS

7600 Glover Rd., Langley, BC V3A 6H4 Tel. (604)888-2246 Fax (604)888-1905
Media Contact, Dist. Exec. Min., Rev. Walter W. Wieser

OFFICERS

Dist. Exec. Min., Rev. Walter W. Weiser

PERIODICAL

B.C. Conference Call

The Bible Holiness Movement

The Bible Holiness Movement, organized in 1949 as an outgrowth of the city mission work of the late Pastor William James Elijah Wakefield, an early-day Salvation Army officer, has been headed since its inception by his son, Evangelist Wesley H. Wakefield, its bishop-general.

It derives its emphasis on the original Methodist faith of salvation and scriptural holiness from the late Bishop R. C. Horner. It adheres to the common evangelical faith in the Bible, the Deity, and the atonement of Christ, and stresses a personal experience of salvation for the repentant sinner, of being wholly sanctified for the believer, and of the fullness of the Holy Spirit for effective witness.

Membership involves a life of Christian love, evangelistic and social activism, and the disciplines of simplicity and separation, including total abstinence from liquor and tobacco, nonattendance at popular amusements, and no membership in secret societies. Divorce and remarriage are forbidden. Similar to Wesley's Methodism, members are, under some circumstances, allowed to retain membership in other evangelical church fellowships. Interchurch affiliations are maintained with a number of Wesleyan-Arminian Holiness denominations.

Year-round evangelistic outreach is maintained through open-air meetings, visitation, literature, and other media. Noninstitutional welfare work, including addiction counseling, is conducted among minorities. There is direct overseas famine relief, civil rights action, environment protection, and antinuclearism. The movement sponsors a permanent committee on religious freedom and an active promotion of Christian racial equality.

The movement has a world outreach with branches in the United States, India, Nigeria, Philippines, Ghana, Liberia, Cameroon, Kenya, Zambia, South Korea, and Haiti. It ministers to 89 countries in 42 languages through literature, radio, and audiocassetes.

HEADQUARTERS

Box 223, Postal Stn. A, Vancouver, BC V6C 2M3 Tel. (604)498-3895

DIRECTORS

Bishop-General, Evangelist Wesley H. Wakefield, (Intl. Leader)
Evangelist M. J. Wakefield, Oliver, BC
Mrs. W. Sneed, Dalhousie Rd., N.W., Calgary, AB
Pastor Vincente & Morasol Hernando, Phillipines
Pastor & Mrs. Daniel Stinnett, 1425 Mountain View W., Phoenix, AZ 85021
Pastor A. Sanon, Port-au-Prince, Haiti
Evangelist I. S. Udoh, Abak, Akwalbom, Nigeria, West Africa
Pastor Augustus Theo Seongbae, Sr., Monrovia, Liberia

Pastor Choe Chong Dee, Cha Pa Puk, S. Korea

PERIODICAL

Hallelujah

Brethren in Christ Church, Canadian Conference

The Brethren in Christ, formerly known as Tunkers in Canada, arose out of a religious awakening in Lancaster County, Pa. late in the 18th century. Representatives of the new denomination reached Ontario in 1788 and established the church in the southern part of the present province. Presently the conference has congregations in Ontario, Alberta, and Saskatchewan. In theology they have accents of the Pietist, Anabaptist, Wesleyan, and Evangelical movements.

HEADQUARTERS

Brethren in Christ Church, Gen. Ofc., P.O. Box 290, Grantham, PA 12027 Tel. (717)697-2634 Fax (717)697-7714

Canadian Headquarters, Bishop's Ofc., 2619 Niagara Pkwy., Ft. Erie, ON L2A 5M4 Tel. (416)871-9991

Media Contact, Mod., Harvey R. Sides, Brethren in Christ Church Gen. Ofc.

OFFICERS

Mod., Bishop R. Dale Shaw, 2619 Niagara Pkwy., Ft. Erie, ON L2A 5M4 Tel. (416)871-9991

Sec., Leonard J. Chester, 5384 Sherkston Rd., Sherkston, ON L0S 1R0

PERIODICAL

Evangelical Visitor

British Methodist Episcopal Church of Canada

The British Methodist Episcopal Church was organized in 1856 in Chatham, Ontario and incorporated in 1913. It has congregations across the Province of Ontario.

HEADQUARTERS

460 Shaw St., Toronto, ON M6G 3L3 Tel. (416)534-3831

OFFICERS

Gen. Supt., Rev. Dr. D. D. Rupwate
Asst. Gen. Supt., Rt. Rev. G. H. Boyce
Gen. Sec./Treas., Rev. M. Hicks

Buddhist Churches of Canada

Founded at Vancouver, British Columbia in 1904. The first minister was the Rev. Senju Sasaki. This body is the Mahayana division of Buddhism, and its sectarian belief is the Pure Land School based on the Three Canonical Scriptures with emphasis on pure faith.

HEADQUARTERS

220 Jackson Ave., Vancouver, BC V6A 3B3 Tel. (604)253-2554 Fax (604)253-7011

OFFICERS

Bishop Toshio Murakami
Pres., Jit Oishi
Vice-Pres., Mitts Sakai
Sec., Mr. Roy Inouye
Treas., Mr. Jim Kitaura
Pres. BCC Min. Assn., Rev. Fujikawa

Canadian and American Reformed Churches

The Canadian and American Reformed Churches accept the Bible as the infallible Word of God, as summarized in The Belgic Confession of Faith (1561), The Heidelberg Cathechism(1563), and The Canons of Dordt (1618-1619). The denomination was founded in Canada in 1950 and American congregations have been formed since 1955.

HEADQUARTERS

Synod: P.O. Box 62053, Burlington, ON L7I 1W5

Canadian Reformed Churches: Ebenezer Canadian Reformed Church, P. O. Box 62053, Burlington, ON L7I 1W5

American Reformed Churches: American Reformed Church, Rev. P. Kingma, 3167-68th St. S.E., Caledonia, MI 46316

PERIODICALS

Preach the Word; In Holy Array; Evangel: The Good News of Jesus Christ

Canadian Baptist Federation

The Canadian Baptist Federation has four federated member bodies: (1) Baptist Convention of Ontario and Québec, (2) Baptist Union of Western Canada, (3) the United Baptist Convention of the Atlantic Provinces, (4) Union d'Églises Baptistes Françaises au Canada (French Baptist Union). Its main purpose is to act as a coordinating agency for the four groups.

HEADQUARTERS

7185 Millcreek Dr., Mississauga, ON L5N 5R4 Tel. (416)826-0191 Fax (416)826-3441

Media Contact, Gen. Sec.-Treas., Dr. Richard C. Coffin

OFFICERS

Pres., Rev. Nelson W. Hooper, 45 Applewood Cres., Cambridge, ON N1S 4K1

Vice-Pres.: Dr. Bruce Milne, 2937 West 16 Ave., Vancouver, BC V6K 3C7; Dr. Joyce Boillat, 2565 Montmartre, Brossard, QC J4Y 1N7; Mrs. Mary Price, P.O. Box 1486, Wolfville, NS B0P 1X0

Gen. Sec.-Treas., Dr. Richard Coffin, 7185 Millcreek Dr., Mississauga, ON L5N 5N4

Canadian Baptist Overseas Mission Bd., Gen. Sec., Rev. R. Berry

PERIODICAL

Enterprise

Baptist Convention of Ontario and Quebec

The Baptist Convention of Ontario and Quebec is a family of 372 churches in Ontario and Quebec, united for mutual support and encouragement and united in missions in Canada and the world.

The Convention was formally organized in 1888. It has two educational institutions—McMaster University, founded in 1887 and the Baptist Leadership Education Centre at Whitby. The Convention works through the all-Canada missionary agency, Canadian Baptist International Ministries. The churches also support the Sharing Way, the relief and development arm of the Canadian Baptist Federation.

HEADQUARTERS

217 St. George St., Toronto, ON M5R 2M2 Tel. (416)922-5163 Fax (416)922-3254

Media Contact, Assoc. Exec. Min., Rev. R. Roger Smith

OFFICERS

Pres., Mr. Donald James
1st Vice-Pres., Rev. Lionel Pye
2nd Vice-Pres., Mrs. Barbara Bell
Treas./Bus. Adm., Mrs. Nancy Bell
Exec. Min., Rev. John Wilton, (Interim)
Assoc. Exec. Min./Div. of Shared Mission, Rev. Robert G. Wilkins
Assoc. Exec. Min./Div. of Cong. Life, ——-
Assoc. Exec. Min./Div. of Pastoral Res., Rev. George W. Scott

PERIODICAL

Canadian Baptist, The

Baptist Union of Western Canada

HEADQUARTERS

202, 838-11th Ave. S.W., Calgary, AB T2R 0E5
Tel. (403)234-9044 Fax (403)269-6755
Media Contact, Exec. Min., Rev. William Cram

OFFICERS

Pres., Rev. Leslie Drew
Exec. Min., Rev. William Cram
Assoc. Exec. Min., Dr. C. Howard Bentall
Area Min., Alberta, Rev. J. Dozois, 43 Strathbury Cir. SW, Calgary, AB T3H 1R9
Area Min., British Columbia, Dr. Don Anderson, 201-7 St., New Westminster, BC V3M 3K2
Area Min., Saskatchewan, Rev. Wayne Larson, 3542 Burns Rd., Regina, SK S4V 2G3
Dir. of Cong. Resources, Rev. Gerald Fisher, 14 Milford Cr., Sherwood Park, AB T8A 3V4
Carey Theological College, Principal & Field Educ. Dir., Rev. Philip Collins, 5920 Iona Dr., Vancouver, BC V6T 1J6
Baptist Leadership Training School (Lay), Principal, Rev. Ken Bellous, 4330-16 Street SW, Calgary, AB T2T 4H9

PERIODICAL

Tidings

United Baptist Convention of the Atlantic Provinces

The United Baptist Convention of the Atlantic Provinces is the largest Baptist Convention in Canada.

Through the Canadian Baptist Federation, it is a member of the Baptist World Alliance.

Work in Canada began in the Atlantic Provinces in the 1700s when Baptists from New England began to migrate into the area. The Rev. Ebenezer Moulton organized a Baptist Church in Horton (now Wolfville, Nova Scotia) in 1763. The present church in Wolfville was formed in 1778 and is Canada's oldest continuing Baptist church. The United Baptist Convention was formed in 1905 when Calvinistic and Free Baptist churches merged; thus the name United Baptist is often used.

The first Baptist Association in Canada met in Nova Scotia in 1800. Today there are 21 Associations (usually comprised of one or two counties) within the convention. Through the Canadian Baptist Overseas Mission Board they support more than 100 missionaries in Kenya, Zaire, Brazil, Bolivia, Indonesia, and Sri Lanka. They have an active program of evangelism, Christian education, and church planting. They own and operate two colleges: Atlantic Baptist College in Moncton, New Brunswick, and Acadia Divinity College in Wolfville, Nova Scotia, which provides training for those entering the ministry and overseas missions. The convention operates six senior citizens' homes and a Christian bookstore.

HEADQUARTERS

1655 Manawagonish Rd., Saint John, NB E2M 3Y2 Tel. (506)635-1922 Fax (506)635-0366

OFFICERS

Pres., Dr. Brian MacArthur, 109 Pleasant St., Moncton, NB E1A 2U3
Exec. Min., Dr. Eugene Thompson
Dir. of Admn. & Treas., Mr. Daryl MacKenzie
Dir. of Evangelism, Rev. Malcolm Beckett
Dir. of Christian Training, Rev. Harold Arbo
Dir. of Home Missions & Church Planting, Rev. Harry Gardner
Dir. of Communications, Rev. Douglas Hapeman

PERIODICAL

Atlantic Baptist, The

Union d'Eglises Baptistes Françaises au Canada

Baptist churches in French Canada first came into being through the labors of two missionaries from Switzerland, Rev. Louis Roussy and Mme. Henriette Feller, who arrived in Canada in 1835. The earliest church was organized in Grande Ligne (now St.-Blaise), Québec in 1838.

By 1900 there were 7 churches in the province of Québec and 13 French-language Baptist churches in the New England states. The leadership was totally French Canadian.

By 1960, the process of Americanization had caused the disappearance of the French Baptist churches. During the 1960s Québec as a society, began rapidly changing in all its facets: education, politics, social values and structures. Mission, evangelism and church growth once again flourished. In 1969, in response to the new conditions, the Grande Ligne Mission passed control of its work to the newly formed Union of French Baptist Churches in Canada, which then included 8 churches. By 1990 the French Canadian Baptist movement had grown to include 25 congregations.

The Union d'Eglises Baptistes Françaises au Canada is a member body of the Canadian Baptist Federation and thus is affiliated with the Baptist World Alliance.

HEADQUARTERS

2285 avenue Papineau, Montreal, QC H2K 4J5 Tel. (514)526-6643
Media Contact, Sec. Gen., John S. Gilmour

OFFICERS

Sec. Gen., Rev. John Gilmour

PERIODICALS

Trait D'Union, Le

Canadian Convention of Southern Baptists

The Canadian Convention of Southern Baptists was formed at the Annual Meeting, May 7-9, 1985, in Kelowna, British Columbia. It was formerly known as the Canadian Baptist Conference, founded in Kamloops, British Columbia, in 1959 by pastors of existing churches.

HEADQUARTERS

Postal Bag 300, Cochrane, AB T0L 0W0 Tel. (403)932-5688 Fax (403)932-4937
Media Contact, Exec. Dir.-Treas., Rev. Allen Schmidt

OFFICERS

Exec. Dir.-Treas., Allen E. Schmidt, Box 7, Site 4, R.R. 1, Cochrane, AB T0L 0W0

Pres., Rev. Don Miller, West Whalley Baptist Church, 13175-107 Ave., Surrey, BC V3T 2G2

PERIODICAL

Baptist Horizon, The

Canadian Yearly Meeting of the Religious Society of Friends

Founded in Canada as an offshoot of the Quaker movement in Great Britain and colonial America. Genesee Yearly Meeting, founded 1834, Canada Yearly Meeting (Orthodox), founded in 1867, and Canada Yearly Meeting, founded in 1881, united in 1955 to form the Canadian Yearly Meeting. The Canadian Yearly Meeting is affiliated with the Friends United Meeting and the Friends General Conference. It is also a member of Friends World Committee for Consultation.

HEADQUARTERS

91A Fourth Ave., Ottawa, ON K1S 2L1 Tel. (613)235-8553

Media Contact, Gen. Sec.-Treas., Anne Thomas

OFFICERS

Gen. Sec./Treas., Anne Thomas

Clk., Elaine Bishop

Archivist, Jane Zavitz Bond

Archives, Arthur G. Dorland, Pickering College, 389 Bayview St., Newmarket, ON L3Y 4X2 Tel. (416)895-1700

PERIODICAL

Canadian Friend, The

Christian and Missionary Alliance in Canada

A Canadian movement, dedicated to the teaching of Jesus Christ the Saviour, Sanctifier, Healer and Coming King, commenced in Toronto in 1887 under the leadership of the Rev. John Salmon. Two years later, the movement united with The Christian Alliance of New York, founded by Rev. A. B. Simpson, becoming the Dominion Auxiliary of the Christian Alliance, Toronto, under the presidency of the Hon. William H. Howland. Its four founding branches were Toronto, Hamilton, Montréal, and Québec. By Dec. 31, 1990, there were 327 churches across Canada, with 1039 official workers, including a worldwide missionary force of 252.

In 1980, the Christian and Missionary Alliance in Canada became autonomous. Its General Assembly is held every two years.

HEADQUARTERS

Natl. Office, #510-105 Gordon Baker Rd., North York, ON M2H 3P8 Tel. (416)492-8775 Fax (416)492-7708

Media Contact, Dir. of Communications, Myrna McCombs

OFFICERS

Pres., Rev. Melvin Sylvester, Box 7900, Postal Sta. B, Willowdale, ON M2K 2R6

Vice-Pres. of Personnel & Missions, Rev. Arnold L. Cook

Vice-Pres. of Fin., Mr. Milton H. Quigg

Vice-Pres. of Canadian Ministries, Rev. C. Stuart Lightbody

Vice-Pres. of Gen. Services, Mr. Kenneth Paton

DISTRICT SUPERINTENDENTS

Canadian Pacific: Rev. Gordon R. Fowler

Western Canadian: Rev. Arnold Downey

Canadian Midwest: Rev. Arnold Reimer

Eastern and Central: Rev. Robert J. Gould

St. Lawrence: Rev. Jesse D. Jespersen

Christian Brethren (also known as Plymouth Brethren)

This orthodox and evangelical movement, which began in the British Isles in the 1820s, is now worldwide. For more detail on the history and theology, see "Religious Bodies in the United States" section of the Yearbook.

In the 1840s the movement divided. The "exclusive" branch, led by John Darby, stressed the interdependence of congregations. Canadian congregations number approximately 150, with an inclusive membership estimated at 11,000. The "open" branch of the movement, stressing evangelism and foreign missions, followed the leadership of George Muller in rejecting the "Exclusive" principle of binding discipline, and has escaped large-scale division.

Canadian congregations number approximately 450, with an inclusive membership estimated at 41,000. There are 250 "commended" full-time ministers, not including foreign missionaries.

HEADQUARTERS

For Quebec, Christian Brethren Church in the Province of Quebec, Norman R. Buchanan, Sec., 222 Alexander St., Sherbrooke, QC J1H 4S7 Tel. (819)562-9198

Correspondent for North America, Interest Ministries, Bruce R. McNichol, Pres., 218 W. Willow, Wheaton, IL 60187 Tel. (708)653-6573

OTHER ORGANIZATIONS

Missionary Service Committee, Exec. Dir., Claude Loney, 1562A Danforth Ave., Toronto, ON M4J 1N4 Tel. (416)469-2012

Vision Ontario, Nelson Annan, 25 Ballyconnor Ct., Willowdale, ON M2M 4B3 Tel. (416)226-6380

PERIODICAL

News of Quebec

Christian Church (Disciples of Christ) in Canada

Disciples have been in Canada since 1810 but were organized nationally in 1922 when the All-Canada Committee was formed. It seeks to serve the Canadian context as part of the whole Christian Church (Disciples of Christ) in the United States and Canada.

HEADQUARTERS

P.O. Box 64, Guelph, ON N1H 6J6 Tel. (519)823-5190

Media Contact, Exec. Minister, Robert W. Steffer

OFFICERS

Mod., Mr. Stan Litke, 255 Midvalley Dr., S.E., Calgary, AB T2X 1K8

Vice-Mod., Rev. Robert Dees, 6 Jedburgh, Toronto, ON M5M 3J6

Exec. Min., Rev. Robert W. Steffer, 7 Lynwood Dr., Guelph, ON N1G 1P8

PERIODICALS

Canadian Disciple

Christian Churches and Churches of Christ in Canada

This fellowship, dedicated to the "restoration of the New Testament Church in doctrine, ordinances and life," has been operating in Canada since 1820. There is no general organization. Each church within the fellowship is completely independent. For detailed information see: *Directory of the Ministry*, Christian Churches and Churches of Christ, 1525 Cherry Rd., Springfield, IL 62704, U.S.A., telephone (217)546-7338.

Christian Reformed Church in North America

The Christian Reformed Church in North America represents the historic faith of Protestantism and is creedally united in the Belgic Confession (1561), the Heidelberg Catechism (1563), and the Canons of Dort (1618-19). The denomination was founded in the U.S. in 1857. Canadian congregations have been formed since 1908.

HEADQUARTERS

United States Office: 2850 Kalamazoo Ave., S.E., Grand Rapids, MI 49560 Tel. (616)246-0744 Fax (616)246-0834

Canadian Office: 3475 Mainway, P.O. Box 5070, Burlington, ON L7R 3Y8 Tel. (416)336-2920 Fax (416)336-8344

Media Contact, Gen. Sec., Leonard J. Hofman, U.S. Office

OFFICERS

Gen. Sec., Rev. Leonard J. Hofman, U.S. Office

Fin. Coord., Harry J. Vander Meer, U.S. Office

Coun. of Christian Ref. Churches in Can., Exec. Sec., Arie G. Van Eek, Canadian Office

Church of God (Anderson, Ind.)

This body is one of the largest of the groups which have taken the name "Church of God." Its headquarters are at Anderson, Ind. It originated about 1880 and emphasizes Christian unity.

HEADQUARTERS

Western Canada Assembly, Chpsn., Jack Wagner, 4717 56th St., Camrose, AB T4V 2C4 Tel. (403)672-0772 Fax (403)672-6888

Ontario Assembly, Chpsn., Rev. John Campbell, 48 Leaside Dr., Welland, ON L3C 6B2

Media Contact for Western Canada, Interim Admn., Lloyd W.E. Moritz

PERIODICALS

Gospel Contact, The; Ontario Messenger

Church of God (Cleveland, Tenn.)

This body began in the United States in 1886 as the outgrowth of the holiness revival under the name Christian Union, and in 1902 it was reorganized as the Holiness Church. In 1907, the church adopted the name Church of God. Its doctrine is fundamental and Pentecostal, and it maintains a centralized form of government and an evangelistic and missionary program.

The first church in Canada was established in 1919 in Scotland Farm, Manitoba. Paul H. Walker became the first overseer of Canada in 1931.

HEADQUARTERS

Intl. Offices: 2490 Keith St., NW, Cleveland, TN 37311 Tel. (615)472-3361

THE YEAR IN IMAGES

Leading the ecumenical movement

In 1991, Rev. Joan B. Campbell became the first ordained woman to serve as the General Secretary of the National Council of Churches of Christ in the U.S.A. At her May 14 installation she said, "The task of our time is to live courageously, strengthen the bonds of unity, and respect and advocate on behalf of one another."

Media Contact, Dir. of Publ. Relations, Lewis J. Willis, P.O. Box 2430, Cleveland, TN 37320-2430 Tel. (615)472-7112 Fax (615)478-7066

OFFICERS

Exec. Office in Canada: Rev. S. A. Lankford, P.O. Box 2036, Bramalea, ON L6T 3S3 Tel. (416)793-2213

Western Canada: Rev. Philip F. Siggelkow, 175 Rogers Rd., Regina, SK S4R 6VI Tel. (306)545-5771

The Church of God of Prophecy in Canada

In the late 19th century, men seeking God's eternal plan as they followed the Reformation spirit began to delve further for scriptural light concerning Christ and his church. On June 13, 1903, a small group gathered in Cherokee County, N.C., for prayer and further study of God's Word.

From that historic meeting, that church has become a visible, organized body, operating in all 50 states of the United States. In 1911, the first missionary effort was launched in the Bahamas; today the church is represented in 91 countries and territories around the world.

In Canada, the first Church of God of Prophecy congregation was organized in Swan River, Manitoba, in 1937. Churches are now established in British Columbia, Manitoba, Alberta, Saskatchewan, Ontario, and Québec.

The church accepts the whole Bible rightly divided, with the New Testament as the rule of faith and practice, government, and discipline. The membership upholds the Bible as the inspired Word of God and believes that its truths are known by illuminative revelation of the Holy Scriptures. The Trinity is recognized as one supreme Godhead in three persons—Father, Son, and Holy Ghost. Jesus Christ, the virgin-born Son of God, lived a sinless life, fulfilled his ministry on earth, was crucified, resurrected, and later ascended to the right hand of God.

HEADQUARTERS

Canadian Headquarters: 1st Line East, RR #2, Brampton, ON L6V 1A1 Tel. (416)843-2379
World Headquarters: Bible Place, Cleveland, TN 37311

OFFICERS

Canada East, Natl. Overseer, Bishop Wade H. Phillips, P.O. Box 457, Brampton, ON L6V 2L4 Tel. (416)843-2379
Canada West, Natl. Overseer, Bishop John Doroshuk, Box 952, Strathmore, AB T0J 3H0 Tel. (403)934-4787

BOARD OF DIRECTORS

Pres., Bishop John Doroshuk
Vice Pres., Bishop Wade H. Phillips
Sec., John Anderson
Members: Bishop M. A. Tomlinson; Bishop Adrian Varlack; Bishop A. R. Morrison; Bishop Leroy V. Greenaway

PERIODICAL

Canadian Trumpeter Canada-West

The Church of Jesus Christ of Latter-day Saints in Canada

This body has no central headquarters in Canada, only stake and mission offices. Elders H. Burke Peterson, Hugh W. Pinnock and F. Enzio Busche of the Quorum of the Seventy oversee the Church's activities in Canada. They reside in Salt Lake City, Utah. All General Authorities may be reached at the headquarters. [See U. S. Directory, "Religious Bodies in the United States" in this edition for further details.] In Canada, there are 34 stakes, 6 missions, 8 districts, and 380 wards/branches (congregations).

HEADQUARTERS

50 East North Temple St., Salt Lake City, UT 84150
Media Contact, Public Affairs Dir., Richard R. Robertson, 7181 Woodbine Ave., #234, Markham, ON L3R 1A3 Tel. (416)477-8595 Fax (416)492-8621

OFFICER

Public Affairs Dir., Richard R. Robertson

Church of the Lutheran Brethren

Organized in Milwaukee, Wisc., in 1900, it adheres to the Lutheran Confessions and accepts into membership those who profess a personal faith in Jesus Christ. It practices congregational autonomy and conducts its services in a nonliturgical pattern. The synod has an advisory rather than ruling function on the congregational level, but in the cooperative efforts of all congregations (Education, American and World Missions, Publications, and Youth Ministries) it exercises a ruling function.

HEADQUARTERS

1007 Westside Dr., P.O. Box 655, Fergus Falls, MN 56538 Tel. (218)739-3336 Fax (218)739-5514
Media Contact, Pres., Rev. Robert Overgaard

OFFICERS

Pres., Rev. Robert M. Overgaard
Vice-Pres., Rev. David Rinden
Sec., Rev. Richard Vettrus, 707 Crestview Dr., West Union, IA 52175
Dir. Fin. Affairs, Bradley E. Martinson

PERIODICAL

Faith and Fellowship

Church of the Nazarene

The first Church of the Nazarene in Canada was organized in November, 1902, by Dr. H. F. Reynolds. It was in Oxford, Nova Scotia. The Church of the Nazarene is Wesleyan Arminian in theology, representative in church government, and warmly evangelistic.

HEADQUARTERS

73800-19 St., N.E., Calgary, AB T2E 6V2
Media Contact, Gen. Sec., Dr. Jack Stone, 6401 The Paseo, Kansas City, MO 64131 Tel. (816)333-7000 Fax (816)361-4983

OFFICERS

Exec. Admn., Neil Hightower
Chmn., Rev. William Stewart, 14 Hollywood Dr., Moncton, NB E1E 2R5
Vice-Chmn., Charles Muxworthy, Ste. 205, 1255 56th St., Delta, BC V4L 2B9

Churches of Christ in Canada

Churches of Christ are autonomous congregations, whose members appeal to the Bible alone to determine matters of faith and practice. There are no central offices or officers. Publications and institutions related to the churches are either under local congregational control or independent of any one congregation.

Churches of Christ shared a common fellowship in the 19th century with the Christian Churches/Churches of Christ and the Christian Church (Disciples of Christ). Fellowship was broken after the introduction of instrumental music in worship and centralization of church-wide activities through a missionary society. Churches of Christ began in Canada soon after 1800, largely in the middle provinces. The few pioneer congregations were greatly strengthened in the mid-1800s, growing in size and number.

Members of Churches of Christ believe in the inspiration of the Scriptures, the divinity of Jesus Christ, and immersion into Christ for the remission of sins. The New Testament pattern is followed in worship and church organization.

MEDIA CONTACT

Media Contact, Man. Ed., Gospel Herald, Eugene C. Perry, 4904 King St., Beansville, ON L0R 1B6 Tel. (416)563-7503

PERIODICALS

Gospel Herald; Good News West

Conference of Mennonites in Canada

The Conference of Mennonites in Canada began in 1902 as an organized fellowship of Mennonite immigrants from Russia clustered in southern Manitoba and around Rosthern, Saskatchewan. The first annual sessions were held in July, 1903. Its members hold to traditional Christian beliefs, believer's baptism, and congregational polity. They emphasize practical Christianity: opposition to war, service to others, and personal ethics. Further immigration from Russia in the 1920s and 1940s increased the group which is now located in all provinces from New Brunswick to British Columbia. This conference is affiliated with the General Conference Mennonite Church whose offices are at Newton, Kan.

HEADQUARTERS

600 Shaftesbury Blvd., Winnipeg, MB R3P 0M4 Tel. (204)888-6781 Fax (204)831-5675
Media Contact, Gen. Sec., Helmut Harder

OFFICERS

Chpsn., Menno Epp, 78 Oak St. E., Leamington, ON N8H 2C6
Vice-Chpsn., George Richert, 3504 Gordon Rd., Regina, SK S4S 2V4
Sec., Ruth Enns, 2425 Haultain Ave., Saskatoon, SK S7J 1R2
Gen. Sec., Helmut Harder

PERIODICALS

Mennonite, The; Mennonite Reporter

Congregational Christian Churches in Canada

This body originated in the early 18th century when devout Christians within several denominations in the northern and eastern United States, dissatisfied with sectarian controversy, broke away from their own denominations and took the simple title "Christians." First organized in 1821 at Keswick, Ontario, these churches became affiliated with the Conservative Congregational Christian Conference in the U.S.A. In doctrine the body is evangelical, being governed by the Bible as the final authority in faith and practice. It believes that Christian character must be expressed in daily living; it aims at the unity of all true believers in Christ that others may believe in Him and be saved. In church polity, the body is democratic and autonomous.

HEADQUARTERS

P.O. Box 4688, Brantford, ON N3T 6H2 Tel. (519)751-0606
Media Contact, Pres., Rev. John Tweedie, 48 Sky Acres Dr., Brantford, ON N3R 1P3 Tel. (519)759-4692

OFFICERS

Pres., Rev. John Tweedie
Exec. Dir., Rev. Walter Riegert
Sec., Mr. Garth McMillan

The Coptic Church in Canada

The Coptic Church in North America was begun in Canada in 1964 and was registered in the province of Ontario in 1965. The Coptic Church has spread since then to a number of locations in North America.

The governing body of each local church is an elected Board of Deacons. The Diocesan Council is the national governing body and meets at least once a year.

OFFICER

Archpriest, Fr. M. A. Marcos, St. Mark's Coptic Orthodox Church, 41 Glendinning Ave., Agincourt, ON M1W 3E2 Tel. (416)494-4449 Fax (416)470-8494

Elim Fellowship of Evangelical Churches and Ministers

The Elim Fellowship of Evangelical Churches and Ministers, a Pentecostal body, was established in 1984 as a sister organization of Elim Fellowship in the U.S.

This is an association of churches, ministers, and missionaries seeking to serve the whole body of Christ. It is Pentecostal and has a charismatic orientation.

OFFICERS

Pres., Errol Alchin, 43 Black Locust Way, Brantford, ON N3R 7C7
Vice-Pres., Winston Nunes, 4 Palamino Cres., Willowdale, North York, ON M2K 1W1 Tel. (416)225-4824
Sec., Paul Heidt, 1303 Murphy Rd., Sarnia, ON N7S 2Y7 Tel. (519)542-8938
Treas., Errol Alchin, 43 Black Locust Way, Brantford, ON N3R 7C7

The Estonian Evangelical Lutheran Church

The Estonian Evangelical Lutheran Church (EELC) was founded in 1917 in Estonia and reorganized in Sweden in 1944. The teachings of the EELC are based on the Old and New Testaments, explained through the Apostolic, Nicean and Athanasian confessions, the unaltered Confession of Augsburg and other teachings found in the Book of Concord.

HEADQUARTERS

383 Jarvis St., Toronto, ON M5B 2C7 Tel. (416)925-5465
Media Contact, Archbishop, Rev. Udo Petersoo

OFFICERS

Archbishop, The Rev. Udo Petersoo
Bishop, Rev. K. Raudsepp, 30 Sunrise Ave., #216, Toronto, ON M4A 2R3
Gen. Sec., Dean Edgar Heinsoo

PERIODICAL

Eesti Kirik

Evangelical Baptist Churches in Canada, The Fellowship of

Founded in 1953 by the merging of the Union of Regular Baptist Churches of Ontario and Quebec with the Fellowship of Independent Baptist Churches of Canada.

HEADQUARTERS

679 Southgate Dr., Guelph, ON N1G 4S2 Tel. (519)821-4830 Fax (519)821-9829

OFFICERS

Pres., Rev. Gabriel Cotnoir
Gen. Sec.-Treas., Dr. R. W. Lawson

PERIODICALS

B.C. Fellowship Baptist; Evangelical Baptist; Intercom

The Evangelical Church in Canada

Founded early in the 19th century by Jacob Albright and William Otterbein in Pennsylvania as the Evangelical Church, this body became known later as the Evangelical United Brethren Church, which in the United States became a part of The United Methodist Church in 1968. This Canadian body is Methodist in organization and Arminian, Wesleyan, and Methodist in doctrine. It was incorporated in 1928 by Dominion Charter as The Northwest Canada Conference Evangelical Church. In 1970, this Canadian Conference was granted autonomy and became a separate denomination. In 1982 The Evangelical Church in Canada joined with The Evangelical Church of North America.

HEADQUARTERS

Evangelical Church Ofc. Bldg., 2805 13th Ave., S.E., Medicine Hat, AB T1A 3R1 Tel. (403)527-4101 Fax (403)526-8402
Media Contact, A. W. Riegel

OFFICERS

Gen. Supt., Dr. John Sills, 4200 S.E. Jennings Ave., Portland, OR 97267 Tel. (503)652-1029
Conf. Supt., Rev. Walter H. Erion, 30 Larkspur Ct. S.E., Medicine Hat, AB T1B 2J7
Conf. Chpsn., Harold Hunter, Box 233, 325 5th Ave. S., Three Hills, AB T0M 2A0 Tel. (503)652-1029
Conf. Sec., Rev. Richard Kopanke, 2300 Gagnon Pl., Richmond, BC V6X 3S6

PERIODICAL

Northwest Canada Echoes

The Evangelical Covenant Church of Canada

A Canadian denomination organized in Canada at Winnipeg in 1904 which is affiliated with the Evangelical Covenant Church of America and with the International Federation of Free Evangelical Churches, which includes churches in 11 European countries.

This body believes in the one triune God as confessed in the Apostles' Creed, that salvation is received through faith in Christ as Saviour, that the Bible is the authoritative guide in all matters of faith and practice. Christian Baptism and the Lord's Supper are accepted as divinely ordained sacraments of the church. As descendants of the 19th century northern European pietistic awakening, the group believes in the need of a personal experience of commitment to Christ, the development of a virtuous life, and the urgency of spreading the gospel to the "ends of the world."

HEADQUARTERS

245 21st St. E., Prince Albert, SK S6V 1L9 Tel. (306)922-3449 Fax (306)922-5414

OFFICERS

Supt., Rev. Jerome Johnson
Chpsn., Les Doell, R.R. #2, Wetaskiwin, AB T9A 1W9
Sec., Melsie Waldner, 415 Perreault La., Saskatoon, SK S7K 6B5
Treas., Grace McKenzie, 60 Bowerman Cres., Prince Albert, SK S6V 6G4

PERIODICAL

Covenant Messenger, The

Evangelical Free Church of Canada

The Evangelical Free Churches in Canada celebrated 50 years of Free Church work under the American Evangelical Free Church by becoming incorporated as a Canadian organization on March 21, 1967. On July 8, 1984, the Evangelical Free Church of Canada was given its autonomy as a self-governing Canadian denomination.

HEADQUARTERS

#200, 20316-56 Ave., Langley, BC V3A 3Y7

OFFICERS

Pres., Rev. Ronald Swanson
Mod., Rev. James Scobbie, Box 778, Steinbach, MB R0A 2A0
Vice-Mod., Mr. Dave Enns, 23 Watercress Rd., Winnipeg, MB R2J 2W2
Fin. Chmn., Mr. Doug Munton, 511-5th St. S., Lethbridge, AB T1J 2B9

Evangelical Lutheran Church in Canada

The Evangelical Lutheran Church in Canada was organized in 1985 through a merger of The Evangelical Lutheran Church of Canada (ELCC) and the Lutheran Church in America—Canada Section.

The merger is a result of an invitation issued in 1972 by the ELCC to the Lutheran Church in America—Canada Section and the Lutheran Church—Canada (LC-MS). Three-way merger discussions took place until 1978 when it was decided that only a two-way merger was possible. The ELCC was the Canada District of the ALC until autonomy in 1967.

The Lutheran Church in Canada traces its history back more than 200 years. Congregations were organized by German Lutherans in Halifax and Lunenburg County in Nova Scotia in 1749. German Lutherans, including many United Empire Loyalists, also settled in large numbers along the St. Lawrence and in Upper Canada. In the late 19th century, immigrants arrived from Scandinavia, Germany, and central European countries, many via the United States. The Lutheran synods in the United States have provided the pastoral support and help for the Canadian church.

HEADQUARTERS

1512 St. James St., Winnipeg, MB R3H 0L2 Tel. (204)786-6707 Fax (204)783-7548
Media Contact, Bishop, Rev. Donald W. Sjoberg

OFFICERS

Bishop, Rev. Donald W. Sjoberg
Vice-Pres., Joan Meyer
Sec., Rev. Leon C. Gilbertson
Treas., Don Rosten

DIVISIONS AND OFFICES

Div. for Canadian Mission, Exec. Dir., Rev. James A. Chell
Div. for Church & Society, Exec. Dir., Rev. Dr. Kenneth C. Kuhn
Div. for College & Univ. Services, Exec. Dir., Rev. Dr. Lawrence Denef
Div. for Parish Life, Exec. Dir.
Div. for Theological Educ. & Leadership, Exec. Dir., Rev. Dr. Lawrence Denef
Div. for World Mission, Exec. Dir., Rev. Peter E. Mathiasen
Ofc. for Communication, ———-
Dept. of Fin. & Admn., Dir., Joan E. Nolting

Ofc. for Resource Dev., Exec. Dir., Rev. Richard Husfloen

Evangelical Lutheran Women, Pres., Joyce Christensen

Exec. Dir., Diane Doth Rehbein

SYNODS

Alberta and the Territories: Bishop, Rev. J. Robert Jacobson, 10014-81 Ave., Edmonton, AB T6E 1W8 Tel. (403)439-2636 Fax (403)433-6623

Eastern: Bishop, Rev. Dr. William D. Huras, 50 Queen St. N., Kitchener, ON N2H 6P4 Tel. (519)743-1461 Fax (519)743-4291

British Columbia: Bishop, Rev. Dr. Marlin Aadland, 80-10th Ave., E., New Westminster, BC V3L 4R5 Tel. (604)524-1318 Fax (604)524-9255

Manitoba/Northwestern Ontario: Bishop, Rev. Dr. G. W. Luetkehoelter, 201-3657 Roblin Blvd., Winnipeg, MB R3G 0E2 Tel. (204)889-3760 Fax (204)869-0272

Saskatchewan: Bishop, Rev. Telmor G. Sartison, Bessborough Towers, Rm. 707, 601 Spadina Cres. E., Saskatoon, SK S7K 3G8 Tel. (306)244-2474 Fax (306)664-8677

PERIODICALS

Canada Lutheran, The; Esprit

The Evangelical Mennonite Conference

The Evangelical Mennonite Conference came about as the result of a renewal movement among a small group of Mennonites in Southern Russia in 1812. Klaas Reimer, a Mennonite minister, had become concerned about the apparent decline of spiritual life in the church, lack of discipline, and the church's backing of the Russian government in the Napoleonic War. Around 1812, Reimer and several others began separate worship services, emphasizing a more strict discipline and separation from the world. By 1814, they were organized as a separate group, called the Kleinegemeinde (small church).

Increasing pressure from the Russian government, particularly in the area of military conscription, finally led to a migration (1874 to 1875) of the entire group to North America. Fifty families settled in Manitoba, and 36 families settled in Nebraska. Ties between the two segments gradually weakened, and eventually the U.S. group gave up its EMC identity.

The church has passed through numerous difficult times and survived several schisms and migrations. Beginning in the 1940s, a growing vision for missions and concern for others fostered a new vitality and growth, reaching people from a variety of cultural backgrounds. Thirty-two of the 50 congregations are in Manitoba. The church has some 146 mission workers in 23 countries of the world.

HEADQUARTERS

Box 1268, 440 Main St., Steinbach, MB R0A 2A0 Tel. (204)326-6401 Fax (204)326-1613

Media Contact, Conf. Sec., Edwin Friesen

OFFICERS

Conf. Mod., Harvey Plett, Box 3271, Steinbach, MB R0A 2A0

Bd. of Missions, Exec. Sec., Henry Klassen

PERIODICAL

Messenger, The

Evangelical Mennonite Mission Conference

Founded in 1936 as the Rudnerweider Mennonite Church in Southern Manitoba and organized as the Evangelical Mennonite Mission Conference in 1959. It was incorporated in 1962. The Annual Conference meeting is held in July.

HEADQUARTERS

526 McMillan Ave., Winnipeg, MB R3L 0N5 Tel. (204)477-1213

Media Contact, Mod., Leonard Sawatzky, Box 2126, Steinbach, MB R0A 2A0 Tel. (204)326-3315 Fax (204)326-2759

OFFICERS

Mod., Rev. Leonard Sawatzky, Box 2126, Steinbach, MB R0A 2A0

Vice-Mod., Frank Zacharias, 14-214 South St. W., Aylmer, ON N5H 3E6

Sec., Mr. Bill Thiessen, Box 12, Randolph, MB R0A 1L0

Exec. Sec., Henry Dueck, Box 126, Winnepeg, MB R3C 2G1 Tel. (204)489-2616

OTHER ORGANIZATIONS

Missions Dir.: Mr. Lawrence Giesbrecht, Box 927, Altona, MB R0G 0B0 Tel. (204)324-6179

The Gospel Message: Box 1622, Saskatoon, SK S7K 3R8 Tel. (306)242-5001; 210-401-33rd St. W., Saskatoon, SK S7L 0V5 Tel. (306)242-5001; Radio Pastor, Rev. John D. Friesen; Radio Pastor, Rev. Ed Martens; Radio Admn., Ernest Friessen

Aylmer Bible School: Principal, Abe Harms, Box 246, Aylmer, ON N5H 2R9 Tel. (519)773-5095

PERIODICAL

EMMC Recorder

Foursquare Gospel Church of Canada

The Western Canada District was formed in 1964 with the Rev. Roy Hicks as supervisor. Prior to 1964 it had been a part of the Northwest District of the International Church of the Foursquare Gospel with headquarters in Portland, Oregon.

A Provincial Society, The Church of the Foursquare Gospel of Western Canada, was formed in 1976; a Federal corporation, the Foursquare Gospel Church of Canada was incorporated in 1981, and a national church formed.

HEADQUARTERS

#200 - 3965 Kingsway, Burnaby, BC V5H 1Y7

Media Contact, Pres. & Gen. Supervisor, Timothy J. Peterson, Tel. (604)439-9567 Fax (604)439-1451

OFFICER

Pres. & Gen. Supervisor, Timothy J. Peterson

Free Methodist Church in Canada

The Free Methodist Church was founded in New York in 1860 and expanded to Canada in 1880. It is Methodist in doctrine, evangelical in ministry, and emphasizes the teaching of holiness of life through faith in Jesus Christ.

The Free Methodist Church in Canada was incorporated in 1927 after the establishment of a Canadian Executive Board. In 1959 the Holiness Movement Church merged with the Free Methodist Church. Full autonomy for the Canadian church was realized in 1990 with the formation of a Canadian General Conference. Mississauga, Ontario, continues to be the location of the Canadian Headquarters.

The Free Methodist Church ministers in 28 countries through its World Ministries Center in Indianapolis, Indiana. Aldersgate College in Moose Jaw, Saskatchewan, is the church's Canadian college.

HEADQUARTERS

4315 Village Centre Ct., Mississauga, ON L4Z 1S2 Tel. (416)848-2600

OFFICERS

Pres., Bishop Donald N. Bastian
Exec. Dir.-Treas., Rev. Paul G. Johnston
Stewardship Dir., Rev. Keith E. Lohnes
Canada East Conference Supt., Rev. Robert J. Buchanan, Box 670 (101-3 Applewood Dr.), Belleville, ON K8N 5B3 Tel. (613)968-8511 Fax (613)968-6190
Canada Great Lakes Conference Supt., Rev. Laverne W. Bates, 30 King St., Brantford, ON N3T 3C5 Tel. (519)753-7390
Canada West Conference Supt., Rev. Dennis H. Camplin, 7-3012 Louise St., Saskatoon, SK S7J 3L8 Tel. (306)955-3320

PERIODICAL

Free Methodist Herald, The

Free Will Baptists

As revival fires burned throughout New England in the mid- and late 1700s, Benjamin Randall proclaimed his doctrine of Free Will to large crowds of seekers. In due time, a number of Randall's converts moved to Nova Scotia. One such believer was Asa McGray, who was to become instrumental in the establishment of several Free Baptist churches. Local congregations were organized in New Brunswick. After several years of numerical and geographic gains, disagreements surfaced over the question of music, Sunday school, church offerings, salaried clergy, and other issues. Adherents of the more progressive element decided to form their own fellowship. Led by George Orser, they became known as Free Christian Baptists.

The new group faithfully adhered to the truths and doctrines which embodied the theological basis of Free Will Baptists. Largely through Archibald Hatfield, contact was made with Free Will Baptists in the United States in the 1960s. The association was officially welcomed into the Free Will Baptist family in July 1981, by the National Association.

HEADQUARTERS

RR #5, Box 355, Hartland, NB E0J 1N0 Tel. (506)375-6735
Media Contact, Promotional Sec., Rev. Fred D. Hanson, Fax (506)375-8473

OFFICER

Mod., Rev. Fred D. Hanson

PERIODICAL

Gospel Standard, The

General Church of the New Jerusalem

The Church of the New Jerusalem is founded on the Writings of Emanuel Swedenborg (1688-1772). These were first brought to Ontario in 1835 by Christian Enslin.

HEADQUARTERS

40 Chapel Hill Dr., Kitchener, ON N2G 3W5 Tel. (519)748-5802
Media Contact, Exec. Vice-Pres., Rev. Louis D. Synnestvedt

OFFICERS

Pres., Rt. Rev. P. M. Buss, Bryn Athyn, PA 19009
Exec. Vice-Pres., Rev. Louis D. Synnestvedt
Sec., Penny Orr, 208-21 Richgrove Dr., Weston, ON M9R 2L2
Treas., Peter Bailey, 36 Moffat Ave., Brampton, ON L6Y 2M8

PERIODICAL

New Church Life

Greek Orthodox Diocese of Toronto (Canada)

Greek Orthodox Christians in Canada under the jurisdiction of the Ecumenical Patriarchate of Constantinople (Istanbul).

HEADQUARTERS

27 Teddington Park Ave., Toronto, ON M4N 2C4 Tel. (416)322-5055
Media Contact, Sec. to the Bishop, Fr. Stavros Moscitos, Tel. (416)485-5929

OFFICERS

Primate of the Archdiocese of North & South America, The Most Rev. Iakovos
Bishop of the Diocese of Toronto, The Rt. Rev. Bishop Sotirios

Independent Assemblies of God—Canada

This fellowship of churches has been operating in Canada for over 25 years. It is a branch of the Pentecostal Church in Sweden. Each church within the fellowship is completely independent.

HEADQUARTERS

1211 Lancaster St., London, ON N5V 2L4 Tel. (519)451-1751

OFFICER

Gen. Sec., Rev. Harry Wuerch

PERIODICAL

Mantle, The

Independent Holiness Church

The former Holiness Movement of Canada merged with the Free Methodist Church in 1958. Some churches remained independent of this merger and they formed the Independent Holiness Church in 1960, in Kingston, Ontario. The doctrines are Methodist and Wesleyan. The General Conference is every three years, next meeting in 1992.

HEADQUARTERS

Rev. R. E. Votary, Box 194, Sydenham, ON K0H 2T0 Tel. (613)376-3114
Media Contact, Gen. Sec., Dwayne Reaney, 5025 River Rd. RR #1, Manotick, ON K4M 1B2 Tel. (613)692-3237

OFFICERS

Gen. Supt., Rev. R. E. Votary, Sydenham, ON K0H 2T0
Gen. Sec., Mr. Dwayne Reaney

The Italian Pentecostal Church of Canada

This body had its beginnings in Hamilton, Ontario, in 1912 when a few people of an Italian Presbyterian Church banded themselves together for prayer and received a Pentecostal experience of the baptism in the Holy Spirit. Since 1912, there has been a close association with the teachings and practices of the Pentecostal Assemblies of Canada.

The work spread to Toronto, then to Montrèal, where it also flourished. In 1959, the church was incorporated in the province of Quèbec. The early leaders of this body were the Rev. Luigi Ippolito and the Rev. Ferdinand Zaffuto. The churches have carried on active missionary work in Italy and among many thousands of immigrants recently arrived in Canada.

HEADQUARTERS

6724 Fabre St., Montreal, QC H2G 2Z6 Tel. (514)593-1944

OFFICERS

Gen. Supt., Rev. Alberico De Vito, 7685 Tremblay St., Brossard, QC J4W 2W2 Tel. (514)465-2846
Gen. Sec., Rev. John DellaForesta, 6550 Maurice Duplesis, Montreal North, QC H1G 6K9 Tel. (514)323-3087
Gen. Treas., Mr. Joseph Manafò
Overseer, Rev. Mario Spiridigliozz, 505 Nanaimo St., Vancouver, BC V5L 4S2 Tel. (604)255-0423
Overseer, Rev. David Mortelliti, 415 rue St. Jacques, St. Pierre, Montreal, QC H8R 1E9 Tel. (514)366-4525

PERIODICALS

Voce Evangelica

Jehovah's Witnesses

For details on Jehovah's Witnesses see the directory in this edition "Religious Bodies in the United States."

Canadian churches: 1292, Inclusive Canadian membership: 105,064, Sunday or Sabbath Schools: none, Total Enrollment: none, Ordained Clergy: none.

HEADQUARTERS

25 Columbia Heights, Brooklyn, NY 11201 Tel. (718)625-3600
Canadian Branch Office: Box 4100, Halton Hills, ON L7G 4Y4

Jewish Organizations in Canada

Jews are spread from coast to coast, with organized communities ranging from Saint John's, Newfoundland, to Victoria, British Columbia. The largest concentration is in Montreal (some 95,000) and in Toronto (approximately 104,000).

The history of the Jewish Community began in 1760 with the conquest of Quebec by the British during the Seven Years War, although a few Jews had come north to Halifax from the Atlantic Colonies as early as 1752. The Colony of Lower Canada (new Quebec) had the first considerable settlement, and it was there that, in 1768, a synagogue was organized, cemeteries established, rabbis were invited to officiate, and the community won its battles for official legal status and civic equality.

The first synagogue, Shearith Israel of Montreal, was affiliated with the Spanish-Portuguese Congregation in London and follows its rite to the present day. In 1846, the east European tradition was formally established, and in 1882 the Reform Temple Emanu-El was organized. In mid-19th century the Toronto and Hamilton communities established facilities for worship and for interment of the dead.

After 1880, a large number of immigrants from eastern Europe came to Canada and the present-day community took shape. Its social history parallels that of the United States, with its story of immigrant reception and settlement, industrial life in the garment industries in large cities, the implantation of synagogues in the Russian tradition, and slow integration and development of the community.

In 1919, the Canadian Jewish community united in the Canadian Jewish Congress (CJC) for a short duration. It was revived in 1934 in the face of the internal threat of anti-semitism and the worldwide problems of Jewry. The Canadian Jewish Congress became a unique nationwide institution which arranged for the reception of over 40,000 immigrants in the years following World War II. The Canadian Jewish Congress fought anti-semitism, coordinated development of a school system and voiced concerns of the Jewish community.

The CJC is active through the National Religious Department, which speaks for the varied religious institutions of the community and participates in their behalf in the tripartite commission. The commission unites Jews, Catholics and Protestants in a common program to make the voice of the community of faith heard in the the nation, and to strengthen the friendship between the adherents of the Judeao-Christian revelation. In addition, a Committee of Dialogue brings together Jews, Protestants, and Catholics, for understanding in the particular context of French Canada.

A census by the Religious Department of the Canadian Jewish Congress indicates 53 of the synagogues are Orthodox, 43 are Conservative, 14 are Reform and two are Reconstructionist. Note: The Congregational and Rabbinical Organizations pertaining to Canada are the same as those for the United States and are listed in "Religious Bodies in the United States," under "Jewish Organizations."

EDUC. & SOCIAL SERVICE ORGANIZATIONS

Canada-Israel Securities, Ltd.: State of Israel Bonds, 1255 University St., #200, Montreal, QC H3B 3B2 Tel. (514)878-1871; Pres., Melvyn A. Dobrin; Natl. Exec. Vice-Pres., Julius Briskin
Canadian Foundation for Jewish Culture: 4600 Bathurst St., Willowdale, ON M2R 3V2 Tel. (416)635-2883; Pres., Mira Koschitzky; Exec. Sec., Edmond Y. Lipsitz
Canadian Jewish Congress: 1590 Ave. Docteur Penfield, Montreal, QC H3G 1C5 Tel. (514)931-7531; Pres., Les Scheininger; Exec. Vice-Pres, Alan Rose
Canadian ORT (Rehab. through Training): 5165 Sherbrooke St. W., Ste. 208, Montreal, QU H4A 1T6 Tel. (514)481-2787; Pres., Bernard Gross; Exec. Dir., Mac Silver
Canadian Sephardi Federation: 210 Wilson Ave., Toronto, ON M5M 3B1 Tel. (416)483-8968; Pres., Maurice Benzacar; Sec., Laeticia Benabou
Canadian Zionist Federation: 5250 Decarie Blvd., Ste. 500, Montreal, QC H3X 2H9 Tel. (514)486-9526; Pres., David J. Azrieli
Hadassah-WIZO Organization of Canada: 1310 Greene Ave., Ste. 900, Montreal, QC H3Z 2B8 Tel. (514)937-9431; Natl. Pres., Naomi Frankenberg; Vice-Pres., Lily Frank

Jewish Immigrant Aid Services of Canada: 5151 Cote St. Catherine Rd., 220 Montreal, QC H3W 1M6 Tel. (514)342-9351; Pres., Sheldon Sper; Exec. Dir., Susan Davis

Jewish Natl. Fund of Canada: 1980 Sherbrooke St. W., Ste. 500, Montreal, QC H3H 1E8 Tel. (514)934-0313; Pres., Neriy J. Bloomfeld; Exec. Vice-Pres., Morris Zilka

Labor Zionist Movement of Canada: 7005 Kildare Rd., Ste. 10, Cote St. Luc, QC H3W 1C1 Tel. (514)484-1789; Pres., David Kofsky; Chmn. Toronto City Committee, Harry Weinstock; Chmn. Montreal City Committee, Harry Froimovitch

Natl. Council of Jewish Women of Canada: 1110 Finch Ave. W., #518, Downsview, ON M3J 2T2 Tel. (416)665-8251

Natl. Council of Jewish Women of Canad: Pres., Gloria Strom

Natl. Council of Jewish Women of Canada: Exec. Dir., Eleanor Appleby

Natl. Joint Community Relations Comm.: Canadian Jewish Congress, 4600 Bathurst St., Willowdale, M2R 3V2 Tel. (416)635-2883; Chpsn., Joseph L. Wilder; Exec. Dir., Manuel Prtuschi

JEWISH WELFARE FUNDS, COMMUNITY COUNCILS

Calgary, Alberta: Calgary Jewish Community Council, 1607 90th Ave., SW, Calgary, AB T2V 4V7 Tel. (403)253-8600; Pres., Hal Joffe; Exec. Dir., Drew Stauffenberg

Edmonton, Alberta: Jewish Federation of Edmonton, 7500-156th St., Edmonton, AB T5R 1X3 Tel. (403)481-3463; Pres., Shelly Maerov; Exec. Dir., Sidney Indig

Hamilton, Ontario: Jewish Fund of Hamilton Wentworth & Area, P.O. Box 7258, 1030 Lower Lion Club Rd., Ancaster, ON L9G 3N6 Tel. (416)648-0605 Fax (416)648-8388; Pres., Gerald Swaye, Q.C.; Exec. Dir., Mark Silverberg

London, Ontario: London Jewish Community Council, 536 Huron St., London, ON N5Y 4J5 Tel. (519)673-1161; Pres., Gloria Gilbert; Exec. Dir., Gerald Enchin

Montreal, Quebec: Allied Jewish Services, 5151 Cote St. Catherine Rd., Montreal, QC H3W 1M6 Tel. (514)735-3541 Fax (514)735-8972; Pres., Maxine Sigman; Vice-Pres., John Fishel

Ottawa, Ontario: Jewish Community Council of Ottawa, 151 Chapel St., Ottawa, ON K1N 7Y2 Tel. (613)232-7306 Fax (613)563-4593; Pres., Dr. Eli Rabin; Exec. Dir., Gerry Koffman

Toronto, Ontario: Toronto Jewish Congress, 4600 Bathurst St., Willowdale, ON M2R 3V2 Tel. (416)635-2883 Fax (416)635-1408; Pres., Charles S. Diamond; Exec. Dir., Steven Ain

Vancouver, British Columbia: Jewish Federation of Greater Vancouver, 950 W. 41st Ave., Vancouver, BC V5Z 2N7 Tel. (604)266-7115; Pres., Daniel U. Pekarsky; Exec. Dir., Steve Drysdale

Windsor, Ontario: Jewish Community Council, 1641 Ouellette Ave., Windsor, ON N8X 1K9 Tel. (519)973-1772 Fax (519)973-1774; Pres., Alan R. Orman; Exec. Dir., Allen Juris

Winnipeg, Manitoba: Winnipeg Jewish Community Council, 370 Hargrave, St., Winnipeg, MB R3B 2K1 Tel. (204)943-0406 Fax (204)956-0609; Pres., Sidney Halpern; Exec. Dir., Robert Freedman

PERIODICALS

Bulletin du Congres Juif Canadien; Canadian Jewish Herald; Canadian Jewish News; Canadian Jewish Outlook; Canadian Zionist; Jewish Eagle; Jewish Post and News; Jewish Standard; Jewish Western Bulletin; Journal of Psychology and Judaism; Ottawa Jewish Bulletin & Review; Undzer Veg; Windsor Jewish Community Council Bulletin

The Latvian Evangelical Lutheran Church in America

This body was organized into a denomination on Aug. 22, 1975, after having existed as the Federation of Latvian Evangelical Lutheran Churches in America since 1955. This church is a regional constituent part of the Lutheran Church of Latvia in Exile, a member of the Lutheran World Federation and the World Council of Churches.

The Latvian Evangelical Lutheran Church in America works to foster religious life, tradition and customs in its congregations in harmony with the Holy Scriptures, the Apostles', Nicene, and Athanasian Creeds, the unaltered Augsburg Confession, Martin Luther's Small and Large Catechisms and other documents of the Book of Concord.

The LELCA is ordered by its Synod, executive board, auditing committee, and district conferences.

HEADQUARTERS

6551 W. Montrose Ave., Chicago, IL 60634-1499 Tel. (312)725-3820 Fax (312)725-3835

Media Contact, Pres., Rev. Vilis Varsbergs

PERIODICAL

Cela Biedrs

Lutheran Church—Canada

Established in 1959 at Edmonton, Alberta, as a federation of Canadian districts of the Lutheran Church, Missouri Synod; constituted in 1988, at Winnipeg, Manitoba, as an autonomous church.

HEADQUARTERS

200-1625 Dublin Ave., Winnipeg, MB R3H 0W3 Tel. (204)772-0676 Fax (204)772-1090

Media Contact, Pres., Dr. Edwin Lehman

OFFICERS

Pres., Rev. Edwin Lehman

Vice-Pres., Rev. Karl Koslowsky, 871 Cavalier Dr., Winnipeg, MB R2Y 1C7

2nd Vice-Pres., Rev. Dennis Putzman, 24 Valencia Dr., St. Catharines, ON L2T 3X8

3rd Vice-Pres., William Ney, 7100 Ada Blvd., Edmonton, AB T5B 4E4

Treas., Mr. Ken Werschler

PERIODICALS

For the Record; Update; Canadian Lutheran

Mennonite Brethren Churches, Canadian Conference of

The conference was incorporated Nov. 22, 1945.

HEADQUARTERS

3-169 Riverton Ave., Winnipeg, MB R2L 2E5 Tel. (204)669-6575 Fax (204)654-1865

Media Contact, Conf. Min., Ike Bergen

OFFICERS

Mod., Abe Konrad, 12404-40 Ave., Edmonton, AB T6J 0S5 Tel. (403)435-1074

Asst. Mod., Roland Marsch, 1420 Portage Ave., Winnipeg, MB R3G 0W2 Tel. (204)774-4414

Sec., Peter Enns, 34676 Skyline Dr., Abbotsford, BC V2S 1H8 Tel. (604)859-5097

PERIODICALS

Mennonite Brethren Herald; Mennonitische Rundschau; IdeaBank; Lien, Le

Metropolitan Community Churches, Universal Fellowship of

The Universal Fellowship of Metropolitan Community Churches is a Christian church which directs a special ministry within, and on behalf of, the gay and lesbian community. Involvement, however, is not exclusively limited to gays and lesbians; U.F.M.C.C. tries to stress its openness to all people and does not call itself a "gay church."

Founded in 1968 in Los Angeles by the Rev. Troy Perry, the UFMCC has 250 member congregations worldwide. Thirteen congregations are in Canada, in Victoria, Vancouver, Edmonton, Calgary, Windsor, London, Kitchener, Toronto, Oshawa, Kingston, and Ottawa.

Theologically, the Metropolitan Community Churches stand within the mainstream of Christian doctrine, being "ecumenical" or "interdenominational" in stance (albeit a "denomination" in their own right).

The Metropolitan Community Churches are characterized by their belief that a) the love of God is a gift, freely offered to all people, regardless of "sexual orientation" and that b) no incompatibility exists between human sexuality and the Christian faith.

The Metropolitan Community Churches in Canada were founded in Toronto in 1973 by the Rev. Robert Wolfe.

OFFICERS

Western Canada District: Rev. Bev Baptiste, 270 Simcoe St., Winnipeg, MB R3G 1W1 Tel. (204)775-4134

Eastern Canada District: Rev. Rod McAvoy, Box 213, Sta. B., London, ON N6A 4V8 Tel. (519)438-9301

The Missionary Church of Canada

This denomination in Canada is affiliated with the worldwide body of the Missionary Church. Historically part of the Anabaptist, Mennonite movement, it changed its name to the United Missionary Church in 1947 and in 1969 it merged with the Missionary Church Association of Fort Wayne, Ind. It is an evangelical, missionary church and became an autonomous national church in Canada in 1987.

MEDIA CONTACT

Media Contact, Asst. to the Pres., Mr. Murray Bennett, 89 Centre Ave., North York, ON M2M 2L7 Tel. (416)223-3019 Fax (416)229-4017

OFFICERS

Pres., Dr. Alfred Rees, 89 Centre Ave., North York, ON M2M 2L7 Tel. (416)223-3019

Canada East District: Dist. Supt., Rev. Lloyd Fretz, 130 Fergus Ave., Kitchener, ON N2A 2H2

Canada West District: Dist. Supt., Rev. David Crouse, #309, 259 Midpark Way S.E., Calgary, AB T2X 1M2

Moravian Church in America, Northern Province, Canadian District of the

The work in Canada is under the general oversight and rules of the Moravian Church, Northern Province, general offices for which are located in Bethlehem, Pa.

HEADQUARTERS

1021 Center St., P.O. Box 1245, Bethlehem, PA 18016-1245

Media Contact, Ed., *The Moravian*, The Rev. Hermann I. Weinlick

OFFICERS

Pres., Rev. Dr. John H. Weinlick, 7310 154 St., Edmonton, AB T5R 1R5 Tel. (403)487-0211

PERIODICAL

Moravian, The

Muslims

The Muslim community in Canada is gathered together by Islamic societies and Muslim Mosques. These societies and other organizations are not regarded as religious sects or divisions. Their multiplication arises from the needs of each group in a given area, long distances between groups, and the absence in Islam of organized hierarchy. All the groups hold the same beliefs, aspire to practice the same rituals; namely prayers, fasting, almsgiving, and pilgrimage to Makkah Almukarramah (Mecca).

HEADQUARTERS

Federation of Islamic Associations in the US and Can., 25351 Five Mile Rd., Redford Twp., MI 48239 Tel. (313)535-0014 Fax (313)535-0015

REGIONAL AND NATIONAL GROUPS

Fed. of Islamic Assn. in the US & Can., Sec. Gen., Nihad Hamed, Fax (313)534-1474

Islamic Society of North America, P.O. Box 38, Plainfield, IN 46168 Tel. (317)839-8157

Council of Muslim Communities of Canada, Dir., Dr. Mir Iqbal Ali, 1250 Ramsey View Ct., Ste. 504, Sudbury, ON P3E 2E7 Tel. (705)522-2948

Council of Masajid (Mosques) in the USA, Sec. Gen., Dawud A. Assad, 99 Woodview Dr., Old Bridge, NJ 08857 Tel. (201)679-8617

Netherlands Reformed Congregations of North America

The Netherlands Reformed Congregations, presently numbering 162 congregations in the Netherlands (90,000 members), 25 congregations in North America (10,000 members), and a handful of congregations in various other countries, organized denominationally in 1907. The so-called Churches Under the Cross (established in 1839 after breaking away from the 1834 secession congregations) and the so-called Ledeboerian churches (established in 1841 under the leadership of Rev. Ledeboer who seceded from the Reformed state church), united in 1907 under the leadership of the then 25-year-old Rev. G. H. Kersten to form the Netherlands Reformed Congregations (Gereformeerde Gemeenten).

Many of the North American congregations left the Christian Reformed Church to join the Netherlands Reformed Congregations after the Kuyperian presupposed regeneration doctrine began making serious inroads into that denomination.

All Netherlands Reformed congregations, office bearers, and members subscribe to three Reformed Forms of Unity: the Belgic Confession of Faith (by DeBres), the Heidelberg Catechism and the Canons of Dordt. The Belgic Confession and Canons of Dordt are read regularly at worship services, and the Heidelberg Catechism is preached weekly except on church feast days.

The NRC stresses the traditional Reformed doctrines of grace, such as the sovereignty of God, responsibility of humankind, the necessity of the new birth, and the experience of God's sanctifying grace.

MEDIA CONTACT

Media Contact, Clk. of Synod, Dr. Joel R. Becker, 2115 Romence NE, Grand Rapids, MI 49503 Tel. (616)459-6565 Fax (616)459-7709

OFFICER

Clk. of Synod, Dr. Joel R. Beeke

PERIODICALS

Banner of Truth; Paul; Insight Into

North American Baptist Conference

Churches belonging to this conference emanated from German Baptist immigrants of more than a century ago. Although scattered across Canada and the U.S., they are bound together by a common heritage, a strong spiritual unity, a Bible-centered faith, and a deep interest in missions.

Note: The details of general organization, officers, and periodicals of this body will be found in the North American Baptist Conference directory in the "Religious Bodies in the United States" section of this Yearbook.

HEADQUARTERS

1 S. 210 Summit Ave., Oakbrook Terrace, IL 60181 Tel. (708)495-2000 Fax (708)495-3301
Media Contact, Dev. Dept. Dir., Rev. Lewis Petrie

OFFICER

Exec. Dir., Dr. John Binder

PERIODICAL

Baptist Herald

The Old Catholic Church of Canada

The church was founded in 1948 in Hamilton, Ontario. The first bishop was the Rt. Rev. George Davis. The Old Catholic Church of Canada accepts all the doctrines of the Eastern Orthodox Churches and, therefore, not Papal Infallibility or the Immaculate Conception. The ritual is Western (Latin Rite) and is in the vernacular language. Celibacy is optional. The Old Catholic Church of Canada is affiliated with the North American Old Roman Catholic Church, whose Presiding Bishop is Most Rev. Theodore Rematt of Chicago (see the directory in the "Religious Bodies in the United States" section of this Yearbook).

HEADQUARTERS

RR #1, Midland, ON L4R 4K3 Tel. (705)835-6865

Media Contact, Bishop, The Most Rev. David Thomson

OFFICER

Bishop, The Most Rev. David Thomson

Old Order Amish Church

This is the most conservative branch of the Mennonite Church and direct descendants of Swiss Brethren (Anabaptists) who emerged from the Reformation in Switzerland in 1525. The Amish, followers of Bishop Jacob Ammann, became a distinct group in 1693. They began migrating to North America about 1720; all of them still reside in the U.S. or Canada. They first migrated to Ontario in 1824 directly from Bavaria, Germany and also from Pennsylvania and Alsace-Lorraine. Since 1953 some Amish have migrated to Ontario from Ohio, Indiana, and Iowa.

In 1990, there were 17 congregations in Ontario, each being autonomous. No membership figures are kept by this group, and no central headquarters. Each congregation is served by a bishop, two ministers, and a deacon, all of whom are chosen from among the male members by lot for life.

CORRESPONDENT

Pathway Publishers, David Luthy, Rte. 4, Aylmer, ON N5H 2R3

PERIODICALS

Blackboard Bulletin; Budget, The; Diary, The; Die Botschaft; Family Life; Herold der Wahrheit; Young Companion

The Open Bible Standard Churches of Canada

This is the Canadian branch of the Open Bible Standard Churches, Inc., USA of Des Moines, Iowa. It is an evangelical, full gospel denomination emphasizing evangelism, missions, and the message of the Open Bible. The Canadian Branch was chartered Jan. 7, 1982.

HEADQUARTERS

62 Overlea Blvd., Toronto, ON M4H 1N9 Tel. (416)429-3882
Media Contact, Gen. Overseer, C. Russell Archer, P.O. Box 518, Vandalia, OH 45377-0518 Tel. (513)898-2864

OFFICERS

Supt. & Gen. Overseer, Dr. C. Russell Archer
Sec.-Treas., Rev. Jaime C. Buslon, 71 Thorncliffe Pk. Dr. #1109, Toronto, ON M4H 1L3 Tel. (416)429-3882
Prov. Supt., Rev. Harry Armoogan, 343 Albert St., Waterloo, ON N2L 3T9 Tel. (519)885-2784

Orthodox Church in America (Canada Section)

The Archdiocese of Canada of the Orthodox Church in America was established in 1926. First organized by St. Tikhon, martyr Patriarch of Moscow, previously Archbishop of North America, it is part of the Russian Metropolia and its successor, the autocephaleous Orthodox Church in America.

The Archdiocesan Council meets twice yearly, the General Assembly of the Archdiocese takes place every three years. The next Assembly will be held in July 1993.

HEADQUARTERS

P.O. Box 179, Spencerville, ON K0E 1X0 Tel. (613)925-5226 Fax (613)925-1521

OFFICERS

Bishop of Ottawa & Canada, The Rt. Rev. Seraphim

Chancellor, V. Rev. John Tkachuk, P.O. Box 1390, Place Bonaventure, Montreal, QC H5A 1H3 Tel. (514)481-5093 Fax same

Treas., Mr. Nikita Lopoukhine, 55 Clarey Ave., Ottawa, ON K1S 2R6

Eastern Sec., Olga Jurgens

Western Sec., Deacon Andrew Piasta, Box 25, Site 5, RR #2, Winterburn, AB T0E 2N0 Tel. (403)987-4500 Fax same

ARCHDIOCESAN COUNCIL

Clergy Members: V. Rev. Nicolas Boldireff; V. Rev. Orest Olekshy; Rev. Lawrence Farley; Rev. Hieromonk Irenee (Rochon); Protodeacon Cyprian Hutcheon

Lay Members: Audrey Ewanchuk; Peter Ferst; Nicholas Ignatieff; Euthymius Katsikas; Constance Kucharczyk; Rhoda Zion

Ex Officio: Chancellor; Treas.; Eastern Sec.; Western Sec.

REPRESENTATIVES TO METROPOLITAN COUNCIL

V. Rev. John Tkachuk
Jim Blizman

The Pentecostal Assemblies of Canada

This body is incorporated under the Dominion Charter of 1919 and is also recognized in the Province of Québec as an ecclesiastical corporation. Its beginnings are to be found in the revivals at the turn of the century, and most of the first Canadian Pentecostal leaders came from a religious background rooted in the Holiness movements.

The original incorporation of 1919 was implemented among churches of eastern Canada only. In the same year, a conference was called in Moose Jaw, Saskatchewan, to which the late Rev. J. M. Welch, general superintendent of the then-organized Assemblies of God in the U.S., was invited. The churches of Manitoba and Saskatchewan were organized as the Western District Council of the Assemblies of God. They were joined later by Alberta and British Columbia. In 1921, a conference was held in Montréal, to which the general chairman of the Assemblies of God was invited. Eastern Canada also became a district of the Assemblies of God, joining Eastern and Western Canada as two districts in a single organizational union.

In 1920, at Kitchener, Ontario, eastern and western churches agreed to dissolve the Canadian District of the Assemblies of God and unite under the name The Pentecostal Assemblies of Canada.

Today, The Pentecostal Assemblies of Canada operate throughout the nation, and religious services are conducted in more than 27 languages, in more than 200 ethnic churches. There are 109 native churches.

HEADQUARTERS

6745 Century Ave., Mississauga, ON L5N 6P7 Tel. (416)542-7400 Fax (416)542-7313

Media Contact, Gen. Supt., Rev. James M. MacKnight

OFFICERS

Gen. Supt., Rev. James M. MacKnight
Gen. Sec., Rev. Charles Yates
Gen. Treas., Rev. Reuben L. Schmunk
Overseas Missions, Exec. Dir., Rev. W. C. Cornelius
Church Ministries, Exec. Dir., Rev. W. A. Griffin
Home Missions & Bible Colleges, Exec. Dir., Rev. Gordon R. Upton
Women's Ministries, Dir., Mrs. Eileen Stewart
Full Gospel Publishing House, Mgr., Mr. Harry E. Anderson

DISTRICT SUPERINTENDENTS

British Columbia: Rev. Lester E. Markham, 5641 176 A St., Surrey, BC V3S 4G8 Tel. (604)576-9421 Fax (604)576-1499

Alberta: Rev. John A. Keys, 10585-111 St., #101, Edmonton, AB T5H 3E8 Tel. (403)426-0084 Fax (403)420-1318

Saskatchewan: Rev. L. Calvin King, 119-C Cardinal Cres., Saskatoon, SK S7L 6H5 Tel. (306)652-6088

Manitoba: Rev. Gordon V. Peters, #201, 3303 Portage Ave., Winnipeg, MB R3K 0W7 Tel. (204)885-2125 Fax (204)888-6319

Western Ontario: Rev. W. D. Morrow, #100, 3410 S. Service Rd., Burlington, ON L7M 3T2 Tel. (416)637-5566 Fax (416)637-7558

Eastern Ontario and Quebec: Rev. E. Stewart Hunter, Box 1600, Belleville, ON K8N 5J3 Tel. (613)968-3422 Fax (613)968-8715

Maritime Provinces: Rev. David C. Slauenwhite, Box 1184, Truro, NS B2N 5H1 Tel. (902)895-4212 Fax (902)897-0705

CONFERENCES

German Conference: Rev. Horst Doberstein, P.O. Box 2310, Stn. B, St. Catharines, ON L2M 7M7

French Conference: Rev. Raymond Lemaire, 4575 Sir Wilfred Laurier Blvd., St. Hubert, QC J3Y 7R6

Slavic Conferences: Eastern District, Rev. Walter Senko, RR 1, Wilsonville, ON N0E 1Z0; Western District, Rev. Michael Brandebura, 4108-134 Ave., Edmonton, AB T5A 3M2

Finnish Conference: Rev. A. Wirkkala, 1920 Argyle Dr., Vancouver, BC V5P 2A8

PERIODICAL

Pentecostal Testimony

Pentecostal Assemblies of Newfoundland

This body began in 1910 and held its first assembly at the Bethesda Pentecostal Mission at St. John's. It was incorporated in 1925 as the Bethesda Pentecostal Assemblies and changed its name in 1930 to the Pentecostal Assemblies of Newfoundland.

HEADQUARTERS

57 Thorburn Rd., St. John's, NF A1B 3N4 Tel. (709)753-6314 Fax (709)753-4945

OFFICERS

Pres. & Gen. Supt., Roy D. King, 50 Brownsdale St., St. John's, NF A1E 4R2

First Asst. Supt., B. Q. Grimes, 14 Chamberlain St., Grand Falls, NF A2A 2G4

Second Asst. Supt., H. E. Perry, P.O. Box 449, Lewisporte, NF A0G 3A0

Gen. Sec.-Treas., F. V. Rideout, 21 Dalhousie Crescent, Mount Pearl, NF A1N 2Y9

DEPARTMENTS
Youth & Sunday School, Dir., Robert H. Dewling,
26 Wicklow St., St. John's, NF A1B 3H2
Literature, Gen. Mgr., Calvin T. Andrews, 28
Royal Oak Dr., St. John's, NF A1G 1S3
Women's Ministries, Dir., Mrs. Sylvia Purchase,
Box 64, R.R. #3, Botwood, NF A0H 1E0
Missionettes, Dir., Mrs. Ivy Stead, Box 8, Spring-
dale, NF A0J 1T0
Men's Fellowship, Dir., Gordon W. Young, P.O.
Box 1090, Windsor, NF A0H 2H0
Central Finance, Dir., Clarence Buckle, Box 2814,
5 Stonehaven Pl., Paradise, NF A1L 1E9

PERIODICALS
Good Tidings; Ambassador, The

Pentecostal Holiness Church of Canada
The first General Conference convened in May,
1971 in Toronto. Prior to this, the Canadian
churches were under the leadership of the Pentecostal Holiness Church in the U.S.A. The General
Conference meets every four years. The next meeting is in 1994.

HEADQUARTERS
Box 442, Waterloo, ON N2J 4A9 Tel. (519)746-
1310

OFFICERS
Gen. Supt., G. H. Nunn
Asst. Supt., Nicholas Murry
Asst. Supt., Vince Brufatto
Asst. Supt., Wayne Longard
Sec.-Treas., Richard Rose

Polish National Catholic Church of Canada
This Diocese was created at the XII General
Synod of the Polish National Catholic Church of
America in October, 1967. Formerly, the Canadian parishes were a part of the Western Diocese
and Buffalo-Pittsburgh Diocese of the Polish National Catholic Church in America.

HEADQUARTERS
186 Cowan Ave., Toronto, ON M6K 2N6 Tel.
(416)532-8249
Media Contact, Bishop, The Rt. Rev. Joseph
Nieminski, 296 Mill Rd. #F-5, Etobicoke, ON
M9C 4X8 Tel. (416)626-1095

OFFICER
Bishop Ordinary, The Rt. Rev. Joseph Nieminski

Presbyterian Church in America (Canadian Section)
Canadian congregations of the Reformed Presbyterian Church, Evangelical Synod, became a
part of the Presbyterian Church in America when
the RPCES joined PCA in June 1982. Some of the
churches were in predecessor bodies of the
RPCES, which was the product of a 1965 merger of
the Reformed Presbyterian Church in North America, General Synod, and the Evangelical Presbyterian Church. Others came into existence later as a
part of the home missions work of RPCES. Congregations are located in six provinces, and the PCA
is continuing church extension work in Canada.
The denomination is committed to world evangelization and to a continuation of historic Presbyterianism. Its officers are required to subscribe to the

Reformed faith as set forth in the Westminster
Confession of Faith and Catechisms.

MEDIA CONTACT
Media Contact, Correspondent, D. Codling, 16292
Glenwood Crescent N., Surrey, BC V4N 1Y1
Tel. (604)589-4438

PERIODICAL
Coast to Coast

The Presbyterian Church in Canada
This is the nonconcurring portion of the Presbyterian Church in Canada that did not become a part
of The United Church of Canada in 1925.

NATIONAL OFFICES
50 Wynford Dr., Don Mills, ON M3C 1J7 Tel.
(416)441-1111 Fax (416)441-2825
Media Contact, Principal Clk., The Rev. Dr. Earle
F. Roberts, 50 Wynford Drive, Dan Mills, ON
M3C 1J7 Tel. (416)441-1111 Fax (416)441-
2825

OFFICERS
Mod., Dr. John R. Cameron
Clks. of Assembly: Principal Clk., Dr. E. F.
Roberts; Dep. Clk., Dr. D. B. Lowry; Dep. Clk.,
Dr. T. Plomp
Admn. Council: Sec., Dr. E. F. Roberts; Treas., Mr.
G. Jones; Comp., Mr. D. A. Taylor

NATIONAL BOARDS
Board of World Missions: Gen. Sec., Rev. Peter
Ruddell; Sec. for Africa, Admn. & Fin., Rev. C.
R. Talbot; Sec., Educ. for Mission, Mrs. Joyce
Hodgson; Sec., Canada Operations, Rev. Ian
Morrison
Board of Congregational Life: Sec. for Lay Minis-
tries & Church Educ., Dr. I. Clark; Sec. for
Church & Society, Dr. R. Hodgson
Communication Services: Consultant, Mr. Donald
Stephens
Board of Ministry: Gen. Sec., Rev. T. Gemmell
Presbyterian World Service & Development: Dir.,
Dr. Marjorie Ross
Presbyterian Church Building Corp.: Dir., Rev. F.
R. Kendall
Women's Missionary Society (WD): Pres., Mrs. J.
Sampson, Ottawa, ON
Women's Missionary Society (ED): Pres., Mrs. W.
Wilson, Rexton, NB
Life and Mission: Gen. Sec., Rev. Glen Davis
Services: Gen. Sec., Rev. Karen Hinke

PERIODICALS
Presbyterian Record, The; Glad Tidings; Vie
Chrétienne, La

Reformed Church in Canada
The Canadian branch of the Reformed Church in
America consists of 36 churches organized under
the Council of the Reformed Church in Canada and
within the classis of Ontario (20 churches), Cascades (15 churches), Lake Erie (one church). The
Reformed Church in America was established in
1628 by the earliest Dutch settlers in America as
the Reformed Protestant Dutch Church. It is evangelical in theology and presbyterian in government.

HEADQUARTERS

Gen. Sec., Rev. Edwin G. Mulder, 475 Riverside Dr., New York, NY 10115 Tel. (212)870-2841 Fax (212)870-2499

Council of the Reformed Church in Canada, Exec. Sec., Rev. Dr. Jonathan N. Gerstner, Reformed Church Center, RR #4, Cambridge, ON N1R 5S5 Tel. (519)622-1777

Media Contact, Dir., Promotion, Comm., & Dev., Rev. E. Wayne Antworth, 475 Riverside Drive, New York, NY 10115 Tel. (212)870-2954 Fax (212)870-2499

Reformed Doukhobors, Christian Community and Brotherhood of

Doukhobors were founded in the late 17th century in Russia. Their doctrine is the "Living Book," which is based on traditional songs and chants and on contents of the Bible. The Living Book is memorized by each generation.

HEADQUARTERS

Site 8, Comp. 50, RR 1, Crescent Valley, BC V0G 1H0

OFFICER

Pastor, Stephan S. Sorokin

The Reformed Episcopal Church

The Canadian jurisdiction of the Reformed Episcopal Church (see U.S. listing in "Religious Bodies in the United States" section of this Yearbook) maintains the founding principles of episcopacy (in historic succession from the apostles), Anglican liturgy, Reformed doctrine and evangelical zeal, and in its practice, continues to recognize the validity of certain nonepiscopal orders of evangelical ministry.

MEDIA CONTACT

Media Contact, Sec., Mrs. B. Gamble, #5-4603 Evergreen La., Ladner, BC V4K 2W7

OFFICERS

Pres., Bishop W. W. Lyle, 1544 Broadview Ct., Coquitlam, BC V3J 5X9

Vice-Pres., Laurence Jackson, 600 Foul Bay Rd., Victoria, BC V8S 4H3

Sec., Miss E. R. MacQueen, 736-13th St., New Westminster, BC V3M 4M7 Tel. (604)521-3580

Treas., Michael Cridge, 1411 Hastings St., Victoria, BC V8X 3X1

Reinland Mennonite Church

This group was founded in 1958 when 10 ministers and approximately 600 members separated from the Sommerfelder Mennonite Church. In 1968, four ministers and about 200 members migrated to Bolivia. The church has work in six communities in Manitoba and one in Ontario.

HEADQUARTERS

Bishop William H. Friesen, P.O. Box 96, Rosenfeld, MB R0G 1X0 Tel. (204)324-6339

Media Contact, Decon, Henry Wiebe, Box 2587, Winkler, MB R6W 4C3 Tel. (204)325-8487

Reorganized Church of Jesus Christ of Latter Day Saints

Founded April 6, 1830, by Joseph Smith, Jr., the church was reorganized under the leadership of the founder's son, Joseph Smith III, in 1860. The Church is established in 38 countries including the United States and Canada, with nearly a quarter of a million members. A biennial world conference is held in Independence, Missouri. The current president is Wallace B. Smith, great-grandson of the founder.

HEADQUARTERS

World Headquarters: RLDS Auditorium, P.O. Box 1059, Independence, MO 64051 Tel. (816)833-1000 Fax Tel+Ext. 307

Ontario Regional Ofc.: 390 Speedvale Ave. E., Guelph, ON N1E 1N5

Media Contact, Public Relations Commissioner, Stephanie Kelley, World Headquarters

CANADIAN REGIONS AND DISTRICTS

North. Plains & Prairie Provinces Region: Regional Admn., Alvin Mogg, #212, 2835 23rd St. NE, Calgary, AB T2A 7A4

No. Plains & Prairie Provinces Region: Alberta District, Donald A. Jenkins, 3144 Palliser Dr. SW, Calgary, AB T2V 4B7; Saskatchewan District, Charles J. Lester, 629 East Place, Saskatoon, SK S7J 2Z1

Pacific Northwest Region: Regional Admn., Raymond Peter, P.O. Box 18469, 4820 Morgan, Seattle, WA 98118; British Columbia District, Dennis L. McKelvie, 2594 Trillium Pl., Coquitlam, BC V3E 2G8

Ontario Region: Regional Admn., Donald H. Comer, 390 Speedvale Ave. E., Guelph, ON N1E 1N5; Chatham District, John S. Scherer, 87 Glenwood Dr., Chatham, ON N7L 3X3; Grand River District, Douglas A. Robinson, 7 Kennedy Drive, Breslau, ON N0B 1M0; London District, Larry Buchanan, Box 59, Straffordsville, ON N0J 1Y0; Northern Ontario District, Donald Arrowsmith, 917 Woodbine Ave., Sudbury, ON P3A 2L8; Ottawa District, Roy A. Young, RR #4, Odessa, ON K0H 2H0; Owen Sound District, Robin M. Duff, 2090 Ninth Ave. E., #15, Owen Sound, ON N4K 3H2; Toronto Metropole, Larry D. Windland, 8142 Islington Ave. N., Woodridge, ON L7L 1B7

The Roman Catholic Church in Canada

The largest single body of Christians in Canada, the Roman Catholic Church is under the spiritual leadership of His Holiness the Pope. Catholicism in Canada dates back to 1534, when the first Mass was celebrated on the Gaspé Peninsula on July 7, by a priest accompanying Jacques Cartier. Catholicism had been implanted earlier by fishermen and sailors from Europe. Priests came to Acadia as early as 1604. Traces of a regular colony go back to 1608 when Champlain settled in Québec City. The Recollets (1615), followed by the Jesuits (1625) and the Sulpicians (1657), began the missions among the native population. The first official Roman document relative to the Canadian missions dates from March 20, 1618. Bishop François de Montmorency-Laval, the first bishop, arrived in Québec in 1659. The church developed in the East, but not until 1818 did systematic missionary work begin in western Canada.

In the latter 1700s, English-speaking Roman Catholics, mainly from Ireland and Scotland, began to arrive in Canada's Atlantic provinces. After 1815 Irish Catholics settled in large numbers in what is now Ontario. The Irish potato famine of 1847 greatly increased that population in all parts of eastern Canada.

By the 1850s the Catholic Church in both English- and French-speaking Canada had begun to erect new dioceses and found many religious communities. These communities did educational, medical, and charitable work among their own people as well as among Canada's native peoples. By the 1890s large numbers of non-English and non-French-speaking Catholics had settled in Canada, especially in the Western provinces. In the 20th century the pastoral horizons have continued to expand to meet the needs of what has now become a very multiracial church.

OFFICERS

General Secretariat of the Episcopacy
Secrétaire général (French Sector), Père Alexandre Taché
General Secretary (English Sector), Rev. V. James Weisgerber
Assistant General Secretary (English Sector), Mr. Bede
Secrétaire général adjoint (French Sector), P. Roland Denis

CANADIAN ORGANIZATION

Canadian Conference of Catholic Bishops: (Conférence des évêques cath. du Canada), 90 Parent Ave., Ottawa, ON K1N 7B1 Tel. (613)236-9461 Fax (613)236-8117

EXECUTIVE COMMITTEE

National Level
Pres., Most Rev. Marcel A. J. Gervais, Archbishop of Ottawa
Vice-Pres., Mgr. Jean-Guy Hamelin, (Rouyn-Noranda)
Co-Treas.: Most Rev., Mgr. Jean-Louis Plouffe, (Sault Ste. Marie); Most Rev. Francis J. Spence, (Kingston)

EPISCOPAL COMMISSIONS

National Level
Social Affairs, Most Rev. J. Faber MacDonald
Canon Law—Inter-rite, Most Rev. Charles A. Halpin
Relations with Assoc. of Priests, Religious, & Laity, Most Rev. Jacques Berthelet
Missions, Most Rev. Jean-Guy Couture
Ecumenism, Most Rev. Donat Chiasson
Theology, Msgr. Brendan O'Brien
Sector Level
Comm. sociales, Msgr. Louis-de-Gonzaque Langevin
Social Comm., Most Rev. John A. O'Mara
Education Chrétien, Msgr. Jean Gratton
Christian Education, Most Rev. Frederick B. Henry
Liturgie, Msgr. Raymond Saint-Gelais
Liturgy, Most Rev. Raymond J. Lahey

OFFICES

Secteur francais
Office des Missions, Dir., Père Lucien Casterman, O.M.I.
Office des communications sociales, Dir., Abbé Lucien Labelle, 4005, rue de Bellechasse, Montréal, QC H1X 1J6 Tel. (514)729-6391 Fax (514)729-7375
Office national de liturgie, coordonnateur, M. l'abbé Paul Boily, 3530, rue Adam, Montréal, QC H1W 1Y8 Tel. (514)522-4930
Service incroyance et foi, Dir., Père Gilles Langevin, s.j., 7400, boulevard Saint-Laurent, Montréal, QC H2R 2Y1 Tel. (514)948-3186

Centre canadien d'oecumenisme, Rev. Thomas Ryan, C.S.P., 2065 ouest, rue Sherbrooke, Montréal, QC H3H 1G6 Tel. (514)937-9176 Fax (514)935-5497
Services des relations publiques, Dir., M. Jacques Binet
Service des Editions, Dir., Mlle Claire Dubé
English Sector
Natl. Liturgical Ofc., Dir., Rev. John Hibbard
Natl. Ofc. of Religious Educ., Dir., Mrs. Bernadette Tourangeau
Ofc. for Missions, Dir., Fr. Lucien Casterman, O.M.I.
Public Information Ofc., Dir., Mr. Dennis Gruending
Social Affairs, Dir., Mr. Tony Clarke

REGIONAL EPISCOPAL ASSEMBLIES

Atlantic Episcopal Assembly: Pres., Msgr. Gérard Dionne; Vice-Pres., Most Rev. J. Edward Troy, C.S.C.; Sec., Rev. Guy Léger, C.S.C., Site 1 Boîte 389, R.R. 1, St. Joseph, NB E0A 2Y0 Tel. (506)758-2531 Fax (506)758-1187
Assemblée des évêques du Que: Prés., Mgr. Bernard Hubert; Vice-Pres., Mgr. Maurice Couture; Sécretaire général, L'abbé Clément Vigneault; Secrétariat, 1225 Boulevard Saint Joseph est, Montréal, QC H2J 1L7 Tel. (514)274-4323 Fax (514)274-4383
Ontario Conference of Catholic Bishops: Pres., Most Rev. John O'Mara; Vice-Pres., Msgr. Eugene LaRocque; Sec., Rev. Angus J. Macdougall, S.J.; Secretariat, 67 Bond St., Ste. 304, Toronto, ON M5B 1X5 Tel. (416)368-1804 Fax (416)368-6687
Western Catholic Conference: Pres., Msgr. Antoine Hacault; Vice-Pres., Most Rev. Maxim Hermaniuk; Sec., Msgr. Peter Sutton, 108-1st St., West, P.O. Box 270, Le Pas, MB R9A 1K4 Tel. (204)623-6152 Fax (204)623-6121

MILITARY ORDINARIATE

Ordinaire aux forces canadiennes: Msgr. André Vallée, p.m.é., National Defense Headquarters, Ottawa, ON K1A 0k2 Tel. (613)992-1261
Canadian Religious Conference: Sec. Gen., Sr. Henriette Laliberte, C.S.C., 324 Laurier Ave. East, Ottawa, ON K1N 6P6 Tel. (613)236-0824 Fax (613)236-0825

LATIN RITE

Alexandria-Cornwall: Msgr. Eugéne P. LaRocque, Centre diocésain, 220 Chemin Montréal, C. P. 1388, Cornwall, ON K6H 5V4 Tel. (613)933-1138
Amos: Evêché, Msgr. Gérard Drainville, 450, Principale Nord, Amos, QC J9T 2M1 Tel. (819)732-6515
Antigonish: Bishop Colin Campbell, Chancery Office, 155 Main St., P.O. Box 1330, Antigonish, NS B2G 2L7 Tel. (902)863-4818
Baie-Comeau: Evêché, Msgr. Pierre Morissette, 639 Rue de Bretagne, Baie-Comeau, QC G5C 1X2 Tel. (418)589-5744
Bathurst: Evêché, Msgr. André Richard, 645, avenue Murray, C.P. 460, Bathurst, NB E2A 3Z4 Tel. (506)546-3493
Calgary: Bishop Paul J. O'Byrne, Bishop's Office, 1916 Second St. S.W., Calgary, AB T2S 1S3 Tel. (403)228-4501
Charlottetown: Most Rev. Joseph Vernon Fougère, D.D., P.O. Box 907, Charlottetown, PE C1A 7L9 Tel. (902)368-8005

Chicoutimi: Evêché, Msgr. Jean-Guy Couture, 602 est, rue Racine, C.P. 278, Chicoutimi, QC G7H 6J6 Tel. (418)543-0783

Churchill-Baie D'Hudson: Evêché, Msgr. Reynald Rouleau, O.M.I., C.P. 10, Churchill, MB R0B 0E0 Tel. (204)675-2541

Archdiocese of Edmonton: Archbishop, Joseph N. MacNeil, Archdiocesan Office, 8421-101st Ave., Edmonton, AB T6A 0L1 Tel. (403)469-1010

Edmundson: Evêché, Msgr. Gérard Dionne, Centre diocésain, Edmundston, NB E3V 3K1 Tel. (506)735-5578

Gaspé: Evêché, Msgr. Bertrand Blanchet, C.P. 440, Gaspé, QC G0C 1R0 Tel. (418)368-2274

Gatineau-Hull: Archévêché, Msgr. Roger Ebacher, 180, boulevard Mont-Bleu, Hull, QC J8X 3J5 Tel. (819)771-8391

Grand Falls: Bishop, Joseph Faber MacDonald, Chancery Office, P.O. Box 397, Grand Falls, NF A2A 2J8 Tel. (709)489-4019

Gravelbourg: Secrétariat, Msgr. Noel Delaquis, C.P. 690, Gravelbourg, SK S0H 1X0 Tel. (306)648-2615

Archidiocèse de Grouard-McLennan: Archévêché, Msgr. Henri Légaré, C.P. 388, McLennan, AB T0H 2L0 Tel. (403)324-3002

Archdiocese of Halifax: Archbishop, Austin E. Burke, Archbishop's Residence, 6541 Coburg Rd., P.O. Box 1527, Halifax, NS B3J 2Y3 Tel. (902)429-9388

Hamilton: Bishop, Bishop Anthony Tonnos, 700 King St. W., Hamilton, ON L8P 1C7 Tel. (416)528-7988

Hearst: Evêché, Msgr. Roger A. Despatie, 76, 7 rue C.P. 1330, Hearst, ON P0L 1N0 Tel. (705)362-4903

Joliette: Evêché, Msgr. Gilles Lussier, 2 rue St.-Charles Borromée, Nord. C.P. 470, Joliette, QC J6E 6H6 Tel. (514)753-7596

Kamloops: Bishop, Lawrence Sabatini, Bishop's Residence, 635A Tranquille Rd., Kamloops, BC V2B 3H5 Tel. (604)376-3351

Archidiocèse de Keewatin-LePas: Archbishop, Peter-Alfred Sutton, Résidence, 108 1st St. W., C.P. 270, Le Pas, MB R9A 1K4 Tel. (204)623-3529

Archdiocese of Kingston: Archbishop, Francis J. Spence, 390 Palace Rd., Kingston, ON K7L 4X3 Tel. (613)548-4461

Labrador City-Schefferville: Evêché, Msgr. Henri Goudreault, 318 Ave. Elizabeth, Labrador City, Labrador, NF A2V 2K7 Tel. (709)944-2046

London: Bishop, John M. Sherlock, Chancery Office, 1070 Waterloo St., London, ON N6A 3Y2 Tel. (519)433-0658

Mackenzie-Fort Smith (T.No.O.): Evêché, Msgr. Denis Croteau, 5117, 52 rue, Bag 8900, Fort Smith, T.N.O, X1A 2R3 Tel. (403)920-2129

Archidiocèse de Moncton: Archévêché, Msgr. Donat Chiasson, C.P. 248, Moncton, NB E1C 8K9 Tel. (506)857-9531

Mont-Laurier: Evêché, Msgr. Jean Gratton, 435 rue de la Madone, C.P. 1290, Mont Laurier, QC J9L 1S1 Tel. (819)623-5530

Archidiocèse de Montréal: Archévêché, Msgr. Jean-Claude Turcotte, 2000 ouest rue Sherbrooke, Montréal, QC H3H 1G4 Tel. (514)931-7311

Monsonee: Msgr. Vincent Cadieux, Résidence, C.P. 40, Moosonee, ON P0L 1Y0 Tel. (705)336-2908

Abbatia Mullius of Muenster: Rt. Rev. Peter Novecosky, OSB, Abbot's Residence, St. Peter's Abbey, Muenster, SK S0K 2Y0 Tel. (306)682-5521

Nelson: Bishop Peter Mallon, Chancery Office, 813 Ward St., Nelson, BC V1L 1T4 Tel. (604)352-6921

Nicolet: Evêché, Msgr. Raymond Saint-Gelais, C.P. 820, Nicolet, QC J0G 1E0 Tel. (819)293-4234

Archidiocèse D'Ottawa: Chancellerie, Msgr. Marcel Gervais, 1247, avenue Kilborn, Ottawa, ON K1H 6K9 Tel. (613)738-5025

Pembroke: Bishop, J. R. Windle, Bishop's Residence, 188 Renfrew St., P.O. Box 7, Pembroke, ON K8A 6X1 Tel. (613)732-3895

Peterborough: Bishop, James L. Doyle, Bishop's Residence, 350 Hunter St. W., Peterborough, ON K9J 6Y8 Tel. (705)745-5123

Prince-Albert: Evêché, Msgr. Blaise Morand, 1415-ouest, 4e Ave. West, Prince-Albert, SK S6V 5H1 Tel. (306)922-4747

Prince-George: ——Chancery Office, 2935 Highway 16 West, P.O. Box 7000, Prince George, BC V2N 3Z2 Tel. (604)964-4424

Archidiocèse de Québec: Archévêché, Msgr. Maurice Couture, 2 rue Port Dauphin, C.P. 459, Québec, QC G1R 4R6 Tel. (418)692-3935

Archdiocese of Regina: Archbishop, Charles A. Halpin, Chancery Office, 455 Broad St. North, Regina, SK S4R 2X8 Tel. (306)352-1651

Archidiocèse de Rimouski: Archévêché, Msgr. Gilles Ouellet, 34 ouest, rue de L'évêché, ouest C.P. 730, Rimouski, QC G5L 7C7 Tel. (418)723-3320

Rouyn-Moranda: Evêché, Msgr. Jean-Guy Hamelin, 515 avenue Cuddihy, C.P. 1060, Rouyn-Noranda, QC J9X 5W9 Tel. (819)764-4660

Ste-Anne de la Pocatière: Evêché, Msgr. André Gaumond, C.P. 430 La Pocatière, Pocatière, QC G0R 1Z0 Tel. (418)856-1811

Archidiocèse de Saint-Boniface: Archévêché, Msgr. Antoine Hacault, 151 ave de la Cathédrale, St-Boniface, MB R2H 0H6 Tel. (204)237-9851

St. Catharine's: Bishop, Thomas B. Fulton, Bishop's Residence, 122 Riverdale Ave., St. Catharines, ON L2R 4C2 Tel. (416)684-0154

St. George's: Bishop, Raymond J. Lahey, Bishop's Residence, 16 Hammond Dr., Corner Brook, NF A2H 2W2 Tel. (709)639-7073

Saint Hyacinthe: Evêché, Msgr. Louis-de-Gonzague Langevin, 1900 ouest Girouard, C. P. 190, Saint-Hyacinthe, QC J2S 7B4 Tel. (514)773-8581

Saint-Jean-de-Longueuil: Evêché, Msgr. Bernard Hubert, 740 boul. Ste-Foy, C.P. 40, Longueuil, QC J4K 4X8 Tel. (514)679-1100

Saint-Jérôme: Evêché, Msgr. Charles Valois, 355 rue St-Georges, C.P. 580, Saint-Jérôme, QC J7Z 5V3 Tel. (514)432-9741

Saint John: Bishop, J. Edward Troy, Chancery Office, 1 Bayard Dr., Saint John, NB E2L 3L5 Tel. (506)632-9222

Archdiocese of St. John's: Archbishop, James H. MacDonald, Archbishop's Residence, P.O. Box 37, Basilica Residence, St. John's, NF A1C 5H5 Tel. (709)726-3660

Saint-Paul: Evêché, Msgr. Raymond Roy, 4410 51e Ave., St-Paul, AB T0A 3A2 Tel. (403)645-3277

Saskatoon: Bishop, James P. Mahoney, Chancery Office, 106 - 5th Ave. N., Saskatoon, SK S7K 2N7 Tel. (306)242-1500

Sault Ste. Marie: Bishop, Jean-Louis Plouffe, Bishop's Residence, 480 McIntyre St., W., P.O. Box 510, North Bay, ON P1B 8J1 Tel. (705)476-1300

Archidiocèse de Sherbrooke: Archévêché, Msgr. Jean-Marie Fortier, 130 rue de la Cathedrale, C.P. 430, Sherbrooke, QC J1H 5K1 Tel. (819)563-9934

Thunder Bay: Bishop, John A. O'Mara, Bishop's Residence, P.O. Box 756, Thunder Bay, ON P7C 4W6 Tel. (807)622-8144

Timmins: Most Rev. Gilles Cazabon, O.M.I., 65, avenue Jubilee est, Timmins, ON P4N 5W4 Tel. (705)267-6224

Archdiocese of Toronto: Archbishop, Aloysius M. Ambrozic, Chancery Office, 355 Church St., Toronto, ON M5B 1Z8 Tel. (416)977-1500

Trois-Rivièrès: Evêché, Msgr. Laurent Noöl, 362 rue Bonaventure, C.P. 879, Trois-Rivièrès, QC G9A 5J9 Tel. (819)374-9847

Valleyfield: Evêché, Msgr. Robert Lebel, 11 rue de l'Eglise, Valleyfield, QC J6T 1J5 Tel. (514)373-8122

Archdiocese of Vancouver: Archbishop, Adam Exner, Chancery Office, 150 Robson St., Vancouver, BC V6B 2A7 Tel. (604)683-0281

Victoria: Bishop, Remi J. De Roo, Bishop's Office, 1 - 4044 Nelthorpe St., Victoria, BC V8X 2A1 Tel. (604)479-1331

Whitehorse (Yukon): Bishop, Thomas Lobsinger, O.M.I. Bishop's Residence, 5119 5th Ave., Whitehorse, YT Y1A 1L5 Tel. (403)667-2052

Archdiocese of Winnipeg: Most Rev. Leonard J. Wall, 1495 Pembina Hwy, Winnipeg, ON R3T 2C6 Tel. (204)452-2227

Yarmouth: —— 53 rue Park, Yarmouth, NS B5A 4B2 Tel. (902)742-7163

EASTErn RITES

Eparchy of Edmonton Eparch: Most Rev. Myron Daciuk, V Eparch's Residence, 6240 Ada Blvd., Edmonton, AB T5W 4P1 Tel. (403)479-0381

Eparchy of New Westminster: Eparch, Most Rev. Jerome I. Chimy, Eparch's Residence, 502 5th Ave., New Westminster, BC V3L 1S2 Tel. (604)521-8015

Eparchy of Saskatoon: Eparch, Most Rev. Basil Filevich, Eparch's Residence, 866 Saskatchewan. Crescent East, Saskatoon, SK S7N 0L4 Tel. (306)653-0138

Eparchy of Toronto: Eparch, Most Rev. Isidore Borecky, Eparch's Residence, 61 Glen Edyth Dr., Toronto, ON M4V 2V8 Tel. (416)924-2381

Archeparchy of Winnipeg: Archeparchy, Most Rev. Maxim Hermaniuk, Archiparch's Residence, 235 Scotia St., Winnipeg, MB R2V 1V7 Tel. (204)339-7457

Toronto, Ontario Eparchy: Eparch, Most Rev. Michael Rusnak, Chancery Office, 223 Carlton Rd., Unionville, ON L3R 3M2 Tel. (416)477-4867

Montréal (Qué) Archéparchie: Archéparque, Msgr. Michel Hakim, Chancelerie: 34 Maplewood, Montréal, QC H2V 2M1 Tel. (514)272-6430

Archéparchie de Montréal: Archéparque, Msgr. Georges Abi-Saber, 12475, rue Grenet, Montréal, QC H4J 2K4 Tel. (514)331-2807

Romanian Orthodox Church in America (Canadian Parishes)

The first Romanian Orthodox immigrants in Canada called for Orthodox priests from their native country of Romania. Between 1902 and 1914, they organized the first Romanian parish communities and built Orthodox churches in different cities and farming regions of western Canada (Alberta, Saskatchewan, Manitoba) as well as in the eastern part (Ontario and Québec).

In 1929, the Romanian Orthodox parishes from Canada joined with those of the United States in a Congress held in Detroit, and asked the Holy Synod of the Romanian Orthodox Church of Romania to establish a Romanian Orthodox Missionary Episcopate in America. The first Bishop, Policarp (Morushca), was elected and consecrated by the Holy Synod of the Romanian Orthodox Church and came to the United States in 1935. He established his headquarters in Detroit with jurisdiction over all the Romanian Orthodox parishes in the United States and Canada.

In 1950, the Romanian Orthodox Church in America (i.e. the Romanian Orthodox Missionary Episcopate in America) was granted administrative autonomy by the Holy Synod of the Romanian Orthodox Church of Romania, and only doctrinal and canonical ties remain with this latter body.

In 1974 the Holy Synod of the Romanian Orthodox Church of Romania recognized and approved the elevation of the Episcopate to the rank of Archdiocese.

HEADQUARTERS

Canadian Office: St. Demetrios Romanian Orthodox Church, 103 Furby St., Winnipeg, MB R3C 2A4 Tel. (204)775-3701

OFFICERS

Archbishop, Most Rev. Archbishop Victorin, 19959 Riopelle St., Detroit, MI 48203 Tel. (313)893-8390

Vicar, V. Rev. Archim., Dr. Vasile Vasilachi, 45-03 48th Ave., Woodside, NY 11377 Tel. (718)784-4453

Cultural Councilor, Very Rev. Fr. Nicolae Ciurea, 19 Murray St. W., Hamilton, ON L8L 1B1 Tel. (416)523-8268

Administrative Councilor, V. Rev. Fr. Mircea Panciuk, 11024-165th Ave., Edmonton, AB T5X 1X9

Sec., V. Rev. Archim. Felix Dubneac, 19959 Riopelle St., Detroit, MI 48203 Tel. (313)892-2402

PERIODICALS

Calendarul Credinta (Yearbook with Church Directory); Credinta—The Faith

The Romanian Orthodox Episcopate of America (Jackson, Mich.)

This body of Eastern Orthodox Christians of Romanian descent was organized in 1929 as an autonomous Diocese under the jurisdiction of the Romanian Patriarchate. In 1951, it severed all relations with the Orthodox Church of Romania. Now under the canonical jurisdiction of the autocephalous Orthodox Church in America, it enjoys full administrative autonomy and is headed by its own Bishop.

HEADQUARTERS

2522 Grey Tower Rd., Jackson, MI 49201 Tel. (517)522-4800 Fax (517)522-5907

Media Contact, Ed./Sec., David Oancea, P.O. Box 185, Grass Lake, MI 49240-0185 Tel. (517)522-3656 Fax (517)522-5907

OFFICERS

Ruling Bishop, Rt. Rev. Nathaniel (Popp)

Dean of all Canada, Rev. Fr. Nicolae Marioncu, Gen. Del., Roblin, MB R0L 1P0 Tel. (204)937-8002

OTHER ORGANIZATIONS

The American Romanian Orthodox Youth: Pres., David Maxim, 3633 22nd St., Wyandotte, MI 48192
Assoc. of Romanian Orthodox Ladies Auxs.: Pauline Trutza, 1446 Waterbury Ave., Lakewood, OH 44107
Orthodox Brotherhood of Canada: Pres., Thrisia Pana, #510-2243 Hamilton St., Regina, SK S4P 4B6
Orthodox Brotherhood, USA: Pres., George Aldea, 824 Mt. Vernon Blvd., Royal Oak, MI 48073

PERIODICAL

Solia/The Herald

Russian Orthodox Church in Canada, Patriarchal Parishes of

Diocese of Canada of the former Exarchate of North and South America of the Russian Orthodox Church. Originally founded in 1897 by the Russian Orthodox Archdiocese in North America.

HEADQUARTERS

St. Barbara's Russian Orthodox Cathedral, 10105 96th St., Edmonton, AB T5H 2G3

OFFICERS

Admn., Archbishop of Klin, Most Rev. Makary, 10812-108 St., Edmonton, AB T5H 3A6

PERIODICAL

Journal Of The Moscow Patriarchate, The

The Salvation Army in Canada

The Salvation Army, an evangelical branch of the Christian Church, is an international movement. The ministry of Salvationists, consisting of clergy (officers) and laity, comes from a commitment to Jesus Christ and is revealed in practical service, regardless of race, color, creed, sex, or age.

The goals of The Salvation Army are to preach the gospel, disseminate Christian truths, instill Christian values, enrich family life, and improve the quality of all life.

To attain these goals, The Salvation Army operates local congregations, provides counseling, supplies basic human needs, and undertakes spiritual and moral rehabilitation of any needy people who come within its influence.

A military system of government was set up in London, England, in 1865, by General William Booth, founder (1829-1912). Converts from England started Salvation Army work in London, Ontario, in 1882. Two years later, Canada was recognized as a Territorial Command, and since 1933 it has included Bermuda. An act to incorporate the Governing Council of The Salvation Army in Canada received royal assent on May 19, 1909.

HEADQUARTERS

Salvation Square, P.O. Box 4021, Postal Sta. A, Toronto, ON M5W 2B1 Tel. (416)598-2071
Media Contact, Asst. Public Rel. Sec. for Comm. & Spec. Events, Major Gary Venables, P.O. Box 4021, Stn. A, Toronto, ON M5W 2B1 Tel. (416)340-2162 Fax (416)598-1672

OFFICERS

Territorial Commander, Commissioner Wesley Harris
Territorial Pres., Women's Organizations, Mrs. Commissioner Margaret Harris
Chief Sec., Col. Arthur E. Waters
Field Sec. for Personnel, Col. Donald Kerr
Program Sec., Col. John Bate
Bus. Adm. Sec., Lt. Col. William Speck
Fin. Sec., Lt. Col. Douglas Kerr
Pub. Relations Sec., Lt. Col. Howard Moore
Property Sec., Lt. Col. Edwin Brown

PERIODICALS

War Cry, The; En Evant!; Young Soldier, The; Edge, The; Sally Ann; Ministry to Women Sketch, The; Horizons

Serbian Orthodox Church in the U.S.A. and Canada, Diocese of Canada

The Serbian Orthodox Church is an organic part of the Eastern Orthodox Church. As a local church it received its autocephaly from Constantinople in A.D. 1219. The Patriarchal seat of the church today is in Belgrade, Yugoslavia. In 1921, a Serbian Orthodox Diocese in the United States of America and Canada was organized. In 1963, it was reorganized into three dioceses, and in 1983 a fourth diocese was created for the Canadian part of the church. The Serbian Orthodox Church is in absolute doctrinal unity with all other local Orthodox Churches.

HEADQUARTERS

5a Stockbridge Ave., Toronto, ON M8Z 4M6 Tel. (416)231-4409

OFFICERS

Serbian Orthodox Bishop of Canada, Rt. Rev. Georgije
Dean of Western Deanery, Rev. Miroslav Dejanov, 620 E. 63rd Ave., Vancouver, BC V5X 2K4 Tel. (604)321-9750
Dean of Eastern Deanery, Rev. Stevo Stojsavljevich, 143 Nash Rd. S., Hamilton, ON L8K 4J9 Tel. (416)560-9424

Seventh-day Adventist Church in Canada

The Seventh-day Adventist Church in Canada is part of the worldwide Seventh-day Adventist Church with headquarters in Washington, D.C. (See "Religious Bodies in the United States" section of this Yearbook for a fuller description.) The Seventh-day Adventist Church in Canada was organized in 1901 and reorganized in 1932.

HEADQUARTERS

1148 King St., E., Oshawa, ON L1H 1H8 Tel. (416)433-0011 Fax (416)433-0982

OFFICERS

Pres., D. D. Devnich
Treas., R. L. Coolen
Sec., O. D. Parchment

DEPARTMENTS

Under Treas., Brian Christenson
Asst. Treas., Sebert Henry
Asst. Treas., Clareleen Ivany
Computer Services, Sebert Henry
Communications, Gerry Karst
Coord. of Ministries, Gerry Karst

Assoc. Coord. of Ministries, Claude Sabot
Education, Jan Saliba
Ministerial Assoc., Gerry Karst
Public Affairs/Religious Liberty Trust, Karnik Doukmetzian
Publishing, George Dronen

PERIODICAL

Canadian Adventist Messenger

Sikh

Sikhism was born in the northwestern part of the Indo-Pakistan sub-continent in Punjab province about 500 years ago. Guru Nanak, founder of the religion, was born in 1469. He was followed by nine successor Gurus. The Guruship was then bestowed on the Sikh Holy Book, popularly known as the Guru Granth. The Granth contains writings of the Sikh Gurus and some Hindu and Muslim saints and was compiled by the fifth Guru, Arjan Dev. For the Sikhs, the Granth is the only object of worship. It contains, mostly, hymns of praise of God, the Formless One.

Sikhs started migrating from India more than 50 years ago. A number of them settled on the West coast of North America, in British Columbia and California. More recently, a sizable group has settled in the eastern part of the continent as well, particularly in Ontario, New York and Michigan. Sikhs are found in all major cities of the United States and Canada.

When Sikhs settle, they soon establish a Gurdwara, or Sikh temple, for worship and social gathering. Gurdwaras are found, among other places, in Toronto, Vancouver, Victoria, and Yuba City, Calif. At other places, they meet for worship in schools and community centers.

The First Sikh Conference was held on March 24-25, 1979 in Toronto. This is the first step in establishing a federation of all the Sikh Associations in Canada, and, if possible, in the United States as well. A Sikh Heritage Conference was held Sept. 19-21, 1981 in Toronto.

There are approximately 200,000 Sikhs in North America.

MEDIA CONTACT

Media Contact, The Sikh Foundation, Mr. Kawad Kohli, 1 Younge St., Ste. 1801, Toronto, ON M5E 5E1 Tel. (416)594-9459

Syrian Orthodox Church of Antioch (Archdiocese of the United States and Canada)

An archdiocese of the Syrian Orthodox Church of Antioch in North America, the Syrian Orthodox Church professes the faith of the first three ecumenical councils of Nicaea, Constantinople, and Ephesus and numbers faithful in the Middle East, India, the Americas, Europe and Australia. It traces its origin to the Patriarchate established in Antioch by St. Peter the Apostle and is under the supreme ecclesiastical jurisdiction of His Holiness the Syrian Orthodox Patriarch of Antioch and All the East, now residing in Damascus, Syria.

The Archdiocese of the Syrian Orthodox Church in the U.S. and Canada was formally established in 1957. The first Syrian Orthodox faithful came to Canada in the 1890s and formed the first Canadian parish in Sherbrooke, Québec. Today five official parishes of the Archdiocese exist in Canada—two in Québec and three in Ontario. There is also an official congregation in Calgary, Alberta.

HEADQUARTERS

Archdiocese of the U.S. and Canada, 49 Kipp Ave., Lodi, NJ 07644 Tel. (201)778-0638 Fax (201)773-7506
Media Contact, Archdiocesan Gen. Sec., Very Rev. Chorepiscopus John Meno, 45 Fairmount Ave., Hackensack, NJ 07601 Tel. (201)646-9443 Fax (201)773-7506

OFFICERS

Primate, Archbishop Mar Athanasius Y. Samuel
Archdiocesan Gen. Sec., Very Rev. Chorepiscopus John Meno, 45 Fairmount Ave., Hackensack, NJ 07601 Tel. (201)646-9443

Ukrainian Orthodox Church of Canada

Toward the end of the 19th century many Ukrainian immigrants settled in Canada—1991 marked the centenary of this immigration. In 1918, these pioneers established the Ukrainian Orthodox Church of Canada, today the largest Ukrainian Orthodox Church beyond the borders of Ukraine.

HEADQUARTERS

Consistory of the Ukrainian Orthodox Church of Canada, 9 St. John's Ave., Winnipeg, MB R2W 1G8 Tel. (204)586-3093 Fax (204)582-5241
Media Contact, V. Rev. Dr. Ihor Kutash, 6270-12th Ave., Montreal, QC H1X 3A5 Tel. (514)727-2236 Fax (514)728-9834

OFFICERS

Presidium, Chpsn., Very Rev. William Makarenko
Primate, Most Rev. Metropolitan Wasyly, 174 Seven Oaks Ave., Winnipeg, MB R2V 0K8

Union of Spiritual Communities of Christ (Orthodox Doukhobors in Canada)

Groups of Canadians of Russian origin living in the western provinces of Canada, their beginnings in Russia are unknown. The name "Doukhobors," or "Spirit Wrestlers," was given in derision by the Russian Orthodox clergy in Russia as far back as 1785. Victims of decades of persecution in Russia, about 7,500 Doukhobors arrived in Canada in 1899.

The teaching of the Doukhobors is penetrated with the Gospel spirit of love. Worshiping God in the spirit they affirm that the outward church and all that is performed in it and concerns it has no importance for them; the church is where two or three are gathered together, united in the name of Christ. Their teaching is founded on tradition, which they call the "Book of Life," because it lives in their memory and hearts. In this book are sacred songs or chants, partly composed independently, partly formed out of the contents of the Bible, and these are committed to memory by each succeeding generation. Doukhobors observe complete pacifism and non-violence.

The Doukhobors were reorganized in 1938 by their leader, Peter P. Verigin, shortly before his death, into the Union of Spiritual Communities of Christ, commonly called Orthodox Doukhobors. It is headed by a democratically elected Executive Committee which executes the will and protects the interests of the people.

At least 99 percent of the Doukhobors are law-abiding, pay taxes, and "do not burn or bomb or parade in the nude" as they say a fanatical offshoot called the "Sons of Freedom" does.

HEADQUARTERS

USCC Central Office, Box 760, Grand Forks, BC
V0H 1H0 Tel. (604)442-8252

OFFICERS

Hon. Chpsn. of the Exec. Comm., John J. Verigin
Chpsn., Andrew Evin
Admn., S. W. Babakaiff

PERIODICAL

Iskra

Unitarian Universalist Association

Three of the twenty-three districts of the Unitarian Universalist Association are located partly or wholly in Canada, as are 40 of the 1,010 congregations. Conseil Unitaire Canadien handles matters of particular concern to Canadian churches and fellowships. See "Religious Bodies in the United States" section of this Yearbook for a fuller description of the history and theology.

HEADQUARTERS

Headquarters: 25 Beacon St., Boston, MA 02108
Tel. (617)742-2100
Conseil Unitaire Canadien: 600 Eglinton Ave.
East, Toronto, ON M4P 1P3 Fax (416)489-4121
Media Contact, Dir. of Public Info., Deborah Weiner, 25 Beacon St., Boston, MA 02108 Tel.
(617)742-2100 Fax (617)367-3237

DISTRICTS AND OFFICERS

Pacific Northwest: Rod Stewart, 370 Mathers
Ave., West Vancouver, BC V7S 1H3
St. Lawrence: Rev. Wendy Colby, 695 Elmwood
Ave., Buffalo, NY 14222
Western Canada: Rev. Stefan Jonasson, 408 Amhurst St., Winnipeg, MB R3J 1Y9
Northeast: Rev. Glenn Turner, 125 Auburn St.,
Portland, ME 04103
Trustee-at-Large from Canada: Dr. Sheilah
Thompson, 930 Whitchurch St., North Vancouver, BC V7L 2A6

United Brethren in Christ, Ontario Conference

Founded in 1767 in Lancaster County, Pa., missionaries came to Canada about 1850. The first class was held in Kitchener in 1855, and the first building was erected in Port Elgin in 1867.

The Church of the United Brethren in Christ had its beginning with Philip William Otterbein and Martin Boehm, who were leaders in the revivalistic movement in Pennsylvania and Maryland during the late 1760s.

HEADQUARTERS

302 Lake St., Huntington, IN 46750

GENERAL OFFICERS

Conf. Supt., Rev. Brian Magnus, 120 Fife Rd.,
Guelph, ON N1H 6Y2 Tel. (519)836-0180
Treas., Mr. Brian Winger, 2233 Hurontario St.,
Apt. 916, Mississauga, ON L5A 2E9

PERIODICAL

United Brethren, The

The United Church of Canada

The United Church of Canada was formed on June 10, 1925, through the union of the Methodist Church, Canada; the Congregational Union of Canada; the Council of Local Union Churches; and 70 percent of the Presbyterian Church in Canada. The union culminated years of negotiation between the churches, all of which had integral associations with the development and history of the nation.

In fulfillment of its mandate to be a uniting as well as a United Church, the denomination has been enriched by other unions during its history. The Wesleyan Methodist Church of Bermuda joined in 1930. On Jan. 1, 1968, the Canada Conference of the Evangelical United Brethren became part of The United Church of Canada. At various times, congregations of other Christian communions have also become congregations of the United Church.

The United Church of Canada is a full member of the World Methodist Council, the World Alliance of Reformed Churches (Presbyterian and Congregational), and the Canadian and World Councils of Churches.

The United Church is the largest Protestant denomination in Canada.

HEADQUARTERS

The United Church House, 85 St. Clair Ave. E.,
Toronto, ON M4T 1M8 Tel. (416)925-5931 Fax
(416)925-3394
Media Contact, Publicist, Mary-Frances Denis

GENERAL COUNCIL

Mod., Rev. Dr. Walter H. Farguharson
Gen. Sec., Rev. Dr. Howard M. Mills
Sec., Management & Personnel, Barbara M. Copp
Sec., Theology, Faith & Ecumenism, Rev. Hallett
E. Llewellyn
Personnel Dir., Margaret C. Scriven
Archivist, Jean E. Dryden, 73 Queen's Park Cr., E.,
Toronto, ON M5C 1K7 Tel. (416)585-4563 Fax
(416)585-4584

ADMINISTRATIVE DIVISIONS

Communications: Gen. Sec., Rev. Randolph L.
Naylor; Dept. of Educ. & Information, Dir.,
Douglas L. Flanders; Dept. of Fin. & Admn.,
Dir., Alice E. Foster; Dept. of Graphics & Print
Production, Dir., Elizabeth J. Parker; Dept. of
Media Resources, Dir., Rev. Rodney M. Booth,
c/o Berkeley Studio, 315 Queen St. E., Toronto,
AB M5A 1S7 Tel. (416)366-9221 Fax (416)368-
9774
The United Church Publishing House, Gen. Mgr.,
Jitu T. Somani
Finance: Gen. Sec., Melanie A. Macdonald; Dept.
of the Treas., Treas., John R. Page; Dept. of
Pensions & Group Ins., Dir., Janet E. Petrie;
Dept. of Stewardship Services, Dir., Rev. Vincent D. Alfano
Ministry Personnel & Education: Gen. Sec.,
Rev. Richard H. Moffat; Theological Educ.,
Rev. Ray Whitehead; Educ. & Ministry Vocations, Rev. Ronald K. Coughlin; Diaconal Ministry & Continuing Educ., K. Virginia Coleman;
Women in Ministry, J. Ann Naylor
Mission in Canada: Gen. Sec., Dr. Gerald A.
Hopkirk; Ofc. of Christian Dev., Dir., S. Ruth
Evans; Ofc. of Church in Society, Dir., Dr.
Bonnie M. Greene; Ofc. of Admn., Dir., T. Lang
Moffat; Adult Resources, Lynda L. Newmarch;
Children, Jean Olthuis; Cong., Mission Support
& Ethnic Ministries, Rev. Roland Kawano; Mission Support & Rural Life, Richard Chambers;
Editor, Mary Rose Donnelly; Family Educ. &
Justice, Rev. A. Jean Ward; Fin. Officer, William
O. Bremner; Health Services, Dr. Peter New-

berry; Energy & Environment, David G. Hallman; Refugees, Racism, Justice, Multiculturalism, Rev. Ellen Turley; Man. Editor, Hymn-Worship Res., John E. Ambrose; Planning Officer, Dixie Kee; Worship, Fred K. Graham; Youth & Young Adults, Raymond D. McGinnis

World Outreach: Gen. Sec., Rev. Frederick M. Bayliss; Africa, Rev. James A. Kirkwood; Africa, Paula J. Butler; Caribbean & Latin America, Rev. Christopher M. Ferguson; East Asia & Pacific, Rhea M. Whitehead; South Asia & Pacific, Jack H. Lakavich; Personnel, Rev. George H. Lavery

Development, Lee R. Holland; Fin. & Admn., Johanna M. Jamieson

Interfaith Dialogue, Rev. Paul W. Newman

CONFERENCE EXECUTIVE SECRETARIES

Alberta and Northwest: Rev. William F. A. Phipps, 9911 48 Ave., Edmonton, AB T6E 5V6 Tel. (403)435-3995 Fax (403)434-0597

All Native Circle: Speaker, Rev. Alfred A. Dumont, 18-399 Berry St., Winnipeg, MB R3J 1N6 Tel. (204)831-0740 Fax (204)837-9703

Bay of Quinte: Rev. David M. Iverson, 218 Barrie St., Kingston, ON K7L 3K3 Tel. (613)549-2503

British Columbia: Rev. Gordon C. How, 1955 W. 4th Ave., Vancouver, BC V6J 1M7 Tel. (604)734-0434 Fax (604)734-7024

Hamilton: Ms. K. Virginia Coleman, Box 100, Carlisle, ON L0R 1H0 Tel. (416)659-3343 Fax (416)659-7766

London: Rev. W. Peter Scott, 359 Windermere Rd., London, ON N6G 2K3 Tel. (519)672-1930 Fax (519)439-2800

Manitoba and Northwestern Ontario: Mrs. H. Dianne Cooper, 120 Maryland St., Winnipeg, MB R3G 1L1 Tel. (204)786-8911 Fax (204)774-0159

Manitou: Rev. J. Stewart Bell, 1402 Regina St., North Bay, ON P1B 2L5 Tel. (705)474-3350 Fax (705)497-3597

Maritime: Rev. Robert H. Mills, Box 1560, Sackville, NS E0A 3C0 Tel. (506)536-1334 Fax (506)536-2900

Montreal and Ottawa: Rev. Tadashi Mitsui, 225-50 Ave., Lachine, QC H8T 2T7 Tel. (514)613-8594 Fax (514)634-2489

Newfoundland and Labrador: Rev. Boyd L. Hiscock, 320 Elizabeth Ave., St. John's, NF A1B 1T9 Tel. (709)754-0386 Fax (709)754-8336

Saskatchewan: Rev. Wilbert R. Wall, 418 A. McDonald St., Regina, SK S4N 6E1 Tel. (306)721-3311 Fax (306)721-3171

Toronto: Dr. Helga Kutz-Harder, Rm. 404, 85 St. Clair Ave., E., Toronto, ON M4T 1L8 Tel. (416)967-1880 Fax (416)925-3394

PERIODICAL

Mandate; Credo; Exchange; Worldwind/Worldview; United Church Observer

United Pentecostal Church in Canada

This body, which is affiliated with the United Pentecostal Church, International with headquarters in Hazelwood, Mo., accepts the Bible standard of full salvation, which is repentance, baptism by immersion in the name of the Lord Jesus Christ for the remission of sins, and the baptism of the Holy Ghost, with the initial signs of speaking in tongues as the Spirit gives utterance. Other tenets of faith include the Oneness of God in Christ, holiness, divine healing, and the second coming of Jesus Christ.

HEADQUARTERS

United Pentecostal Church Intl., 8855 Dunn Rd., Hazelwood, MO 63042 Tel. (314)837-7300 Fax (314)837-4503

Media Contact, Gen. Sec./Treas., Rev. C. M. Becton

DISTRICT SUPERINTENDENTS

Atlantic: Rev. R. A. Beesley, Box 965, Sussex, NB E0E 1P0

British Columbia: Rev. Paul V. Reynolds, 13447-112th Ave., Surrey, BC V3R 2E7

Canadian Plains: Rev. Johnny King, 1840 38th St., SE, Calgary, AB T2B 0Z3

Central Canadian: Rev. Clifford Heaslip, 4215 Roblin Blvd., Winnipeg, MB R3R 0E8

Nova Scotia-Newfoundland: Rev. John D. Mean, P.O. Box 2183, D.E.P.S., Dartmouth, NS B2W 3Y2

Ontario: Rev. William V. Cooling, Box 1638, Brighton, ON K0K 1H0

PERIODICALS

Pentecostal Herald, The

The Wesleyan Church of Canada

The Canadian portion of The Wesleyan Church which consists of the Atlantic and Central Canada districts. The Central Canada District of the former Wesleyan Methodist Church of America was organized at Winchester, Ontario, in 1889 and the Atlantic District was founded in 1888 as the Alliance of the Reformed Baptist Church, which merged with the Wesleyan Methodist Church in July, 1966.

The Wesleyan Methodist Church and the Pilgrim Holiness Church merged in June, 1968, to become The Wesleyan Church. The doctrine is evangelical and Arminian and stresses holiness beliefs. For more details, consult the U.S. listing under The Wesleyan Church.

HEADQUARTERS

The Wesleyan Church Intl. Center, P.O. Box 50434, Indianapolis, IN 46250-0434

Media Contact, Dist. Supt., Central Canada, Rev. S. Allan Summers, 3 Applewood Dr. Ste. 102, Belleville, ON K8P 4E3 Tel. (613)966-7527 Fax (613)968-6190

DISTRICT SUPERINTENDENTS

Central Canada: Rev. S. Allan Summers

Atlantic: Rev. Ray Barnwall, P.O. Box 20, 41 Summit Ave., Sussex, NB E0E 1P0 Tel. (506)433-1007

PERIODICALS

Atlantic Wesleyan; Central Canada Clarion; Wesleyan Advocate, The

OTHER RELIGIOUS BODIES IN CANADA

Although the majority of Canadian church members belong to the religious bodies listed in the preceding section, a number of important groups have not yet provided complete directory information. They are listed below.

African Methodist Episcopal Church in Canada, 765 Lawrence Ave. W., Toronto, ON M6A 1B7. Rev. L. O. Jenkins (9 churches)

Beachy Amish Mennonite Churches, 9675 Iams Rd., Plain City, OH 43064. Tel. (614)873-8140 (3 congregations, 378 members)

Bergthaler (Mennonite) Congregations, John Neudorf, LaCrete, AB T0H 2H0

Chortitzer (Mennonite) Conference, Bishop Wilhelm Hildebrandt, Box 452, Steinbach, MB R0A 2A0 (11 Congregations, 2,000 members)

Christadelphians in Canada, P.O. Box 221, Weston, ON M9N 3M7

Christian Science in Canada, Mr. J. Donald Fulton, 339 Bloor St. West, Suite 215 Toronto, ON M5S 1W7. Tel. (416)593-1031

Church of God in Christ, Mennonite (Holdeman), P. O. Box 313, Moundridge, KS 67107. Tel. (316)345-2533 (34 congregations, 3,341 members)

Fellowship of Evangelical Bible Churches, P.O. Box 2858, Steinbach, MB R0A 2A0. Tel. (204)326-3380 (19 congregations, 1,892 members)

Hutterian Brethren, Elder Jacob Kleinsasser, Crystal Sprint Colony, Ste. Agatha, MB R0G 1Y0 (246 congregations, 9,213 members)

New Apostolic Church Canada, Admn. Ofc., c/o Rev. Michael Kraus, Pres., 65 Northfield Drive West, Box 1615, Waterloo, ON N2J 4J2. Tel. (519)884-2862. Fax. (519)884-3438

Old Colony Mennonite Church in Canada, Alberta, Deacon Herman Geisbrecht, La Crete, AB T0H 2H0 (650 members); British Columbia, Deacon Jacob Giesbrecht, Ft. St. John, BC V0C P20 (320 members); Manitoba, Deacon Abram Driedger, Box 601, Winkler, MB R0G 2X0 (930 members); Ontario, Bishop Henry Reimer, R. R. 3, Wheatley, ON N0P 2P0 (260 members); Saskatchewan, Deacon Klass Dyck, R. R. 4, Saskatoon, SK (1,087 members)

Ontario Old Roman Catholic Church (Christ Catholic Church in Canada). The Most Rev. Frederick P. Dunleavy, 1062 Woodbine Ave., Toronto, ON M4C 4C5 (1 congregation, 153 members)

Reformed Presbyterian Church of North America, Louis D. Hutmire, 7408 Penn. Ave., Pittsburgh, PA 15208. Tel. (412)731-1177

Sommerfelder (Mennonite) Church, Bishop John A. Friesen, Lowe Farm, MB R0G 1E0 (13 congregations, 3,650 members)

RELIGIOUS BODIES IN CANADA ARRANGED BY FAMILIES

The following list of religious bodies appearing in preceding directory, "Religious Bodies in Canada," including "Other Religious Bodies in Canada," shows the "families" or related clusters into which Canadian religious bodies can be grouped. For example, there are many bodies that can be grouped under the heading "Baptist" for historical and theological reasons. It is not to be assumed, however, that all denominations under one family heading are necessarily similar in belief or practice. Often any similarity is purely coincidental since ethnicity, theological divergence, and even political and personality factors have shaped the directions denominational groups have taken.

Family categories provide one of the major pitfalls of church statistics because of the tendency to combine statistics by "families" for analytical and comparative purposes. Such combined totals are almost meaningless, although often used as variables for sociological analysis.

Religious bodies not grouped under family headings appear alphabetically and are not indented in the following list.

The Anglican Church of Canada
Apostolic Christian Church (Nazarene)
Armenian Evangelical Church
Associated Gospel Churches
Bahá'í Faith

Baptist Bodies
The Association of Regular Baptist Churches (Canada)
Baptist General Conference of Canada
The Central Canada Baptist Conference
Baptist General Conference of Alberta

British Columbia Baptist Conference
Canadian Baptist Federation
Baptist Convention of Ontario and Quebec
Baptist Union of Western Canada
Union of French Baptist Churches in Canada
United Baptist Convention of the Atlantic Provinces
Canadian Convention of Southern Baptists
Evangelical Baptist Churches in Canada, The Fellowship of
Free Will Baptists
North American Baptist Conference

Bible Holiness Movement
Brethren in Christ Church, Canadian Conference
Buddhist Churches of Canada
The Canadian Yearly Meeting of the Religious Society of Friends
Christadelphians in Canada
The Christian and Missionary Alliance in Canada
Christian Brethren (aka Plymouth Brethren)
Christian Science in Canada
Church of God, (Anderson, Ind.)
Church of the Nazarene

Churches of Christ--Christian Churches

Christian Church (Disciples of Christ) in Canada
Christian Churches and Churches of Christ in Canada
Churches of Christ in Canada
Congregational Christian Churches in Ontario, The Conference of

Doukhobors

Reformed Doukhobors, Christian Community and Brotherhood of
Union of Spiritual Communities of Christ (Orthodox Doukhobors in Canada)

Eastern Churches

The Antiochian Orthodox Christian Archdiocese of North America
The Armenian Church of North America, Diocese of Canada
The Coptic Church in Canada
Greek Orthodox Diocese of Toronto, Canada
Orthodox Church in America (Canada Section)
Romanian Orthodox Church in America (Canadian Parishes)
The Romanian Orthodox Episcopate of America (Jackson, Michigan)
Russian Orthodox Church in Canada, Patriarchal Parishes of the
Serbian Orthodox Church in the U.S.A. and Canada, Diocese of Canada
Syrian Orthodox Church of Antioch (Archdiocese of the United States and Canada)
Ukrainian Greek-Orthodox Church of Canada

The Evangelical Covenant Church of Canada
Evangelical Free Church of Canada
General Church of the New Jerusalem
Gospel Missionary Association
Independent Holiness Church
Jehovah's Witnesses
Jewish Organizations in Canada

Latter Day Saints

The Church of Jesus Christ of Latter-day Saints
Reorganized Church of Jesus Christ of Latter Day Saints

Lutherans

Church of the Lutheran Brethren
The Estonian Evangelical Lutheran Church
The Evangelical Lutheran Church in Canada
The Latvian Evangelical Lutheran Church in America
Lutheran Church--Canada

Wisconsin Evangelical Lutheran Synod

Mennonite Bodies

Beachy Amish Mennonite Churches
Bergthaler Congregations
Chortitzer Mennonite Conference
Church of God in Christ, Mennonite (Holdeman)
Conference of Mennonites in Canada
The Evangelical Mennonite Conference
Evangelical Mennonite Mission Conference
Hutterian Brethren
Fellowship of Evangelical Bible Churches
Mennonite Brethren Churches, Canadian Conference of
Mennonite Church (Canada)
Old Colony Mennonite Church in Canada
Old Order Amish Church
Old Order Mennonite Church
Reinlaender Mennonite Church
Sommerfelder (Mennonite) Church

Methodist Bodies

African Methodist Episcopal Church in Canada

THE YEAR IN IMAGES

Grappling with sexuality

The ordination of The Rev. James Williams 1989 touch off a controversy in the Episcopal Church that did not go away. Debates over sexuality ripped through several denominations during 1991 and early 1992. The General Convention of the Episcopal Church affirmed traditional standards, while acknowledging a "discontinuity" between them and the experience of many church members. The Presbyterian Church (U.S.A.), The Southern Baptist Convention, and The United Methodist Church all struggled with the homosexual questions during 1991.

British Methodist Episcopal Church of Canada
The Evangelical Church in Canada
Free Methodist Church in Canada
The Wesleyan Church of Canada

Metropolitan Community Churches, Universal Fellowship of
The Missionary Church of Canada
Moravian Church in America, Northern Province
Muslims
New Apostolic Church of North America in Canada
The Old Catholic Church of Canada
Ontario Old Roman Catholic Church

Pentecostal Bodies

The Apostolic Church in Canada
Apostolic Church of Pentecost of Canada
Church of God (Cleveland, Tenn.)
The Church of God of Prophecy in Canada
Elim Felowship of Evangelical Churches and Ministers
Foursquare Gospel Church of Canada
Independent Assemblies of God--Canada
The Italian Pentecostal Church of Canada
The Open Bible Standard Churches of Canada
The Pentecostal Assemblies of Canada
Pentecostal Assemblies of Newfoundland
Pentecostal Holiness Church of Canada

United Pentecostal Church in Canada

Polish National Catholic Church of Canada

Presbyterian Bodies

Presbyterian Church in America (Canadian Section)
The Presbyterian Church in Canada
Reformed Presbyterian Church of North America

Reformed Bodies

Canadian and American Reformed Churches
Christian Reformed Church in North America
Netherlands Reformed Congregations of North America
Reformed Church in Canada
The United Church of Canada

The Reformed Episcopal Church
The Roman Catholic Church in Canada
The Salvation Army in Canada
Seventh-day Adventist Church in Canada
Sikhs
Standard Church of America (Canadian Section)
Unitarian Universalist Association
United Brethren in Christ, Ontario Conference

167

5. INTERNATIONAL AGENCIES: CONFESSIONAL, INTERDENOMINATIONAL, COOPERATIVE

A listing of major confessional, interdenominational and cooperative international agencies follows. Organizations that primarily work in Canada or the United States can be found in the listings of Cooperative Organizations for those countries.

INTERNATIONAL AGENCIES

Alliance World Fellowship

The Alliance World Fellowship, founded in 1975 at Nyack, NY, is a nonlegislative body composed of 71 national churches raised up through the ministry of The Christian and Missionary Alliance and found under a variety of names in 41 nations of the world.

The purpose of the Fellowship is to provide a means of fellowship, consultation, cooperation and encouragement in the task of missions and evangelism, which we understand to be the special calling of the church.

The AWF has a plenary convocation quadrennially. The first was in Nyack, NY, in 1975; the second in Hong Kong in 1979; the third in Lima, Peru, in 1983; the fourth in St. Paul, MN, in 1987; the fifth in Yamoussoukro, Cote d'Ivoire in 1991; and the sixth to be held in Seoul, Korea, in 1995.

HEADQUARTERS

37 Sta. Monica, Pasig, Metro Manila, Phillipines, Tel. 673-3179

OFFICERS

Exec. Dir., Dr. Benjamin de Jesus
Pres., Rev. Roger Lang, P.O. Box 336, Curtin, ACT, Australia, 2605
Vice-Pres., Rev. Luis Palomino, Apartado 18-1054, Lima 18 (Miraflores) Peru
Sec., Rev. David Kennedy, P. O. Box 35000, Colorado Springs, CO 80935
Treas., Mr. Phillip Margesson, P. O. Box 320, Oxford, 0X4 2DE, England

Anglican Consultative Council

The Anglican Consultative Council is the central council for the worldwide Anglican Communion. Its creation was proposed by the Lambeth Conference of Bishops of the Anglican Communion in 1968, and came into being by the end of 1969 with the consent of all the Provinces (or member Churches). Council meetings are held in different parts of the world. Its first meeting was held in Limuru, Kenya, in 1971; the second in Dublin, Ireland, in July 1973; the third in Trinidad, April 1976; the fourth in Canada May 1979; the fifth in Newcastle, England, September 1981; the sixth meeting in Badagry, Nigeria, July, 1984. The seventh meeting was held in Singapore, April 25 - May 7, 1987. Its report is titled "Many Gifts, One Spirit." The eighth meeting was held in Wales, July 21-August 4, 1990. The next meeting will be held in South Africa.

The membership includes bishops, priests, and lay people. Each Province (or member Church) is represented by up to three members and meetings are held every second or third year; the Standing Committee meets every year.

True to the Anglican Communion's style of working, the Council has no legislative powers. It fills a liaison role, consulting and recommending, and at times representing the Anglican Commun-

ion. Among its functions are "to share information about developments in one or more provinces with the other parts of the Communion and to serve as needed as an instrument of common action"; "to develop as far as possible agreed Anglican policies in the world mission of the Church and to encourage national and regional Churches to engage together in developing and implementing such policies by sharing their resources of manpower, money, and experience to the best advantage of all"; "to encourage and guide Anglican participation in the Ecumenical Movement and the ecumenical organizations." It is responsible for international dialogues with other world communions.

OFFICERS

Pres. The Archbishop of Canterbury, Most Rev. George Carey, Lambeth Palace, London SE1 7JU, England
Chpsn., Rev. Canon Colin Craston
Vice-Chpsn., Rev. Canon Simon Chiwanga
Sec. Gen., Rev. Canon Samuel Van Culin, Partnership House, 157 Waterloo Rd., London SE1 8UT, England, Tel. 071-620-1110 Fax 071-620-1070

Baptist World Alliance

The Baptist World Alliance is a voluntary association of Baptist conventions and unions which was formed at the first world gathering of Baptists in Exeter Hall, London, England, July 11-18, 1905. There have been 16 meetings of the Alliance's Baptist World Congress, the most recent of which was held in Seoul, Korea, August 1990.

One hundred fifty-seven national bodies around the world participate in the Alliance, representing approximately 36 million church members baptized upon their personal, conscient profession of faith in Jesus Christ. Along with children in member families, sympathizers and others considered under pastoral care, the Alliance world community would number more than seventy million persons.

BWA functions as: (1) A means of contact among world Baptists through publications, news, representational visits, correspondence and other communications; (2) A forum for study and fraternal discussion of doctrines, practice and ways of witness to the world; (3) A channel of world aid to the hungry and victims of disaster, for development projects and fraternal assistance to those in need; (4) An agency for monitoring and safeguarding religious liberty and other God-given rights; (5) A sponsor of regional and worldwide gatherings for the furtherance of the gospel; (6) An agency for consultation and cooperation among Baptists worldwide; (7) An agency for encouraging evangelism and education; and (8) A sponsor of programs for lay development, including conferences for Christian women, men, and youth.

6733 Curran St., McLean, VA 22101 Tel. (703)790-8980 Fax (703)593-5160

OFFICERS

Pres., Dr. Knud Wumpelman Villavej 8, DK 4340 Tollose, Denmark
Gen. Sec.-Treas., Rev. Dr. Denton Lotz
Treas., Mr. John R. Jones, Falls Church, VA
Division Dirs.: Evangelism & Educ., Study & Research, Rev. Tony Cupit; Baptist World Aid, Mr. Paul Montacute, Tel. (703)790-8980; Communications, Wendy Ryan; Women's Dept., Beth MacClaren
Secs. of Regional Fellowships: Africa, Dr. Samuel T. Ola, Akande, Nigeria; Asia, Rev. Edwin I. Lopez, Philippines; Caribbean, Rev. Azariah McKenzie, Jamaica; Europe, Rev. Karl-Heinz Walter, West Germany; North America, Mrs. Carolyn Weatherford-Crumpler, U.S.A.; Latin America, Rev. Jose Missena, Paraguay

Disciples Ecumenical Consultative Council (DECC)

The Disciples Ecumenical Consultative Council is an international body of Disciples of Christ Churches, established in 1975, which has four major objectives: (1) to deepen the fellowship of Disciples with each other and with other Churches on the way to the visible unity God wills for his people; (2) to encourage participation in the ecumenical movement through joint theological study, church union conversations and other forms of dialogue, and programs of joint action and witness; (3) to gather, share and evaluate information about Disciples' ecumenical activities in local, national and regional situations around the world; (4) to appoint fraternal representatives of Disciples to the assemblies of ecumenical bodies such as the World Council of Churches, and of other world families of churches, including the Roman Catholic Church.

OFFICERS

Mod., Dr. Trevor A. Banks, 13 Eton Rd., Belmont 3216, Victoria, Australia
Gen. Sec., Dr. Paul A. Crow, Jr., P.O. Box 1986, Indianapolis, IN 46206 Tel. (317)353-1491
Advisory Committee: Dr. Trevor Banks, Australia; Ms. Hazel Byfield, Jamaica; Rev. Carmelo Alvarez, Puerto Rico; Dr. Paul A. Crow, Jr., U.S.A.

MEMBERSHIP

Disciples of Christ Churches in: Argentina; Australia; Canada; Great Britain/Ireland; Jamaica; Mexico; New Zealand; Paraguay; Puerto Rico; Southern Africa; United States of America; Vanuatu; Zaire

Friends World Committee for Consultation (Section of the Americas)

The Friends World Committee for Consultation (FWCC) was formed in 1937. There has been an American Section as well as a European Section from the early days and an African Section was organized in 1971. In 1974 the name Section of the Americas was adopted by that part of the FWCC with constituency in North, Central and South America and in the Caribbean area. In 1985 the Asia-West Pacific Section was organized. The purposes of the Section of the Americas can be summarized as follows: to facilitate loving understanding of diversities among Friends while discovering together, with God's help, a common spiritual ground; and to facilitate full consideration of the Quaker witness in response to today's issues of peace and social justice.

HEADQUARTERS

1506 Race St., Philadelphia, PA 19102 Tel. (215)241-7250

OTHER OFFICES

P.O. Box 751, Wilmington, OH 45177 Tel. (513)382-6914
P.O. Box 18510, Denver, CO 80218-0510 Tel. (303)393-8757
P.O. Box 923, Oregon City, OR 97045 Tel. (503)655-3779
Latin American Office: Casa de los Amigos, Ignacio Mariscal 132, Mexico 06030, Mexico, Tel. (905)705-0521

Heads of Orthodox Churches

Among the churches that are referred to as "Orthodox" there are three distinct groups defined by the recognition of different ecumenical councils. Divisions of this family of churches stem from seven ecumenical councils held from the fourth to the eighth centuries. The Apostolic and Catholic Assyrian Church of the East accepts the first two ecumenical councils. The Oriental Orthodox Churches, The Armenian Apostolic Church, the Coptic Orthodox Church of Alexandria (Egypt), the Ethiopian Orthodox Church and the Syrian Orthodox Church accept the first three ecumenical councils. The 18 local churches referred to as Eastern Orthodox embody the teachings of all the seven ecumenical councils. The Ecumenical Patriarch of Constantinople is regarded by all as "first among equals," the first in honor and distinction without direct authority over churches other than his own.

ASSYRIAN CHURCH OF THE EAST

Patriarch, His Holiness Mar Dinka IV, 7444 North Kildare, Chicago, IL 60076

ORIENTAL ORTHODOX CHURCHES

Armenian Apostolic Church, Supreme Patriarch & Catholicos of All Armenia, His Holiness Vazken I, Etchmiadzin, Armenia
Armenian Apostolic Ch., See of Cilicia, Catholicos of Cilicia Antelias, His Holiness Karekin II, Lebanon
Coptic Orthodox Church, Pope of Alexandria & Patriarch of the See of St. Mark, His Holiness Pope Shenouda III, Anba Rueiss Bldg., Ramses St., Abbasyia, Cairo, Arab Republic of Egypt
Ethiopian Orthodox Church, Patriarch, His Holiness Abuna Tekle Haimanot, P.O. Box 1283, Addis Ababa, Ethiopia
Syrian Orthodox Church, Patriarch of Antioch & All the East, His Holiness Moran Mor Ignatius Zakka I, Bab Tooma, Damascus, Syria

EASTErn ORTHODOX CHURCHES

Ecumenical Patriarchate: Archbishop of Constantinople & Ecumenical Patriarch, His All-Holiness Bartholomew I, Rum Patrikhanesi, Fener, Istanbul, Turkey
Patriarch of Alexandria, Greek Orthodox Patriarchate, His Beatitude Parthenios, P. O. Box 2006, Alexandria, Egypt

Patriarch of Antioch, Greek Orthodox Patriarchate, His Beatitude Ignatius IV, P. O. Box 9, Damascus, Syria

Patriarch of Jerusalem, His Beatitude Diodorus, P.O. Box 19, Jerusalem, Old City, Israel

Patriarch of Moscow & All Russia, Alexy II, 5 Tchisty Pereulok, Moscow 34, Russia

Patriarch of the Serbian Orthodox Church, His Holiness Pave I, 7 Juli 5, Belgrade, Yugoslavia

Patriarch of Romania, His Holiness Teoctist, 29 Strada Antim, Bucharest. Romania

Patriarch of the Bulgarian Orthodox Church, His Holiness Maxim, The Orthodox Patriarchate, Sofia, Bulgaria

Church of Georgia: Catholicos Patriarch of Georgia, His Holiness Ilya II, Tiflis, Georgia

Church of Cyprus: Archbishop of Cyprus, His Beatitude Chrysostomos, Nicosia, Cyprus

Church of Greece: Archbishop of Athens & All Greece, His Beatitude Seraphim, Athens, Greece

Church of Albania: -----, Tirana, Albania

Church of Poland: Metropolitan of Warsaw & All Poland, His Beatitude Vasilios, Aleja Generala K, Swiercewskiego 52, Warsaw 4, Poland

Church of Czechoslovakia: Metropolitan of Prague & All Czechoslovakia, His Beatitude Dorotheos, V Jame 6, Prague 1, Czechoslovakia

Orthodox Church in America: Metropolitan of All America & Canada, His Beatitude Metropolitan Theodosius, P.O. Box 675, Syosset, NY 11791

Church of Sinai: The Archbishop Abbott Damian, Mt. Sinai, Egypt

Church of Finland: Archbishop of Karelia & All Finland, Most Rev. Archbishop John, Kupio, Finland

Church of Japan: Metropolitan of All Japan, His Eminence Metropolitan Theodosius, 3-1-4 Surugadai Kanda, Chiyoda Ku, Tokyo, Japan

Hierarchy of the Roman Catholic Church

The Hierarchy of the Roman Catholic Church consists of His Holiness, the Pope, Supreme Pastor of the Roman Catholic Church, and the various bishops from around the world joined with the Pope in one apostolic body to care for the Church. Cardinals, now always bishops, number about 150. They serve as the chief counselors to the Pope.

The Supreme Pastor is further assisted by the Roman Curia, which consists of the Secretariat of State or the Papal Secretariat, and the Council for the Public Affairs of the Church, various Sacred Congregations, Secretariats, Tribunals, and Offices. The bishops, some bearing the title of Patriarch or Archbishop, are united with the Supreme Pastor in the government of the whole Church. The bishops, when assigned to particular sees, are individually responsible for the teaching, sanctification, and governance of their particular jurisdictions of the Church.

The Papal territorial possessions are called the State of Vatican City, situated within the city of Rome and occupying 108.7 acres. It is the smallest sovereign state in the world. Papal authority is recognized as supreme by virtue of a Concordat reached with the Italian state and ratified June 7, 1929. Included in Vatican City are the Vatican Palace, various museums, art galleries, libraries, apartments, officers, a radio station, post office, and St. Peter's Basilica.

HIS HOLINESS THE POPE

John Paul II, Karol Wojtyla, Supreme Pastor of the Roman Catholic Church (born May 18, 1920; installed Oct. 22, 1978)

THE ROMAN CURIA

Pontifical Council for Christian Unity. This Council has responsibility for relations with non-Roman Catholic Christian religious bodies; is concerned with the observance of the principles of ecumenism; promotes bilateral conversations on Christian unity both on national and international levels; institutes colloquies on ecumenical questions and activities with churches and ecclesiastical communities separated from the Holy See; deputes Catholic observers for Christian congresses; invites to Catholic gatherings observers of the separated churches and orders into practice conciliar degrees on ecumenical matters. The Pontifical Council for Promoting Christian Unity deals with all questions concerning religious relations with Judaism. Cardinal Praeses: Pres., Most Rev. Edward Cassidy; Pres. Emeritus, Jan Cardinal Willebrands; Sec., Most Rev. Pierre Duprey. Office: 1 via dell'Erba, Rome, Italy.

Pontifical Council for Inter-Religious Dialog. This Council deals with those who are outside the Christian religion, profess some religion, or have a religious sense. It fosters studies and promotes relations with non-Christians to bring about an increase in mutual respect and seeks ways to establish a dialogue with them. President, Francis Cardinal Arinze; Sec., Most Rev. Michael Louis Fitzgerald. Office: 1 via dell'Erba, Rome, Italy.

Pontifical Council For Dialog with Non-Believers. This Council studies atheism in order to explore more fully its nature and to establish a dialogue with non-believers who sincerely wish to collaborate. President, Paul Cardinal Poupard; Sec., Franc Rode, C.M. Office: 16 Palazza S. Calisto, Vatican City State.

(Note: For a complete description and listing of the Hierarchy of the Roman Catholic Church, see the Official Catholic Directory, 1992, P. J. Kenedy & Sons, 121 Chanlon Rd., New Providence, NJ 07974. For a description of the Roman Catholic Church in the United States and in Canada, see "Religious Bodies in the United States" and "Religious Bodies in Canada" in this Yearbook.)

International Bible Society

International Bible Society was founded in 1809 in New York City by a small group of evangelism-minded Christians who wanted to "extend the knowledge of the Holy Scriptures in which God has revealed . . . salvation." At that time it was the New York Bible Society and its ministry centered on that city--distributing Bibles in hotels, hospitals, and jails, aboard ships and to immigrants. Over the years it has expanded into an international ministry. To date, International Bible Society has published God's Word in more than 480 languages on six continents. Overseas, the majority of its Scriptures are provided free of charge through gifts from Christians in America. These Scriptures are distributed by workers from dozens of evangelical organizations. In the United States most of the Bible Society's Scriptures are sold at cost for use in local evangelism.

As part of its efforts to make God's Word as clear as possible, International Bible Society sponsored the translation of the New International Version. Over 100 evangelical scholars worked to produce this highly accurate version of the Bible in modern English.

Throughout its history, International Bible Society's purpose has remained the same: to serve the Church in evangelism by translating, publishing and distributing God's Word so that all people everywhere may come to a saving faith in Jesus Christ. In keeping with this purpose, the Bible Society's main functions are:

--Assisting in the translating and publishing of new Scripture translations, in partnership with Wycliffe Bible Translators, New Tribes Mission and others.

--Providing Scriptures for areas where God's Word is most needed but evangelism is taking place, such as Eastern Europe and Asia.

--Supporting evangelism projects and opportunities around the world with Scriptures. Examples include: supplying Scriptures for Billy Graham and Luis Palau crusades and U.S. campus ministries, and placing Bibles in Africa's public schools.

--Selling Bibles, New Testaments and portions at or below cost to individuals, churches and organizations such as the military for use in evangelism and worship. Helping believers use God's Word more effectively through the sponsorship of evangelism/church growth seminars.

--International Bible Society is an independent, non-profit organization with membership in the Evangelical Council for Financial Accountability, the National Association of Evangelicals and the Evangelical Fellowship of Mission Agencies.

HEADQUARTERS
1820 Jet Stream Dr., Colorado Springs, CO 80921 Tel. (719)488-9200 Fax (719)488-3840

OFFICERS
Chmn., Bd. of Directors, John H. Pinkham
Pres., James R. Powell
Vice-Pres. & Publisher, John Cruz
Vice-Pres./Ministries, Dr. Eugene F. Rubingh
Intl. Bible Soc. Foundation, Pres., Robert Horan
New York Bible Soc., Dir., Charles S. Rigby

International Congregational Fellowship

ICF is a voluntary association, first formed at a world gathering of Congregationalists in Chrislehurst, England, in 1975. It is a successor to the International Congregational Council (formed in London in 1891 and merged into the World Alliance of Reformed Churches in 1966, during which time it held 10 international meetings). The ICF has held additional meetings, the most recent at Leeuwen Horst Congres Center, Noordwijkerhout, The Netherlands. It is in contact with Congregational-related bodies and individuals, each autonomous, in 52 countries.

ICF functions as: 1) an agency of communication between Congregationalists through publications, dissemination of news, personal visits, and correspondence; 2) a forum for study and fraternal discussion of doctrines, practice, and ways of witnessing to the world; 3) a channel of cooperation in extending help to one another and those in need; 4) a vigilant force for safeguarding religious liberty and other God-given rights; 5) a sponsor of regional and worldwide gatherings for the furtherance of the gospel; 6) an agency for promotion, consultation, and cooperation among Congregationalists.

HEADQUARTERS
6807 East Bayley, Wichita, KS 67207

OFFICERS
Co-Chpsns.: Rev. John Travell, 44 Cornwall Rd., Dorchester DT1 1RY, United Kingdom; Dr. Donald Ward, Park Alhambra 56, 999 E. Valley Blvd., Alhambra, CA 91801

Regional Secretaries: United Kingdom, Rev. D. Gwylfa Evans, 58 Bonnersfield La., Harrow HA1 2LE, UK; North America, Paul Miller, 6807 East Bayley, Wichita, KS 67207; Pacific & Australia, Rev. Jim Chambers, P.O. Box 2047, Raumati Beach, New Zealand; Central & Southern America, Pastor Teodoro Stricker, 25 de Mayo 1259, Casilla de Correo 57, 3315 Leandro N, Alem, Misiones, Argentina; Africa & Central Europe, Rev. Phaedon Cambouropoulos, 46 Moulopoulou St., GR-17455 Alimos, Athens, Greece

International Council of Christian Churches

Founded in 1948 and consisting of denominations of Bible-believing churches throughout the world, the ICCC promotes worldwide fellowship of evangelical churches and councils, encourages member bodies to foster a loyal and aggressive revival of Bible Christianity, seeks to awaken Christians to the dangers of modernism and to call them to unity of mind and effort against unbelief and compromise with modernism.

HEADQUARTERS
756 Haddon Ave., Collingswood, NJ 08108 Tel. (609)858-0700

OFFICER
Assoc. Sec., John Nillheim

ORGANIZATIONS
Commissions: Christian Educ.; Evangelism; Information & Publication; Intl. Affairs; Intl. Christian Youth; Justice & Freedom; Missions; New Contacts; Radio; Social & Relief

Lambeth Conference of Bishops of the Anglican Communion

The Lambeth Conference consists of all the diocesan bishops and a limited number of other members of the Anglican Communion, and is called together by the personal invitation of the Archbishop of Canterbury.

The first Lambeth Conference was held in 1867 at the request of the bishops in Canada and the United States, and it became a recurring event at approximately 10-year intervals.

The Anglican Communion has no central legislative body but in 1968 the Lambeth Conference agreed to the formation of the Anglican Consultative Council, a body with a permanent office in London. It brings together clergy, lay, and episcopal representatives once every two or three years. This practice of consultation and acknowledged interdependence ensures the validity of the Anglican Communion as a worldwide family of autonomous churches and provinces in communion with the See of Canterbury.

After the Lambeth Conference of 1958, a full-time officer, who became known as the Anglican Executive Officer, was appointed "to collect and disseminate information, keep open lines of communication, and make contact when necessary with responsible authority." The next Lambeth Conference in 1968 proposed the setting up of an Anglican Consultative Council, which, with the consent of all the provinces (or member churches), came into being at the end of 1969. The appointment of Secretary General of the Council replaced that of Anglican Executive Officer. The Lambeth Conference of 1978 proposed regular meetings of the Primates of the Anglican Communion. These have taken place in England in 1979, in America in 1981, in Kenya in 1983, in Canada in 1986, in Cyprus in 1989 and in Ireland in 1991.

OFFICERS

Pres., The Archbishop of Canterbury, Most Rev. George Carey, Lambeth Palace, London SE1 7JU, England

Sec. Gen., Rev. Canon Samuel Van Culin, 157 Waterloo Rd., London SE1 8UT, England, Tel. (01)620-1110.

Lutheran World Federation

The Lutheran World Federation was organized on July 1, 1947, at Lund, Sweden, succeeding the Lutheran World Convention which had been organized in Eisenach, Germany, in 1923. In the aftermath of World War II, the Federation plunged into programs of emergency relief, interchurch aid, and studies. Currently it functions between assemblies through major departments of Theology and Studies, Mission and Development and World Service. The most recent assembly in 1990 provided for a restructuring that is now complete. The 1989 membership consists of 107 member churches from all parts of the world with constituencies approaching 55 million persons.

The LWF is incorporated under Swiss law and has its headquarters in Geneva. Its constitution stipulates that it is a free association of Lutheran churches, acting as their agent in such matters as they assign to it; "it shall not exercise churchly functions on its own authority, nor shall it have power to legislate for the Churches belonging to it or to limit the autonomy of any Member Church."

The LWF constitution says it shall:

"(a) Further a united witness before the world to the Gospel of Jesus Christ as the power of God for salvation.

(b) Cultivate unity of faith and confession among the Lutheran Churches of the world.

(c) Develop fellowship and cooperation in study among Lutherans.

(d) Foster Lutheran interest in, concern for, and participation in ecumenical movements.

(e) Support Lutheran Churches and groups as they endeavor to extend the gospel and carry out the church's mission.

(f) Help Lutheran churches and groups, as a sharing community, to serve human need and to promote social and economic justice and human rights."

HEADQUARTERS

150 Route de Ferney 1211, Geneva 2, Switzerland

OFFICERS

Pres., Rev. Gotfried Brakemeier, Rua Senhor dos Passos 202, Caixa Postal 2876, 90.001 Porto Alegre, RS, Brazil

Vice-Pres.: Rev. Herbert W. Chilstrom, Bishop, ECLA, 8765 W. Higgins Rd., Chicago, IL 60631; Rt. Rev. Horst Hirshler, Bishop, Evangelical Lutheran Ch. of Hannover, Haarstrasse 6,3000, Hannover, Germany; Ms. Martina Huhn, Evangelical Lutheran Church of Saxony, Dorfstrass 6 B, 7231 Hopfgarten, Germany; Mr. Francis Stephanos, Pres., Ethiopian Evang. Ch. Mekame Yesus, P.O. Box 2087, Addis Ababa, Ethiopia; Ms. Sophia Tung, Taiwan Lutheran Church, 86 Section 3, Hsin Sheng South Rd., Taipei 10769, Taiwan, Republic of China

Treas., Ms. Christian Rogestam, Church of Sweden, Tosse Prastgaard, Pl 5169, 66200 Amaal, Sweden

Gen. Sec., Rev. Dr. Gunnar Staalsett, Route de Ferney 150, P.O. Box 2100, CH 1211, Geneva 2, Switzerland

Exec. Dir., USA Natl. Comm., Rev. Dr. William G. Rusch, Ofc. for Ecumenical Affairs, ECLA, 8765 W. Higgins Rd., Chicago, IL 60631 Tel. (312)380-2700

Mennonite World Conference

Mennonite World Conference (MWC) began with a small meeting in Basel, Switzerland, in 1925. Today, all the major Mennonite and related church conferences around the world participate in the program of the MWC. These bodies represent approximately 856,600 baptized members. The three-fold purpose of the organization is communication, fellowship, and facilitation. MWC normally sponsors an assembly (worldwide people's meeting) every six years. Assembly 13 is tentatively planned for 1996/7 in India.

HEADQUARTERS

North America Office, P.O. Box 88836, Carol Stream, IL 60188-0836 Fax (708)690-9691

OFFICERS

Pres., Raúl O GarcÀa, Godoy 448, Pehuajó 6450, Argentina

Exec. Sec., Larry Miller, 7 ave. la Forêt-Noire, 67000 Strasbourg, France, Fax (33)88.61.57.17

Pentecostal World Conference

The Pentecostal World Conference was organized in 1947 at Zurich, Switzerland, where Pentecostal leaders met in conference seeking ways to help bring about greater understanding and cooperation among their churches.

Formed and continuing as a nonlegislative body, the conference provides a forum for exchanging ideas, sharing information, and participating in fellowship together.

The main event of the organization is the triennial worldwide convention. Past conventions have been in Paris, London, Stockholm, Toronto, Jerusalem, Helsinki, Rio de Janeiro, Dallas, Seoul, Vancouver, Nairobi, Zurich and Singapore. The 1992 conference will be held in Norway.

Between conventions the World Conference Advisory Committee supervises the work of the conference and plans the next convention. The 29-member committee is elected at each Pentecostal World Conference and has members from around the world.

OFFICERS

Chpsn., Dr. Ray H. Hughes, P.O. Box 4815, Cleveland, TN 37320-4815

Vice-Chpsn., Rev. James MacKnight, 6745 Century Ave., Mississauga, ON L5N 6P7

Sec., Rev. Jakob Zopfi, Heimstatte SPM, 6376 Emmetten NW, Switzerland

United Bible Societies

The United Bible Societies is a world fellowship of 77 national Bible Societies and 33 Bible Society national offices which coordinates the efforts of Bible Societies in over 180 countries and territories.

The UBS was founded in 1946 to facilitate consultation and mutual support between its then 16 member Societies, thus helping them to carry out the translation, production and distribution of the Scriptures with ever-increasing effectiveness. In fulfilling this purpose, the UBS has evolved over the years and is now a single partnership of Societies responsible corporately through national and regional representation in the operation of a World Service program for planning, policy making, financing and carrying out the worldwide work.

The UBS has functional subcommittees and a team of technical consultants working in its four regions of Africa, Americas, Asia/Pacific and Europe/Middle East. The UBS organizes training institutes and publishes technical helps for translators, coordinates and advises on the most efficient and economical production of the Scriptures, makes known and stimulates new methods of Scripture distribution, undergirds work on the New Readers Projects, a graded series of Scriptures for beginning readers, represents Bible Society interests at world and regional interdenominational conferences and committees, and when necessary coordinates arrangements to provide Scriptures in emergency situations.

The American Bible Society is the UBS member in the United States. (See separate listing.)

HEADQUARTERS
Office of the Gen. Sec., 7th Fl., Reading Bridge House, Reading RG1 8PJ, England

OFFICERS
Pres., Rt. Rev. Dr. Eduard E. Lohse
Gen. Sec., Rev. Dr. John D. Erickson
Council Chm., Rev. Prof. Samuel Escobar
Gen. Comm. Chm., Bishop George Phimphisan

World Alliance of Reformed Churches (Presbyterian and Congregational)

The World Alliance of Reformed Churches (Presbyterian and Congregational) was formed in 1970 at Nairobi, Kenya, with the union of the former World Alliance of Reformed Churches and the former International Congregational Council. Both organizations were composed of member churches whose origins lie mainly in the Reformation with which the names of Calvin and Zwingli are linked.

Member churches constituent to WARC number 175 in more than 76 countries with a total estimated 70 million people as members.

The constitution provides that ordinarily once in five years delegates from member churches will meet in General Council (Assembly). Only this Assembly has the authority to make and administer policies and plans, and to speak as the Alliance. Between Assemblies, the Executive Committee exercises general oversight of the Alliance work; it meets annually.

The Executive Committee consists of the president, three vice-presidents, department heads, and 25 members. WARC headquarters are in the ecumenical center in Geneva, Switzerland, and its staff members maintain close contact with departments and agencies of the World Council of Churches and with the executives of other world confessional organizations.

Regional needs and growing membership in all parts of the world have produced area organizations within the Alliance. Three areas are fully organized: the European, the South African, and the Caribbean and North American; currently an area council in Latin America is being explored. The major objective of such area organizations is to provide means of cooperation, fellowship, and study in specific regions of the world.

OFFICERS
Pres., Rev. James Dempsey Douglass, Princeton Theological Sem., CN 821, Princeton, NJ 08542
Vice-Pres.: Dr. Chung Hyun Ro, Korea; Rev. Abival Pieres da Silveira, Brazil; Mr. Benjamin Masilo, Kenya
Gen. Sec., Dr. Milan Opocensky, 150 route de Ferney, 1211 Geneva 2, Switzerland, Fax (022)791-03-61
Gen. Treas., Mr. Jean Francois Rochette, 11, Corraterie, 1204 Geneva, Switzerland

CARIBBEAN & NO. AMERICAN AREA OFFICERS
Mod., Rev. J. Dorcas Gordon, 79 Merkley Sq., Scarborough, ON M1G 2YN
Vice-Mod., Dr. Wilbur T. Washington, 159-29 90th Ave., Jamaica, NY 11432
Area Sec., Rev. Margrethe B. J. Brown, 88 Gramercy Park, Rochester, NY 14610
Rec. Clk., Ms. Bette Duff, 1813 Camelot Dr., Madison, WI 53705
Area Treas., Mr. John A. MacFarlane, 99 Acacia Ave., Ottawa, ON K1M 0P8

World Alliance of Young Men's Christian Associations

The World Alliance of YMCAs links about 100 national YMCA movements into a world movement.

Today there are 10,000 local associations in 97 countries. Through them, about 26 million men and women, boys and girls are involved in various programs and services tailored to meet specific needs. YMCAs around the world are united by a common mission: the extension of the Kingdom of God, as expressed in the Paris Basis:

"The Young Men's Christian Associations seek to unite those young men who regarding Jesus Christ as their God and Saviour, according to the Holy Scriptures, desire to be His disciples in their faith and in their life, and to associate their efforts for the extension of His Kingdom amongst young men."

The role of the World Alliance is to interpret and express the Christ-centered nature of the YMCA; to help, encourage and inspire the world YMCA in its constant search for unity in Christ, and in its mission to work together for the extension of His Kingdom amongst people living in different circumstances and conditions; and to promote ecumenical understanding and action.

The World Alliance has been promoting an action-oriented study process on the YMCA's tasks, to arrive at a common understanding of the YMCA as a world-wide lay Christian ecumenical movement today.

World Alliance work also centers on mobilizing

world YMCA action with regard to international issues such as racism, particularly apartheid, Central America, the Palestinian problem, migrant workers and human rights, peace concerns, development issues, and health. The World Alliance promotes youth leadership development and addresses issues affecting women in society. Work with refugees is part of the YMCA's involvement in peace and justice issues. The World Alliance's task is to connect global awareness on refugee issues with the institutional resources of local YMCAs.

The World Alliance coordinates the appropriate sharing of resources within the context of international cooperation. Leadership development is central to all collaborative efforts. It also represents the YMCA at the United Nations and its agencies, and cooperates with churches and other world Christian bodies.

HEADQUARTERS

37 Quai Wilson, 1201 Geneva, Switzerland, Tel. (022)732-31-00 Fax (022)738-40-15

OFFICERS

Pres., Garba A. Yaroson
Sec. Gen., John W. Casey

World Association for Christian Communication

The World Association for Christian Communication (WACC) is a professional service organization working with churches and other groups in more than 84 countries to use media for the proclamation of the Christian values in their relevance to all of life.

WACC channels nearly $3 million yearly to more than 100 communication projects, mainly in developing nations, as well as providing professional services for management, planning and coordination. Funds come from churches and development agencies.

WACC also helps communicators improve skills through training, consultations, research, and information exchange.

WACC's 240 corporate members include Protestant, Catholic and Orthodox churches and related groups as well as secular organizations. (WACC also has more than 300 personal members.) Members are divided into regional associations: Africa, Asia, Europe, Latin America-Caribbean, Middle East, Pacific and North America.

HEADQUARTERS

357 Kennington Lane, London SE11 5QY, England, Tel. (01)582-9139

OFFICERS

Pres., Rev. Randy Naylor, Canada
Vice Pres., Rev. Hilmar Kannenberg, Brazil
Treas., Rev. Kevin Engel, Australia
Sec., Murri Selle, Germany
Chpsns. of Regional Associations: Africa, Rev. Samuel Dossou, Benin; Asia, Rev. Dr. James Massey, India; Europe, Dr. Hans Wolfgang Hessler, Germany; Latin America-Caribbean, Rev. Hilmar Kannenberg, Brazil; Middle East, Gabriel Habib, Lebanon; Pacific, Seru Verebalavu, Fiji; North America, John Peterson, U.S.A.

STAFF

Gen. Sec., Rev. Carlos Valle, Argentina
Dir., Funding, Dr. Ole van Luyn, Netherlands

Dir., Project Evaluation, Rev. Horace Etemesi, Kenya
Dir., Forum & Advocacy, Dr. Michael Traber, Switzerland
Dir., Communication Educ., Teresita Hermano, Philippines
Regional Coords.: Latin America, Ramon Orellano, Chile; Asia, Dr. Pradip Thomas, India
Information Coord., Ann Shakespeare, U.K.
Fin. Controller, Richard Cridlan, U.K.

World Conference on Religion and Peace International

The World Conference on Religion and Peace (WCRP) promotes interreligious encounter and cooperation throughout the world with participation of its constituent religions: Baha'ism; Buddhism; Christianity; Confucianism; Hinduism; Islam; Jainism; Judaism; Shintoism; Sikhism; Taoism; Traditionalism of the indigenous cultures in Africa, the Americas, Asia, Australia and Oceania; and Zoroastrianism. On local, national, regional and global levels, WCRP convenes periodic meetings and assemblies, gathering religious leaders and representatives for the purpose of exploring urgent issues, sharing experiences in working for peace with justice, and making interreligious commitment for common actions to promote peace and harmony between religious bodies, nations, and ethnic groups, as well as between human beings and the natural environment. WCRP is committed to working actively on the following issues: conflict resolution, disarmament, peace education, human rights, children and youth, refugees, economic and social development, and environmental protection.

HEADQUARTERS

WCRP/USA Office: 777 United Nations Plaza, New York, NY 10017 Tel. (212)687-2163 Fax (212)983-0566

OFFICERS

Intl. Secretariat:
Australia, Assoc. Sec. Gen., Rev. John Baldock, 5 Barkly Ave., Armadale, Victoria, Australia Tel. 61-3-688-4188 Fax 61-3-688-4808
Japan, Assoc. Sec. Gen., Priest Kiyotoshi Kawai, Fuman Hall, 2-11-1 Wada, Suginami-ku, Tokyo 166, Japan Tel. 81-3-3384-2337 Fax 81-3-3383-7993
Switzerland, Sec. Gen., Dr. John B. Taylor, 14 ch. Auguste-Vilbert, 1218 Grand-Saconnex, Geneva, Switzerland, Tel. 41-22-7698-5162 Fax 41-22-791-0034
USA, Assoc. Sec. Gen., Dr. William F. Vendley
Presidents: President Nikkyo Niwano, (Buddhist), Japan; Mr. Zhao Puchu, (Buddhist), People's Republic of China; Archbishop Angelo Fernandes, (Christian); India; Metropolitan Filaret of Kiev, (Christian), Soviet Union; The Right Reverend Sir Paul Reeves, (Christian), New Zealand; Mme. Jacqueline Rouge, (Christian), France; Ms. Hannah Stanton, (Christian), United Kingdom; Archbishop Desmond Tutu, (Christian), Republic of South Africa; Dr. M. Aram, (Hindu), India; Dr. Inamullah Khan, (Islam), Pakistan; Dr. Abdullah Bin Omar Nasseef, (Islam), Saudi Arabia; Dr. Adamou N'dam N'joya, (Islam), Cameroon; Mrs. Norma Levitt, (Jewish), USA; Rev. Toshio Miyake, (Shintoist), Japan; Mr. Tarlok S. Nandhra, (Sikh), Kenya; Maj. Gen. S. S. Uban, (Sikh), India

Officers of WCRP/USA: Pres., Ms. Mary Jane Patterson; Sec. Gen., Dr. William F. Vendley; Vice-Pres.: Dr. Viqar A. Hamdani, Ms. Judith M. Hertz, Rev. Malcolm R. Sutherland, Rev. Robert Smylie; Sec., Ms. Edna McCallion; Treas., Rev. Robert McClean; Officer Ex Officio, Mrs. Norma U. Levitt, Intl. Pres.; Officer Ex Officio, The Right Rev. Sir Paul Reeves, Intl. Pres.; Exec. Cmte. Officers: Dr. John Borelli, Mr. Edward Doty, Dr. Jane Evans, Ms. Betty Golomb, Dr. Anand Mohan, Sr. Mary Beth Reissen, Rev. Katsuji Suzuki

World Convention of Churches of Christ

The World Convention of Churches of Christ was organized in 1930 in Washington, D.C. It normally meets every four years and is an international confessional grouping including churches and work in 60 countries of the world. It uses the name "Churches of Christ" because it is the name used by many of its churches in various parts of the world. The World Convention is aligned with the Christian Church (Disciples of Christ), Christian Churches/Churches of Christ.

This organization, according to its constitution, "may in no way interfere with the independence of the churches or assume the administrative functions of existing ongoing organizations among us." It exists "in order, more fully to show the essential oneness of the churches in the Lord Jesus Christ; impart inspiration to the world brotherhood; cultivate the spirit of fellowship; provide unity among the churches; and to cooperate with Christians everywhere toward the unity of the Church upon the basis of the New Testament."

HEADQUARTERS

First City Bank Center, 100 N. Central Expressway, Ste. 804, Richardson, TX 75080

OFFICERS

Pres., Harold R. Watkins, Indianapolis, In
First Vice-Pres., Mrs. Donald I. Black, Guelph, ON
Gen. Sec., Dr. Allan W. Lee, Richardson, TX

World Council of Churches

The World Council of Churches is a fellowship of more than 300 churches of the Protestant, Anglican, Orthodox, and Old Catholic traditions banded together for study, witness, service, and the advancement of unity. It includes in its membership churches in more than 100 countries with various forms of government, and its life reflects the immense richness and variety of Christian faith and practice. The World Council of Churches came into being after many years of preparation on August 23, 1948, when its First Assembly was held in Amsterdam, The Netherlands.

The basis for World Council membership is: "The World Council of Churches is a fellowship of Churches which confess the Lord Jesus Christ as God and Saviour according to the Scriptures and therefore seek to fulfill together their common calling to the glory of the one God, Father, Son, and Holy Spirit."

Membership is open to churches which express their agreement with this basis and satisfy such criteria as the Assembly or Central Committee may prescribe.

HEADQUARTERS

150 route de Ferney, P.O. Box 2100, 1211 Geneva 2, Switzerland. Tel. (022)791 61 11; Telex: 415 730 OIK CH; Fax (022)791 03 61
U.S. Office: 475 Riverside Dr., Rm. 915, New York, NY 10115. Tel. (212)870-2533
New York Office, CCIA: 777 United Nations Plz., New York, NY 10017. Tel. (212)867-5890; Fax (212) 870-2528

PRESIDIUM

Prof. Anne-Marie Aagaard, Denmark
Bishop Vinton Anderson, USA
Bishop Leslie Boseto, Solomon Islands
Dr. Priyanka Mendis, Sri Lanka
His Beatitude Parthenios of Alexandria, Egypt
His Holiness Pope Shenouda, Egypt
The Rev. Dr. Eunice Santana, Puerto Rico
Dr. Aaron Tolen, Cameroon

CENTRAL COMMITTEE

Mod., Archbishop Aram Keshishian, Lebanon
Vice-Mods.: Ephorus Dr. S. A. E. Nababan, Indonesia; Pastóra Nélida Ritchie, Argentina

GENERAL SECRETARIAT

Gen. Sec., Rev. Dr. Emilio Castro, Uruguay
Dep. Gen. Secs.: Ms. Mercy Oduyoye; Prof. Todor Sabev; Asst. Gen. Sec. for Finance & Admn., Rev. Michael Davies; Asst. to Gen. Sec., Ms. Jean Stromberg
Librarian, Mr. Pierre Beffa
Personnel Dir., Rev. Carlos Sintado
Ecumenical Institute, Dir., Rev. Dr. Jacques Nicole
Communication, Mr. Jan Kok
U. S. Office, Interim Dir., Rev. Dr. Donald Black

PROGRAM UNIT I--UNITY and RENEWAL

Unity and Renewal brings together the concern for the search for visible unity, the search for inclusive community; renewal through worship and spirituality; ecumenical formation and theological education, including the work of the Ecumenical Institute Bossey; theological reflection and inter-faith dialogue; reflection on justice, peace and the integrity of creation.

PROGRAM UNIT II--MISSION, EDUCATION and WITNESS

Mission, Education and Witness focuses on unity in mission, gospel and culture, evangelism, healing and transformation, education for all God's people, education in mission, and the theological significance of religions.

PROGRAM UNIT III--JUSTICE, PEACE and CREATION

Justice, Peace and Creation is the base for concerns relating to justice, peace and the integrity of creation as a conciliar process; for theological, ethical, socioeconomic and ecological analysis; economic justice; peace ministries and conflict resolution; human rights; issues of indigenous peoples and land rights; continuing emphasis on combating racism; the churches' response to international affairs; concerns and perspectives of women; concerns and perspectives of youth; education for justice, peace and creation; communication as power.

PROGRAM UNIT IV--SHARING and SERVICE

Sharing and Service is concerned with the service of human need, solidarity by sharing of resources, comprehensive diakonia, development of human resources, new models for sharing and service, biblical and theological analysis in partnership with those concerned with mission and diakonia.

MEMBER CHURCHES

Africa

African Christian Church and Schools [Kenya]
African Church of the Holy Spirit [Kenya]*
African Israel Church, Nineveh [Kenya]
African Protestant Church [Cameroon]*
Baptist Community of Western Zaire
Church of Jesus Christ in Madagascar
Church of Jesus Christ on Earth by the Prophet Simon Kimbangu [Zaire]
Church of the Brethren in Nigeria
Church of the Lord Aladura [Nigeria]
Church of the Province of Burundi, Rwanda and Zaire [Burundi]
Church of the Province of Central Africa [Botswana]
Church of the Province of Kenya
Church of the Province of Nigeria
Church of the Province of Southern Africa [South Africa]
Church of the Province of Tanzania
Church of the Province of the Indian Ocean [Seychelles]
Church of the Province of West Africa [Liberia]
Church of Uganda
Community of Disciples of Christ [Zaire]
Community of Light [Zaire]
Dutch Reformed Mission Church of South Africa
Episcopal Baptist Community [Zaire]
Ethiopian Evangelical Church Mekane Yesus
Ethiopian Orthodox Church
Evangelical Church of Cameroon
Evangelical Church of Gabon
Evangelical Church of the Congo
Evangelical Church of Togo
Evangelical Community [Zaire]
Evangelical Congregational Church in Angola
Evangelical Lutheran Church in Southern Africa [South Africa]
Evangelical Lutheran Church in Tanzania
Evangelical Lutheran Church in Zimbabwe
Evangelical Pentecostal Church of Angola*
Evangelical Presbyterian Church [Ghana]
Evangelical Presbyterian Church in South Africa
Lesotho Evangelical Church
Lutheran Church in Liberia
Malagasy Lutheran Church
Mennonite Community [Zaire]
Methodist Church, Ghana
Methodist Church in Kenya
Methodist Church in Zimbabwe
Methodist Church, Nigeria
Methodist Church of Southern Africa [South Africa]
Methodist Church Sierra Leone
Moravian Church in Southern Africa [South Africa]
Moravian Church in Tanzania
Nigerian Baptist Convention
Presbyterian Church in Cameroon
Presbyterian Church in the Sudan
Presbyterian Church of Africa [South Africa]
Presbyterian Church of Cameroon
Presbyterian Church of East Africa [Kenya]
Presbyterian Church of Ghana
Presbyterian Church of Mozambique*
Presbyterian Church of Nigeria
Presbyterian Church of Rwanda
Presbyterian Church of Southern Africa [South Africa]
Presbyterian Community [Zaire]

Presbytery of Liberia*
Protestant Church of Algeria*
Protestant Methodist Church in Benin and Togo [Benin]
Protestant Methodist Church, Ivory Coast
Province of the Episcopal Church of the Sudan
Reformed Church in Zambia
Reformed Church in Zimbabwe
Reformed Church of Equatorial Guinea*
Reformed Presbyterian Church of Southern Africa [South Africa]
Union of Baptist Churches of Cameroon
United Church of Zambia
United Congregational Church of Southern Africa [South Africa]
United Evangelical Church of Angola*

Asia

Anglican Church of Australia
Anglican-Episcopal Church in Japan
Associated Churches of Christ in New Zealand
Bangladesh Baptist Sangha
Baptist Union of New Zealand
Batak Christian Community Church [Indonesia]*
Batak Protestant Christian Church [Indonesia]
Bengal-Orissa-Bihar Baptist Convention [India]*
China Christian Council
Christian Church of Central Sulawesi [Indonesia]
Christian Evangelical Church in Minahasa [Indonesia]
Christian Protestant Angkola Church [Indonesia]*
Christian Protestant Church in Indonesia
Church of Bangladesh*
Church of Ceylon
Church of Christ in China, The Hong Kong Council
Church of Christ in Thailand
Church of North India
Church of Pakistan
Church of South India
Church of the Province of Burma
Church of the Province of New Zealand
Churches of Christ in Australia
East Java Christian Church
Evangelical Christian Church in Halmahera [Indonesia]
Evangelical Christian Church in Irian Jaya [Indonesia]
Evangelical Church of Sangir Talaud [Indonesia]
Evangelical Methodist Church in the Philippines
Indonesian Christian Church (GKI)
Indonesian Christian Church (HKI)
Japanese Orthodox Church
Javanese Christian Churches
Kalimantan Evangelical Church [Indonesia]
Korean Christian Church in Japan*
Karo Batak Protestant Church [Indonesia]
Korean Methodist Church
Malankara Orthodox Syrian Church [India]
Mar Thoma Syrian Church of Malabar [India]
Methodist Church in India
Methodist Church in Malaysia
Methodist Church in Singapore*
Methodist Church of New Zealand
Methodist Church [Sri Lanka]
Methodist Church, Upper Burma
Myanmar Baptist Convention
Nias Protestant Christian Church [Indonesia]
Pasundan Christian Church [Indonesia]
Philippine Episcopal Church
Philippine Independent Church
Presbyterian Church in Taiwan
Presbyterian Church in the Republic of Korea
Presbyterian Church of Korea
Presbyterian Church of New Zealand
Protestant Christian Church in Bali*

Protestant Church in Indonesia
Protestant Church in Sabah [Malaysia]*
Protestant Church in the Moluccas [Indonesia]
Protestant Church in South-East Sulawesi
Protestant Church in West Indonesia
Protestant Evangelical Church in Timor [Indonesia]
Samavesam of Telugu Baptist Churches [India]
Simalungun Protestant Christian Church [Indonesia]
Toraja Church [Indonesia]
United Church of Christ in Japan
United Church of Christ in the Philippines
United Evangelical Lutheran Churches in India
United Presbyterian Church of Pakistan
Uniting Church in Australia
Caribbean
Church in the Province of the West Indies [Barbados]
Methodist Church in Cuba*
Methodist Church in the Caribbean and the Americas [Antigua]
Moravian Church, Eastern West Indies Province [Antigua]
Moravian Church in Jamaica
Moravian Church in Surinam
Presbyterian Church in Trinidad & Tobago
Presbyterian Reformed Church in Cuba*
United Church of Jamaica and Grand Cayman
United Protestant Church [Netherlands Antilles]*
Europe
Armenian Apostolic Church
Autocephalic Orthodox Church in Poland
Baptist Union of Denmark
Baptist Union of Great Britain
Baptist Union of Hungary
Bulgarian Orthodox Church
Catholic Diocese of the Old Catholics in Germany
Church in Wales
Church of England
Church of Greece
Church of Ireland
Church of Norway
Church of Scotland
Church of Sweden
Congregational Union of Scotland
Czechoslovak Hussite Church
Ecumenical Patriarchate of Constantinople
Estonian Evangelical Lutheran Church
European Continental Province of the Moravian Church -- Western District [Bad Boll, Germany]
Evangelical Baptist Union of Italy*
Evangelical Christian Baptist Union of the USSR
Evangelical Church in Germany
-Church of Lippe
-Evangelical Church in Baden
-Evangelical Church in Berlin-Brandenburg
-Evangelical Church in Hesse and Nassau
-Evangelical Church in Württemberg
-Evangelical Church of Anhalt
-Evangelical Church of Bremen
-Evangelical Church of Hesse Electorate-Waldeck
-Evangelical Church of the Görlitz Region
-Evangelical Church of the Palatinate
-Evangelical Church of the Province of Saxony
-Evangelical Church of the Rhineland
-Evangelical Church of Westphalia
-Evangelical Lutheran Church in Bavaria
-Evangelical Lutheran Church in Brunswick
-Evangelical Lutheran Church in Oldenburg
-Evangelical Lutheran Church in Thuringia
-Evangelical Lutheran Church of Hanover

-Evangelical Lutheran Church of Mecklenburg
-Evangelical Lutheran Church of Saxony
-Evangelical Lutheran Church of Schaumburg-Lippe
-Evangelical Reformed Church in Northwestern Germany
-North Elbian Evangelical Lutheran Church
-Pomeranian Evangelical Church
Evangelical Church of Czech Brethren [Czechoslovakia]
Evangelical Church of the Augsburg and Helvetic Confession [Austria]
Evangelical Church of the Augsburg Confession in Poland
Evangelical Church of the Augsburg Confession in Romania
Evangelical Church of the Augsburg Confession of Alsace and Lorraine [France]
Evangelical Lutheran Church [Netherlands]
Evangelical Lutheran Church of Denmark
Evangelical Lutheran Church of Finland
Evangelical Lutheran Church of France
Evangelical Lutheran Church of Iceland
Evangelical Lutheran Church of Latvia
Evangelical Methodist Church of Italy
Evangelical Presbyterian Church of Portugal*
Evangelical Synodal Presbyterial Church of the Augsburg Confession in Romania
Georgian Orthodox Church
Greek Evangelical Church
Lusitanian Catholic-Apostolic Evangelical Church [Portugal]*
Lutheran Church in Hungary
Mennonite Church [Germany]
Mennonite Church in the Netherlands
Methodist Church [UK]
Methodist Church in Ireland
Mission Covenant Church in Sweden
Moravian Church [Herrnhut, Germany]
Moravian Church in Great Britain and Ireland
Netherlands Reformed Church
Old Catholic Church of Austria
Old Catholic Church of Switzerland
Old Catholic Church of the Netherlands
Old Catholic Mariavite Church in Poland
Orthodox Church of Czechoslovakia
Orthodox Church of Finland
Polish Catholic Church in Poland
Presbyterian Church of Wales
Reformed Christian Church in Slovakia [Czechoslovakia]
Reformed Christian Church in Yugoslavia
Reformed Church in Hungary
Reformed Church of Alsace and Lorraine [France]
Reformed Church of France
Reformed Church of Romania
Reformed Churches in the Netherlands
Remonstrant Brotherhood [Netherlands]
Romanian Orthodox Church
Russian Orthodox Church
Scottish Episcopal Church
Serbian Orthodox Church [Yugoslavia]
Silesian Evangelical Church of the Augsburg Confession [Czechoslovakia]
Slovak Evangelical Church of the Augsburg Confession [Czechoslovakia]
Slovak Evangelical Church of the Augsburg Confession in Yugoslavia
Spanish Evangelical Church
Spanish Reformed Episcopal Church*
Swiss Protestant Church Federation
Union of Welsh Independents
United Free Church of Scotland
United Protestant Church of Belgium

177

United Reformed Church in the United Kingdom
Waldensian Church [Italy]

Latin America
Baptist Association of El Salvador*
Baptist Convention of Nicaragua
Bolivian Evangelical Lutheran Church*
Church of God [Argentina]*
Church of the Disciples of Christ [Argentina]*
Episcopal Anglican Church of Brazil
Evangelical Church of Lutheran Confession in Brazil
Evangelical Church of the River Plate [Argentina]
Evangelical Lutheran Church in Chile
Evangelical Methodist Church in Bolivia*
Evangelical Methodist Church in Uruguay*
Evangelical Methodist Church of Argentina
Evangelical Methodist Church of Costa Rica*
Free Pentecostal Mission Church of Chile
Latin American Reformed Church [Brazil]
Methodist Church in Brazil
Methodist Church of Chile*
Methodist Church of Mexico
Methodist Church of Peru*
Moravian Church in Nicaragua
Pentecostal Church of Chile
Pentecostal Mission Church [Chile]
Salvadorean Lutheran Synod*
United Evangelical Lutheran Church [Argentina]*
United Presbyterian Church of Brazil*

Middle East
Apostolic Catholic Assyrian Church of the East [Iraq]
Armenian Apostolic Church [Lebanon]
Church of Cyprus
Coptic Orthodox Church [Egypt]
Episcopal Church in Jerusalem and the Middle East
Greek Orthodox Patriarchate of Alexandria and All Africa [Egypt]
Greek Orthodox Patriarchate of Antioch and All the East [Syria]
Greek Orthodox Patriarchate of Jerusalem
National Evangelical Synod of Syria and Lebanon [Lebanon]
Syrian Orthodox Patriarchate of Antioch and All the East
Synod of the Evangelical Church of Iran
Synod of the Nile of the Evangelical Church [Egypt]
Union of the Armenian Evangelical Churches in the Near East [Lebanon]

North America
African Methodist Episcopal Church [USA]
African Methodist Episcopal Zion Church [USA]
American Baptist Churches in the USA
Anglican Church of Canada
Canadian Yearly Meeting of the Religious Society of Friends
Christian Church (Disciples of Christ) [Canada]
Christian Church (Disciples of Christ) [USA]
Christian Methodist Episcopal Church [USA]
Church of the Brethren [USA]
Episcopal Church [USA]
Estonian Evangelical Lutheran Church [Canada]
Evangelical Lutheran Church in America
Evangelical Lutheran Church in Canada
Evangelical Lutheran Church of Latvia in Exile [Canada]
Hungarian Reformed Church in America
International Council of Community Churches [USA]
International Evangelical Church [USA]
Moravian Church in America (Northern Province)

Moravian Church in America (Southern Province)
National Baptist Convention of America
National Baptist Convention, USA, Inc.
Orthodox Church in America
Polish National Catholic Church [USA]
Presbyterian Church in Canada
Presbyterian Church (USA)
Progressive National Baptist Convention, Inc. [USA]
Reformed Church in America
Religious Society of Friends: Friends General Conference and Friends United Meeting [USA]
United Church of Canada
United Church of Christ [USA]
United Methodist Church [USA]

Pacific
Church of Melanesia [Solomon Islands]
General Assembly, Congregational Christian Church in American Samoa
Congregational Christian Church in Samoa
Cook Islands Christian Church
Evangelical Church in New Caledonia and the Loyalty Isles [New Caledonia]
Evangelical Church of French Polynesia
Evangelical Lutheran Church of Papua New Guinea
Kiribati Protestant Church
Methodist Church in Fiji
Methodist Church in Samoa
Methodist Church in Tonga
Presbyterian Church of Vanuatu
Tuvalu Christian Church
United Church in Papua New Guinea and the Solomon Islands

Names and locations of churches are given according to information available to the WCC at the time of publication. The name of the country appears in square brackets where it is not obvious from the name of the church. Geographical references are provided only where they are necessary to identify the church of when they indicate the location of headquarters of churches with regional or world membership. The mention of a country in this list does not imply any political judgment on the part of the WCC.

*Associate member church

World Council of Synagogues (Conservative)

The World Council of Synagogues (Conservative) was organized in 1957 as an alliance of Conservative synagogues and synagogue organizations throughout the world. Its purpose is to extend fellowship and mutual aid to each other and to foster the growth and development of Conservative Judaism abroad.

OFFICERS

Pres., Rabbi Zachary I. Heller, 744 Avenue A, Bayonne, NJ 07002 Tel. (201)436-4499
Exec. Vice-Chmn., Rabbi Benjamin Z. Kretman, 155 Fifth Ave., New York, NY 10010 Tel. (212)533-7800
Exec. Dir., Bernard Barsky, 155 Fifth Ave., New York, NY 10010 Tel. (212)533-7693

World Evangelical Fellowship

Founded in 1951 in the Netherlands, the World Evangelical Fellowship traces its roots to the Evangelical Alliance founded in 1846 in Britain. It is an international alliance of autonomous national and regional bodies serving as a resource and catalyst through these bodies to encourage, motivate, and help the local church fulfill its scriptural mandate.

HEADQUARTERS
Intl. Headquarters, 141 Middle Rd. #05-05 GSM Bldg., Singapore 0718
European Ofc., 2 Molenstraat, B-1560, Hoeilaart, Belgium, Tel. 2-657-18-01
No. American Ofc., P. O. Box WEF, Wheaton, IL 60189 Tel. (708)668-0440

OFFICERS
Intl. Dir., Dr. David M. Howard
Executive Council: Chpsn., Dr. Tokunboh Adeyemo, Nigeria; Pres., Dr. Theodore Williams, India; Sec., Rev. Alfred C. H. Yeo, Singapore; Treas., Mr. John E. Langlois, Channel Islands; Rev. David Ho, Jamaica; Dr. Emilio A. Nunez C., Guatemala; Pfarrer Hans-Winrich Scheffbuch, Germany; Dr. Brian C. Stiller, Canada; Dr. Agustin B. Vencer, Jr., Phillipines; Dr. Raymond V. J. Windsor, New Zealand

REGIONAL MEMBERS
Assoc. of Evangelicals of Africa & Madagascar
Evangelical Assoc. of the Caribbean
Evangelical Fellowship of Asia
European Evangelical Alliance
Latin American Evangelical Fellowship (CONELA)

WORLD EVANGELICAL FELLOWSHIP MEMBERS
Assoc. of Evangelicals of Angola
Argentine Alliance of Evangelical Churches
Australian Evangelical Alliance
National Christian Fellowship of Bangladesh
Evangelical Fellowship of Botswana
Fed. of Evangelical Churches & Missions in Burkina Faso
Myanmar Evangelical Christian Fellowship
Evangelical Fellowship of Canada
Assoc. of Central African Evangelical Churches
China Evangelical Fellowship (Taiwan)
Evangelical Alliance of Denmark
(Dutch) Evangelical Alliance
Fellowship of Evangelicals in Egypt
French Evangelical Alliance
German Evangelical Alliance
Natl. Assoc. of Evangelicals of Ghana
Evangelical Alliance of Great Britain
Evangelical Alliance of Guatemala
Assoc. of Evangelical Churches & Missions of Guinea
Guyana Evangelical Fellowship
Council of Evangelical Churches of Haiti
Pan-Hellenic Evangelical Alliance
Evangelical Fellowship of India
Indonesia Evangelical Fellowship
United Christian Council in Israel
Italian Evangelical Alliance
Evangelical Federation of the Ivory Coast
Jamaica Assoc. of Evangelicals
Japan Evangelical Assoc.
Evangelical Fellowship of Kenya
Korea Evangelical Fellowship
Assoc. of Evangelicals of Liberia
Evangelical Fellowship of Malawi
Natl. Evangelical Christian Fellowship, Malaysia
Assoc. of Evangelical Protestants of Mali
Mexican Evangelical Confraternity
Nepal Christian Fellowship
Evangelical Fellowship of New Zealand
Nigeria Evangelical Fellowship

Evangelical Fellowship of Pakistan
Natl. Council of Evangelical Ch. of Papua, New Guinea
Philippine Council of Evangelical Churches
Portugese Evangelical Alliance
Evangelical Alliance of Romania
Evangelical Fraternity of Senegal
Evangelical Fellowship of Singapore
Evangelical Fellowship, Sierra Leone
Evangelical Fellowship of South Africa
Spanish Evangelical Alliance
Evangelical Alliance of Sri Lanka
Swaziland Conference of Churches
Swiss Evangelical Alliance
Evangelical Fellowship of Thailand
Trinidad & Tobogo Council of Evangelical Churches
Natl. Assoc. of Evangelicals (U.S.A.)
Christian Assoc. of Evangelical Churches of Uruguay
Evangelical Council of Venezuela
Evangelical Fellowship of Zambia
Evangelical Fellowship of Zimbabwe

World Jewish Congress

The World Jewish Congress was organized in 1936 and, in the United States, in 1939. The WJC seeks to intensify bonds of world Jewry with Israel as a cultural force in Jewish life; to strengthen solidarity among Jews everywhere and secure their rights, status, and interests as individuals and communities; to encourage development of Jewish social, religious and cultural life throughout the world and coordinate efforts by Jewish communities and organizations to cope with any Jewish problems; to work for human rights generally.

HEADQUARTERS
501 Madison Ave., 17th Floor, New York, NY 10022 Tel. (212)755-5770 Fax (212)755-5883

OFFICERS
Pres., Edgar M. Bronfman
American Section: Chpsn., Ms. Evelyn Sommer; Dir., Elan Steinberg
Sec.-Gen., Israel Singer

World Methodist Council

The World Methodist Council is one of about 30 families of churches known as "Christian World Communions." These communions share a general tradition which is common to all Christians, but each has specific traditions which have grown out of spiritual crises in the history of the Church.

The World Methodist Council is comprised of 68 churches with common roots in the Methodist tradition, including a number of united churches in which a significant number of former Methodists were part of the union. Member churches of the Council are each autonomous in their government. Council decisions and directives do not encroach on this autonomy, but are derived from the churches themselves, carrying moral suasion and inspiring united witness where common endeavor seems desirable.

Although the name World Methodist Council was adopted in 1951 at Oxford, England, the Council dates from 1881 when the first Ecumenical Methodist Conference met in London. This world organization convened at ensuing 10-year intervals with the exception of the 1941 Conference, which was not held until 1947 because of World War II. Since 1951, meetings of the Council, and the Conference it convenes, have been held every five years.

The World Methodist Council seeks to deepen the fellowship of the Methodist peoples over the barriers of race, nationality, color and language; to foster Methodist participation in the ecumenical movement; to conduct bilateral dialogues on an international level with other Christian World Communions; and to advance the unity of theological and moral standards in the churches. The Council suggests priorities in Methodist activity; promotes the most effective use of Methodist resources in the Christian mission throughout the world; encourages evangelism in every land; promotes Christian education and the church's concern for youth; seeks to uphold and relieve persecuted or needy Christian minorities; and arranges for the exchange of ministers, youth and laity through an extensive program of world exchange. Through its program of World Evangelism, the Council trains and equips men and women to be evangelists in their own culture. In addition, an ongoing program of international institutes and area evangelism seminars is conducted by the World Methodist Evangelism Institute, a joint venture of the Council and Emory University in Atlanta, GA.

A North American Section of the World Methodist Council provides a regional focus for the Council in the United States, Canada and Mexico.

Methodist churches are at work in 93 countries and have approximately 26,000,000 members with the sphere of influence reaching a community of more than 54 million.

HEADQUARTERS

P.O. Box 518, Junaluska, NC 28745 Tel. (704)456-9432 Fax (704)456-9433

OFFICERS

Chpsn., Exec. Comm., Rev. Dr. Donald English, United Kingdom
Vice-Chpsn., Mrs. Betty Davis, Australia
Honorary Pres., Bishop Lawi Imathiu, Kenya
Treas., Mr. Ewing Werlein, Jr., U.S.A.
Asst. Treas., Mrs. Edna Alsdurf, U.S.A.
Presidium: Mrs. Frances M. Alguire, U.S.A.; Bishop Heinrich Bolleter, Switzerland; Miss Alka Edwards, India; Bishop Ho Chee-Sin, Singapore; Bishop Nathaniel Linsey, U.S.A./West Africa; His Eminence S. C. Mbang, Nigeria; Bishop Raul Ruiz Avila, Mexico; Ms. Mary Um, Korea; Mrs. Edith Loane, WFMW President, Ireland
Gen. Sec., Dr. Joe Hale
Geneva Sec., Mr. Ralph C. Young, Box 2100 CH1211, Geneva 2, Switzerland, Tel. (22)791-6231
Past Chpsns.: Bishop William R. Cannon; Dr. Kenneth G. Greet; Bishop Prince A. Taylor, Jr.
Gen. Sec. Emeritus, Dr. Lee F. Tuttle

OFFICERS, NORTH AMERICAN SECTION

Pres., Bishop L. Bevel Jones, United Methodist
First Vice-Pres., Bishop Herman L. Anderson, African Methodist Episcopal Zion
Vice-Pres.: Pbro. Abner Alaniz, Methodist Church in Mexico; Bishop Richard A. Hildebrand, African Methodist Episcopal Church; Bishop Richard O. Bass, Christian Methodist Episcopal Church; Dr. Earle Wilson, Wesleyan Church

World Student Christian Federation

The World Student Christian Association was founded in 1895 by a group of Student Christian Movement leaders, John R. Mott prominent among them.

WSCF now has movements in more than 90 countries with constituency at all levels of education: secondary schools, university and graduate institutions and the wider academic community. For many years, WSCF published the quarterly *Student World*, which has been replaced by regional publications, the *WSCF Journal*, and the quarterly *Federation News*. Information and subscriptions can be obtained by contacting the WSCF interregional office in Geneva, Switzerland

At the General Assembly in Helsinki, Finland, in 1968, a decision was made to regionalize the WSCF. Now six regional, continental offices serve to coordinate regional and interregional programs which seek to promote Christian community and a just world.

At the General Assembly in San Francisco, California in August 1981, the WSCF adopted four major foci for the next quadrennium: education, human rights and solidarity, theology and ecumenism, and women. These program areas are a further development of WSCF's previous commitment to provide Christian witness in the struggle for liberation. Further development of these four program areas occurred at the XXIX WSCF General Assembly in Mexico City, March 1986, under the theme "That They May Have Life in All Its Fullness: Our Commitment to Peace with Justice." Continued and vigorous commitment to theological reflection and involvement in the church universal undergirds the programs. The XXX General Assembly was held in 1990 in Chantilly, France, under the theme: ."You Shall Be My Witnesses-- Student witness in Pluralist Societies." The XXXI General Assembly will take place in Africa in 1995, to coincide with the Centenary Celebrations of the Federation.

HEADQUARTERS

Interregional Ofc., 5, Route des Morillons, 1218 Grand-Saconnex, Switzerland, Tel. (022)798-89-53 Fax (4122)798-23-70

OFFICERS

Co-Gen. Secs.: Jean-Francois Delteil, France; Clarissa Balan-Sycip, Phillipines
Chpsn., Marshal Fernando, Sri Lanka

World Union for Progressive Judaism

The World Union for Progressive Judaism was established in London in 1926, by representatives of Liberal, Progressive, and Reform congregational associations and individual synagogues from six nations. Today the World Union stimulates the development of a worldwide movement and its congregations in 25 countries. The membership of these congregations totals approximately 1.1 million Jewish men, women, and children.

The World Union operates a secondary school in Haifa, Israel and a college for training rabbis in London. It extends organizational and financial assistance to new congregations in many countries, assigns and employs rabbis wherever Jews are in search of their religious heritage, operates religious and social youth programs in Israel and Europe, publishes prayer books and other texts in many languages, holds biennial conferences for Jewish leaders and scholars from all corners of the world.

13 King David St., Jerusalem, Israel, Tel. 02-203-447

838 5th Ave., New York, NY 10021 Tel. (212)249-0100

OFFICERS

Pres., Mr. Donald Day
Exec. Dir., Rabbi Richard G. Hirsch
No. American Dir., Mr. Martin Strelzer
Intl. Affairs & Dev., Dir., Rabbi Clifford Kulwin

World Young Women's Christian Association

The World YWCA was founded in 1894 by four of the existing National YWCAs: the Associations of Great Britain, Norway, Sweden, and the United States. During the first years of its history the world movement, reflecting the patterns of its national affiliates, was primarily made up of members of various Protestant denominations. However, as the work spread around the world, Roman Catholic and Orthodox Christians joined the Association and the World YWCA became consciously ecumenical. Today it includes large numbers of women from all confessions and serves women and girls of many faiths. The World YWCA constitution, adopted in 1955, expresses the functions of the World Association as follows:

"The World YWCA provides a channel for the sharing of resources and the exchange of experience among its affiliated associations.

It helps its affiliated associations with the development of their leadership and programme.

It surveys new fields and promotes work to meet the needs therein.

It acts in cooperation with world voluntary movements and with intergovernmental organizations in matters of common concern.

It works for international understanding for improved social and economic conditions and for basic human rights for all people.

In times of emergency it undertakes and sponsors international humanitarian, welfare, and relief work, in accordance with Christian principles, irrespective of religious, social, political, national or racial differences."

The YWCA is now at work in 88 countries with programs including a variety of development projects with emphasis on self-reliance and appropriate technology, educational activities, vocational training programs for women and girls, hostels, rural projects, and programs of study and action in relation to social and economic issues. A wide network of sharing of financial resources and personnel between Associations and of financial aid from other sources forms the World YWCA program of development aid. The World YWCA also carries on refugee services in cooperation with other international agencies and with its own member associations.

The World YWCA has a legislative Council which brings together representatives of its na-

tional affiliates every four years and an Executive Committee made up of 20 members from all parts of the world which meets annually. An international staff works at the headquarters in Geneva.

HEADQUARTERS

37 Quai Wilson, 1201 Geneva, Switzerland, Tel. (022)732-31-00

OFFICERS

Pres., Razia S. Ismail
Gen. Sec., Elaine Hesse Steel

World's Christian Endeavor Union (Presbyterian and Congregational)

Christian Endeavor is a Christ-centered youth-oriented ministry which is committed to assisting local churches reach young people with the Gospel of Jesus Christ, disciple them in the Christian faith, equip them for ministry, and involve them in the life of their church and community. Christian Endeavor also encourages each young person to become involved in the shaping of the youth program at his/her level of interest and ability. It is multi-church, cross-cultural, global in its outreach.

Christian Endeavor groups usually are organized locally under the direction of the church, which determines the theology, program, activities and relationships of the group. Materials are produced for program enrichment, seminars provided for equipping youth leaders for effective ministry, and conferences and conventions sponsored for inspiration, spiritual growth and fellowship.

Christian Endeavor was organized Feb. 2, 1881, in Portland, Maine. Dr. Frances E. Clark, pastor of the Williston Congregational Church, challenged the young people to develop a Christian lifestyle and become involved in the ministry of the local church. The concept spread rapidly, and by 1895 Christian Endeavor had become a worldwide movement and the World's Christian Endeavor Union organized. As the movement spread to other lands, many national unions were formed. There are now over 50 groups worldwide with over 2 million members.

World Conventions are held quadrennially and regional conferences in the intervening years. The World's Union is governed by a Council which meets every four years, a Board of Trustees which meets annually, and an Executive Committee which meets on call. There are no full-time paid employees with most of the work is carried out through volunteer service.

HEADQUARTERS

1221 E. Broad St., P.O. Box 1110, Columbus, OH 43216 Tel. (614)258-9545 Fax (614)258-1834

OFFICERS

Pres., Rev. Konrad Brandt
Exec. Dir., Rev. David G. Jackson

INTERNATIONAL AGENCIES

6. NATIONAL CHRISTIAN COUNCILS AND REGIONAL AND INTERREGIONAL CONFERENCES

The following material is taken from the *Directory of Christian Councils, Fourth Edition, 1985,* published by the World Council of Churches, 150 route de Ferney, 1211 Geneva 2, Switzerland. Supplementary material supplied by the WCC was also used. This directory is produced in this abridged form by permission of the World Council of Churches.

Listings below follow a geographical arrangement and, within geographical area, alphabetically by country. Each listing gives the name and address of the Christian Council or Interregional Conference, telephone number, cable and/or Telex, name of chief executive officer, president, or other responsible person.

AFRICA

Angola—Conselho Angolano de Igrejas Evangelicas (Angolan Council of Evangelical Churches), Caixa Postal 1659, Rua Amilcar Cabral No. 182, 1 andar 11, Luanda, People's Republic of Angola. Cable: CAIE, Luanda. Gen. Sec., Rev. Augusto Chipesse.

Botswana—Botswana Christian Council, P.O. Box 355, Gaborone, Botswana. Tel. 51981, Cable: KOPANYO. Acting Gen. Sec., Churchill Grape.

Burundi—Conseil National des Eglises du Burundi (National Council of Churches of Burundi), B.P. 17, Bujumbura, Burundi. Tel. 24216. Gen. Sec., Rev. Nimpe Sylvère.

Cameroun—Fédération des Eglises et Missions Evangéliques du Cameroun (Federation of Protestant Churches and Missions in Cameroun), B.P. 491, Yaoundé, Cameroun. Tel. 22 30 78, Cable: FEMEC B.P. 491 Yaoundé. Gen. Sec., Rev. Woongli-Massaga.

The Gambia—The Gambia Christian Council, P.O. Box 27, Banjul, The Gambia, West Africa. Gen. Sec., Ms. H. A. Peters.

Ghana—Christian Council of Ghana, P.O. Box 919, Accra, Ghana. Tel. 76678/76725; Cable: CHRISTCON. Gen. Sec., Rev. David A. Dartey.

Kenya—National Council of Churches of Kenya, P.O. Box 45009, Church House, Moi Avenue, Nairobi, Kenya, East Africa. Tel. 338211/336763, Cable: OIKOUMENE. Gen. Sec., Rev. Samuel Kobia.

Lesotho—Christian Council of Lesotho, P.O. Box 547, 100 Maseru, Lesotho. Tel. 323639, Cable: CHRISTCOL Maseru. Gen. Sec., Mr. Ramolulela Michael Taole.

Liberia—Liberian Council of Churches, 182 Tubman Blvd., P.O. Box 10-2191, Monrovia, Liberia. Tel. 262820. Gen. Sec., Rev. Steven W. Muin.

Madagascar—Fiombonan'ny Fiangonana Protestanta eto Madagascar, Federation des Eglises Protestantes à Madagascar (Federation of the Protestant Churches in Madagascar), Vohipiraisana Ambohijatovo-Atsimo, 101-Antananarivo, Madagascar. Tel. 201.44. Gen. Sec., Pasteur Charles Rakotoson. Fiombonan'ny Fiangonana Kristiana eto Madagasikara (Christian Council of Churches in Madagascar), B.P. 798, 101-Antananarivo, Madagascar. Tel. 290.52. Exec. Sec., Rev. Lala Andriamiharisoa.

Malawi—Christian Council of Malawi, P.O. Box 30068, Capital City, Lilongwe 3, Malawi. Tel. 730499, Cable: EKLESIAS. Gen. Sec., Rev. Dr. Overtoun Mazunda.

Mozambique—Christian Council of Mozambique, Av. Ahmed Sekou Touré No. 1822, P.O. Box 108, Maputo, Mozambique. Tel. 25103-3,22836, Cable: COCRIMO, Maputo. Telex: 6-199 cocri mo. Maputo. Gen. Sec., Rev. Filipe Sique Banze.

Namibia—Council of Churches in Namibia, Mashego St. 8521, P.O. Box 41, Windhoek 9000, Namibia. Tel. 37510/36511/37512/32976, Telex: 56834 wk. Gen. Sec., Dr. A. Shejavali.

Nigeria—Christian Council of Nigeria, 139 Ogunlana Dr., Surulere, P.O. Box 2838, Marina, Lagos, Nigeria. Tel. Lagos 836019, Cable: CHURCHCON, Lagos. Gen. Sec., Mr. C. O. Williams.

Rwanda—Conseil Protestant du Rwanda (Protestant Council of Rwanda) B.P. 79, Kigali, Rwanda. Tel. 5825. Gen. Sec., Mr. Jean Utumbahutu.

Sierra Leone—Council of Churches in Sierra Leone, 4 A Kingharman Rd., Brookfields, P.O. Box 404, Freetown, Sierra Leone. Tel. 40568, Cable: UNCED, Freetown. Gen. Sec., Rev. Mr. Amadu F. Kamara.

South Africa—South African Council of Churches, Khotso House, 62 Marshall Street, Johannesburg 2001, P.O. Box 4921, Johannesburg, 2000, South Africa. Tel. (011)492-1380/96, Fax (011)492-1448. Cable: Ecunews, Johannesburg. Teletex: 450614. Gen Sec., Rev. Frank Chikane.

Sudan—New Sudan Council of Churches, P.O. Box 14894, Nairobi, Kenya. Exec. Sec., Mr. Roger Schrock; Sudan Council of Churches, P.O. Box 469 Khartoum. Sudan. Tel. 42859/42855/ 41137, Cable: SUDCHURCH, Khartoum. Telex: 24099 scc, sd. Khartoum. Gen. Sec., Rev. Ezekiel Kutjok.

Swaziland—Council of Swaziland Churches, P.O. Box 1095, Manzini, Swaziland. Gen. Sec., Mrs. Eunice Nokuthula Sowazi.

Tanzania—Christian Council of Tanzania, P.O. Box 1454, Dodoma, Tanzania. Tel. 20445, Cable: UNITAS. Sec., Rev. Bella Ben Mlewa.

Uganda—Uganda Joint Christian Council, P.O. Box 30154, Kampala, Uganda. Gen. Sec. Rev. J. Ndyabahika.

Zaïre—Eglise du Christ au Zaïre (Church of Christ in Zaïre), B.P. 4938, Kinshas-Gome, Zaïre. President: Mgr., I.B. Bokeleale.

Zambia—Christian Council of Zambia, P.O. Box 30315, Lusaka, Zambia. Tel. 214308/219379/219380. Telex: 45160 christ 2a. Gen. Sec., ———.

Reuter photo

Opening up the Dead Sea scrolls

The decades-long scholarly monopoly over access to the Dead Sea scrolls was broken when two researchers reconstructed some of the ancient texts with the help of a concordance and a computer. The Israeli Antiquities Authority finally decided to give all scholars free access to the scrolls. William A. Moffett (left) and Bob Schlosser, of the Huntington Library in Pasadena, view slides of the scrolls. This sample shows text from Leviticus.

Zimbabwe—Zimbabwe Council of Churches, 128 Victoria St., P.O. Box 3566, Harare, Zimbabwe. Tel. 791208; Cable: OIKOUMENE; Telex: 4752 C CARE ZW. Gen. Sec., Rev. M. C. Kuchera.

ASIA

Bangladesh—Jatiya Church Parishad, Bangladesh (National Council of Churches, Bangladesh), 395 New Eskaton Rd., P.O. Box 220, Dhaka-1000, Bangladesh. Tel. 402869, Cable: CHURCHSERV Dhaka. Gen Sec., Mr. Subodh Adhikary

Burma—(see: Union of Myanmar)

Hong Kong—Hong Kong Christian Council, 33 Granville Rd., Tsim Sha Tsui, Kowloon, Hong Kong. Tel. 3-670071. Gen. Sec., Rev. Dr. Manking TSO.

India—National Council of Churches in India, Christian Council Lodge, Post Bag 105, Nagpur 440001, M. S. India. Tel. 31312, Cable: AIKYA. Gen. Sec., Mr. K. LungMuana.

Indonesia—Communion of Churches in Indonesia, Jalan Salemba Raya 10, Jakarta Pusat 10430, Indonesia. Tel. 884321, Cable.: OIKOUMENE Jakarta. Gen. Sec., Rev. Dr. J. M. Pattiasina.

Japan—National Christian Council in Japan, Japan Christian Center, 2-3-18-24 Nishiwaseda, Shinjuku-ku, Tokyo 160, Japan. Tel. (03)203-0372 to 4, Cable: JAPACONCIL Tokyo; Telex: 27890 ccrai-j. Gen. Sec., Rev. Maejima Munetoshi.

Korea—National Council of Churches in Korea, Rm. 706 Christian Building, 136-46 Yonchi-Dong, Chongno-Ku, Seoul 110-701, Korea. Tel. 763-8427, 763-7323, Cable: KOCOUNCIL, Telex: Korencc K 26840. Gen. Sec., Rev. Kwon Ho Kyung.

Malaysia—Majlis Gereja-Gereja Malaysia (Council of Churches of Malaysia), 26 Jalan University, 46200 Petaling Jaya, Selangor, Malaysia. Tel. 03.567092, Cable: ECUMENICAL PETALING JAYA. Hon. Gen. Sec., Mr. Varghese George.

Pakistan—National Council of Churches in Pakistan, P.O. Box 357, 32-B Shar-e-Fatima Jinnah, Lahore-4, Pakistan. Tel. 57307, Cable: ECUMENICAL, Lahore. Exec. Sec., Mr. Yousaf Saroia.

Philippines—National Council of Churches in the Philippines (Sangguniang Pambansa ng mga Simbahan sa Pilipinas) 879 Epifanio de los Santos Ave., Quezon City (P.O. Box 1767, Manila D-406), Republic of the Philippines. Tel. 99-86-36, Cable: OIKOUMENE, Manila. Gen. Sec., Dr. Feliciano Carino.

Singapore—National Council of Churches, Singapore, Sophia Road #04-34, Peace Centre, Singapore 0922. Gen. Sec., Mr. P. S. George. Tel. 337-2150

Sri Lanka—National Christian Council of Sri Lanka, 368/6 Bauddhaloka Mawalta, Colombo, Sri Lanka. Tel. 587285/7. Gen. Sec., Mr. Shirley J. S. Peiris.

Thailand—Church of Christ in Thailand, 14 Pramuan Road, Bangkok 10500, Thailand Gen. Sec. Boonratna Boayen.

Union of Myanmar—Myanmar Council of Churches, 263 Maha Bandoola St. Central YMCA Building, GPO Box 1400, Yangon, Union of Myanmar. Tel. 73290, Cable: OIK-OUMENE, Yangon. Gen. Sec., U Win Tin; Yangon, Pres., Rev. Canon A. Mya Han.

AUSTRALASIA

Australia—Australian Council of Churches, 379 Kent St., Sydney, N.S.W. 2000, P.O. Box C 199 Clarence St., Sydney, N.S.W.2000. Tel. (02) 29.2215, Cable: ECUMENICAL, Sydney, Telex: aa 171715 Sydacc, Sydney. Fax: (02)262-4514 Gen. Sec., Rev. David Gill.

New Zealand—Conference of Churches in Aotearoa New Zealand and Te Runanga Whakawhanaunga I Nga Haahi O Aotearoa (Maori Council of Churches), P.O. Box 9573, Newmarket, Auckland, New Zealand. Tel. (09)520-5499.

CARIBBEAN, CENTRAL AMERICA & MEXICO

Antigua—Antigua Christian Council, P.O. Box 863, St. John's, Antigua, West Indies. Tel. 20261. Exec. Sec., Rev. Lloyd Kitson.

Bahamas—The Bahamas Christian Council, P.O. Box SS-5863, The Shirley Street Post Office, Nassau, Bahamas. West Indies. Tel. 32153/31441 Sec., Rev. Charles A. Sweeting.

Belize—Belize Christian Council, P.O. Box 508, 149 Allenby St., Belize City, Belize, C.A. Tel. 02-7077. Exec. Sec., Ms. J. A. Jeffries.

Cuba—Consejo Ecuménico de Cuba (Ecumenical Council of Cuba), Calle 6, No. 273, entre 12 y 13, Vedado, Apartado 4179, La Habana 4, Cuba. Tel. 3-7404, Cable: IGLEPICUBA. Gen. Sec., Rev. Raul Suarez Ramos.

Curaçao—Curaçao Council of Churches, Barantslaan, 11, Curaçao, Netherlands Antilles. Tel. 611139. Pres. Dr. G. J. Schüssler.

Jamaica—The Jamaica Council of Churches, 14 South Avenue, P.O. Box 30, Kingston 10, Jamaica, West Indies. Tel. 092-60974; Cable: CIL-CHURCH. Gen. Sec., Mrs. Rubye Gayle.

Mexico—Federacion Evangélica de Mexico (Evangelical Federation of Mexico) Apartado 1830, Motolinia 8-107, Mexico 06001, D.F., Mexico. Tel. 585-0594. Exec. Sec., Rev. Israel Ortiz Murrieta.

Puerto Rico—(See under "United States Regional and Local Ecumenical Agencies" in this Yearbook.

St. Vincent—St. Vincent Christian Council, P.O. Box 445, Kingstown, St. Vincent, W.I. Tel. 71809. Exec. Sec., Mr. Liley Cato.

Trinidad & Tobago—Christian Council of Trinidad & Tobago, Hayes Court, Hayes St., Port-of-Spain, Trinidad and Tobago. Tel. 809-622-2863. Exec. Sec., Mrs. Grace Steele.

EUROPE

Austria—Ökumenischer Rat der Kirchen in Oesterreich (Ecumenical Council of Churches in Austria), Hamburgerstr. 3, A-1050 Vienna, Austria. Tel. (0222)587 31 41. Supt., Mag. Werner Horn.

Czechoslovakia— Czechoslovak Ecumenical Council of Churches, 18600 Prague 8—Karlin, Vitkova 13. Tel. 227581. Sec., Rev. Pavel Vychopen.

Denmark—Ecumenical Council of Denmark, Skindergade 24, DK-1159 Copenhagen K. Tel. 01-15 59 27. Sec., Mr. Jorgen Thomsen.

Finland—Ecumenical Council of Finland, Luotsikatu la, PL 185, SF-00161 Helsinki 16, Finland. Tel. 3580-18021; Telex: infic 122357. Gen. Sec., Rev. Jaakko Rusama.

France—Fédération Protestante de France (French Protestant Federation), 47 rue de Clichy, Paris F-75009, France. Tel. 1/4874. Telex: 642 380 f paribip., Gen. Sec., Rev. Louis Schweitzer

Germany—Arbeitsgemeinschaft christlicher Kirchen in Deutschland (Council of Christian Churches in Germany), Neue Schlesingergasse 22-24, Postfach 10 17 62, D-W-6000 Frankfurt/Main 1, Tel. (069) 20334. Gen. Sec., Dr. Athanasios Basdekis; Auguststrasse 80, D-O-1040 Berlin. Tel. Berlin 28860. Gen. Sec., Rev. Martin Lange.

Hungary—Magyarorszagi Egyhazak Okumenikus Tanacsa (Ecumenical Council of Churches in Hungary), Szabadsag têr 2, H-1054 Budapest V, Hungary. Tel. (36-1) 114-862, Cable: OIKOUMENE Budapest. Gen. Sec., Rev. Laszlo Lehel.

Ireland—The Irish Council of Churches, Inter-Church Centre, 48 Elmwood Ave., Belfast, BT9 6AZ, Northern Ireland, Tel.: Belfast 663145. Gen. Sec., Rt. Hon. David W. Bleakley.

Italy—Federazione delle Chiese Evangeliche in Italia (Federation of Protestant Churches in Italy), via Firenze 38, 00184 Rome, Italy. Tel. 47 55 120. Exec. Sec., Dr. Renato Maiocchi.

Netherlands, Raad van Kerken in Nederland (Council of Churches in The Netherlands), Kon. Wilhelminalaan 5, 3818 HN Amersfoort, The Netherlands. Tel. (033)633844, Fax (033)613-995. Gen. Sec., Rev. W. R. van der Zee.

Poland—Polska Rada Ekumeniczna (Polish Ecumenical Council), ul. Willowa 1, 00-790 Warszawa Poland. Tel. 49 96 79/497343, Cable: OIKUMENE Warsaw, Telex: 817 875 pec pl, Warszawa. Gen. Sec., Rev. Zdzislaw Pawlik.

Portugal—Conselho Portugués de Igrejas Christas (Portuguese Council of Christian Churches), Rua de Lapa 9, Sala I, 3080 Figueira da Foz, Portugal. Tel. 033-28279. Gen. Sec., Rev. Manuel Pedro Cardoso.

Sweden—Swedish Ecumenical Council, Stortorget 3, 11129 Stockholm, Sweden. Tel. 08/10.12.35. Sec., Rev. Rune Forsbeck

United Kingdom—Council of Churches for Britain and Ireland (CCBI), Inter-Church House, 35-41 Lower Marsh, London SE1 7RL, Tel. 071-620-4444. Gen. Sec., Rev. John Reardon; Churches Together in England, Inter-Church House, 35/41, Lower Marsh, Waterloo, London SE1 7RL. 071-620-4444, Cable; KOINONIA London, Telex: 916504 CHRAID G. Gen. Sec., Canon Martin Reardon. Isle of Man Council of Churches—Sec., Rev. J. C. Walne, St. Olave's Vicarage, Ramsey, Isle of Man, U.K. Action of Churches Together in Scotland (ACTS):—Scottish Churches' House, Dunblane, Perthshire, FK15 OAJ, Scotland, UK. Tel. Dunblane 823588. Gen. Sec., Rev. Maxwell Craig. Cytun (Churches Together in Wales) 21 St. Helen's Rd., Swansea, West Glamorgan SA1 4AP, Wales, UK. Tel. (0792)460876. Gen. Sec., Rev. Noel A. Davies.

Yugoslavia—Ecumenical Council of Churches in Yugoslavia, Secretariat, Fah 182, 1101 Belgrade, Yugoslavia. Gen. Sec., Deacon Radomir Rakic.

MIDDLE EAST

Israel—International Christian Committee in Israel, P.O.B. 304, Nazareth 16102, Israel; Chpsn., Dr. Sami Geraisy, United Christian Council in Israel; Gen. Sec., Mr. Charles Kopp, Box 546, Jerusalem 91004.

Jerusalem—International Christian Committee and Jerusalem Inter-Church Aid Committee, Sec., Mr. Elias Khouri, P.O. Box 19195, Jerusalem.

NORTH AMERICA

Canada—(See Canadian Council of Churches in "Canadian Cooperative Organizations, National" in this Yearbook for complete details.)

United States—(See National Council of the Churches of Christ in the U.S.A. in "United States Cooperative Organizations, National" in this Yearbook for complete details.)

PACIFIC

American Samoa—National Council of Christian Churches of American Samoa, P.O. Box 849, Pago Pago, American Samoa 96799. Gen. Sec., Rev. Mauala Sanerivi.

Cook Islands—Religious Advisory Council of the Cook Islands, P.O. Box 886, Rarotonga, Cook Islands. Tel. 22851. Gen. Sec., Bishop Robin Leamy.

Fiji—Fiji Council of Churches, Actg. Sec., Mr. Are Wakowako, P.O. Box 2300, Government Buildings, Suva, Fiji.

Papua New Guinea—Papua New Guinea Council of Churches, P.O. Box 1015, Boroko, Port Moresby, Papua New Guinea. Tel. 256410; Cable: Melcon Boroko; Telex: c/o 22213 Wantok. Gen. Sec., Rev. Leva Kila Pat.

Samoa—Samoa Council of Churches, P.O. Box 574, Apia, Western Samoa. Sec., Rev. Oka Fau'olo.

Solomon Islands—Solomon Islands Christian Association, P.O. Box 520, Honiara, Solomon Islands. Tel. 22898; Cable: SICA Honiara. Sec., Mr. P. Bochaligana.

Tonga—Tonga National Council of Churches, P.O. Box 1205, Nuku'alofa, Tonga. Tel. 21177; Cable: UNICIL Nuku'alofa; Telex: 66237 lipons ts. Exec. Sec., Mr. Laitia Fifita.

Vanuatu—Vanuatu Christian Council, P.O. Box 379, Port Vila, Vanuatu. Tel. 2161. Sec., Rev. N. Aiong.

SOUTH AMERICA

Argentina—Federacion Argentina de Iglesias Evangélicas (Argentine Federation of Evangelical Churches) José Maria Moreno 873, 1424 Buenos Aíres, Argentina. Tel. 922-5356. Pres., Rev. Juan van der Velde.

Brazil—Conselho Nacional de Igrejas Cristas do Brasil (The National Council of Christian Churches in Brazil), C.P. 2876, 90.020 Porto Alegre, R.S., Brazil. Sec., Rev. Godofredo G. Boll. Tel. (0512) 24.50.10-1, Cable: ECLESIA; Telex: 512332

Guyana—The Guyana Council of Churches, 71 Murray St., P.O. Box 10864, Georgetown, Guyana. Tel. 66610. Sec., Mr. Michael McCormack

Uruguay—Federacion de Iglesias Evangélicas del Uruguay (Federation of Evangelical Churches of Uruguay), Av. 8 de Octubre 3324, Montevideo, Uruguay. Tel. 81.33.16; Cable: OIKOUMENE, Montevideo. Exec. Sec., Mr. Lothar J. Driedger.

REGIONAL AND INTER-REGIONAL CONFERENCES

Africa—All Africa Conference of Churches (Conférence des Eglises de Toute l'Afrique), Waiyaki Way, P.O. Box 14205, Nairobi, Kenya. Tel. 441483/441338/44133. Fax (2542) 443241. Cable: CHURCHCON, Nairobi, Telex: 22175 AACC Nairobi. Gen. Sec., Rev. José Chipenda

Asia—Christian Conference of Asia, 2, Jordan Rd., Ground Floor, Kowloon, Hong Kong. Gen. Sec., Bishop John Samuel.

Caribbean—Caribbean Conference of Churches, P.O. Box 616, Bridgetown, Barbados. Tel. (809) 42-72681, Cable: CHRISTOS, Telex: 2335 CADEC WB. Gen. Sec., Rev. Allan F. Kirton.

Europe—Conference of European Churches, P.O. Box 2100, 150 route de Ferney, 1211 Geneva 2, Switzerland. Tel. 791 61 11, Cable: OIK-OUMENE Geneva, Telex: 415 730 OIK CH; Fax: (022)791-03-61. Gen. Sec., Mr. Jean Fischer.

Latin America—Consejo Latinoamericano de Iglesias (CLAI), Latin American Council of Churches, Casilla, 85-22, Quito, Ecuador, South America. Tel. 238.220; Telex: clai 2316 ietel ed. Gen. Sec., Rev. Felipe Adolf.

Middle East—The Middle East Council of Churches, Mail to: c/o P.O. Box 4259, Limassol, Cyprus. Tel. (51) 26 022, Telex: 5378 oik cy; Telex West Beirut Office: 22662 oik le; East Beirut Office: 22054 telesco le for mecc. Gen. Sec., Mr. Gabriel Gergi Habib.

Pacific—Pacific Conference of Churches, P.O. Box 208, 4 Thurston St., Suva, Fiji, South Pacific. Tel. 302-332, Cable: PACFICONS, Suva. Gen. Sec., Mr. S. K. Motu'ahala.

7. UNITED STATES REGIONAL AND LOCAL ECUMENICAL AGENCIES

One of the many ways Christians and Christian churches relate to one another locally and regionally is through ecumenical agencies. The membership in these ecumenical organizations is diverse. Historically, councils of churches were formed primarily by Protestants, but many local and regional organizations now include Orthodox and Roman Catholics. Many are made up of congregations or judicatory units of churches. Some have a membership-base of individuals. Others foster cooperation between ministerial groups, community ministries, coalitions, or church agencies. While Councils of Churches is a term still commonly used to describe this form of cooperation, other terms such as "conference of churches," "ecumenical councils," "churches united," "metropolitan ministries," are coming into use.

An increasing number of ecumenical agencies have been exploring ways to strengthen the interreligious aspect of life in the context of religious pluralism in the U.S. today. Some organizations in this listing are interfaith agencies primarily through the inclusion of Jewish congregations in their membership. Other organizations are considering ways to nurture partnership with a broader base of religious groups in their communities, especially in the areas of public policy and interreligious dialogue.

This list does not include all local and regional ecumenical and interfaith instrumentalities in existence today. No such compilation currently exists. However, the Ecumenical Networks Working Groups of the National Council of Churches of Christ in the U.S.A. and the National Association of Ecumenical Staff (NAES), are cooperating on the compilation of such data.

The terms regional and local are sometimes relative, making identification somewhat ambiguous. Regional councils may cover sections of large states or cross state borders. Local councils may be made up of several counties, towns, or clusters of congregations. State councils or state-level ecumenical contacts exist in 45 of the 50 states. One of these, at the state level, is an interfaith council—the Arkansas Interfaith Council.

For additional information about community ministries, ecumenical agencies with voluntary leadership, covenant congregations, or new developments within a specific area, consult the state or local councils.

For information concerning this listing or to report changes in staff, officers, mailing addresses, and program emphases for the agencies listed here, contact: Dr. Kathleen Hurty, Dir. for Ecumenical Networks, National Council of the Churches of Christ in the USA, 475 Riverside Dr., rm. 868, New York, NY 10115. Tel. (212)870-2155.

Information concerning NAES, a professional association for persons engaged in ecumenical service—local, state, regional, national—may be obtained through Ecumenical Networks at the address and phone listed above.

Other agencies of interest may appear in other sections of this book. Consult the index to find them.

REGIONAL

Appalachian Ministries Educational Resource Center (AMERC)
518 Second Ave., South Charleston, WV 25303 Tel. (304)744-7410 Fax (304)744-7411
Exec. Dir., Rev. Dr. Mary Lee Daughtery, 518 2nd Ave., South Charleston, WV 25303 Tel. (304)744-7410
Chair, AMERC Bd., Dr. Richard Reid, O.F.M.
Office Admin., Ruby Provance
AMERC Staff: E. David DuBois, United Methodists; David Deaderick, Presbyterian Church (USA); Sr. Jane McDowell, Roman Catholic Church; Nancy Conway, Episcopal Church
Major Activities: Education and Training for Seminarians; Small-town and Rural Churches in Appalachia; Travel Seminar; Intensive Summer Term; Scholarships

INTERFAITH IMPACT for Justice and Peace
110 Maryland Ave., N.E., Washington, DC 20002 Tel. (202)543-2800 Fax (202)547-8107
Executive Dir., James M. Bell

National Farm Worker Ministry
1337 W. Ohio, Chicago, IL 60622 Tel. (312)829-6436 Fax (312)829-8915
Exec. Dir., Sr. Patricia Drydyk

Assoc. Dir., Dr. Jon Lacy, Midwest Office, P.O. Box 4897, East Lansing, MI 48226 Tel. (517)332-0869
Major Activities: Ministry Among Pesticide Victims; UFW Table Grape Boycott; Farm Worker Week; Farm Labor Organizing Committee Support; Witness for Farm Worker Justice Delegation; Grape Free Zone Campaign; Support of UFW of WA State boycott of Ste. Michelle wines

North America Interfaith Network (NAIN)
Sec., Dr. Peter Laurence, Cathedral of St. John Divine, 1047 Amsterdam Ave., New York, NY 10025 Tel. (212)865-9117
Co-Chair & Exec. Dir., Rev. Dr. Charles R. White, Buffalo Area Metropolitan Ministries, 775 Main St., Ste. 405, Buffalo, NY 14203 Tel. (716)854-0822
Major Activities: Interfaith Directory; Interfaith Conferences; Networking between Interfaith Organizations

The Commission on Religion in Appalachia, Inc. (AMERC)
864 Weisgarber Rd., NW, P.O. Box 10867, Knoxville, TN 37909 Tel. (615)584-6133 Fax (615)584-8114
Exec. Coord., Jim Sessions
Admin. Sec., Linda Selfridge
Financial Sec., Pearl Jones
Stewardship Coord., Jim Rugh

Coord. Appalachian Dev. Proj. Committee, Gaye Evans
Prgm. Chpsn. Appalachian Dev Proj. Comm., Jean Stone
Prgm. Chpsn. Appalachian Dev. Proj. Comm., Marty Zinn
Coord., Coop. Congregational Dev., Tena Willemsma
Prgm. Chpsn. Coop. Cong. Dev., Gladys Campbell
Coord. Volunteer Prog., John MacLean
Coord. Volunteer Prog., Chickie MacLean
Prog. Chpsn. Volunteer Prog., Dory Campbell
Consultant, Northn Appalachian Comm., Douglas Macneal
Prog. Chpsn. Northn App. Comm., Ron Evans
Communications Consultant, Jamie Harris
Tennessee Industrial Renewal Netwk. on Assgn. from CORA, Bill Troy
Major Activities: A 13-state regional ecumenical agency composed of 17 communions and 10 state councils of churches

ALABAMA

Greater Birmingham Ministries
1205 N. 25th St., Birmingham, AL 35234-3197 Tel. (205)326-6821 Fax (205)326-6823
Exec. Dir., Doug Mitchell
Co-Chair, Economic Justice: Hattie Belle Lester; Scott Douglas
Chair, Direct Services, Janine Hagan
Chair, Faith in Community, Peggy Miller
Chair, Finance & Fund-Raising, Dick Sales
Pres., Richard Johnson
Sec., Carolyn Higgins
Treas., Ed Wilson
Major Activities: Direct Service Ministries (Food, Utilities, Rent, and Nutrition Education, Shelter); ALABAMA ARISE (Statewide legislative network focusing on low income issues); Economic Justice Issues (Low Income Housing and Advocacy, Health Care, Community Development, Jobs Creation); Faith in Community Ministries (Interchurch Forum, Interpreting and Organizing, Bible Study)

Interfaith Mission Service
411-B Holmes Ave., Huntsville, AL 35801 Tel. (205)536-2401
Exec. Min., Rev. Robert Loshuertos
Pres., Rev. Harold Dowler
Major Activities: Food Pantry and Emergency Funds; Interfaith Dialogue; Harvest of Food; Ministry Development; Clergy Luncheon; Workshops; Evaluation of Member Ministries; Response to Community Needs; Information and Referral; Police Department Chapl; Interfaith Understanding

ALASKA

Alaska Christian Conference
3031 LaTouche, Anchorage, AK 99508
Pres., Rev. Wesley Veatch
Vice-Pres., Mrs. Betty Taylor, 1307 Grenac Rd., Fairbanks, AK 99701
Sec., Rev. David Fison, 6800 O'Malley Rd., Anchorage, AK 99516
Treas., Mary Kron, 9650 Arlene Dr., Anchorage, AK 99515

Major Activities: Legislative & Social Concerns; Resources and Continuing Education; New Ecumenical Ministries; Communication; Alcoholism (Education & Prevention); Family Violence (Education & Prevention); Native Issues; Ecumenical/Theological Dialogue; HIV/AIDS Education and Ministry; Criminal Justice

ARIZONA

Arizona Ecumenical Council
4423 N. 24th St., Ste. 750, Phoenix, AZ 85016 Tel. (602)468-3818 Fax (602)955-4540
Admn., Dr. Arlo Nau
Pres., Dr. Carl Wallen, 525 E. Alameda Dr., Tempe, AZ 85282
Major Activities: Donohoe Ecumenical Forum Series; Political Action Team; Legislative Workshop; Arizona Ecumenical Indian Concerns Committee; Biomedical Ethics Project; Mexican/American Border Issues; VISN-TV; AZ Volunteer Organizations; Disaster Relief

ARKANSAS

Arkansas Interfaith Conference
16th & Louisiana, P.O. Box 164073, Little Rock, AR 72216 Tel. (501)375-1553
Conf. Exec., Mimi Dortch
Pres., Rev. Bryan Fulwider, P.O. Box 6594, Sherwood, AR 72116
Sec., Joy Greer, 6904 Burton, Little Rock, AR 72204
Treas., Mr. Jim Davis, Box 7239, Little Rock, AR 72217
Major Activities: Task Force on Hunger; Institutional Ministry; Interfaith Executives' Advisory Council; T.V. Awareness; Drug Abuse, Interfaith Relations; Church Women United; IMPACT; AIDS Task Force; Public Schools Committee; Our House-Shelter; Governor's Task Force on Education; Statewide Fair Trial Committee Legislation

CALIFORNIA

California Council of Churches, Office for State Affairs
1300 N. St., Sacramento, CA 95814 Tel. (916)442-5447 Fax (916)442-3036
Exec. Dir., Patricia Whitney-Wise
Major Activities: Monitoring State Legislation; Calif. IMPACT Network; Legislative Principles; Food Policy Advocacy; Family Welfare Issues; Health; Church/State Issues

Council of Churches of Contra Costa County
1543 Sunnyvale Ave., Walnut Creek, CA 94596 Tel. (510)933-6030
Dir., Rev. Machrina L. Blasdell
Chaplains: Rev. Keith Spooner; Rev. Jana L. Johnsen; Rev. Duane Woida; Rev. Harold Wright
Pres., Rev. Shirley Sherrill
Treas., Mr. Bertram Sturm
Major Activities: Institutional Chaplaincies, Community Education

US ECUMENICAL AGENCIES

187

Fresno Metropolitan Ministry

1055 N. Van Ness, Ste. H, Fresno, CA 93728 Tel. (209)485-1416
Exec. Dir., Rev. Walter P. Parry
Admn. Asst., Sandy Sheldon
Pres., Rev. Betty Pingel
Major Activities: Hunger Relief Advocacy; Homelessness, Human Relations and Anti-Racism; Cross Cultural Mental Health; Health Care Advocacy; Public Education Concerns; Environment; Biblical and Theological Education For Laity; Refugee Advocacy;; Ecumenical & Interfaith Celebrations & Cooperation

Interfaith Service Bureau

3720 Folsom Blvd., Sacramento, CA 95816 Tel. (916)456-3815
Exec. Dir., Ron Holehouse
Pres., Rev. Lloyd Hansen
Major Activities: Chaplaincy; Interfaith Food Closet Network; Clergy Concerns Committee; Religious Cable Television; Brown Bag Network (ages 60 & up); Faith in Crisis

Marin Interfaith Council

35 Mitchell Blvd., Ste. 13, San Rafael, CA 94903 Tel. (415)492-1052
Exec. Dir., Rev. Linda Compton
Major Activities: Basic Human Needs—Homelessness; Interfaith Dialogue; Education & Advocacy; Religious Leadership and Values; Community-wide Interfaith Worship Services & Commemorations

Northern California Ecumenical Council

942 Market St., No. 702, San Francisco, CA 94102 Tel. (415)434-0670
Exec. Dir., Rev. Ben Fraticelli
Dir., Nicaragua Interfaith Committee for Action, Janine Chagoya
Dir., Refugee Community Programs, Rod Miller
Vice-Pres., Sydney Brown
Sec., Rev. Phil Lawson
Treas., Rev. Michael Cooper-White
Pres., Rev. Timothy Boeve
Major Activities: Peace with Justice; Faith and Witness; Ministry; Communications

Pacific and Asian American Center for Theology and Strategies (PACTS)

1798 Scenic Ave., Berkeley, CA 94709 Tel. (710)849-0653
Dir., Julia K. Estrella
Pres., Rev. Diana Akiyama
Fin. Sec., Rev. Daniel Maedjaja
Major Activities: Collect and Disseminate Resource Materials; Training Conferences; Public Seminars; Women in Ministry; Human Rights; Racial and Ethnic Minority Concerns; Journal and Newsletter; Sadao Watanabe Calendars; Pacific Ecumenical Forum

Pomona Valley Council of Churches

1753 N. Park Ave., Pomona, CA 91768 Tel. (714)622-3806
Pres., Rev. Jonathan Glass
Exec. Dir., Ms. Pat Irish
Sec., Ms. Becky Ewing

Treas., Ms. Dorothy Becker
Major Activities: Advocacy and Education for Social Justice; Ecumenical Celebrations; Hunger Advocacy; Emergency Food and Shelter Assistance; Farmer's Market; Affordable Housing

San Diego County Ecumenical Conference

4075 Park Blvd., P.O. Box 3628, San Diego, CA 92163 Tel. (619)296-4557
Exec. Dir., Rev. E. Vaughan Lyons
Dir. of Communication, Rev. Bernard Filmyer, S.J.
Admin., Patricia R. Munley
Pres., Rev. Glenn Allison
Treas., Mr. Joseph Ramsey
Major Activities: Interfaith Shelter Network/Transitional Housing for the Homeless: Emerging Issues; Communications; Faith Order & Witness; Worship & Celebration; Ecumenical Tribute Dinner; Advent Prayer Breakfast; AIDS Chaplaincy Program; Third World Opportunies Seafarer's Mission; "Sunday Focus" TV News; Seminars and Workshops

San Fernando Valley Interfaith Council

10824 Topanga Canyon Blvd., No. 7, Chatsworth, CA 91311 Tel. (818)718-6460 Fax (818)718-8694
Exec. Dir., Barry Smedberg
Pres., Rev. Charlotte Shivvers
Major Activities: Seniors' Multi-Purpose Centers; Nutrition & Services; Meals to the Homebound and Meals on Wheels; "Interfaith Reporter"; Interfaith Relations; Interfaith AIDS Committee; Social Adult Day Care; Hunger/Homelessness; Volunteer Care-Givers; Clergy Gatherings; Food Pantries and Outreach; Peace and Justice, Aging, Hunger; Human Relations

South Coast Ecumenical Council

3326 Magnolia Ave., Long Beach, CA 90806 Tel. (310)595-0268
Exec. Dir., Rev. Ginny Wagener
Interfaith Action for the Aging, Cathy Trott
Centro Shalom, Olivia Herraka
Counseling Ministries, Dr. Lester Kim
Farmers' Markets, Rev. Dale Whitney
Job Center (South Bay), Michelle May
Mid-Cities Help Center, Sherrie Walker
Pres., Rev. M. E. Kilsby
Major Activities: Homeless, Immigration and Refugee Support Services; Interfaith Action for Aging; Farmers' Markets; Hunger Projects; Lay Academy of Religion; Church Athletic Leagues; Community Action; Hunger Walks; Christian Unity Worships; Interreligious Dialogue

Southern California Ecumenical Council

1010 S. Flower, Ste. 403, Los Angeles, CA 90015 Tel. (213)746-7677 Fax (213)748-2432
Exec. Dir., Mr. Charles L. Jones
Admn. Coord., Magaly Sevillano
Pres., Rev Canon D. Bruce MacPherson
Ed. Hope Publishing, Ms. Faith Sand
Dir., Interfaith Hunger Coalition, Ms. Elizabeth Riley

Dir., Interfaith Taskforce on Cent. Am., Ms. Mary Brent Wehrli
Dir., Witness for Peace, ——-
Dir., Peace with Justice, Rev. Ignacio Custuera
Dir., Witness Life, Rev. Al Cowen
Dir., Faith & Order, Rev. Barbara Mudge
Dir., Ecology Task Force, Rev. Gary Herbertson
Dir., L.A.N.D., Mr. Bruce Young
Major Activities: Communications Div. (ECU-MEDIA, Hope Publ. House, ECUNEWS newsletter); Faith and Order (Faith and Order Comm. Celebrations Cmte.); Witness Life (Clergy and Laity Concerned, Disaster Response, Econ. Devel., Ecology Task Force, Interfaith Hunger, LAND); Peace with Justice (Southern Calif. Interfaith Task Force on Central Am.; Southern Calif. Ecumenical Task Force on South Africa; Witness for Peace

The Council of Churches of Santa Clara County
1229 Naglee Ave., San Jose, CA 95126 Tel. (408)297-2660
Exec. Dir., Rev. Hugh Wire
Sec., Mary Jo Cloe
Affordable Housing, Gertrude Welsh
Interpretation & Dev., Paul Burks
Pres., Rev. John Freesemann
Major Activities: Social Education/Action; Ecumenical and Interfaith Witness; Affordable Housing; Emergency Food Supply

The Ecumenical Council of the Pasadena Area Churches
P.O. Box 41125, Pasadena, CA 91114-8125 Tel. (818)797-2402
Exec. Dir., Donald R. Locher
Pres., Lyn Caulfield
Major Activities: Christian Education; Community Worship; Community Concerns; Christian Unity; Ethnic Ministries; Hunger; Peace; Food, Clothing Assistance for the Poor; Emergency Shelter Line

Westside Ecumenical Conference
P.O. Box 1402, Santa Monica, CA 90406 Tel. (213)394-1518
Exec. Dir., Rev. Gregory Garland
Major Activities: Convalescent Hospital Visiting; Meals on Wheels; Community Religious Services; Convalescent Hospital Chaplaincy; Shelter Coordinator

COLORADO

Colorado Council of Churches
1370 Pennsylvania, Ste. 100, Denver, CO 80203-2476 Tel. (303)861-1884 Fax (303)861-1884
Pres., Rev. William Crowl
Exec. Dir., Rev. Gilbert Horn
Major Activities: Ecumenical Witness and Religious Dialogue; Institutional Ministries; Human Needs and Economic Issues (Includes Homelessness, Migrant Ministry, Justice in the Workplace); World Peace and Global Affairs; Communication, Media and the Arts; Interfaith Child Care Network

Interfaith Council of Boulder
2650 Table Mesa Dr., Boulder, CO 80303 Tel. (303)499-5611
Exec. Dir., Ms. Marsha Caplan
Major Activities: Interfaith Dialogue and Programs; Thanksgiving Worship Services; Food for the Hungry; Share-A-Gift; Monthly Newsletter

CONNECTICUT

Association of Religious Communities
213 Main St., Danbury, CT 06810 Tel. (203)792-9450
Exec. Dir., Samuel E. Deibler, Jr.
Pres., Rev. Mary Lou Howson
Major Activities: Refugee Resettlement, Family Counseling; Family Violence Prevention; Affordable Housing

Center City Churches
170 Main St., Hartford, CT 06106 Tel. (203)728-3201
Exec. Dir., Paul C. Christie
Pres., Rev. Charlotte Lohrenz
Sec., Suzanne Jacobson
Treas., Peter Grant
Major Activities: Aging; Social services; Youth and Community Resources; Tutorial Program; Food Pantry; Community Mental Health; Indigent; Advocacy; AIDS Residence; Energy Bank

Christian Community Action
98 S. Main St., South Norwalk, CT 06854 Tel. (203)854-1811
Dir., Jacquelyn P. Miller
Major Activities: Emergency Food Program; Used Furniture & Clothing; Loans for Rent, Security, and Fuel

Christian Community Action
168 Davenport Ave., New Haven, CT 06519
Exec. Dir., The Rev. Bonita Grubbs
Major Activities: Emergency Food Program; Used Furniture & Clothing; Loans for Rent, Security, & Fuel; Emergency Housing for Families; Advocacy

Christian Conference of Connecticut (CHRISCON)
60 Lorraine St., Hartford, CT 06105 Tel. (203)236-4281 Fax (203)236-9977
Exec. Dir., Rev. Stephen J. Sidorak, Jr.
Exec. Asst., Sharon Anderson
Admn. Asst., Mildred Robinson
Pres., Rev. Geroge B. Elia
Vice-Pres., Ms. Elisabeth C. Miller
Sec., Rev Walter M. Elwood
Treas., Mr. Thomas F. Sarubbi
Major Activities: Communications; Institutional Ministries; Conn. Bible Society; Conn. Council on Alcohol Problems; Ecumenical Forum; Faith & Order; Social Concerns; Public Policy

Council of Churches and Synagogues of Lower Fairfield County
628 Main St., Stamford, CT 06901 Tel. (203)348-2800

Exec. Dir., Rev. Dr. Brenda J. Stiers
Program Assoc., Deborah Goldberg
Program Assoc., Terry Andrews
Communications, Sally Bassler
Hospital Chaplain, Rev. William Scott
Pres., Rev. Ralph Ahlberg
Treas., Don Rider
Major Activities: Prison Visitation; Senior Neighborhood Support Services; Ecumenical Services; Interfaith Dialogue; Food Bank; Fuel Assistance; Interfaith AIDS Ministry; Elderly Visitation Programs; Adopt-A-House; Friendship House; Homeless Planning

Council of Churches of Greater Bridgeport, Inc.
126 Washington Ave., Bridgeport, CT 06604 Tel. (203)334-1121
Exec. Dir., Rev. John S. Kidd
Pres., Rev. Don Studer
Sec., Mrs. Dorothy Allsop
Treas., Thomas Holloway
Major Activities: Youth in Crisis; Youth Shelter; Criminal Justice; Hospital, Nursing Home and Jail Ministries; Local Hunger; Ecumenical Relations, Prayer and Celebration; Covenantal Ministries

Manchester Area Conference of Churches
736 East Middle Tpke., P.O. Box 773, Manchester, CT 06040 Tel. (203)649-2093
Exec. Dir., Christina B. Edelwich
Dir., Dept. of Sheltering Ministries, Denise Cabrana
Dir., Dept. of Human Needs, Elizabeth Harlow
Dir., Project Reentry, Joseph M. Piescik
Pres., Rev. Dr. Bill Scott
Treas., Florence Noyes
Major Activities: Provision of Basic Needs (Food, Fuel, Clothing, Furniture); Emergency Aid Assistance; Emergency Shelter; Soup Kitchen; Reentry Assistance to Ex-Offenders; Pastoral Care in Local Institutions; Interfaith Day Camp; Advocacy for the Poor; Ecumenical Education and Worship

New Britain Area Conference of Churches (NEWBRACC)
19 Chestnut St., New Britain, CT 06051 Tel. (203)229-3751
Exec. Minister, Rev. Dr. David D. Mellon
Pastoral Care/Chaplaincy, Rev. Susan Gregory-Davis
Pastoral Care/Chaplaincy, Rev. Will Baumgartner
Pres., Joanne Dimauro-Staves
Treas., Margaret Fletcher
Major Activities: Worship; Social Concerns; Emergency Food Bank Support; Communications-Mass Media; Hospital and Nursing Home Chaplaincy; Elderly Programming; Homelessness and Hunger Programs; Telephone Ministry; Urban Sisters Center; Thanksgiving Vou

The Capitol Region Conference of Churches
30 Arbor St., Hartford, CT 06106 Tel. (203)236-1295
Exec. Dir., Rev. Roger W. Floyd
Dir. Pastoral Care & Training, Rev. John Swift

Dir. Social Concerns, Rev. William Watson
Dir. Aging Project, Rev. Robert Feldmann
Community Organizer, Mr. Joseph Wasserman
Educ. Advocate, Ms. Annette Carter
Hartford Correctional Center Chaplain, Rev. Raymond Sailor
Broadcast Ministry Consultant, Ivor T. Hugh
Pres., Rev. King T. Hayes
Major Activities: Organizing for Peace and Justice; Aging; Legislative Action; Cooperative Broadcast Ministry; Ecumenical Cooperation; Interfaith Reconciliation; Chaplaincies; Affordable Housing; Low-Income Senior Empowerment; Anti-Racism Education

The Downtown Cooperative Ministry in New Haven
57 Olive St., New Haven, CT 06511 Tel. (203)776-9526
Coord., Rev. Samuel N. Slie
Co-Pres., Rev. Kate Latimer, 343 Litchfield Turnpike, Bethany, CT 06525
Co-Pres., Rev. Florestine Taylor, 485 George St., Apt. 1, New Haven, CT 06511
Treas., Murray Harrison, 264 Curtis St., Meriden, CT 06450
Major Activities: Mission to Poor and Dispossessed; Criminal Justice; Elderly; Sheltering Homeless; Soup Kitchen; Low Income Housing; AIDS Residence

Waterbury Area Council of Churches
24 Central Ave., Waterbury, CT 06702 Tel. (203)756-7831
Coord., Mrs. Virginia B. Tillson
Admn. Asst., Susan Girdwood
Pres., Rev. Peter Marsden
Major Activities: Emergency Food Program; Emergency Fuel Program; Soup Kitchens; Ecumenical Worship; Christmas Toy Sale

DELAWARE

The Christian Council of Delaware and Maryland's Eastern Shore
1626 N. Union St., Wilmington, DE 19806 Tel. (302)655-6151
Admin. Sec., Mrs. Judith G. Berry
Interfaith Resource Center, Dir., Mrs. Elaine B. Stout
Pres., Rev. Msgr. Paul J. Schierse, 10 Old Church Rd., Greenville, DE 19807 Tel. (302)658-7017
Major Activities: Facilitates the work of member denominations in shared ministry, specifically public policy, faith and order, and religious education. Supports local ecumenical efforts.

DISTRICT OF COLUMBIA

Interfaith Conference of Metropolitan Washington
1419 V St., NW, Washington, DC 20009 Tel. (202)234-6300
Exec. Dir, Rev. Dr. Clark Lobenstine
Ofc. Mgr., Ms. Kadija Ash
Staff Assoc., Ms. Amy J. Nelson Kehret
Sec., Najla Robinson
Pres., Rabbi Andrew Baker

1st Vice Pres., Bishop J. Clinton Hoggard
Vice Pres., Elder Raul McQuivey
Vice Pres., Dr. Ibrahim M. Fofanah
Vice Pres., James Cardinal Hickey
Vice Pres., Dr. Amrit Kaur
Sec., Rev. John O'Conner, SJ
Treas., Mr. Harminder Singh Jassal
Major Activities: Interfaith Dialogue; Interfaith Concert; Racial and Ethnic Polarization; Drugs; AIDS; Hunger; Homelessness

FLORIDA

Christian Service Center for Central Florida, Inc.

808 West Central Blvd., Orlando, FL 32805-1809 Tel. (407)425-2523
Exec. Dir., Dr. Patrick J. Powers
Assoc. Dir, Terry Laugherty
Dir. Family Emergency Services, Andrea Evans
Dir. Marriage & Family Therapy Center, Dr. Gloria Lobnitz
Dir. Daily Bread, Rev. James Blount
Dir. Alzheimers Respite, Mary Ellen Ort-Marvin
Dir. Fresh Start, Rev. Fred Robinson
Dir. of Mktg., Margaret Ruffier-Farris
Pres., Robert Bryan
Pres.-Elect, W. Marvin Hardy, III
Treas., Terry Bitner
Sec., Barbara Lehman
Major Activities: Provision of Basic Needs (food, clothing, shelter); Emergency Assistance; Professional Counseling. Noon-time Meals; Sunday Church Services at Walt Disney World; Collection and Distribution of Used Clothing; Shelter for Homeless; Training for Homeless; Respite for caregivers of Alzheimers

Florida Council of Churches

924 N. Magnolia Ave., Ste. 236, Orlando, FL 32803 Tel. (407)839-3454 Fax (407)246-0019
Exec. Dir., Walter F. Horlander
Admn. Asst., Mrs. Kay Stewart
Staff Assoc., Refugee Services, Orlando Offc., Joyce L. Voorhees
Staff Assoc., Refugee Services, Tallahassee Offc., Mary Jane Barabash
Staff Assoc., Disaster Response, William Nix
Staff Assoc., Program Development, Richard Walker
Assoc. for Haitian Issues, Jean Claude Picard
Major Activities: Faith and Order; Education and Renewal; Evangelism and Mission; Justice and Peace Refugee Resettlement; Disaster Response; Legislation & Public Policy

GEORGIA

Christian Council of Metropolitan Atlanta

465 Boulevard, S.E., Atlanta, GA 30312 Tel. (404)622-2235 Fax (404)627-6626
Exec. Dir., Dr. Robert P. Reno
Assoc. Dir., Mr. Neal P. Ponder, Jr.
Pres., Very Rev. John C. Sanders
Treas., Ms. June B. Debatin

Major Activities: Refugee Services; Emergency Assistance; Voluntary Service; Employment; Racism; Homeless; Ecumenical and Interreligious Events; Computerized Action-Information Ministry and Human Needs Network; Interchurch Ministry Planning; Persons with Handicapping Conditions; Women's Concerns; Seminary Student Internship Program

Georgia Christian Council

P.O. Box 7193, Macon, GA 31209 Tel. (912)474-3906
Exec. Dir., F. Thomas Scholl, Jr.
Pres., David L. Alexander, 2370 Vineville Ave., Macon, GA 31104 Tel. (912)743-8649
Treas., Rev. Gordon Reinersten, 3264 Northside Pkwy. NW, Atlanta, GA 30327
Major Activities: Local Ecumenical Support and Resourcing; Legislation (GRAIN); Rural Development; Racial Justice; Networking for Migrant Coalition and Aging Coalition

HAWAII

Hawaii Council of Churches

1300 Kailua Rd., B-1, Kailua, HI 96734 Tel. (808)263-9788 Fax (808)262-8915
Exec. Dir., Ms. Patricia Mumford
Major Activities: Laity and Clergy Education; Ecumenical Worship; Religious Art, Music, Drama; Legislative Concerns; Interfaith TV and Radio Ministry; Social Action; AIDS Education; Advocacy for Peace with Justice

IDAHO

The Regional Council for Christian Ministry, Inc.

P.O. Box 2236, Idaho Falls, ID 83403 Tel. (208)524-9935
Exec. Sec., Wendy Schoonmaker
Major Activities: Island Park Ministry; Community Food Bank; Community Observances; Community Information and Referral Service; F.I.S.H.

ILLINOIS

Churches United of the Quad City Area

630 - 9th St., Rock Island, IL 61201 Tel. (309)786-6494
Exec. Dir., ———-
Assoc. Exec. Dir., Sheila D. Fitts
Pres., The Very Rev. John L. Hall
Treas., Dortha Hoy
Major Activities: Jail Ministry; Hunger Projects; Minority Enablement; Criminal Justice; Radio-TV; Peace; Local Church Development

Contact Ministries of Springfield

401 E. Washington, Springfield, IL 62701 Tel. (217)753-3939
Dir., Ethel Butcher
Major Activities: Information; Referral and Advocacy; Ecumenical Coordination; Low Income Housing Referral; Food Pantry Coordination; Low Income Budget Counseling; 24 hours on call

Evanston Ecumenical Action Council

P.O. Box 1414, Evanston, IL 60204 Tel. (708)475-1150

Exec. Dir., Tecla Sund Reklau

Dir. Hospitality Cntr. for the Homeless, Patricia Johnson

Pres., Charles Underwood

Treas., Ann C. Campbell

Major Activities: Interchurch Communication and Education; Peace and Justice Ministries; Coordinated Social Action; Soup Kitchens; Multi-Purpose Hospitality Center for the Homeless; Worship and Renewal

Greater Chicago Broadcast Ministries

112 E. Chestnut St., Chicago, IL 60611-2014 Tel. (312)988-9001

Chairman of Development Committee, David Hardin

Exec. Dir., Lydia Talbot

Admn. Asst., Margaret Early

Major Activities: Television, Cable, Interfaith/Ecumenical Development; Social/Justice Concerns

Illinois Conference of Churches

615 S. 5th St., Springfield, IL 62703 Tel. (217)544-3423

Gen. Sec., Rev. Dr. Carol M. Worthing

Dir., IMPACT, Rev. Dr. George Ogle

Dir., Farm Worker Ministry, Ms. Olgha Sandman, 935 Curtiss, Rm. 8, Downers Grove, IL 60515 Tel. (312) 964-7474

Dir., Refugee & Immigration Prog., Ms. Mary Caroline Dana, Tel. (217)522-9942

Supervisor Chicago Refugee Services Ofc., Ms. May Campbell, 2320 W. Peterson, Ste. 505, Chicago, IL 60659 Tel. (312)764-0008

Dir., Domestic Violence Prog., Mrs. Jacqueline Clingan

Dir., Human Services Ministry, ——

Pres., Dr. David MacDonna, 1360 W. Main, Decatur, IL 62521 Tel. (217)423-1396

Treas., Rev. Daniel Holland, P.O. Box 3786, Springfield, IL 62708 Tel. (217)525-1386

Major Activities: Migrant & Farm Worker Ministry; Chaplaincy in Institutions; Governmental Concerns and Illinois Impact; Ecumenical Courier; Ministry to Developmentally Disabled; Ministry with Aging;; Immigration and Refugee Resettlement; Domestic Violence

Oak Park-River Forest Community of Congregations

324 N. Oak Park Ave., Oak Park, IL 60302

Exec. Sec., D. Laini Zinn

Vice-Pres., Mrs. Kathleen Lobato-Martinez

Pres., Rev. Thomas Cross

Major Activities: Community Affairs; Ecumenical/Interfaith Affairs; Youth Education; Food Pantry; Senior Citizens Worship Services; Interfaith Thanksgiving Services; Good Friday Services; UNICEF Children's Fund Drive; ASSIST (Network); Blood Drive; Literacy Training; Christian Unity Week Pulpit Exchange; CROP/CWS Hunger Walkathon; Austin Community Table (feeding hungry); Work with Homeless Commission; Unemployed Task Force

Peoria Friendship House of Christian Service

800 N.E. Madison Ave., Peoria, IL 61603 Tel. (309)671-5200

Exec. Dir., Rev. Cheryl F. Dudley

Dir. of Community Dev., Ms. Nora Vogt

Dir. of Prog. & Spiritual Nurture, Rev. Beth Hennessey

Pres. of Board, Ms. Nora Sullivan

Major Activities: Children's after-school activities; Teen Programs; Parenting Groups; Recreational Leagues; Senior Citizens Activities; Emergency Food/Clothing Distribution; Emergency Payments for prescriptions, utilities, and transportation cost; Community/Neighborhood Development in Terms of Housing Advocacy, Economic Development, and Grass Roots Community Organizing

The Hyde Park & Kenwood Interfaith Council

1448 East 53rd St., Chicago, IL 60615 Tel. (312)363-1620

Exec. Dir., Mr. Werner H. Heymann

Pres., Rev. Lawrence R. Hamilton

Treas., Ms. Barbara Krell

Major Activities: Interfaith Work; Hunger Projects; Community Development

INDIANA

Christian Ministries of Delaware County

806 W. White River Blvd., Muncie, IN 47303-4868 Tel. (317)288-0601

Exec. Dir., Sallie Maish

Pres., Dr. Thomas Rough

Treas., Jack Carmichael

Major Activities: Migrant Ministry; Christian Education; Feed-the-Baby Program; Youth Ministry at Detention Center; Community Church Festivals; Community Pantry; Community Assistance Fund; CROP Walk; Social Justice; Quality of Homelife

Church Community Services

1703 Benham Ave., Elkhart, IN 46516 Tel. (219)295-3673

Exec. Dir., Mary Jane Carpenter

Major Activities: Advocacy Program, Emergency Housing, Financial Assistance, Transportation, Educational Classes, Food Pantry

Ecumenical Assembly of Bartholomew County Churches

P.O. Box 1421, Love Chapel, 311 Center St., Columbus, IN 47202 Tel. (812)372-9421

Exec. Dir., Marjorie Wilson

Major Activities: Emergency Assistance Fund: FISH (Food and Prescriptions)

Evansville Area Council of Churches, Inc.

414 N.W. Sixth St., Evansville, IN 47708-1332 Tel. (812)425-3524

Exec. Dir., Rev. Joseph N. Peacock

Weekday Supervisor, Ms. Linda M. Schenk

Office Mgr., Ms. Barbara Gaisser

Pres., Rev. Conrad Grosenick

Sec., The Rev. Dennis Hollinger-Laut
Fin. Chpsn., Rev. Will Jewsbury
Major Activities: Christian Education; Community Responsibility & Service; Public Relations; Interpretation; Church Women United; Institutional Ministries; Interfaith Dialogue; Ethics in care of the Earth; Churches in support of public education; Disaster preparedness for churches

Indiana Council of Churches

1100 W. 42nd St., Rm. 225, Indianapolis, IN 46208-3383 Tel. (317)923-3674 Fax (317)924-4859
Exec. Dir., Rev. Scott J. Schiesswohl
Program Dir. & Legislative Assoc., Rev. Karen S. Smith
Refugee Resettlement Facilitator, Ms. Sylvia J. Robles
Peace with Justice Facilitator, Rev. John E. Gaus
Pres., Mrs. Edith M. Jones
Vice Pres., Bishop Ralph A. Kempski
Sec., Rev. Bryon Rose
Treas., Mr. David F. Rees
Major Activities: Educational Ministries; Communications and Public Media; Social Ministries; Peace and Justice; Farmworker Ministries; Institutional Ministries; Ecumenical Concerns; Indiana Rural Justice Network; Refugee Resettlement; NAESNET; IMPACT

Indiana Interreligious Commission on Human Equality

1100 W. 42nd St., Ste. 320, Indianapolis, IN 46208 Tel. (317)924-4226 Fax (317)924-4859
Pres., Rev. Thomas J. Murphy
Treas., Dr. Ralph Quellhorst
Major Activities: Human Rights; Anti-Racism Training; Racism/Sexism Inventory; Cultural and Religious Intolerance; South Africa Consultations; Interfaith Dialogue

Interfaith Community Council, Inc.

702 E. Market St., New Albany, IN 47150 Tel. (812)948-9248
Exec. Dir., Rev. Dr. George Venable Beury
Dir. of Finance, Mary Ann Sodrel
Dir., Child Dev. Center, Carol Welsh
Dir., Deaf Relay, Susan Wagner
Dir., Hedden House, Hope LaChance
Dir., RSVP, Matie Watts
Chpsn., Ms. Jane Harmon
Treas., Dick Peterson
Major Activities: Child Development Center; Deaf Relay Teletype Center; Emergency Assistance; Hedden House (Half Way Home for Recovering Alcoholic Women); Retired Senior Volunteer Program; New Clothing and Toy Drives; Convalescent Sitter & Mother's Aides; Senior Day College; Emergency Food Distribution; Homeless Prevention

Lafayette Urban Ministry

12 North 8th St., Lafayette, IN 47901 Tel. (317)423-2691
Dir., Joseph Micon
Advocate Coord., Jean Stearns
Public Policy Coord., Jo Johannsan
Pres., Lee Ann Duffy
Major Activities: Social Justice Ministries With and Among the Poor

The Associated Churches of Fort Wayne & Allen County, Inc.

602 E. Wayne St., Fort Wayne, IN 46802 Tel. (219)422-3528
Exec. Pastor, Rev. Vernon R. Graham
Sec., Pat Arthur
Foodbank Staff: Ellen Graham; Rev. Ed. Pease
WRE Coord., Ruth Proctor
Prog. Development, Ellen Graham
Pres., Marilyn Rousseau, 3228 Glencairn Dr., Fort Wayne, IN 46815
Treas., Jean Streicher, 436 Downing Avenue, Fort Wayne, IN 46807
Major Activities: Weekday Religious Ed.; Radio & TV; Church Clusters; Church and Society Commission; Ed. for Christian Life Division; Clergy United for Action; Faith and Order Commission; Christian Ed.; Widowed-to-Widowed; CROP; Campus Ministry; Feeding the Babies; Food Bank System; Peace Education; Welfare Reform; Endowment Development; Habitat for Humanity; Child Care Advocacy; Project 25; Ecumenical Dialogue; Feeding Children; Vincent House (Homeless); A Learning Journey (Literacy); Reaching Out in Love

The Church Federation of Greater Indianapolis, Inc.

1100 W. 42nd St., Ste. 345, Indianapolis, IN 46208 Tel. (317)926-5371
Exec. Dir., Rev. C. Bruce Naylor
Dir., Social Ministries, James E. Morgan, III
Dir., Development, Carol J. Blinzinger
Dir., Communications, Donald M. Frick
Pres., Rev. Darin Moore
Treas., William Bell
Major Activities: Celebrations and Unity; Ministries in Media; Ministries in Specialized Settings; Ministries in Society; Education and Training

United Religious Community of St. Joseph County

2015 Western Ave., South Bend, IN 46629 Tel. (219)282-2397
Exec. Dir., Dr. James J. Fisko
Pres., Robert Curtis
Coord., State Prison Visitation, Sr. Susan Kinzele, CSC
Coord. Victim Offender Reconciliation Prog. (VORP), Ruth Andrews
Coord., Volunteer Advocacy Project, Sara Goetz
Major Activities: Religious Understanding; Social and Pastoral Ministries; Congregational Ministries

West Central Neighborhood Ministry, Inc.

1210 Broadway, Fort Wayne, IN 46802-3304 Tel. (219)422-9319
Exec. Dir., Andrea S. Thomas
Ofc. Mgr., Frances Bruce
Food Bank Coord., Doras Bailey
Youth Dir., Gary Cobb
Independent Living Dir., Ranelle Melton
Senior Citizens Dir., Gayle Mann

Major Activities: After-school tutoring, crafts, recreation; Teen Drop-In Center; Church League Basketball; Summer Day Camp; Summer Overnight Camps; Information and Referral Services; Food Pantry; Nutrition Program for Senior Citizens; Educational, Recreational, and Field Trip Activities for Senior Citizens; Homemaker and Handyperson Services for Homebound Senior Citizens; Vocational Development for Teens/Young Adults

IOWA

Churches United, Inc.
222 29th St. Drive S.E., Cedar Rapids, IA 52403 Tel. (319)366-7163

Admn. Sec., Mrs. Marcey Luxa

Pres., Rev. Lloyd Brockmeyer

Treas., Christian Davies, 221 3rd Ave. SE, Town Center, Ste. 300, Cedar Rapids, IA 52403

Major Activities: Community Food Bank; LEAF (Local Emergency Assistance Fund; CROP; Co-operative Low Income Store (ONE Store); Community Information and Referral; Jail Chaplaincy; World Hunger; Nursing Home Ministry; Radio and TV Ministry; Ecumenical City-Wide Celebrations

Des Moines Area Religious Council
3816 - 36th St., Des Moines, IA 50310 Tel. (515)277-6969

Exec. Dir., Forrest Harms

Pres., David Bear

Treas., Bill McGill

Major Activities: Outreach and Nurture; Education; Social Concerns; Mission; Worship; Emergency Food Pantry; Ministry to Widowed; Child Care Assistance

Ecumenical Ministries of Iowa (EMI)
3816 - 36th St., Ste. 202, Des Moines, IA 50310 Tel. (515)255-5905

Admn. Coord., Wendy E. Hanson Wagner

Major Activities: A forum dialogue related to theological faith issues and social concerns; Opportunity to develop responses to discern needs and join in common mission; Communication, Global, Justice and Unity

KANSAS

Cross-Lines Cooperative Council
1620 S. 37th St., Kansas City, KS 66106 Tel. (913)432-5497 Fax None

Exec. Dir., David Schmidt Shulman

Dir. of Programs, Rev. Robert L. Moore

Board Pres., Larry Leighton

Board Treas., Phil Woodworth

Major Activities: Emergency Assistance; Family Support Advocacy; Crisis Heating/Plumbing Repair; Thrift Store; Workcamp Experiences; Adult Education (GED and Basic English Literacy Skills); School Supplies (served 550 student in August/September 1991); Christmas Store (550 families registered to shop December 1991); Institute for Poverty and Empowerment Studies (Education on poverty for the non-poor); Business Incubator (Entrepeneurial assistance for the poor)

Inter-Faith Ministries—Wichita
334 N. Topeka, Wichita, KS 67202-2410 Tel. (316)264-9303 Fax (316)264-2233

Exec. Dir., Rev. Sam Muyskens

Ofc. Mgr., Virginia Courtright

Dir. of Community Min., Patrick Cameron

Community Min., Ann Gay-Bishop

Dir., Inter-Faith Inn (Homeless Shelter), Sandy Swank

Dir., Operation Holiday, Sally Dewey

Pres., Lois Ruby

Major Activities: Communications; Urban Education; Inter-religious Understanding; Community Needs and Issues; Theology and Worship; Hunger; Advocacy

Kansas Ecumenical Ministries
3615 S.W. 29th St., Topeka, KS 66614 Tel. (913)272-9531

Exec. Dir., Rev. Alden Hickman

Pres., Rev. John Tomlonson

Vice-Pres., Mrs. Winnie Crapson

Sec., Rev. George Harvey

Treas., Rev. Kathy Timpany

Rural Life Worker, Del Jacobsen

Major Activities: Legislative Activities; Program Facilitation and Coordination; World Hunger; Higher Education Concerns; Interfaith Rural Life Committee; Education; Mother-to-Mother Program; Peacemaking

KENTUCKY

Fern Creek/Highview United Ministries
P.O. Box 91372, Louisvlle, KY 40291 Tel. (502)239-4967

Exec. Dir., Darla A. Bailey

Pres., Elizabeth A. Sneed

Major Activities: Ecumenically supported social service agency providing services to the community, including Emergency Financial Assistance, Food/Clothes Closet, Health Aid Equipment Loans, Information/Referral, Advocacy, Monthly Blood-Pressure Checks; Holiday Programs, Adult Day-Care Program, Life Skills Training, and Intensive Care Management

Hazard-Perry County Community Ministries, Inc.
P.O. Box 1506, Hazard, KY 41701 Tel. (606)436-5043

Exec. Dir., Ms. Gerry Feamster-Martin

Chpsn., Rev. Terry Reffett

Treas., Mrs. Margaret Adams

Major Activities: Food Pantry/Crisis Aid Program; Day Care; Summer Day Camp; After-school Program; Christmas Tree

Highlands Community Ministries

1140 Cherokee Rd., Louisville, KY 40204 Tel. (502)451-3695
Exec. Dir., Stan Esterle
Pres., Rev. Dick Teaford
Vice-Pres., Rev. Jack Oliver
Sec./Treas., Sandy Hoover
Major Activities: Welfare Assistance; Day Care; Counseling with Youth, Parents and Adults; Adult Day Care; Social Services for Elderly; Housing for Elderly and Handicapped; Ecumenical Programs; Community Classes; Activities for Children; Neighborhood and Business

Kentuckiana Interfaith Community

1115 South 4th St., Louisville, KY 40203 Tel. (502)587-6265
Exec. Dir., Rev. Dr. Gregory C. Wingenbach
Pres., Rev. Deacon David Kannapell
Vice-Pres., Rev. Dr. Curtis Miller
Sec., Ms. Sara Klein Wagner
Treas., Rev. Wallace Garner
Admn. Sec., Mrs. Sue Weatherford
Major Activities: Ecumenical Ministries, Consensus Advocacy; Inter-Christian/Interfaith dialogue; Interpastoral/Ministry Support; Religion & Race, Education & Civil Rights Forums; Network for Neighborhood-based Community Ministries; "Community *Winterhelp*"; LUAH/Hunger & Justice Concerns Commission; "Intermedia": Radio & TV, HORIZON Bimonthly Newspaper; Ecumenical/Interfaith Research & Planning; Institutional Chaplaincy & Ministry Support; Liaison, Networking with Seminaries & Religious-affiliated Colleges

Kentucky Council of Churches

1039 Goodwin Dr., Lexington, KY 40505 Tel. (606)253-3027 Fax (606)231-5028
Exec. Dir., Rev. Nancy Jo Kemper
Coord., Disaster Recovery Prog., C. Nelson Hostetter
Ed., INTERCOM, Dr. David Berg
Pres., Rev. William Brown, P.O. Box 12350, Lexington, KY 40582-2350
Major Activities: Christian Unity; Hunger; Church and Government; Disaster Response; Peace Issues; Racism; Health Care Issues; Local Ecumenism; Rural Land/Farm Issues

Northern Kentucky Interfaith Commission, Inc.

601 Greenup St., Covington, KY 41011 Tel. (606)581-2237
Exec. Dir., Rev. William C. Neuroth
Major Activities: Understanding faith traditions; meeting spiritual and human needs in area

Paducah Cooperative Ministry

1359 S. 6th St., Paducah, KY 42003 Tel. (502)442-6795
Dir., Jo Ann Ross
Chpsn., Rev. Brian Cope
Major Activities: The P.C.M. is a cooperative venture of 36 local churches and six denominational judicatories, serving the community's hungry, elderly, poor, prisoners, homeless, handicapped and undereducated

South East Associated Ministries (SEAM)

2125 Goldsmith Ln., Louisville, KY 40218 Tel. (502)454-0380
Exec. Dir., Mary Beth Helton
Dir., Life Skills Center, Martha Hinson
Dir., Volunteers, ——-
Dir., Youth Services, John Hamric
Pres., Rob Nash
Treas., Joe Hays
Major Activities: Emergency Food and Financial Assistance; Life Skills Center (Programs of Prevention and Self-Sufficiency Through Education, Empowerment, Support Groups, etc.); Juvenile Court Diversion Program; Bloodmobile; Ecumenical Education and Worship; Family Counseling

South Louisville Community Ministries

801 Camden Ave., Louisville, KY 40215 Tel. (502)367-6445
Exec. Dir., J. Michael Jupin
Bd. Chair., Rev. Levan Luker
Bd. Vice-Chair., Rev. Lloyd Spencer
Bd. Treas., Eugene Wells
Major Activities: Food, Clothing & Financial Assistance; Home Delivered Meals, Transportation, Refugee Resettlement; Ecumenical Worship; Juvenile Diversion Program; Affordable Housing; Adult Day Care

St. Matthews Area Ministries

309 Browns La., Louisville, KY 40207 Tel. (502)893-0205
Exec. Dir., Rev. A. David Bos
Dir., Youth Services, Liza Murray
Dir., Emergency Fin. Assis., Linda Leeser
Dir., After-School Care Centers, Janet Hennessey
Dir. of Volunteers, Karen DeFazio
Major Activities: After-School Care; Youth Services; Interchurch Worship and Education; Emergency Financial Assistance

LOUISANA

Louisiana Interchurch Conference

440 N. Foster Dr., Ste. 106, Baton Rouge, LA 70806 Tel. (504)924-0213
Exec. Dir., The Very Rev. C. Dana Krutz
Pres., The Rt. Rev. James B. Brown
Major Activities: Ministries to Aging; Prison Reform; Liason with State Agencies; Ecumenical Dialogue; Institutional Chaplains; Racism

Greater Baton Rouge Federation of Churches and Synagogues

P.O. Box 626, Baton Rouge, LA 70821 Tel. (504)356-6985
Exec. Dir., Rev. Jeff Day
Admn. Asst., Mrs. Marion Zachary
Pres., Dr. William Staats
Vice-Pres., Mr. Richard K. Goldberger
Treas., Mr. E. Cole Thornton
Major Activities: Combating Hunger; Housing (Helpers for Housing); Lay Academy of Religion (training); Interfaith Relations

Greater New Orleans Federation of Churches

4545 Magnolia St., #206, New Orleans, LA 70115 Tel. (504)897-4488

Major Activities: Radio-TV Programs; Central Business District Ministries; Regional Suburban Network; Leadership Training; Senior Citizens; Social Action; Public Information; Religious Census and Survey; Literacy; Counseling Coordination; Cable T.V. Channel; Emergency

MAINE

Maine Council of Churches

15 Pleasant Ave., Portland, ME 04103 Tel. (207)772-1918

Pres., Rev. David Glusker

Exec. Dir., Thomas C. Ewell

Major Activities: Legislative Issues; Criminal Justice; Concern for the Vulnerable; Environmental Issues

MARYLAND

Central Maryland Ecumenical Council

Cathedral House, 4 E. University Pkwy., Baltimore, MD 21218 Tel. (301)467-6194

Exec. Dir., The Rev. Roy W. Cole, III

Pres., The Rev. Barbara Sands

Major Activities: Interchurch Communicationis and Collaboration; Information Systems; Ecumenical Relations; Urban Mission and Advocacy; Staff Judicatory Leadership Council; Commission on Dialogue; Commission on Church & Society; Commission on Admin. & Dev.; Annual Ecumenical Choral Concert; Annual Ecumenical Service

Community Ministries of Rockville

114 West Montgomery Ave., Rockville, MD 20850 Tel. (301)762-8682

Exec. Dir., Mansfield M. Kaseman

Assoc. Dir., Hune Allred

Major Activities: Shelter Care; Emergency Assistance; Elderly Home Care; Affordable Housing; Political Advocacy

Community Ministry of Montgomery County

114 West Montgomery Ave., Rockville, MD 20850 Tel. (301)762-8682 Fax (301)762-2939

Exec. Dir., Lincoln S. Dring, Jr.

Major Activities: Interfaith Clothing Center; Grant Assistance Program; Manna Food Center; The Advocacy Function; Thanksgiving in February; Information and Referral Services; Friends in Action; The Thanksgiving Hunger Drive; Montgomery Habitat for Humanity

MASSACHUSETTS

Attleboro Area Council of Churches, Inc.

505 N. Main St., Attleboro, MA 02703 Tel. (508)222-2933

Exec. Dir., Carolyn L. Bronkar

Admn. Sec., Joan H. Lindstrom

Ofc. Asst., Roberta Kohler

Hosp. Chpln., Rev. Linnea Prefontaine

Pres., Rev. Carole Baker, P.O. Box 1319, Attleboro Falls, MA 02760

Treas., David Quinlan, 20 Everett St., Plainville, MA 02762

Major Activities: Hospital Chaplaincy; Radio Ministry; Personal Growth/Skill Workshops; Ecumenical Worship; Media Resource Center; Referral Center; Communications/Publications; Community Social Action; Food'n Friends Kitchens; Emergency Food and Shelter Fund; Nursing Home Volunteer Visitation Program

Cooperative Metropolitan Ministries

474 Centre St., Newton, MA 02158 Tel. (617)244-3650

Exec. Dir., Claire Kashuck

Cncl. Chpsn., Dani Danzig

Board Pres., Carolyn Panasevich

Treas., Archie Morrison

Sec., Mary Morrison

Major Activities: Low Income, Elderly, Affordable Housing; Legislative Advocacy; Hunger; Networking; Volunteerism; Publication on Elder Housing Alternatives

Council of Churches of Greater Springfield

152 Sumner Ave., Springfield, MA 01108 Tel. (413)733-2149

Exec. Dir., Rev. Ann Geer

Dir. of Community Min., Mr. Arthur Serota, Esq.

Dir., Nursing Home Min., Patrick McMahon

Pres., The Rev. Dr. Rolf Hedburg

Treas., Mr. Jerre Hoffman

Major Activities: Christian Education Resource Center; Advocacy; Emergency Fuel Fund; Peace and Justice Division; Community Ministry; Visitor Ombudspersons to Nursing Homes; Task Force on Aging; Hospital and Jail Chaplaincies; Pastoral Service; Crisis Counseling; Christian Social Relations; Relief Collections; Ecumenical and Interfaith Relations; Ecumenical Dialogue with Roman Catholic Diocese; Mass Media; Church/Community Projects and Dialog

Greater Lawrence Council of Churches

117A S. Broadway, Lawrence, MA 01843

Major Activities: Ecumenical Worship; Radio Ministry; Hospital and Nursing Home Chaplancy; Church Women United; Afterschool Children's Program; Educational Programs

Inter-Church Council of Greater New Bedford

412 County St., New Bedford, MA 02740 Tel. (508)993-6242

Acting Exec. Min., Rev. Dr. John Douhan

Pres., Rev. Christopher Drew

Treas., William Reed

Major Activities: Pastoral Counseling; Chaplaincy; Housing for Elderly; Urban Affairs; Parent-Child Center; Social Rehabilitation Club

Massachusetts Commission on Christian Unity

82 Luce St., Lowell, MA 01852 Tel. (508)453-5423

Exec. Sec., Rev. K. Gordon White
Major Activities: Faith and Order Dialogue with Church Judicatories

Massachusetts Council of Churches

14 Beacon St., Boston, MA 02108 Tel. (617)532-2771
Exec. Dir., Rev. Diane C. Kessler
Assoc. Dir. for Public Policy, Dr. Ruy Costa
Assoc. Dir., Ecumenical Development, Rev. David A. Anderson
Major Activities: Christian Unity Through Education and Evangelism; Defend Social Justice & Individual Rights; Ecumenical Worship; Services and Resources for Individuals and Churches

The Cape Cod Council of Churches, Inc.

142 Corporation Rd., Hyannis, MA 02601 Tel. (508)775-5073
Exec. Dir., Rev. Ellen C. Chahey
Admn. Asst., Muriel L. Eggers
Pres., Rev. John H. Williams
Chaplain, Cape Cod Hospital, Rev. William Wilcox
Chaplain, Barnstable County Hospital, Elizabeth Stommel
Chaplain, Falmouth Hospital, Rev. Allen Page
Chaplain, House of Correction & Jail, Rev. Thomas Shepherd
Dir., Service Center & Thrift Shop, Joan McCurdy, P.O. Box 125, Dennisport, MA 02639 Tel. (508)394-6361
Asst. to Dir., Service Center & Thrift Shop, Merilyn Lansing
Major Activities: Pastoral Care; Social Concerns; Religious Education; Emergency Distribution of Food, Clothing, Furniture; Referral and Information; Church World Service; Interfaith Relations; Media Presence

Worcester County Ecumenical Council

25 Crescent St., Worcester, MA 01605 Tel. (508)757-8385
Exec. Dir., Rev. Richard A. Hennigar
Program Asst., Richard Monroe
Pres., Rev. Clifford Gerber
Major Activities: Clusters of Churches; Electronic Media; Economic Justice; Youth Ministries; Ecumenical Worship and Dialogue; Interfaith Activities; Nursing Home Chaplaincies; Assistance to Churches; Peace; Hunger Ministries; AIDS Pastoral Care Network; Mental Illness; Group Purchasing Consortium

MICHIGAN

ACCORD—Area Churches Together . . .Serving

312 Capital Ave., NE, Battle Creek, MI 49017 Tel. (616)966-2500
Exec. Dir., Patricia A. Staib
Pres., Rev. David Morton
Vice-Pres./Church, Rev. Charles Sandum
Vice-Pres./Admn., David Lucas
Vice-Pres./Community, Rev. Joseph Bistayi

Major Activities: CROP Walk; Thanksgiving International Student Homestay; Food Closet; Christian Sports; Week of Prayer for Christian Unity; Nursing Home Vesper Services; Ecumenical Worship

Christian Communication Council of Metropolitan Detroit

1300 Mutual Building, 28 W. Adams, Detroit, MI 48226 Tel. (313)962-0340
Exec. Dir., Rev. Edward Willingham
Assoc. Dir., Mrs. Angie Willingham
Media Assoc., Mrs. Tawnya Bender
Prog. Dir., Meals for Shut-ins, Mr. John Simpson
Coord., Summer Feeding Prog., Ms. Sabrina Brentz
Major Activities: Theological and Social Concerns; Ecumenical Worship; Educational Services; Electronic Media; Print Media; Meals for Shut-Ins; Summer Feeding Program

Grand Rapids Area Center for Ecumenism (GRACE)

38 W. Fulton, Grand Rapids, MI 49503 Tel. (616)774-2042
Exec. Dir., Rev. David P. Baak
Prog. Dir., Ms. Betty Zylstra
Major Activities: Hunger Walk; November Hunger and Shelter Awareness Week; Shelter Forum; Aging Committee; AIDS Pastoral Care Network; Clergy Interracial Forum; Annual Week of Prayer for Christian Unity; Ecumenical Eucharist and Pentecost Services, Educational Forums.; Affiliates: ACCESS (All County Churches Emergency Support System); FISH for My People (Transportation); Habitat for Humanity/GR; Grace Notes

Greater Flint Council of Churches

927 Church St., Flint, MI 48502 Tel. (313)238-3691
Major Activities: Christian Education; Christian Unity; Christian Missions; Hospital and Nursing Home Visitors; Church in Society; American Bible Society Materials; Interfaith Dialogue; Church Visitor Exchange Sunday; Directory of Area Faiths and Clergy;; Operation Brush-up; Thanksgiving & Easter Sunrise Services

Michigan Ecumenical Forum

809 Center St., Ste. 7-B, Lansing, MI 48906 Tel. (517)485-4395
Coord./Exec. Dir., Rev. Steven L. Johns-Boehme
Major Activities: Communication and Coordination; at State Level; Support and Development of Network of Regional Ecumenical Fora; Ecumenical Studies; Fellowship and Celebration; Church and Society Issues; Continuing Education

The Jackson County Interfaith Council

425 Oakwood, P.O. Box 156, Clarklake, MI 49234-0156
Exec. Dir., Rev. Loyal H. Wiemer

US ECUMENICAL AGENCIES

197

Major Activities: Chaplaincy at County Institutions and Senior Citizens Residences; Martin L. King, Jr. Day Celebrations; Ecumenical Council Representation; Radio and Television Programs; Food Pantry; Interreligious Events

MINNESOTA

Arrowhead Council of Churches

230 E. Skyline Pkwy., Duluth, MN 55811 Tel. (218)727-5020
Exec. Dir., Joel E. Huenemann
Pres., Tab Baumgartner
Major Activities: Inter-Church Evangelism; Community Concerns; Joint Religious Legislative Coalition; Downtown Ecumenical Good Friday Service; Corrections Chaplaincy; CROP Hunger Walk; Forum for Interfaith Dialogue; Church Women United; Community Seminars

Community Emergency Assistance Program (CEAP)

7231 Brooklyn Blvd., Brooklyn Center, MN 55429 Tel. (612)566-9600 Fax (612)566-9604
Exec. Dir., Edward T. Eide
Major Activities: Provision of Basic Needs (Food, Clothing, Furniture); Emergency Financial Assistance for Shelter; Home Delivered Meals; Chore Services and Homemaking Assistance; Single Parent Loan Program; Volunteer Services

Greater Minneapolis Council of Churches

122 W. Franklin Ave., Rm. 218, Minneapolis, MN 55404 Tel. (612)870-3660 Fax (612)870-3663
Exec. Dir., Rev. Dr. Gary B. Reierson
Assoc. Exec. Dir., Indian Work, Mary Ellen Dumas
Dir., Twin Cities Metropolitan Church Comm., Rev. Sally Hill
Dir., Meals on Wheels, Barbara Green
Dir., Minnesota FoodShare, Rev. Peg Chemberlin
Correctional Chaplain, Rev. Norman Menke
Correctional Chaplain, Rev. Susan Allers Hatlie
Correctional Chaplain, Rev. Thomas Van Leer
Dir., Congregations Concerned for Childre, Carolyn Hendrixson
Dir., Dr. Richard Green Tutoring Program, Rev. Belinda Green
Dir., Metro Paint-A-Thon, Jodi Young
Dir., Chore/Housekeeping Services, DeLaine Brown
Pres., Larry Haeg
Treas., Mike McCarthy
Major Activities: Indian Work (Emergency Assistance, Youth Leadership, Teen Indian Parents Program, and Family Violence Program); Minnesota FoodShare; Metro Paint-A-Thon; Meals on Wheels; Dr. Richard Green Tutoring Program; Congregations Concerned for Children; Correctional Chaplaincy Program; Chore/Housekeeping Services; Education and Celebration; Church Women United

Minnesota Council of Churches

122 W. Franklin Ave., #100, Minneapolis, MN 55404
Dir. of Life & Work, Louis S. Schoen
Dir. of Hispanic Ministry, Carlos Mariani-Rosa
Dir. of Faith & Order, Rev. Molly M. Cox
Dir., Refugee Services, Shannon Bevans
Caseworker, Ge Cheuthang Yang
Case Mgr./Sponsor Developer, Brenda Otterson
Dir. of Indian Concerns, Mary Ann Walt
Dir. of Facilities, Cynthia Darrington-Ottinger
Dir., Twin Cities Metropolitan Church Com, Rev. Sally L. Hill
Dir., Joint Religious Legislative Coalition, Brian A. Rusche
Pres., Rev. Dean Larson
Major Activities: Minnesota Church Center; Local Ecumenism; Life & Work: Hispanic Ministries, Indian Concerns; Legislative Advocacy, Refugee Services, Service to Newly Legalized/Undocumented Persons, Sexual Exploitation within the Religious Community; State Fair Ministry; Faith & Order: Consultation on Church Union, Ecumenical Dialogue, Jewish Christian Relations, Spirituality

St. Paul Area Council of Churches

1671 Summit Ave., St. Paul, MN 55105 Tel. (612)646-8805
Exec. Dir., Rev. Thomas Duke
Chaplaincy, Dr. Fred A. Hueners
Ecumenical Relations, Rev. Sally Hill
Congregations Concerned for Children, Ms. Peg Wangensteen
Volunteer Care Ministries, Ms. Pat Argyros
Coop. Ministries for Children/Youth, Ms. Robin Hickman
Dept. of Indian Work, Ms. Sheila WhiteEagle
Pres., Mr. James Redman
Treas., Arthur Sternberg
Sec., Ms. Kay O'Keefe
Major Activities: Chaplaincy at Detention and Corrections Authority Institutions; Police Chaplaincy; Education and Advocacy Regarding Children and Poverty; Assistance to Churches Developing Child Care Services; Ecumenical Encounters and Activities; Indian Ministries; Leadership in Forming Cooperative Ministries for Children and Youth; Parent Befriender Ministry

The Joint Religious Legislative Coalition

122 West Franklin Ave., Rm. 315, Minneapolis, MN 55404 Tel. (612)870-3670
Exec. Dir., Brian Rusche
Research Dir., Jim Casebolt
Major Activities: Lobbying at State Legislature; Researching Social Justice Issues and Preparing Position Statements; Organizing Grassroots Citizen's Lobby

Twin Cities Metropolitan Church Commission

122 W. Franklin, Rm. 100, Minneapolis, MN 55404 Tel. (612)870-3600 Fax (612)870-3663
Exec. Dir., Rev. Sally L. Hill
Pres., Rev. Tom Duke, 1673 Summet Ave., St. Paul, MN 55105
Major Activities: Education; Criminal Justice Committee; Peace Education Project; Interreligious Committee on Central America; Ecumenical Decade; Churches in Solidarity with Women; US/USSR Religious Exchanges

MISSISSIPPI

Mississippi Religious Leadership Conference
P.O. Box 68123, Jackson, MS 39286-8123 Tel. (601)948-5954 Fax (601)345-3401

Exec. Dir., Rev. Thomas E. Tiller, Jr.

Chair, Rabbi Eric Gurvis

Treas., Mrs. Barbara Barnes

Co-Treasurer, Rev. Tom Clark

Major Activities: Foster trust, understanding and cooperation among religious leaders; Lay/Clergy Retreats; Social Concerns Seminars; Disaster Task Force; Advocacy for Disadvantaged

MISSOURI

Council of Churches of the Ozarks
P.O. Box 3947, Springfield, MO 65808-3947 Tel. (417)862-3586 Fax (417)862-2129

Exec. Dir., Dr. Dorsey E. Levell

Assoc. Dir., Rosanna Bradshaw

Major Activities: Ministerial Alliance; Hospital Chaplains' Fellowship; Retired Sr. Volunteer Prog.; Treatment Center for Alcoholics and Drug Abuse; Helping Elderly Live More Productively; Daybreak Adult Day Care Services; Ombundsman for Nursing Homes; Homesharing; Family Day Care Homes; USDA Food Program; Youth Ministry; Disaster Aid and Counseling; Homebound Shoppers; Alternatives to Incarceration; Food and Clothing Pantry; Ozarks Food Harvest; Spiritual Care Chaplains; Parenting Life Family Skills

Ecumenical Ministries
#2 St. Louis Ave., Fulton, MO 65251 Tel. (314)642-6065

Exec. Dir., Jack W. Rogers

Pres., Rev. Cynthia Ray

Major Activities: Kingdom Hospice; CROP Hunger Walk; Little Brother and Sister; Older Kids Partnership; Summer Youth Day Camps; Widow to Widow Support; Christmas Bookmobile; Unity Service; Family Ministry; Inmate and Family Counseling; Criminal Justice Advocacy; AIDS Prison Counseling and Education; Community Pastor Study; BRIDGE College-to-Senior Program; Senior Center Bible Study; Older Adult Connection; Senior Advocacy and Study Seminars

Interfaith Community Services
200 Cherokee St., P.O. Box 4038, Joseph, MO 64504-0038 Tel. (816)238-4511

Exec. Dir., David G. Berger

Major Activities: Child Development; Neighborhood Family Services; Group Home for Girls; Retired Senior Volunteer Program; Nutrition Program; Mobile Meals; Southside Youth Program; Church and Community; Housing Development

MONTANA

Montana Association of Churches
Andrew Square, Ste. G, 100 24th St. W., Billings, MT 59102 Tel. (406)656-9779

Exec. Dir., Margaret E. MacDonald

Admn. Asst., Larry D. Drane

Pres., Rev. Paul Everett, 1301 Ave. D, Billings, MT 59102

Treas., Don Patterson, East Lake Shore Rd., Big Fork, MT 59911

Rural Ministry Coord., Mary Lou Heiken, 935 S. 72nd St. W., Billings, MT 59106

Legislative Liaison, Harley Warner, 901 Elm, Helena, MT 59601

Campus Ministries Program Assoc., Rev. Kent Elliot, P.O. Box 389, Boulder, MT 59632

Major Activities: Christian Education; Montana Religious Legislative Coalition; Christian Unity; Junior Citizen Camp; Public Information; Ministries Development; Social Ministry; Rural Ministry

NEBRASKA

Interchurch Ministries of Nebraska
215 Centennial Mall S., Rm. 411, Lincoln, NE 68508-1888 Tel. (402)476-3391 Fax (402)476-9310

Exec. Sec., Dr. Mel H. Luetchens

Admin. Asst., Sharon K. Kalcik

Pres., Rev. Dr. Roger Harp

Treas., Rev. "Clip" Higgins

Major Activities: Interchurch Planning and Development; Comity; Indian Ministry; Rural Church Strategy; World Hunger; Refugee Resettlement Coordination; United Ministries in Higher Education; Disaster Response; Christian in Society Forum; Clergy Consultations; Farm Families Crisis Response Network; Video Technology; Interim Ministry Network; Pantry Network; Farm Mediation Services; Hispanic Ministry; the Church & Mental Illness Program; Conflict Management

Lincoln Interfaith Council
215 Centennial Mall South, Rm. 411, Lincoln, NE 68508 Tel. (402)474-3017 Fax (402)476-9310

Exec. Dir., Rev. Dr. Norman E. Leach

Pres., Attorney Beverly Evans Grenier

Treas., Ms. Nancy Glaesemann

Media Specialist, Mr. David Hancock

Urban Ministires, Rev. Nancy Erickson

PEP Coord., Dawn Schmidt

Admin. Asst., Marge Daugherty

Fiscal Mgr., Sharon Kalchik

Jail Chaplain, Cantor Michael Weisser

Communities of Hope, Rev. Otto Schultz

Major Activities: Media Ministry; Emergency Food Pantry; Partnership Empowerment Program (PEP); Communites of Hope; Jail Chaplaincy; Day Watch for Homeless; Spiritual Growth; Clergy Fellowship; Clergy Connection for Non-Lincoln Patients; Prayer Breakfast; Refugee Work; Clergy Orientation; Directory of Clergy, Congregations & Religious Resrouces; Anti-Drug & Gang activities; Boy-Girl Scouts/Campfire/4-H Religious Awards Programs; HS Baccalaureate; UNICEF; Festival of Faith; Holocaust Memorial Obseration; King Observance

NEW HAMPSHIRE

New Hampshire Council of Churches
24 Warren St., P.O. Box 1107, Concord, NH 03302 Tel. (603)224-1352
Exec. Sec., Mr. David Lamarre-Vincent
Pres., Rev. Robert Witham, P.O. Box 465, Concord, NH 03302
Treas., Richard Edmunds, P.O. Box 136, Concord, NH 03302
Major Activities: Facilitating cooperative work of member denominations

NEW JERSEY

Bergen County Council of Churches
165 Burton Ave., Hasbrouck Hts., NJ 07604 Tel. (201)288-3784
Exec. Sec., Neila Vander Vliet

Council of Churches of Greater Camden
P.O. Box 1208, Merchantville, NJ 08109 Tel. (609)985-7724
Exec. Sec., Dr. Samuel A. Jeanes
Pres., Rev. Lawrence L. Dunn
Treas., Mr. William G. Mason
Major Activities: Radio & T.V.; Hospital Chaplaincy; United Services; Good Friday Breakfast; Mayors' Prayer Breakfast; Public Affairs; Easter Sunrise Service

Metropolitan Ecumenical Ministry
525 Orange St., Newark, NJ 07107 Tel. (201)481-6650
Exec. Dir., C. Stephen Jones
Major Activities: Community Advocacy (education, housing, environment); Church Mission Assistance; Community and Clergy Leadership Development

New Jersey Council of Churches
116 N. Oraton Pkwy., East Orange, NJ 07017 Tel. (201)675-8600 Fax (201)675-0620
176 W. State St., Trenton, NJ 08608 Tel. (609)396-9546
Commission on Impact & Public Witness, Rev. Steven C. Case
Commission on Mission Planning & Strategy, Rev. Robert K. Stuhlmann
Commission on Theology & Interreligious Relations, Rev. Betty Jane Bailey

Dir., IMPACT, Ms. Joan Diefenbach
Pres., Rev. William F. Freeman
Treas., Rev. Barry Sziklay
Major Activities: Racial Justice; AIDS Education; Ethics Public Forums; Advocacy

Trenton Ecumenical Area Ministry (TEAM)
2 Propsect St., Trenton, NJ 08618
Exec. Dir., Rev. David A. Gibbons
Chpsn., Rev. Ronald Bagnall
Hospital Chaplains: Rev. Leo Forsberg; Ms. Lee Carol S. Hollendonner; Rev. Jessie L. Irvin
Campus Chaplains: Rev. Wayne Griffith; Rev. Nancy Schulter
Sec., Ms. Tina Swan
Major Activities: Racial Justice; Children & Youth Ministries; Advocacy; CROP Walk; Ecumenical Worship; Hospital Chaplaincy; Church Women United; Campus Chaplaincy; T.V. Program; Congregational Empowerment

NEW MEXICO

Inter-Faith Council of Santa Fe, New Mexico
818 Camino Sierra Vista, Santa Fe, NM 87501 Tel. (505)983-2892
Pres., Hib Sabin
Chpsn., Peace with Justice Task Force, Marjorie Schuckman
Chpsn., Hunger/Shelter Task Force, Br. Jim Brown
Major Activities: Faith Community Assistance Center; Hunger Walk, Interfaith Dialogues/Celebrations/Visitations; Peace Projects; Understanding Hispanic Heritage; Newsletter

New Mexico Conference of Churches
124 Hermosa S.E., Albuquerque, NM 87108-2610 Tel. (505)255-1509 Fax (505)256-0071
Exec. Sec., Dr. Wallace Ford
Pres., Rev. Minerva Carcano, 700 Granite N.W., Albuquerque, NM 87102-4190
Treas., Mr. John Wright, P.O. Box 25707, Albuquerque, NM 87125
Major Activities: State Task Forces: Peace With Justice, Poverty, Caring Inclusive Congregations, Legislative Concerns/Impact, Faith and Order, AIDS, Correctional Ministries, Public Education, Eco-Justice, Ecumenical Continuing Education; Regional Task Forces: Aging, Ecumenical Worship, Refugees, Emergency Care, Alcoholism; Church's Solidarity with Women; Marriage and Family Life

NEW YORK

Allied Christians of Tioga
228 Main Street, Owega, NY 13827 Tel. (607)687-6919
Exec. Dir., Al Smith, Jr.
Pres., Jack Checchia
Major Activities: Jail Ministry; Soup Kitchen; Food Pantry; Coordinate Special Events

Bronx Division of the Council of Churches of the City of New York

39 W. 190th St., P.O. Box 144, Bronx, NY 10468 Tel. (212)367-0612
Pres., Rev. Robert L. Foley, Sr.
Exec. Dir.,————-
Major Activities: Pastoral Care; Christian Education & Youth Ministry; Welfare & Advocacy; Substance Abuse

Brooklyn Council of Churches

125 Ft. Greene Pl, Brooklyn, NY 11217 Tel. (718)625-5851
Dir., Mr. Charles Henze
Pres., Rev. Richard A. Miller
Treas., Rev. Albert J. Berube
Major Activities: Education Ministry; Justice Ministry; Hunger Ministry; Local Ecumenism; Pastoral Care; Community Issues

Broome County Council of Churches, Inc.

81 Main St., Binghamton, NY 13905 Tel. (607)724-9130
Exec. Dir., Mr. William H. Stanton
Admin. Asst., Ms. Joyce M. Kirby
Hospital Chaplain, Rev. LeRoy Flohr
Hospital Chaplain, Mrs. Betty Pomeroy
Jail Chaplain, Rev. Philip Singer
Aging Ministry Coord., Mrs. Dorothy Myers
CHOW Prog. Coord., Mrs. Billie L. Briggs
Pres., Mr. Ray A. Hull
Treas., Mrs. Rachel Light
Major Activities: Hospital and Jail Chaplains; Youth and Aging Ministries; CHOW (Emergency Hunger Program); Christian Education; Ecumenical Worship and Fellowship; Media; Community Affairs; Peace

Buffalo Area Council of Churches

1272 Delaware Ave., Buffalo, NY 14209 Tel. (716)882-4793
Exec. Dir., Rev. Dr. G. Stanford Bratton
Coord., Church Women United, Mrs. Sally Giordano
Coord., Radio/TV, Ms. Linda Velazquez
Pres., The Rev. Ronald Tryon
Pres., Pastor Virginia Williams
1st Vice-Pres., Mr. Charles Banks
Sec., Rev. Karen Lipinczyk
Treas., Rev. Kenneth Neal
Chpsn of Trustees, Rev. Dr. Robert Graham
Pres. Church Women United, Mrs. Bobbie Campbell
Chpsn., Ecumenical Events, Dr. Marie Coles Baker
Chpsn., Community Ministry, Mrs. Miriam Kennedy
Chpsn, Lay/Clergy Education, Rev. James Blackburn
Chpsn., Public Policy, Father Julius Jackson
Major Activities: Radio-TV; Social Services; Chaplains; Church Women United; Ecumenical Relations; Refugees; Public Policy; Community Development; Lay/Clergy Education; Interracial Dialogue

Buffalo Area Metropolitan Ministries, Inc.

775 Main St., Ste. 203, Buffalo, NY 14203-1310 Tel. (716)854-0822
Exec. Dir., Rev. Dr. Charles R. White
Pres., Rev. Francis X. Mazur
Vice-Pres. for Plng. & Prog., Rev. Steven Metcalfe
Vice-Pres. for Admn. & Fin., Rev. Richard Zajac
Sec., Dr. R. Parthasarathy
Treas., Rev. Richard E. McFail
Chair, Food for All Prog., Maureen Gensler
Major Activities: An association of religious communities in Western New York with Jewish, Muslim, Christian, Unitarian, Univeralist, Hindu, and Jain membership providing a united religious witness through these major activities: Shelter; Hunger; Economic Issues; Interreligious Dialogue; Interfaith AIDS Network

Capital Area Council of Churches, Inc.

646 State St., Albany, NY 12203 Tel. (518)462-5450
Exec. Dir., Rev. Edgar N. Kemp, Jr.
Admn. Asst., Ms. Renee Kemp
Pres., Rev. Dr. S. Albert Newman
Treas., Mr. Alan Spencer
Major Activities: Hospital Chaplaincy; Food Pantries; CROP Walk; Jail and Nursing Home Ministries; Martin Luther King Memorial Service and Scholarship Fund; Emergency Shelter for the Homeless; Campus Relations; Forums on Social Concerns; Community Worship; Peace and Justice Education; Inter-Faith Programs; Legislative Concerns; Half-Way House for Ex-Offenders; Annual Ecumenical Musical Celebration

Chautauqua County Rural Ministry

127 Central Ave., P.O. Box 362, Dunkirk, NY 14048 Tel. (716)366-1787
Exec. Dir., Mr. Christopher J. Owens
Major Activities: Chautauqua County Food Bank; Collection/Distribution of Furniture, Clothing, & Appliances; Homeless Services; Building & Refurbishing Housing; Summer Work Camps

Christians United in Mission, Inc.

40 N. Main Ave., Albany, NY 12203 Tel. (518)453-6795
Prog. Dir., Mr. Ronald K. Willis
Communications Dir., Mr. Stephen Esker
Major Activities: Promote Cooperation/Coordination Among Member Judicatories in Urban Ministries, Media Communications, Social Action, Criminal Justice; Emergency Food; AIDS; Homelessness

Concerned Ecumenical Ministries of West Side Buffalo

286 LaFayette Ave., Buffalo, NY 14213 Tel. (716)882-2442
Exec. Dir., Mr. Cliff Whitman
Assoc. Dir., Mr. Robert Adler
Pres., Ellen Kennedy
Major Activities: Community center serving aging seniors

Council of Churches of Chemung County, Inc.

330 W. Church St., Elmira, NY 14901 Tel. (607)734-7622

Exec. Dir., Mrs. Joan Geldmacher

Pres., Rev. Curtis Coley

Chaplain, Lee Griffith, Elmira College, Tel. (607)734-3911

Major Activities: CWS Clothing Collection; CROP Walk; UNICEF; Institutional Chaplaincies; Radio, Easter Dawn Service; Communications Network; Representation on Community Boards and Agencies; Meals on Wheels; Campus Ministry; Food Cupboards; Ecumenical Services; Amerasian Resettlement

Dutchess Interfaith Council, Inc.

9 Vassar St., Poughkeepsie, NY 12601 Tel. (914)471-7333

Exec. Dir., Ms. Gail Burger

Pres., Timmian C. Massie

Treas., Elizabeth M. DiStefano

Major Activities: County Jail Chaplaincy; Radio; CROP Hunger Walk; Interfaith Music Festival; Public Worship Events; Interfaith Dialog; Christian Unity; Interfaith Youth Evening; Oil Purchase Group; Interfaith Volunteer Caregivers Program

East Harlem Interfaith

2050 - 2nd Ave., New York, NY 10029 Tel. (212)427-1500 Fax (212)427-1636

Dir., Charlotte Spence

Bd. Chmn., Rev. Robert Lott

Major Activities: Ecumenical Worship; Welfare and Hunger Advocacy; AIDS Advocacy; Community Organizing; Economic Development (Community Reinvestment)

Genesee County Churches United, Inc.

P.O. Box 547, Batavia, NY 14020 Tel. (716)343-9002

Pres., Mrs. Captain Lucy Jordan

Exec. Sec., M. Deloris Cooper

Chaplain, Rev. Arthur Dolch

Major Activities: Jail Ministry.; Food Pantries; Serve Needy Families; Radio Ministry; Pulpit Exchange; Community Thanksgiving; Ecumenical Services at County Fair

Genesee-Orleans Ministry of Concern

118 S. Main St., Box 245, Albion, NY 14411

Exec. Dir., Marian Adrian, G.N.S.H., P.O. Box 245, Albion, NY 14411 Tel. (716)589-9210

Advocates: Jeannette Winiarz; Robert Fleming

Pres., Betsy Dexheimer

Chaplains: Orleans County Jail, Rev. Wilford Moss; Orleans Albion Correctional Facility, Sr. Dolores O'Dowd

Major Activities: Advocacy Services for the Disadvantaged, Homeless, Ill, Incarcerated, and Victims of Family Violence; Emergency Food, Shelter, Utilities, Medicines

Greater Rochester Community of Churches

17 S. Fitzhugh St., Rochester, NY 14614-1488 Tel. (716)232-6530

Exec. Dir., Rev. Lawrence E. Witmer

Admin. Asst., Marie E. Gibson

Fin. Admn., Ilse Kearney

Pres., Rev. J. Paul Womack

Treas., Lovetta Darling

Major Activities: Criminal Justice (Alternatives to Incarceraton); Legislative IMPACT Network; Mission Education & Training; Refugee Resettlement; Hospital Chaplaincies; Hunger and Food policies; Habitat for Humanity; Respite Cares (developmental disabilities)

Interreligious Council of Central New York

910 Madison St., Syracuse, NY 13210 Tel. (315)476-2001

Exec. Dir., Dorothy F. Rose

Pres., Rev. Msgr. Ronald C. Bill

Assoc. Dir., Rev. Dale Hindmarsh

Assoc. Dir., Rev. Robert Stoppert

Dir. of Refugee Resettlement, Nona Stewart

Dir. Senior Companion Prog., Virginia Frey

Dir. Hunger Outreach Services, Dawn Burk

Dir. Project Exodus Re-entry Program, Raheem Jami

Bus. Mgr., Arthur A. West

Major Activities: Interreligious Relations; Education, Worship; Institutional Pastoral Care; Children/Youth Ministry; Low Cost Housing Program; Community Advocacy and Planning

Jamestown Area Ministry Association

SS Peter & Paul Church, 508 Cherry St., Jamestown, NY 14701 Tel. (716)664-5703

Dir., Rev. James E. Wall

Chaplain, Rev. John Kuhlmann

Chaplain Mayville Jail, Sr. Mary Elligan

Major Activities: Food Vouchers; Homeless/Needy Program; Jail Ministry

Livingston County Coalition of Churches

P.O. Box 548, Lakeville, NY 14480 Tel. (716)658-2122

Coord., Rev. Robert Booher, The United Church of Mount Morris, Stanley St., Mount Morris, NY 14510

Pres., Stephanie Sauve

Major Activities: Hospice Program; Jail Ministry; Visitors' Center at Groveland Correctional Facility; Food Pantries; Gateways Family Service; Parents Anonymous; Alternative Sentencing Program; Coordinate Services for Aging and Rural Poor; Christian Education Learning Fair; Lecture Series and Chaplain at SUNY Geneseo

Mid-Hudson Catskill Rural Migrant Ministry

415 Lattintown Rd., Marlboro, NY 12542 Tel. (914)255-0993

Exec. Dir., Rev. Gail Keeney-Mulligan

Pres., Mary Sherwig

Chaplain, Sr. Maria Theresa De'Bourbon

Major Activities: Serving the rural poor and migrants through pastoral work and social programs; Women's Support Group; Youth Program; Men's Soccer League; Latino Committee; Organization and advocacy with and for rural poor; Jail Ministry

New York State Council of Churches, Inc.

362 State St., Albany, NY 12210 Tel. (518)436-9319 Fax (518)436-6705

Exec. Dir., Rev. Dr. Arleon L. Kelley

Coord., New York State IMPACT, Edward J. Bloch

Pres., Rev. J. Fay Cleveland

1st Vice-Pres., Rev. Allen A. Stanley

2nd Vice-Pres., Rev. Marian Shearer

Sec., Isabel Morrison

Treas., Dr. George H. DeHority

Consultant for Resource Development, Mary Lu Bowen

Assoc. for Admn. Services, Ms. Sylvenia Cochran

Assoc. for Finance & Personnel, Helen Vault

Assoc. for Admn. & Communications, Thila A. Bell

Consultant for Resource Development, George Black

Program Assoc. for Chaplaincy, Rev. Frank Snow

Progam Assoc. for Issues Research & Advocacy, Dr. Sabine O'Hara

Major Activities: Public Policy and Ecumenical Ministries; Chaplaincy in State Institutions; Rural Poor and Migrants; Homeless; AIDS; Universal Health Care; Life and Law; U.S.-Canadian Border Concerns; Single Parent Families; Faith and Order; Environmental Issues; The Family, Education, Violence; Covenanting Congregations

Niagara County Migrant Rural Ministry

5465 Upper Mountain Rd., Lockport, NY 14094 Tel. (716)433-4070

Coord., Ms. Barbara Meeks

Sec./Asst., Grayce Dietz

Seasonal Outreach Worker, Jesse Garcia, (bi-lingual)

Seasonal Outreach Worker, Ofelia Carmona, (bilingual)

Seasonal Outreach Worker, Deborah Hill

Seasonal Outreach Worker, Grayce Dietz

Major Activities: Migrant Farm Worker Program; Primary Health Clinic; Assist with immigration problems and application process for social services; Emergency Food Pantry; "Rummage Room" for clothing and household goods; Monitor Housing Conditions; Assist Rural Poor; Referrals to appropriate service agencies

Queens Federation of Churches

86-17 105th St., Richmond Hill, NY 11418-1597 Tel. (718)847-6764 Fax (718)847-7392

Exec. Dir., Rev. N. J. L'Heureux, Jr.

Exec. Asst., Kevin Murphy

York College Chaplain, Rev. Dr. Hortense Merritt

Pres., John W. Jerome

Treas., Lloyd W. Patterson, Jr.

Major Activities: Emergency Food Service; York College Campus Ministry; Blood Bank; Scouting; Christian Education Workshops; Planning and Strategy; Church Women United; Community Consultations; Seminars for Church Leaders; Directory of Churches and Synagogues; Christian Relations (Prot/RC); Chaplaincies; Public Policy Issues; N.Y.S. Interfaith Commission on Landmarking of Religious Property; Queens Interfaith Hunger Network

Schenectady Inner City Ministry

5 Catherine St., Schenectady, NY 12307 Tel. (518)374-2683

Urban Agent, Rev. Phillip N. Grigsby

Admn. Asst., Ms. Elaine MacKinnon

Emergency Food Liaison, Ms. Patricia Obrecht

Nutrition Dir., Diane Solomon

Project SAFE/Safehouse Dir., Ms. Delores Edmonds-McIntosh

Church/Community Worker, Jim Murphy

Learning Tree Nursery Coords.: Kathy Stuitje; Audrey Yanis

Pres., Sr. Stella Dillon

Bethesda House, Rev. Paul Fraser

Save and Share, Nilda Colon

Major Activities: Emergency Food; Advocacy; Housing; Child Care; Alternatives to Prostitution for Runaway and At-Risk Youth; Shelter for Runaway/Homeless Women; Neighborhood and Economic Issues; Ecumenical Worship and Fellowship; Community Research; Education in Churches on Faith Responses to Social Concerns; Legislative Advocacy; Nutrition Outreach Program; Hispanic Community Ministry; Food Buying Club; Day Shelter

Southeast Ecumenical Ministries

25 Westminister Rd., Rochester, NY 14607 Tel. (716)271-5350

Dir., Laura Julien

Mgr., Food Cupboard, Martin Edic

Pres., Eileen Thomas-Poehner

Major Activities: Food Cupboard; Transportation of Elderly

Staten Island Council of Churches

2187 Victory Blvd., Staten Island, NY 10314 Tel. (718)761-6782

Ofc. Mgr., Mrs. Marjorie R. Bergendale

Pres., Rev. Donald C. Mullen

Vice-Pres., Rev. William E. Merryman

Sec., Mrs. Mildred J. Saderholm

Major Activities: Support; Christian Education; Pastoral Care; Congregational Concerns; Urban Affairs

The Cortland County Council of Churches, Inc.

7 Calvert St., Cortland, NY 13045 Tel. (607)753-1002

Exec. Dir., Rev. Donald M. Wilcox

Major Activities: College Campus Ministry; Jail Ministry; Hospital Chaplaincy; Nursing Home Ministry; Newspaper Column; Interfaith Relationships; Hunger Relief; UNICEF; CWS; Leadership Education; Community Issues; Criminal Justice; Mental Health Chaplaincy

The Council of Churches of the City of New York

475 Riverside Dr., Rm. 439, New York, NY 10015 Tel. (212)870-2120 Fax (212)870-2025
Exec. Dir., Rev. Patricia A. Reeberg
Pres., Bishop Norman N. Quick
First Vice-Pres., Rev. N. J. L'Heureux, Jr.
Second Vice-Pres., Rev. Robert L. Foiley, Sr.
Third Vice-Pres., Rev. Edward Earl Johnson
Sec., Ms. Paule Alexander
Treas., Dr. John E. Carrington
Major Activities: Radio & TV; Pastoral Care; Protestant Chapel, Kennedy International Airport; Coordination and Strategic Planning; Religious Conferences; Referral & Advocacy

The Long Island Council of Churches

1644 Denton Green, Hempstead, NY 11550 Tel. (516)565-0290
Exec. Dir., Rev. Robert L. Pierce
Exec. Asst., Rev. Ruth Phillips-Huyck
Admn. Asst., Ms. Barbara McLaughlin
Int. Dir., Pastoral Care, Rev. Walter Baepler
Dir., Clinical Pastoral Educ., Rev. Kai Borner
Dir., Social Services, Mrs. Lillian Sharik, Tel. (516)565-0390
Dir., Project REAL, Mr. Stephen Gervais
Dir., Counseling Services, Rev. S. Bruce Wagner
Dir. of Development, Rev. Arnold C. Miller
Nassau Cnty. Ofc.: Social Services Sec., Ms. Mary Johnson
Suffolk Cnty. Ofc.: Family Support, Mrs. Deborah Scott
Food Prog., Mrs. Carolyn Gumbs
Food Prog., Mrs. Millie McSteen
Blood Prog. Coord., Ms. Leila Truman
Blood Prog. Coord., Mrs. Audry Wolf
Coord. for Training in Caring Ministry, Ms. Barbara Mathews
Major Activities: Pastoral Care in Hospitals and Jails; Clinical Pastoral Education; Emergency Aid and Food; Advocacy for Domestic and International Peace & Justice; Blood Donor Coordination; Church World Service; Inter-faith Cooperation; Radio Program; Newsletter; Church Directory; Counseling Service; Community Residences for Adults with Psychiatric Disabilities; Project REAL; AIDS Education Projects; Special Projects

The Niagara Council of Churches Inc.

Rainbow Blvd. at Second St., Niagara Falls, NY 14303 Tel. (716)285-7505
Exec. Dir., Prof. Caroline C. Latham
Pres., Mr. Paul Wilson, 1556 101st St., Niagara Falls, NY 14304
Treas., Mr. Edward Weber, 1306 Maple Ave., Niagara Falls, NY 14305
Major Activities: Ecumenical Worship; Bible Study; Christian Ed. & Social Concerns; Church Women United; Evangelism & Mission; Institutional Min. Youth Activities; Hymn Festival; Week of Prayer for Christian Unity; CWS Projects; Audio-Visual Library; UNICEF; Food Pantries and Kitchens; Community Missions, Inc.; Political Refugees; Eco-Justice Task Force; Migrant/rural Ministries; Interfaith Coalition on Energy

Troy Area United Ministries

12 King St., Troy, NY 12180 Tel. (518)274-5920
Exec. Dir., Mrs. Margaret T. Stoner
Pres., Rev. James E. Robinson
Chaplain, R.P.I., Rev. Donald Stroud
Chaplain, Russell Sage College, Cheryl Donkin
Chaplain, Russell Sage
Major Activities: Community Dispute Settlement (mediation) Program; College Ministry; Nursing Home Ministry; CROP Walk; Homeless and Housing Concerns; Weekend Meals Program at Homeless Shelter; Community Worship Celebrations; Racial Relations; and Bias Awareness

Wainwright House Interfaith Center

260 Styvesant Ave., Rye, NY 10580 Tel. (914)967-6080
Exec. Dir., Susan Collett
Major Activities: Educational program and conference center with a special focus on interdisciplinary programming; provides support for those in search of intellectual, psychological, physical, and spiritual growth

NORTH CAROLINA

Asheville-Buncombe Community Christian Ministry (ABCCM)

24 Cumberland Ave., Asheville, NC 28801 Tel. (704)259-5300 Fax (704)259-5316
Exec. Dir., Rev. Scott Rogers
Pres., Mr. James A. Lee
Major Activities: Crisis Ministry; Jail/Prison Ministry; Transitional Housing; Shelter Ministry; Medical Ministry

Greensboro Urban Ministry

407 N. Eugene St., Greensboro, NC 27401 Tel. (919)271-5959 Fax (919)271-5920
Exec. Dir., Rev. Mike Aiken
Major Activities: Emergency Financial Assistance; Housing; Hunger Relief; Inter-Faith and Inter-Racial Understanding; Justice Ministry; Indigent Health Care

North Carolina Council of Churches

Methodist Bldg., 1307 Glenwood Ave., Ste. 162, Raleigh, NC 27605-3258 Tel. (919)828-6501
Exec. Dir., Rev. S. Collins Kilburn
Program Assoc., Jimmy Creech
Pres., Rev. Raymon E. Hunt, 5905 Rockwell Church Rd., Charlotte, NC 28269
Treas., Dr. James W. Ferree, P.O. Box 11772, Winston-Salem, NC 27116
Major Activities: AIDS Ministry; Christian Unity; Equal Rights; Legislative Program; Criminal Justice; Farmworker Ministry; Peace; Rural Crisis; Racism; Disaster Response; Caring Program for Children

NORTH DAKOTA

North Dakota Conference of Churches

227 W. Broadway, Bismarck, ND 58501 Tel. (701)255-0604 Fax (701)222-8543
Pres., Bishop Wesley N. Haugen

Treas., Rev. Charles R. Freuden
Ofc. Mgr., Eunice Brinckerhoff
Major Activities: Prison Chaplaincy; Rural Life Ministry; Interfaith Dialogue; BEM Study; Faith and Order

OHIO

Akron Area Association of Churches
750 Work Dr., Akron, OH 44320 Tel. (216)535-3112
Exec. Dir., Rev. Harry Eberts, Jr.
Pres. Bd. of Trustees, Dr. Arthur Kemp
Vice-Pres.: Rev. Jan Walker; Mrs. Katherine Chapman
Sec., Rev. Dan Petry
Treas., Dr. Stephen Laning
Program Dir., Elsbeth Fritz
Chpsn. Educ. Dir., Mrs. Kimberly Porter
Major Activities: Messiah Sing; Interfaith Council; Newsletters; Resource Center; Community Worship; Training of Local Church Leadership; Radio Programs; Clergy and Lay Fellowship Breakfasts; Cable TV; Interfaith Caregivers; Neighborhood Development; Community Outreach

Alliance of Churches
470 E. Broadway, Alliance, OH 44601 Tel. (216)821-6648
Dir., Richard A. Duro
Pres., Rev. Robert Stewart
Treas., Betty Rush
Major Activities: Christian Education; Community Relations & Service; Ecumenical Worship; Community Ministry; Peacemaking; Medical Transportation for Anyone Needing It; Job Placement Service

Churchpeople for Change and Reconciliation
326 W. McKibben, Box 488, Lima, OH 45802 Tel. (419)229-6949
Exec. Dir., Richard Keller
Major Activities: New programs for minorities, poor, alienated, and despairing and spinning them off as independent agencies; Community and soup kitchens

Council of Christian Communions of Greater Cincinnati
2439 Auburn Ave., Cincinnati, OH 45219 Tel. (513)579-0099
Exec. Dir., Joellen W. Grady
Assoc. Dir. for Justice Chaplaincy, Rev. Jack Marsh
Assoc. Dir. for Educ., Sharon D. Jones
Asst. Dir. Communication, John H. Gassett
Pres., Rev. Esther Chandler
Major Activities: Christian Unity & Interfaith Cooperation; Justice Chaplaincies; Police-Clergy Team; Adult and Juvenile Jail Chaplains; Religious Education; Broadcasting and Communications; Information Service; Social Concerns

Ecumenical Communication Commission of N.W. Ohio, Inc.
1011 Sandusky, Ste. M, P.O. Box 351, Perrysburg, OH 43551 Tel. (409)874-3932
Dir., Ms. Margaret Hoepfl
Major Activities: Ecumenical/Cooperative Communication; TV and Radio Production

Greater Dayton Christian Council
212 Belmonte Park E., Dayton, OH 45405 Tel. (513)222-8654
Exec. Dir., Dr. Richard C. Duncan
Coord., Montgomery Cty. Vol. Jail Program, Nancy Haas
Pres., Rev. Don Dixon
Major Activities: Communications: Service to the Churches and Community; Housing Advocacy; Race Relations Advocacy; Substance Abuse Prevention

Inner City Renewal Society
2230 Euclid Ave., Cleveland, OH 44115 Tel. (216)781-3913
Exec. Dir., Myrtle L. Mitchell
Major Activities: Friendly Town; Urban Ministries Training and Community Development Center; Drug and Alcohol Education; Juvenile Opportunity and Involvement Network (J.O.I.N.); Project Chore; Career Beginnings; AIDS Education, Scholarship; Burial Aid

Interchurch Council of Greater Cleveland
2230 Euclid Ave., Cleveland, OH 44115-2499 Tel. (216)621-5925 Fax (216)621-0588
Exec. Dir., Rev. Thomas Olcott
Assoc. Dir. & Dir., Church and Society, Ms. Mylion Waite
Assoc. Dir. & Dir., Communications, Ms. Janice Giering
Pres., Frank Rasmussen
Chmn. of the Assembly, Mildred McFarland
Major Activities: Church and Society; Communications; Hunger; Christian Education; Legislation; Faith and Order; Public Education; Interchurch News; Tutoring; Parent-Child Books Program; Shelter for Homeless Women and Children; Radio & T.V.; Interracial Cooperation; Interfaith Cooperation; Adaopt-A-School; Women of Hope; Leadership Development; Religious Education; Center for Peace & Reconciliation—Youth and the Courts

Mahoning Valley Association of Churches
631 Wick Ave., Youngstown, OH 44502 Tel. (216)744-8946
Exec. Dir., Elsie L. Dursi
Pres., Rev. William Brewster, St. John's Epis. Ch., 323 Wick Ave., Youngstown, OH 44503
Treas., Mr. Paul Fryman, 42 Venloe Dr., Poland, OH 44514
Major Activities: Communications; Christian Education; Ecumenism; Social Action; Advocacy

Metropolitan Area Church Board

760 E. Broad St., Columbus, OH 43205 Tel. (614)461-7103

Exec. Dir., Rev. Dr. Robert Lee Erickson
Support Service Coord., Rebecca S. Trover
Chmn. of Bd., Mrs. Marilyn Shreffler
Vice Chmn., Dr. Luther Holland
Sec., Mrs. Juanita Bridges
Treas., Rev. Dean Bright
Major Activities: Newsletter; Liaison with Other Community Organizations; Week of Prayer for Christian Unity; Support for Ministerial Associations and Church Councils; Enrichment Seminars; Prayer Groups; "Emerging Social Issues Forums;" CROP Walk; Habitat for Humanity; School of Religion; Orientation for New Clergy; Church Leader Packet

Metropolitan Area Religious Coalition of Cincinnati

1035 Enquirer Bldg., 617 Vine St., Cincinnati, OH 45202 Tel. (513)721-4843

Dir., Rev. Duane Holm
Pres., Rabbi Samuel Joseph
Major Activities: Children-At-Risk; Public Education; Food & Welfare; Housing

Ohio Council of Churches, Inc.

89 E. Wilson Bridge Rd., Columbus, OH 43085-2391 Tel. (614)885-9590 Fax (614)885-6097

Exec. Dir., ———-
Dir. for Ecumenical Relations, Mr. David A. Leslie
Dir. for Public Policy, Rev. David O. McCoy
Dir. for Church & Community Issues, Mr. Raymond S. Blanks
Pres., Rev. Kenneth Sauer
Treas., Ms. Dolores Eyerman
Major Activities: Economic Justice; Minority Church Empowerment; Ecumenical Development; Public Policy Issues; Criminal Justice Issues; World Peace and Justice

Pike County Outreach Council

122 E. Second St., Waverly, OH 45690 Tel. (614)947-7151

Dir., Judy Dixon

Toledo Ecumenical Area Ministries

444 Floyd St., Toledo, OH 43620 Tel. (419)242-7401

Admn., Metro-Toledo Churches United, Nancy Lee Atkins
Exec. Dir., Toledo Campus Ministry, Rev. Glenn B. Hosman, Jr.
Exec. Dir., Toledo Metropolitan Mission, Ms. Nancy Atkins
Major Activities: Ecumenical Relations; Interfaith Relations; Food Program; Campus Ministry; Social Action (Public Education; Health Care; Urban Ministry; Employment; Community Organization; Welfare Rights; Housing; Refugee Assistance; Mental Retardation; Voter Registration/Education)

Tuscarawas County Council for Church and Community

120 First Dr. SE, New Philadelphia, OH 44663 Tel. (216)343-6012

Exec. Dir., Barbara E. Lauer
Pres., Mr. Thomas L. Kane, Jr., 1221 Crater Ave., Dover, OH 44622
Treas., Mr. James Barnhouse, 120 N. Broadway, New Phladelphia, OH 44663
Major Activities: Human Services; Health; Family Life; Child Abuse; Housing; Educational Programs; Emergency Assistance; Legislative Concerns; Juvenile Prevention Program; Teen Pregnancy Prevention Program; Prevention Program for High Risk Children (the Council acts as a facilitator of the above); Bimonthly newsletter The Pilot

West Side Ecumenical Ministry

4315 Bridge Ave, Cleveland, OH 44113 Tel. (216)651-2037 Fax (216)651-4145

Exec. Dir., Robert T. Begin
Major Activities: Emergency Food Centers; Senior Meals Programs; Youth Services; Advocacy, Empowerment Programs; Church Clusters; Drug Rehabilitation Program; Head Start Centers; Theatre

OKLAHOMA

Oklahoma Conference of Churches

P.O. Box 60288, Oklahoma City, OK 73146 Tel. (405)525-2928 Fax (405)557-0023

Exec. Dir., The Rev. Dr. William Moorer
Pres., Mrs. Rebecca Markham, 1912 S. 69th East Ave., Tulsa, OK 74112
Treas., Mrs. Ann Fent
Major Activities: Priority is Christian Unity issues and COCU "Covenanting"; community building among 16 member communions; Farm Crisis; Ecumenical Decade with Women ; Children's Advocacy; Refugee Resettlement; Day at the Legislature

Tulsa Metropolitan Ministry

221 S. Nogales, Tulsa, OK 74127 Tel. (918)582-3147 Fax (918)582-3159

Exec. Dir., Sr. Sylvia Schmidt, S.C.C.
Assoc. Dir., Rev. Gerald L. Davis
Resident Service Dir., Shanita Spencer
Dir., Day Center for the Homeless, Marcia Sharp
Dir., (Housing Outreach Services of Tulsa), Rev. Charles Boyle
Advocacy Program Director, Rev. Larry Cowan
Pres., Rev. LeRoy K. Jordan
Vice-Pres., Sylvia Tuers
Sec., Dr. Rita Cowan
Treas., Joe Unger
Major Activities: Corrections Ministry; Jewish-Christian Understanding; Police-Community Relations; Shelter for the Homeless; Women's Issues; Shelter for Mentally Ill; Outreach and Advocacy for Public Housing; Spirituality and Aging; Legislative Issues; Interfaith Dialogue TV Series; Christian Issues/Justice and Peace Issues; Central America Concerns & Events; Eco-Spirituality; Environmental Concerns; Communications

OREGON

Ecumenical Ministries of Oregon

0245 S.W. Bancroft St., Ste. B, Portland, OR 97201
Tel. (503)221-1054 Fax (503)223-7007
Exec. Dir., Rev. Rodney I. Page
Dep. Dir., Barbara J. George
Dir. of Center for Urban Education, Rodney I. Page
Dir., Legis. & Govt. Ofc., Ellen C. Lowe
Comptroller, Gary B. Logsdon
Dir., Clinical Services, Cindy Klug
Med. Dir., Neal Rendleman, M.D.
Hopewell House Dir., Judith Kenning
Alternative Break Coalition, Eric Massanari
Dir., Hope Haven, Skip Amos
Dirs., Hemophilia NW: Larkey DeNeffe; Beth Weinstein
Drug Educ. Proj., Bob McNeil
Dirs., Sophia Center: Judith Meckling; Kathryn Knoll
Alcohol & Drugs Min., Nancy Anderson
Police Chaplain, Rev. Greg Kammann
Sponsors Organized to Assist Refugees, Gary Gamer, Fax (503)284-6445
Dir., Emergency Food, Britt Olson
Dir., Folk-Time (Soc. Prog. for Mentally Ill), Susan Alperin
Dir., Job Opportunity Bank, Noreen Goplen, Fax (503)249-2857
Dir., HIV Day Center, Tina Tommaso-Jennings
Pres., The Rev. Richard Osburn
Pres.-Elect, The Rev. William Creevey
Treas., Ron Means
Major Activities: Educational Ministries; Legislation; Urban Ministries; Refugees; Chaplaincy; Social Concerns; Direct Services; Jewish-Christian Relations; Farm Ministry; Alcohol and Drug Ministry; Welfare Advocacy; Faith & Order; Peace Ministries; IMPACT; Communications; AIDS Ministry; Prostitution Ministry; Farm and Rural Ministries; Racism; Religious Education; Health and Human Ministries

PENNSYLVANIA

Allegheny Valley Association of Churches

1333 Freeport Road, Natrona Heights, PA 15065
Tel. (412)226-0606
Dir., Luella H. Barrage
Pres., Rev. Dr. W. James Legge, RR #4, Box 186, Tarentum, PA 15084
Treas., Mrs. Libby Grimm, RR #2, Box 36, Tarentum, PA 15084
Major Activities: Education Evangelism Workshops; Ecumenical Services; Dial-a-Devotion; Youth Activities; CROP Walk; Food Bank; Super Cupboard; Emergency Aid; Cross-on-the-Hill

Christian Associates of Southwest Pennsylvania

239 Fourth Ave., #1817, Pittsburgh, PA 15222-1769 Tel. (412)288-4020 Fax (412)288-4023
Exec. Dir., Rev. Donald Leiter
Assoc. Exec. Dir., Rev. Bruce H. Swenson
Cable TV Co-ordinator, Mr. Ron Bocchi
Admn. Asst., Mrs. Barbara Irwin
Pres., Rev. Robert Rigg
Treas., Rev. David Zubik

Communications Coord., Mr. Bruce J. Randolph
Major Activities: Communications; Planning; Church and Community; Leadership Development; Theological Dialogue; Evangelism/Church Growth; Racism

Christian Churches United of the Tri-County Area

900 S. Arlington Ave., Rm. 128, Harrisburg, PA 17109 Tel. (717)652-2771 Fax (717)545-7777
Exec. Dir., Rev. Michael Morrill
Pres., Rev. Jay Wesley House
Treas., Rev. Lawrence Jones
Major Activities: Volunteer Ministries to Prisons, Hospitals, Institutionalized Aged, AIDS and for Christian Education; Harrisburg Area Emergency Life Survival Project (Housing, Rent, Food, Medication, Transportation, Home Heating, Clothing);; La Casa de Amistad (The House of Friendship), same services as above but in the Hispanic area; Accredited Clinical Pastoral Care Program; Lay Institute of Pastoral Care

Christians United in Beaver County

1098 Third Street, Beaver, PA 15009 Tel. (412)774-1446
Exec. Sec., Mrs. Lois L. Smith
Chaplain, Rev. Samuel Ward
Chaplain, Mrs. Erika Bruner
Chaplain, Rev. Anthony Massey
Chaplain, Rev. Frank Churchill
Chaplain, Mr. Jack Kirkpatrick
Pres., Rev. Jonathan T. Carlisle, 426 4th Avenue, Beaver Falls, PA 15010 Tel. (412)774-1446
Treas., Mr. William Young, 2903-20th St., Beaver Falls, PA 15010
Major Activities: Christian Education; Evangelism; Radio; Social Action; Church Women United; United Church Men; Ecumenism; Hospital, Detention Home, and Jail Ministry

Delaware Valley Media Ministry

1501 Cherry St., Philadelphia, PA 19102 Tel. (215)563-7854 Fax (215)864-0104
Exec. Dir., Ms. Nancy Nolde
Major Activities: Interfaith Communication and Television Production Agency

East End Cooperative Ministry

250 N. Highland Ave., Pittsburgh, PA 15206 Tel. (412)361-5549
Exec. Dir., Mrs. Judith Marker
Major Activities: Food Pantry; Soup Kitchen; Men's Emergency Shelter; Meals on Wheels; Casework and Supportive Services for Elderly; Information and Referral; Program for Children and Youth; Bridge Housing Program for Men and Women in Recovery and their Children

Easton Area Interfaith Council

330 Ferry St., Easton, PA 18042 Tel. (215)258-4955
Admn. Sec., Mirian Fretzo
Major Activities: Food Bank; Hospital and Nursing Home Chaplaincy; Center for Mentally Handicapped; Homeless

Ecumenical Conference of Greater Altoona

1208 - 13th St., P.O. Box 305, Altoona, PA 16603 Tel. (814)942-0512

Exec. Dir., Mrs. Eileen Becker

Major Activities: Religious Education; Workshops; Ecumenical Activities; Religious Christmas Parade; Campus Ministry; Community Concerns; Peace Forum; Religious Education for Mentally Handicapped

Ecumenical Urban Ministries

100 N. Bellefield at Fifth Ave., Pittsburgh, PA 15213 Tel. (412)682-2751

Exec. Dir., Rev. James C. Faltot

Pres. of EUM Bd., Dr. Walter Wiest

Major Activities: Training Programs Focused on Increasing the Effectiveness of the Urban Church; Advocacy on Social Justice Matters

Greater Bethlehem Area Council of Churches

520 E. Broad St., Bethlehem, PA 18018 Tel. (215)867-8671

Exec. Dir., Mrs. Audrey Bertsch

Pres., Rev. Dr. William Matz, 3130 Patterson Dr., Bethlehem, PA 18017

Treas., Mrs. Polly McClure, 7 W. Washington Ave., Bethlehem, PA 18018

Major Activities: Support Ministry; Institutional Ministry to Elderly and Infirm; Family Concerns; Scripture Center; Social Concerns; World Local Hunger Projects; Elderly Ministry

Hanover Area Council of Churches

120 York St., Hanover, PA 17331 Tel. (717)633-6353

Exec. Dir., Nancy M. Hewitt

Major Activities: Meals on Wheels, Provide a Lunch Program, Fresh Air Program, Clothing Bank, Hospital Chaplaincy Services Congregational & Interfaith Relations, Public Ecumenical Programs and Services, State Park Chaplaincy Services & Children's Program

Inter-Church Ministries of Erie County

252 W. 7th St., Erie, PA 16501 Tel. (814)454-2411

Exec. Dir., Rev. Willis J. Merriman

Assoc. Dir., Rev. Deborah R. Dockstader

Adjunct Staff: Pastoral Counseling, Dr. David J. Sullivan; Aging Prog., Ms. Carolyn A. DiMattio

Pres., The V. Rev. John P. Downey, 134 W. 7th St., Erie, PA 16501

Treas., The Rev. Victoria Wood Parrish, 538 E. 10th St., Erie, PA 16503

Major Activities: Local Ecumenism; Ministry with Aging; Social Ministry; Pastoral Counseling; Continuing Education; N.W. Pa. Conf. of Bishops and Judicatory Execs.; Institute of Pastoral Care; Theological Dialogue; AIDS Ministry and Interracial Sharing of Families Ministry

Lancaster County Council of Churches

447 E. King St., Lancaster, PA 17602 Tel. (717)291-2261

Exec. Dir., Rev. James Hughes

Prison Chaplain, Rev. David F. Myer

Dir. Prescott House, Casey Jones

Asst. Admn., Kim Y. Wittel

Dir. Child Abuse, Ursula Wanner

Dir. CONTACT, Rhoda Mull

Pres., Rev. Charlotte Whiting

Dir., Service Ministry, Adela Dohner

Major Activities: Social Ministry; Residential Ministry to Youthful Offenders; Prison Ministry; CONTACT; Advocacy; Child Abuse Prevention

Lebanon County Christian Ministries

818 Water St., P.O. Box 654, Lebanon, PA 17042 Tel. (717)274-2601

Exec. Dir., Mrs. Elizabeth F. Greer

Food & Clothing Bank Dir., Sherry A. Wallis

H.O.P.E. Services, P. Richard Forney

Noon Meals Coord., Mrs. Glenda Wenger

Major Activities: H.O.P.E. (Helping Our People in Emergencies—Emergency Material Needs Services and Clearinghouse); Food & Clothing Bank; Free Noon Meal Program; Surplus Federal Commodity Distribution Program; Ecumenical Events; Chaplaincy and Support Services

Lehigh County Conference of Churches

534 Chew St., Allentown, PA 18102 Tel. (215)433-6421

Exec. Dir., Rev. William A. Seaman

Pres., Rev. Dr. Iris Simpson

Treas., Mr. James G. Hottenstein

Major Activities: Chaplaincy Program; Migrant Ministry; Social Concerns and Action; Clergy Dialogues; Drop-In-Center for De-Institutionalized Adults; Ecumenical Food Kitchen; Housing Advocacy Program; Pathways (Reference to Social Services)

Metropolitan Christian Council of Philadelphia

1501 Cherry St., Philadephia, PA 19102 Tel. (215)563-7854 Fax (215)864-0104

Exec. Dir., Rev. C. Edward Geiger

Assoc. Communications, Ms. Nancy L. Nolde

Admn. Asst., Mrs. Joan G. Shipman

Pres., Dr. William J. Shaw

Vice-Pres., Rt. Rev. Allen L. Bartlett, Jr.

Treas., John A. Clark, 1 Liberty Pl., Philadelphia, PA 19103

Major Activities: Congregational Clusters; Public Policy Advocacy; Communication; Interfaith Dialogue

North Hills Youth Ministry

1566 Northway Mall, Pittsburgh, PA 15237 Tel. (412)366-1300

Exec. Dir., Ronald B. Barnes

Major Activities: Junior and Senior High School Family and Individual Counseling; Pre-Adolescent Youth Early Intervention Counseling; Educational Programming for Churches and Schools; Youth Advocacy

Northside Common Ministries

P.O. Box 99861, Pittsburgh, PA 15233 Tel. (412)734-3663

Exec. Dir., Rev. Robert J. Wilde, MSW

Pres., Rev. Thomas Moog

Major Activities: Pleasant Valley Shelter for Homeless Men: Capacity 25 men each night of the year (food, laundry, clothes, bed) plus extensive counseling program; Advocacy around Hunger, Housing, Poverty, and Racial Issues; Community Service Center and Pantry: Provides one week's supply of food to 1000 persons each month, distributes TEFAP (government surplus food) to 10 pantries, offers community social services to clients

Northwest Interfaith Movement

Greene St. at Westview, Philadelphia, PA 19119 Tel. (215)843-5600 Fax (215)843-2755
Exec. Dir., Rev. Richard R. Fernandez
Dir., Long Term Care Connection, Valerie Pogozelski
Chpsn., Dr. Phillip Welser
Dir., Northwest Child Care Resource Prog., Amy Gendall
Dir., Neighborhood Child Care Resource Program, Amy Gendall
Major Activities: Community Development & Community Reinvestment; Older Adult Concerns; Nursing Home Program; Unemployment; Economic Issues; Public Education; Peace; Racism; Poverty Issues

Pennsylvania Conference on Interchurch Cooperation

P.O. Box 2835, 223 North St., Harrisburg, PA 17105 Tel. (717)545-4761 Fax (717)238-1473
900 S. Arlington Ave., Harrisburg, PA 17109
Co-Staff, Dr. Howard Fetterhoff
Co-Staff, Rev. Albert E. Myers
Co-Chairpersons, Bishop Nicolas Datillo
Co-Chairpersons, Bishop Guy S. Edmiston, Jr.
Major Activities: Theological Consultation; Social Concerns; Inter-Church Planning; Conferences and Seminars; Disaster Response Preparedness

Reading Urban Ministry

230 N. Fifth St., Rm. 300, Reading, PA 19601 Tel. (215)374-6917
Exec. Dir., Beth Bitler
Pres., Mark C. Potts
Vice-Pres., Rev. Lydia A. Speller
Sec., Sarah Boyd
Treas., Raymond Drain
Major Activities: Community Clothing Center; Friendly Visitor Program to Elderly; Caring When It Counts (Emergency Intervention with Elderly); Summer Youth Program; Family Action Support Team (For Single-Parent Families)

South Hills Interfaith Ministries

5171 Park Ave., Bethel Park, PA 15102 Tel. (412)833-6177 Fax (412)833-5212
Exec. Dir., Robert Laird Brashear
Psychological Services, Mr. Don Zandier
Psychological Services, Ms. Hilda Schorr-Ribera
Cmty. Services, Mr. Thomas Tompkins
Cmty. Services, Mrs. Mary Ethel Patterson
Admn. Operations Dir., Ms. Jacqueline Riebel
Interfaith Reemployment Job Advocate, Mr. David Bates
Pres., Rev. Dan Merry
Treas., Mr. Jerry Sherman

Community Dev. Dir., Rev. Sharon Williams-Gebhard
Major Activities: Basic Human Needs; Unemployment; Community Organization and Development; Inter-Faith Cooperation; Family Hospice; Personal Growth

The Greater Reading Council of Churches

54 N. 8th St., Reading, PA 19601 Tel. (215)375-6108
Exec. Dir., Rev. Larry T. Nallo
Admn. Asst., Constance B. Fegley
Pres., Rev. Edward Ward
Rec. Sec., Rev. Thomas Ross
Treas., Mr. Lee M. LeVan
Major Activities: Institutional Ministry; CWU; Social Action; Migrant Ministry; CWS; CROP Walk for Hunger; Emergency Assistance; Furniture Bank; Prison Chaplaincy; AIDS Hospice Development; Hospital Chaplaincy

The Pennsylvania Council of Churches

900 S. Arlington Ave., Ste. 100, Harrisburg, PA 17109 Tel. (717)545-4761
Exec. Dir., Rev. Albert E. Myers
Asst. Exec. Dir., Ethnic Coop & Institutional Min., Rev. Debra L. Moody
Asst. Exec. Dir., Soc. Min., Rev. Paul D. Gehris
Asst. Exec. Dir., Special Min., Rev. Charles E. Dorsey
Pres., Bishop Charles F. McNutt, Jr., 221 N. Front St., P.O. Box 11937, Harrisburg, PA 17108
Vice-Pres., Hon. Gorham L. Black, Jr.
Sec., Mrs. Pearl Veronis
Treas., Robert Ziegler
Bus. Mgr., Marjorie Maddison
Major Activities: Institutional Ministry; Migrant Ministry; Truck Stop Chaplaincy; Social Ministry; Park Ministry; Inter-Church Planning and Dialog; Conferences; Disaster Response; Trade Association Activities; Church Education; Ethnic Cooperation

United Churches of Williamsport and Lycoming County

202 E. Third St., Williamsport, PA 17701 Tel. (717)322-1110
Exec. Dir., Mrs. Gwen Nelson Bernstine
Ofc. Sec., Mrs. Linda Winter
Pres., Rev. Robert M. Logan, 369 Broad St., Montoursville, PA 17754
Treas., Mr. Russell E. Tingue, 1987 Yale Ave., Williamsport, PA 17701
Shepherd of the Streets, Rev. Joseph L. Walker, 130 E. 3rd St., Williamsport, PA 17701
Dir., Ecumenism, Msgr. Wm. J. Fleming, 410 Walnut St., Williamsport, PA 17701
Dir., Educ. Ministries, Rev. George E. Doran, Jr., 122 S. Main St., Hughesville, PA 17737
Dir., Institutional Ministry, Rev. Wilbur L. Scranton III, 207 E. Water St., Box 504, Muncy, PA 17756
Dir., Radio-TV, Rev. Michael D. Gingerich, P.O. Box 366, Picture Rocks, PA 11762
Dir., Social Concerns, Rev. Mark A. Santucci, 426 Mulberry St., Williamsport, PA 17701
Dir., Prison Ministry, Rev. John N. Mostoller, 1200 Almond St., Williamsport, PA 17701

Major Activities: Ecumenism; Educational Ministries; Church Women United; Church World Service and CROP; Prison Ministry; Radio-TV; Nursing Homes; Fuel Bank; Food Pantry; Family Life; Shepherd of the Streets Urban Ministry; Peace Concerns; Hospitality Network for Homeless

Willkinsburg Community Ministry

710 Mulberry St., Pittsburgh, PA 15221 Tel. (412)241-8072 Fax (412)241-8315
Dir., Ms. Vivian Lovingood
Atn. Coord., Victor Evans
Pres. of Bd., Raymond Touvell
Major Activities: Hunger and Clothing Ministry; After School Youth Programs, Including Child Care for Working Parents; Summer Bible School; Teen-Moms Infant Care; Support Programs for Single Parents and Pregnant Teens; Meals on Wheels; Tape Ministry; Community Activities and Events; Fundraising

Wyoming Valley Council of Churches

35 S. Franklin Sts., Wilkes-Barre, PA 18701 Tel. (717)825-8543
Exec. Dir., Rev. Lynn P. Lampman
Ofc. Sec., Mrs. Sandra Karrott
Pres., William E. Bachman
Treas., Miss Marjorie Trethaway
Major Activities: Hospital and Nursing Home Chaplaincy; Church Women United; High Rise Apartment Ministry; Hospital Referral Service; Emergency Response; Food Bank; Migrant Ministry; Meals on Wheels; Dial-A-Driver; Radio and TV; Leadership Schools; Interfaith Programs; Night Chaplain Ministry; Area Hospitals; CROP Hunger Walks; Pastoral Care Ministries

York County Council of Churches

104 Lafayette St., York, PA 17403 Tel. (717)854-9504
Int. Exec. Dir., Patrick Rooney
CONTACT-York Teleministry Dir., Mrs. Lois Wetzler
Pres., Dr. Florence Ames
Treas., Mr. William Anderson
Major Activities: Educational Development; Spiritual Growth and Renewal; Worship and Witness; Congregational Resourcing; Outreach and Mission

RHODE ISLAND

The Rhode Island State Council of Churches

734 Hope St., Providence, RI 02906 Tel. (401)861-1700 Fax (401)331-3080
Exec. Minister, Rev. James C. Miller
Admn. Asst., Ms. Peggy Macnie
Pres., Mr. George Weavill, Jr.
Treas., Mr. Robert A. Mitchell
Major Activities: Urban Ministries; TV; Institutional Chaplaincy; Advocacy/Justice & Service; Legislative Liaison; Faith & Order; CWS; Leadership Development; Campus Ministries

SOUTH CAROLINA

South Carolina Christian Action Council, Inc.

P.O. Box 3663, Columbia, SC 29230 Tel. (803)786-7115 Fax (803)786-7116
Exec. Minister, Dr. L. Wayne Bryan
Pres., Ms. Betty Park
Major Activities: Advocacy and Ecumenism; Continuing Education; Interfaith Dialogue; Citizenship and Public Affairs; Publications

United Ministries

606 Pendleton St., Greenville, SC 29601 Tel. (803)232-6463
Exec. Dir., Rev. Beth Templeton
Pres., Mr. Bobby Carpenter
Vice-Pres., Rev. Baxter Wynn
Sec., Ms. Mack Pazdan
Treas., Mr. Bill Kellett
Major Activities: Volunteer Programs: Volunteers work in all components as well as through Adopt-A-House and Spend a Day, Building Wheelchair Ramps; Emergency Assistance with Rent, Utilities, Medication, Heating, Food, Shelter Referrals; Homeless Programs: Place of Hope-Day Shelter for Homeless People; Employement Readiness; Travelers Aid; Magdalene Project; Case Management

SOUTH DAKOTA

Association of Christian Churches

1320 S. Minnesota Ave., Ste. 210, Sioux Falls, SD 57105 Tel. (605)334-1980
Exec. Dir., ——
Pres., Rev. R. William Ingvoldstad
Ofc. Mgr., Pat Willard
Major Activities: Ecumenical Forums; Continuing Education for Clergy; Legislative Information; Resourcing Local Ecumenism; Native American Issues; Ecumenical Fields Ministries; Rural Economic Development

TENNESSEE

Metropolitan Inter Faith Association (MIFA)

P.O. Box 3130, Memphis, TN 38173-0130 Tel. (901)527-0208 Fax (901)527-3202
Exec. Dir., Mr. Allie Prescott
Dir. of Urban Ministries, Sara Holmes
Major Activities: Emergency Housing; Emergency Services (Rent, Utility, Food, Clothing Assistance); Home-Delivered Meals and Senior Support Services; Youth Services

Tennessee Association of Churches

413 Moss Creek Ct., Nashville, TN 37221 Tel. (615)646-8106
Exec. Dir., Dr. C. Ray Dobbins
Pres., Rev. James L. Rogers
Major Activities: Faith and Order; Christian Unity; Social Concern Ministries; Legislative Concerns

TEXAS

Austin Metropolitan Ministries
44 East Ave., Ste. 302, Austin, TX 78701 Tel. (512)472-7627
Exec. Dir., Patrick Flood
Pres., Roy Kimble
Treas., Shaun P. O'Brien
Chaplain, Rev. Charles I. Fay, Travis Co. Jails
Chaplain, Rev. Tommy MacIntosh, Travis Co. Jails
Chaplain, Rev. Floyd Vick, Gardner-Betts Juvenile Home
Chaplain, Rev. Don Bobb, Program Staff
Chaplain, Rev. Valerie Bridgeman-Davis, Program Staff
Office Admn., Carole Hatfield
Major Activities: Pastoral Care in Jails; Broadcast Ministry; Emergency Assistance; Older Persons Task Force; Housing Task Force; Peace and Justice Commission; Youth at Risk; AIDS Service; Commission on Racism; Interfaith Dialogues; Economy and Jobs Issues

Border Association for Refugees from Central America
P.O. Box 715, Edinburg, TX 78540 Tel. (512)631-7447 Fax (512)687-9266
Exec. Dir, Ninfa Ochoa-Krueger
Dir. Refugee Children Serv., Kathleen Grace
Major Activities: Food, Shelter, Clothing, to Central Americans; Medical and Other Emergency Aid; Legal Advocacy; Special Services to Children; Speakers on Refugee Concerns for Church Groups

Corpus Christi Metro Ministries
1919 Leopard St., P.O. Box 4899, Corpus Christi, TX 78469-4899 Tel. (512)887-0151
Exec. Dir., Rev. Edward B. Seeger
Dir.,Admn., Daniel D. Scott
Dir., Volunteers, Ann Schiro
Fin. Coord., Sue McCown
Dir., Loaves & Fishes, Ray Gomez
Dir., Counseling, Amie Harrell
Dir., Rustic House, Amie Harrell
Dir., Employment, Curtis Blevins
Dir., Bethany House, Mike Swearingen
Dir., Rainbow House, Judy Fuhrman
Dir., Child Abuse Prevention, Judy Fuhrman
Major Activities: Food Center; Shelters; Counseling; Job Readiness; Job Placement; Abuse Prevention and Intervention; Adult Day Care; Primary Health Care; Community Service Restitution

East Dallas Cooperative Parish
P.O. Box 64725, Dallas, TX 75206 Tel. (214)823-9149 Fax (214)823-2015
Pres., Roy H. Harrell
Sec., Elizabeth Blessing
Major Activities: Emergency Food, Clothing, Job Bank; Pediatric Medical Clinic; Legal Clinic, Tutorial Education; Home Companion Service; Pre-School Education; Learning Center; Asian Ministry; Hispanic Ministry; Activity Center for Low Income Older Adults; Pastoral Counseling

Greater Dallas Community of Churches
2800 Swiss Ave., Dallas, TX 75204 Tel. (214)824-8680 Fax (214)824-8726
Exec. Dir., Rev. Thomas H. Quigley
Assoc. Dirs., Church & Comm.: Rev. Holsey Hickman; John Stoez
Dir., Community College Min., Dr. Philip del Rosario
Dev. Dir., Carole Rylander
Pres., Rev. Joel Martinez
Treas., Gilbert Hernandez
Program Assoc., Child Advocacy, Rev. Carolyn Bullard-Zerweck
Major Activities: Hospital Chaplaincy; Community College Ministry; Housing; Hunger; Peacemaking; Faith and Life; Jewish-Christian Relations; Racial Ethnic Justice; Child Advocacy

Interfaith Ministries for Greater Houston
3217 Montrose Blvd., Houston, TX 77006 Tel. (713)522-3955 Fax (713)520-4663
Exec. Dir., Betty K. Mathis
Assoc. Exec. Dirs.: Kassie Larson; Douglass L. Simmons
Dir. of Dev., Lisa Estes
Dir. of Congregational Dev., Rev. C. Elaine Smith
Dir., Family Connection, Larry Norton
Dir., Hunger Coalition, Barbara McCormick
Dir., Jail Chaplaincy, Rev. Freddie Wier
Dir., Meals on Wheels/Senior Health, Evelyn Velasquez
Dir., Refugee Services, David Deming
Dir. Retired Sr. Volunteer Svcs (RSVP), Candice Twyman
Dir. Youth Victim/Witness, Pamela Hobbs
Comm. Coord., James L. Maxwell
Pres., Rev. James L. Tucker
Treas., Rev. John T. King
Major Activities: Community concerns in areas of: hunger, older adults, families, youth, child abuse, refugee services, jail chaplaincy, congregational and interfaith development

North Dallas Shared Ministries
2526 Manana #203A, Dallas, TX 75220 Tel. (214)353-0495 Fax (214)351-3899
Exec. Dir., Rev. Matt English
Pres., Edward St. John
Major Activities: Emergency Assistance; Job Counseling; Advocacy for Homeless

Northside Inter-Church Agency (NICA)
506 N.W. 15th St., Fort Worth, TX 76106 Tel. (817)626-1102
Dir., Francine Esposito Pratt

San Antonio Community of Churches
1101 W. Woodlawn, San Antonio, TX 78201 Tel. (512)733-9159
Exec. Dir., Dr. Kenneth Thompson
Pres., Mrs. Rene Silk
Pres.-Elect, Rev. C. W. Ganrath
Vice-Pres., Rev. Dan McLendon
Sec., Mrs. Marilyn Pistel
Treas., Rev. Dr. Michael Beaugh

Major Activities: Christian Educ.; Missions; Radio-TV; Resource Center Infant Formula and Medical Prescriptions for Children of Indigent Families; Continuing Education For Clergy; Media Resource Center; Social Issues; Aging Concerns; Youth Concerns

San Antonio Urban Ministries
2002 W. Olmos Dr., San Antonio, TX 78201 Tel. (512)733-5080
Exec. Dir., Mr. L. C. Harrier
Pres., Mr. Chris McDaniel
Major Activities: Homes for Discharged Mental Patients; After School Care for Latch Key Children; Christian Based Community Ministry; San Antonio Legalization Education Coalition

Southeast Area Churches (SEARCH)
P.O. Box 51256, Fort Worth, TX 76105 Tel. (817)531-2211
Dir., Ms. Dorothy Anderson
Major Activities: Emergency Assistance; Advocacy; Information and Referral; Community Worship

Southside Area Ministries (SAM)
305 W. Broadway, Fort Worth, TX 76104 Tel. (817)332-3778
Exec. Dir., Diane Smiley
Major Activities: Assisting those for whom English is a second language; Tutoring grades K-12; Mentoring Grades 6-9; Programs for Senior Citizens and Refugees

Tarrant Area Community of Churches
801 Texas St., Fort Worth, TX 76102 Tel. (817)335-9341
Pres., Rev. Dr. John Tietjen
Treas., Mr. Mark Wells
Exec. Dir., Rev. M. Gayland Pool
Major Activities: Convene four councils: church, community-based, interfaith, pastoral ministry. Sponsor: Jail and elderly ministry

Texas Conference of Churches
6633 Hwy. 290 East, Ste. 200, Austin, TX 78723-1157 Tel. (512)451-0991 Fax (512)451-2904
Exec. Dir., Rev. Dr. Frank H. Dietz
Church & Society Asst., Mary Berwick
Dir., Addictions Min., Ms. Trish Merrill
Dir., Texas Regional AIDS Interfaith Network, Rev. Robert Huie
Pres., Rev. A.M. Hart
Major Activities: Church and Society; Ecumenism; Christian-Jewish Relations; Domestic Violence; Peace; Disaster Response; BARCA; Texas Church World Service/CROP; Alcoholism-Addiction Education; Church Woman United In Texas; Central American Issues; Texas IMPACT; AIDS

United Board of Missions
1701 Bluebonnet Ave., P.O. Box 3856, Port Arthur, TX 77643-3856 Tel. (409)982-9412 Fax (409)985-3668
Exec. Dir., Clark Moore
Pres., Rev. Gene Easterly

Major Activities: Emergency Assistance (i.e., Food and Clothing, Rent and Utility, Medical, Dental, Transportation); Share a Toy at Christmas; Counseling; Back to School Clothing Assistance; Information and Referral; Hearing Aid Bank; Meals on Wheels; Super Panty; Energy Conservation Programs

UTAH

The Shared Ministry
175 W. 200 S., Ste. 3006, Salt Lake City, UT 84101 Tel. (801)355-0168
Exec. Min., Rev. Dr. Max E. Glenn
Major Activities: Poverty, Hunger, and Homelessness; Legislation Concerns; Family Counseling; Peacemaking; Prison Youth and Singles Ministries

VERMONT

Vermont Ecumenical Council and Bible Society
285 Maple St., Burlington, VT 05401 Tel. (802)864-7723
Exec. Sec., Rev. John E. Nutting
Pres., Rev. James M. MacKellar
Treas., Rev. Louis Drew, Jr.
Major Activities: Christian Unity; Bible Distribution; Social Justice; Committees on Peace, Life and Work, Faith and Order, and Bible

VIRGINIA

Community Ministry of Fairfax County
1920 Association Dr., Rm. 505, Reston, VA 22091 Tel. (703)620-5014 Fax (703)264-9494
Exec. Dir., Rev. Frederick S. Lowry
Newsletter Ed., James Vining
Chpsn., Nancy Wormeli
Sec., Marge DeBlaay
Treas., Robert Hunt
Major Activities: Ecumenical Social Ministry; Elderly; Criminal Justice; Housing; Public Education

Virginia Council of Churches, Inc.
1214 W. Graham Rd., Richmond, VA 23230-1409 Tel. (804)321-3300 Fax (804)329-5066
Gen. Min., Rev. James McDonald
Prog. Assoc., Rev. Judith Bennett
Dir., Migrant Head Start, Rev. Myron Miller
Dir., Refugee Resettlement, Rev. David Montanye
Coord., Weekday Rel. Ed., Ms. Evelyn W. Simmons, P.O. Box 245, Clifton Forge, VA 24422
Coord., Campus Ministry Forum, Rev. Robert Thomason, 5000 Echols Ave., Alexandria, VA 22304
Major Activities: Faith and Order; Network Building & Coordination; Ecumenical Communications; Justice and Legislative Concerns; Educational Development; Rural Concerns; Refugee Resettlement; Migrant Ministries and Migrant Day Care; Disaster Coordination

WASHINGTON

Associated Ministries of Tacoma-Pierce County
1224 South "I" St., Tacoma, WA 98405 Tel. (206)383-3056 Fax (206)572-3193
Exec. Dir., Rev. David T. Alger, 4510 Defiance, Tacoma, WA 98407
Assoc. Dir., Janet E. Leng, 1809 N. Lexington, Tacoma, WA 98406
Pres., Virginia Gilmore
Sec., Betty Tober
Treas., Mr. Dennis Paul
Vice-Pres., Danna Clancy
Major Activities: FISH/Food Banks; Hunger Awareness; Economic Justice; Christian Education; Shalom (Peacemaking) Resource Center; Social Service Program Advocacy; Communication and Networking of Churches; Housing; Paint Tacoma/Pierce Beautiful; Interfaith Task Force on Safe Streets

Associated Ministries of Thurston County
P.O. Box 895, Olympia, WA 98507 Tel. (206)357-7224
Exec. Dir., Ken Schwilk
Pres., Jim Castrolang
Treas., Carroll Dick
Major Activities: Church Information and Referral; Interfaith Worship; Workshops; Social and Health Concerns

Center for the Prevention of Sexual and Domestic Violence
1914 N. 34th St., Ste. 105, Seattle, WA 98103 Tel. (206)634-1903 Fax (206)634-0115
Exec. Dir., Rev. Marie M. Fortune
Video Project Coordinator, Jean Anton
Program Specialist, Rev. Thelma B. Burgonio-Watson
Program Assoc., Sandra Barone
Clerical Asst., Lorna Newgent
Devel. Assoc., Lennie Ziontz
Program Specialist, Elizabeth A. Stellas, M.Div.
Fin. & Dev. Direct, Nan Stoops
Mission Intern, Dina Hall
Major Activities: Educational Ministry; Clergy and Lay Training; Social Action.

Church Council of Greater Seattle
4759 - 15th Ave., NE, Seattle, WA 98105 Tel. (206)525-1213 Fax (206)524-5856
Pres.-Dir., Rev. Elaine J. W. Stanovsky
Assoc. Dir.-Urban Min., Rev. David C. Bloom
Assoc. Dir.-Admn., Alice M. Woldt
Exec. Asst., Angela W. Ford
Dir. Emerg. Feeding Prog., Arthur Lee
Dir. Friend-to-Friend, Marilyn Soderquist
Dir. Youth Service Chaplaincy, Terri Ward
Dir. Mental Health Chaplaincy, Rev. Craig Rennebohm
Dir., Native Am. Task Force, Ron Adams
Dir., The Sharehouse, Mike Buckman
Dir. Homelessness Project, Nancy Dorman
Dir., Mission for Music & Healing, Esther "Little Dove" John
Dir., Seattle Displacement Coalition, John Fox
Staff, Church Relations, June Whitson

Dir., Task force on Aging, Mary Liz Chaffee
Dir., ACTfra, Gloria Yamato
Dir., Public Education Task Force, Rev. Joyce Manson
Dir., Housing & Homelessness Task Force, Josephine Archuleta
Vice-Pres., Rev. Rodney Romney
Treas., Dorothy Eley
Ed., Source, Marge Lueder
Major Activities: Racial Justice; Peace Action; Pastoral Ministry; Hunger; Public Education; Housing; Mental Health; Gay Rights; Aging; Latin America; Asia Pacific; South Africa; Native Americans; Jewish-Christian Relations; Ecology; Homelessness; Labor & Economic Justice; Children, Youth & Families; Race Relations; International Relations

Ecumenical Metropolitan Ministry
P.O. Box 12272, Seattle, WA 98102 Tel. (206)625-0755 Fax (206)625-7518
Exec. Dir., Ruth M. Velozo
Chpsn., Rev. Henry F. Seaman
Major Activities: Northwest Harvest (Hunger Response); Northwest Infants Corner (Special Nutritional Products for Infants and Babies); Northwest Caring Ministry (Individuals and Family Crisis Intervention and Advocacy); E.M.M. (Advocacy, Education, Communications Relative to Programs and Economic Justice).

North Snohomish County Association of Churches
2301 Hoyt, P.O. Box 7101, Everett, WA 98201 Tel. (206)252-6672
Exec. Dir., Rev. Lisa Jankanish
Pres., Rev. Edwin C. Coon
Major Activities: Housing and Shelter; Economic Justice; Hunger; Family Life. The Association also sponsors ecumenical and interfaith worship experiences for the community.

Spokane Christian Coalition
E. 245-13th Ave., Spokane, WA 99202 Tel. (509)624-5156
Exec. Dir., Rev. John A. Olson
Pres., Rev. Jim Burford
Treas., Lula Hage, N. 1413 Superior, Spokane, WA 99202
Admn. Coord. & Ed., Mary Stamp Haworth
Major Activities: Greater Spokane Coalition Against Poverty; Multi-Cultural Human Relations Camp for High School Youth; Night Walk Ministry; Calling and Caring Training; Fig Tree Newspaper; Solidarity with Women Task Force; Dir. of Churches & Community Agencies; Interfaith Thanksgiving Worship; Community Easter Sunrise Service; Forums on Issues; Friend to Friend Visitation with Nursing Home Patients; Interstate Task Force on Human Relations

Washington Association of Churches
4759 - 15th Ave. N.E., Seattle, WA 98105 Tel. (206)525-1988 Fax (206)524-5886
Exec. Min., Rev. John C. Boonstra
Dir., Legislative, Tony Lee
Dir., Immigration & Refugee Prog., Leah Iraheta, 233 Sixth Ave. N., Ste. 110, Seattle, WA 98103 Tel. (206)443-9219

Pres., Bishop Calvin McConnell
Treas., Rev. David T. Alger
Major Activities: Faith and Order; Poverty and Justice Advocacy; Hunger Action; Legislation; Denominational Ecumenical Coordination; Theological Formation; Leadership Development; Refugee Resettlement; Racial Justice Advocacy; Immigration; International Solidarity

WASHINGTON, D.C.

The Council of Churches of Greater Washington
411 Rittenhouse St., NW, Washington, DC 20011 Tel. (202)722-9240
Exec. Dir., Rev. Rodney L. Young
Asst. Dir. for Prog., City, Mr. Daniel Thompson
D.C. Communities Ministries, Rev. George N. Bolden
Prog. Coord., Hope Valley Camp, Mr. Daniel Thompson
Pres., Rev. Lincoln Dring
Major Activities: Development of Group and Community Ministries; Church Development and Redevelopment; Liaison with Public Agencies; In-school Youth Employment; Summer Youth Employment; Hope Valley Camp; Institutional Ministry; Hunger Relief; Vision to Action—Community Revitalization; Health Ministries; Cluster of Store Front Churches

WEST VIRGINIA

Greater Fairmont Council of Churches
P.O. Box 108, Fairmont, WV 26554
Exec. Sec., Nancy Hoffman
Major Activities: Community Ecumenical Services; Youth and Adult Sports Leagues; CROP Walk Sponsor; Weekly Radio Broadcasts

The Greater Wheeling Council of Churches
110 Methodist Bldg., Wheeling, WV 26003 Tel. (304)232-5315
Exec. Dir., Kathy J. Burley
Hospital Notification Sec., Mrs. Ruth Fletcher
Pres., Rev. Charles Ellwood
Treas., Mrs. Naoma Boram
Major Activities: Christian Education; Evangelism; Summer Vespers; Television; Institutional Ministry; Religious Film Library; Church Women United; Volunteer Pastor Care at OVMC Hospital; School of Religion; Hospital Notification; Hymn Sing in the Park; Flood Relief Network; Pentecost Celebration; Clergy Council, Easter Sunrise Service; Community Seder

West Virginia Council of Churches
1608 Virginia St. E., Charleston, WV 25311 Tel. (304)344-3141
Exec. Dir., Rev. James M. Kerr
Pres., Bishop L. Alexander Black, ELCA Synod of WV-MD, 502 Morgantown Ave., Atrium Mall, Ste. 100, Fairmont, WV 26554
Vice-Pres., Mary Virginia DeRoo, 2006 Northwood Rd., Charleston, WV 25314
Sec., Sr. Marguerite St. Amand, 63 Elk River Rd., Clendinin, WV 25045

Treas., Rev. Richard Flowers, P.O. Box 667, Scott Depot, WV 25560
Major Activities: Leisure Ministry; Disaster Response; Faith and Order; Family Concerns; Inter-Faith Relations; Peace and Justice; Government Concerns; Support Sevices Network

WISCONSIN

Center for Community Concerns
1501 Villa St., Racine, WI 53403 Tel. (414)637-9176
Exec. Dir., Mrs. Jean Mandli
Skillbank Coord., Eleanor Sorenson
Volunteer Prog. Coord., Chris Udell-Solberg
RSVP (Retired Senior Volunteer Program), Laurie Defatte
Admn. Asst., Bonnie Wrixton
Major Activities: Advocacy; Direct Services; Research; Community Consultant; Criminal Justice; Volunteerism; Senior Citizen Services

Christian Youth Council
1715-52nd St., Kenosha, WI 53140 Tel. (414)652-9543
Exec. Dir., Ron Stevens
Sports Dir., Krisp Jensen
Outreach Dir., Linda Osborne
Pres., Floyd Wilkinson
Major Activities: Leisure Time Ministry; Institutional Ministries; Ecumenical Committee; Social Concerns

Interfaith Conference of Greater Milwaukee
1442 N. Farwell Ave., Ste. 200, Milwaukee, WI 53202 Tel. (414)276-9050 Fax (414)224-0243
Exec. Dir., Mr. Jack Murtaugh
First Vice-Chair, Bishop Peter Rogness
Second Vice-Chair, Archbishop Rembert Weakland
Sec., Rev. Paul Bodine, Jr.
Treas., Rev. Mary Ann Neevel
Prog. Coord. on Poverty Issues: Mrs. Donna Ferency; Mr. Marcus White
Dir. of Dev., Mrs. Donna Ferency
Ofc. Admn., Mrs. Frankie Mason-McCain
Prog. Coord. for Public Educ., Mrs. Charlotte Holloman
Consultant in Communications, Rev. Robert Seater
Chpsn., Bishop Peter Rogness
Major Activities: Economic Issues - Unemployment; Emergency Assistance - Public Policy; Religion and Labor Committee; Economic Concerns - Private Sector Committee; Public Education Committee; TV Programming; Peace and International Issues Committee; Annual Membership Luncheon

Madison Urban Ministry
1127 University Ave., Madison, WI 53715 Tel. (608)256-0906
Exec. Dir., Charles Pfeifer
Office/Program Mgr., Margaret Tanaka
Admn. Asst./Community Liaison, Cynthia Adams
Major Activities: Develop Community Projects; Race Relations Task Force; Housing Coalition

Wisconsin Conference of Churches

1955 W. Broadway, Ste. 104, Madison, WI 53713 Tel. (608)222-9779 Fax (608)222-2854

Exec. Dir., Rev. John D. Fischer

Office Mgr., Ms. Linda Spilde

Dir., Public Policy & IMPACT, Ms. Bonnee Voss

Dir. Broadcasting Ministry Commission, Rev. Robert P. Seater, 2717 E. Hampshire, Milwaukee, WI 53211 Tel. (414)332-2133

Co-Dir., Peace & Justice Ecumenical Partnership, Jane Hammatt-Kavaloski, Rt. #3, Box 228E, Dodgeville, WI 53533

Co-Dir., Peace & Justice Ecumenical Partnership, Vincent Kavaloski, Rt. #3, Box 228E, Douglasville, WI 53533

Chaplaincy Coord., Rev. M. Charles Davis, 1221 Jackson St., Oshkosh, WI 54901

Pres., Bishop David Lawson

Treas., Mr. Chester Spangler, 625 Crandall, Madison, WI 53711

Major Activities: Church and Society; Migrant Ministry; Broadcasting Ministry; Aging; IMPACT; Institutional Chaplaincy; Peace and Justice; Faith and Order; Rural Concerns Forum; American Indian Ministries Council; Park Ministry

WYOMING

Wyoming Church Coalition

P.O. Box 990, Laramie, WY 82070 Tel. (307)745-6000

Admn. Coord., Melissa Sanders

Chair, Rev. Warren Murphy, P.O. Box 1718, Cody, WY 82414

Penitentiary Chaplain, Rev. Lynn Schumacher, P.O. Box 400, Rawlins, WY 82301

Major Activities: Death Penalty; Empowering the Poor and Oppressed; Peace and Justice; Prison Ministry

8. CANADIAN REGIONAL AND LOCAL ECUMENICAL AGENCIES

Most of the organizations listed below are councils of churches in which churches participate officially, whether at the parish or judicatory level. They operate at either the city, metropolitan area, or county level. Parish clusters within urban areas are not included.

Canadian local ecumenical bodies operate without paid staff, with the exception of a few which have part-time staff. In most cases the name and address of the president or chairperson is listed. As these offices change from year to year, some of this information may be out of date by the time the *Yearbook of American and Canadian Churches* is published. However, a letter to the address listed will be forwarded. Up-to-date information may be secured from the Canadian Council of Churches, 40 St. Clair Ave., E., Toronto, Ontario M4T 1M9.

ALBERTA

Calgary Inter-Faith Community Association
Rev. V. Hennig, 7515 7th St., Calgary, Alberta T2V 1G1

Calgary Inter-Faith Sawdap
Mrs. Caroline Brown, #106-1916-2 St., S.W., Calgary, Alberta T2S 1S3

Calgary Council of Churches
Box 7550, Stn. E., Calgary, Alberta T3C 3M3

Edmonton & District Council of Churches
Rev. John Bergman, 13340-96th St., Edmonton, Alberta T5E 4B3

ATLANTIC PROVINCES

Atlantic Ecumenical Council of Churches
Pres., Rev. John E. Boyd, Box 637, 90 Victoria St., Box 637, Amherst, Nova Scotia B4H 4B4

BRITISH COLUMBIA

Canadian Ecumenical Action
Coordinator, 1410 West 12th Ave., Vancouver, British Columbia V6H 1M8

Greater Victoria Council of Churches
Pres., Mr. H. De Zwager, 1457 Clifford St., Victoria, British Columbia V8S 1M1

MANITOBA

Association of Christian Churches in Manitoba
240 Home St., Winnipeg, Manitoba R3G 1X3

Manitoba Provincial Interfaith Council
Rev. Canon W. J. G. Ayers, #8 - 400 Carpathia St., Winnipeg, Manitoba R3N 1Y4

NEW BRUNSWICK

Moncton Area Council of Churches
Ms. Faye L. MacKay, Site 9. Comp. 7, R.R. #1, Hillsborough, New Brunswick E0A 1X0

First Miramichi Inter-Church Council
Mrs. Victor Ross, Boiestown, New Brunswick E0H 1A0

NOVA SCOTIA

Amherst and Area Council of Churches
Mr. Ron Esta Brooks, RR#6, Amherst, Nova Scotia B3H 3Y4

Annapolis Royal Council of Churches
Rev. David Stokes, P. O. Box 7, Annapolis Royal, Nova Scotia B0S 1A0

Atlantic Baptist Fellowship
Rev. Donald Jackson, Tideways, Apt. 207, Wolfville, Nova Scotia B0P 1X0

Bedford and Sackville Church Association
Ms. Dianne Swineman, P. O. Box 585, Lower Sackville, Nova Scotia B4C 3J1

Bridgewater Inter-Church Council
Pres., Ms. Carroll Young, 159 High St., Bridgewater, Nova Scotia B4V 1W2

Cornwallis District Inter-Church Council
Pres., Mr. Tom Regan, Centreville, R.R. #2, Kings County, Nova Scotia B0T 1J0

Halifax-Dartmouth Council of Churches
Rev. Robert L. Johnson, 2021 Oxford St., Halifax, Nova Scotia B3L 2T3

Industrial Cape Breton Council of Churches
Mr. J. Redmond O'Keefe, 56 Rosewood Dr., Sydney, Nova Scotia B1P 1P4

Kentville Council of Churches
Rev. Canon S.J.P. Davies, 325 Main St., Kentville, Nova Scotia B4N 1C5

Mahone Bay Inter-Church Council
Mrs. Phyllis Smeltzer, R. R. 1, Mahone Bay, Nova Scotia B0J 2E0

Queen's County Council of Churches
Rev. Robert L. Johnson, P.O. Box 394, Milton, Nova Scotia B0T 1P0

Wolfville Inter-Church Council
Rev. Douglass Hergett, Box 786, Wolfville, Nova Scotia B0P 1X0

ONTARIO

Brockville & District Inter-Church Council
Rev. George Clifford, 5 Wall St., Brockville, Ontario K6V 4R8

Burlington Inter-Church Council
Mr. Fred Townsend, 425 Breckenwood, Burlington, Ontario L7L 2J6

Ottawa Christian Council of the Capital Area
1247 Kilborn Ave., Ottawa, Ontario K1H 6K9

Glengarry-Prescott-Russell Christian Council
Pres., Rev. G. Labrosse, St.-Eugene, Prescott, Ontario K0B 1P0

Hamilton and District Christian Churches Association
Chpsn., Rev. Dr. John A. Johnston, 147 Chedoke Ave., Hamilton, Ontario L8P 4P2

Ignace Council of Churches
Box 5, 205 Pine St., St. Ignace, Ontario P0T 1H0

Kitchener-Waterloo Council of Churches
Rev. Clarence Hauser, CR, 53 Allen St. E., Waterloo, Ontario N2J 1J3

London Inter-Church Council
Rev. R. Breitwieser, 172 High St., London, Ontario N6C 4K6

London Inter-City Faith Team
c/o United Church, 711 Colfourne St., London, Ontario N6A 3Z4

Reuter photo

Leaning on the everlasting arms
An old Serbian woman leans on the cross as she cries over the grave of her son, in the village of Mirkovci, Yugoslavia. Her son was killed during fighting with Croatian forces in February, 1992. Throughout late 1991 and early 1992, Serbs and Croats fought for control of newly contested territories.

Manitoulin West Inter-Church Council
Mr. Douglas Wismer, Silver Water, Ontario P0P 1Y0

Massey Inter-Church Council
Rev. Hope Jackson, Box 248, Massey, Ontario P0P 1P0

Oshawa Ecumenical Group
Rev. James A. McKay, 333 Rossland Rd., N., Oshawa, Ontario L1J 3G4

Ecumenical Committee
Rev. William B. Kidd, 76 Eastern Ave., Sault Ste., Marie, Ontario P6A 4R2

Stratford District Council of Churches
Rev. N. S. Gibson, 20 Manning Ave., Stratford, Ontario N5A 5M9

Thorold Inter-Faith Council
1 Dunn St., St. Catharines, Ontario L2T 1P3

Thunder Bay Council of Churches
Rev. Richard Darling, 1800 Moodie St., E., Thunder Bay, Ontario P7E 4Z2

Waterloo Clergy Fellowship
50 Erb St., W., Waterloo, Ontario N2L 1T1

PRINCE EDWARD ISLAND

Charlottetown Christian Council
Rev. H. M. D. Westin, 21 Fitzroy St., Charlottetown, Prince Edward Island C1A 3K9

Summerside Christian Council
Mr. Paul H. Scherman, 181 Green St., Summerside, Prince Edward Island C1N 1Y8

West Prince Christian Council
Rev. Kenneth C. Jones, Box S, Ellerslie, Prince Edward Island C0B 1J0

QUEBEC

Hemmingford Ecumenical Committee
c/o Catherine Priest, Box 300, Hemmingford, Quebec J0L 1H0

Montreal Council of Churches
Rev. Stéphane Valiquette, 2065 Sherbrooke St., W., Montréal, Québec H3H 1G6

Montreal Ecumenical Association
Rev. William Derby, Box 158, Sta. B, Montreal, Quebec H3B 3J5

Centre for Ecumenism/Centre d'oecuménisme
Rev. Tom Ryan, 2065 Sherbrooke St., West, Montreal, Quebec H3H 1G6

Ecumenical Council of Churches/Downtown Montreal
Rev. Vernon Wishart, 3407 Avenue de Musee, Montréal, Québec H3G 2C6

The Ecumenical Group
c/o Mrs. C. Haten, 1185 Ste. Foy, St. Bruno, Quebec J3V 3C3

SASKATCHEWAN

Humboldt Clergy Council
Fr. Leo Hinz, O. S. B., Box 1989, Humboldt, Saskatchewan S0K 2A0

Melville Association of Churches
Attn., Catherine Gaw, Box 1078, Melville, Saskatchewan S0K 2A0

Inter-City Church Council
James Tait, 805 7th Ave., Saskatoon, Saskatchewan S7K 2V5

Saskatoon Council of Churches
816 Spadina Cres., E., Saskatoon, Saskatchewan S7K 3H4

Centre for Ecumenism—Saskatoon
Rev. Bernard de Margerie, 1006 Broadway Ave., Saskatoon, Saskatchewan S7N 1B9

9. THEOLOGICAL SEMINARIES AND BIBLE COLLEGES IN THE UNITED STATES

The following list includes theological seminaries and departments in colleges and universities in which ministerial training is given. Many denominations have additional programs. The lists of Religious Bodies in the United States should be consulted for the address of denominational headquarters.

Inclusion in or exclusion from this list implies no judgment about the quality or accreditation of any institution.

The listing includes the institution name, denominational sponsor when appropriate, location, head, telephone number, and fax number when known.

Abilene Christian University, (Churches of Christ), ACU Station, Box 7000, Abilene, TX 79699. Royce Money. Tel. (915)674-2412. Fax (915)674-2958

Academy of the New Church (Theol. Sch.), (General Church of the New Jerusalem), 2815 Huntingdon Pk., Box 717, Bryn Athyn, PA 19009. Daniel W. Goodenough. Tel. (215)947-4200. Fax (215)938-2616

Alabama Christian School of Religion, (Churches of Christ), 7500 Taylor Rd., P.O. Box 17096, Montgomery, AL 36117. Rex A. Turner. Tel. (205)277-2277

Alaska Bible College, (Nondenominational), P.O. Box 289, Glennallen, AK 99588. Dr. Gary J. Ridley, Sr. Tel. (907)822-3201. Fax (907)822-3290

Alliance Theological Seminary, (Christian and Missionary Alliance), Alliance Theological Seminary, Nyack, NY 10960. Paul F. Bubna. Tel. (914)358-1710. Fax (914)358-2651

American Baptist College, (Natl. Bapt., USA, Inc.; So. Bapt. Conv.), 1800 Baptist World Center Dr., Nashville, TN 37207. Odell McGlothian, Sr. Tel. (615)262-1369

American Baptist Seminary of the West, (American Baptist Churches), 2606 Dwight Way, Berkeley, CA 94704. Theodore Keaton. Tel. (510)841-1905

Anderson University School of Theology, (Church of God), Anderson University, Anderson, IN 46012. James Earl Massey. Tel. (317)641-4032. Fax (317)641-3851

Andover Newton Theological School, (Amer. Bapt.; United Church of Christ), 210 Herrick Rd., Newton Centre, MA 02159. David T. Shannon. Tel. (617)964-1100. Fax (617)965-9756

Appalachian Bible College, (Independent), P.O. Box ABC, Bradley, WV 25818. Daniel L. Anderson. Tel. (304)877-6428

Aquinas Institute of Theology, 3642 Lindell Blvd., St. Louis, MO 63108. Charles E. Bouchard. Tel. (314)658-3882

Arizona College of the Bible, (Nondenominational), 2045 W. Northern Ave., Phoenix, AZ 85021. Robert W. Benton. Tel. (602)995-2670

Arlington Baptist College, 3001 W. Division, Arlington, TX 76012. Wayne Martin. Tel. (817)461-8741

Asbury Theological Seminary, (Interdenominational), 204 N. Lexington Ave., Wilmore, KY 40390. David McKenna. Tel. (606)858-3581. Fax (606)858-3581

Ashland Theological Seminary, (Brethren Church (Ashland, OH)), 910 Center St., Ashland, OH 44805. Joseph R. Schultz. Tel. (419)289-4142. Fax (419)289-5333

Assemblies of God Theological Seminary, (Assemblies of God), 1445 Boonville Ave., Springfield, MO 65802. Del Tarr. Tel. (417)862-3344. Fax (417)862-3214

Atlanta Christian College, (Christian Churches/Church of Christ), 2605 Ben Hill Rd., East Point, GA 30344. James C. Donovan. Tel. (404)761-8861. Fax (404)669-2024

Austin Presbyterian Theological Seminary, (PCUSA), 100 E. 27th St., Austin, TX 78705. Jack L. Stotts. Tel. (512)472-6736. Fax (512)479-0738

Azusa Pacific University, (Interdenominational), 901 E. Alosta, P.O. Box APU, Azusa, CA 91702. Richard Felix. Tel. (818)969-3434. Fax (818)969-7180

Bangor Theological Seminary, (United Church of Christ), 300 Union St., Bangor, ME 04401. Malcolm Warford. Tel. (207)942-6781. Fax (207)942-4914

Baptist Bible College, (Baptist), 628 E. Kearney, Springfield, MO 65803. Leland Kennedy. Tel. (417)869-9811. Fax (417)831-8029

Baptist Bible College and Seminary, (Baptist), 538 Venard Rd., Clarks Summit, PA 18411. Milo Thompson, D.D. Tel. (717)587-1172. Fax (717)586-1753

Baptist Missionary Association Theological Seminary, (Baptist Missionary Assoc. of America), 1410 Pine St., Jacksonville, TX 75766. Philip R. Bryan. Tel. (903)586-2501

Barclay College, (Friends), P.O. Box 288, Haviland, KS 67059. Robin W. Johnson. Tel. (316)862-5252

Bay Ridge Christian College, (Church of God (Anderson, IN)), P.O. Box 726, Kendleton, TX 77451. Wilfred Jordan. Tel. (409)532-3982

Berean Christian College, (Interdenominational), 6801 Millmark Ave., Long Beach, CA 90805. A. A. Bachman. Tel. (213)428-0030

Berkeley Divinity School at Yale, (Episcopalian), 363 St. Ronan St., New Haven, CT 06511. Dean Philip Turner. Tel. (203)432-6106. Fax (203)432-6110

Bethany College, (Assemies of God), 800 Bethany Dr., Scotts Valley, CA 95066. Richard Foth. Tel. (408)438-3800. Fax (408)438-1621

Bethany Lutheran Theological Seminary, (Evangelical Lutheran Synod), 447 N. Division St., Mankato, MN 56001. W. W. Petersen. Tel. (507)625-2977. Fax (507)625-1849

Bethany Theological Seminary, (Church of the Brethren), Butterfield and Meyers Rd., Oak Brook, IL 60521. Wayne L. Miller. Tel. (708)620-2200. Fax (708)620-9014

Bethel Theological Seminary, (Baptist General Conference), Bethel Theological Seminary, St. Paul, MN 55112. George K. Brushaber. Tel. (612)638-6230. Fax (612)638-6002

Beulah Heights Bible College, (Pentecostal), 892 Berne St. SE, Atlanta, GA 30316. James B. Keiller. Tel. (404)627-2681

Biblical Theological Seminary, (Interdenominational), 200 N. Main St., Hatfield, PA 19440. David G. Dunbar. Tel. (215)368-5000. Fax (215)368-7002

Boise Bible College, (Independent), 8695 Marigold St., Boise, ID 83714. Charles A. Crane. Tel. (208)376-7731

Boston University (School of Theology), (United Methodist Church), 745 Commonwealth Ave., Boston, MA 02215. Dean Robert E. Neville. Tel. (617)353-3051. Fax (617)353-2053

Brite Divinity School, Texas Christian University, (Christian Church (Disciples of Christ)), P.O. Box 32923, TCU, Ft. Worth, TX 76129. Leo G. Perdue. Tel. (817)921-7575. Fax (817)921-7333

Calvary Bible College, (Nondenominational), 15800 Calvary Rd., Kansas City, MO 64147. Donald A. Urey. Tel. (800)326-3960

Calvin Theological Seminary, (Christian Reformed Church), 3233 Burton St. SE, Grand Rapids, MI 49546. J. A. DeJong. Tel. (616)957-6036. Fax (616)957-8551

Catholic Theological Union, (Catholic), 5401 S. Cornell Ave., Chicago, IL 60615. Donald Senior. Tel. (312)324-8000

Catholic University of America (Theological College), (Catholic), 401 Michigan Ave. NE, Washington, DC 20017. Lawrence B. Terrien. Tel. (202)319-5900. Fax (202)319-5967

Central Baptist College, (Baptist), 1501 College Ave., Conway, AR 72032. Charles Attebery. Tel. (501)329-6872. Fax (501)329-2941

Central Baptist Theological Seminary, (American Baptists), 741 N. 31st St., Kansas City, KS 66102. John R. Landgraf. Tel. (913)371-5313. Fax (913)371-8110

Central Baptist Theological Seminary in Indiana, (Natl. Bapt., USA, Inc; Natl. Bapt. Conv.), 1535 Dr. A. J. Brown Ave. N, Indianapolis, IN 46202. F. Benjamin Davis. Tel. (317)636-6622

Central Bible College, (Assemblies of God), 3000 N. Grant Ave., Springfield, MO 65803. Dr. H. Maurice Lednicky. Tel. (417)833-2551. Fax (417)833-5141

Central Christian College of the Bible, (Christian Church), 911 E. Urbandale, Moberly, MO 65270. Lloyd M. Pelfrey. Tel. (816)263-3900

Central Indian Bible College, (Assembies of God), P.O. Box 550, Mobridge, SD 57601. Howard Hodson. Tel. (605)845-7801

Central Wesleyan College, (Wesleyan Church), One Wesleyan Dr., Central, SC 29630. John Newby. Tel. (803)639-2453. Fax (803)639-0826

Chicago Theological Seminary, (United Church of Christ), 5757 University Ave., Chicago, IL 60637. Kenneth B. Smith. Tel. (312)752-5757. Fax (312)752-5925

Christ the King Seminary, (Catholic), 711 Knox Rd., P.O. Box 607, East Aurora, NY 14052. Dr. Frederick D. Leising. Tel. (716)652-8900. Fax (716)652-8903

Christ the Savior Seminary, (Amer. Carpatho-Russ. Orth. Greek Cath.), 225 Chandler Ave., Johnstown, PA 15906. Bishop Nicholas Smisko. Tel. (814)539-8086

Christian Theological Seminary, (Christian Church (Disciples of Christ)), 1000 W. 42nd St., Indianapolis, IN 46208. Richard D. N. Dickinson. Tel. (317)924-1331. Fax (317)923-1961

Church Divinity School of the Pacific, (Episcopalian), 2451 Ridge Rd., Berkeley, CA 94709. Charles A. Perry. Tel. (415)848-3282. Fax (415)644-0712

Cincinnati Bible College and Seminary, 2700 Glenway Ave., Cincinnati, OH 45204. C. Barry McCarty. Tel. (513)244-8100. Fax (513)244-8140

Circleville Bible College, (Churches of Christ in Christian Union), P.O. Box 458, Circleville, OH 43113. David Van Hoose. Tel. (614)474-8896

Clear Creek Baptist Bible College, (Southern Baptist), 300 Clear Creek Rd., Pineville, KY 40977. Bill Whittaker. Tel. (606)337-3196

Colegio Biblico Pentecostal de Puerto Rico, (Church of God (Cleveland, TN)), P.O. Box 901, Saint Just, PR 00750. Ernesto L. Rodriquez. Tel. (809)761-0640

Colgate Rochester Divinity School/Crozer Theological Sem., (Multidenominational), 1100 S. Goodman St., Rochester, NY 14620. James H. Evans, Jr. Tel. (716)271-1320. Fax (716)271-2166

College of the Bible, (Independent), 1515 S. 10th St., Omaha, NE 68108. Warren E. Bathke. Tel. (402)449-2800

Colorado Christian University, (Interdenominational), 180 S. Garrison St., Lakewood, CO 80226. Dr. L. David Beckman. Tel. (303)238-5386. Fax (303)234-1217

Columbia Bible College and Seminary, (Interdenominational), P.O. Box 3122, Columbia, SC 29230. Johnny Miller. Tel. (803)754-4100. Fax (803)786-4209

Columbia Theological Seminary, (PCUSA), P.O. Box 520, Decatur, GA 30031. Douglas Oldenburg. Tel. (404)378-8821. Fax (404)377-9696

Concordia Sem., (Lutheran Church - Missouri Synod), 801 DeMun, St. Louis (Clayton), MO 63105. John F. Johnson. Tel. (314)721-5934. Fax (314)721-5902

Concordia Theolical Seminary, (Lutheran Church - Missouri Synod), 6600 N. Clinton St., Ft. Wayne, IN 46825. Dr. Norbert H. Mueller. Tel. (219)481-2100. Fax (219)481-2121

Covenant Theological Seminary, (Presbyterian), 12330 Conway Rd., St. Louis, MO 63141. Paul Kooistra. Tel. (314)434-4044. Fax (314)434-4819

Cranmer Seminary, (Anglican Orthodox Church), P.O. Box 329, 323 Walnut St., Statesville, NC 28677. James P. Dees. Tel. (704)873-8365

Crichton College, (Independent), 6655 Winchester Rd., Memphis, TN 38175. Dr. James M. Latimer. Tel. (901)367-9800. Fax (901)375-8198

Criswell Center for Biblical Studies, (Baptist), 4010 Gaston Ave., Dallas, TX 75246. W. A. Criswell. Tel. (214)821-5433

Criswell College, The, (Baptist), 4010 Gaston Ave., Dallas, TX 75246. Paige Patterson. Tel. (214)818-1300. Fax (214)818-1320

Dallas Christian College, (Christian Churches), 2700 Christian Pky., Dallas, TX 75234. Gene Shepherd. Tel. (214)241-3371. Fax (214)241-8021

Dallas Theological Seminary, (Interdenominational), 3909 Swiss Ave., Dallas, TX 75204. Donald K. Campbell. Tel. (214)824-3094. Fax (214)841-3642

De Sales School of Theology, (Catholic), 721 Lawrence St. NE, Washington, DC 20017. John W. Crossin. Tel. (202)269-9412

Denver Conservative Baptist Seminary, (Conservative Baptist), Box 10,000, Denver, CO 80210. -----. Tel. (303)761-2482. Fax (303)761-8060

Disciples Divinity House, University of Chicago, (Christian Church (Disciples of Christ)), 1156 E. 57th St., Chicago, IL 60637. Kristie A. Culp. Tel. (312)643-4411

Dominican House of Studies (Pontifical Faculty of the Immacu, (late Conception), 487 Michigan Ave. NE, Washington, DC 20017-1585. Philip Smith. Tel. (202)529-5300. Fax (202)636-4460

Drew University (Theological School), (United Methodist), 36 Madison Ave., Madison, NJ 07940-4010. Robin Warren Lovin. Tel. (201)408-3258. Fax (201)408-3939

Dubuque, University of (Theological Seminary), (PCUSA), 2000 University, University of Dubuque, Dubuque, IA 52001. Dr. John J. Agria. Tel. (319)589-3222. Fax (319)556-8633

Duke University (Divinity School), (United Methodist), Duke University Divinity School, Durham, NC 27706. Dennis M. Campbell. Tel. (919)660-3400

Earlham School of Religion, (Friends (Quakers)), 228 College Ave., Richmond, IN 47374. Andrew P. Grannell. Tel. (800)432-1377. Fax (317)983-1304

East Coast Bible College, (Church of God), 6900 Wilkinson Blvd., Charlotte, NC 28214. Ronald Martin. Tel. (704)394-2307. Fax (704)394-2308

Eastern Baptist Theological Seminary, (American Baptist), P.O. Box 12438, Philadelphia, PA 19151-0438. Manfred T. Brauch. Tel. (215)896-5000. Fax (215)649-3834

Eastern Mennonite Seminary, (Mennonite Churches), Eastern Mennonite Seminary, Harrisonburg, VA 22801. George R. Brunk III. Tel. (703)432-4260. Fax (703)432-4444

Eden Theological Seminary, (United Church of Christ), 475 E. Lockwood Ave., St. Louis, MO 63119. Dr. Eugene S. Wehrli. Tel. (314)961-3627. Fax (314)961-5738

Emmanuel College School of Chrisitian Ministries, (Pentecostal Holiness Church), P.O. Box 129, Franklin Springs, GA 30639. David Hopkins. Tel. (404)245-7226. Fax (404)245-4424

Emmanuel School of Religion, (Christian Churches & Churches of Christ), One Walker Dr., Johnson City, TN 37601. Calvin L. Phillips. Tel. (615)926-1186. Fax (615)461-1556

Emmaus Bible College, (Independent), 25720 Asbury Rd., Dubuque, IA 52001. Daniel Smith. Tel. (319)588-8000. Fax (319)588-1216

Emory University (The Candler School of Theology), (United Methodist), Bishops Hall 202, Emory University, Atlanta, GA 30322. R. Kevin LaGree. Tel. (404)727-6324

Episcopal Divinity School, (Episcopalian), 99 Brattle St., Cambridge, MA 02138. Otis Charles. Tel. (617)868-3450. Fax (617)864-5385

Episcopal Theological Seminary of the Southwest, (Episcopalian), P.O. Box 2247, Austin, TX 78768-2247. Rev. Durstan R. McDonald. Tel. (512)472-4133. Fax (512)472-3098

Erskine Theological Seminary, (Associate Reformed Presbytarian Church), Drawer 668, Due West, SC 29639. R. T. Ruble. Tel. (803)379-8885. Fax (803)379-8759

Eugene Bible College, 2155 Bailey Hill Rd., Eugene, OR 97405. Jeffrey E. Farmer. Tel. (503)485-1780. Fax (503)485-1782

Evangelical School of Theology, (Evangelical Congregational Ch.), 121 S. College St., Myerstown, PA 17067. Ray A. Seilhamer. Tel. (717)866-5775. Fax (717)866-4667

Evangelical Theological Seminary, Inc., 2302-2400 E. Ash St., Goldsboro, NC 27530. William Ralph Painter. Tel. (919)735-0831

Faith Baptist Bible College and Seminary, (Baptist), 1900 NW 4th St., Ankeny, IA 50021. Robert Domokos. Tel. (515)964-0601. Fax (515)964-1638

Florida Bible College, (Ind. Fundamental Churches of America), 1701 N. Poinciana Blvd., Kissimmee, FL 32758. Ron Von Behren. Tel. (407)933-4500

Florida Christian College, (Christian Church), 1011 Osceola Blvd., Kissimmee, FL 34744. A. Wayne Lowen. Tel. (407)847-8966

Franciscan School of Theology, (Catholic), 1712 Euclid Ave., Berkeley, CA 94709. William J. Short. Tel. (510)848-5232

Free Will Baptist Bible College, (Free Will Baptist), 3606 West End Ave., Nashville, TN 37205. Tom Malone. Tel. (615)383-1340

Fuller Theological Seminary, (Multidenominational), 135 N. Oakland Ave., Pasadena, CA 91182. David A. Hubbard. Tel. (818)584-5200. Fax (818)795-8767

Garrett-Evangelical Theological Seminary, (United Methodist), 2121 Sheridan Rd., Evanston, IL 60201. Neal F. Fisher. Tel. (708)866-3900. Fax (708)866-3957

General Theological Seminary, (Episcopalian), 175 Ninth Ave., New York, NY 10011. James C. Fenhagen. Tel. (212)243-5150. Fax (212)727-7880

George Mercer, Jr., Memorial School of Theology, (Episcopalian), 65 Fourth St., Garden City, NY 11530. Dr. Lloyd A. Lewis, Jr. Tel. (516)248-4800. Fax (516)248-4883

God's Bible School and College, (Independent), 1810 Young St., Cincinnati, OH 45210. Bence Miller. Tel. (513)721-7944

Golden Gate Baptist Theological Seminary, (Southern Baptist), Strawberry Point, Mill Valley, CA 94941. William O. Crews. Tel. (415)388-8080. Fax (415)383-0723

Gordon-Conwell Theological Seminary, (Interdenominational), 130 Essex St., South Hamilton, MA 01982. Robert E. Cooley. Tel. (508)468-7111. Fax (508)468-6691

Goshen Biblical Seminary, (Mennonite), 3003 Benham Ave., Elkhart, IN 46517-1999. Marlin E. Miller. Tel. (219)295-3726. Fax (219)295-0092

Grace Bible College, (Grace Gospel Fellowship), P.O. Box 910, Grand Rapids, MI 49509. Samuel R. Vinton, Jr. Tel. (616)538-2330

Grace College of the Bible, (Independent), 1515 S. 10th St., Omaha, NE 68108. Warren E. Bathke. Tel. (402)449-2800

Grace Theological Seminary, (Fellowship of Grace Brethren), 200 Seminary Dr., Winona Lake, IN 46590. John J. Davis. Tel. (219)372-5100. Fax (219)372-5265

Graduate Theological Union, (Nondenominational), 2400 Ridge Rd., Berkeley, CA 94709. Robert Barr. Tel. (415)647-2412

Grand Rapids School of the Bible and Music, (Independent), 109 School St. NE, Comstock Park, MI 49321. Dr. Ronald Chadwick. Tel. (616)785-8703. Fax (616)785-8708

Great Lakes Bible College, (Church of Christ/Christian Church), 6211 W. Willow Hwy., Lansing, MI 48917. Rex Dye. Tel. (517)321-0242. Fax (517)321-5902

Greenville College, (Free Methodist Church of North America), 315 E. College Ave., Greenville, IL 62246. W. Richard Stephens. Tel. (800)345-4440. Fax (618)664-4084

Harding University Graduate School of Religion, (Churches of Christ), 1000 Cherry Rd., Memphis, TN 38117. C. Philip Slate. Tel. (901)761-1352. Fax (901)761-1358

Hartford Seminary, (Interdenominational), 77 Sherman St., Hartford, CT 06105. Barbara Brown Zikmund. Tel. (203)232-4451

Harvard Divinity School, (Nondenominational), 45 Francis Ave., Cambridge, MA 02138. Ronald F. Thiemann. Tel. (617)495-5761. Fax (617)495-9489

Hebrew Union College--Jewish Inst. of Religion, (Jewish), 1 W. 4th St., New York, NY 10012. Tel. (212)674-5300. Fax (212)533-0129

Hebrew Union College--Jewish Inst. of Religion, (Jewish), 3077 University, Los Angeles, CA 90007. Tel. (213)749-3424. Fax (213)747-6128

Hebrew Union College--Jewish Inst. of Religion, (Jewish), 13 King David St., Jerusalem, Israel, Alfred Gottschalk. Tel. 02-232444

Hebrew Union College--Jewish Institute of Religion, (Jewish), 3101 Clifton Ave., Cincinnati, OH 45215. Tel. (513)221-1875. Fax (513)221-2810

Hobe Sound Bible College, (Independent), P.O. Box 1065, Hobe Sound, FL 33475. Robert E. Whitaker. Tel. (407)546-5534. Fax (407)546-9379

Holy Cross Gk. Orthodox School of Theology (Hellenic College), (Greek Orthodox), 50 Goddard Ave., Brookline, MA 02146. Alkiviadis Calivas. Tel. (617)731-3500. Fax (617)738-9169

Holy Trinity Orthodox Seminary, (Russian Orthodox), P.O. Box 36, Jordanville, NY 13361. Archbishop Laurus (Skurla). Tel. (315)858-0940. Fax (315)858-0505

Hood Theological Seminary, (A.M.E. Zion), 800 W. Thomas St., Salisbury, NC 28144. Dr. James R. Samuel. Tel. (704)638-5505

Howard University School of Divinity, (Interdenominational), 1400 Shepherd St. NE, Washington, DC 20017. Clarence G. Newsome. Tel. (202)806-0500. Fax (202)806-0711

Huntington College, Graduate School of Christian Ministries, (United Brethren in Christ), 2303 College Ave., Huntington, IN 46750. Paul R. Fetters. Tel. (800)642-6493. Fax (219)356-9448

Iliff School of Theology, The, (United Methodist), 2201 S. University Blvd., Denver, CO 80210. Dr. Donald E. Messer. Tel. (303)744-1287. Fax (303)744-3387

Immaculate Conception Sem. Sch. of Theol. of Seton Hall Univ, (Catholic), 400 S. Orange Ave., South Orange, NJ 07079. Rev. Robert E. Harahan. Tel. (201)761-9575. Fax (201)761-9577

Indiana Wesleyan University, (Wesleyan Church), 4201 S. Washington, Marion, IN 46953. Joseph W. Seaborn. Tel. (317)677-2241. Fax (317)677-2499

Interdenominational Theological Center, (Interdemoninational), 671 Beckwith St. SW, Atlanta, GA 30314. James H. Costen. Tel. (404)527-7702. Fax (404)527-0901

Jesuit School of Theology at Berkeley, (Catholic), 1735 LeRoy Ave., Berkeley, CA 94709. Rev. Thomas F. Gleeson, SJ. Tel. (415)841-8804. Fax (415)841-8536

Jewish Theological Seminary of America, (Jewish), 3080 Broadway, New York, NY 10027. Ismar Schorsch. Tel. (212)678-8000. Fax (212)678-8947

John Wesley College, 2314 N. Centennial St., High Point, NC 27265. Brian C. Donley. Tel. (919)889-2262

Johnson Bible College, (Christian Chs.), 7900 Johnson Dr., Knoxville, TN 37998. David L. Eubanks. Tel. (615)573-4517. Fax (615)579-2336

222

Kansas City College and Bible School, (Church of God-Holiness), 7401 Metcalf, Overland Park, KS 66204. Dr. Noel Scott. Tel. (913)722-0272

Kenrick-Glennon Seminary, (Catholic), 5200 Glennon Dr., St. Louis, MO 63119. Ronald W. Ramson. Tel. (314)644-0266. Fax (314)644-3079

Kentucky Christian College, (Christian Chs.), 617 N. Carol Malone Blvd., Grayson, KY 41143-1199. Keith P. Keeran. Tel. (606)474-6613. Fax (606)474-3502

Kentucky Mountain Bible College, (Kentucky Mountain Holiness Assn.), Box 10, Vancleve, KY 41385. Wilfred Fisher. Tel. (606)666-5000

L.I.F.E. Bible College, (Intnatl. Church Foursquare Gospel), 1100 Covina Blvd., San Dimas, CA 91773. Jack E. Hamilton. Tel. (714)599-5433. Fax (714)599-6690

La Sierra University, (Seventh-day Adventist), 4700 Pierce St., Riverside, CA 92515-8247. Fritz Guy. Tel. (714)785-2041. Fax (714)785-2199

Lancaster Bible College, (Nondenominational), 901 Eden Rd., Lancaster, PA 17601. Gilbert A. Peterson. Tel. (717)569-7071. Fax (717)560-8213

Lancaster Theological Seminary of the Unit. Church of Christ, (United Church of Christ), 555 W. James St., Lancaster, PA 17603-2897. Peter M. Schmiechen. Tel. (717)393-0654

Lexington Theological Seminary, (Christian Church (Disciples of Christ)), 631 S. Limestone St., Lexington, KY 40508. William O. Paulsell. Tel. (606)252-0361

Lincoln Christian College and Seminary, (Church of Christ/Christian Churches), 100 Campus View Dr., Lincoln, IL 62656. Charles A. McNeely. Tel. (217)732-3168. Fax (217)732-5914

Louisville Presbyterian Theological Seminary, (PCUSA), 1044 Alta Vista Rd., Louisville, KY 40205. John M. Mulder. Tel. (502)895-3411. Fax (502)895-1096

Luther Northwestern Theological Seminary, (Evangelical Lutheran Church in America), 2481 Como Ave., St. Paul, MN 55108. David L. Tiede. Tel. (612)641-3456. Fax (612)641-3425

Lutheran Bible Institute in California, (Lutheran), 641 S. Western Ave., Anaheim, CA 92804. Clifton Pederson. Tel. (714)827-1940

Lutheran Bible Institute of Seattle, (Lutheran), 4221 - 228th Ave. SE, Issaquah, WA 98027. Trygve R. Skarsten. Tel. (206)392-0400. Fax (206)392-0404

Lutheran Brethren Seminary, (Church of the Luteran Brethren), 815 W. Vernon, Fergus Falls, MN 56537. Rev. Joel Egge. Tel. (218)739-3375

Lutheran School of Theology at Chicago, (Evangelical Lutheran Church in America), 1100 E. 55th St., Chicago, IL 60615. William E. Lesher. Tel. (312)753-0700

Lutheran Theological Seminary, (Evangelical Lutheran Church in America), 61 NW Confederate Ave., Gettysburg, PA 17325. Darold H. Beekmann. Tel. (717)334-6286. Fax (717)334-3469

Lutheran Theological Seminary at Philadelphia, (Evangelical Church in America), 7301 Germantown Ave., Philadelphia, PA 19119. Rev. Dr. Robert G. Hughes. Tel. (215)248-4616. Fax (215)248-4577

Lutheran Theological Southern Seminary, (Evangelical Lutheran Church in America), Lutheran Theological Southern Seminary, Columbia, SC 29203. Mack C. Branham, Jr.. Tel. (803)786-5150

Magnolia Bible College, (Churches of Christ), P.O. Box 1109, Kosciusko, MS 39090. Cecil May, Jr.. Tel. (601)289-2896

Manhattan Christian College, (Christian Churches), 1415 Anderson Ave., Manhattan, KS 66502. Kenneth Cable. Tel. (913)539-3571

Manna Bible Institute, (Independent), 700 E. Church La., Philadelphia, PA 19144. Raymond Thomas. Tel. (215)843-3600

Mary Immaculate Seminary, (Catholic), 300 Cherryville Rd., Box 27, Northampton, PA 18067. Richard J. Kehoe. Tel. (215)262-7866

Maryknoll School of Theology, (Cath. Foreign Miss. Soc. of Amer., Inc.), Maryknoll School of Theology, Maryknoll, NY 10545. John K. Halbert. Tel. (914)941-7590. Fax (914)941-5753

McCormick Theological Seminary, (PCUSA), 5555 S. Woodlawn Ave., Chicago, IL 60637. David Ramage, Jr.. Tel. (312)947-6300. Fax (312)947-6273

Meadville/Lombard Theological School, (Unitarian Universalist Assoc.), 5701 S. Woodlawn Ave., Chicago, IL 60637. Spencer Lavan. Tel. (312)753-3195

Memphis Theol. Sem. of the Cumberland Presbyterian Church, (Cumberland Presbyterian), 168 E. Parkway S, Memphis, TN 38104. J. David Hester. Tel. (901)458-8232. Fax (901)452-4051

Mennonite Biblical Seminary, (General Conference Mennonite), 3003 Benham Ave., Elkhart, IN 46517-1999. Marlin E. Miller. Tel. (219)295-3726. Fax (219)295-0092

Mennonite Brethren Biblical Seminary, (Mennonite Brethren Church), 4824 E. Butler Ave. (at Chestnut Ave.), Fresno, CA 93727. Larry D. Martens. Tel. (209)251-8628

Methodist Theological School in Ohio, (United Methodist), 3081 Columbus Pk., P.O. Box 1204, Delaware, OH 43015-0931. Norman E. Dewire. Tel. (614)363-1146. Fax (614)362-3135

Miami Christian College, (Interdenominational), 500 NE 1st Ave., P.O. Box 019674, Miami, FL 33101-9674. V. Eugene Goldy. Tel. (305)577-4600. Fax (305)577-4612

Mid-America Bible College, (Church of God), 3500 SW 119th St., Oklahoma City, OK 73170. Forrest R. Robinson. Tel. (405)691-3800

Midwestern Baptist Theological Seminary, (Southern Baptist), 5001 N. Oak St., Kansas City, MO 64118. Milton Ferguson. Tel. (816)453-4600

Minnesota Bible College, (Church of Christ), 920 Mayowood Rd. SW, Rochester, MN 55902. Donald Lloyd. Tel. (507)288-4563

Moody Bible Institute, (Interdenominational), 820 N. La Salle Dr., Chicago, IL 60610. Joseph M. Stowell III. Tel. (312)329-4000

Moravian Theological Seminary, (Moravian), 60 W. Locust St., Bethlehem, PA 18018. David A. Schattschneider. Tel. (215)861-1516. Fax (215)861-3919

Moreau Seminary (Holy Cross Fathers), (Catholic), Moreau Seminary, Notre Dame, IN 46556. Thomas K. Zurcher. Tel. (219)283-7735

Morehouse School of Religion, (Amer.Bapt.;Prog.Natl.Bapt;Natl.Bapt.Conv), USA, So.Bapt.Conv.), 645 Beckwith St.SW, Atlanta, GA 30314. Rev. Hezekiah Benton, Jr. Tel. (404)527-7777. Fax (404)527-0901

Mt. Angel Seminary, (Catholic), Mount Angel Seminary, St. Benedict, OR 97373. Patrick S. Brennan. Tel. (503)845-3951. Fax (503)845-3126

Mt. St. Mary's Seminary, (Catholic), Emmitsburg, MD 21727. Kenneth W. Roeltgen. Tel. (301)447-5295

Mt. St. Mary's Seminary of the West, (Catholic), 6616 Beechmont Ave., Cincinnati, OH 45230. Robert J. Mooney. Tel. (513)231-2223. Fax (513)231-3254

Multnomah Graduate School of Ministry, (Interdenominational), 8435 NE Glisan St., Portland, OR 97220. Joseph C. Aldrich. Tel. (503)255-0332. Fax (503)254-1268

Mundelein Seminary of the Univ. of St. Mary-of-the-Lake, (Catholic), Mundelein Seminary, Mundelein, IL 60060. Gerald F. Kicanas. Tel. (708)566-6401. Fax (708)566-7330

Nashotah House (Theological Seminary), (Episcopalian), 2777 Mission Rd., Nashotah, WI 53058. Jack C. Knight. Tel. (414)646-3371. Fax (414)646-2215

Nazarene Bible College, (Nazarene), Box 15749, Colorado Springs, CO 80935. Jerry Lambert. Tel. (719)596-5110. Fax (719)550-9437

Nazarene Theological Seminary, (Nazarene), 1700 E. Meyer Blvd., Kansas City, MO 64131. Terrell C. Sanders, Jr.. Tel. (816)333-6254. Fax (816)822-9025

Nebraska Christian College, (Christian Church), 1800 Syracuse Ave., Norfolk, NE 68701. Richard E. Brown, Dean. Tel. (402)371-5960

New Brunswick Theological Seminary, (Reformed American), 17 Seminary Pl., New Brunswick, NJ 08901-1107. Robert A. White. Tel. (908)247-5241. Fax (908)249-5412

New Orleans Baptist Theological Seminary, (Southern Baptist), 3939 Gentilly Blvd., New Orleans, LA 70126. Landrum P. Leavell II. Tel. (504)282-4455. Fax (504)944-4455

New York Theological Seminary, (Interdenominational), Five W. 29th St., 9th Floor, New York, NY 10001. M. William Howard, Jr.. Tel. (212)532-4012. Fax (212)684-0757

North American Baptist Seminary, (North American Baptist Conference), 1321 W. 22nd St., Sioux Falls, SD 57105. Charles M. Hiatt. Tel. (605)336-6588. Fax (605)355-9090

North Central Bible College, (Assemblies of God), 910 Elliot Ave. S, Minneapolis, MN 55404. Don Argue. Tel. (612)332-3491. Fax (612)343-4778

North Park Theological Seminary, (Evangelical Covenant Church), 3225 W. Foster Ave., Chicago, IL 60625. David G. Horner. Tel. (312)583-2700. Fax (312)583-0858

Northern Baptist Theological Seminary, (American Baptist), 660 E. Butterfield Rd., Lombard, IL 60148. Ian M. Chapman. Tel. (312)620-2100

Northwest Col. of the Assembies of God, (Assemblies of God), 5520 108th Ave. NE, P.O. Box 579, Kirkland, WA 98083. Dennis A. Davis. Tel. (206)822-8266. Fax (206)827-0148

Notre Dame Seminary, (Catholic), 2901 S. Carrollton Ave., New Orleans, LA 70118. Rev. Gregory M. Aymond. Tel. (504)866-7426

Oak Hills Bible College, (Independent), 1600 Oak Hills Rd. SW, Bemidji, MN 56601. Mark Hovestol. Tel. (218)751-8670

Oblate College, (Catholic), 391 Michigan Ave. NE, Washington, DC 20017. Dennis Cooney. Tel. (202)529-6544

Oblate School of Theology, (Catholic), 285 Oblate Dr., San Antonio, TX 78216. Patrick Guidon. Tel. (512)341-1366. Fax (512)341-4519

Ozark Christian College, (Churches of Christ/Christian Churches), 1111 N. Main St., Joplin, MO 64801. Ken Idleman. Tel. (417)624-2518

Pacific Christian College, (Nondenominational), 2500 E. Nutwood Ave., Fullerton, CA 92631. E. Leroy Lawson. Tel. (714)879-3901. Fax (714)526-0231

Pacific Lutheran Theological Seminary, (Evangelical Lutheran Church in America), 2770 Marin Ave., Berkeley, CA 94708. Jerry L. Schmalenberger. Tel. (415)524-5264. Fax (415)524-2408

Pacific School of Religion, (Interdenominational), 1798 Scenic Ave., Berkeley, CA 94709. Eleanor Scott Meyers. Tel. (510)848-0528. Fax (510)845-8948

Payne Theological Seminary, (A.M.E.), P.O. Box 474, Wilberforce, OH 45384. Louis-Charles Harvey. Tel. (513)376-2946

Pepperdine University, (Churches of Christ), Pepperdine University, Religion Division, Malibu, CA 90263. Thomas H. Olbricht, Chair. Tel. (213)456-4352. Fax (213)456-4314

Perkins School of Theology (Southern Methodist University), (United Methodist), Perkins School of Theology, Kirby Hall, Dallas, TX 75275-0133. Dr. James E. Kirby, Jr.. Tel. (214)692-2138. Fax (214)692-4295

Philadelphia College of Bible, (Interdenominational), 200 Manor Ave., Langhorne, PA 19047-2990. W. Sherrill Babb. Tel. (215)752-5800. Fax (215)752-5812

Philadelphia Theological Seminary, (Reformed Episcopal Church), 4225 Chestnut St., Philadelphia, PA 19104. Milton C. Fisher. Tel. (215)222-5158. Fax (215)222-5164

Phillips Graduate Seminary, (Christian Church (Disciples of Christ)), Box 2335, University Sta., Enid, OK 73702. William Tabbernee. Tel. (405)237-4433

Piedmont Bible College, (Baptist), 716 Franklin St., Winston-Salem, NC 27101. Howard L. Wilburn. Tel. (919)725-8344

Pittsburgh Theological Seminary, (PCUSA), 616 N. Highland Ave., Pittsburgh, PA 15206. Carnegie Samuel Calian. Tel. (412)362-5610. Fax (412)363-3260

Point Loma Nazarene College, (Nazarene), 3900 Lomaland Dr., San Diego, CA 92106. Jim Bond. Tel. (619)221-2200. Fax (619)221-2579

Pontifical College Josephinum, (Catholic), 7625 N. High St., Columbus, OH 43235. Blase J. Cupich. Tel. (614)885-5585. Fax (614)885-2307

Pope John XXIII National Seminary, (Catholic), 558 South Ave., Weston, MA 02193. Cornelius M. McRae. Tel. (617)899-5500. Fax (617)899-9057

Practical Bible Training School, (Independent Baptist), Box 601, Bible School Park, NY 13737. Dale E. Linebaugh. Tel. (607)729-1581

Presbyterian School of Christian Education, (PCUSA), 1205 Palmyra Ave., Richmond, VA 23227. Heath K. Rada. Tel. (804)359-5031. Fax (804)254-8060

Princeton Theological Seminary, (PCUSA), Box 552, Princeton, NJ 08542-0803. Thomas W. Gillespie. Tel. (609)921-8300. Fax (609)924-2973

Protestant Episcopal Theolopgical Seminary in Virginia, (Episcopal), 3737 Seminary Rd., Alexandria, VA 22304. Rev. Richard Reid. Tel. (703)370-6600. Fax (703)370-6234

Puget Sound Christian College, (Christian Church), 410 Fourth Ave. N, Edmonds, WA 98020-3171. Glen R. Basey. Tel. (206)775-8686

Rabbi Isaac Elchanan Theol. Sem. (affil. of Yeshiva Univ.), (Orthodox Jewish), 2540 Amsterdam Ave., New York, NY 10033. Zevulun Charlop. Tel. (212)960-5344

Reconstructionist Rabbinical College, (Jewish), Church Rd. and Greenwood Ave., Wyncote, PA 19095. Dr. Arthur Green. Tel. (215)576-0800. Fax (215)576-6143

Reformed Bible College, (Interdenominational), 3333 East Beltline NE, Grand Rapids, MI 49505. Edwin D. Roels. Tel. (616)363-2050. Fax (616)363-9771

Reformed Presbyterian Theological Seminary, (Reformed Presb. Church of North America), 7418 Penn Ave., Pittsburgh, PA 15208. Dr. Bruce C. Stewart. Tel. (412)731-8690

Reformed Theological Seminary, (Independent), 5422 Clinton Blvd., Jackson, MS 39209. Luder G. Whitlock, Jr.. Tel. (601)922-4988. Fax (601)922-1153

Roanoke Bible College, (Churches of Christ), 714 First St., Elizabeth City, NC 27909. William A. Griffin. Tel. (919)338-5191

Saint Bernard's Institute, (Catholic), 1100 S. Goodman St., Rochester, NY 14620. Sebastian A. Falcone. Tel. (716)271-1320. Fax (716)271-2166

St. Charles Borromeo Seminary, (Catholic), 1000 East Wynnewood Rd., Overbrook, PA 19096. Daniel A. Murray. Tel. (215)667-3394

St. Francis Seminary, (Catholic), 3257 S. Lake Dr., Milwaukee, WI 53207. Daniel J. Packenham. Tel. (414)747-6400. Fax (414)747-6442

St. John's Seminary, (Catholic), St. John's Seminary, Brighton, MA 02135. Thomas J. Daly. Tel. (617)254-2610

St. John's Seminary College, (Catholic), 5118 E. Seminary Rd., Camarillo, CA 93010. Rev. Rafael Luevano. Tel. (805)482-2755. Fax (805)987-5097

St. John's University, School of Theology, (Catholic), St. John's University, Collegeville, MN 56321. Dale Launderville. Tel. (612)363-2100. Fax (616)363-2115

St. Joseph's Seminary, (Catholic), 201 Seminary Ave., (Dunwoodie) Yonkers, NY 10704. Raymond T. Powers. Tel. (914)968-6200

St. Louis Christian College, (Christian Churches), 1360 Grandview Dr., Florissant, MO 63033. Thomas W. McGee. Tel. (314)837-6777

St. Mary Seminary, (Catholic), 28700 Euclid Ave., Wickliffe, OH 44092. Allan R. Laubenthal. Tel. (216)943-7600. Fax (216)585-3528

St. Mary's Seminary, (Catholic), 9845 Memorial Dr., Houston, TX 77024. Rev. Chester L. Borski. Tel. (713)686-4345. Fax (713)681-7550

St. Mary's Seminary and University, (Catholic), 5400 Roland Ave., Baltimore, MD 21210. Robert F. Leavitt. Tel. (301)323-3200. Fax (301)323-3554

St. Meinrad School of Theology, (Catholic), St. Meinrad Seminary, St. Meinrad, IN 47577. Eugene Hensell. Tel. (812)357-6611. Fax (812)357-6964

St. Patrick's Seminary, (Catholic), 320 Middlefield Rd., Menlo Park, CA 94025. Gerald D. Coleman. Tel. (415)325-5621. Fax (415)322-0997

St. Paul Bible College, (Christian and Missionary Alliance), 6425 County Rd., 30, St. Bonifacius, MN 55375. Bill W. Lanpher. Tel. (612)446-4100. Fax (612)446-4149

Saint Paul School of Theology, (United Methodist), 5123 Truman Rd., Kansas City, MO 64109. Lovett H. Weems, Jr.. Tel. (816)483-9600. Fax (816)483-9605

St. Paul Seminary School of Divinity, (Catholic), 2260 Summit Ave., St. Paul, MN 55105. Charles Froehle. Tel. (612)647-5715. Fax (612)647-4361

Saint Thomas Theological Seminary, (Catholic), 1300 S. Steele St., Denver, CO 80210. John E. Rybolt. Tel. (303)722-4687. Fax (303)722-7422

St. Tikhon's Orthodox Theological Seminary, (Russian Orthodox), South Canaan, PA 18459. Bishop Herman. Tel. (717)937-4686

St. Vincent Seminary, (Catholic), St. Vincent Seminary, Latrobe, PA 15650. Thomas Acklin. Tel. (412)537-4592

St. Vincent de Paul Regional Seminary, (Catholic), 10701 S. Military Trail, Boynton Beach, FL 33436. Rev. Arthur Bendixen. Tel. (407)732-4424. Fax (407)737-2205

St. Vladimir's Orthodox Theological Seminary, (Eastern Orthodox), 575 Scarsdale Rd., Crestwood, NY 10707. John Meyendorff. Tel. (914)961-8313. Fax (914)961-4507

SS. Cyril and Methodius Seminary, (Catholic), St. Mary's College, Orchard Lake, MI 48324. Stanley E. Milewski. Tel. (313)682-1885. Fax (313)683-0402

San Francisco Theological Seminary, (PCUSA), 2 Kensington Rd., San Anselmo, CA 94960. J. Randolph Taylor. Tel. (415)258-6500. Fax (415)454-2493

San Jose Christian College, (Nondenominational), 790 S. 12th St., P.O. Box 1090, San Jose, CA 95108. Bryce L. Jessup. Tel. (408)293-9058

Savonarola Theological Seminary, (Polish National Catholic), 1031 Cedar Ave., Scranton, PA 18505. John F. Swantek. Tel. (717)343-0100

School of Theology at Claremont, (United Methodist), 1325 N. College Ave., Claremont, CA 91711. Robert W. Edgar. Tel. (714)626-3521. Fax (714)626-7062

Seabury-Western Theological Seminary, (Episcopal), 2122 N. Sheridan Rd., Evanston, IL 60201. M. S. Sisk. Tel. (708)328-9300. Fax (708)328-9624

Seminario Evangelico de Puerto Rico, (Interdemoninational), 776 Ponce de Leon Ave., Hato Rey, PR 00918. Luis Fidel Mercado. Tel. (809)751-6483. Fax (809)751-0847

Seminary of the Immaculate Conception, (Catholic), 440 West Neck Rd., Huntington, NY 11743. John J. Strynkowski. Tel. (516)423-0483. Fax (516)423-2346

Seventh Day Baptist Center on Ministry, (Seventh Day Baptist General Conference), 3120 Kennedy Rd., P.O. Box 1678, Janesville, WI 53546. Rodney Henry. Tel. (608)752-5055. Fax (608)752-7711

Seventh-day Adventist Theological Seminary, Andrews Univ., (Seventh-day Adventist), Berrien Springs, MI 49104. Raoul Dederen. Tel. (616)471-3536

Shaw Divinity School, (National Baptist), P.O. Box 2090, Raleigh, NC 27102. Joseph C. Paige. Tel. (919)832-1701

Simpson College, (Christian and Missionary Alliance), 2211 College View Dr., Redding, CA 96003. Francis Grubbs. Tel. (916)222-6360. Fax (916)222-0709

Southeastern Baptist College, (Baptist Missionary Assn. of Mississippi), P.O. Box 8276, Laurel, MS 39941. A. M. Wilson. Tel. (601)426-6346

Southeastern Baptist Theological Seminary, (Southern Baptist Convention), 222 N. Wingate, P.O. Box 1889, Wake Forest, NC 27587. Lewis A. Drummond. Tel. (919)556-3101. Fax (919)556-3101

Southeastern Bible College, (Interdenomational), 3001 Highway 280 E, Birmingham, AL 35243. John D. Talley, Jr.. Tel. (205)969-0880

Southeastern College of the Assemblies of God, (Assemblies of God), 1000 Longfellow Blvd., Lakeland, FL 33813. James L. Hennesy. Tel. (813)665-4404. Fax (813)666-8103

Southern Baptist Theological Seminary, (Southern Baptist Convention), 2825 Lexington Rd., Louisville, KY 40280. Roy Lee Honeycutt, Jr.. Tel. (502)897-4011. Fax (502)897-4202

Southwestern Assemblies of God College, (Assemblies of God), 1200 Sycamore St., Waxahachie, TX 75165. Delmer R. Guynes. Tel. (214)937-4010. Fax (214)923-0488

Southwestern Baptist Theological Seminary, (Southern Baptist Convention), P.O. Box 22000, Fort Worth, TX 76122. Russell H. Dilday. Tel. (817)923-1921. Fax (817)923-0610

Southwestern College, (Baptist), 2625 E. Cactus Rd., Phoenix, AZ 85032. Wesley A. Olsen. Tel. (602)992-6101

Starr King School for the Ministry, (Unitarian), Starr King School for the Ministry, Berkely, CA 94709. Rebecca Parker. Tel. (415)845-6232

Summit Christian College, (Missionary Church), 1025 W. Rudisill Blvd., Ft. Wayne, IN 46807. Dr. Donald D. Gerig. Tel. (219)456-2111. Fax (219)456-2117

Swedenborg Sch. of Religion (formerly New Church Theol. Sch., (Gen. Conv. of the Swedenborgian Church), 48 Sargent St., Newton, MA 02158. Mary Kay Klein. Tel. (617)244-0504. Fax (617)964-3258

Talbot School of Theology, (Interdenominational), 13800 Biola Ave., La Mirada, CA 90639. W. Bingham Hunter. Tel. (213)903-4816. Fax (213)903-4759

Tennessee Temple University, (Baptist), 1815 Union Ave., Chattanooga, TN 37404. Dr. L. W. Nichols. Tel. (615)698-4100. Fax (615)493-4497

Theological School of the Protestant Reformed Churches, (Protestant Reformed Churches in America), 4949 Ivanrest Ave., Grandville, MI 49418. Robert D. Decker. Tel. (616)531-1490. Fax (616)531-3033

Toccoa Falls College, (Christian and Missionary Alliance), Toccoa Falls College, Toccoa Falls, GA 30598. Paul L. Alford. Tel. (404)886-6831. Fax (404)886-0210

Trevecca Nazarene College (Religion Dept.), (Nazarene), 333 Murfreesboro Rd., Nashville, TN 37210. Don W. Dunnington. Tel. (615)248-1200

Trinity Bible College, (Assemblies of God), Trinity Bible College, Ellendale, ND 58436. Ray W. Trask. Tel. (800)523-1603. Fax (701)349-5443

Trinity College of Florida, (Independent), P.O. Box 9000, Holiday, FL 34690. Barry Banther. Tel. (813)376-6911

Trinity Evangelical Divinity School, (Evangelical Free Church of America), 2065 Half Day Rd., Deerfield, IL 60015. Kenneth M. Meyer. Tel. (708)945-8800. Fax (708)317-8090

Trinity Lutheran Seminary, (Evangelical Lutheran Church in America), 2199 E. Main St., Columbus, OH 43209. Dennis A. Anderson, Jr.. Tel. (614)235-4136. Fax (614)238-0263

Union Theological Seminary, (Interdenominational), 3041 Broadway, New York, NY 10027. Holland L. Hendrix. Tel. (212)662-7100

Union Theological Seminary in Virginia, (PCUSA), 3401 Brook Rd., Richmond, VA 23227. T. Hartley Hall IV. Tel. (804)355-0671. Fax (804)355-3919

United Theological Seminary, (United Methodist), 1810 Harvard Blvd., Dayton, OH 45406. Leonard I. Sweet. Tel. (513)278-5817. Fax (513)278-1218

United Theological Seminary of the Twin Cities, (United Church of Christ), 3000 Fifth St. NW, New Brighton, MN 55112. Benjamin Griffin. Tel. (612)633-4311. Fax (612)633-4315

University of Chicago (Divinity School), (Interdenominational), 1025 E. 58th St., Chicago, IL 60637. W. Clark Gilpin. Tel. (312)702-8221. Fax (312)702-6048

University of Notre Dame, Dept. of Theology, (Catholic), University of Notre Dame, Notre Dame, IN 46556. Richard P. McBrien. Tel. (219)239-7811

University of the South (School of Theology), (Episcopal), School of Theology, Sewanee, TN 37375-4001. Guy Fitch Lytle III. Tel. (615)598-1000. Fax (615)598-1165

Valley Forge Christian College, (Assemblies of God), Charlestown Rd., Phoenixville, PA 19460. Wesley W. Smith. Tel. (215)935-0450

Vanderbilt University (Divinity School), (Interdenominational), Vanderbilt University, Nashville, TN 37240. Joseph C. Hough, Jr.. Tel. (615)322-2776. Fax (615)343-9957

Vennard College, (Interdenominational), P.O. Box 29, University Park, IA 52595. Warthen T. Israel. Tel. (515)673-8391

Virginia Union University (School of Theology), (Baptist), 1601 W. Leigh St., Richmond, VA 23220. John W. Kinney. Tel. (804)257-5715

Walla Walla College (School of Theology), (Seventh-day Adventist), Walla Walla College, College Place, WA 99324. Douglas Clark. Tel. (509)527-2194. Fax (509)527-2253

Wartburg Theological Seminary, (Evangelical Lutheran Church in America), 333 Wartburg Pl., Dubuque, IA 52003-7797. Roger Fjeld. Tel. (319)589-0200. Fax (319)589-0333

Wash. Theological Consortium & Washington Inst. of Ecumenics, 487 Michigan Ave. NE, Washington, DC 20017. David Trickett. Tel. (202)832-2675

Washington Bible College/Capital Bible Seminary, (Interdenominational), 6511 Princess Garden Pkwy., Lanham, MD 20706. John A. Sproule. Tel. (301)552-1400. Fax (301)552-2775

Washington Theological Union, (Catholic), 9001 New Hampshire Ave., Silver Springs, MD 20903. Vincent D. Chushing. Tel. (301)439-0551. Fax (301)445-4929

Wesley College, (Cong. Methodist), P.O. Box 70, Florence, MS 39073. David Coker. Tel. (601)845-2265

Wesley Theological Seminary, (United Methodist), 4500 Massachusetts Ave. NW, Washington, DC 20016. Douglass Lewis. Tel. (202)885-8600. Fax (202)885-8605

West Coast Christian College, (Church of God), 6901 N. Maple Ave., Fresno, CA 93710. H. B. Thompson, Jr.. Tel. (209)299-7201. Fax (209)299-0932

Western Baptist College, (Baptist), 5000 Deer Park Dr. SE, Salem, OR 97301. David F. Miller. Tel. (503)581-8600. Fax (503)585-4316

Western Conservative Baptist Seminary, (Conservative Baptist Assoc.), 5511 SE Hawthorne Blvd., Portland, OR 97215. -----. Tel. (503)233-8561. Fax (503)239-4216

Western Evangelical Seminary, (Interdenominational), 4200 SE Jennings Ave., Portland, OR 97267. David LeShana. Tel. (503)654-5466. Fax (503)654-5469

Western Theological Seminary, (Reformed Church in America), 86 E. 12th St., Holland, MI 49423. Marvin D. Hoff. Tel. (616)392-8555. Fax (616)392-7717

Westminster Theological Seminary, (PCUSA), Chestnut Hill, P.O. Box 27009, Philadelphia, PA 19118. Samuel T. Logan, Jr.. Tel. (215)887-5511. Fax (215)887-5404

Weston School of Theology, (Catholic), 3 Phillips Pl., Cambridge, MA 02138. Edward M. O'Flaherty. Tel. (617)492-1960. Fax (617)492-5833

William Tyndale College, (Interdenominational), 35700 W. Twelve Mile Rd., Farmington Hills, MI 48331. James C. McHann, Jr.. Tel. (313)553-7200. Fax (313)553-5963

Winebrenner Theological Seminary, (Churches of God, General Conference), 701 E. Melrose Ave., P.O. Box 478, Findlay, OH 45839. David E. Draper. Tel. (419)422-4824

Wisconsin Lutheran Seminary, (Lutheran (Wisconsin)), 11831 N. Seminary Dr., 65W, Mequon, WI 53092. Armin Panning. Tel. (414)242-7200. Fax (414)242-7255

Yale University (Divinity School), (Nondenominatinal), 409 Prospect St., New Haven, CT 06511-2167. Thomas Ogletree. Tel. (203)432-5303. Fax (203)432-5756

10. THEOLOGICAL SEMINARIES AND BIBLE SCHOOLS IN CANADA

The following list includes theological seminaries and departments in colleges and universities in which ministerial training is given. Many denominations have additional programs. The lists of Religious Bodies in Canada should be consulted for the address of denominational headquarters.

The list has been developed from direct correspondence with the institutions. Inclusion in or exclusion from this list implies no judgment about the quality or accreditation of any institution.

The listing includes the institution name, denominational sponsor when appropriate, location, head, telephone number, and fax number when known.

Acadia Divinity College, (Un. Bapt. Conv. of Atlantic Provinces), Acadia University, Wolfville, NS B0P 1X0. Andrew D. MacRae. Tel. (902)542-2285. Fax (902)542-7527

Alberta Bible College, 599 Northmount Dr. N.W., Calgary, AB T2K 3J6. Ronald A. Fraser. Tel. (403)282-2994

Aldersgate College, (Free Methodist Church in Canada), Box 460, MooseJaw, SK S6H 4P1. Joseph F. James. Tel. (306)693-7773. Fax (306)692-8821

Arthur Turner Training School, (The Anglican Church of Canada), Pangnirtung, NT X0A 0R0. Rev. Roy Bowkett. Tel. (819)473-8375

Atlantic Baptist College, (Un. Bapt. Conv. of the Atlantic Province), Box 6004, Moncton, NB E1C 9L7. W. Ralph Richardson. Tel. (506)858-8970. Fax (506)858-9694

Atlantic School of Theology, (ecumenical), 640 Francklyn St., Halifax, NS B3H 3B5. Gordon MacDermid. Tel. (902)423-6801. Fax (902)422-5825

Baptist Leadership Training School, (Bapt. Un. of Western Canada), 4330 16th St. S.W., Calgary, AB T2T 4H9. Kenneth W. Bellous. Tel. (403)243-3770. Fax (403)287-1930

Bethany Bible College—Canada, 26 Western St., Sussex, NB E0E 1P0. David S. Medders. Tel. (506)432-4400. Fax (506)432-4425

Bethany Bible Institute, (Mennonite Brethren Church, Can. Con. of), Box 160, Hepburn, SK S0K 1Z0. Dr. James Nikkel. Tel. (306)947-2175. Fax (306)947-2182

Briercrest Bible College and Biblical Seminary, (Interdenominational), 510 College Dr., Caronport, SK S0H 0S0. John Barkman. Tel. (306)756-3200. Fax (306)756-3366

Brockville Bible College, (Stand. Ch. of Am.), Box 1900, Brockville, ON K6V 6N4. Tel. (613)345-5001

Canadian Bible College, (Chr. and Miss. All.), 4400-4th Ave., Regina, SK S4T 0H8. Robert A. Rose. Tel. (306)545-1515. Fax (306)545-0210

Canadian Lutheran Bible Institute, (Lutheran), 4837 52A St., Camrose, AB T4V 1W5. Tel. (403)672-4454

Canadian Mennonite Bible College, 600 Shaftesbury Blvd., Winnipeg, MB R3P 0M4. John H. Neufeld. Tel. (204)888-6781

Canadian Nazarene College, (Church of the Nazarene), 1301 Lee Blvd., Winnipeg, MB R3T 2P7. Riley Coulter. Tel. (204)269-2120. Fax (204)269-7772

Canadian Reformed Churches, Theol. College of the, (Can. Ref. Chs), 110 West 27th St., Hamilton, ON L9C 5A1. L. C. Van Dam

Canadian Theological Seminary, (Chr. and Miss. All.), 4400-4th Ave., Regina, SK S4T 0H8. Robert A. Rose. Tel. (306)545-1515. Fax (306)545-0210

Catherine Booth Bible College, (Salvation Army), 447 Webb Pl., Winnipeg, MB R3B 2P2. Major Earl Robinson. Tel. (204)947-6701. Fax (204)942-3856

Central Baptist Seminary, (Fell. of Evan. Bapt. Chs. in Canada), 6 Gormley Industrial Ave., Box 28, Gormley, ON L0H 1G0. Stan Fowler. Tel. (416)888-9600. Fax (416)888-9603

Central Pentecostal College, University of Saskatchewan, (Pentecostal Assemblies of Canada), 1303 Jackson Ave., Saskatoon, SK S7H 2M9. J. Harry Faught. Tel. (306)374-6655

Centre d'Etudes Theologiques Evangeliques, (Un. d'Eglises Bapt. Françaises au Canada), 2285, avenue Papineau, Montreal, QC H2K 4J5. Dr. Nelson Thomson. Tel. (514)526-6643

Centre for Christian Studies, (Ang. Ch. of Canada; Un. Ch. of Canada), 77 Charles St. W., Toronto, ON M5S 1K5. Trudy Lebans. Tel. (416)923-1168

Christianview Bible College, (Pent. Holiness Chs. of Canada), 164 George St., ON N0M 1A0. Alisa Graig. Tel. (519)293-3506

Church Army College of Evangelism, (Anglican Church of Canada), 397 Brunswick Ave., Toronto, ON M5R 2Z2. Capt. Roy Dickson. Tel. (416)924-9279

College Dominicain de Philosophie et de Theologie, (Catholic), 96 avenue Empress, Ottawa, ON K1R 7G3. Michel Gourgues. Tel. (613)233-5696. Fax (613)233-6064

College of Emmanuel and St. Chad, (Anglican Church of Canada), 1337 College Dr., Saskatoon, SK S7N 0W6. J. Russell Brown. Tel. (306)975-3753

Columbia Bible College, (Menn. Breth.; Gen. Conf. Menn), 2940 Clearbrook Rd., Clearbrook, BC V2T 2Z8. Walter Unger. Tel. (604)853-3358. Fax (604)853-3063

Concordia Lutheran Seminary, (Lutheran Church—Canada), 7040 Ada Blvd., Edmonton, AB T5B 4E3. Dr. Milton L. Rudnick. Tel. (403)474-1468. Fax (403)479-3067

Concordia Lutheran Theological Seminary, (Lutheran Church—Canada), 470 Glenridge Ave., Box 1117, St. Catharines, ON L2R 7A3. Jonathan Grothe. Tel. (416)688-2362. Fax (416)688-9744

Covenant Bible College, (Evangelical Covenant Church of Canada), 245-21st St. E., Prince Albert, SK S6V 1L9. W. B. Anderson. Tel. (306)922-3443

Eastern Pentecostal Bible College, (Pentecostal Assemblies of Canada), 780 Argyle St., Peterborough, ON K9H 5T2. R. W. Taitinger. Tel. (705)748-9111. Fax (705)748-3931

Emmanuel Bible College, (Missionary Church of Canada), 100 Fergus Ave., Kitchener, ON N2A 2H2. Dr. Thomas E. Dow. Tel. (519)894-8900

Emmanuel College, (United Church of Canada), 75 Queen's Park Crescent, Toronto, ON M5S 1K7. John C. Hoffman. Tel. (416)585-4539. Fax (416)585-4584

Full Gospel Bible Institute, (Apostic Church of Pentecost), Box 579, Eston, SK S0L 1A0. Alan B. Mortensen. Tel. (306)962-3621. Fax (306)962-3810

Gardner Bible College, (Church of God (Anderson, IN)), 4704 55th St., Camrose, AB T4V 2B6. Bruce Kelly. Tel. (403)672-0171. Fax (403)672-6888

Great Lakes Bible College, (Churches of Christ), 4875 King St. E., Beamsville, ON L0R 1B0. Dave McMillan. Tel. (416)563-5374. Fax (416)563-0818

Hillcrest Christian College, (Evangelical Church), 2801-13th Ave. S.E., Medicine Hat, AB T1A 3R1. Kervin Raugust. Tel. (403)526-6951. Fax (403)526-8404

Huron College, (Ang. Ch. of Canada, Faculty of Theology), 1349 Western Rd., London, ON N6G 1H3. Dr. Charles J. Jago. Tel. (519)438-7224. Fax (519)438-3938

Institut Biblique Bethel, (Interdenominational), 1175 Chemin Woodward, RR1, Lennoxville, QC J1M 2A2. Richard Strout. Tel. (819)823-8435

Institut Biblique Laval, (Mennonite Brethren), 1775, boul. Edouard-Laurin, Ville Saint-Laurent, QC H4L 2B9. Tel. (514)331-0878

International Bible College, (Church of God (Cleveland, TN)), 401 Trinity La., Moose Jaw, SK S6H 0E3. Tel. (306)692-4041

Knox College, (Presbytarian Church in Canada), 59 St. George St., Toronto, ON M5S 2E6. Iain G. Nicol. Tel. (416)978-4500

London Baptist Bible College, (Indep. Baptist), 30 Grand Ave., London, ON NGC 1K8. Marvin Brubacher. Tel. (519)434-6801

Lutheran Theological Seminary, (Evangelical Lutheran Church in Canada), 114 Seminary Crescent, Saskatoon, SK S7N 0X3. Roger Nostbakken. Tel. (306)975-7004. Fax (306)975-0084

Maritime Christian College, Box 1145, 223 Kent St., Charlottetown, PE C1A 7M8. Stewart J. Lewis. Tel. (902)894-3828. Fax (902)892-3959

McMaster Divinity College, (Baptist Convention of Ontario and Quebec), McMaster Divinity College, Hamilton, ON L8S 4K1. Dr. William H. Brackney. Tel. (416)525-9140. Fax (416)577-4782

Mennonite Brethren Bible College, (Mennonite Brethren), 1-169 Riverton Ave., Winnipeg, MB R2L 2E5. James N. Pankratz. Tel. (204)669-6575. Fax (204)654-1865

Montreal Diocesan Theological College, (Anglican Church of Canada), 3473 University St., Montreal, QC H3A 2A8. John Simons. Tel. (514)849-3004

Mountain View Bible College, (Missionary Church of Canada), Box 190, Didsbury, AB T0M 0W0. Dr. Virgil Stauffer. Tel. (403)335-3337

Newman Theological College, (Catholic), 15611 St. Albert Trail, Edmonton, AB T5L 4H8. D. MacDonald. Tel. (403)447-2993. Fax (403)447-2685

Nipawin Bible Institute, (Interdenominational), Box 1986, Nipawin, SK S0E 1E0. Mark Leppington. Tel. (306)862-3651

North American Baptist College and Edmonton Baptist Seminary, (North American Baptist Conference), 11525 - 23rd Ave., Edmonton, AB T6J 4T3. Paul Siewert. Tel. (403)437-1960. Fax (403)436-9416

Northwest Baptist Theological College and Seminary, (Fell. Bapt.), 22606 76A Ave., P.O. Box 790, Langley, BC V3A 8B8. Doug Harris. Tel. (604)888-3310. Fax (604)888-3354

Northwest Bible College, (Pentecostal Assemblies of Canada), 11617-106 Ave., Edmonton, AB T5H 0S1. G. K. Franklin. Tel. (403)452-0808. Fax (403)452-5803

Okanagan Bible College, (Interdenominational), Box 407, Kelowna, BC V1Y 7N8. Dr. Stewart Simpson. Tel. (604)768-4410. Fax (604)763-7580

Ontario Christian Seminary, P.O. Box 324, Stn. D; 260 High Park Ave., Toronto, ON M6P 3J9. Nelson Deuitch. Tel. (416)769-7115. Fax (416)769-7115

Ontario Theological Seminary, (Multidenominatinal), 25 Ballyconnor Ct., Willowdale, ON M2M 4B3. Dr. Wm. J. McRae, Chancellor. Tel. (416)226-6380. Fax (416)226-6746

Peace River Bible Institute, Box 99, Sexsmith, AB T0H 3C0. Reuben Kvill. Tel. (403)568-3962

Prairie Bible Institute, (Interdenominational), Box 4000, Three Hills, AB T0M 2A0. Ted S. Rendall. Tel. (403)443-5511. Fax (403)443-5540

Presbyterian College, 3495 University St., Montreal, QC H3A 2A8. W. J. Klempa. Tel. (514)288-5256

Queen's College, (Anglican Church of Canada), Queen's College, St. John's, NF A1B 3R6. Rev. Canon Frank Cluett. Tel. (709)753-0640. Fax (709)753-1214

Queen's Theological College, (United Church of Canada), Queen's Theological College, Kingston, ON K7L 3N6. Tel. (613)545-2110. Fax (613)545-6879

Regent College, (Transdenominational), 5800 University Blvd., Vancouver, BC V6T 2E4. Walter C. Wright, Jr.. Tel. (800)663-8664. Fax (604)224-3097

Regis College, (Catholic), 15 St. Mary St., Toronto, ON M4Y 2R5. John E. Costello. Tel. (416)922-5474. Fax (416)922-2898

St. **Andrew's College**, (United Church of Canada), 1121 College Dr., Saskatoon, SK S7N 0W3. Tel. (306)966-8970

St. **Augustine's Seminary of Toronto**, (Catholic), 2661 Kingston Rd., Scarborough, ON M1M 1M3. Rev. James M. Wingle. Tel. (416)261-7207. Fax (416)261-2529

St. **John's College, Univ. of Manitoba, Faculty of Theology**, (Anglican Church of Canada), St. John's College, Univ. of Manitoba, Winnipeg, MB R3T 2M5. Tel. (204)474-8543

St. **Peter's Seminary**, (Catholic), 1040 Waterloo St., London, ON N6A 3Y1. Patrick W. Fuerth. Tel. (519)432-1824

St. **Stephen's College, Grad. and Continuing Theological Ed.**, (United Church of Canada), St. Stephen's College, 8810 112th St., Edmonton, AB T6G 2J6. Garth I. Mundle. Tel. (403)439-7311. Fax (403)433-8875

Salvation Army College for Officer Training, The, (Salvation Army), 2130 Bayview Ave., Toronto, ON M4N 3K6. Shirley Rowsell. Tel. (416)481-6131

Steinbach Bible College, (Mennoniete-Anabaptist), Box 1420, Steinbach, MB R0A 2A0. Gordon Daman. Tel. (204)326-6451. Fax (204)326-6908

Swift Current Bible Institute, (Mennonite), Box 1268, Swift Current, SK S9H 3X4. Ray Friesen. Tel. (306)773-0604

Toronto Baptist Seminary and Bible College, (Baptist), 130 Gerrard St., E., Toronto, ON M5A 3T4. Norman Street. Tel. (416)925-3263

Toronto School of Theology, (Federation of 7 theol colleges (4 denom)), 47 Queens Park Crescent E., Toronto, ON M5S 2C3. E. James Reed. Tel. (416)978-4039. Fax (416)978-7821

Trinity College, Faculty of Divinity, (Anglican Church of Canada), 6 Hoskin Ave., Toronto, ON M5S 1H8. R. H. Painter. Tel. (416)978-2370

United Theological College/Le Séminaire Uni, (United Church of Canada), 3521 rue Université, Montréal, QC H3A 2A9

Université Laval, Faculté de théologie, (Catholic), Cité Universitaire Ste-Foy, Ste-Foy, QC G1K 7P4. Rene-Michel Roberse. Tel. (418)656-7823

Université Saint-Paul, Faculté de théologie, (Catholic), 223 rue Main, Ottawa, ON K1S 1C4. M. Hubert Doucet. Tel. (613)236-1393. Fax (713)782-3004

Université de Montréal, Faculté de théologie, (Catholic), C. P. 6128, Montréal, QC H3C 3J7. Laval Letourneau, Dean. Tel. (514)343-7167. Fax (514)343-5738

Université de Sherbrooke, Faculté de théologie,, (Catholic), 2500 boul. Université, Sherbrooke, QC J1K 2R1. Lucien Vachon. Tel. (819)821-7600

University of St. Michael's College, Faculty of Theology, (Catholic), 81 St. Mary St., Toronto, ON M5S 1J4. Michael A. Fahey. Tel. (416)926-7140. Fax (416)926-7276

University of Winnipeg, Faculty of Theology, (Interdenominational), 515 Portage Avenue, Winnipeg, MB R3B 2E9. H. J. King. Tel. (204)786-9390. Fax (204)786-1824

Vancouver School of Theology, (Interdenominational), 6000 Iona Dr., Vancouver, BC V6T 1L4. Arthur Van Seters. Tel. (604)228-9031. Fax (604)228-0189

Waterloo Lutheran Seminary, (Evangelical Lutheran Church in Canada), 75 University Avenue West, Waterloo, ON N2L 3C5. Richard C. Crossman. Tel. (519)884-1970. Fax (519)725-2434

Western Christian College, (Churches of Christ), Box 5000, Dauphin, MB R7N 2V5. V. V. Anderson

Western Pentecostal Bible College, (Pentecostal Assemlies of Canada), Box 1000, Clayburn, BC V0X 1E0. James G. Richards. Tel. (604)853-7491. Fax (604)853-8951

Winkler Bible Institute, (Mennonite Brethren), 121 7th St., South, Winkler, MB R6W 2N4. Eldon DeFehr. Tel. (204)325-4242

Winnipeg Bible College and Theological Seminary, Providence College and Theological Sem., Otterburne, MB R0A 1G0. William R. Eichhorst. Tel. (204)284-2923. Fax (204)433-7158

Wycliffe College, (Anglican Church of Canada), 5 Hoskin Ave., Toronto, ON M5S 1H7. P. R. Mason. Tel. (416)979-2870. Fax (416)979-0471

11. RELIGIOUS PERIODICALS IN THE UNITED STATES

This list of religious periodicals does not include all publications prepared by religious bodies. The listing of religious bodies includes the titles of publications found in this list.

Probably the most inclusive list of religious periodicals published in the United States can be found in *Gale Directory of Publications and Broadcast Media, 1992*, (Gale Research, Inc., P.O. Box 33477, Detroit MI 48232-5477).

Each entry lists the title of the periodical, frequency of publication, religious affiliation, editor's name, address, telephone number and fax number when known.

21st Century Christian (m), Churches of Christ, M. Norvel Young, Box 40526, Nashville, TN 37204

A.M.E. Christian Recorder, African Methodist Episcopal Church, Dr. Robert H. Reid, 500 8th Ave., S., Nashville, TN 37203. Tel. (615)256-8548

A.M.E. Review, African Methodist Episcopal Church, Dr. Jamye Coleman Williams, 500 Eighth Ave., S., Nashville, TN 37203. Tel. (615)320-3500

ADRIS Newsletter (q), Independent, Richard F. Smith, 3601 Lindell Blvd., St. Louis, MO 63108. Tel. (314)658-2588

ALERT (m), Metropolitan Community Churches, Universal Fellowship of, Rev. Stephen Pieters, 5300 Santa Monica Blvd., Los Angeles, CA 90029

Action (m), Churches of Christ, Tex Williams, Box 9346, Austin, TX 78766

Adult Quarterly, The, Associate Reformed Presbyterian Church (General Synod), Mr. W. H. F. Kuykendall PhD., One Cleveland St., Greenville, SC 29601

Advance (m), Assemblies of God, Harris Jansen, Gospel Publishing House, 1445 Boonville Ave., Springfield, MO 65802

Advancer, The (m), Baptist Missionary Association of America, Larry Slivey, P.O. Box 7270, Texarkana, TX 75502

Advent Christian News (m), Advent Christian Church, Rev. Robert Mayer, P.O. Box 23152, Charlotte, NC 28212

Advent Christian Witness, The (m), Advent Christian Church, Rev. Robert Mayer, P.O. Box 23152, Charlotte, NC 28212

Adventist Review (w), Seventh-day Adventist Church, W. G. Johnson, 12501 Old Columbia Pike, Silver Spring, MD 20904-6600. Tel. (301)680-6561. Fax (301)680-6638

Advocate, The (m), Baptist Missionary Association of America, Ronald J. Beasley, 8101 Joffree Dr., Jacksonville, FL 32210

Allegheny Wesleyan Methodist, The (m), Allegheny Wesleyan Methodist Connection (Original Allegheny Conference), Rev. John B. Durfee, 1827 Allen Dr., Salem, OH 44460

Alliance Life (bi-w), The Christian and Missionary Alliance, Maurice Irvin, P.O. Box 35000, Colorado Springs, CO 80935. Tel. (719)599-5999

America (W), Catholic, George W. Hunt, 106 W. 56th St., New York, NY 10019. Tel. (212)581-4640. Fax (212)399-3596

American Baptist Quarterly (q), American Baptist Churches, William R. Millar, P.O. Box 851, Valley Forge, PA 19482

American Baptist, The (10/yr), American Baptist Churches, Philip E. Jenks, P.O. Box 851, Valley Forge, PA 19482. Tel. (215)768-2301. Fax (215)768-2275

American Bible Society Record (10/yr), Nondenominational, Clifford P. Macdonald, 1865 Broadway, New York, NY 10023. Tel. (212)408-1480. Fax (212)408-1456

American Jewish History, Jewish, Marc Lee Raphael, 2 Thornton Rd., Waltham, MA 02154. Tel. (617)891-8110. Fax (617)899-9208

American Presbyterians: Journal of Presbyterian History (q), Presbyterian Church (U.S.A.), Rev. James H. Smylie, 425 Lombard St., Philadelphia, PA 19147. Tel. (215)627-1852. Fax (215)627-0509

Anglican Theol. Review (q), The Episcopal Church, Rev. W. Taylor Stevenson, 600 Haven St., Evanston, IL 60201

Anglican and Episcopal History (q), Episcopal, John F. Woolverton, P. O. Box 261, Center Sandwich, NH 03227

Associate Reformed Presbyterian, The, Associate Reformed Presbyterian Church (General Synod), Mr. Ben Johnston, One Cleveland St., Greenville, SC 29601

At Ease (bi-m), Assemblies of God, Lemuel McElyea, Gospel Publishing House, 1445 Boonville Ave., Springfield, MO 65802

Banner of Truth, The (m), Netherlands Reformed Congregations, Dr. Joel R. Beeke, 2115 Romence Ave., N.E., Grand Rapids, MI 29503

Banner, The (w), Christian Reformed Church in North America, John H. Kromminga Harvey A. Smit, 2850 Kalamazoo Ave., S.E., Grand Rapids, MI 49560. Tel. (616)246-0732. Fax (616)246-0834

Baptist Beacon, Southern Baptist Convention, Elizabeth Young, 4520 N. Central Ave., Ste. 550, Phoenix, AZ 85013. Tel. (602)264-9421

Baptist Bible Tribune, The (m), Baptist Bible Fellowship International, James O. Combs, P.O. Box 309 HSJ, Springfield, MO 65801. Tel. (417)831-3996

Baptist Bulletin (m), General Association of Regular Baptist Churches, Vernon D. Miller, 1300 N. Meacham Rd., Schaumburg, IL 60173-4888. Tel. (708)843-1600. Fax (708)843-3757

Baptist Courier (w), Southern Baptist Convention, John E. Roberts, P.O. Box 2168, Greenville, SC 29602. Tel. (803)232-8736

Baptist Digest, Southern Baptist Convention, John Hopkins, 5410 W. 7th, Topeka, KS 66606. Tel. (913)273-4880

Baptist Herald (m), Baptist Missionary Association of America, Jerry Derfelt, P.O. Box 218, Galena, KS 66739

Baptist Herald, The (10/yr.), North American Baptist Conference, Barbara J. Binder, 1 S. 210 Summit Ave., Oakbrook Terrace, IL 60181

Baptist History and Heritage (q), Lynn E. May Jr., 901 Commerce St., Ste. 400, Nashville, TN 37203-3630. Tel. (615)244-0344

Baptist Leader (q), American Baptist Churches, Linda Isham, P.O. Box 851, Valley Forge, PA 19842-0851. Tel. (215)768-2153. Fax (215)768-2056

Baptist Message, Southern Baptist Convention, Lynn Clayton, Box 311, Alexandria, LA 71309. Tel. (318)442-7728

Baptist Messenger (w), Southern Baptist Convention, Glenn A. Brown, Box 12130, Oklahoma City, OK 73157. Tel. (405)942-3800. Fax (405)947-7170

Baptist Program, Southern Baptist Convention, Ernest E. Mosley, SBC, 901 Commerce St., Nashville, TN 37203. Tel. (615)244-2355

Baptist Progress (w), Baptist Missionary Association of America, Danny Pope, P.O. Box 2085, Waxahachie, TX 85165

Baptist Record (w), Southern Baptist Convention, Guy Henderson, Box 530, Jackson, MS 39205. Tel. (601)968-3800. Fax (601)968-3928

Baptist Standard (w), Southern Baptist Convention, Presnall H. Wood, P.O. Box 660267, Dallas, TX 75266. Tel. (214)630-4571. Fax (214)638-8535

Baptist True Union, Southern Baptist Convention, Robert Allen, 10255 Old Columbia Rd., Columbia, MD 21046. Tel. (301)290-5290

Baptist Trumpet (w), Baptist Missionary Association of America, David Tidwell, P.O. Box 19084, Little Rock, AR 72219

Baptist Witness, Primitive Baptists, L. Bradley Jr., Box 17037, Cincinnati, OH 45217

Baptist and Reflector (w), Southern Baptist Convention, W. Fletcher Allen, P.O. Box 728, Brentwood, TN 37024. Tel. (615)371-2003. Fax (615)371-2014

Being In Touch (q), Mennonite Church, The General Conference, David Linscheid, Box 347, 722 Main St., Newton, KS 67114

Bible Advocate (m), The Church of God (Seventh Day), Denver, Colo., Roy Marrs, 330 W. 152 Ave., Denver, CO 80233

Bible College Bulletin (m), Free Will Baptists, National Association of, Bert Tippett, 3606 West End Ave., Nashville, TN 37205

Biblical Recorder (w), Southern Baptist Convention, R. Eugene Puckett, P.O. Box 26568, Raleigh, NC 27611. Tel. (919)847-2127. Fax (919)847-6939

Bread (m), Church of the Nazarene, Karen DeSollar, Nazarene Publishing House, Box 419527, Kansas City, MO 64141

Brethren Evangelist, The (m), Brethren Church (Ashland, Ohio), Rev. Richard C. Winfield, 524 College Ave., Ashland, OH 44805

Brethren Journal (m), Unity of Brethren, Rev. Milton Maly, Rte. 3, Box 558N, Brenham, TX 77833

Brethren Missionary Herald, Grace Brethren Churches, Fellowship of, Rev. Charles Turner, P.O. Box 544, Winona Lake, IN 46590

Bridegroom's Messenger, The, The International Pentecostal Church of Christ, Janie Boyce, 121 W. Hunters Trail, Elizabeth City, NC 27909. Tel. (919)338-3003

Builder (m), Mennonite Church, David R. Heibert, 616 Walnut Ave., Scottdale, PA 15683

Burning Bush, The (bi-m), The Metropolitan Church Association, Inc., Rev. E. L. Adams, The Publishing House, The Metropolitan Church Assoc., Lake Geneva, WI 53147

C.L.C. Directory (a), Church of the Lutheran Confession, Rollin Reim, 994 Emerald Hill Rd., Redwood City, CA 94061

Calendarul Credinta (a), The Romanian Orthodox Church in America, V. Rev. Archim. Dr. Vasile Vasilachi, 19959 Riopelle St., Detroit, MI 48203

Calvary Messenger, The, Beachy Amish Mennonite Churches, Ervin N. Hershberger, Rt. 1, Box 176, Meyersdale, PA 15552

Campus Life,, Independent, Roy Coffman, 465 Gunderson Dr., Carol Stream, IL 60188. Tel. (312)260-6200. Fax (708)260-0114

Capital Baptist, Southern Baptist Convention, Victor Tupitza, 1628 16th St. NW, Washington, DC 20009. Tel. (202)265-1526

Capsule (m), General Baptists, Rev. Charles Carr, 100 Stinson Dr., Poplar Bluff, MO 63901

Caring (8/yr.), Assemblies of God, Owen Wilkie, Gospel Publishing House, 1445 Boonville Ave., Springfield, MO 65802

Cathedral Age, The Episcopal Church, Nancy Montgomery, Mt. St. Albans, Washington, DC 20016

Catholic Chronicle (bi-w), Catholic, Richard S. Meek, Jr., P.O. Box 1866, 2130 Madison Avenue, Toledo, OH 43603. Tel. (419)243-4178. Fax (419)243-4235

Catholic Digest (m), Catholic, Henry Lexau, P. O. Box 64090, St. Paul, MN 55164. Tel. (612)647-5296. Fax (612)647-4346

Catholic Herald (w), Catholic, Ethel M. Gintoft, 3501 S. Lake Dr., Milwaukee, WI 53207. Tel. (414)769-3500. Fax (414)769-3468

Catholic Light (bi-w), Catholic, Arthur F. Perry, 300 Wyoming Ave., Scranton, PA 18503

Catholic Review, The (w), Catholic, Daniel L. Medinger, P.O. Box 777, Baltimore, MD 21203. Tel. (301)547-5327

Catholic Standard and Times (w), Catholic, Rev Paul S. Quinter, 222 N. 17th St., Philadelphia, PA 19103. Tel. (215)587-3660. Fax (215)587-3979

Catholic Transcript, The (w), Catholic, David M. Fortier, 785 Asylum Ave., Hartford, CT 06105. Tel. (203)527-1175. Fax (203)541-6110

Catholic Universe Bulletin (bi-w), Catholic, Michael G. Dimengo, 1027 Superior Ave., N.E., Cleveland, OH 44114. Tel. (216)696-6525. Fax (216)696-6525

Catholic Worker (8/yr), Catholic, Jo Roberts, 36 E. First St., New York, NY 10003. Tel. (212)254-1640

Catholic World, The (bi-m), Catholic, Laurie Felknor, 997 Macarthur Blvd., Mahwah, NJ 07430

Cela Biedrs (10/yr.), The Latvian Evangelical Lutheran Church in America, Rev. Eduards Putnins, 1468 Hemlock St., Napa, CA 94559. Tel. (707)252-1809

Celebration! (m), Seventh-day Adventist Church, Jack Calkins, 55 W. Oak Ridge Dr., Hagerstown, MD 21740

Celebration: An Ecumenical Worship Resource (m), Catholic, William Freburger, P.O. Box 419493, Kansas City, MO 64141. Tel. (816)531-0538

Cerkovnyj Vistnik--Church Messenger (bi-w), The American Carpatho-Russian Orthodox Greek Catholic Church, Very Rev. James S. Dutko, 280 Clinton St., Binghamton, NY 13905

Charisma Courier, The, Full Gospel Assemblies International, C. E. Strauser, P.O. Box 1230, Coatesville, PA 19320. Tel. (215)857-2357

Childlife (q), Independent, Terry Madison, 919 W. Huntington Dr., Monrovia, CA 91016. Tel. (818)357-7979. Fax (818)357-0915

Christadelphian Advocate, Christadelphians, Alex T. Kay, Jr. Edward W. Farrar, 1023 Green Hill Rd., South Hill, VA 23970

Christadelphian Tidings (m), Christadelphians, Donald H. Styles, 30480 Oakleaf Ln., Franklin, MI 48025

Christadelphian Watchman (m), Christadelphians, George Booker, 2500 Berwyn Cir., Austin, TX 78745

Christian Baptist (m), Primitive Baptists, S. T. Tolly, P.O. Box 68, Atwood, TN 38220

Christian Bible Teacher (m), Churches of Christ, J. J. Turner, Box 1060, Abilene, TX 79604

Christian Century, The (40/yr), Independent, James M. Wall, 407 S. Dearborn St., Chicago, IL 60605. Tel. (312)427-5380. Fax (312)427-1302

Christian Chronicle (m), Churches of Christ, Howard W. Norton, Box 11000, Oklahoma City, OK 73136

Christian Community, The (m), Community Churches, International Council of, J. Ralph Shotwell, 7808 College Dr., Suite 2SE, Palos Heights, IL 60463. Tel. (708)361-2600. Fax (708)361-3649

Christian Echo, The (m), Churches of Christ, R. N. Hogan, Box 37266, Los Angeles, CA 90037

Christian Endeavor World, The (q), Independent, David G. Jackson, P.O. Box 1110, 1221 E. Broad St., Columbus, OH 43216. Tel. (614)258-9545. Fax (614)258-1834

Christian Herald (bi-m), Independent, Bob Chuvala, 40 Overlook Dr., Chappaqua, NY 10514. Tel. (914)769-9000. Fax (914)238-5393

Christian Index, The (bi-m), Christian Methodist Episcopal Church, Rev. Lawrence Reddick III, P.O. Box 665, Memphis, TN 38101. Tel. (901)345-1173

Christian Index, The (w), Southern Baptist Convention, R. Albert Mohler, Jr., 2930 Flowers Rd., S., Atlanta, GA 30341. Tel. (404)936-5312. Fax (404)936-5160

Christian Living (m), Mennonite Church, David Graybill, 616 Walnut Ave., Scottdale, PA 15683

Christian Ministry, The (6/yr), Independent, James M. Wall, 407 S. Dearborn St., Chicago, IL 60605. Tel. (312)427-5380. Fax (312)427-1302

Christian Monthly (m), Apostolic Lutheran Church of America, Alvar Helmes, Apostolic Lutheran Book Concern, P.O. Box 537, Brush Prairie, WA 98606

Christian Outlook (m), Pentecostal Assemblies of the World, Inc., Jane Sims, 3939 Meadow Dr., Indianapolis, IN 46208

Christian Pathway (m), Primitive Baptists, Elder Harold Hunt, Hwy. 172, Crockett, KY 41413

Christian Reader, The (BI-M), Independent, James Kraus, P.O. Box 220, Wheaton, IL 60189. Tel. (708)668-8300. Fax (708)668-8905

Christian Record (m), Seventh-day Adventist Church, R. J. Kaiser Jr., P.O. Box 6097, Lincoln, NE 68506

Christian Science Journal, The (m), Church of Christ, Scientist, William E. Moody, One Norway St., Boston, MA 02115. Tel. (617)450-2000

Christian Science Monitor, The (d & w), Church of Christ, Scientist, Richard Cattani, One Norway St., Boston, MA 02115

Christian Science Quarterly (q), Church of Christ, Scientist, William E. Moody, One Norway St., Boston, MA 02115

Christian Science Sentinel (w), Church of Christ, Scientist, William E. Moody, One Norway St., Boston, MA 02115. Tel. (617)450-2000

Christian Social Action (m), The United Methodist Church, Lee Ranck, 100 Maryland Ave. NE, Washington, DC 20002. Tel. (202)488-5632

Christian Standard (w), Christian Churches and Churches of Christ, Sam E. Stone, 8121 Hamilton Ave., Cincinnati, OH 45231. Tel. (513)931-4050. Fax (513)931-0904

Christianity and Crisis (bi-w), Independent, Leon Howell, 537 W. 121st St., New York, NY 10027. Tel. (212)662-5907

Church & Society Magazine (bi-m), Presbyterian Church (U.S.A.), Kathy Lancaster, 100 Witherspoon St., Louisville, KY 40202. Fax (502)569-5018

Church Advocate, The (m), Churches of God, General Conference, Mrs. Linda Draper, P.O. Box 926, 700 E. Melrose Ave., Findlay, OH 45839

Church Herald, The (11/yr), Reformed Church in America, Jeffrey Japinga, 6157-28th St., SE, Grand Rapids, MI 49546. Tel. (616)957-1351

Church History (q), Independent, Martin E. Marty, and Jerald C. Brauer, The Univ. of Chicago, Chicago, IL 60637. Tel. (312)702-8215. Fax (312)702-6048

Church Management: The Clergy Journal (10/yr), Independent, Manfred Holck, Jr, P.O. Box 162527, Austin, TX 78716. Tel. (512)327-8501

Church School Herald (q), African Methodist Episcopal Zion Church, Ms. Mary A. Love, P.O. Box 31005, Charlotte, NC 28231

Church of God Missions (m), Church of God (Anderson, Ind.), Dondeena Caldwell, Box 2337, Anderson, IN 46018

Church of God Progress Journal (bi-m), Church of God General Conference (Oregon, Ill.), David Krogh, Box 100,000, Morrow, GA 30260

Church of God Quarterly, The (q), The Church of God, Voy M. Bullen, Box 13036, 1207 Willow Brook, Apt. #2, Huntsville, AL 35802

Churchman's Human Quest, The (m), The Episcopal Church, Edna Ruth Johnson, 1074 23rd Ave. N., St. Petersburg, FL 33704. Tel. (813)894-0097

Churchwoman (bi-m), Church Women United, Margaret Schiffert, 475 Riverside Dr., New York, NY 10115. Tel. (212)870-2344. Fax (212)870-2338

Clarion Herald (bi-w), Catholic, Emile M. Comar Jr., P. O. Box 53247, 100 Howard Ave. Suite 400, New Orleans, LA 70153. Tel. (504)596-3030. Fax (504)596-3032

Co-Laborer (bi-m), Free Will Baptists, National Association of, Lorene Miley, Woman's Natl. Auxiliary Convention, P.O. Box 5002, Antioch, TN 37011-5002

Collegiate Quarterly (q), Seventh-day Adventist Church, Gary B. Swanson, P.O. Box 7000, Boise, ID 83707

Columbia (m), Catholic, Richard McMunn, One Columbus Plz., New Haven, CT 06507. Tel. (203)772-2130. Fax (203)777-0114

Commission, The, Southern Baptist Convention, Leland F. Webb, The, Box 6767, Richmond, VA 23230

Commonweal (bi-w), Catholic, Margaret O'Brien Steinfels, 15 Dutch St., New York, NY 10038. Tel. (212)732-0800

Congregational Journal (3/yr), Congregational Christian Churches, American Congregational Center, Henry David Gray, P.O. Box 6040, Ventura, CA 93004. Tel. (805)644-3397

Congregationalist, The (bi-m), Congregational Christian Churches, National Association of, Joseph B. Polhemus, 1105 Briarwood Rd., Mansfield, OH 44907. Tel. (419)756-5526

Congregationalist, The, Louis B. Gerhardt, P. O. Box 9397, Fresno, CA 93792. Tel. (209)227-6936

Conqueror, United Pentecostal Church International, Rev. Darrell Johns, 8855 Dunn Rd., Hazelwood, MO 63042

Conservative Judaism, Jewish, Rabbi Shamai Kanter, 3080 Broadway, New York, NY 10027. Tel. (212)678-8060. Fax (212)749-9166

Contact (m), Free Will Baptists, National Association of, Jack Williams, P.O. Box 5002, Antioch, TN 37011-5002

Contempo, Southern Baptist Convention, Ela Clay, P.O. Box 830010, Birmingham, AL 35283

Cornerstone Connections International (q), Seventh-day Adventist Church, Mrs. Lyndelle Chiomenti, 55 W. Oak Ridge Dr., Hagerstown, MD 21740

Courage in the Struggle for Justic and Peace (10/yr), Office for Church in Society, Rubin Tendai, 110 Maryland Ave., NE, Washington, DC 20002. Tel. (202)543-1517. Fax (202)543-5994

Covenant Companion (m), Evangelical Covenant Church, Rev. James R. Hawkinson, 5101 N. Francisco Ave., Chicago, IL 60625

Covenant Home Altar (Q), Evangelical Covenant Church, Rev. James R. Hawkinson, 5101 N. Francisco Ave., Chicago, IL 60625

Covenant Quarterly (q), Evangelical Covenant Church, Dr. James C. Weld, 5101 N. Francisco Ave., Chicago, IL 60625

Covenanter Witness, The (m), Reformed Presbyterian Church of North America, James Pennington, 7408 Penn Ave., Pittsburgh, PA 15208. Tel. (412)241-0436

Credinta--The Faith (m), The Romanian Orthodox Church in America, V. Rev. Archim. Dr. Vasile Vasilachi, 19959 Riopelle St., Detroit, MI 48203

Criterion, The (w), Catholic, John F. Fink, P. O. Box 1717, 1400 N. Meridian, Indianapolis, IN 46206. Tel. (317)236-1570

Cumberland Flag, The, Second Cumberland Presbyterian Church in U.S., Rev. Robert Stanley Wood, 226 Church St., Huntsville, AL 35801

Cumberland Presbyterian, The (m), Cumberland Presbyterian Church, Mark Brown, 1978 Union Ave., Memphis, TN 38104. Tel. (901)276-4572. Fax (901)276-4578

Currents in Theology and Mission (6/yr), Lutheran School of Theology, Ralph W. Klein, 1100 E. 55th St., Chicago, IL 60615. Tel. (312)753-0751. Fax (312)753-0782

Curriculum Publications (q), Assemblies of God, Gary Leggett, Gospel Publishing House, 1445 Boonville Ave., Springfield, MO 65802

Decision (11/yr), Billy Graham Evangelistic Assn., Roger C. Palms, 1300 Harmon Pl., Minneapolis, MN 55403. Tel. (612)338-0500. Fax (612)335-1299

Directory of the Ministry (a), Christian Churches and Churches of Christ, Zella M. McLean, 1525 Cherry Rd., Springfield, IL 62704. Tel. (217)546-7338

Disciple, The (m), Christian Church (Disciples of Christ), Robert L. Friedly, Box 1986, Indianapolis, IN 46206. Tel. (317)353-1491. Fax (317)359-7546

Doors and Windows (q), The Evangelical Church, Revs. Dirk Pogue and Timothy Christman, E.C. Church Center, Myerstown, PA 17067

EMC Today (m), Evangelical Mennonite Church, Donald W. Roth, 1420 Kerrway Ct., Fort Wayne, IN 46805

Ecumenical Trends (m), William Carpe, 475 Riverside Dr., Rm. 528, New York, NY 10115. Tel. (212)870-2330. Fax (212)870-2001

El Interprete (q Spanish), The United Methodist Church, Edith LaFontaine, P.O. Box 320, Nashville, TN 37202

Eleventh Hour Messenger (bi-m), Wesleyan Holiness Association of Churches, Rev. J. Stevan Manley, 108 Carter Ave., Dayton, OH 45405

Emphasis on Faith and Living (bi-m), The Missionary Church, Rev. Robert Ransom, 3901 S. Wayne Ave., Ft. Wayne, IN 46807

Ephphatha, The (Deaf Ministry), United Pentecostal Church International, Billie Savoie, 8855 Dunn Rd., Hazelwood, MO 63042

Episcopal Church Annual, The, The Episcopal Church, E. Allen Kelly, 78 Danbury Rd., Wilton, CT 06897

Episcopal Life (m), The Episcopal Church, Jerrold Hames, 815 Second Ave., New York, NY 10017. Tel. (212)867-8400. Fax (212)949-8059

Episcopal Recorder (m), Reformed Episcopal Church, Rev. Walter G. Truesdell, 4225 Chestnut St., Philadelphia, PA 19104. Tel. (212)222-5158

Evangel, The (m), Lutheran Churches, The American Association of, Dr. Christopher Barnekov, 214 South St., Waterloo, IA 50701

Evangelical Beacon (m), The Evangelical Free Church of America, Ms. Carol Madison, 901 East 78th St., Minneapolis, MN 55420-1300

Evangelical Visitor (m), Brethren in Christ Church, Glen A. Pierce, P.O. Box 189, Nappanee, IN 46550

Evangelist, The (w), Catholic, James Breig, 40 N. Main Ave., Albany, NY 12203. Tel. (518)453-6688. Fax (518)453-6793

Extension (9/yr), Catholic, Bradley Collins, 35 East Wacker Dr., Chicago, IL 60601. Tel. (312)236-7240. Fax (312)236-5276

FOCUS (2/yr.), Friends General Conference, Meredith Walton, 1216 Arch St., 2B, Philadelphia, PA 19107. Tel. (215)561-1700

FORESEE (bi-m), Conservative Congregational Christian Conference, Mrs. Wanda Evans, 7582 Currell Blvd., #108, St. Paul, MN 55125

Faith and Truth, Pentecostal Fire-Baptized Holiness Church, Edgar Vollrath, P.O. Box 212, Nicholson, GA 30565

Faith-Life (bi-m), The Protestant Conference (Lutheran), Inc., Pastor Marcus Albrecht, P.O. Box 2141, LaCrosse, WI 54601

Fellowscript (q), Assemblies of God, Dennis Gaylor, Gospel Publishing House, 1445 Boonville Ave., Springfield, MO 65802

Fellowship Magazine, The, Assemblies of God International Fellowship (Independent/Not affiliated), Rev. T. A. Lanes, 8504 Commerce Ave., San Diego, CA 92121

Firm Foundation (m), Churches of Christ, H. A. Dobbs, P.O. Box 690192, Houston, TX 77269-0192

First Things: A Monthly Journal of Religion and Public, Independent, Richard J. Neuhaus, 156 Fifth Ave., Ste. 400, New York, NY 10010. Tel. (212)627-2288. Fax (212)627-2184

Flaming Sword, The (m), The Fire Baptized Holiness Church (Wesleyan), Susan Davolt, 10th St. & College Ave., Independence, KS 67301

For the Poor (m), Primitive Baptists, W. H. Cayce, Hwy. 172, Crockett, KY 41413

Forum Letter (m), Lutheran, Russell E. Saltzman, P.O. Box 327, Delhi, NY 13753. Tel. (607)746-7511

Forward, United Pentecostal Church International, Rev. J. L. Hall, 8855 Dunn Rd., Hazelwood, MO 63042

Forward Movement Publications, The Episcopal Church, Rev. Charles H. Long, 412 Sycamore St., Cincinnati, OH 45202. Tel. (513)721-6659

Foursquare World Advance (6/yr.), International Church of the Foursquare Gospel, Rev. Ron Williams, 1910 W. Sunset Blvd., Ste 200, Los Angeles, CA 90026

Free Will Baptist Gem (m), Free Will Baptists, National Association of, Rev. Clarence Burton, P.O. Box 991, Lebanon, MO 65536

Free Will Baptist, The (w), Original Free Will Baptist, Janie Jones Sowers, P.O. Box 159, Ayden, NC 28513. Tel. (919)746-6128. Fax (919)746-9248

Friends Journal (m), Vinton Deming, 1501 Cherry St., Philadelphia, PA 19102-1497. Tel. (215)241-7277. Fax (215)568-1377

Gem, The (w), Churches of God, General Conference, Pastor Marilyn Rayle Kern, P.O. Box 926, Findlay, OH 45839

General Baptist Messenger (m), General Baptists, Rev. Wayne Foust, 100 Stinson Dr., Poplar Bluff, MO 63901

Gleaner, The (m), Baptist Missionary Association of America, F. Donald Collins, 721 Main St., Little Rock, AR 72201

Global Witness, The, United Pentecostal Church International, Rev. Mervyn Miller, 8855 Dunn Rd., Hazelwood, MO 63042

God's Field (bi-w), Polish National Catholic Church of America, Rt. Rev. Anthony M. Rysz, 1002 Pittston Ave., Scranton, PA 18505

Gospel Advocate (m), Churches of Christ, Furman Kearley, Box 150, Nashville, TN 37202. Tel. (615)254-8781

Gospel Herald (w), Mennonite Church, J. Lorne Peachey, 616 Walnut Ave., Scottdale, PA 15683. Tel. (412)887-8500. Fax (412)887-3111

Gospel Herald, The, Church of God, Mountain Assembly, Inc., Rev. Dennis McClanahan, P.O. Box 157, Jellico, TN 37762

Gospel Messenger, The (m), Congregational Holiness Church, Mr. Franklin Creswell, 3888 Fayetteville Hwy., Griffin, GA 30223

Gospel News, The (m), The Church of Jesus Christ (Bickertonites), Anthony Scolaro, 15843 Manning, Detroit, MI 48205

Gospel Tidings, Fellowship of Evangelical Bible Churches, Robert L. Frey, 5800 S. 14th St., Omaha, NE 68107

Guardian of Truth (m), Churches of Christ, Mike Willis, Box 9670, Bowling Green, KY 42101

Guide (w), Seventh-day Adventist Church, Jeannette R. Johnson, 55 W. Oak Ridge Dr., Hagerstown, MD 21740

Happenings (q), Free Will Baptists, National Association of, Vernie Hersey, P.O. Box 5002, Antioch, TN 37011-5002

Harvest Field Messenger (bi-m), The Church of God (Seventh Day), Denver, Colo., Gina Tolbert, 330 W. 152 Ave., Colorado, CO 80233

Heartbeat, Free Will Baptists, National Association of, Don Robirds, Foreign Missions Office, P.O. Box 5002, Antioch, TN 37011-5002

Helping Hand (bi-m), Pentecostal Holiness Church, International, Mrs. Doris Moore, P.O. Box 12609, Oklahoma City, OK 73157

Herald of Christian Science, The (m), Church of Christ, Scientist, William E. Moody, One Norway St., Boston, MA 02115. Tel. (617)450-2000

Herald of Holiness (m), Church of the Nazarene, Wesley D. Tracy, 6401 The Paseo, Kansas City, MO 64131. Tel. (816)333-7000. Fax (816)333-1748

Heritage (q), Wayne E. Warner, 1445 Boonville Ave., Springfield, MO 65802. Tel. (417)862-2781. Fax (417)862-8558

High Adventure (q), Assemblies of God, Marshall Bruner, Gospel Publishing House, 1445 Boonville Ave., Springfield, MO 65802

Historical Magazine (q), The Episcopal Church, Rev. J. F. Woolverton, Box 2247, Austin, TX 78705

Holiness Union, The (m), United Holy Church of America, Inc., Dr. Joseph T. Durham, 13102 Morningside La., Silver Spring, MD 20904

Homelife, United Pentecostal Church International, Rev. Mark Christian, 8855 Dunn Rd., Hazelwood, MO 63042

Homiletic and Pastoral Review (m), Kenneth Baker, 86 Riverside Dr., New York, NY 10024. Tel. (212)799-2600

Horizons (bi-m), Presbyterian Church (U.S.A.), Barbara A. Roche, Presbyterian Women, 100 Witherspoon St., Louisville, KY 40202. Tel. (502)569-5367

Horizons (bi-w), Christian Churches and Churches of Christ, Norman L. Weaver, Box 2427, Knoxville, TN 37901. Tel. (615)577-9740

Image (m), Churches of Christ, Denny Boultinghouse, 115 Warren Dr., Ste. D, West Monroe, LA 71291. Tel. (318)396-4366

Insight (w), Seventh-day Adventist Church, J. Christopher Blake, 55 W. Oak Ridge Dr., Hagerstown, MD 21740

Insight (q), Advent Christian Church, Millie Griswold, P.O. Box 23152, Charlotte, NC 28212

Insight Into (bi-m), Netherlands Reformed Congregations, Rev. H. Hofman, 905 4th Ave., N.E., Sioux Center, IA 51250

Interest (m), Christian Brethren, William W. Conrad, 218 W. Willow, Wheaton, IL 60187. Tel. (708)653-6573. Fax (708)653-6595

International Bulletin of Missionary Research (q), Independent, Gerald H. Anderson, 490 Prospect St., New Haven, CT 06511. Tel. (203)624-6672. Fax (203)865-2857

Interpretation (q), Jack D. Kingsbury, 3401 Brook Rd., Richmond, VA 23227. Tel. (804)355-0671. Fax (804)355-3919

Interpreter (m), The United Methodist Church, Laura Okumu, P.O. Box 320, 810 Twelfth Ave. S., Nashville, TN 37203. Tel. (615)742-5104. Fax (615)742-5469

Jewish Action (q), Jewish, Charlotte Friedland, 333 Seventh Avenue, 18th Floor, New York, NY 10001. Tel. (212)244-2011. Fax (212)564-9058

Jewish Education (q), Jewish, Alvin I. Schiff, 426 W. 58th St., New York, NY 10019. Tel. (212)713-0290

John Three Sixteen (w), The Fire Baptized Holiness Church (Wesleyan), Mary Cunningham, 10th St. & College Ave., Independence, KS 67301

Journal of Adventist Education (5/yr.), Seventh-day Adventist Church, Beverly Rumble, 12501 Old Columbia Pike, Silver Spring, MD 20904-6600

Journal of Christian Education, African Methodist Episcopal Church, Kenneth H. Hill, 500 Eighth Ave., S., Nashville, TN 37203. Tel. (615)242-1420. Fax (615)726-1866

Journal of Ecumenical Studies (q), Independent, Leonard Swidler, Temple Univ. (022-38), Philadelphia, PA 19122. Tel. (215)787-7714

Journal of Pastoral Care, The (q), Independent, Orlo Strunk Jr., 1549 Clairemont Rd., Ste. 103, Decatur, GA 30030-4611

Journal of Reform Judaism (q), Jewish, Samuel Stahl, 192 Lexington Ave., New York, NY 10016. Tel. (212)684-4990

Journal of Theology (4/yr.), Church of the Lutheran Confession, Prof. John Lau, Immanuel Lutheran College, Eau Claire, WI 54701

Journal of the American Academy of Religion (q), Independent, William Scott Green, Univ. of Rochester, Rochester, Rochester, NY 14627. Tel. (716)275-5415

Judaism (q), Ruth B. Waxman, 15 E. 84th St., New York, NY 10028. Tel. (212)879-4500. Fax (212)249-3672

Keeping in Touch (m), Metropolitan Community Churches, Universal Fellowship of, Rev. Kittredge Cherry, 5300 Santa Monica Blvd, #304, Los Angeles, CA 90029

Leadership: A Practical Journal for Church Leaders (q), Independent, Marshall Shelley, 465 Gundersen Dr., Carol Stream, IL 60188. Tel. (708)260-6200. Fax (708)260-0114

Leaves of Healing (bi-m), Christian Catholic Church (Evangelical-Protestant), Roger W. Ottersen, 2500 Dowie Memorial Dr., Zion, IL 60099

Liberty (bi-m), Seventh-day Adventist Church, R. R. Hegstad, 55 W. Oak Ridge Dr., Hagerstown, MD 21740-6600

Light of Hope, The (bi-m), Apostolic Faith Mission of Portland, Oregon, Rev. Loyce C. Carver, 6615 S.E. 52nd Ave., Portland, OR 97206. Tel. (503)777-1741

Liguorian (m), Roman Catholic Church, Allen J. Weinert, 1 Liguori Dr., Liguori, MO 63057. Tel. (314)464-2500. Fax (314)464-8449

Listen (m), Seventh-day Adventist Church, Lincoln E. Steed, P.O. Box 7000, Nampa, ID 83707

Living Church, The (w), The Episcopal Church, David A. Kalvelage, 816 E. Juneau Ave., Milwaukee, WI 53202. Tel. (414)276-5420

Long Island Catholic, The (51/yr), Roman Catholic Church, Francis J. Maniscalco, P. O. Box 700, 115 Greenwich St., Hempstead, NY 11551. Tel. (516)538-8858. Fax (516)292-9372

Lookout, The (w), Christian Churches and Churches of Christ, Simon J. Dahlman, 8121 Hamilton Ave., Cincinnati, OH 45231. Tel. (513)931-4050. Fax (513)931-0904

Lutheran Ambassador, The (bi-w), Free Lutheran Congregations, The Association of, Rev. Laurel Udden, 3110 East Medicine Lake Blvd., Minneapolis, MN 55441

Lutheran Educator, The, Wisconsin Evangelical Lutheran Synod, Prof. John R. Isch, 2929 N. Mayfair Rd., Wauwatosa, WI 53222

Lutheran Forum (q), Independent, Paul R. Hinlicky, P.O. Box 327, Delhi, NY 13753. Tel. (607)746-7511

Lutheran Sentinel (m), Evangelical Lutheran Synod, Rev. P. Madson, 813 S. Willow Ave., Sioux Falls, SD 57104

Lutheran Spokesman, The (m), Church of the Lutheran Confession, Rev. Paul Fleischer, 238 Nicollet Ave., North Mankato, MN 56003

Lutheran Synod Quarterly (q), Evangelical Lutheran Synod, W. W. Peterson, Bethany Lutheran College, 734 Marsh St., Mankato, MN 56001

Lutheran Witness, The (m), The Lutheran Church--Missouri Synod, Rev. David Mahsman, 1333 S. Kirkwood Road, St. Louis, MO 63122. Tel. (314)965-9917. Fax (314)822-8307

Lutheran, The (s-m), Evangelical Lutheran Church in America, Rev. Dr. Edgar R. Trexler, 8765 W. Higgins Rd., Chicago, IL 60631. Tel. (312)380-2540. Fax (312)380-1465

Lutherans Alert-National (q), World Confessional Lutheran Association, Michael Adams, P.O. Box 7186, Tacoma, WA 98407

MORAVIAN, THE (m), Moravian Church in America (Unitas Fratrum), Rev. Herman I. Weinlick, 1021 Center St., P.O. Box 1245, Bethlehem, PA 18016. Tel. (215)867-7566. Fax (215)866-9223

Magyar Egyhaz (6/yr.), Hungarian Reformed Church in America, Stefan Torok, 331 Kirkland Pl., Perth Amboy, NJ 08861

Majallat Al-Masjid, Muslims, Dawud Assad, 99 Woodview Dr., Old Bridge, NJ 08857. Tel. (201)679-8617

Maranatha (q), Advent Christian Church, Rev. Robert Mayer, P.O. Box 23152, Charlotte, NC 28212

Marriage Partnership (q), Independent, Ron Lee, 465 Gundersen Dr., Carol Stream, IL 60188. Tel. (708)260-6200. Fax (708)260-0114

Maryknoll (m), Ronald R. Saucci, Maryknoll Fathers and Brothers, Maryknoll, NY 10545. Tel. (914)941-7590. Fax (914)945-0670

Mature Years (q), The United Methodist Church, Don Donnall, 201 Eighth Ave. S, Nashville, TN 37202

Media & Values (q), Independent, Elizabeth Thoman, 1962 S. Shenandoah St., Los Angeles, CA 90034. Tel. (213)559-2944. Fax (213)559-9396

Mennonite Brethren Herald, General Conference of Mennonite Brethren Churches, Ron Geddert, 3-169 Riverton Ave., Winnipeg, MB R2L 2E5

Mennonite Quarterly Review (q), Mennonite Church, John S. Oyer, 1600 S. Main St., Goshen, IN 46526

Mennonite Yearbook (a), Mennonite Church, James E. Horsch, 616 Walnut Ave., Scottdale, PA 15683

Mennonite, The (semi-m), Mennonite Church, The General Conference, Muriel Thiessen Stackley, Box 347, 722 Main St., Newton, KS 67114. Tel. (316)283-5100. Fax (316)283-0454

Message Magazine, The (bi-m), Seventh-day Adventist Church, Delbert W. Baker, 55 West Oak Ridge Dr., Hagerstown, MD 21740. Tel. (301)791-7000. Fax (301)791-7012

Message of the Open Bible (m), Open Bible Standard Churches, Inc., Delores A. Winegar, 2020 Bell Ave., Des Moines, IA 50315-1096

Messenger (m), Church of the Brethren, Kermon Thomasson, 1451 Dundee Ave., Elgin, IL 60120. Tel. (708)742-5100. Fax (708)742-6103

Messenger of Truth (bi-w), Church of God in Christ (Mennonite), Gladwin Koehn, P.O. Box 230, Moundridge, KS 67107

Messenger, The, The (Original) Church of God, Inc., Rev. Johnny Albertson, 2214 E. 17th St., Chattanooga, TN 37404. Tel. (615)629-4505

Messenger, The (m), Presbyterian Church in America, Rev. Robert G. Sweet, 1852 Century Pl., Ste. 101, Atlanta, GA 30345. Tel. (404)320-3388. Fax (404)320-7964

Messenger, The (m), The Swedenborgian Church, Mrs. Patte LeVan, 1592 N. 400 W., LaPorte, IN 46350. Tel. (219)325-8209

Messenger, The (m), Pentecostal Free Will Baptist Church, Inc., Mrs. Donna Hammond, P.O. Box 1568, Dunn, NC 28335

Methodist History (q), The United Methodist Church, Charles Yrigoyen Jr., P.O. Box 127, Madison, NJ 07940

Mid-Stream: An Ecumenical Journal (q), Christian Church (Disciples of Christ), Paul A. Crow Jr., P.O. Box 1986, Indianapolis, IN 46206. Tel. (317)353-1491. Fax (317)359-7546

Midwest Missionary Baptist (m), Baptist Missionary Association of America, Bill Brevette, 202 Romona Ave., Portage, MI 49002

Ministry (m), Seventh-day Adventist Church, J. David Newman, 55 W. Oak Ridge Dr., Hagerstown, MD 21740

Ministry Today (bi-m), The Missionary Church, Rev. Robert Ransom, 3901 S. Wayne Ave., Ft. Wayne, IN 46807

Mission Grams, Free Will Baptists, National Association of, Pat Thomas, Home Missions Office, P.O. Box 5002, Antioch, TN 37011-5002

Mission Herald (bi-m), National Baptist, William J. Harvey III, 701 S. 19th Street, Philadelphia, PA 19146. Tel. (215)878-2854. Fax (215)735-1721

Mission, Adult and Junior (q), Seventh-day Adventist Church, Janet Kangas, 55 W. Oak Ridge, Hagerstown, MD 21740

Missionary Messenger, The (m), Christian Methodist Episcopal Church, Mrs. P. Ann Pegues, 2309 Bonnie Ave., Bastrop, LA 71220. Tel. (318)281-3044

Missionary Messenger, The (m), Cumberland Presbyterian Church, Rev. Clay J. Brown, 1978 Union Ave., Memphis, TN 38104

Missionary Seer (m), African Methodist Episcopal Zion Church, Rev. Kermit J. DeGraffenreidt, 475 Riverside Dr., Rm. 1935, New York, NY 10115. Tel. (212)870-2952

Missionettes Memos (q), Assemblies of God, Linda Upton, Gospel Publishing House, 1445 Boonville Ave., Springfield, MO 65802

Missions, USA, William Junker, 1350 Spring St., N.W., Atlanta, GA 30367. Tel. (404)873-4041

Missions USA (m), Southern Baptist Convention, Phyllis Thompson, 1350 Spring St. NW, Atlanta, GA 30367. Tel. (404)898-7000. Fax (404)898-7228

Monday Morning (bi-m), Presbyterian Church (U.S.A.), Theodore A. Gill Jr., 100 Witherspoon St., Louisville, KY 40202

Moody Magazine (m), Independent, Dennis Shere, 820 N. LaSalle Dr., Chicago, IL 60610. Tel. (312)329-2163. Fax (312)329-2144

Mother Church, The (m), Armenian Church of America, Diocese of the, Rev. Fr. Sipan Mekhsian, 1201 N. Vine St., Hollywood, CA 90038

Mountain Movers (m), Assemblies of God, Joyce Wells Booze, Gospel Publishing House, 1445 Boonville Ave., Springfield, MO 65802

Muslim World, The, Independent, Ernest Hamilton, 77 Sherman St., Hartford, CT 06105. Tel. (203)232-4451

National Baptist Voice (s-m), National Baptist Convention, U.S.A., Inc., Dr. Roscoe Cooper, 2800 Third Ave., Richmond, VA 23222. Tel. (804)321-5115

National Catholic Reporter, Roman Catholic Church, Thomas C. Fox, P.O. Box 419281, Kansas City, MO 64141. Tel. (816)531-0538. Fax (816)931-5082

National Spiritualist Summit, The (m), National Spiritualist Association of Churches, Sandra Pfortmiller, 2020 W. Turney Ave., Phoenix, AZ 85015

New Church Life (m), General Church of the New Jerusalem, Rev. Donald L. Rose, Box 277, Bryn Athyn, PA 19009

New Oxford Review (10/yr), Dale Vree, 1069 Kains Ave., Berkeley, CA 94706. Tel. (510)526-5374

New World Outlook (m), The United Methodist Church, Alma Graham, 475 Riverside Dr., Rm. 1351, New York, NY 10115

New World, The, Cathy Campbell, 1144 W. Jackson Blvd., Chicago, IL 60607. Tel. (312)243-1300

News, The (m), The Anglican Orthodox Church, Mrs. Margaret D. Lane, P.O. Box 128, Statesville, NC 28677. Tel. (704)873-8365

Newscope (w), The United Methodist Church, Tom Tozer, P.O. Box 801, Nashville, TN 37202

North American Catholic, The (m), North American Old Roman Catholic Church, Mrs. Nan Simpson, 4200 N. Kedvale Ave., Chicago, IL 60641

Northwest Baptist Witness, Southern Baptist Convention, James L. Watters, 1033 NE 6th Ave., Portland, OR 97232. Tel. (503)238-4545

Northwest Profile (m), Baptist Missionary Association of America, Leo Hornaday, 5575 Barger St., Eugene, OR 97402

Northwestern Lutheran (semi-m), Wisconsin Evangelical Lutheran Synod, Rev. James P. Schaefer, 2929 N. Mayfair Rd., Milwaukee, WI 53222. Tel. (414)771-9357. Fax (414)771-9357

On the Line (w), Mennonite Church, Mary C. Meyer, 616 Walnut Ave., Scottdale, PA 15683

One Church (bi-m), Russian Orthodox Church in the U.S.A., Patriarchal Parishes of the, Rt. Rev. Feodor Kovalchuk, 727 Miller Ave., Youngstown, OH 44502

Orthodox Observer, The (m), Greek Orthodox Archdiocese of North and South America, Jim Golding, 8 E. 79th St., New York, NY 10021. Tel. (212)628-2590

Orthodox Tradition (4/yr.), True (Old Calendar) Orthodox Church of Greece (Synod of Metropolitan Cyprian), American Exarchate, Bishop Auxentios and Fr. James Thornton, St. Gregory Palamas Monastery, Etna, CA 96027

Our Daily Bread (m), General Convention of the Swedenborgian Church, Rev. Richard H. Tafel Jr., 9685 Lagoon Rd., Ft. Myers Beach, FL 33931

Our Family (m), New Apostolic Church of North America, Verlag Friedrich Bischoff GmbH, Gutleutstrasse 298, 6000 Frankfurt am Main, Germany

Our Little Friend (w), Seventh-day Adventist Church, Aileen Andres Sox, P.O. Box 7000, Nampa, ID 83707

Our Sunday Visitor (w), Roman Catholic Church, Robert Lockwood, 200 Noll Plaza, Huntington, IN 46750. Tel. (219)356-8400. Fax (219)356-8472

Outreach (m), Armenian Apostolic Church of America, Iris Papazian, 138 E. 39th St., New York, NY 10016

Outreach Magazine (semi-m), Open Bible Standard Churches, Inc., Paul V. Canfield, 2020 Bell Ave., Des Moines, IA 50315-1096

Outreach, The, United Pentecostal Church International, Rev. J. L. Fiorino, 8855 Dunn Rd., Hazelwood, MO 63042

Paraclete (q), Assemblies of God, David Bundrick, Gospel Publishing House, 1445 Boonville Ave., Springfield, MO 65802

Pastor's Journal, The (q), Community Churches, International Council of, Robert Puckett, 7808 College Dr., 2 SE, Palos Heights, IL 60463

Pastoral Life (m), Roman Catholic Church, Anthony Chenevey, Rte. 224, Canfield, OH 44406. Tel. (216)533-5503. Fax (216)533-1076

Path of Orthodoxy (Eng.), The, Serbian Orthodox Church in the U.S.A. and Canada, Rev. Rade Merick and Mirko Dobrijevich, P.O. Box 36, Leetsdale, PA 15056. Tel. (412)741-8660

Path of Orthodoxy (Serbian), The, Serbian Orthodox Church in the U.S.A. and Canada, V. Revs. Uros Ocokoljich and Nedeljko Lunich, P.O. Box 36, Leetsdale, PA 15056

Paul (bi-m), Netherlands Reformed Congregations, Dr. J. R. Beeke, 2115 Romence Ave., N.E., Grand Rapids, MI 29503

Pedagogic Reporter, The, Jewish, Mordecai H. Lewittes, 730 Broadway, New York, NY 10003. Tel. (212)529-2000

Pentecost Today, Full Gospel Assemblies International, C. E. Strauser, P.O. Box 1230, Coatesville, PA 19320. Tel. (215)857-2357

Pentecostal Evangel (w), Assemblies of God, Richard G. Champion, Gospel Publishing House, 1445 Boonville Ave., Springfield, MO 65802. Tel. (417)862-2781. Fax (417)862-8558

Pentecostal Herald, The, United Pentecostal Church International, Rev. J. L. Hall, 8855 Dunn Rd., Hazelwood, MO 63042

Pentecostal Holiness Advocate, The (m), Pentecostal Holiness Church, International, Mrs. Shirley Spencer, P.O. Box 12609, Oklahoma City, OK 73157

Pentecostal Interpreter, The, The Church of God in Christ, Bishop H. Jenkins Bell, P.O. Box 320, Memphis, TN 38101

Pentecostal Messenger, The (m), Pentecostal Church of God, Donald K. Allen, P.O. Box 850, Joplin, MO 64802

Perspectives on Science and Christian Fa (q), Independent, J. W. Haas Jr., P.O. Box 668, Ipswich, MA 01938. Tel. (508)356-5656

Pilot, The (w), Roman Catholic Church, Leila H. Little, 49 Franklin St., Boston, MA 02110. Tel. (617)482-4316. Fax (617)482-5647

Pockets (m), The United Methodist Church, Janet McNish Bugg, P.O. Box 189, Nashville, TN 37202

Polka (q), Polish National Catholic Church of America, Cecelia Lallo, 1002 Pittston Ave., Scranton, PA 18505

Power for Today (q), Churches of Christ, Steven S. and Emily Y. Lemley, Box 40536, Nashville, TN 37204

Praying (bi-m), Roman Catholic Church, Art Winter, P.O. Box 419335, 115 E. Armour Blvd., Kansas City, MO 64111. Tel. (816)531-0538. Fax (816)931-5082

Preacher's Magazine (m), Church of the Nazarene, Randal Denney, Nazarene Publishing House, Box 419527, Kansas City, MO 64141

Preacher, The (bi-m), Baptist Bible Fellowship International, James O. Combs, P.O. Box 309 HSJ, Springfield, MO 65801. Tel. (417)831-3996

Presbyterian Layman, The (6/yr), Independent, Parker Williamson, 1489 Baltimore Pike, Ste. 301, Springfield, PA 19064. Tel. (215)543-0227. Fax (215)543-2759

Presbyterian Outlook (w), Independent, Robert H. Bullock Jr., Box C-32071, Richmond, VA 23261-2071. Tel. (804)359-8442. Fax (804)353-6369

Presbyterian Survey (m), Presbyterian Church, U.S.A., Kenneth Little, 100 Witherspoon St., Louisville, KY 40202-1396. Tel. (502)569-5637. Fax (502)569-5018

Primary Treasure (w), Seventh-day Adventist Church, Aileen Andres Sox, P.O. Box 7000, Nampa, ID 83707

Primitive Baptist (m), Primitive Baptists, W. H. Cayce, Hwy. 172, Crockett, KY 41413

Priority (m), The Missionary Church, Rev. Ken Stucky, 3901 S. Wayne Ave., Ft. Wayne, IN 46807

Providence Visitor (w), Roman Catholic Church, Father Stanley T. Nakowicz, 184 Broad St., Providence, RI 02903. Tel. (401)272-1010

Pulpit Digest, The, Independent, David Albert Farmer, 151 Union St., Icehouse One-401, San Francisco, CA 94111

Purity Guide, The Church of God in Christ, Mrs. Pearl McCullom, P.O. Box 1526, Gary, IN 46407

Purpose (w), Mennonite Church, James E. Horsch, 616 Walnut Ave., Scottdale, PA 15683

Qala min M'Dinkha (Voice from the East) (q), Apostolic Catholic Assyrian Church of the East, North American Dioceses, Mr. Akhitiar Moshi, Diocesan Offices, 7201 N. Ashland, Chicago, IL 60626. Tel. (312)465-4777. Fax (312)465-0776

Quaker Life (m), Friends United Meeting, James R. Newby, 101 Quaker Hill Dr., Richmond, IN 47374. Tel. (317)962-7573. Fax (317)966-1293

Quarterly Review (q), The United Methodist Church, Sharon Hels, Box 871, Nashville, TN 37202. Tel. (615)340-7334. Fax (615)340-7048

Quarterly Review (q), African Methodist Episcopal Zion Church, Rev. James D. Armstrong, P.O. Box 31005, Charlotte, NC 28231

Reconstructionist, The (bi-m), Jewish, Joy Levitt, Church Rd. & Greedwood Ave., Wycote, PA 19095. Tel. (215)887-1988

Reflections, United Pentecostal Church International, Melissa Anderson, 8855 Dunn Rd., Hazelwood, MO 63402

Reform Judaism (4/yr), Jewish, Aron Hirt-Manheimer, 838 Fifth Ave., New York, NY 10021. Tel. (212)249-0100. Fax (212)734-2857

Reformation Today (bi-m), Sovereign Grace Baptists, Erroll Hulse, c/o Tom Lutz, 3743 Nichol Ave., Anderson, IN 46011

Reformed Herald, The (m), Reformed Church in the United States, Rev. P. Grossmann, Box 362, Sutton, NE 68979

Rejoice! (q), Mennonite Church, Katie Funk Wiebe, 836 Amidon, Wichita, KS 67203

Religious Broadcasting (11/yr), National Religious Broadcasters, Ron J. Kopczick, 299 Webro Road, Parsippany, NJ 07054. Tel. (201)428-5400. Fax (201)428-1814

Religious Education, Independent, Jack D. Spiro, Virginia Commonwealth Univ., Richmond, VA 23284. Tel. (804)257-1224

Religious Herald, Southern Baptist Convention, Michael Clingenpeel, P.O. Box 8377, Richmond, VA 23226. Tel. (804)672-1973

Reporter (24/yr), The Lutheran Church--Missouri Synod, David Mahsman, 1333 S. Kirkwood Rd., St. Louis, MO 63122. Tel. (314)965-9000. Fax (314)822-8307

Rescue Herald, The (q), American Rescue Workers, Col. Robert N. Coles, 1209 Hamilton Blvd., Hagerstown, MD 21742

Response (m), The United Methodist Church, Carol M. Herb, 475 Riverside Dr., Room 1363, New York, NY 10115. Tel. (212)870-3755

Restitution Herald, The (bi-m), Church of God General Conference (Oregon, Ill.), Hollis Partlowe, Box 100, Oregon, IL 61061

Restoration Herald (m), Christian Churches and Churches of Christ, Thomas D. Thurman, 5664 Cheviot Rd., Cincinnati, OH 45247-7071. Tel. (513)385-0461

Restoration Quarterly (q), Churches of Christ, Everett Ferguson, Box 8227, Abilene, TX 79699

Restoration Witness (bi-m), Reorganized Church of Jesus Christ of Latter Day Saints, Barbara Howard, P.O. Box 1059, Independence, MO 64051

Review for Religious (bi-m), Roman Catholic Church, David L. Fleming, 3601 Lindell Blvd., St. Louis, MO 63108. Tel. (314)535-3048

Review of Religious Research (4/yr), Independent, D. Paul Johnson, Texas Tech. Univ., Lubbock, TX 79409. Tel. (806)742-2400

Rocky Mountain Christian, Churches of Christ, Jack W. Carr, 2247 Highway 86 E., Castlerock, CO 80104

Sabbath Recorder (m), Seventh Day Baptist General Conference, USA and Canada, Rev. Kevin J. Butler, 3120 Kennedy Rd., P.O. Box 1678, Janesville, WI 53547. Tel. (608)752-5055. Fax (608)752-7711

Saint Anthony Messenger (m), Roman Catholic Church, Norman Perry, 1615 Republic St., Cincinnati, OH 45210. Tel. (513)241-5616. Fax (513)241-0399

Saints Herald (m), Reorganized Church of Jesus Christ of Latter Day Saints, McMurray, Sheehy, Smith & Yarrington, P.O. Box HH, Independence, MO 64055. Tel. (816)252-5010. Fax (816)252-3976

Salt (m), Catholic, Mark J. Brummel, 205 W. Monroe St., Chicago, IL 60606. Tel. (312)236-7782. Fax (312)236-7230

Schwenkfeldian, The (q), The Schwenkfelder Church, Nancy M. Byron, 1 Seminary Street, Pennsburg, PA 18073

Second Century, The (q), Independent, W. Everett Ferguson, Box 8227, Abilene, TX 79699

Secret Chamber, African Methodist Episcopal Church, Dr. Yale B. Bruce, 5728 Major Blvd., Orlando, FL 82819. Tel. (305)352-6515

Secret Place, The, American Baptist Churches, Phyllis DeMott, P.O. Box 851, Valley Forge, PA 19482

Shabat Shalom (q), Seventh-day Adventist Church, Clifford Goldstein, 55 W. Oak Ridge Dr., Hagerstown, MD 21740

Sharing (q), Mennonite Church, Steve Bowers, P.O. Box 438, Goshen, IN 46526

Shiloh's Messenger of Wisdom (m), Israelite House of David, William Robertson, P.O. Box 1067, Benton Harbor, MI 49023

Signs of the Times (m), Seventh-day Adventist Church, Gregory Brothers, P.O. Box 7000, Boise, ID 83707. Tel. (208)465-2577. Fax (208)465-2531

Skopeo (q), Fellowship of Fundamental Bible Churches, Rev. A. Glenn Doughty, Rev. Mark Franklin & Rev. James Korth, 134 Delsea Dr., Westville, NJ 08093

Social Questions Bulletin (bi-m), Independent, Rev. George McClain, 76 Clinton Ave., Shalom House, Staten Island, NY 10301. Tel. (718)273-6372. Fax (718)273-6372

Sojourners (10/yr), Independent, Jim Wallis, Box 29272, Washington, DC 20017. Tel. (202)636-3637

Southwestern News, John Earl Seelig, Box 22,00-3E, Fort Worth, TX 76122

Spirit of Truth Magazine (m), House of God, Which is the Church of the Living God, the Pillar and Ground of the Truth, Inc., Bishop Raymond A. White, 3943 Fairmont Ave., Philadelphia, PA 19104

Spirituality Today, Richard Woods, 7200 W. Division St., River Forest, IL 60305. Tel. (312)771-4270

St. Willibrord Journal, Christ Catholic Church, Dr. Charles E. Harrison, P.O. Box 271751, Houston, TX 77277-1751

Standard, The (m), Baptist General Conference, Donald E. Anderson, 2002 S. Arlington Heights Rd., Arlington Heights, IL 60005. Tel. (312)228-0200. Fax (708)228-5376

Star of Zion (w), African Methodist Episcopal Zion Church, Rev. Morgan W. Tann, P.O. Box 31005, Charlotte, NC 28231. Tel. (704)377-4329

Stewardship USA, Independent, Raymond Barnett Knudsen II, P.O. Box 9, Bloomfield Hills, MI 48303. Tel. (313)737-0895. Fax (313)737-0895

Story Friends (w), Mennonite Church, Marjorie Waybill, 616 Walnut Ave., Scottdale, PA 15683

Sunday (q), Interdenominational, James P. Wesberry, 2930 Flowers Rd., S., Atlanta, GA 30341. Tel. (404)451-7315

Sunday School Counselor (m), Assemblies of God, Sylvia Lee, Gospel Publishing House, 1445 Boonville Ave., Springfield, MO 65802

Sunday School Literature, Pentecostal Holiness Church, International, Shirley Spencer, P.O. Box 12609, Oklahoma City, OK 73157

Sunday School Literature, The Church of God in Christ, Bishop Roy L. H. Winbush, Church of God in Christ, 272 S. Main St., Memphis, TN 38103

Sunshine Band Topics, The Church of God in Christ, Mrs. Mildred Wells, 648 Peart St., Benton Harbor, MI 29022

Tablet, The (w), Catholic, Ed Wilkinson, 653 Hicks St., Brooklyn, NY 11231. Tel. (718)858-3838. Fax (718)858-2112

Theological Education (semi-a), Undenominational, James Waits, 10 Summit Park Dr., Pittsburgh, PA 15275. Tel. (412)788-6505

Theology Digest (q), Catholic, Bernhard A. Asen & Rosemary Jermann, 3634 Lindell Blvd., St. Louis, MO 63108. Tel. (314)658-2857

Theology Today (q), Undenominational, Hugh T. Kerr, P.O. Box 29, Princeton, NJ 08542. Tel. (609)497-7714. Fax (609)924-2973

These Days (bi-m), Presbyterian Church (U.S.A.), Arthur M. Field, 100 Witherspoon St., Louisville, KY 40202

Thought (q), Catholic, G. Richard Dimler, Fordham Univ., Bronx, NY 10458. Tel. (212)579-2322. Fax (212)579-2708

Tidings, Dr. Chester P. Jenkins, 4325 W. Ledbetter Dr., Dallas, TX 75233

Tidings, The, Alfred Doblin, 1530 W. Ninth St., Los Angeles, CA 90015. Tel. (213)251-3360

Today's Christian Woman (6/yr), Independent, Julie A. Talerico, 465 Gunderson Dr., Carol Stream, IL 60188. Tel. (708)260-6200. Fax (708)260-0114

Tradition: A Journal of Orthodox Jewish Thought (q), Jewish (Rabbinical Council of America), Rabbi Emanuel Feldman, 275 Seventh Ave., New York, NY 10001. Tel. (212)807-7888. Fax (212)727-8452

Truth (bi-m), Grace Gospel Fellowship, Roger G. Anderson, 2125 Martindale SW, Grand Rapids, MI 49509

U.S. Catholic (m), Mark J. Brummel, 205 W. Monroe St., Chicago, IL 60606. Tel. (312)236-7782. Fax (312)236-7230

Ubique: American Province (q), The Liberal Catholic Church--Province of the United States of America, Rt. Rev. Joseph Tisch, P.O. Box 1117, Melbourne, FL 32901

Ukrainian Orthodox Herald, Ukrainian Orthodox Church in America (Ecumenical Patriarchate), Rev. Dr. Anthony Ugolnik, c/o St. Mary's Church, 1031 Fullerton Ave., Allentown, PA 18102

United Brethren, The (m), United Brethren in Christ, Steve Dennie, 302 Lake St., Huntington, IN 46750

United Evangelical ACTION (bi-m), Interdenominational, Donald R. Brown, 450 E. Gundersen Drive, Carol Stream, IL 60188. Tel. (708)665-0500. Fax (708)665-8575

United Foursquare Women's Magazine, International Church of the Foursquare Gospel, Rev. Beverly Brafford, 1910 W. Sunset Blvd., Los Angeles, CA 90026

United Methodist Reporter, The (bi-w), Methodist, Ronald P. Patterson, P.O. Box 660275, Dallas, TX 75266. Tel. (214)630-6495. Fax (214)630-0079

United Synagogue Review (bi-a), Jewish, Lois Goldrich, 155 - 5th Ave., New York, NY 10010. Tel. (212)533-7800

Upreach (semi-m), Churches of Christ, Randy Becton, Box 2001, Abilene, TX 79604

Vanguard, Christian Church (Disciples of Christ), Ann Updegraff Spleth, 222 S. Downey Ave., Box 1986, Indianapolis, IN 46206-1986

Vibrant Life (bi-m), Seventh-day Adventist Church, Barbara L. Jackson-Hall, 55 W. Oak Ridge Dr., Hagerstown, MD 21740

Vindicator, The, Old German Baptist Brethren, M. Keith Skiles, 1876 Beamsville-Union City Rd., Union City, OH 45390

Vineyard (Vreshta), The (q), Albanian Orthodox Archdiocese in America, Rev. Dennis J. Schutte, 30 Willow St., Wollaston, MA 02170

Vista (m), Christian Church of North America, General Council, Rev. David Perrello, Box 141-A RD 1, Transfer, PA 16148

Vital Christianity (15/yr), Church of God (Anderson, Ind.), Arlo F. Newell, Box 2499, Anderson, IN 46018. Tel. (317)644-7721. Fax (317)649-3664

Voice, General Baptists, Rev. Gene Koker, 100 Stinson Dr., Poplar Bluff, MO 63901

Voice (11/yr.), Mennonite Church, Eve MacMaster, 421 S. 2nd St., Ste. 600, Elkhart, IN 46516

Voice of Missions, African Methodist Episcopal Church, Maeola Herring, 475 Riverside Dr., Rm. 1926, New York, NY 10115. Tel. (212)870-2258

Voice of Missions, The, The Church of God in Christ, Ms. Jenifer James, 1932 Dewey Ave., Evanston, IL 60201

Voice, The (m), Independent Fundamental Churches of America, Rev. Paul J. Dollaske, P.O. Box 810, Grandville, MI 49418

Voice, The, The Bible Church of Christ, Inc., Montrose Bushrod, 1358 Morris Ave., Bronx, NY 10456. Tel. (212)588-2284

WAVE, General Baptists, Mrs. Sandra Trivitt, 100 Stinson Dr., Poplar Bluff, MO 63901

WSBC Horizons, Southern Baptist Convention, John Thomason, P.O. Box 3074, Casper, WY 82602. Tel. (307)472-4087

War Cry, The (w), The Salvation Army, Col. Henry Gariepy, 615 Slaters Lane, Alexandria, VA 22313. Tel. (703)684-5500. Fax (703)684-5539

Wesleyan Advocate, The (m), The Wesleyan Church, Dr. Wayne E. Caldwell, P.O. Box 50434, Indianapolis, ID 46250. Tel. (317)576-1314. Fax (317)842-9188

Wesleyan Woman, The (q), The Wesleyan Church, Karen Disharoon, P.O. Box 50434, Indianapolis, IN 46250. Tel. (317)576-1312. Fax (317)573-0679

Wesleyan World (m), The Wesleyan Church, Stanley K. Hoover, P.O. Box 50434, Indianapolis, IN 46250. Tel. (317)576-8172. Fax (317)841-1125

Western Recorder (w), Southern Baptist Convention, Marv Knox, Box 43969, Louisville, KY 40253. Tel. (502)244-6470

White Wing Messenger, The (bi-w), Church of God of Prophecy, Billy Murray, P.O. Box 2910, Cleveland, TN 37320-2910. Fax (615)476-6108

Whole Truth, The, The Church of God in Christ, Dr. David Hall, P.O. Box 2017, Memphis, TN 38101

Window to Mission (q), Mennonite Church, The General Conference, Lois Deckert, 722 Main St., Newton, KS 67114

Wisconsin Lutheran Quarterly (q), Wisconsin Evangelical Lutheran Synod, Prof. Wilbert R. Gawrisch, 11831 N. Seminary Dr., 65 W. Mequon, WI 53092

With (m), Mennonite Church, Eddy Hall &. Carol Duerksen, P.O. Box 347, Newton, KS 67114

241

Witness (m), Pentecostal Holiness Church, International, Rev. Joe Iaquinta, P.O. Box 12609, Oklahoma City, OK 73157

Woman's Touch (bi-m), Assemblies of God, Sandra Clopine, Gospel Publishing House, 1445 Boonville Ave., Springfield, MO 65802

Women's Missionary Magazine, African Methodist Episcopal Church, Mrs. Bertha O. Fordham, 800 Risley Ave., Pleasantville, NJ 08232

Word and Way, Southern Baptist Convention, Bob Terry, 400 E. High, Jefferson City, MO 65101. Tel. (314)635-7931

Word and Work, Independent, Alex V. Wilson, 2518 Portland Ave., Louisville, KY 40212

Word, The (m), The Antiochian Orthodox Christian Archdiocese of North America, V. Rev. George S. Corey, 52 78th St., Brooklyn, NY 11209

Workman, The (q), Churches of God, General Conference, Pastor Marilyn Rayle Kern, P.O. Box 926, Findlay, OH 45839

World Missions (m), Church of the Nazarene, Robert H. Scott, Nazarene Publishing House, Box 419527, Kansas City, MO 64141

World Monitor Mazagine (m), Church of Christ, Scientist, Earl W. Foell, One Norway St., Boston, MA 02115

World Parish (s-m), The United Methodist Church, Joe Hale, P.O. Box 518, Lake Junaluska, NC 28745

World Partners (bi-m), The Missionary Church, Rev. Charles Carpenter, 3901 S. Wayne Ave., Ft. Wayne, IN 46807

World Vision (m), Open Bible Standard Churches, Paul V. Canfield, 2020 Bell Ave., Des Moines, IA 50315-1096

World Vision (bi-m), Nondenominational, Terry Madison, 919 W. Huntington Dr., Monrovia, CA 91016. Tel. (818)357-7979. Fax (818)357-0915

World, The (6/yr.), Unitarian Universalist Association, Ms. Linda C. Beyer, 25 Beacon St., Boston, MA 02108. Tel. (617)742-2100. Fax (617)367-3637

Worldorama (m), Pentecostal Holiness Church, International, Rev. Jesse Simmons, P.O. Box 12609, Oklahoma City, OK 73157

Worship (6/yr), Catholic, R. Kevin Seasoltz, St. John's Abbey, Collegeville, MN 56321. Tel. (612)363-2600. Fax (612)363-2504

Y.P.W.W. Topics, The Church of God in Christ, Elder James L. Whitehead Jr., 67 Tennyson, Highland Park, MI 48203

Young Salvationist (m), The Salvation Army, Col. Henry Gariepy, National Publications Dept., 799 Bloomfield Ave., Verona, NJ 07044

Young Soldier, The (m), The Salvation Army, Col. Henry Gariepy, National Publications Dept., 799 Bloomfield Ave., Verona, NJ 07044

Youth Ministry Accent (q), Seventh-day Adventist Church, Michael H. Stevenson, 12501 Old Columbia Pike, Silver Spring, MD 20904-6600

Youth Ministry Quarterly (q), Lutheran (Mo. Synod), Karen Jurgensen, 1333 S. Kirkwood Rd., St. Louis, MO 63122. Tel. (314)965-9000. Fax (314)822-8307

Zion's Advocate, Church of Christ, Gary Housknecht, P.O. Box 472, Independence, MO 64051

Zion's Herald, United Zion Church, Miss Martha Harting, 75 Hickory Rd., Denver, PA 17517

12. RELIGIOUS PERIODICALS IN CANADA

The religious periodicals below constitute a basic core of important newspapers, journals, and periodicals circulated in Canada. The list does not include all publications prepared by religious bodies. The listing of religious bodies in Canada includes the titles of publications found in this list.

Each entry lists the title of the periodical, frequency of publication, religious affiliation, editor's name, address, telephone number and fax number when known.

Advance (q), Assoc. Gospel Chs., Wayne Foster, 8 Silver St., Paris, ON N3L 1T6. Tel. (519)442-6220

Alberta Alert, The, Baptist Gen. Conf. of Alberta, Virgil Olson, 10727 - 114 St., Edmonton, AB T5H 3K1. Tel. (403)424-8440

Ambassador, The (m), Pentecostal Assemblies of Newfoundland, R. H. Dewling, 57 Thorburn Rd., St. John's, NF A1B 3N4

Anglican Journal/Journal Anglican (m), Anglican Ch. of Canada, Carolyn Purden, 600 Jarvis St., Toronto, ON M4Y 2J6. Tel. (416)924-9192. Fax (416)921-4452

Anglican Magazine: Living Message (7/yr.), Ang. Ch. of Can., John Bird, 600 Jarvis St., Toronto, ON M4Y 2J6. Tel. (416)924-9192. Fax (412)968-7983

Anglican, The (10/yr.), Vivian Snead, 135 Adelaide St. E, Toronto, ON M5C 1L8. Tel. (416)363-6021. Fax (416)363-7678

Atlantic Baptist, The (m), Un. Bapt. Conv. of the Atlantic Provinces, Rev. Michael Lipe, Box 756, Kentville, NS B4N 3X9. Tel. (902)678-6868

Atlantic Wesleyan (m), Atlantic Dist. of The Wesleyan Ch., Rev. Ray E. Barnwell Sr., P.O. Box 20, Sussex, NB E0E 1P0. Tel. (506)433-1007. Fax (506)432-6668

B.C. Conference Call, British Columbia Baptist Conference, Rev. Walter W. Wieser, 7600 Glover Rd., Langley, BC V3A 6H4

B.C. Fellowship Baptist (m), Evang. Bapt. Chs. in B.C. and Yukon, Gordon Reeve, Box 800, Langley, BC V3A 3C9. Tel. (604)888-3616. Fax (604)888-3601

BGC Canada NEWS (4/yr), Baptist General Conference of Canada, Rev. Abe Funk, 4306 97th St., Edmonton, ON AB T6E 5R9. Tel. (403)438-9127. Fax (403)435-2478

Banner of Truth (m), Netherlands Reformed Congregations of North America, Dr. Joel R. Beeke, 2115 Romence NE, Grand Rapids, MI 49503

Baptist Herald (10/yr), North American Bapt. Conference, Mrs. Barbara J. Binder, 1 S. 210 Summit Ave., Oakbrook Terrace, IL 60181

Baptist Horizon, The, Canadian Conv. of Southern Baptists, Nancy McGough, Postal Bag 300, Cochrane, AB T0L 0W0

Blackboard Bulletin, Old Order Amish Church, Elizabeth Wengerd, Rt. 4, Aylmer, ON N5H 2R3

Briercrest Echo, The (q), Mark Fowke, Briercrest Schools, Caronport, SK S0H 0S0. Tel. (306)756-3200. Fax (306)756-3366

British Columbia Catholic, The (w), Cath., Vincent J. Hawkswell, 150 Robson St., Vancouver, BC V6B 2A7. Tel. (604)683-0281. Fax (604)683-8117

Budget, The, Old Order Amish Church, George R. Smith, P.O. Box 249, Sugarcreek, OH 44681

Bulletin du Congres Juif Canadien (irreg.), Jewish, French Canadian Jewish Congress, 1590 Ave. Docteur Penfield, Montréal, QC H3G 1C5. Tel. (514)931-7531

Cahiers de Josephologie (2/yr), Catholic, Roland Gauthier, Centre de recherche, 3800 Ch. Reine-Marie, Montréal, QC H3V 1H6. Tel. (514)733-8211. Fax (514)733-9735

Calendarul Credinta (Yearbook with Church Directory), Romanian Orthodox Ch. in America (Canadian Parishes), V. Rev. Archim, Dr. Vasile Vasilachi, 19959 Riopelle St., Detroit, MI 48203

Calvinist Contact (w), Reform, Bert Witvoet, 261 Martindale Rd., Unit 4, St. Catharines, ON L2W 1A1. Tel. (416)682-8311. Fax (416)682-8313

Canada Armenian Press (q), Armenian Evangelical Church, Rev. Y. Sarmazian, 42 Glenforest Rd., Toronto, ON M4N 1Z8

Canada Lutheran, The (11/yr), Ev. Luth. Ch. in Canada, Kenn Ward, 1512 St. James St., Winnipeg, MB R3H 0L2. Tel. (204)786-6707. Fax (204)783-7548

Canadian Adventist Messenger (12/yr), Seventh-day Adv. Ch. in Canada, J. Polishuk, Maracle Press, 1156 King St. E, Oshawa, ON L1H 7N4. Tel. (416)723-3438. Fax (416)428-6024

Canadian Baptist, The (10/yr.), Canadian Baptist Federation, Bapt. Conf. of Ontario & Quebec, Larry Matthews, 217 St. George St., Toronto, ON M5R 2M2. Tel. (416)922-5163. Fax (416)922-4369

Canadian Bible Society Quarterly Newsletter (q), Floyd Babcock, 10 Carnforth, Toronto, ON M4A 2S4. Tel. (416)757-4171. Fax (416)757-3376

Canadian Disciple (4/yr.), Christian Church (Disciples of Christ) in Canada, Rev. Raymond Cuthbert, 240 Home St., Winnipeg, MB R3G 1X. Tel. (204)783-5881

Canadian Friend, The, Canadian Yearly Mtg. of the Religious Soc. of Friends, Dorothy Parshall, General Delivery, Highland Grove, ON K0L 2A0

Canadian Jewish Herald (irreg.), Jewish, Dan Nimrod, 17 Anselme Lavigne Blvd., Dollard des Ormeaux, QC H9A 1N3. Tel. (514)684-7667

Canadian Jewish News (w), Jewish, Patricia Rucker, 10 Gateway Blvd., Don Mills, ON M3C 3A1. Tel. (416)422-2331

Canadian Jewish Outlook (m), Jewish, Henry M. Rosenthal, 6184 Ash St., #3, Vancouver, BC V5Z 3G9. Tel. (604)324-5101

Canadian Lutheran (bi-m), Lutheran Church--Canada, Frances A. Wershler, Box 163, Sta. A, Winnipeg, MB R3K 2A1. Tel. (204)832-0123. Fax (204)888-2672

Canadian Trumpeter Canada-West, Church of God of Prophecy in Canada, John Doroshuk, Box 952, Strathmore, AL TOJ 3HO. Tel. (403)934-4787. Fax (403)934-5011

Canadian Zionist (5/yr.), Jewish, Rabbi Meyer Krentzman, 5250 Decarie Blvd., Ste. 550, Montréal, QC H3X 2H9. Tel. (514)486-9526

Caravan: A Resource for Adult Religious Education (q), Joanne Chafe, 90 Parent Ave., Ottawa, ON KIN 7BI. Tel. (613)236-9461. Fax (613)236-8117

Catalyst (6/yr.), Citizens for Public Justice, Harry J. Kits, 229 College Street, #311, Toronto, ON M5T 1R4. Tel. (416)979-2443

Catholic New Times (bi-w), Catholic, Anne O'Brien, 80 Sackville St., Toronto, ON M5A 3E5. Tel. (416)361-0761

Catholic Register, The (w), Catholic, Rev. Carl Matthews, 67 Bond St., Toronto, ON M5B 1X6. Tel. (416)362-6822. Fax (416)362-6822

Cela Biedrs (10/yr.), Latvian Evangelical Luth. Ch. in America, Rev. Edwards Putnins, 1468 Hemlock St., Napa, CA 94559. Tel. (707)252-1809

Central Canada Clarion (bi-m), Weslyan Ch., S. A. Summers, 3 Applewood Dr., Ste. 102, Belleville, ON K8P 4E3

Channels (q), Renewal Fellowship, Presby. Ch. in Canada, J. H. Kouwenberg, 5800 University Blvd., Vancouver, BC V6T 2E4. Tel. (604)224-3245

China and Ourselves (q), Ecum., Canada China Prog., Cynthia K. McLean, 40 St. Clair Ave. E, Ste. 201, Toronto, ON M4T 1M9. Tel. (416)921-4152. Fax (416)921-7478

Coast to Coast (bi-m), Presbyterian Ch. in America (Canadian Section), J. Cameron Fraser, Box 490, Sechelt, BC V0N 3A0

College News & Updates (6/yr), Gardner Bible College, Bruce Kelly, 4704 - 55 St., Camrose, AB T4V 2B6. Tel. (403)672-0171. Fax (403)672-6888

Communauté Chrétienne (8/yr), unaffil., Richard Guimoud, Pères Dominicains, 2715 chemin de la Côte, Ste. Catherine, Montréal, QC H3T 1B6. Tel. (514)739-9797. Fax (514)739-1664

Communicator, The (4/yr), Assoc. of R.C. Communicators of Can., Ron Pickersgill, Box 2400, London, ON N6A 4G3. Tel. (519)439-7211. Fax (519)439-0207

Connexions (4/yr), Ulli Diemer, 427 Bloor St. W, Toronto, ON M5S 1X7. Tel. (416)460-3903

Contact, The, Menn. Breth., George Dirks, Bethany Bible Institue, Box 160, Hepburn, SK S0K 1Z0. Tel. (306)947-2175

Covenant Messenger, The (m), Evangelical Cov. Ch. of Canada, Elizabeth A. Stroman, 245 21st St. E, Prince Albert, SK S6V 1L9. Tel. (306)922-3449

Credinta--The Faith (m), Romanian Orthodox Ch. in America (Canadian Parishes), V. Rev. Archim., Dr. Vasile Vasilachi, 19959 Riopelle St., Detroit, MI 48203

Credo (French m), Église unie du Canada (United Church of Canada), Gérard Gautier, 132 Victoria, Greenfield Park, QC J4V 1L8. Tel. (514)466-7733

Crosstalk (10/yr), Anglican Diocese of Ottawa, J. R. Maybee, 71 Bronson Ave., Ottawa, ON K1R 6G6. Tel. (613)232-1451

Crusader, The (2/yr), Anglican Ch. of Canada, Capt. W. Marshall, 397 Brunswick Ave., Toronto, ON M5R 2Z2. Tel. (416)924-9279

Crux (q), Donald Lewis, Regent College, 5800 University Blvd, Vancouver, BC V6T 2E4. Tel. (604)224-3245. Fax (604)224-3097

Diary, The, Old Order Amish Ch., Joseph Beiler, 3981 E. Newport Rd., Gordonville, PA 17529

Die Botschaft, Old Order Amish Church, James Weaver, Brookshire Pub, Inc., 200 Hazel St., Lancaster, PA 17603

Discover the Bible (w), Cath., Walter Bedard, 2000 Sherbrooke St. W, Montréal, QC H3H 1G4. Tel. (514)931-7311

EMMC Recorder (m), Mennonite, Adina Kehler, Box 126, Winnipeg, MB R3C 2G1. Tel. (204)477-1213

Ecumenism/Oecuménisme (q), Canadian Centre for Ecumenism, Thomas Ryan, 2065 Sherbrooke St. W, Montréal, QC H3H 1G6. Tel. (514)937-9176. Fax (514)935-5497

Edge, The, Salvation Army in Canada, Maj. David Hammond, 455 N. Service Rd. E, Oakville, ON L6H 1A5. Tel. (416)845-9235. Fax (416)845-1966

Eesti Kirik, Estonian Evangelical Luth. Ch., Bishop K. Raudsepp, 30 Sunrise Ave., #216, Toronto, ON M4A 2R3

Eglise et Theologie: Review of the Faculty of Theology (3/yr-bil), Cath., bi-lingual, Leo Laberge, St. Paul University, 223 Main St., Ottawa, ON K1S 1C4. Tel. (613)236-1393. Fax (613)782-3005

En Evant!, Salvation Army in Canada, Maj. David Hammond, 455 N. Service Rd. E, Oakville, ON L6H 1A5. Tel. (416)845-9235. Fax (416)845-1966

End Times' Messenger (m), Apost. Ch. of Pent. of Canada, I. W. Ellis, 105, 807 Manning Rd. NE, Calgary, AB T2E 7M8

Enterprise (q), Canadian Bapt. Intl. Ministries, Rev. Frank Byrne, 7185 Millcreek Dr., Mississauga, ON L5N 5R4. Tel. (416)821-3533. Fax (416)826-3441

Entre-nous (q), Canadian Council of Chs., James Hodgson, 40 St. Clair Ave. E, Toronto, ON M4T 1M9. Tel. (416)921-4152. Fax (416)921-7478

Esprit (bi-m), Evangelical Luth. Church in Canada, Gwen Hawkins, Box 19, RR #1, Madeira Park, BC V0N 2H0. Tel. (604)883-2778. Fax (604)885-2900

Evangelical Baptist (m), Evangelical Bapt. Church in Canada, Dr. Roy W. Lawson, 679 Southgate Dr., Guelph, ON N1G 4S2. Tel. (519)821-4830. Fax (519)821-9829

Exchange (3/yr), United Ch. of Canada, Lynda Newmarch, Div. of Mission in Canada, 85 St. Clair Ave. E, Toronto, ON M4T 1M8. Tel. (416)925-5931. Fax (416)925-3394

Expression (q), Menn. Breth. Chs. of Canada, Dan Block, Box 2, Sta. F, Winnipeg, MB R2L 2A5. Tel. (204)667-9576

Faith Today (bi-m), Evang. Fell. of Canada, Brian C. Stiller, Box 8800, Sta. B, Willowdale, ON M2K 2R6. Tel. (416)479-5885. Fax (416)479-4742

Faith and Fellowship (bi-m), Church of the Lutheran Breth., Rev. David Rinden, 704 Vernon Ave. W, Fergus Falls, MN 56537

Family Life, Old Order Amish Ch., Joseph Stoll, Rt. 4, Aylmer, ON N5H 2R3

For the Record, Luth. Church--Canada, John M. Cobb, Canadian Luth. Hist. Assn., Box 86, Wildwood, AB T0E 2M0. Tel. (403)325-2247

Free Methodist Herald, The (m), Free Meth., D. G. Bastian, 69 Browning Ave., Toronto, ON M4K 1W1. Tel. (416)463-4536

Free Methodist Herald, The (m), Free Methodist Ch. in Canada, Donald G. Bastian, 69 Browning Ave., Toronto, ON M4K 1W1. Tel. (416)463-4536

Glad Tidings (10/yr), Presbyterian Ch. in Canada, Women's Mission Soc., L. June Stevenson, 50 Wynford Dr., Rm. 100, Don Mills, ON M3C 1J7. Tel. (416)441-2840. Fax (416)441-2825

Global Village Voice (q), Canadian Cath. Org. for Development and Peace, Jack J. Panozzo, 3028 Danforth Ave., Toronto, ON M4C 1N2. Tel. (416)698-7770. Fax (416)698-8269

Good News West (bi-m), Chs. of Christ in Canada, Kelly Carter, 3460 Shelbourne St., Victoria, BC V8P 4G5

Good Tidings (m), Pent. Assemb. of Newfoundland, Roy D. King, 57 Thorburn Rd., P.O. Box 8895, Sta. A, St. John's, NF A1B 3N4. Tel. (709)753-6314. Fax (709)753-4945

Gospel Contact, The (10/yr), Ch. of God in Western Canada (Anderson, IN), Lloyd Moritz, 4717 56th St., Camrose, AB T4V 2C4. Tel. (403)672-0772. Fax (403)672-6888

Gospel Herald (m), Churches of Christ in Canada, Eugene C. Perry, 4904 King St., Beamsville, ON L0R 1B6. Tel. (416)563-7503

Gospel Standard, The, Free Will Bapts., Rev. Fred D. Hanson, Box 355, Hartland, NB E0J 1N0

Gospel Standard, The (m), Fund., Perry F. Rockwood, Box 1660, Halifax, NS B3J 3A1. Tel. (902)423-5540

Grail (q), Ecum., Michael W. Higgins, Univ. of St. Jerome's College, Waterloo, ON N2L 3G3. Tel. (519)884-8110

Guide, The (9/yr.), Christian Labour Assoc. of Canada, Edward Vanderkloet, 5920 Atlantic Dr., Mississauga, ON L4W 1N6. Tel. (416)670-7383. Fax (416)670-8416

Hallelujah (bi-m), Bible Holiness Movement, W. H. Wakefield, Box 223, Postal Stn. A, Vancouver, BC V6C 2M3. Tel. (604)498-3895

Herold der Wahrheit, Old Order Amish Church, Cephas Kauffman, 1829 110th St., Kalona, IA 52247

Horizons, Salvation Army in Canada, Maj. David Hammond, 455 N. Service Rd. E., Oakville, ON L6H 1A5. Tel. (416)845-9235. Fax (416)845-1966

Huron Church News (10/yr), Ang. Ch. of Canada, Rev. Roger W. McCombe, 220 Dundas St., 4th Fl., London, ON N6A 1H3. Tel. (519)434-6893. Fax (519)673-4151

IdeaBank (q), Menn. Breth. Churches, Canadian Conf., David Wiebe, Christian Ed. Office, 3-169 Riverton Ave., Winnipeg, MB R2L 2E5. Tel. (204)669-6575. Fax (204)654-1865

In Holy Array, Canadian and American Ref. Chs., c/o Rev. E. Kampen, Canadian Ref. Young Peoples' Societies, 21112 35th Ave. NW, Edmonton, AB T5P 4B7

Insight Into (bi-m), Netherlands Ref. Cong. of North America, Rev. H. Hofman, 46660 Ramona Dr., Chilliwack, BC V2P 7W6

Insight: A Resource for Adult Religious Education, CCCB, Joanne Chafe, 90 Parent Ave., Ottawa, ON K1N 7B1. Tel. (613)236-9461. Fax (613)236-8117

Intercom (q), Evang. Bapt. Chs. in Canada, Dr. R. W. Lawson, 679 Southgate Dr., Guelph, ON N1G 4S2. Tel. (519)821-4830. Fax (519)821-9829

Iskra (bi-w), Un. of Spiritual Communities of Christ (Orth. Doukhobors in Canada), D. E. Popoff, Box 760, Grand Forks, BC V0H 1H0. Tel. (604)442-8252. Fax (604)442-3433

Jewish Eagle (w), Jewish, in Yiddish, Hebrew, French, B. Hirshtal, 4180 De Courtrai, Rm. 218, Montréal, QC H3S 1C3. Tel. (514)735-6577

Jewish Post and News (w), Jewish, Matt Bellan, 117 Hutchings St., Winnipeg, MB R2X 2V4. Tel. (204)694-3332

Jewish Standard (semi-m), Jewish, Julius Hayman, 77 Mowat Ave., Ste. 016, Toronto, ON M6K 3E3. Tel. (416)537-2696

Jewish Western Bulletin (w), Jewish, Samuel Kaplan, 3268 Heather St., Vancouver, BC V5Z 3K5. Tel. (604)879-6575

Journal Of The Moscow Patriarchate, The (m), Russian Orthodox Ch. in Canada, Metropolitan Pitirim of Volokolamsk, P.O. Box 624, Moscow, Russia, 119435

Journal of Psychology and Judaism (q), Jewish, Reuven P. Bulka, 1747 Featherston Dr., Ottawa, ON K1H 6P4. Tel. (613)731-9119

Journal of the Canadian Church Historical Society (2/yr), Angl. Ch. of Canada, Dorothy Kealey, c/o The General Synod Archives, 600 Jarvis St., Toronto, ON M4Y 2J6. Tel. (416)924-9192

Kerygma (2/yr), Cath. (bilingual), Martin Roberge, St. Paul Univ., Inst. of Mission Studies, 223 Main St., Ottawa, ON K1S 1C4. Tel. (613)236-1393. Fax (613)782-3005

L'Église Canadienne (15/y), Cath., Rolande Parrot, 1073 boul. St-Cyrille ouest, Québec, QC G1S 4R5. Tel. (418)688-1211. Fax (418)681-0304

Laval Théologique et Philosophique (3/yr), Cath., René Michael Roberge, Pavillon Félix-Antoine Savard, Université Laval, Québec, QC G1K 7P4. Tel. (418)656-4115

Lien, Le, Menn. Breth. Ch., Canadian Conf., Annie Brosseau, 1775 Edouard-Laurin, St. Laurent, QC H4L 2B9. Tel. (514)331-0878

Mandate (6/yr), United Ch. of Canada, Rebekah Chevalier, Div. of Communications, 85 St. Clair Ave. E, Toronto, ON M4T 1M8. Tel. (416)925-5931. Fax (416)925-3394

Mantle, The (m), Ind. Assemblies of God--Canada, Rev. A. W. Rassmussen, 24411 Ridge Route Dr., Ste. 230, Laguna Hills, CA 92653

Marketplace, The: A Magazine for Christians in Business (m), Menn., Wally Kroeker, 420-280 Smith St., Winnipeg, MN R3C 1K2. Tel. (204)944-1995. Fax (204)942-4001

Mennonite Brethren Herald (bi-w), Menn. Breth. Ch., Canadian Conf., Ron Geddert, 3-169 Riverton Ave., Winnipeg, MB R2L 2E5. Tel. (204)669-6575. Fax (204)654-1865

Mennonite Mirror (10/yr), Inter-Menn., Ruth Vogt, 207-1317A Portage Ave., Winnipeg, MB R3G 0V3. Tel. (204)786-2289

Mennonite Reporter (bi-w), Conf. of Mennonites in Canada, Ron Rempel, 3-312 Marsland Dr., Waterloo, ON N2J 3Z1. Tel. (519)884-3810

Mennonite, The (semi-m), Conf. of Mennonites in Canada, Muriel T. Stackley, Box 347, 722 Main, Newton, KS 67114. Tel. (316)283-5100. Fax (316)283-0454

Mennonitische Post, Die (bi-m), Inter-Menn., Isbrand Hiebert, Box 1120, Steinbach, MB R0A 2A0. Tel. (204)326-6790

Mennonitische Rundschau (bi-w), Menn. Breth. Ch., Canadian Conf., Lorina Marsch, 3-169 Riverton Ave., Winninpeg, MB R2L 2E5. Tel. (204)669-6575. Fax (204)654-1865

Messenger (of the Sacred Heart) (m), Cath, F. J. Power, Apostleship of Prayer, 661 Greenwood Ave., Toronto, ON M4J 4B3. Tel. (416)466-1195

Messenger, The (bi-w), Evangelical Menn. Conf., Menno Hamm, Bd. of Church Ministries, Box 1268, Steinbach, MB R0A 2A0

Ministry to Women Sketch, The, Salvation Army in Canada, Maj. David Hammond, 455 N. Service Rd. E, Oakville, ON L6H 1A5. Tel. (416)845-9235. Fax (416)845-1966

Monitor, The (m), Cath., Patrick J. Kennedy, P.O. Box 986, St. John's, NF A1C 5M3. Tel. (709)739-6553. Fax (709)726-8021

Montreal Churchman (m), Ang. Ch. of Can., Joan Shanks, Cathedral Place, 1444 Union Ave., Montréal, QC H3A 2B8. Tel. (514)843-6577

Moravian, The, Rev. Hermann I. Weinlick, P.O. Box 1245, Bethlehem, PA 18016-1245. Tel. (215)867-7566. Fax (215)866-9223

National Bulletin on Liturgy (4/yr), Cath., J. Frank Henderson, Novalis, P.O. Box 990, Outremont, QC H2V 4S7. Tel. (514)948-1222

New Church Life (m), General Ch. of the New Jerusalem, Rev. Donald L. Rose, Box 277, Bryn Athyn, PA 19009

New Freeman, The (w), Cath., Robert G. Merzetti, One Bayard Dr., Saint John, NB E2L 3L5. Tel. (506)632-9226. Fax (506)632-9272

News of Quebec (q), Christian Breth. (aka Plymouth Breth.), Richard Strout, 222 Alexander St., P.O. Box 1054, Sherbrooke, QC J1H 4S7

Newsletter (3/yr), Faith at Work, E. Milliken, 29 Albion St., Belleville, ON K8N 3R7. Tel. (613)968-7409

Newsletter of the Diocese of London (q), Cath., Ron Pickersgill, P.O. Box 2400, London, ON N6A 4G3. Tel. (519)439-7211. Fax (519)439-0207

Northwest Canada Echoes (m), Evangelical Church in Canada, A. W. Riegel, c/o 2805-13th Ave. SE, Medicine Hat, AB T1A 3R1

Ontario Messenger (m), Ch. of God (Anderson, IN), Paul Kilburn, 85 Emmett Ave., #1109, Toronto, ON M6M 5A2

Ottawa Jewish Bulletin & Review (bi-w), Jewish, Cynthia Engel, 151 Chapel St., Ottawa, ON K1N 7Y2. Tel. (613)232-7306

PMC: The Practice of Ministry in Canada (5/yr.), PMC Board, Editor Jim Taylor, 60 St. Clair Ave. E, Ste. 500, Toronto, ON M4T IN5. Tel. (416)928-3223

Paul (bi-m), Netherlands Ref. Congregations of North America, Dr. Joel R. Beeke, 50420 Castleman Rd., Chilliwack, BC V2P 6H4

Pentecostal Herald, The (m), United Pentecostal Ch. in Canada, Rev. J. L. Hall, 8855 Dunn Rd., Hazelwood, MO 63042. Tel. (314)837-7300. Fax (314)837-4503

Pentecostal Testimony (m), Pent. Assemblies of Canada, R. J. Skinner, 6745 Century Ave., Mississauga, ON L5N 6P7. Tel. (416)542-7400. Fax (416)542-7313

Peoples Magazine, The, Peoples Church, Paul B. Smith, 374 Sheppard Ave. E, Toronto, ON M2N 3B6. Tel. (416)222-3341

Prairie Messenger (w), Cath., Art B. Babych, Box 190, Muenster, SK S0K 2Y0. Tel. (306)682-5215. Fax (306)682-5285

Preach the Word, Canadian and American Ref. Chs., Rev. J. Visscher, 5734-191A St., Surrey, BC V3S 4N9

Presbyterian Record, The (m), Presbyterian Ch. in Canada, John Congram, 50 Wynford Ave., Don Mills, ON M3C 1J7. Tel. (416)441-1111. Fax (416)441-2825

Relations (m), Cath., Compagnie de Jésus, Giselle Turcot, 25 ouest, Jarry, Montréal, QC H2P 156. Tel. (514)387-2541

Religious Studies and Theology (5/yr), P. Joseph Cahill, Religious Studies, University of Alberta, Edmonton, AB T6G 2E5. Tel. (403)492-2174

Rivers of Living Water (q), Interdenom., Mark Leppington, Box 1986, Nipawin, SK S0E 1E0. Tel. (306)862-3651

Rupert's Land News (10/yr), Ang. Ch. of Can., J. D. Caird, 935 Nesbitt Bay, Winnipeg, MB R3T 1W6. Tel. (214)453-6130

SR: Studies in Religion: Sciences réligieuses (q), Peter Richardson, c/o Wilfrid Laurier University Press, Waterloo, ON N2L 3C5. Tel. (416)978-7149. Fax (416)978-8854

Sally Ann, Salvation Army in Canada, Maj. David Hammond, 455 N. Service Rd. E, Oakville, ON L6H 1A5. Tel. (416)845-9235. Fax (416)845-1966

Saskatchewan Anglican (10/yr), Ang. Diocs. of Saskatchewan, Saskatoon and Qu'appelle, Patrick Tomalin, 1501 College Ave., Regina, SK S4P 1B8. Tel. (306)522-1608. Fax (306)352-6808

Scarboro Missions (9/yr), Scarboro For. Miss. Soc., G. Curry, 2685 Kingston Rd., Scarborough, ON M1M 1M4. Tel. (416)261-7135

Servant Magazine, Interdenom., Phil Callaway, Prairie Bible Inst., Three Hills, AB T0M 2A0. Tel. (403)443-5511

Servant, The (bi-m), Inter-Menn., Gordon Daman, Steinbach Bible College, Box 1420, Steinbach, MB R0A 2A0

Shantyman, The (bi-m), Non-denom., Arthur C. Dixon, 6981 Millcreek Dr., Unit 17, Mississauga, ON L5N 6B8. Tel. (416)821-1175. Fax (416)821-8400

Solia/The Herald (m), Romanian Orth. Episcopate of America (Jackson, MI), David Oancea, P.O. Box 185, Grass Lake, MI 49240-0185

Studia Canonica (semi-a), Cath., Francis G. Morrisey, Faculty of Canon Law, Saint Paul Univ., 223 Main Street, Ottawa, ON K1S 1C4. Tel. (613)236-1393. Fax (613)782-3005

TRAIT D'UNION, Le (q), Union d'Églises Baptistes Françaises, Dr. Amar Djaballah, 2285 Ave. Papineau, Montréal, QC H2K 4J5. Tel. (514)526-6643

Tidings (10/yr), Canadian Bapt. Fed., Atlantic Prov., Bapt. Women's Missions, H. May Bartlett, 225 Massey St., Fredericton, NB E3B 2Z5. Tel. (506)455-9674

Touchstone (3/yr), A. M. Watts, Faculty of Theology, Univ. of Winnipeg, Winnipeg, MB R3B 2E9. Tel. (204)786-9390

Undzer Veg (irreg.), (Yiddish, English) Jewish, Joseph Kage, 272 Codsell Ave., Downsview, ON M3H 3X2. Tel. (416)636-4024

United Brethren, The (m), Un. Breth. in Christ, Ontario Conf., Steve Dennie, 302 Lake St., Huntington, IN 46750

United Church Observer (m), United Ch. of Canada, Muriel Duncan, 84 Pleasant Blvd., Toronto, ON M4T 2Z8. Tel. (416)960-8500. Fax (416)960-8477

Update (q), Multidenom., William J. McRae, Ontario Bible College and Theological S., 25 Ballyconnor Ct., Willowdale, ON M2M 4B3. Tel. (416)226-6380. Fax (416)226-6746

Update (bi-m), Lutheran Church--Canada, Frances A. Wershler, Box 163, Sta. A, Winnipeg, MB R3K 2A1. Tel. (204)832-0123. Fax (204)888-2672

Vie Chrétienne, La (French, m), Presbyterian Ch. in Canada, Jean Porret, 2302 Goyer, Montréal, QC H3S 1G9. Tel. (514)737-4168

Vie des Communautés religieuses, La (5/yr), Cath., Laurent Boisvert, 5750 boul. Rosemont, Montréal, QC H1T 2H2. Tel. (514)259-6911

Voce Evangelica (q), Italian Pent. Ch. of Canada, Joseph Manafo, Daniel Ippolito, 6724 Fabre St., Montréal, QC H2G 2Z6. Tel. (416)766-8014. Fax (514)593-1835

War Cry, The (w), Salv. Army in Canada & Bermuda, Maj. David Hammond, 455 N. Service Rd. E, Oakville, ON L6H 1A5. Tel. (416)845-9235. Fax (416)845-1966

Wesleyan Advocate, The (m), Wesleyan Ch., Wayne Caldwell, P.O. Box 50434, Indianapolis, IN 46250-0434. Tel. (317)576-1313. Fax (317)842-9188

Western Catholic Reporter (w), Cath., Glen Argan, Great Western Press, 8421-101 Avenue, Edmonton, AB T6A 0L1. Tel. (403)465-8030

Windsor Jewish Community Council Bulletin (irreg.), Jewish, Allen Juris, 1641 Ouellette Ave., Windsor, ON N8X 1K9. Tel. (519)973-1772

Word, The (10/yr), Antiochian Ortho. Christian Archdioc. of North America, V. Rev. George S. Corey, 52 78th St., Brooklyn, NY 11209. Tel. (718)748-7940. Fax (201)871-7954

Worldwind/Worldview (2/yr), United Ch. of Can., Rebekah Chevalier, 85 St. Clair Ave. E, Toronto, ON M4T 1M8. Tel. (416)925-5931. Fax (416)925-3394

Young Companion, Old Order Amish Ch., Joseph Stoll, Rt. 4, Aylmer, ON N5H 2R3

Young Soldier, The, Salvation Army in Canada, Maj. David Hammond, 455 N. Service Rd. E, Oakville, ON L6H 1A5. Tel. (416)845-9235. Fax (416)845-1966

13. UNITED STATES SERVICE AGENCIES: SOCIAL, CIVIC, RELIGIOUS

The Yearbook of American and Canadian Churches offers the following selected list of Service Agencies for two purposes. The first is to direct attention to a number of major agencies which can provide resources of information and service to the churches. No attempt is made to produce a complete listing of such agencies. The second purpose is to illustrate the types of resources that are available. There are many agencies providing services which can be of assistance to local, regional or national church groups. It is suggested that a valuable tool in locating such service agencies is *The Encyclopedia of Associations, Vol. I, National Organizations of the United States*. The organizations are listed in Parts 1 and 2, and Part 3 is a name and keyword index. It is published by Gale Research Co., P.O. Box 33477, Detroit, MI 48232-5477.

ADRIS (Association for the Development of Religious Information Systems), Dept. Social & Cultural Sciences, Marquette U., Milwaukee, WI 53233. Tel. (414)288-6838. Coord., Dr. David O. Moberg

Alban Institute, 4125 Nebraska Ave. NW, Washington, DC 20016. Tel. (202)244-7320. President, Loren B. Mead

American Academy of Political and Social Science, The, 3937 Chestnut St., Philadelphia, PA 19104. Tel. (215)386-4594. Pres., Marvin E. Wolfgang

American Association for Adult and Continuing Education, 1112 Sixteenth St. NW, Ste. 420, Washington, DC 20036. Tel. (202)463-6333. Exec. Dir., Judith Ann Koloski

American Association of Bible Colleges, P.O. Box 1523, Fayetteville, AR 72702. Tel. (501)521-8164. Fax (501)521-9202. Exec. Dir., Randall E. Bell

American Association of Retired Persons, 1909 K St. NW, Washington, DC 20049. Tel. (202)872-4700. Fax (202)728-4573. Exec. Dir., Horace Deets

American Civil Liberties Union, 132 West 43rd St., New York, NY 10036. Tel. (212)944-9800. Pres., Nadine Strossen

American Council on Alcohol Problems, 3426 Bridgeland Dr., Bridgeton, MO 63044. Tel. (314)739-5944. Exec. Dir., Curt Scarborough

American Farm Bureau Federation, 225 Touhy Ave., Park Ridge, IL 60068. Tel. (202)484-3600. Pres. and Admn., Dean R. Kleckner

American Federation of Labor and Congress of Industrial Organizations, AFL-CIO Bldg., 815 16th St. NW, Washington, DC 20006. Tel. (202)637-5000. Fax (202)637-5058. Pres., Lane Kirkland

American Friends Service Committee, 1501 Cherry St., Philadelphia, PA 19102. Tel. (215)241-7000. Clerk, Dulany Bennett

American Library Association, 50 E. Huron St., Chicago, IL 60611. Tel. (312)944-6780. Fax (312)440-9374. Exec. Dir., Linda Crismond

American Medical Association, 515 N. State St., Chicago, IL 60610. Tel. (312)464-5000. Exec. Vice-Pres., James S. Todd

American Protestant Health Association, 1701 E. Woodfield Rd., Ste. 311, Schaumburg, IL 60173. Tel. (708)240-1010. Fax (708)240-1015. Pres., Rev. L. James Wylie

American Public Health Association, 1015 15th St. NW, Washington, DC 20005. Tel. (202)789-5600. Fax (202)789-5661. Exec. Dir., William H. McBeath M.D.

American Public Welfare Association, 810 First St. NE, Ste. 500, Washington, DC 20002. Tel. (202)682-0100. Fax (202)289-6555. Exec. Dir., A. Sidney Johnson III

American Red Cross, The, 17th & D Sts. NW, Washington, DC 20006. President, Elizabeth Dole

American Theological Library Association, 820 Church St., Ste. 300, Evanston, IL 60201. Pres., James W. Dunkly

American Waldensian Society, The, Rm. 1850, 475 Riverside Dr., New York, NY 10115. Tel. (212)870-2671. Exec. Dir., Rev. Frank G. Gibson, Jr.

Americans United for Separation of Church and State, 8120 Fenton St., Silver Spring, MD 20910. Tel. (301)589-3707. Exec. Dir., Robert L. Maddox

Association for Clinical Pastoral Education, 1549 Clairmont Rd., Ste. 103, Decatur, GA 30030. Tel. (404)320-1472. Fax (404)320-0849. Exec. Dir., Duane F. Parker

Association of Catholic Diocesan Archivists, Dio. of Lansing, 955 Alton Road, East Lansing, MI 48823. Tel. (517)351-7215. President, Rev. George C. Michalek

Association of Jewish Chaplains of the Armed Forces, 15 E. 26th St., New York, NY 10010. Tel. (212)532-4949. Fax (212)481-4174. Pres., Rabbi Jacob J. Greenberg

Association of Theological Schools in the United States and Canada, 10 Summit Park Drive, Pittsburgh, PA 15275-1103. Tel. (412)788-6505. President, Robert Cooley

B'nai B'rith International, 1640 Rhode Island Ave. NW, Washington, DC 20036. Tel. (202)857-6600. Fax (202)857-1099. Pres., Kent E. Schiner

Baptist Joint Committee, 200 Maryland Ave. NE, Washington, DC 20002. Tel. (202)544-4226. Fax (202)544-2094. Exec. Dir., James M. Dunn

Bible Sabbath Association, RD 1, Box 222, Fairview, OK 73737. Tel. (405)227-3200. Exec. Dir., Richard A. Wiedenheft

Boy Scouts of America, 1325 W. Walnut Hill La., P.O. Box 152079, Irving, TX 75015. Tel. (214)580-2000. Fax (214)580-2502. Pres., Richard H. Leet

Boys & Girls Club of America, 771 First Ave., New York, NY 10017. Tel. (212)351-5900. Fax (212)351-5972. Chmn. of Bd., Jeremiah Milbank

Bread for the World, 802 Rhode Island Ave. NE, Washington, DC 20018. Tel. (202)269-0200. Pres., David Beckmann

CARE, 660 First Ave., New York, NY 10016. Tel. (212) 686-3110. Pres., Philip Johnston

CONTACT USA, Inc., Pouch A, Harrisburg, PA 17105. Tel. (717)232-3501.

Camp Fire Inc., 4601 Madison Ave., Kansas City, MO 64112. Tel. (816)756-1950. Natl. Exec. Dir., David W. Bahlmann

Campus Crusade for Christ International, Arrowhead Springs, San Bernardino, CA 92414. Tel. (714)886-5224. Pres., William R. Bright

Carnegie Council on Ethics and International Affairs, 170 E. 64th St., New York, NY 10021. Tel. (212)838-4120. Chpsn., Maurice Spanbach

Center for Applied Research in the Apostolate (CARA), Georgetown University, PO Box 1601, Washington, DC 20057. Tel. (207)6878080. Fax (202)687-8083. Exec. Dir., Msgr. Edward C. Foster

Center for Parish Development, 5407 S. University Ave., Chicago, IL 60615. Tel. (312)752-1596. Dir., Paul Dietterich

Christian Camping International (USA), P.O. Box 646, 2100 Manchester, Ste. 605, Wheaton, IL 60189. Tel. (708)462-0300. Exec. Dir., Robert Kobielush

Christian Children's Fund, Inc., P.O. Box 26227, Richmond, VA 23261. Tel. (804)756-2700. Fax (804)756-2718. Exec. Dir., Dr. Paul McCleary

Christian Management Association, P.O. Box 4638, Diamond Bar, CA 91765. Tel. (714)861-8861. Chief Exec. Officer, Sylvia Nash

Church Growth Center, Corunna, IN 46730. Tel. (219) 281-2452. Dir., Dr. Kent R. Hunter

Churches' Center for Theology and Public Policy, 4500 Massachusetts Ave. NW, Washington, DC 20016. Tel. (202)885-9100. Exec. Dir., James A. Nash

College of Chaplains of APHA, 701 E. Woodfield Rd., Ste. 311, Schaumburg, IL 60173. Tel. (708)240-1014. Fax (708)240-1015. Exec. Dir., Rev. Dr. Arne K. Jessen

Congress of National Black Churches Inc., The, 1225 Eye Street NW, Ste. 750, Washington, DC 20005-3914. Tel. (202)371-1091. Fax (202)371-0908. Chairman, Dr. Charles W. Butler

Council for Health and Human Service Ministries, The, 700 Prospect Ave., Cleveland, OH 44115. Tel. (216)736-2250. Fax (216)736-2251. Exec. Dir., Bryan W. Sickbert

Counselor Association, Inc., The, P.O. Box 9, Bloomfield Hills, MI 48303. Tel. (313)737-0895. Fax (313)737-0895. Pres., Raymond Barnett Knudsen II

Credit Union National Association, P.O. Box 431, Madison, WI 53701. Tel. (608)231-4000.

Evangelical Council for Financial Accountability (ECFA), P.O. Box 17456, Washington, DC 20041. Tel. (703)435-8888. Fax (703)787-0834. Pres., Clarence Reimer

Fellowship of Reconciliation, The, Box 271, Nyack, NY 10960. Tel. (914)358-4601. Fax (914)358-4924. Exec. Sec., Doug Hostetter

Foreign Policy Association, 729 Seventh Ave., New York, NY 10019. Tel. (212)764-4050. Fax (212)302-6123. Pres. and C.E.O., R. T. Curran

Friends Committee on National Legislation, 245 Second St. NE, Washington, DC 20002. Tel. (202)547-6000. Exec. Sec., Joe Volk

General Federation of Women's Clubs, 1734 N St. NW, Washington, DC 20036. Tel. (202)347-3168. Pres., Phyllis J. Dudenhoffer

Girl Scouts of the U.S.A., 830 Third Ave., New York, NY 10022. Tel. (212)940-7500. Fax (212)940-7859. Pres., Ms. B. LaRue Orullian

Glenmary Research Center, 750 Piedmont Ave. NE, Atlanta, GA 30308. Tel. (404)876-6518. Dir., Lou McNeil

Healing Community, 521 Harrison Ave., Claremont, CA 91711. Tel. (714) 621-6808. Dir., Dr. Harold Wilke

Institute of International Education, 809 United Nations Plaza, New York, NY 10017. Tel. (212)883-8200. Pres., Richard M. Krasno

Institutes of Religion and Health, 3 W. 29th St., New York, NY 10001. Tel. (212)725-7850. Pres., Anne E. Impellizzeri

Interfaith Forum on Religion, Art and Architecture, 1913 Architects Bldg., Philadelphia, PA 19103. Tel. (215)568-0960. Dir., Henry Jung

Japan International Christian University Foundation, Inc., c/o Quentin Squires, Davies & Davies, 521 Fifth Avenue, Ste 1600, New York, NY 10175. Tel. (212)687-5341. Fax (212)986-4998. Pres., Dr. Paul R. Gregory

John Milton Society for the Blind: A Worldwide Ministry, 475 Riverside Dr., Rm. 455, New York, NY 10115. Tel. (212)870-3335. Exec. Dir., Richard R. Preston

LAOS Inc., P.O. Box 1437, Ocean Springs, MS 39564-1437. Exec. Dir., Penny Penrose

Laymen's National Bible Association, 1865 Broadway, 12th Fl., New York, NY 10123. Tel. (212)408-1390. Fax (212)408-1448. Pres., Victor W. Eimicke

League of Women Voters of the U.S., 1730 M St. NW, Washington, DC 20036. Tel. (202)429-1965. Pres., Susan S. Lederman

Lutheran Church Library Association, 122 West Franklin Ave., Minneapolis, MN 55404. Tel. (612)870-3623. Exec. Dir., Leanna D. Kloempken

Lutheran Educational Conference of North America, 122 C St. NW, Ste. 300, Washington, DC 20001. Tel. (202)783-7505. Exec. Dir., Don Stoike

Lutheran Immigration and Refugee Service, 390 Park Ave. S, New York, NY 10016. Tel. (212)532-6350. Exec. Dir., Mr. Ralston H. Deffenbaugh, Jr.

Lutheran Resources Commission, 5 Thomas Circle NW, Washington, DC 20005. Tel. (202)667-9844. Chpsn., Charles Miller ELCA

US SERVICE AGENCIES

249

Lutheran World Relief, 390 Park Ave. S, New York, NY 10016. Tel. (212)532-6350. Fax (212)213-6081. Pres., Robert J. Marshall

National Assoc. of Pastoral Musicians, 225 Sheridan St. NW, Washington, DC 20011. Tel. (202)723-5800. Pres., Rev. Virgil C. Funk

National Association for the Advancement of Colored People, 4805 Mt. Hope Dr., Baltimore, MD 21215. Tel. (301)358-8900. Fax (301)358-2332. Exec. Dir., -----

National Association of Church Business Administration, Inc., 7001 Grapevine Hwy., #324, Ft. Worth, TX 76180. Tel. (817)284-1732. Exec. Dir., F. Marvin Myers

National Association of Human Rights Workers (NAHRW), c/o NC Human Relations Council, 121 W. Jones St., Raleigh, NC 27603. Tel. (919)733-7996. Pres., Mr. James Stowe

National Association of Social Workers, Inc., 7981 Eastern Ave., Silver Springs, MD 20910. Tel. (301)565-0333. Fax (301)589-9340. Pres., Barbara W. White

National Catholic Educational Association, 1077 30th St. NW, Ste. 100, Washington, DC 20007. Tel. (202)337-6232. Pres., Catherine T. McNamee

National Consumers League, 815 15th St. NW, Ste. 928-N, Washington, DC 20005. Tel. (202)639-8140. Pres., Jack A. Blum

National Cooperative Business Association, 1401 New York Ave. NW, Ste. 1100, Washington, DC 20005. Tel. (202)638-6222. Fax (202)638-1374. Pres., Robert D. Scherer

National Council on Alcoholism and Drug Dependence, 12 W. 21st. St., New York, NY 10010. Tel. (212)206-6770. Fax (212)645-1690. Pres., Paul Wood Ph.D.

National Council on Crime and Delinquency, 685 Market St., San Francisco, CA 94105. Tel. (415)896-6223. Pres., Barry Krisberg

National Education Association, 1201 16th St. NW, Washington, DC 20036. Tel. (202)833-4000. Fax (202)822-7974. Exec. Dir., Don Cameron

National Farmers Union, 10065 E. Harvard Ave., Denver, CO 80251. Tel. (303)337-5500. Fax (303)368-1390. Pres., Leland H. Swenson

National Federation of Business and Professional Women's Clubs, Inc., 2012 Massachusetts Ave. NW, Washington, DC 20036. Tel. (202)293-1100. Exec. Dir., Sana Shtasel

National Grange, 1616 H Street NW, Washington, DC 20006. Tel. (202)628-3507. Master, Robert E. Barrow

National Housing Conference, 1126 16th St. NW, Ste. 211, Washington, DC 20036. Tel. (202)223-4844. Exec. Dir., Philip A. Sampson

National Mental Health Association, The, 1021 Prince St., Alexandria, VA 22314. Tel. (703)684-7722. Fax (703)684-5968. Pres. & CEO, John Horner

National PTA, The (National Congress of Parents and Teachers), 700 N. Rush St., Chicago, IL 60611. Tel. (312)787-0997. Fax (312)787-8342. Pres., Mrs. Pat Henry

National Planning Association, 1414 16th St. NW, Ste. 700, Washington, DC 20036. Tel. (202)265-7685. Pres., Edward E. Masters

National Urban League, Inc., 500 E. 62nd St., New York, NY 10021. Tel. (212)310-9000. Chmn. of Bd., Robert C. Larson

OXFAM--America, 115 Broadway, Boston, MA 02116. Tel. (617)482-1211. Fax (617)556-8925. Exec., John Hammock

THE YEAR IN IMAGES

Reuter photo

Church battles over war

In January of 1991 United Nations troops attacked Iraqi positions in the Gulf region. Churches in the United States, Canada and around the world debated and prayed. The war was denounced by most mainline Protestant bodies, and the U.S. Catholic bishops issued a statement based on several "just war" principles challenging the use of military force against Iraq.

Planned Parenthood Federation of America, Inc., 810 Seventh Ave., New York, NY 10019. Tel. (212) 541-7800. Pres., Faye Wattleton

Protestant Health and Human Service Assembly, 8765 W. Higgins Road, Ste. 410, Chicago, IL 60631. Exec. Dir., David A. Johnson

Protestant Radio and TV Center, 1727 Clifton Rd. NE, Atlanta, GA 30329. Tel. (404)634-3324. Fax (404)634-3326. Pres., William Horlock

Religious Education Association, The, 409 Prospect St., New Haven, CT 06511. Tel. (203)865-6141. Pres/Bd. Chpsn., Dr. Mary Elizabeth Moore

Religious News Service, P.O. Box 1015, Radio City Station, New York, NY 10101. Tel. (212)315-0870. Ed. and Dir., Judith L. Weidman

Religious Research Association, Inc., Marist Hall, Rm. 108, Cath. Univ. of Am., Washington, DC 20064. Tel. (202)319-5447. Pres., Wade Clark Roof

Society for Values in Higher Education, Georgetown Univ., Washington, DC 20057. Tel. (202)687-3653. Fax (202)687-7084. Exec. Dir., Charles Courtney

Southern Christian Leadership Conference, 334 Auburn Ave. NE, Atlanta, GA 30312. Tel. (404)522-1420. Pres., Joseph E. Lowery

Southern Regional Council, 134 Peachtree St. NW, Atlanta, GA 30303-1825. Tel. (404)522-8764. Fax (404) 522-8791. Pres., Lottie Shackelford

Theos Foundation, 1301 Clark Bldg., 717 Liberty Ave., Pittsburgh, PA 15222. Tel. (412)471-7779. Contact, Cathy Smith

USO World Headquarters, 601 Indiana Ave. NW, Washington, DC 20004. Tel. (202)783-8121. Fax (202)638-4716. Pres., Chapman B. Cox

United Nations Association of the U.S.A., 485 Fifth Ave., New York, NY 10017. Tel. (212)697-3232. Chpsn. of the Assn., John C. Whitehead

United Way of America., 701 North Fairfax St., Alexandria, VA 22314. Tel. (703)836-7100. Pres., -----

Vellore Christian Medical College Board Inc., 475 Riverside Dr., Rm. 243, New York, NY 10115. Tel. (212)870-2640. Fax (212)870-2173. Exec. Dir., Linda L. Pierce

Woman's Christian Temperance Union (National), 1730 Chicago Ave., Evanston, IL 60201. Tel. (708)864-1396. Pres., Mrs. Rachel Bubar Kelly

Women's International League for Peace and Freedom, 1213 Race St., Philadelphia, PA 19107. Tel. (215) 563-7110. Pres., Mary Zepernick

World Conference on Religion and Peace, 777 United Nations Plaza, New York, NY 10017. Tel. (212)687-2163.

World Peace Foundation, 22 Batterymarch St., Boston, MA 02109. Tel. (617)482-3875. Exec. Dir., Richard J. Bloomfield

World Vision, Inc., 919 W. Huntington Dr., Monrovia, CA 91016. Tel. (818)357-7979. Fax (818)303-7651. Pres. and CEO, Dr. Robert A. Seiple

14. CANADIAN SERVICE AGENCIES: SOCIAL, CIVIC, RELIGIOUS

The following list of Canadian service agencies is offered for purposes of directing the reader's attention to a number of major Canadian agencies that can provide resources of information and service to the churches. No attempt is made to produce a complete listing of such agencies.

Listings are alphabetical by name of institution and have the following order: Name of institution, address, telephone number, fax number and contact person.

Aboriginal Rights Coalition (Project North), 151 Laurier, East Ottawa, ON K1N 6N8. Tel. (613)235-9956. Fax (613)235-1302. Staff Contact, Lorna Schwartzentruber

Alcohol and Drug Concerns, 11 Progress Ave., Ste. 200, Scarborough, ON M1P 4S7. Tel. (416)293-3400. Fax (416)293-1142. Exec. Dir., Rev. Karl Burden

Alcoholics Anonymous, 234 Eglinton Ave. E., Ste. 502, Toronto, ON M4P 1K5. Tel. (416)487-5591. Fax (416)487-5855. Exec. Sec., Carole Blais

Alliance for Life, B1 - 90 Garry St., Winnipeg, MB R3C 4H1. Tel. (204)942-4772. Fax (204)943-9283

Association of Canadian Bible Colleges, The, Prairie Bible College, Box 173, Three Hills, AB T0M 2A0. Tel. (403)443-5511. Fax (403)443-5540. Dr. C. Kinvig-Bates

Association of Universities and Colleges of Canada, 151 Slater, Ottawa, ON K1P 5N1. Tel. (613)563-1236. Fax ((613)563-9745. Pres., Claude Lajeunesse

B'nai B'rith Canada, The League for Human Rights of, 15 Hove St., Downsview, ON M3H 4Y8. Tel. (416)633-6224. Exec. Vice-Pres., Frank Dimant

Boys and Girls Clubs of Canada, 7030 Woodbine Ave., Ste. 703, Markham, ON L3R 6G2. Tel. (416)477-7272. Fax (416)477-2056. Natl. Exec. Dir., Robert T. Duck

Boys' Brigade in Canada, The, 115 St. Andrews Rd., Scarborough, ON M1P 4N2. Tel. (416)431-6052. Pres., Don Moore

CARE Canada, 1550 Carling Ave., P.O. Box 9000, Ottawa, ON K1G 4X6. Tel. (613)724-1122. Fax (613)724-1284. Exec. Dir., A. John Watson

CUSO, 135 Rideau St., Ottawa, ON K1N 9K7. Tel. (613)563-1264. Fax (613)563-8068. Communications Officer, Maureen Johnson

Canada China Programme, 40 St. Clair Ave. E., Ste. 201, Toronto, ON M4T 1M9. Tel. (416)921-4152. Fax (416)921-7478. Dir., Cynthia K. McLean

Canadian Alliance in Solidarity with the Native Peoples (CASNP), P.O. Box 574, Stn. P, Toronto, ON M5S 2T1. Tel. (416)972-1573. Fax (416)972-6232

Canadian Association for Adult Education, 29 Prince Arthur Ave., Toronto, ON M5R 1B2. Tel. (416)964-0559. Fax (416)964-9226. Exec. Dir., Ian Morrison

Canadian Association for Community Living, Kinsmen Bldg., York Univ., 4700 Keele St, Downsview, ON M3J 1P3. Tel. (416)661-9611. Fax (416)661-5701

Canadian Association for Pastoral Education, P.O. Box 96, Roxboro, QU H8Y 3E8. Tel. (514)624-0382. Business Mgr., Mrs. Verda Rochon

Canadian Association of Social Workers, 55 Parkdale Ave., Ottawa, ON K1Y 1E5. Tel. (613)729-6668. Fax (613)725-3720

Canadian Book Publishers' Council, 250 Merton St., Ste. 203, Toronto, ON M4S 1B1. Tel. (416)322-7011. Fax (416)322-6999. Exec. Dir., Jacqueline Hushion

Canadian Catholic Organization for Development and Peace, 5633, Sherbrooke est, Montréal, QU H1N 1A3. Tel. (514)257-8711. Fax (514)257-8497. Exec. Dir., Gabrielle Lachance

Canadian Center for Ecumenism, 2065 Sherbrooke St. W, Montréal, QU H3H 1G6. Tel. (514)937-9176. Dir., Thomas Ryan

Canadian Chamber of Commerce, The, 55 Metcalfe St., Ste. 1160, Ottawa, ON K1P 6N4. Tel. (613)238-4000. Pres., Timothy Reid

Canadian Civil Liberties Association, 229 Yonge St., Ste. 403, Toronto, ON M5B 1N9. Tel. (416)363-0321. Fax (416)861-1291. Gen. Counsel, A. Alan Borovoy

Canadian Co-operative Credit Society Limited, 300 The East Mall, Islington, ON M9B 6B7. Tel. (416)232-1262. Fax (416)232-9196. National Credit Union CEO, Brian F. Downey

Canadian Council of Crisis Centres, c/o DistressCentre, Box 393, Postal Sta.K, Toronto, ON M4P 2G7. Tel. (416)486-6766. Exec. Dir., Patricia Harnisch

Canadian Council on Social Development, The, 55 Parkdale Ave., Box 3505, Sta. C, Ottawa, ON K1Y 4G1. Tel. (613)728-1865. Exec. Dir., Patrick Johnston

Canadian Ecumenical Action, 1410 W. 12th Ave., Vancouver, BC V6H 1M8. Tel. (604)736-1613. Pres., Dr. Bryan Colwell

Canadian Education Assoc./Association canadienne d'éducation, Ste. 8-200, 252 Bloor St. W, Toronto, ON M5S 1V5. Tel. (416)924-7721. Fax (416)924-3188. Exec. Dir., Robert Blair

Canadian Evangelical Theological Assoc.: Ontario Theological Seminary, 25 Ballyconnor Ct., Willowdale, ON M2M 4B3. Tel. (416)226-6380. Pres., John Vissers

Canadian Girls in Training, Rm. 200, 40 St. Clair Ave. E, Toronto, ON M4T 1M9. Tel. (416)961-2036. Fax (416)921-7478. Natl. Co-ord., Ruth Dobrensky

Canadian Institute of Planners, 404-126 York St., Ottawa, ON K1N 5T5. Tel. (613)233-2105. Fax (613)233-1984. Exec. Dir., David Sherwood

Canadian Institute of Religion and Gerontology, 40 St. Clair Ave. E, Ste. 203, Toronto, ON M4T 1M9. Tel. (416)924-5865. Dir., Rev. Donald H. Powell

Canadian Labour Congress, 2841 Riverside Dr., Ottawa, ON K1V 8X7. Tel. (613)521-3400. Fax (613)521-4655. Pres., Shirley G. E. Carr

Canadian Medical Association, The, 1867 Alta Vista Dr., Box 8650, Ottawa, ON K1G 0G8. Tel. (613)731-9331. Fax (613)731-9013. Sec. Gen., Leo Paul Landry, M.D.

Canadian Mental Health Association, 2160 Yonge St., Toronto, ON M4S 2Z3. Tel. (416)484-7750. Fax (416)484-4617. Gen. Dir., Edward J. Pennington

Canadian Red Cross Society, 1800 Alta Vista Dr., Ottawa, ON K1G 4J5. Tel. (613)739-3000. Sec. Gen., George Weber

THE YEAR IN IMAGES

Religious News Service photo

Light of new life

These young Ukrainian children look to the light during a Mass in the midst of revolution in the former Soviet Union. The new climate brought money and missionaries from churches in other parts of the world, while some old conflicts between Catholic and Orthodox churches re-emerged. Organized religion saw a resurgence in the Soviet Union during the Mikhail Gorbachev era and returned to prominence when Boris Yeltsin came to power and the union dissolved. What role will it play in the new order of reorganized republics of the former Soviet Union?

Canadian Society of Biblical Studies, Dept of Religious Studies, U. of Calgary, Calgary, AL T2N 1N4. Tel. (403)261-4827. Exec. Sec., Wayne O. McCready

Canadian UNICEF Committee, 443 Mount Pleasant Rd., Toronto, ON M4S 2L8. Tel. (416)482-4444. Fax (416)482-8035. Exec. Dir., Harry S. Black

Canadian Unitarian Council, 175 St. Clair Ave. W, Toronto, ON M4V 1P7. Tel. (416)921-4506. Exec. Dir., Ellen K. Campbell

Canadian Woman's Christian Temperance Union, #302 - 30 Gloucester St., Toronto, ON M4Y 1L6. Tel. (416)921-4909. Natl. Pres., Ms. Barbara Taylor

Catholic Women's League of Canada, The, 1-160 Murray Rd., Winnipeg, MB R3J 3X5. Tel. (204)885-4856. Fax (204)831-9507. Exec. Dir., Miss Valerie J. Fall

Christian Service Brigade of Canada, 1254 Plains Rd. E., Burlington, ON L7S 1W6. Tel. (416)634-1841. Fax (416)634-7643. Gen. Dir., Robert A. Clayton

Church Army in Canada, The, 397 Brunswick Ave., Toronto, ON M5R 2Z2. Tel. (416)924-9279. Dir., Capt. Walter Marshall

Church Council on Justice and Corrections, The, 507 Bank St., 2nd Fl., Ottawa, ON K2P 1Z5. Tel. (613)563-1688. Fax (613)237-6129. Mgmt. Coord., Ms. Jean Somers

Churches and Corporate Responsibility, The Taskforce on, 129 St. Clair Ave. W, Toronto, ON M4V 1N5. Tel. (416)923-1758. Fax (416)927-7554. Coord., Bill Davis

Churches' Council on Theological Education in Canada: An Ecumenical Foundation, The, 60 St. Clair Ave. E, Ste. 500, Toronto, ON M4T 1M5. Tel. (416)928-3223. Fax (416)928-3223. Chpsn., Rev. Howard Mills

Consumers' Association of Canada, 307 Gilmour St., Ottawa, ON K2P 0P7. Tel. (613)238-2533. Pres., Marilyn Lister

Couchiching Institute on Public Affairs, 250 Consumers Rd., Ste. 301, Willowdale, ON M2J 4V6. Tel. (416)494-1440. Fax (416)495-8723. Exec. Dir., Brian Lechem

Ecumenical Coalition for Economic Justice (formerly GATT-Fly), 11 Madison Ave., Toronto, ON M5R 2S2. Tel. (416)921-4615. Fax (416)924-5356. Coord., John Dillon

Elizabeth Fry Society of Toronto (Prisoner's Aid), 215 Wellesley St. E, Toronto, ON M4X 1G1. Tel. (416)924-3708. Exec. Dir., Ms. Darlene Lawson

Frontiers Foundation/Operation Beaver, 2615 Danforth Ave., Ste. 203, Toronto, ON M4C 1L6. Tel. (416)690-3930. Fax (416)690-3934. Exec. Dir., Charles R. Catto

Gideons International in Canada, 501 Imperial Rd. N, Guelph, ON N1H 7A2. Tel. (519)823-1140. Fax (519)767-1913. Exec. Dir., Graham Sawer

Girl Guides of Canada - Guides du Canada, 50 Merton St., Toronto, ON M4S 1A3. Tel. (416)487-5281. Fax (416)487-5570. Exec. Dir., Mrs. Margaret Ringland

Institute for Christian Studies, 229 College St., Toronto, ON M5T 1R4. Tel. (416)979-2331. Fax (416)979-2332. Pres., Dr. Harry Fernhout

Inter-Church Committee for Refugees, 40 St. Clair Ave. E, Toronto, ON M4T 1M9. Tel. (416)921-4152. Fax (416)921-7478. Officer:, Dr. Tom Clark

Inter-Church Committee on Human Rights in Latin America, 40 St. Clair Ave. E, Ste. 201, Toronto, ON M4T 1M9. Tel. (416)921-4152. Fax (416)921-7478. Exec. Dir., Bill Fairbairn

Inter-Church Communication: Berkeley Studio, The United Church of Canada, 315 Queen St. E, Toronto, ON M5A 1S7. Tel. (416)366-9221. Fax (416)368-9774. Chmn., Donald Stephens

Inter-Church Fund for International Development (ICFID), 85 St. Clair Ave. E, Ste. 204, Toronto, ON M4T 1M8. Tel. (416)968-1411. Fax (416)925-3394. Exec. Sec., Dr. Robert Fugere

Interchurch Committee for World Development Education (Ten Days for World Development), 85 St. Clair Ave. E, Toronto, ON M4T 1M8. Natl. Coord., Jeanne Moffat

John Howard Society of Ontario (Prisoner's Aid), 6 Jackson Place, Toronto, ON M6P 1T6. Tel. (416)604-8412. Fax (416)604-8948. Exec. Dir., Graham Stewart

John Milton Society for the Blind in Canada, 40 St. Clair Ave. E, Ste. 202, Toronto, ON M4T 1M9. Tel. (416)960-3953

L'Association canadienne des périodiques catholiques, 9795 boul. Ste-Anne-de-Beaupré, CP100, Ste-Anne-de-Beaupré, QU G0A 3C0. Tel. (418)827-4538. Fax (418)827-4530. Prés., Jerome Martineau

OXFAM - Canada/National Office, 251 Laurier W, Ste. 301, Ottawa, ON K1P 5J6. Tel. (613)237-5236. Fax (613)237-0524

Organisation Catholique Canadienne pour le Developpement et la paix, (See Canadian Catholic Organization for Development and Peace)

PLURA (Inter-Church Association to Promote Social Justice in Canada), Box 1023, New Hamburg, ON N0B 2G0. Tel. (519)662-3450. Sec., Roy Shepherd

Pioneer Clubs Canada, Inc., Box 5447, Burlington, ON L7R 4L2. Tel. (416)681-2883. Natl. Dir., Richard G. Beurling

Planned Parenthood Federation of Canada, 1 Nicholas St., Ste. 430, Ottawa, ON K1N 7B7. Tel. (613)238-4474. Fax (613)238-1162. Exec. Dir., Bonnie Johnson

Project Ploughshares, Conrad Grebel College, Waterloo, ON N2L 3G6. Tel. (519)888-6541. Res. Coord., Ernie Regehr

Religious Television Associates, Berkeley Studio, 315 Queen St. E, Toronto, ON M5A 1S7. Tel. (416)366-9221. Fax (416)368-9774. Dir., Rev. Rod Booth

Save the Children Canada/Aide à l'enfance Canada, 3080 Yonge St., Ste. 6020, Toronto, ON M4N 3P4. Tel. (416)488-0306. Fax (416)483-4430. Acting Natl. Dir., Richard Hutchison

Scouts Canada, National Council, 1345 Baseline Rd., P.O. Box 5151, Sta. F, Ottawa, ON K2C 3G7. Tel. (613)224-5131. Fax (613)224-3571. Chief Exec., J. Blain

Scripture Union, 1885 Clements Rd., Unit 226, Pickering, ON L1W 3V4. Tel. (416)427-4947. Fax (416)427-0334. Gen. Dir., John F. Booker

Shantymen International, 6981 Millcreek, Unit 17, Mississauga, ON L5N 6B8. Tel. (416)821-1175. Fax (416)821-8400. Pres., W. D. Morrison

Social Science Federation of Canada and Canadian Federation for the Humanities, 151 Slater St., Ste. 415, Ottawa, ON K1P 5H3. Tel. (613)238-6112. Fax (613)238-6114. Exec. Dir., Dr. Ayman Yassini

TELECARE Teleministries of Canada, Inc., P.O. Box 695, Midland, ON L4R 4P4. Tel. (705)526-8058. Exec. Dir., Rev. James Manuel

The St. Leonard's Society of Canada (Prisoner's Aid), 3 Robert Speck Pkwy, Ste. 900, Mississauga, ON L4Z G5. Tel. (416)566-1360. Fax (416)273-4162. Int. Exec. Dir., E. T. Gurney

Unitarian Service Committee of Canada, 56 Sparks St., Ottawa, ON K1P 5B1. Tel. (613)234-6827. Fax (613)234-6842. Founder, Dir., Lotta Hitschmanova

United Nations Association in Canada, 63 Sparks St., Ste. 808, Ottawa, ON K1P 5A6. Tel. (613)232-5751. Fax (613)563-2455. Pres., Geoffrey Grenville-Wood

Vanier Institute of the Family, Institut Vanier de la famille, 120 Holland Ave., Ste. 300, Ottawa, ON K1Y 0X6. Tel. (613)722-4007. Fax (613)729-5249. Coord., Admn. & Commun., Alan Mirabelli

Voice of Women for Peace/La Voix des Femmes pour la Paix - Canada, 736 Bathurst St., Toronto, ON M5S 2R4. Tel. (416)537-9343. Fax (416)531-6214. Natl. Staff, Carolyn Langdon

World Relief Canada, 250 Consumers Rd., Ste. 1002, Willowdale, ON M2J 4V6. Tel. (416)494-9930. Fax (416)494-2611. Pres., Reg Reimer

World University Service of Canada, P.O. Box 3000, Stn. C., Ottawa, ON K1Y 4M8. Tel. (613)798-7477. Fax (613)798-0990. Exec. Dir., Mr. Ed Barisa

World Vision Canada, 6630 Turner Valley Rd., Mississauga, ON L5N 2S4. Tel. (416)821-3030. Fax (416)821-1354. Pres., J. Don Scott

Youth for Christ/Canada, 220 Attwell Dr., #1, Rexdale, ON M9W 5B2. Tel. (416)674-0466. Fax (416)674-0616. Pres., Robert E. Simpson

15. INTERNATIONAL CONGREGATIONS

This directory lists International Congregations seeking to serve an international and ecumenical constituency using the English Language.

The churches are listed within global regions, and then alphabetically by country.

This list was provided by INTERNATIONAL CONGREGATIONS/Christians Abroad, 475 Riverside Dr., 6th Floor, New York, NY 10115-0050. Tel. (212)870-2463. Fax (212)870-3112.

EUROPE

Austria
Vienna Community Church, Dorotheergasse 16, A-1010 Vienna. Tel. (0222)50 55 233

United Methodist Church, Sechshauser Strasse 56, A-1150 Vienna. Tel. (01)83 62 67

Belgium
American Protestant Church, Antwerp International School, Veltwijklaan 180, B-2070 Ekeren, Antwerp. Tel. (03)665 37 05

International Protestant Church, Kattenberg, 19 (campus of Int'l School), B-1170 Brussels. Tel. (02)673 05 81 or 660 27 10

Czechosoivakia
International Church of Prague, Czech Brethren Church, Vrazova 4, Praha 5. Tel. (02) 35-38-096

Denmark
International Church, Vartov Church, Farvergade 27 Copenhagen. Tel. (031) 62 47 85

England
American Church in London, Whitefield Memorial Church, Tottenham Court Road, 79 London WIP 9HB. Tel. (071) 580 2791 or 722 58 46 Fax (071)580 5013

St. Anne & St. Agnes Church, Gresham Street, London EC2V 7BX. Tel. (071) 373 5566 or (081) 769 2677

International Community Church, Rydens School, Hersham, Surrey. Tel. (0932) 868 283 or 222 781

Estonia
International Christian Fellowship, Meeting at Puhavaium Church, Tallinn. Tel. (358) (090) 446 776

Finland
International Evangelical Church, Runeberginkatu 39 A 56 SF-00100 Helsinki. Tel. (0) 90-406 091 or 684 8051

France
Holy Trinity Episcopal Church, 11 rue de la Buffa, F-06000 Nice. Tel. (093) 87 19 83

American Cathedral of the Holy Trinity, 23 Avenue George V, F-75008 Paris. Tel. (01) 4720 17 92

American Church in Paris, 65 Quai d'Orsay, F-75007 Paris. Tel. (01) 47 05 07 99 or 45 55 98 48

Germany
American Church in Berlin, Alte Dorfkirche, Potsdamer Str. & Clayaliee, D-1000 Berlin 37. Tel. (030) 813 2021

American Protestant Church of Bonn, Kennedy Alle 150, D-5300 Bonn 2. Tel. (0228) 374 193 or 373 393

Church of Christ the King, Sebastian Rinzstrasse 22, D-6000 Frankfurt am Main 1. Tel. (069) 550 184

Trinity Lutheran Church, Am Schwalbenschwanz 37, D-6000 Frankfurt am Main 50. Tel. (069) 599 478, 512 552 or 598 602. Fax (069) 599 845

United Methodist Church, Ministries with Laity Abroad, Kirchenkanzlei, Wilhelm-Leuschner 8, D-6000 Frankfurt (M) 1. Tel. (069) 239 373 or (06192) 41554. Fax (069) 239 375

Kaiserslautern Lutheran Church, Bruchstrasse 10, D-6750 Kaiserslautern. Tel. (0631) 92 210

Church of the Ascension, Seyboth Strasse 4, D-8000 Munich 90. Tel. (089) 648 185

Friedenskirke/English Congregation, Frauenlobstrasse 5, D-8000 Munich 2. Tel. (089) 265 091 or 300 6100

Greece
St. Andrew's Protestant Church, Xenopoulou 5, GR-15451 New Psychiko, Athens. Tel. (01) 647 9585 or 652 1401. Fax (01) 652 8191

Hungary
International Church, Budapest Cultural Center, Budapest I. Corvin ter 8. Tel./Fax (01) 176 4815

Italy
St. James Episcopal Church, Via Bernardo Rucellai 13, Florence, I-50123. Tel. (055) 294 417

All Saints Anglican Church, Via del Babuino 153B 00187, Rome. Tel. (06) 679 4357

St. Andrew's Church, Via XX Settembre 7, I-00187, Rome. Tel. (06) 482 7627

Ponte Sant'Angelo Methodist Church, Via del Banco di Santo Spirito, 3 I-00186, Rome. Tel. (06) 475 1627

Rome Baptist Church, Piazza San Lorenzo in Lucina, 351-00186, Rome. Tel. (06) 892 6487 or 687 6652

St. Paul's Within the Walls, Via Napoli 58, Rome I-00184. Tel. (06) 474 3569 or 463 339

Protestant English Church, Chiesa Evanglica Valdese, Corso Vittorio Emanuele 23, Turin. Tel. (011) 669 28 38 or 65 26 01 Fax (011) 650 75 42

The Netherlands
Trinity Church Eindhoven, Pensionaat Eikenburg Chapel, Aalstereweg 289, Eindhoven. Tel. (040) 512 580

American Protestant Church, Esther de Boer Van Rijklaan, 20, NL-2597 TJ The Hague. Tel. (070) 324 44 90 or 324 44 91

Norway
American Lutheran Congregation, Fritznersgate 15, Oslo 2. Tel. (02) 44 35 84 or 53 26 17

Stavenger International Church, Hetland Church, Storhaugveien, 2 at Breibakken, Stavanger. Tel. (0474) 56 48 43 or 52 21 21

Poland
Warsaw International Church, ul. Obserwatorow 13, 02-714 Warszawa. Tel. 43 29 70

Russia
Moscow Protestant Chaplaincy Anglo-American School, Leninskiy Prospekt 78. Tel. (095) 143 35 62

Spain
Community Church of Madrid, Colegio de los Sogrades Corazones, Padre Damian, 34, Madrid E-28016. Tel. (01) 302 0176

Sweden
Immanuel International Church, Kungstensgatan 17, S-113 57 Stockholm. Tel. (08) 15 12 25 or 673 68 03 Fax (08) 31 53 25

United Christian Congregation Stockholm, Klara Ostra Kyrkogata 8, S-111 52 Stockholm. Tel. (08) 723 3029 Fax (08) 21 31 09

Switzerland
Emmanuel Episcopal/American Church, 3 rue de Monthoux, CH-1201 Geneva. Tel. (022) 732 8078

Evangelical Lutheran Church, 20 rue Verdaine, CH- 1204 Geneva. Tel. (022) 320 50 89 or 348 75 95 Fax (022) 798 86 16

Intenational Church, Swiss Methodist Church, Zaehringerstrasse 7, CH-6003 Luzern Tel. (041)44 39 16

Intenational Protestant Church/Zurich, French Reformed Church, Schanzengasse and Promenadengasse. Tel. (01) 262 5525 or (01) 825 6483

MIDDLE EAST

Bahrain
National Evangelical Church, P.O. Box 1, Manama. Tel. 254 508

Egypt
Alexandria Community Church, Schutz American School 51 Schutz St., Alexandria. Tel. (03) 857 525

Heliopolis Community Church, No.8 Seti Street, Heliopolis, Cairo. Tel. (02) 290 9885

St. Andrew's United Church, 38 26th of July Street, Cairo. Tel. (02) 759 451 or 360 3527

Maadi Community Church, Sharia Port Said & Roads 82 & 17, Cairo. Tel. (02) 351 2755 or 353 2118

Jerusalem
Church of the Redeemer, Muristan Road, Old City, Jerusalem. Tel. (02) 89 47 50 or 82 84 01 Fax (02) 89 46 10

Kuwait
National Evangelical Church, P.O. Box 80 Safat, 13001 Kuwait. Tel. 243 1087

Libya
Union Church of Tripoli, Box 6397, Tripoli. Tel. (021) 70531

Oman
Protestant Church in Muscat, P.O. Box 4982 Ruwi. Tel. 70 23 72

Salalah English-Speaking Congregation, Salalah Christian Centre, P.O. Box 19742, Salalah. Tel. 23 56 77

Tunisia
Community Church in Tunis, 5 rue des Protestants, 1006 Tunis, Bab Souika. Tel. (01) 24 36 48

Turkey
Union Church of Istanbul, Istiklal Caddesi 485 TR-80050 Beyoglu, Istanbul. Tel. (01) 144 5212 or 144 5763

AFRICA

Kenya
Uhuru Hiway Lutheran Church, P.O. Box 44685, Nairobi

Methodist Community Church, P.O. Box 25030, Nairobi

South Africa
St. Peter's by the Lake, 43 Lower Drive, Parkview, Johannesburg. Tel. (011) 646 5740

Tanzania
International English Congregation, Azania Front Lutheran Church, P.O. Box 1594, Dar es Salaam. Tel. (051) 25127

NORTH AMERICA

Canada
Chalmers-Wesley United Church, 78 rue Ste-Ursule, Quebec City. Tel. (418) 692-2640 or 692-0431 Fax (418) 692-3876

Illinois
O'Hare Airport Interdenominational Chapel, Mezzanine level/Terminal 2, P.O. Box 66353, Chicago, IL 60666. Tel. (708) 596-3050 or 333-0020

CENTRAL AMERICA/CARIBBEAN

Costa Rica
Escazu Christian Fellowship, Country Day School, Escazu. Tel. (506) 32-14-07 or 34-32-92

Union Church of San Jose, Apartado 4456, San Jose

Dominican Republic
Union Church of Santo Domingo with Epiphany Episcopal Church, Avenida Independencia No. 253, Santo Domingo. Tel. (809) 689-2070 or 687-3707 Fax (809) 685-1635 or 541-6550

El Salvador
Union Church of San Salvador, Calle 4, Colonia La Mascota, San Salvador. Tel. (503) 23 5505

Guatemala

Church Union of Guatemala, Apartado Postal 6-A, Guatemala City. Tel. (502) 2-316904

Honduras

Union Christian Church, Colonia las Lomas enfrente de Parque Espana. Tel. (504) 32 3386 or 32-4454

Mexico

Union Evangelical Church, Reforma 1870-Lomas Chapultepec, Mexico City 11000 D.F. Tel. (05)520-0436 or 520-9931

Union Church of Monterrey, Oscar F. Castillon 200, Col. Chepe Vera, Monterrey. Tel. (083) 46-05-41 or 47-17-27

Panama

Balboa Union Church, Box 3664, Balboa. Tel. (507) 52-2295

Margarita Union Church, Apartado 2401, Cristobel. Tel. (507) 89 39 54 or 46 44 98

Gamboa Union Church, Apartado 44, Gamboa. Tel. (507) 56 64 70 or 56 68 30

Puerto Rico

Wesleyan Community Church, Lopetegui Street, Guaynabo. Tel.(809) 720-2595 or 790-4818

Second Union Church of San Juan, Apolo Avenue & Mileto Street, Guaynabo 00969. Tel. (809) 720-4423 or 789-7178 Fax (809) 789-1380

Grace Lutheran Church, Calle del Parque 150, Santurce 00911. Tel. (809) 722-5372 or 722-1137

St. John's Episcopal Cathedral, 1401 Ave. Ponce de Leon, Santurce. Tel. (809)722-3254 or 784 7883

Union Church of San Juan, 2310 Lauel Street, Punta Las Marias, Santurce 00913. Tel. (809) 726-0280

SOUTH AMERICA

Argentina

United Community Church, Avenida Santa Fe 839, Acassuso (1640), Buenos Aires. Tel. (01) 792 1375

Bolivia

Community Church, Castilla 4718, La Paz. Tel. (02) 78-6515 or 78-6525

Brazil

Campinas Community Church, Rua Barbosa da Cunha 562, Jardim Guanabara, Campinas.

Union Church of Rio, Av. Alvorada 600, 22600 Barra da Tijuca. Tel. (021) 325-8601

Fellowship Community Church, Rua Carlos Sampaio, 107, 01333 Bela Vista, Sao Paulo S.P. Tel. (011) 287-2294 or 844-1153

Chile

Santigo Community Church, Avenida Holanda 151, Santiago, 9

Columbia

Union Church of Bogota, Carrera 3a No. 69-06, Bogota. Tel.(01)248-5115

Ecuador

Advent-St. Nicholas Lutheran/Episcopal Church, Ave. Isabel la Catolica 1837, Quito. Tel. (02) 23 43 91

English Christian Fellowship, Casilla 691, Quito

Peru

Union Church of Lima, Av. Angamos (Oeste)1155, Miraflores. Tel. (14) 41-1472 or 41-4882

Uruguay

Christ Church, Arocena 1907, Montevideo. Tel. (02) 61 03 00 or 60 27 11

Venezuela

United Christian Church, Av. La Arboleda - El Bosque, Caracas. Tel. (02) 71 39 01, 71 39 02 or 751-6438

Christ Church, Calle 74 & Ave. 8, Maracaibo. Tel. (061) 77 548

Protestant Church of Puerto Ordaz, Apartado 229, Estado Bolivar, Puerto Ordaz, 8015A. Tel. (086) 22 89 48

ASIA

Bangladesh

Dhaka International Christian Church, American International School, United Nations Road, Baridhara, Dhaka.

Hong Kong

Church of All Nations (Lutheran), 8 Repulse Bay, Hong Kong. Tel. 812-0375 Fax 812-9508

Hong Kong Union Church, 22A Kennedy Road, Victoria. Tel. 522-1515 or 523-7247

Kowloon Union Church, 4 Jordan Road, Kowloon. Tel. 367-2585

India

St. Andrew's Church, 15 B.B.D. Bag, Calcutta 700 001. Tel. (033) 20-1994

St. Paul's Cathedral, Cathedral Road, Calcutta 700 001. Tel.(033) 28-2801 or 28-5127

Church of the Redemption, Church Road (North Avenue), New Delhi 110 001. Tel. (011) 301-4458

Centenary Methodist Church, 25, Lodi Road at Flyover, New Delhi 110003. Tel. (011) 36-5396

Free Church, 10, Sansad Marg, New Delhi 110 001. Tel. (011) 31-1331

Free Church Green Park, A24 Green Park, New Delhi 110 016. Tel. (011) 66-4574

Indonesia

Jakarta Community Church, Jalan Iskandarsyah II/176, Jakarta 12160. Tel. (021) 7723325

Japan

Kobe Union Church, 6-15 Ikuta-cho 4-chome, Chuo-ku, Kobe 651. Tel.(078) 221-4733 or 221 4791

All Soul's Episcopal Church, 935 Makiminato, Urasoe City, Okinawa 901-21

Nagoya Union Church, Kinjo Church UCC, Tatedaikan-cho 17, Higashi-ku, Nagoya 461. Tel.(052) 932-1066 or 772-3043 Fax (052) 931-6421

St. Alban's Anglican/Episcopal Church, 6-25 Shiba-koen 3-chome, Minato-ku, Tokyo 105. Tel.(03) 431-8534 or 432-6040 Fax (03) 5472-4766

Tokyo Union Church, 7-7, Jingumae 5-chome, Shibuya-ku, Tokyo 150. Tel.(03) 3400-0047 or 3461-4537 Fax (03) 3400-1942

West Tokyo Union Church, Lutheran Theological College, 3-10-20, Osawa, Mitaka-shi, Tokyo 181. Tel. (0422) 33-0993

St. Paul International Lutheran Church, 1-2-32. Fujimi, 1-chome, Chiyoda-ku, Tokyo 102. Tel.(03) 261-3740 or 262-8623

Yokohama Union Church, 66 Yamate-cho, Naka-ku, Yokohama 231. Tel.(045) 651-5177 Fax (045) 625-4656

Korea

Seoul Union Church, Memorial Chapel at Foreigners' Cemetery Park, Seoul. Tel.(02) 333-7393 or 333-0838

International Lutheran Church, 726-39 Hannam-2 Dong, Yongsan-ku, Seoul 140-212. Tel.(02) 794-6274

Malaysia

St. Andrew's Presbyterian International Church, 31 Jalan Raja Chulan. 50200 Kuala Lumpur. Tel. (03) 232-5687

Nepal

International Protestant Congregation, Lincoln School, Raki Bahwan, Box 654, Kathmandu. Tel.(01) 270 966

Pakistan

Protestant International Congregation, No. 21A, St 55, F-7/4, Isalamabad. Tel(051) 818 397

International Church of Karachi, 61/1 25th Street, Phase 5, Defense Housing Authority, Karachi. Tel. (021) 57 07 76

International Christian Fellowship, 11 Forman Christian College, Lahore. Tel. (041) 879955 or 305867

Philippines

Union Church of Manila, Legaspi & Radfa St., Makati. Tel.(02) 818-1634 or 817-4474 Fax (01) 818-2888

Singapore

Lutheran Church of Our Redeemer, 28-30 Dukes Road, Singapore 1026. Tel. (65)466-45590 or 467-5093

Orchard Road Presbyterian Church, 3 Orchard Road, Singapore 0923. Tel. (65)337-6681

St. George's Church (Anglican), Minden Road, Tanglin, Singapore 1024. Tel. (65)473-2783

Sri Lanka

St. Andrew's Church, 73 Galle Road, Colombo 3. Tel.(01) 23765

Taiwan

Kaohsiung Community Church, Kwang Hwa First Road #138-38. Tel. (07) 331-8131

Taipei International Church, Taipei American School, 800 Chung Shan North Road, Sec. 6, Tienmou, Taipei. Tel.(02) 872-4073

Thailand

International Church of Bangkok, 73 Soi 19 Sukhumvit, Bangkok 10110. Tel.(02) 258-5821 Fax (02) 253-7291

Chiang Mai Community Church, Cort Hall, Chiang Mai. Tel. (053) 242661

OCEANIA

American Samoa

Community Christian Church, P.O. Box 1016, Pago Pago. Tel. (684) 699-1544 or 699-9184

Guam

Guam United Methodist Church, P.O. Box 20279 GMF, Barrigada 96291. Tel. (761) 734-3251 or 477-8357

16. DEPOSITORIES OF CHURCH HISTORY MATERIAL

Kenneth E. Rowe
Neil Semple

Most American denominations have established central archival-manuscript depositories. In addition, many large communions have formed regional (conference, diocesan, synodical, or provincial) depositories. Denominations with headquarters in the United States may also have churches in Canada. Historical material on Canadian sections of these denominations will occasionally be found at the various locations cited below. The reader is also referred to the section "In Canada," which follows.

The section for the United States was compiled by Kenneth E. Rowe. The Canadian section was compiled by Neil Semple.

IN THE UNITED STATES

The most important general guide is *Directory of Archives and Manuscript Repositories* in the United States, 2d edition, compiled by the National Historical Publications and Records Commission. New York: Oryx Press, 1988.

Major Ecumenical Collections:

American Antiquarian Society, 185 Salisbury St., Worcester, MA 01609 Tel (617)755-5221

American Bible Society Library, 1865 Broadway, New York, NY 10023-9980. Tel (212)408-1495 FAX (212)408-1512. Peter Wosh

Amistad Research Center, Old U.S.Mint Building, 400 Esplanade Ave., New Orleans, LA 70116. Tel (504)522-0432

Billy Graham Center Archives, Wheaton College, 510 College Ave., Wheaton, IL 60187-5593. Tel (708)752-5910. Robert Schuster

Boston Public Library, Copley Square, Boston, MA 02117-0286. Tel (617)536-5400 FAX (617)236-4306

Graduate Theological Union Library, 2400 Ridge Road, Berkeley, CA 94709 Tel (415)649-2540 FAX (415)649-1417. Oscar Burdick

Harvard University (Houghton Library) Cambridge, MA 02138 Tel (617)495-2440

Howard University, Moorland-Springarn Research Center, 500 Howard Place, N.W., Washington, DC 20059 Tel (202)636-7480

Huntingdon Library, 1151 Oxford Road, San Marino, CA 91108 Tel (213)792-6141.

National Council of Churches Archives, in Presbyterian Church USA Office of History Library, 425 Lombard St., Philadelphia, Pa 19147. Tel (215)627-0509. FAX (215)627-0509. Gerald W. Gillette

Newberry Library, 60 W. Walton St., Chicago, IL 60610-3394. Tel (312)943-9090.

New York Public Library, Fifth Ave. & 42nd St. New York, NY 10018. Tel (212)930-0800 FAX (212)921-2546.

Schomburg Center for Research in Black Culture, 515 Malcolm X Blvd., New York, NY 10037. Tel (212)862-4000. Howard Dodson

Union Theological Seminary (Burke Library) 3041 Broadway, New York, NY 10027. Tel (212)280-1505 FAX (212)280-1416. Richard D. Spoor. Includes Missionary Research Library

University of Chicago (Regenstein Library) 1100 E.57th St. Chicago, IL 60637-1502. Tel (312)702-8740 Curtis Bochanyin

University of Texas Libraries, P.O. Box P, Austin, TX 78713-7330. Tel (512)471-3811 FAX (512)471-8901.

Yale Divinity School Library, 409 Prospect St. New Haven, CT 06510 Tel (203)432-5291. Includes Day Missions Library

Yale University (Sterling Memorial Library) 120 High St., P.O. Box 1603A Yale Station, New Haven, CT 06520. Tel (203)432-1775. FAX (203)432-7231 Katharine D. Morton

Adventist:

Andrews University (James White Library), Berrien Springs, MI 49104 Tel (616) 471-3264. Mr. Warren Johns.

Auroro University (Charles B. Phillips Library) 347 S. Gladstone, Aurora, IL 60506 Tel (708) 844-5437. Ken VanAndel. Advent Christian Church archives

Berkshire Christian College (Linden J. Carter Library) Lenox, MA 01240

Seventh Day Adventists General Conference Archives, 6840

Eastern Ave. NW, Washington, DC 20012 Tel (212)722-6000

Baptist:

American Baptist-Samuel Colgate Historical Library, 1106 S. Goodman St., Rochester, NY 14620-2532. Tel (716)473-1740. James R. Lynch.

Andover Newton Theological School, (Franklin Trask Library) 169 Herrick Road, Newton Centre, MA 02159 Tel (617) 964-1100. Ms. Sharon A. Taylor. Includes Backus Historical Library.

Bethel Theological Seminary Library, 3949 Bethel Dr., St. Paul, MN 55112 Tel (612)638-6184. Dr. Norris Magnuson. Swedish Baptist collection.

Elon College (Iris Holt McEwen Library) P.O. Box 187, Elon, NC 27244-2010 Tel (919)584-2479. Diane Gill, archivist. Primitive Baptist Archives.

Seventh Day Baptist Historical Society Library, 3120 Kennedy Rd., P.O. Box 1678, Janesville, WI 53547 Tel (608)752-5055. Janet Thorngate.

Southern Baptist Historical Library & Archives, 901 Commerce St., Suite 400, Nashville TN 37203-3620. Tel (615)244-0344. FAX 615-242-2153. Pat Brown

Brethren in Christ:

Messiah College (Murray Learning Resources Center) Grantham, PA 17027-9990 Tel (717)691-6042. E. Morris Sider.

Church of the Brethren:

Bethany Theological Seminary Library, Butterfield and Meyers Roads, Oak Brook, IL 60521. Tel (708) 620-2214. Dr. Helen K. Mainelli.

Brethren Historical Library and Archives, 1451 Dundee Ave., Elgin, IL 60120 Tel (708)742-5100. Kenneth M. Shaffer Jr.

Juniata College (L. A. Beeghly Library) 18th & Moore, Huntingdon, PA 16652. Tel (814)314-6286. Peter Kupersmith.

Churches of Christ:

Abilene Christian University (Brown Library) 1700 Judge Ely Blvd., ACU Station, P.O. Box 8177, Abilene, TX 79699-8177. Tel (915)674-2344. Marsha Harper

Harding Graduate School of Religion (L.M.Graves Memorial Library) 1000 Cherry Rd., Memphis, TN 38117. (901)761-1354. Don Meredith.

Pepperdine University (Payson Library) Malibu, CA 90263. Tel (213)456-4243. Harrold Holland

Churches of God, General Conference:

University of Findlay (Shafer Library) 1000 N. Main St., Findlay, OH 45840-3695. Tel (419)424-4612. FAX (419)424-4757. Robert W. Shirmer. Archives/Museum of the Churches of God in North America.

Congregational: (See United Church of Christ)

Disciples of Christ:

Brite Divinity School Library, Texas Christian University, P.O. Box 32904, Fort Worth, TX 76219. Tel (817)921-7106. FAX (817) 921-7110. Robert Olsen, Jr.

Christian Theological Seminary Library, P.O. Box 88267, 1000 W. 42nd St., Indianapolis, IN 46208. Tel (317)924-1331. David Bundy.

Culver-Stockton College (Johnson Memorial Library) College Hill, Canton, MO 63435. Tel (314)288-5221. FAX (314)288-3984. John Sperry, Jr.

Disciples Divinity House, University of Chicago,1156 E. 57th St., Chicago, IL 60637 Tel (312)643-4411

Disciples of Christ Historical Society Library, 1101 Nineteenth Ave., S., Nashville, TN 37212-2196. Tel (615)327-1444. David I. McWhirter.

Lexington Theological Seminary (Bosworth Memorial Linbrary) 631 South Limestone St., Lexington, KY 40508 Tel (606)252-0361 FAX (606)281-6042. Philip N. Dare

Episcopal:

Archives of the Episcopal Church, P.O. Box 2247 606 Rathervue Pl., Austin, TX 78768 Tel (512)472-6816. V. Nelle Bellamy

Episcopal Divinity School Library, 99 Brattle St. Cambridge, MA 02138 Tel (617)868-3450. James Dunkly

General Theological Seminary (Saint Mark's Library) 175 Ninth Ave., New York, NY 10011. Tel (212)243-5150. David Green.

Nashotah House Library, 2777 Mission Road, Nashotah, WI 53058-9793. Tel (414)646-3371 FAX (414)646-2215 Mike Tolan.

National Council, The Episcopal Church, 815 2nd Ave., New York, NY 10017. Tel (212)867-8400.

Yale Divinity School Library, 409 Prospect Street, New Haven, CT 06510 Tel (203)432-5291. Berkeley Divinity School Collection.

Evangelical United Brethren:

(see United Methodist Church)

Evangelical Congregational Church:

Evangelical School of Theology (Rostad Library), 121 S. College St., Myerstown, PA 17067. Tel (717)866-5775. FAX (717) 866-4667. Terry Heisey. Historical Society Library of the Evangelical Congregational Church

Friends:

Friends' Historical Library, Swarthmore College, 500 College Ave., Swarthmore, PA 19081. Tel (215)328-8557. FAX (215)328-8673. J. William Frost.

Haverford College (Magill Library) Haverford, PA 19041-1392. Tel (215)-896-1175. FAX (215)896-1224. Edwin Bronner

Jewish:

American Jewish Archives, 3101 Clifton Ave., Cincinnati, OH 45220 Tel (513)221-1875.

Friedman Memorial Library, American Jewish Historical Society, 2 Thornton Rd., Waltham, MA 02154 Tel (617)891-8110. FAX (617)899-9208. Nathan M. Kaganoff.

YIVO Institute for Jewish Research, Library & Archives, 1048 Fifth Ave., New York, NY 10028. Tel (212)535-6700. Zachary Baker, librarian; Marek Weber, archivist.

Latter-Day Saints:

Church of Jesus Christ of the Latter-Day Saints Library-Archives, Historical Department, 50 E. North Temple St., Salt Lake City, UT 84150. Tel (801)240-2745. Steven Sorenson

Family History Library, 35 North West Temple St., Salt Lake City, UT 84150. Tel (801) 240-2331 FAX (801)240-5551 David M. Mayfield.

Lutheran:

Augustana College (Swenson Swedish Immigration History Center) Box 175, Rock Island, IL 61201. Tel (309)794-7221. Kermit Westerberg.

Evangelical Lutheran Church in American Archives, 8765 West Higgins Road, Chicago, IL 60631-4198.Tel 1-800-NET-ELCA or (312)380-2818. Elisabeth Wittman

Region 1 (Alaska, Idaho, Montana, Oregon and Washington) Pacific Lutheran University (Mortvedt Library) Tacoma, WA 98447 Tel (206)535-7587 Kerstin Ringdahl

Region 2 (Arizona, California, Colorado, Hawaii, New Mexico, Nevada, Utah, Wyoming) Pacific Lutheran Theological Seminary, 2770 Marin Ave., Berkeley, CA, 94708; contact Ray Kibler III, 4249 N. LaJunta Drive, Claremont, CA 91711-3199.

Region 3 (Minnesota, North Dakota, South Dakota) Paul Daniels, Region 3 Archives, ELCA, 2481 Como Avenue West, Saint Paul, MN 55108-1445. Tel (612)641-3205

Region 4 (Arkansas, Kansas, Louisiana, Missouri, Nebraksa, Oklahoma, Texas) No archives esablished by 1992.

Region 5 (Illinois, Iowa, Wisconsin, Upper Michigan) Robert C. Wiederaenders, Region 5 Archives, ELCA, 333 Wartburg Place, Dubuque, IA 52001

Region 6 (Indiana, Kentucky, Michigan, Ohio) No archives established by 1992

Region 7 (New York, New Jersey, Eastern Pennsylvania, New England and the non-geographic Slovak-Zion Synod) John E. Peterson, Region 7 Archives, ELCA, 7301 Germantown Ave., Philadelphioa, PA 19119 Tel (215)248-4616. For Metropolitan New York Synod : David Gaise, 32 Neptune Road, Toms River, NJ 08753

Region 8 (Delaware, Maryland, Central and Western Pennsylvania, West Virginia, Washington, DC) Paul A. Mueller, Thiel College, Greenville, PA 16125 Tel (412)588-7000; (Central Pennsylvania, Delaware, Eastern Maryland, and Washington, DC) Lutheran Theological Seminary (Wentz Library) 66 Confederate Ave., Gettysburg, PA 17325 Tel (717)334-6286. Donald Matthews

Region 9 (Alabama, North and South Carolina, Florida, Georgia, Mississippi, Tennessee, Virginia, and the Caribbean Synod) Lutheran Theological Southern Seminary, 4201 N. Main St., Columbia, SC 29203-5898. Tel (803)786-5150. Lynn A. Feider

Concordia Historical Institute (Dept. of Archives and History, Lutheran Church-Missouri Synod) 801 De Mun Ave., St. Louis, MO 63105-3199. Tel (314)721-5934, Ext 320,321. August R. Suelflow

Concordia Seminary (Fuerbringer Hall library) 801 DeMun Avenue, St. Louis, MO 63105. Tel (314) 721-5934. David O. Berger.

Finnish-American Historical Archives, Suomi College, Hancock, MI 49930. Tel (906)482-5300, ext 273.

Luther College (Preus Library) Decorah, IA 52101. Tel (319)387-1191. FAX (319)382-3717. Ted Stark.

Lutheran School of Theology at Chicago (Jesuit/Kraus/ McCormick Library) 1100 East 55th St., Chicago, IL 60615 Tel (312)753-0739. Mary R. Bischoff

Saint Olaf College (Rolvaag Memorial Library) 1510 St. Olaf Ave., Northfield, MN 55057-1097. Tel (507)663-3225 Joan Olson. Norwegian Lutheran collection.

Wisconsin Lutheran Seminary Archives, 11831 N. Seminary Drive, 65W, Mequon, WI 53092. Tel (414)272-7200. Martin Westerhaus

Mennonite:

Archives of the Mennonite Church, 1700 South Main, Goshen, IN 46526. Tel (219)533-3161, Ext 477

Associated Mennonite Biblical Seminaries, Library, 1445 Boonville Ave, Northwest Dock, Springfield, MO 65802. Tel (417)862-3344. Joseph F Marics, Jr.

Bethel College, Historical Library, P.O. Dramer A, North Newton, KS 67117-9998. Tel (316)283-2500, Ext 366. FAX (316)284-5286. Dale R. Schrag.

Bluffton College (Mennonite Historical Library) Bluffton, OH 45817 Tel (419)358-8015, ext 271.

Center for Mennonite-Brethren Studies, 4824 E. Butler, Fresno, CA 93727 Tel (209)251-7194, Ext 1055.

Eastern Mennonite College (Menno Simons Historical Library and Archives) Eastern Mennonite College, Harrisonburg, VA 22801 Tel (703)433-2771, ext 177

Goshen College (Mennonite Historical Library) Goshen, IN 46526 Tel (219)535-7418

Mennonite Historians of Eastern Pennsylvania Library and Archives, P.O. Box 82, 656 Yoder Road, Harleysville, PA 19438. Tel (215)256-3020. Joel D. Alderfer

Methodist:

Asbury Theological Seminary (B.L.Fisher Library) Wilmore, KY 40390-1199. Tel (606)858-3581. David W. Faupel

Boston University School of Theology (New England Methodist Historical Society Library) 745 Commonwealth Ave., Boston, MA 02215. Tel (615)353-3034. Myra V. Siegenthaler.

Cincinnati Historical Society (Nippert German Methodist Collection) The Museum Center, Cincinnati Union Terminal, 1301 Western Ave., Cincinnati, OH 45403. Tel (513)287-7068. Jonathan Dembo

Drew University Library, Madison, NJ 07940. Tel (201) 408-3590. Kenneth E. Rowe, Methodist Librarian.

Duke Divinity School Library, Duke University, Durham, NC 27706. Tel (919)684-3234. Roger Loyd

Emory University, Candler School of Theology (Pitts Theology Library) Atlanta, GA 30322. Tel (404)727-4166. Channing Jeschke

Free Methodist World Headquarters (Marston Memorial Historical Center) Winona Lake, IN 46590. Tel (219)267-7656. Frances Haslam

Garrett-Evangelical Theological Seminary (United Library) 2121 Sheridan Rd, Evanston, IL 60201. Tel (708)866-3900. David Himrod

General Commission on Archives and History, The United Methodist Church, PO Box 127, Madison, NJ 07940. Tel (201) 822-2787 FAX (201)408-3909 Susan M. Eltscher, Asst. Gen. Sec.

Indiana United Methodist Archives, DePauw University (Roy O. West Library) Greencastle, IN 46135. Tel (317)658-4434. FAX (317)658-4789. Wesley Wilson.

Interdenominational Theological Center (Woodruff Library) 6111 James P. Brawley Drive, S.W., Atlanta, GA 30314. Tel (404)522-8980. Joseph E. Troutman. African American Methodist collection

Livingstone College and Hood Theological Seminary (William J. Walls Heritage Center) 701 W. Monroe St., Salisbury, NC 28144 Tel (704)638-5500 A.M.E.Zion collection

Miles College (W.A.Bell Library) 5500 Avenue G., Birmingham, AL 35208 Tel (205)923-2771. C.M.E. collection

Mother Bethel African Methodist Episcopal Church, 419 South 6th St., Philadelphia, PA 19147 Tel (215)925-0616

Paine College (Candler Library) Augusta, GA 30910 Tel (404)722-4471 C.M.E. collection

Perkins School of Theology (Bridwell Library Center for Methodist Studies) Southern Methodist University, Dallas, TX 75275-0476. Tel (214)692-3483. Dr. Richard P. Heitzenrater

United Methodist Historical Library, Beeghley Library, Ohio Wesleyan University, 43 University Ave., Delaware, OH 43015. Tel (614)369-4431, Ext 3245 FAX (614)363-0079.

United Methodist Publishing House Library, Room 122, 201 Eighth Ave., South, Nashville, TN 37202. Tel (615)749-6437. Rosalyn Lewis

United Theological Seminary (Center for Evangelical United Brethren Studies) 1810 Harvard Blvd., Dayton, OH 45406. Tel (513)278-5817. Elmer J. O'Brien

Upper Room Library, 1908 Grand Avenue, P.O. Box 189, Nashville, TN 37202-0189. Tel (615)340-7204. FAX (615)340-7006. Sarah Schaller-Linn.

Vanderbilt University, Divinity Library, 419 21st Avenue, South, Nashville, TN 37240-0007 Tel (615)322-2865. William J. Hook

Wesley Theological Seminary Library, 4500 Massachusetts Ave., NW, Washington, DC 20016 Tel (202)885-8691 Allen Mueller. Methodist Protestant Church collection

Wesleyan Church Archives & Historical Library, International Center Wesleyan Church, P.O. Box 50434, Indianapolis, IN 46250-0434 Tel (317)842-0444. Daniel L. Burnett

Wilberforce University and Payne Theological Seminary (Rembert E. Stokes Learning Resources Center) Wilberforce, OH 45384-1003 Tel (513)376-2911 ext 628 A.M.E. Archives

World Methodist Council Library, P.O. Box 518, Lake Junaluska, NC 28745 Tel (704)456-9432. Evelyn Sutton

For United Methodist annual conference depositories, see *United Methodist Church Archives and History Directory 1989-1992*. Madison, NJ : General Commission on Archives and History, UMC, 1989.

Moravian:

The Archives of the Moravian Church, 41 W. Locust St., Bethlehem, PA 18018 Tel (215)866-3255 Vernon H. Nelson

Moravian Archives, Southern Province of the Moravian Church, 4 East Bank St., Winston-Salem, NC 27101 Tel (919) 722-1742

Nazarene:

Nazarene Archives, International Headquarters, Church of the Nazarene, 6401 The Paseo, Kansas City, MO 64131. Tel (816) 333-7000, Ext 437 Stan Ingersoll

Nazarene Theological Seminary (Broadhurst Library) 1700 East Meyer Blvd., Kansas City, MO 64131. Tel (816)333-6254 William C. Miller

Pentecostal:

Assemblies of God Archives, 1445 Boonville Ave., Springfield, MO 65802.Tel (417)862-2781. Wayne Warner

Oral Roberts University Library, P.O. Box 2187,777 S. Lewis, Tulsa, OK 74171 Tel (918)495-6894. Oon-Chor Khoo

Pentecostal Research Center, Church of God (Cleveland, Tenn.), P. O. Box 3448, Cleveland, TN 37320. Tel (615)472-3361 FAX (615)478-7052. Joseph Byrd

Polish National Catholic:

Commission on History and Archives, Polish National Catholic Church, 1031 Cedar Ave., Scranton, PA 18505. Chmn., Joseph Wielczerzak

Presbyterian:

Department of History, Presbyterian Church (USA) Library, 425 Lombard St., Philadelphia, PA 19147 Tel (215)627-1852 FAX (215)627-0509. Gerald W. Gillette.

Department of History, Presbyterian Church (USA), Historical Foundation Library, P.O. Box 847, Montreat, NC 28757. Tel (704)669-7061 FAX (704)669-5369. Robert Benedetto

McCormick Theological Seminary (Jesuit/Kraus/McCormick Library) 1100 East 55th St., Chicago, IL 60615 (312)753-0739 Mary R.Bischoff

Princeton Theological Seminary (Speer Library) Library Place and Mercer St., P.O. Box 111, Princeton, NJ 08540 Tel (609)497-7940. James S. Irvine

Presbyterian Church in America, Historical Center,12330 Conway Rd., St. Louis, MO 63141

Reformed:

Calvin College and Seminary Library, 3207 Burton St, S.E., Grand Rapids, MI 49546 Tel (616)949-4000. Harry Boonstra (Christian Reformed)

Commission on History, Reformed Church in America, Gardner A. Sage Library, New Brunswick Theological Seminary, 21 Seminary Place, New Brunswick, NJ 08901-1159. Tel (908)247-5243 FAX (908)249-5412 Russell Gassaro

Lancaster Theological Seminary, Evangelical and Reformed Historical Society (Philip Schaff Library) 555 West James St., Lancaster, PA 17603. Tel (717)393-0654. Richard R. Berg. Reformed in the U.S., Evangelical and Reformed)

Roman Catholic:

Archives of the American Catholic Historical Society of Philadelphia, Ryan Memorial Library, St. Charles Boromeo Seminary, 1000 E. Wynnewood Rd., Overbrook, Philadelphia, PA 19096-3012. Tel (215)667-3394. FAX (215)664-7913. Joseph S. Casino

Catholic University of America (Mullen Library) 620 Michigan Ave., NE Washington, DC 20064 Tel (202)319-5055. Carolyn T. Lee.

Georgetown University (Lauinger Library) P.O.Box 37445, Washington, DC 20013-7445. Tel (202)687-7425 Eugene Rooney

St. Louis University (Pius XII Memorial Library) 3650 Lindell Blvd., St. Louis, MO 63108 Tel (314)658-3100 Thomas Tolles

St. Mary's Seminary & University (Knott Library) 5400 Roland Ave, Baltimore, MD 21210-1994. Tel (301)323-3200, Ext 64. David P. Siemsen

University of Notre Dame Archives (Hesburg Library) Box 513, Notre Dame, IN 46556 Tel (219)239-5252. Sophia K. Jordan.

Salvation Army:

The Salvation Army Archives and Research Center, 615 Slaters Lane, Alexandria, VA 22313. Tel (703)684-5500, Ext 669. Connie Nelson

Schwenkfelder:

Schwenkfelder Library, 1 Seminary Ave., Pennsburg, PA 18073. Tel (215)679-3103. Dennis Moyer

Shaker:

Ohio Historical Society, Archives Library, 1982 Velma Ave., Columbus, OH 43211-2497. Tel (614)297-2510. Wendy Greenwood

Western Reserve Historical Society,10825 E. Blvd. Cleveland, OH 44106-1788. Tel (216)721-5722 FAX (216)721-0645. Kermit J. Pike

Swedenborgian:

Academy of the New Church Library, 2815 Huntingdon Pike, P.O. Box 278-68, Bryn Athyn, PA 19009. Tel (215)938-2547. Carroll C. Odhner

Unitarian and Universalist:

Harvard Divinity School (Andover-Harvard Theological Library) 45 Francis Ave., Cambridge, MA 02138 Tel (617)495-5770. Alan Seaburg

Meadville/Lombard Theological School Library, 5701 S. Woodlawn Ave., Chicago, IL 60637. Tel (312)753-3196 Neil W. Gerdes

Rhode Island Historical Society Library, 121 Hope St., Providence, RI 02906. Tel (401)331-8575. FAX (401)751-7930. Madeleine Telfeyan

Unitarian-Universalist Association Archives Library, 25 Beacon St., Boston, MA 02108 Tel (617)742-2100. Deborah Weiner

The United Church of Christ:

Chicago Theological Seminary (Hammond Library) 5757 University Ave., Chicago, IL 60637 Tel (312)752-5757. Neil W. Gerdes

Congregational Library, 14 Beacon St., Boston, MA 02108 Tel (617)523-0470. Harold Worthley

Eden Archives, 475 E. Lockwood Ave., Webster Groves, MO 63119-3192. Tel (314)961-3627. Lowell H. Zuck.

Evangelical and Reformed

Hartford Seminary (Educational Resources Center) 77 Sherman St., Hartford, CT 06105 Tel (203)232-4451. William Peters

Harvard Divinity Schol (Andover Harvard Theological Library) 45 Francis Ave., Cambridge, MA 02138. Tel (617)495-5770. Russell O. Pollard.

Lancaster Theological Seminary, Archives of the United Church of Christ (Philip Schaff Library) Lancaster Theological Seminary, 555 W. James St., Lancaster, PA 17603 Tel (717)393-0654. Richard R. Berg

Yale Divinity School Library, 409 Prospect Street, New Haven, CT 06510. Tel (203)432-5291

Yale University (Sterling Memorial Library) Yale University, 120 high St., Box 1603A Yale Station, New Haven, CT 06520 Tel (203)436-0907

Wesleyan, see Methodist

STANDARD GUIDES TO CHURCH ARCHIVES

William Henry Allison, Inventory of Unpublished Material for American Religious History in Protestant Church Archives and other Depositories (Washington, D. C., Carnegie Institution of Washington, 1910, 254 pp.).

John Graves Barrow, A Bibliography of Bibliographies in Religion (Ann Arbor, Mich., 1955), pp. 185-198.

Edmund L. Binsfield, "Church Archives in the United States and Canada: a Bibliography," in American Archivist, V. 21, No. 3 (July 1958) pp. 311-332, 219 entries.

Nelson R. Burr, "Sources for the Study of American Church History in the Library of Congress," 1953. 13 pp. Reprinted from Church History, Vol. XXII, No. 3 (Sept. 1953).

Homer L. Calkin, Catalog of Methodist Archival and Manuscript Collections. Mont Alto, PA: World Methodist Historical Society, 1982—(4 vols. to date)

Church Records Symposium, American Archivist, Vol. 24, October 1961, pp. 387-456.

Mable Deutrich, "Supplement to Church Archives in the United States and Canada, a Bibliography," Washington, DC: 1964.

Andrea Hinding, ed. Women's History Sources: A Guide to Archives and Manuscript Collections in the U.S. New York: Bowker, 1979. 2 vols.

E. Kay Kirkham, A Survey of American Church Records, for the Period Before The Civil War, East of the Mississippi River (Salt Lake City, 1959-60, 2 vols.). Includes the depositories and bibliographies.

Peter G. Mode, Source Book and Bibliographical Guide for American Church History (Menasha, Wisc., George Banta Publishing Co., 1921, 735 pp.).

Society of American Archivists. American Archivist, 1936/37 (continuing). Has articles on church records and depositories.

Aug. R. Suelflow, A Preliminary Guide to Church Records Repositories, Society of American Archivists, Church Archives Committee, 1969. Lists more than 500 historical-archival depositories with denominational and religious history in America.

U. S. National Historical Publications and Records Commission, Directory of Archives and Manuscript Repositories in the United States. 2d edition. New York: Oryx Press, 1988.

United States, Library of Congress, Division of Manuscripts, Manuscripts in Public and Private Collections in the United States (Washington, D.C., 1924).

U. S. Library of Congress, Washington, D. C.: The National Union Catalog of Manuscript Collections, A59—22 vols., 1959-1986. Based on reports from American repositories of manuscripts. Contains many entries for collections of church archives. This series is continuing. Extremely valuable collection. Researchers must consult the cumulative indexes.

IN CANADA

A few small Canadian religious bodies have headquarters in the United States, and therefore the reader is advised to consult "Main Depositories of Church History Material and Sources in the United States," which immediately precedes this section for possible sources of information on Canadian religious groups. Another source: Directory of Canadian Archives, edited by Marcel Caya.

The use of the term "main" depositories in this section implies that there are some smaller communions with archival collections not listed below and also that practically every judicatory of large religious bodies (e.g., diocese, presbytery, conference) has archives excluded from this listing. For information on these collections, write directly to the denominational headquarters or to the judicatory involved.

The major libraries in the United States listed

above "Major Ecumenical Collections" contain material relating to Canadian church history.

Most American Protestant denominational archives have important primary and secondary source material relating to missionary work in Canada during the pioneer era.

Ecumenical:

Canadian Council of Churches Archives, on deposit in Public

Archives of Canada, 395 Wellington, Ottawa, Ontario K1A 0N3. Some records remain at the Canadian Council of Churches office located at 40 St. Clair Ave. E., Toronto, Ontario M4T 1M9. The Public Archives of Canada also contains a large number of records and personal papers related to the various churches.

Anglican:

General Synod Archives, 600 Jarvis St., Toronto, Ontario M4Y 2J6. Archivist: Mrs. Terry Thompson.

Baptist:

Canadian Baptist Archives, McMaster Divinity College, Hamilton, Ontario L8S 4K1. Librarian: Judith Colwell

Evangelical Baptist Historical Library, 3034 Bayview Ave., Willowdale, Ontario M2N 6J5

Baptist Historical Collection, Vaughan Memorial Library, Acadia University, Wolfville, Nova Scotia B0P 1X0. Archivist: Mrs. Pat Thompson

Disciples of Christ:

Canadian Disciples Archives, 39 Arkell Rd., R.R. 2, Guelph, Ontario N1H 6H8. Archivist: James A. Whitehead

Reuben Butchart Collection, Victoria University, Toronto, Ontario M5S 1K7

Jewish:

Jewish Historical Society of Western Canada, 404-365 Hargrave St., Winnipeg, Manitoba R3B 2K3. Archivist: Dorothy Hershfield

Canadian Jewish Congress (Central Region) Archives, 4600 Bathurst St., Toronto, Ontario M5T 1Y6. Archivist: Stephen A. Speisman

Lutheran:

Lutheran Council in Canada, 500-365 Hargrave St., Winnipeg, Manitoba R3B 2K3. Archivist: Rev. N. J.Threinen

Evangelical Lutheran Church in Canada, 1512 St. James St., Winnipeg, Manitoba R3H 0L2. Archivist: Rev. Leon C. Gilbertson (incorporating archives of the Evangelical Lutheran Church of Canada, the Lutheran Church in America—Canada Section's Central Synod Archives and those of the Western Canada Synod) The Eastern Synod Archives are housed at Wilfrid Laurier University, Waterloo, Ontario N2L 3C5. Archivist: Rev. Erich R.W. Schultz.

Lutheran Church—Canada, Ontario District, 149 Queen St., S., Kitchener, Ontario N2H 1W2. Archivist: Rev. W. W. Wentzlaff; Manitoba-Saskatchewan District, 411 Leighton Ave., Winnipeg, Manitoba R2K 0J8. Archivist Mr. Harry Laudin.

Concordia College, Edmonton, Alberta T5B 4E4. Archivist: Mrs. Hilda Robinson.

Mennonite:

Conrad Grebel College, Archives Centre, Waterloo, Ontario N2L 3G6. Archivist: Sam Steiner

Mennonite Brethren Bible College, Center for Mennonite Brethren Studies in Canada, 1-169 Riverton Ave., Winnipeg, Manitoba R2L 2E5. Archivist: Kenneth Reddig

Mennonite Heritage Centre. Archives of the General Conference of Mennonites in Canada, 600 Shaftesbury Blvd., Winnipeg, Manitoba R3P 0M4. Tel (204)888-6781. Historian-archivist: Lawrence Klippenstein

Free Methodist:

4315 Village Centre Ct., Mississauga, Ontario L4Z 1S2

Pentecostal:

The Pentecostal Assemblies of Canada, 10 Overlea Blvd., Toronto Ontario M4H 1A5.

Presbyterian:

Presbyterian Archives, Knox College, University of Toronto, 59 St. George St., Toronto, Ontario M5S 2E6. Archivist: Rev. T. M. Bailey; Deputy Archivist, Mrs. Kim Moir

Roman Catholic:

For guides to many Canadian Catholic diocesan religious community, and institutional archives, write: Rev. Pierre Hurtubise, O.M.I., Dir. of the Research Center in Religious History in Canada, St. Paul University, 223 Main St., Ottawa, Ontario K1S 1C4.

Salvation Army:

The George Scott Railton Heritage Centre, 2130 Bayview Ave., Toronto, Ontario M4N 3K6. Contact: Catherine Sequin.

The United Church of Canada:

Central Archives, Victoria University, Toronto, Ontario M5S 1K7. Archivist-Historian: Miss Jean Dryden. (Methodist, Presbyterian, Congregational, Evangelical United Brethren.) Also Regional Conference Archives.

## III

STATISTICAL SECTION

GUIDE TO STATISTICAL TABLES

Earl Brewer

Since there are no religious questions in the U.S. census, the Yearbook of American and Canadian Churches becomes as near an "official" record of denominational statistics as is available. It is often supplemented by several sample studies, such as Gallup, National Opinion Research Center, and others.

Students, denominational, ecumenical, or congregational policy-makers may use these statistics to gain insights for program planning. Trends in religious adherents and the population of the countries may be related to these statistics.

In spite of these and other values, there are limitations of these statistics which need to be kept in mind by users:

1. The data are not for a single year. Each year the Yearbook staff sends questionnaires to appropriate officers of religious bodies in Canada and the United States. The responses are shown in Tables 1-4.

Denominations have different report schedules and some do not report on a regular basis. The Yearbook tables identifies the most current data (received for 1990 or 1991) with boldface type. Data dated 1989 or earlier are in light type.

2. The statistics are not comparable in all cases. Definitions of membership and other important characteristics differ from denomination to denomination. In Tables 1-4 of this section, full or confirmed membership refers to those with full, communicant, or confirmed status. Inclusive membership refers to those who are full communicants or confirmed members plus other members baptized, non-confirmed or non-communicant.

3. The data are incomplete. Different methods and times are used in collecting them. Some denominations don't keep or report statistics in some of the categories listed in the tables.

4. This statistical information is based on reports made by denominational leaders rather than "head counts" of the population.

The Yearbook staff wants to make every effort to improve the quality and the quantity of the statistics of the vast number of religious bodies. It is hoped that continued cooperation of religious bodies and ecumenical groups will enhance and make more useful this part of the Yearbook.

Statistics collected from other sources than the questionnaire are often included in the Yearbook.

Tables 1-4 are based largely on the responses to the questionnaires mailed to appropriate officials in all known religious bodies in Canada and the United States. The religious bodies are listed alphabetically. The financial data are based on the currency of the country.

TABLE 1: CANADIAN CURRENT AND NON-CURRENT STATISTICS

Fifty-three of the 87 religious bodies in Canada reported current statistics, with 34 non-current in 1991. The same number of bodies reported for the past two years. Fifty-five of the 87 denominations reported fewer than 100 churches, 22 fewer than 25. This is a clue to the size of membership, number of pastors and enrollment in Sunday or Sabbath Schools. Data for the latter are not shown for non-current reports.

Religious Body	Year Reported	No. of Churches	Inclusive Membership	Full, Communicant or Confirmed Members	No. of Pastors Serving Parishes	Total No. of Clergy	No. of Sunday or Sabbath Schools	Total Enrollment
THE ANGLICAN CHURCH OF CANADA	1990	1,767	848,256	529,943	1,907	3,463	1,623	82,022
The Antiochian Orthodox Christian Archdiocese of North America	1989	12	20,000		25	25		
Apostolic Christian Church (Nazarene)	1985	14	830		49	49		
Apostolic Church in Canada	1989	14	1,600		14	19		
Apostolic Church of Pentecost of Canada	1989	123	11,306		176	265		
Armenian Church of North America, Diocese of Canada	1979	7	25,000		3	3		
ASSOCIATED GOSPEL CHURCHES	1991	124	19,342	9,152	109	209	91	6,970
Baptist General Conference of Canada	1987	70	6,066		80	84	NR	NR
BIBLE HOLINESS MOVEMENT	1991	14	904	358	6	11		
BRETHREN IN CHRIST CHURCH, CANADIAN CONFERENCE	1990	36	3,069	3,069	51	100	32	2,293
British Methodist Episcopal Church	1978	13	2,000		9	9		
Buddist Churches of Canada	1979	15	2,543		10	10		
The Canadian and American Reformed Churches	1989	41	18,944		37	55		
CANADIAN BAPTIST FEDERATION	1990	1,100	130,000	130,000	715	1,274	NR	NR
CANADIAN CONVENTION OF SOUTHERN BAPTISTS	1990	104	6,001	6,001	NR	NR	104	6,482
CANADIAN YEARLY MEETING OF THE RELIGIOUS SOCIETY OF FRIENDS	1990	23	1,150	1,150	None	None	12	121
CHRISTIAN AND MISSIONARY ALLIANCE IN CANADA	1990	325	74,286	26,784	450	1,039	NR	33,962
Christian Brethren (a.k.a. Plymouth Brethren)	1985	600	52,000		NR	250		
CHRISTIAN CHURCH (DISCIPLES OF CHRIST) IN CANADA	1990	36	4,251	2,496	25	48	36	1,006
Christian Churches and Churches of Christ	1989	140	7,500		95	100		
CHRISTIAN REFORMED CHURCH ON NORTH AMERICA	1990	240	88,892	50,927	202	276	NR	NR
CHURCH OF GOD (ANDERSON, IND.)	1990	50	3,151	3,151	39	57	44	2,639
CHURCH OF GOD (CLEVELAND, TENN.)	1991	98	5,958	5,958	NR	NR	NR	NR
THE CHURCH OF GOD OF PROPHECY OF CANADA	1991	50	2,915	2,915	114	114	49	2,644
THE CHURCH OF JESUS CHRIST OF LATTER-DAY SAINTS IN CANADA	1990	380	126,000	126,000	380	380	380	NR

TABLE 1: CANADIAN CURRENT AND NON-CURRENT STATISTICS--Continued

Religious Body	Year Reported	No. of Churches	Inclusive Membership	Full, Communicant or Confirmed Members	No. of Pastors Serving Parishes	Total No. of Clergy	No. of Sunday or Sabbath Schools	Total Enrollment
CHURCH OF THE LUTHERAN BRETHREN.	1990	7	514	309	6	8	7	590
CHURCH OF THE NAZARENE.	1991	161	10,951	10,915	117	243	159	15,957
CHURCHES OF CHRIST IN CANADA.	1991	147	7,181	7,181	133	NR	108	NR
Conference of Mennonites in Canada.	1989	157	28,688		200	335		
CONGREGATIONAL CHRISTIAN CHURCHES IN ONTARIO, THE CONFERENCE OF.	1990	5	258	258	5	13	4	105
The Coptic Church in Canada.	1987	7	40,000		7	7		
THE ESTONIAN EVANGELICAL LUTHERAN CHURCH.	1990	13	6,478	6,268	13	15	NR	NR
Evangelical Baptist Churches in Canada, The Fellowship of.	1989	484	57,780		NR	NR		
THE EVANGELICAL CHURCH IN CANADA.	1990	46	3,688	3,688	46	79	39	3,431
THE EVANGELICAL COVENANT CHURCH OF CANADA	1990	23	1,286	1,286	17	31	16	1,392
EVANGELICAL FREE CHURCH OF CANADA.	1991	124	13,299	6,358	51	126	124	NR
THE EVANGELICAL LUTHERAN CHURCH IN CANADA	1991	655	206,024	149,059	485	849	486	2,744
EVANGELICAL MENNONITE CONFERENCE.	1990	50	6,000	6,000	175	200	50	NR
EVANGELICAL MENNONITE MISSION CONFERENCE.	1990	28	3,559	3,528	25	51	25	3,092
FOURSQUARE GOSPEL CHURCH OF CANADA.	1990	46	2,019	2,019	78	94		1,375
Free Methodist Church in Canada.	1989	147	7,479		132	235		
FREE WILL BAPTIST.	1991	19	2,225	1,375	6	8	13	1,199
GENERAL CHURCH OF THE NEW JERUSALEM.	1991	3	826	275	4	6	3	185
The Gospel Missionary Association.	1981	13			10	44		
Greek Orthodox Diocese of Toronto (Canada).	1984	58	230,000		45	49		
Independent Assemblies of God--Canada.	1977	45	4,500		125	166		
Independent Holiness Church.	1987	13	600		13	21		
THE ITALIAN PENTECOSTAL CHURCH OF CANADA.	1990	21	3,300	3,300	20	24	NR	NR
JEHOVAH'S WITNESSES.	1990	1,270	101,713	101,713	NR	NR	NR	NR
Jews.	1981	112	296,425		None	None		
THE LATVIAN EVANGELICAL LUTHERAN.	1990	8	2,380	2,200	6	8	5	NR
LUTHERAN CHURCH--CANADA.	1990	330	80,240	60,760	250	387	298	17,997
MENNONITE BRETHREN CHURCHES CANADIAN CONFERENCE OF.	1990	190	27,288	NR	89	187	22,541	NR
MENNONITE CHURCH (CANADA).	1990	111	9,779	9,779	158	158	NR	NR
Metropolitan Community Churches, Universal Fellowship of	1984	11	1,600		10	10		
The Missionary Church of Canada.	1984	92	6,431		73	129		

TABLE 1: CANADIAN CURRENT AND NON-CURRENT STATISTICS--Continued

Religious Body	Year Reported	No. of Churches	Inclusive Membership	Full, Communicant or Confirmed Members	No. of Pastors Serving Parishes	Total No. of Clergy	No. of Sunday or Sabbath Schools	Total Enrollment
MORAVIAN CHURCH IN AMERICA–NORTHERN PROVINCE, CANADIAN DISTRICT.	1990	9	2,157	1,482	10	13	9	508
NETHERLANDS REFORMED CONGREGATIONS OF NORTH AMERICA.	1990	9	4,560	2,080	1	2	NR	NR
NORTH AMERICAN BAPTIST CONFERENCE.	1990	105	15,825	15,825	88	189	105	None
The Old Catholic Church of Canada.	1989	2	110		2	3	None	None
The Open Bible Standard Churches of Canada.	1987	4	1,000		5	6		
ORTHODOX CHURCH IN AMERICA (CANADA SECTION).	1991	59	NR	NR	37	41	13	NR
THE PENTECOSTAL ASSEMBLIES OF CANADA.	1990	976	194,972	192,706	1,372	1,593	NR	NR
PENTECOSTAL ASSEMBLIES OF NEWFOUNDLAND.	1990	160	31,719	15,707	243	405	156	13,340
Polish National Catholic Church.	1982	13	6,000		11	14		
PRESBYTERIAN CHURCH IN AMERICA (CANADIAN SECTION).	1990	16	886	538	17	23	NR	392
THE PRESBYTERIAN CHURCH IN CANADA.	1990	1,023	245,883	156,513	1,218	1,218	637	35321
REFORMED CHURCH IN CANADA.	1990	36	6,831	4,129	35	71	33	1,953
Reformed Doukhobors, Christian Community and Brotherhood.	1986	1	2,108		None	None		
Reformed Episcopal Church, the First Synod in the Dominion of Canada.	1989	3	770		9	13		
Reinlaender Mennonite Church.	1987	7	800		10	10		
REORGANIZED CHURCH OF JESUS CHRIST OF LATTER DAY SAINTS.	1990	83	12,258	12,258	1,088	1,088	NR	NR
The Roman Catholic Church in Canada.	1989	5,922	11,375,914		6,749	11,302		
The Romanian Orthodox Church in America (Canadian Parishes).	1972	19	16,000		19	19		
THE ROMANIAN ORTHODOX EPISCOPATE OF AMERICA (JACKSON, MI).	1990	13	8,600	8,600	11	12	10	663
RUSSIAN ORTHODOX CHURCH IN CANADA PATRIARCHAL PARISHES OF THE.	1991	24	7,000	6,000	4	5	3	46
The Salvation Army in Canada.	1988	398	88,899		732	2008		
Serbian Orthodox in the U.S.A. and Canada Diocese of Canada.	1983	17	18,494		11	13		
SEVENTH-DAY ADVENTIST CHURCH IN CANADA.	1990	317	40,047	40,047	167	286	348	26,529
Ukrainian Greek-Orthodox Church of Canada.	1988	258	120,000		75	91		
Union of Spiritual Communities of Christ (Orthodox Doukhobors in Canada).	1972	25	21,300		None	None		

TABLE 1: CANADIAN CURRENT AND NON-CURRENT STATISTICS--Continued

Religious Body	Year Reported	No. of Churches	Inclusive Membership	Full, Communicant or Confirmed Members	No. of Pastors Serving Parishes	Total No. of Clergy	No. of Sunday or Sabbath Schools	Total Enrollment
UNITARIAN UNIVERSALIST ASSOCIATION.	1990	40	6,003	60,003	20	20	34	1,303
UNITED BRETHREN IN CHRIST, ONTARIO CONFERENCE	1990	9	864	864	8	14	9	448
THE UNITED CHURCH OF CANADA.	1990	4,081	2,049,923	808,441	2,169	3,888	3,409	192,385
UNITED PENTECOSTAL CHURCH IN CANADA.	1991	197	NR	NR	327	NR	NR	NR
THE WESLEYAN CHURCH.	1991	83	5,143	4,925	81	131	83	17,010
WISCONSIN EVANGELICAL LUTHERAN SYNOD.	1990	10	1,357	907	11	11	10	276

TABLE 2: UNITED STATES CURRENT AND NON-CURRENT STATISTICS

Of the 219 bodies listed in this table, 118 reported current statistics and 101 did not, as in the previous year. For current reports, there was an increase from 113,575,941 to 132,694,380 inclusive members. The number of pastors serving parishes in current denominations increased from 238,298 to 299,836. The total number of clergy moved from 394,045 to 431,555.

Eighty-six of the 219 denominations show fewer than 100 churches and 36 had fewer than 25, pointing to the large number of small religious bodies in the United States.

Religious Body	Year Reported	No. of Churches	Inclusive Membership	Full, Communicant or Confirmed Members	No. of Pastors Serving Parishes	Total No. of Clergy	No. of Sunday or Sabbath Schools	Total Enrollment
ADVENT CHRISTIAN CHURCH.	**1990**	**334**	**27,590**	**27,590**	**257**	**491**	**330**	**16,045**
African Methodist Episcopal Church.	1981	6,200	2,210,000	1,000,000	6,050	6,550		
AFRICAN METHODIST EPISCOPAL ZION CHURCH.	**1991**	**3,000**	**1,200,000**	**1,000,000**	**2,500**	**2,686**	**1,556**	**50,046**
Alaska Moravian Church.	1987	23	5,159		11	15		
Albanian Orthodox Archdiocese in America.	1978	16	40,000		18	25		
ALBANIAN ORTHODOX DIOCESE OF AMERICA.	**1991**	**2**	**1,870**	**325**	**2**	**3**	**2**	**134**
ALLEGHENY WESLEYAN METHODIST CONNECTION (ORIGINAL ALLEGHENY CONFERENCE).	**1990**	**120**	**2,155**	**2,037**	**96**	**204**	**120**	**6,974**
AMANA CHURCH SOCIETY.	**1990**	**1**	**450**	**400**	**NR**	**NR**	**1**	**44**
American Baptist Association.	1986	1,705	250,000		1,740	1,760	NR	
AMERICAN BAPTIST CHURCHES IN THE U.S.A.	**1990**	**5,808**	**1,535,971**	**1,535,971**	**5,351**	**8,356**	**NR**	**299,609**
AMERICAN CARPATHO-RUSSIAN ORTHODOX GREEK CATHOLIC CHURCH.	**1990**	**72**	**14,058**	**14,058**	**75**	**83**	**71**	**NR**
American Rescue Workers.	1984	20	2,700		35	53		
The Anglican Orthodox Church.	1983	40	6,000		8	8		
The Antiochian Orthodox Christian Archdiocese of North America.	1989	160	350,000		250	325		
Apostolic Catholic Assyrian Church of the East North American Diocese.	1989	22	120,000		92	109		
Apostolic Christian Church (Nazarene).	1985	48	2,799		178	178		
Apostolic Christian Churches of America.	1989	80	11,450		300	340		
APOSTOLIC FAITH MISSION OF PORTLAND OR.	**1990**	**50**	**4,100**	**4,100**	**76**	**86**	**50**	**6,600**
Apostolic Faith Mission Church of God.	1989	18	6,200		27	32		
Apostolic Lutheran Church of America.	1989	53	7,583		29	34		
Apostolic Overcoming Holy Church of God.	1988	177	12,479		127	130		
ARMENIAN APOSTOLIC CHURCH OF AMERICA.	**1991**	**28**	**150,000**	**20,000**	**22**	**29**	**22**	**1,100**
Armenian Church of America, Diocese of.	1979	66	450,000		45	61		
ASSEMBLIES OF GOD.	**1990**	**11,353**	**2,181,502**	**1,298,121**	**16,336**	**30,524**	**10,958**	**1,403,168**
Assemblies of God, International Fellowship (Independent/Not Affiliated)	1962	136	NR		136	367		

TABLE 2: UNITED STATES CURRENT AND NON-CURRENT STATISTICS--Continued

Religious Body	Year Reported	No. of Churches	Inclusive Membership	Full, Communicant or Confirmed Members	No. of Pastors Serving Parishes	Total No. of Clergy	No. of Sunday or Sabbath Schools	Total Enrollment
ASSOCIATED REFORMED PRESBYTERIAN CHURCH GENERAL SYNOD	**1990**	**189**	**37,988**	**32,787**	**158**	**247**	**172**	**16,892**
Baptist Bible Fellowship, International.	1986	3,449	1,405,900		3,400	4,500		
BAPTIST GENERAL CONFERENCE.	**1991**	**799**	**134,717**	**134,717**	**1,200**	**1,700**	**799**	**79,181**
BAPTIST MISSIONARY ASSOCIATION OF AMERICA.	**1990**	**1,372**	**229,166**	**229,166**	**1,232**	**2,557**	**1,330**	**98,337**
Beachy Amish Mennonite Church.	1989	99	6,872		376	376		
BEREAN FUNDAMENTAL CHURCH.	**1991**	**51**	**2,768**	**2,768**	**60**	**60**	**51**	**4,063**
THE BIBLE CHURCH OF CHRIST INC.	**1991**	**6**	**6,812**	**4,270**	**8**	**51**	**6**	**740**
Bible Way Church of Our Lord Jesus Christ World Wide. Inc.	1970	350	30,000		350	350		
BRETHREN CHURCH (ASHLAND, OHIO).	**1990**	**124**	**13,060**	**13,060**	**90**	**175**	**118**	**6,784**
BRETHREN IN CHRIST CHURCH.	**1990**	**189**	**17,277**	**17,277**	**252**	**486**	**165**	**12,818**
Buddhist Churches of America.	1989	67	19,441		65	107		
BULGARIAN EASTERN ORTHODOX CHURCH (DIOCESE OF N. & S. AMERICA AND AUSTRALIA).	**1991**	**9**	**10,000**	**10,000**	**15**	**20**	**6**	**230**
CHRIST CATHOLIC CHURCH.	**1990**	**12**	**1,444**	**1,193**	**10**	**15**	**1**	**9**
Christadelphians.	1964	850	15,800		None	None		
THE CHRISTIAN AND MISSIONARY ALLIANCE.	**1990**	**1,856**	**279,207**	**138,071**	**1,596**	**2,385**	**1,686**	**193,500**
Christian Brethren.	1984	1,150	98,000		NR	500		
CHRISTIAN CATHOLIC CHURCH (EVANGELICAL PROTESTANT).	**1990**	**6**	**2,500**	**2,500**	**10**	**19**	**6**	**1,000**
CHRISTIAN CHURCH (DISCIPLES OF CHRIST).	**1990**	**4,069**	**1,039,692**	**678,750**	**3,744**	**6,899**	**4,069**	**308,804**
Christian Church of North America General Council.	1985	104	13,500		107	169		
Christian Churches and Churches of Christ.	1988	5,579	1,070,616		5,525	6,596		
THE CHRISTIAN CONGREGATION.	**1990**	**1,453**	**109,919**	**109,919**	**1,451**	**1,455**	**1,307**	**48,070**
Christian Methodist Episcopal Church.	1983	2,340	718,922		2,340	2,650		
Christian Nation Church, USA.	1989	5	200		4	23		
CHRISTIAN REFORMED CHURCH IN NORTH AMERICA	**1990**	**715**	**226,163**	**146,402**	**634**	**1,176**	**NR**	**NR**
Christian Union.	1984	114	6,000		80	114		
Church of Christ.	1972	32	2,400		169	188		
Church of Daniel's Band.	1951	4	200		4	10		
The Church of God.	1978	2,035	75,890		1,910	2,737		
CHURCH OF GOD (ANDERSON, IND.).	**1990**	**2,339**	**205,884**	**205,884**	**2,126**	**3,504**	**2,185**	**168,918**
CHURCH OF GOD BY FAITH.	**1991**	**145**	**8,235**	**6,819**	**155**	**170**	**NR**	**NR**
CHURCH OF GOD (CLEVELAND, TN).	**1990**	**5,841**	**620,393**	**620,393**	**4,665**	**6,585**	**5,514**	**389,093**

STATISTICAL SECTION

TABLE 2: UNITED STATES CURRENT AND NON-CURRENT STATISTICS--Continued

Religious Body	Year Reported	No. of Churches	Inclusive Membership	Full, Communicant or Confirmed Members	No. of Pastors Serving Parishes	Total No. of Clergy	No. of Sunday or Sabbath Schools	Total Enrollment
CHURCH OF GOD GENERAL CONFERENCE (OREGON, IL).................	1991	89	5,688	4,375	60	79	89	3,278
THE CHURCH OF GOD IN CHRIST..........	1991	15,300	5,499,875	5,499,875	28,988	33,593	NR	NR
The Church of God in Christ International....	1982	300	200,000		700	1,600	NR	NR
CHURCH OF GOD IN CHRIST (MENNONITE)......	1990	76	9,684	9,684	341	341	1,824	NR
CHURCH OF GOD OF PROPHECY........	1991	2,096	72,904	72,904	7,015	10,151	103	90,357
CHURCH OF GOD MOUNTAIN ASSEMBLY......	1991	103	4,938	4,938	266	272	NR	5,202
CHURCH OF GOD (SEVENTH DAY) DENVER, CO....	1990	153	5,749	5,749	NR	127	NR	NR
CHURCH OF GOD (WHICH HE PURCHASED WITH HIS OWN BLOOD)........	1991	7	800	800	NR	16	7	22
Church of Illumination.............	1983	4	9,000		60	60		
The Church of Jesus Christ (Bickertonites).......	1989	63	2,707		183	262		
CH. OF THE LORD JESUS CHRIST OF LATTER-DAY SAINTS..........	1990	9,213	4,267,000	3,736,000	27,639	31,059	9,213	3,380,000
Church of Our Lord Jesus Christ of the Apostolic Faith...........	1954	155	45,000		150	185		
CHURCH OF THE BRETHREN........	1990	1,095	148,253	148,253	1,084	1,541	NR	NR
Church of the Living God (C.W.F.F.).......	1985	170	42,000		NR	170		
CHURCH OF THE LUTHERAN BRETHREN OF AMERICA.................	1990	111	12,220	7,715	115	207	111	10,979
CHURCH OF THE LUTHERAN CONFESSION........	1990	69	8,753	6,397	57	82	64	1,487
CHURCH OF THE NAZARENE..........	1991	5,172	573,834	572,153	4,416	9,363	4,945	860,099
CHURCHES OF CHRIST............	1990	13,134	1,683,346	1,282,972	NR	NR	12,030	8,000
CHURCHES OF CHRIST IN CHRISTIAN UNION......	1990	214	9,221	9,221	115	474	214	11,349
CHURCHES OF GOD, GENERAL CONFERENCE........	1990	349	33,371	33,371	258	437	NR	27,697
COMMUNITY CHURCHES, INTL. COUNCIL OF......	1991	398	250,000	250,000	NR	NR	NR	NR
CONGREGATIONAL CHRISTIAN CHURCHES, NATIONAL ASSOCIATION OF........	1991	400	90,000	90,000	550	650	NR	NR
Congregational Holiness Church........	1981	174	8,347		176	488		
Conservative Baptist Association of America......	1989	1,126	210,000		1,126	1,324		
CONSERVATIVE CONGREGATIONAL CHRISTIAN CONFERENCE.................	1990	178	28,355	28,355	289	485	168	11,444
COPTIC ORTHODOX CHURCH...........	1990	42	165,000	150,000	49	49	NR	6,600
CUMBERLAND PRESBYTERIAN CHURCH.....	1990	796	98,891	91,857	571	799	NR	45,226
Duck River (and Kindred) Association of Baptists.....	1975	85	8,632		148	148		
ELIM FELLOWSHIP................	1990	177	20,000	NR	151	272	NR	NR
THE EPISCOPAL CHURCH............	1990	7,354	2,446,050	1,698,240	8,040	14,878	NR	568,205

TABLE 2: UNITED STATES CURRENT AND NON-CURRENT STATISTICS--Continued

Religious Body	Year Reported	No. of Churches	Inclusive Membership	Full, Communicant or Confirmed Members	No. of Pastors Serving Parishes	Total No. of Clergy	No. of Sunday or Sabbath Schools	Total Enrollment
The Estonian Evangelical Lutheran Church.	1989	24	7,298		17	19		
The Ethical Culture Movement.	1988	21	3,212		19	43		
THE EVANGELICAL CHURCH.	1990	185	16,398	16,398	240	349	185	17,428
EVANGELICAL CONGREGATIONAL CHURCH.	1990	155	32,700	24,437	141	222	153	17,100
THE EVANGELICAL COVENANT CHURCH.	1990	590	89,735	89,735	824	1,267	506	76,923
EVANGELICAL FREE CHURCH OF AMERICA.	1991	1,087	192,352	NR	NR	1,863	NR	NR
EVANGELICAL FRIENDS INTERNATIONAL	1991	246	26,322	NR	NR	455	246	14,881
EVANGELICAL LUTHERAN CHURCH IN AMERICA.	1990	11,087	5,240,739	3,898,478	10,083	17,402	10,054	1,160,694
EVANGELICAL LUTHERAN SYNOD.	1990	128	21,630	16,181	100	148	116	3,926
EVANGELICAL MENNONITE CHURCH.	1991	26	3,958	3,958	31	51	26	4,512
Evangelical Methodist Church.	1987	130	8,282		151	238		
EVANGELICAL PRESBYTERIAN CHURCH.	1991	155	52,645	49,286	233	313	155	NR
Fellowship of Evangelical Bible Churches.	1988	14	1,925		18	47		
FELLOWSHIP OF FUNDAMENTAL BIBLE CHURCHES.	1991	25	1,482	1,482	36	48	25	1,426
THE FIRE BAPTIZED HOLINESS CHURCH (WESLEYAN)	1991	49	695	695	49	64	NR	NR
Free Christian Zion Church of Christ.	1956	742	22,260		321	420		
FREE LUTHERAN CONGREGATIONS, THE ASSOCIATION OF.	1991	210	27,650	21,150	114	170	182	8,705
FREE METHODIST CHURCH OF NORTH AMERICA.	1990	1,096	74,313	58,084	NR	1,805	NR	98,005
FREE WILL BAPTISTS, NATIONAL ASSOCIATION OF.	1990	2,506	197,206	197,206	2,800	2,900	2,506	145,704
Friends General Conference.	1987	505	31,690		None	None		
FRIENDS UNITED MEETING.	1990	526	54,945	45,691	306	585	480	17,244
Full Gospel Assemblies, International.	1984	150	3,800		122	399		
Full Gospel Fellowship of Churches and Ministers, International.	1985	450	65,000		850	850		
FUNDAMENTAL METHODIST CHURCH, INC.	1990	12	1,075	675	14	25	12	431
GENERAL ASSOCIATION OF REGULAR BAPTIST CHURCHES.	1990	1,574	168,068	168,068	NR	NR	NR	NR
GENERAL BAPTISTS (GENERAL ASSOCIATION OF).	1990	876	74,156	74,156	1,384	1,384	NR	NR
General Church of the New Jerusalem.	1971	33	2,143		17	31		
General Conference of the Evangelical Baptist Ch.	1952	31	2,200		22	37		
General Six Principle Baptists.	1970	7	175		4	7		
Grace Brethren Churches, Fellowship of.	1989	319	39,481		NR	653		
GRACE GOSPEL FELLOWSHIP.	1990	50	4,500	2,500	68	120	50	NR
Greek Orthodox Archdiocese of North & South Amer.	1977	535	1,950,000		610	655		
The Holiness Church of God, Inc.	1968	28	927		25	36		
Holy Ukrainian Autocephalic Church in Exile.	1965	10	4,800		15	24		

273

TABLE 2: UNITED STATES CURRENT AND NON-CURRENT STATISTICS--Continued

Religious Body	Year Reported	No. of Churches	Inclusive Membership	Full, Communicant or Confirmed Members	No. of Pastors Serving Parishes	Total No. of Clergy	No. of Sunday or Sabbath Schools	Total Enrollment
House of God, Which is the Church of the Living God the Pillar and Ground of the Truth, Inc.	1956	107	2,350		80	120		
Hungarian Reformed Church in America	1989	27	9,780		29	32		
HUTTERIAN BRETHREN	1990	375	38,000		600	600	375	14,300
INDEPENDENT FUNDAMENTAL CHURCHES OF AMERICA	1991	700	78,174	78,174	745	1,510	700	74,566
INTERNATIONAL CHURCH OF THE FOURSQUARE GOSPEL	1990	1,451	199,385	194,880	NR	4,505	1,017	NR
INTERNATIONAL PENTECOSTAL CHURCH OF CHRIST	1991	76	3,995	2,610	76	181	76	3,995
JEHOVAH'S WITNESSES	1991	9,347	858,367	858,367	None	None	None	None
JEWS*	1990	3,416	5,981,000	3,750,000	NR	6,500	NR	NR
Kodesh Church of Immanuel	1980	5	326		2	28		
Korean Presbyterian Church in America General Assembly of the	1986	180	24,000		200	225		
LATVIAN EVANGELICAL LUTHERAN CHURCH IN AMERICA, THE	1990	56	12,553	11,423	34	48	19	NR
Liberal Catholic Church--Province of the United States of America	1987	34	2,800		64	127		
LIBERTY BAPTIST FELLOWSHIP	1990	600	180,000	180,000	2,000	3,500	600	NR
THE LUTHERAN CHURCH--MISSOURI SYNOD	1990	5,296	2,602,849	1,954,350	5,347	8,301	5,746	673,432
Lutheran Churches, The American Association of	1988	78	15,150		63	80		
Mennonite Brethren Churches, The United States Conference of	1989	130	16,794		181	181		
MENNONITE CHURCH	1990	1,034	92,517	92,517	1,504	2,545	NR	NR
MENNONITE CHURCH, THE GENERAL CONFERENCE	1990	218	33,535	33,535	214	409	218	16,165
Metropolitan Church Association	1958	15	443		13	62		
METROPOLITAN COMMUNITY CHURCHES, UNIVERSAL FELLOWSHIP OF	1990	195	25,076	12,576	276	304	NR	NR
THE MISSIONARY CHURCH	1990	302	26,910	26,910	273	578	286	27,790
MORAVIAN CHURCH IN AMERICA--NORTHERN	1990	98	31,032	23,526	86	167	95	7,129
MORAVIAN CHURCH IN AMERICA--SOUTHERN	1990	55	21,269	17,146	56	87	55	8,702
National Baptist Convention of America	1956	11,398	2,668,799		7,598	28,574		
NATIONAL BAPTIST CONVENTION, U.S.A., INC.	1991	30,000	7,800,000	NR	30,000	NR	30,000	NR
National Primitive Baptist Convention, Inc.	1975	616	250,000		460	636		
NATIONAL SPIRITUALIST ASSOCIATION OF CH	1990	120	3,406	3,406	186	218	49	478
NETHERLANDS REFORMED CONGREGATIONS	1990	15	5,212	2,780	5	7	NR	NR

TABLE 2: UNITED STATES CURRENT AND NON-CURRENT STATISTICS--Continued

Religious Body	Year Reported	No. of Churches	Inclusive Membership	Full, Communicant or Confirmed Members	No. of Pastors Serving Parishes	Total No. of Clergy	No. of Sunday or Sabbath Schools	Total Enrollment
NEW APOSTOLIC CHURCH OF NORTH AMERICA	**1990**	**506**	**38,612**	**NR**	**756**	**839**	**NR**	**2,276**
NORTH AMERICAN BAPTIST CONFERENCE	**1990**	**279**	**44,493**	**44,493**	**135**	**341**	**279**	**24,503**
NORTH AMERICAN OLD ROMAN CATHOLIC Church	1986	133	62,611		109	150		
NORTH AMERICAN OLD ROMAN CATHOLIC CHURCH (ARCHDIOCESE OF NEW YORK)	**1990**	**6**	**650**	650	13	14	2	**29**
OLD GERMAN BAPTIST BRETHREN	**1990**	**55**	**5,439**	5,439	233	233	**NR**	**NR**
Old Order Amish Church	1989	785	70,650		3,140	3,140		
Old Order (Wisler) Mennonite Church	1980	36	9,731		NR	NR		
OPEN BIBLE STANDARD CHURCHES, INC.	**1990**	**335**	**41,000**	33,000	525	994	**NR**	**NR**
The (Original) Church of God	1971	70	20,000		50	124		
Orthodox Church in America	1978	440	1,000,000		457	531		
The Orthodox Presbyterian Church	1987	188	19,094		160	334		
Pentecostal Assemblies of the World, Inc.	1960	550	4,500		450	600		
PENTECOSTAL CHURCH OF GOD, INC.	**1990**	**1,174**	**91,300**	40,000	NR	1,634	**NR**	**74,125**
Pentecostal Fire-Baptized Holiness Church	1969	41	545		80	80		
THE PENTECOSTAL FREE WILL BAPTIST CHURCH, INC.	**1991**	**141**	**11,757**	11,757	163	228	**141**	**11,734**
Pentecostal Holiness Church, International	1989	1,475	119,073		1,583	2,095		
Pillar of Fire	1949	61	5,100		NR	NR		
Polish National Catholic Church of America	1960	162	282,411		141	141		
PRESBYTERIAN CHURCH IN AMERICA	**1990**	**1,167**	**223,935**	185,526	1,204	2,073	**NR**	**112,282**
PRESBYTERIAN CHURCH (U.S.A.)	**1990**	**11,501**	**3,788,009**	2,847,437	10,308	20,338	**9,881**	**1,143,506**
PRIMITIVE ADVENT CHRISTIAN CHURCH	**1991**	**10**	**339**	339	10	10	**8**	**324**
Primitive Baptists	1960	1,000	72,000		NR	NR		
Primitive Methodist Church, U.S.A.	1989	85	8,244		54	84		
PROGRESSIVE NATL. BAPTIST CONVENTION, INC.	**1991**	**1,400**	**2,500,000**	2,500,000	1,400	1,400	**1,400**	**NR**
THE PROTESTANT CONFERENCE (LUTHERAN)	**1990**	**7**	**1,086**	816	9	9	**6**	**152**
Protestant Reformed Churches in America	1980	21	4,544		19	31		
REFORMED CHURCH IN AMERICA	**1990**	**924**	**326,850**	197,154	860	1,729	**NR**	**105,483**
Reformed Church in the United States	1985	34	3,778		28	34		
REFORMED EPISCOPAL CHURCH	**1990**	**83**	**6,565**	5,882	88	147	**72**	**2,938**
Reformed Mennonite Church	1970	12	500		18	21		
Reformed Methodist Union Episcopal Church	1983	18	3,800		24	33		
Reformed Presbyterian Church of North America	1988	68	5,174		59	127		
Reformed Zion Union Apostolic Church	1965	50	16,000		28	NR		
Religious Society of Friends (Conservative)	1984	28	1,744		NR	17		

TABLE 2: UNITED STATES CURRENT AND NON-CURRENT STATISTICS--Continued

Religious Body	Year Reported	No. of Churches	Inclusive Membership	Full, Communicant or Confirmed Members	No. of Pastors Serving Parishes	Total No. of Clergy	No. of Sunday or Sabbath Schools	Total Enrollment
Religious Society of Friends (Unaffiliated Meetings)	1980	112	6,386					
REORGANIZED CHURCH OF JESUS CHRIST OF LATTER DAY SAINTS	1990	1,025	189,524	189,524	16,666	16,666	NR	NR
THE ROMAN CATHOLIC CHURCH	1990	23,685	58,568,015	NR	34,598	53,088	NR	7,301,930
THE ROMANIAN ORTHODOX EPISCOPATE OF AMERICA	1990	37	65,000	65,000	37	81	30	1,800
Russian Orthodox Church in the U.S.A., Patriarchal Parishes	1985	38	9,780		37	45		
The Russian Orthodox Church Outside of Russia	1955	81	55,000		92	168		
THE SALVATION ARMY	1990	1,133	445,991	132,489	3,540	5,120	1,166	111,510
THE SCHWENKFELDER CHURCH	1990	5	2,488	2,488	9	11	5	834
Second Cumberland Presbyterian Church in the U.S.	1959	121	30,000		121	125		
Separate Baptists in Christ	1988	101	10,000		101	165		
Serbian Eastern Orthodox Church in the U.S.A. and Canada	1986	68	67,000		60	82		
SEVENTH-DAY ADVENTIST CHURCH	1990	4,217	717,446	717,446	2,316	4,582	4,295	440,733
SEVENTH DAY BAPTIST GENERAL CONFERENCE	1991	86	5,200	5,200	48	77	86	NR
Social Brethren	1975	40	1,784		47	47		
SOUTHERN BAPTIST CONVENTION	1990	37,922	15,038,409	15,038,409	37,800	64,500	36,439	8,003,918
THE SOUTHERN METHODIST CHURCH	1991	130	7,572	7,572	98	133	NR	NR
SOVEREIGN GRACE BAPTISTS	1990	275	3,000	3,000	350	450	275	1,900
The Swedenborgian Church	1988	50	2,423		45	54		
Syrian Orthodox Church of Antioch (Archdiocese of the U.S.A. and Canada)	1988	28	30,000		20	25		
Triumph the Church and Kingdom of God in Christ (International)	1972	475	54,307		860	1,375		
TRUE (OLD CALENDAR) ORTHODOX CHURCH OF GREECE (SYNOD OF METROPOLITAN CYPRIAN) AMERICAN EXARCHATE	1991	8	900	900	6	12	NR	NR
Ukrainian Orthodox Church in the U.S.A.	1966	107	87,745		107	131		
Ukrainian Orthodox Church of America (Ecumenical Patriarchate)	1986	27	5,000		36	37		
UNITARIAN UNIVERSALIST ASSOCIATION	1991	1,020	141,315	141,315	650	1,210	NR	48,888

TABLE 2: UNITED STATES CURRENT AND NON-CURRENT STATISTICS--Continued

Religious Body	Year Reported	No. of Churches	Inclusive Membership	Full, Communicant or Confirmed Members	No. of Pastors Serving Parishes	Total No. of Clergy	No. of Sunday or Sabbath Schools	Total Enrollment
UNITED BRETHREN IN CHRIST.	**1990**	**260**	**25,775**	**25,775**	**320**	**382**	**260**	**14,748**
United Christian Church.	1987	12	420		8	11		
UNITED CHURCH OF CHRIST.	**1990**	**6,260**	**1,599,212**	**1,599,212**	**4,813**	**9,635**	**NR**	**425,929**
United Holy Church of America.	1960	470	28,890		379	400		
The United Methodist Church.	1989	37,407	8,904,824		20,774	38,359		
UNITED PENTECOSTAL CHURCH, INTERNATIONAL.	**1991**	**3,626**	**500,000**	**500,000**	**NR**	**7,464**	**NR**	**NR**
United Zion Church.	1987	13	850		19	20		
UNITY OF THE BRETHREN.	**1990**	**25**	**3,196**	**2,750**	**22**	**28**	**23**	**1,701**
Vedanta Society.	1988	13	2,500		14	14		
Volunteers of America.	1978	607	36,634		704	704		
THE WESLEYAN CHURCH.	**1990**	**1,628**	**110,561**	**102,838**	**1,857**	**3,048**	**1,628**	**121,219**
WISCONSIN EVANGELICAL SYNOD.	**1990**	**1,211**	**420,039**	**316,813**	**1,167**	**1,607**	**1,173**	**49,395**
World Confessional Lutheran Association.	1987	12	1,530		18	27		

*Inclusive membership represents estimates of the total number of Jews seen as an ethnic, social and religious community. Full membership is the number of Jews estimated to be associated with synagogues and temples of the Orthodox, Conservative and Reformed branches by officials of the congregational organizations of these three groups.

Table 3: SOME STATISTICS OF CHURCH

Communion	Year	Full or Confirmed Members	Inclusive members	Total Contributions	Per Capita Full or Confirmed Members	Per Capita Inclusive Members
The Anglican Church of Canada	1990	529,943	848,256	203,946,617	384.84	240.43
Associated Gospel Churches	1991	9,152	19,342	13,534,426	1,478.84	699.74
Baptist Convention of Ontario and Quebec	1990	33,000	3,000	39,036,700	1,182.93	1,182.93
Baptist Union of Western Canada	1990	15,651	20,867	22,340,757	1,427.43	1,070.62
Bible Holiness Movement	1991	358	904	162,301	453.35	179.53
Brethren in Christ Church	1990	3,069	3,069	4,089,420	1,332.49	1,332.49
The Christian and Missionary Alliance in Canada	1990	26,784	74,286	64,097,550	2,393.12	862.84
Christian Church (Disciples of Christ) in Canada	1990	2,496	4,251	2,007,071	804.11	472.14
Church of the Nazarene	1991	10,915	10,951	10,207,965	935.22	932.14
Conference of Mennonites in Canada	1989	28,689	28,689	22,006,773	767.08	767.08
Congregational Christian Churches in Canada	1990	258	258	309,344	1,199.00	1,199.00
The Evangelical Covenant Church of Canada	1990	1,286	1,286	1,846,999	1,436.23	1,436.23
The Evangelical Lutheran Church in Canada	1991	149,059	206,024	54,295,178	364.25	263.53
Foursquare Gospel Church of Canada	1990	2,019	2,019	2,968,100	1,470.08	1,470.08
Latvian Evangelical Lutheran Church in America	1990	2,200	2,380	380,000	172.72	159.66
Lutheran Church-Canada	1990	60,760	80,240	5,800,000	95.45	72.28
Mennonite Brethren Churches Canadian Conference of	1990	27,288	27,288	35,088,863	1,285.87	1,285.87
Mennonite Church (Canada)	1990	9,779	9,779	11,263,513	1,151.80	1,151.80
Moravian Church in America Northern Province Canadian District	1990	1,482	2,157	939,214	633.74	435.42
North American Baptist Conference	1990	15,825	15,825	18,439,364	1,165.20	1,165.20
Presbyterian Church in America (Canadian Section)	1990	538	886	754,115	1,401.70	851.14
The Presbyterian Church in Canada	1990	156,513	245,883	70,529,716	450.63	286.84
Reformed Church in Canada	1990	4,129	6,831	5,285,653	1,280.12	773.77
Russian Orthodox Church in Canada, Patriarchal Parishes	1991	6,000	700	310,800	51.8	
Seventh-day Adventist Church in Canada	1990	40,047	40,047	46,135,253	1,152.02	1,152.02
United Baptist Convention of the Atlantic Provinces	1990	65,346	65,346	29,965,013	458.55	458.55
The United Brethren in Christ Ontario Conference, Church	1990	864	864	886,387	1,025.91	1,025.91
The United Church of Canada	1990	808,441	2,049,923	243,168,533	300.78	118.62
The Wesleyan Church	1991	4,925	5,143	8,023,384	1,629.11	1,560.05
Wisconsin Evangelical Lutheran Synod	1990	907	1,357	634611	699.68	467.65

Table 4: SOME STATISTICS OF CHURCH

Communion	Year	Full or Confirmed Members	Inclusive members	Total Contributions	Per Capita Full or Confirmed Members	Per Capita Inclusive Members
African Methodist Episcopal Zion Church	1991	1,000,000	1,200,000	71,895,244	71.90	59.91
Albanian Orthodox Diocese of America	1991	325	1,870	179,850	553.38	96.18
Allegheny Wesleyan Methodist Connection (Original Allegheny Conference	1990	2,037	2,155	3,948,995	1,938.63	1,832.48
American Baptist Churches in the USA	1990	1,535,971	1,535,971	359,952,372	234.35	234.35
Apostolic Lutheran Church of America	1989	3,351	7,583	93,428	27.88	12.32

NANCES—CANADIAN CHURCHES

	CONGREGATIONAL FINANCES			BENEVOLENCES			
	Total Congregational Contributions	Per Capita Full or Confirmed Members	Per Capita Inclusive Members	Total Benevolences	Per Capita Full or Confirmed Members	Per Capita Inclusive Members	Benevolences As a Percentage of Total Contributions
	159,699,148	301.35	188.26	44,247,469	83.49	52.16	21.69
	10,928,298	1,194.08	565.00	2,606,128	284.76	134.73	19.25
	34,096,700	1,033.23	1,033.23	4,190,000	126.96	126.96	10.73
	17,997,310	1,149.91	862.47	4,343,447	277.51	208.14	19.44
	25,301	70.67	27.98	137,000	382.68	151.54	84.41
	3,211,101	1,046.30	1,046.30	878,319	286.19	286.19	21.47
	52,890,205	1,974.69	711.98	11,207,345	418.43	150.86	17.48
	1,777,158	712.00	418.05	229,913	92.11	54.08	11.45
	9,091,902	832.97	830.23	1,116,063	102.25	101.91	10.93
	12,809,243	446.48	446.48	9,197,530	320.59	320.59	41.79
	271,928	1,053.98	1,053.98	37,416	145.02	145.02	12.09
	1,507,290	1,172.07	1,172.07	339,709	264.15	264.15	18.39
	46,367,143	311.06	225.05	7,928,035	53.18	38.48	14.60
	2,835,618	1,404.46	1,404.46	132,483	65.61	65.61	4.46
	300,000	136.36	126.05	80,000	36.36	33.61	21.05
	4,500,000	74.06	56.08	1,300,000	21.39	16.20	22.41
	25,137,738	921.20	921.20	9,951,125	364.67	364.67	28.35
	7,116,278	727.71	727.71	4,147,235	424.09	424.09	36.82
	819,756	553.14	380.04	119,458	80.60	55.38	12.71
	14,111,353	891.71	891.71	4,328,011	273.49	273.49	23.47
	604,728	1,124.02	682.53	149,388	277.67	168.60	19.80
	59,268,267	378.67	241.04	11,261,449	71.95	45.80	15.96
	4,710,480	1,140.82	689.57	575,173	139.30	84.20	10.88
	300,000	50	428.57	10,800	1.8		3.47
	12,273,145	306.46	306.46	33,862,107	845.55	845.55	73.39
	24,116,340	369.05	369.05	5,848,673	89.50	89.50	19.51
	623,930	722.14	722.14	262,457	303.76	303.76	29.60
	202,243,845	250.16	98.65	40,924,688	50.62	19.96	16.82
	6,648,806	1,350.01	1,292.78	1,374,578	279.10	267.27	17.13
	515,765	568.64	380.07	118,846	131.03	87.57	18.72

NANCES—UNITED STATES CHURCHES

	CONGREGATIONAL FINANCES			BENEVOLENCES			
	Total Congregational Contributions	Per Capita Full or Confirmed Members	Per Capita Inclusive Members	Total Benevolences	Per Capita Full or Confirmed Members	Per Capita Inclusive Members	Benevolences As a Percentage of Total Contributions
	69,178,114	69.18	57.65	2,717,130	2.72	2.26	3.78
	173,000	532.31	92.51	6,850	21.08	3.66	3.81
	3,063,230	1,503.79	1,421.45	885,765	434.84	411.03	22.43
	305,212,094	198.71	198.71	54,740,278	35.64	35.64	15.21
	23,410	6.99	3.09	70,018	20.89	9.23	74.94

Table 4: SOME STATISTICS OF CHURC

				TOTAL CONTRIBUTIONS		
Communion	Year	Full or Confirmed Members	Inclusive Members	Total Contributions	Per Capita Full or Confirmed Members	Per Capita Inclusive Members
Associate Reformed Presbyterian Church (General Synod)	1990	32,787	37,988	21,984,152	670.51	578.71
Baptist General Conference	1991	134,717	134,717	123,180,155	914.36	914.36
Baptist Missionary Association of America	1990	229,166	229,166	55,558,469	242.44	242.44
Berean Fundamental Church Council Inc	1991	2,768	2,768	37,63,620	1,359.69	1,359.69
Brethren in Christ Church	1990	17,277	17,277	16,663,994	964.52	964.52
Christian and Missionary Alliance	1990	138,071	279,207	168,255,859	1,218.62	602.62
Christian Church (Disciples of Christ)	1990	678,750	1,039,692	364,176,916	536.54	350.27
Church of God (Anderson IN)	1990	205,884	205,884	162,462,531	789.10	789.10
Church of God General Conference (Oregon,IL)	1991	4,375	5,688	3,419,151	781.52	601.12
Church of the Brethren	1990	148,253	148,253	69,024,463	465.59	465.59
Church of the Lutheran Confession	1990	6,397	8,753	3,081,917	481.78	352.10
Church of the Nazarene	1991	572,153	573,834	403,923,855	705.97	703.90
Churches of God General Conference	1990	33,371	33,371	18,583,217	556.87	556.87
Conservative Congregational Christian Conference	1990	28,355	28,355	21,138,261	745.49	745.49
Cumberland Presbyterian Church	1990	91,857	98,891	32,720,167	356.21	330.87
The Episcopal Church	1990	1,698,240	2,446,050	1,377,794,610	811.31	563.27
The Evangelical Church	1990	16,398	16,398	14,497,946	884.13	884.13
Evangelical Congregational Church	1990	24,437	32,700	12,389,360	506.99	378.88
Evangelical Covenant Church	1990	89,735	89,735	86,170,275	960.27	960.27
Evangelical Lutheran Church in America	1990	3,898,478	5,240,739	1,503,058,833	385.55	286.80
Evangelical Lutheran Synod	1990	16,181	21,630	7,720,865	477.15	356.95
Evangelical Mennonite Church	1991	3,958	3,958	5,184,678	1,309.92	1,309.92
Evangelical Presbyterian Church	1991	49,286	52,645	47,685,179	967.52	905.79
Fellowship of Fundamental Bible Churches	1991	1,482	1,482	1,862,061	1,256.45	1,256.45
Fire Baptized Holiness Church	1991	695	695	784,000	1,128.06	1,128.06
Free Methodist Church of North America	1990	58,084	74,313	65,347,686	1,125.05	879.36
Free Will Baptists National Association Inc	1990	197,206	197,206	55,500,000	281.43	281.43
Friends United Meeting	1990	45,691	54,945	12,547,146	274.61	228.36
General Association of General Baptists	1990	74,156	74,156	24,896,639	335.30	335.30
General Association of Regular Baptist Churches	1990	168,068	168,068	116,171,637	691.22	691.22
International Pentecostal Church of Christ	1991	2,610	3,995	2,289,435	877.18	573.08
The Latvian Evangelical Lutheran Church in America	1990	11,423	12,553	2,546,000	222.88	202.82
Lutheran Church-Missouri Synod	1990	1,954,350	2,602,849	841,464,284	430.56	323.29
Mennonite Church	1990	92,517	92,517	94,106,910	1,017.19	1,017.19
Mennonite Brethren Churches United States Conference of	1989	16,794	16,794	28,118,881	1,674.34	1,674.34
Mennonite Church, The General Conference	1990	33,535	33,535	22,118,683	659.57	659.57
Metropolitan Community Churches Universal Fellowship of	1990	12,576	25,076	7,414,949	589.61	295.70
Missionary Church Inc	1990	26,910	26,910	35,541,201	1,320.74	1,320.74
Moravian Church in America Northern Province	1990	23,526	31,032	11,442,653	486.38	368.74
North American Baptist Conference	1990	44,493	44,493	38,803,791	872.13	872.13
Presbyterian Church in America	1990	185,526	223,935	227,082,419	1,223.99	1,014.06
Presbyterian Church (USA)	1990	2,847,437	3,788,009	1,825,332,148	641.04	481.87
Reformed Church in America	1990	197,154	326,850	172,066,651	872.75	526.44
The Schwenkfelder Church	1990	2,488	2,488	953,456	383.22	383.22
Seventh-day Adventist Church	1990	717,446	717,446	628,089,298	875.45	875.45
Seventh day Baptist General Conference USA and Canada	1991	5,200	5,200	3,084,307	593.14	593.14
Southern Baptist Convention	1990	15,038,409	15,038,409	4,864,460,435	323.47	323.47
True (Old Calendar) Orthodox Church of Greece	1991	900	900	67,700	75.22	75.22
Unitarian Universalist Association	1991	141,315	141,315	89,817,968	635.59	635.59
United Brethren in Christ	1990	25,775	25,775	16,187,703	628.04	628.04

	CONGREGATIONAL FINANCES			BENEVOLENCES		
Total Congregational Contributions	Per Capita Full or Confirmed Members	Per Capita Inclusive Members	Total Benevolences	Per Capita Full or Confirmed Members	Per Capita Inclusive Members	Benevolences As a Percentage of Total Contributions
16,666,990	508.34	438.74	5,317,162	162.17	139.97	24.19
102,021,709	757.30	757.30	21,158,446	157.06	157.06	17.18
44,170,711	192.75	192.75	11,387,758	49.69	49.69	20.50
3,085,281	1,114.62	1,114.62	678,339	245.06	245.06	18.02
13,327,414	771.40	771.40	3,336,580	193.12	193.12	20.02
136,639,430	989.63	489.38	31,616,429	228.99	113.24	18.79
321,569,909	473.77	309.29	42,607,007	62.77	40.98	11.70
141,375,027	686.67	686.67	21,087,504	102.43	102.42	12.98
2,756,651	630.09	484.64	662,500	151.43	116.47	19.38
54,832,226	369.86	369.86	14,192,237	95.73	95.73	20.56
2,571,777	402.03	293.82	510,140	79.75	58.28	16.55
352,654,251	616.36	614.56	51,269,604	89.61	89.35	12.69
15,536,694	465.57	465.57	3,046,523	91.29	91.29	16.39
16,964,128	598.28	598.28	4,174,133	147.21	147.21	19.75
28,364,344	308.79	286.82	4,355,823	47.42	44.05	13.31
1,147,118,051	675.47	468.97	230,676,559	135.83	94.31	16.74
11,412,700	695.98	695.98	3,085,246	188.15	188.15	21.28
9,946,582	407.03	304.18	2,442,778	99.96	74.70	19.72
70,568,800	786.41	786.41	15,601,475	173.86	173.86	18.11
1,318,884,279	338.31	251.66	184,174,554	47.24	35.14	12.25
6,527,076	403.38	301.76	1,193,789	73.78	55.19	15.46
3,394,563	857.65	857.65	1,790,115	452.28	452.28	34.53
42,413,030	860.55	805.64	5,272,149	106.97	100.15	11.06
1,556,962	1,050.58	1,050.58	305,099	205.87	205.87	16.39
712,000	1,024.46	1,024.46	72,000	103.60	103.60	9.18
55,229,181	950.85	743.20	10,118,505	174.20	136.16	15.48
43,800,000	222.10	222.10	11,700,000	59.33	59.33	21.08
10,036,083	219.65	182.66	2,511,063	54.96	45.70	20.01
23,127,835	311.88	311.88	1,737,011	23.42	23.42	6.99
94,430,756	561.86	561.86	21,740,881	129.36	129.36	18.71
1,806,641	692.20	452.23	482,794	184.98	120.85	21.09
2,160,000	189.09	172.07	386,000	33.79	30.75	15.16
712,235,204	364.44	273.64	129,229,080	66.12	49.65	15.36
65,709,827	710.25	710.25	28,397,083	306.94	306.94	30.18
21,169,039	1,260.51	1,260.51	6,949,842	413.83	413.83	24.72
13,669,288	407.61	407.61	8,449,395	251.96	251.96	38.20
6,611,603	525.73	263.66	803,346	63.88	32.04	10.83
29,835,730	1,108.72	1,108.72	5,705,471	212.02	212.02	16.05
10,105,037	429.53	325.63	1,337,616	56.86	43.10	11.69
31,103,672	699.07	699.07	7,700,119	173.06	173.06	19.84
164,813,870	888.36	735.99	62,268,549	335.63	278.07	27.42
1,530,341,707	537.45	404.00	294,990,441	103.60	77.87	16.16
144,357,947	732.21	441.66	27,708,704	140.54	84.77	16.10
732,573	294.44	294.44	220,883	88.78	88.78	23.17
195,054,218	271.87	271.87	433,035,080	603.58	603.58	68.94
2,329,822	448.04	448.04	754,485	145.09	145.09	24.46
4,146,285,561	275.71	275.71	718,174,874	47.76	47.76	14.76
57,000	63.33	63.33	10,700	11.89	11.89	15.81
87,084,115	616.24	616.24	2,733,853	19.35	19.35	3.04
13,251,867	514.14	514.14	2,935,836	113.90	113.90	18.14

Table 4: SOME STATISTICS OF CHURCH

Communion	Year	Full or Confirmed Members	Inclusive Members	TOTAL CONTRIBUTIONS Total Contributions	Per Capita Full or Confirmed Members	Per Capita Inclusive Members
United Church of Christ	1990	1,599,212	1,599,212	599,363,294	374.79	374.79
The United Methodist Church	1989	8,904,824	8,904,824	2,845,998,177	319.60	319.60
Unity of the Brethren	1990	2,750	3,196	1,348,185	490.25	421.85
The Wesleyan Church	1990	102,838	110,561	114,856,003	1,116.86	1,038.85
Wisconsin Evangelical Lutheran Synod	1990	316,813	420,039	158,408,452	500.01	377.13

SUMMARY STATISTIC

Communion	Number Reporting	Full or Confirmed Members	Inclusive members	TOTAL CONTRIBUTIONS Total Contributions	Per Capita Full or Confirmed Members	Per Capita Inclusive Members
Canadian Communions	30	2,017,723	3,807,851	918,453,620	455.19	241.20
United States Communions	60	43,514,781	48,264,056	17,866,548,721	410.59	370.18

CONGREGATIONAL FINANCES			BENEVOLENCES			
Total Congregational Contributions	Per Capita Full or Confirmed Members	Per Capita Inclusive Members	Total Benevolences	Per Capita Full or Confirmed Members	Per Capita Inclusive Members	Benevolences As a Percentage of Total Contributions
527,378,397	329.77	329.77	71,984,897	45.01	45.01	12.01
2,207,326,260	247.88	247.88	638,671,917	71.72	71.72	22.44
1,260,785	458.47	394.49	87,400	31.78	27.35	6.48
95,278,783	926.49	861.78	19,577,220	190.37	177.07	17.05
134,319,884	423.97	319.78	24,088,568	76.03	57.35	15.21

CHURCH FINANCES

CONGREGATIONAL FINANCES			BENEVOLENCES			
Total Congregational Contributions	Per Capita Full or Confirmed Members	Per Capita Inclusive Members	Total Benevolences	Per Capita Full or Confirmed Members	Per Capita Inclusive Members	Benevolences As a Percentage of Total Contributions
716,798,776	355.25	188.24	200,904,845	99.57	52.76	21.87
14,613,623,118	335.83	302.78	3,252,925,603	74.75	67.40	18.21

TABLE 5: CONSTITUENCY OF THE NATIONAL COUNCIL OF THE CHURCHES IN THE U.S.A.

A separate tabulation has been made of the constituent bodies of the National Council of Churches of Christ in the U.S.A.

Religious Body	Year	Number of Churches	Inclusive Membership	Pastors Serving Parishes
African Methodist Episcopal Church.	1981	6,200	2,210,000	6,050
African Methodist Episcopal Zion Church.	1991	3,000	1,200,000	2,500
American Baptist Churches in the USA.	1990	5,808	1,535,971	5,351
The Antiochian Orthodox Christian Archdiocese of N. America.	1989	160	350,000	250
Armenian Church of America, Diocese of the	1979	66	450,000	45
Christian Church (Disciples of Christ).	1990	4,069	1,039,692	3,744
Christian Methodist Episcopal Church.	1983	2,340	718,922	2,340
Church of the Brethren.	1990	1,095	148,253	1,084
Community Churches, International Council of.	1991	398	250,000	NR
Coptic Orthodox Church.	1990	42	165,000	49
The Episcopal Church.	1990	7,354	2,446,050	8,040
Evangelical Lutheran Church in America	1990	11,087	5,240,739	10,083
Friends United Meeting.	1991	526	54,945	306
General Convention, the Swedenborgian Church.	1988	50	2,423	45
Greek Orthodox Archdiocese of North and South America.	1977	535	1,950,000	610
Hungarian Reformed Church in America.	1989	27	9,780	29
Korean Presbyterian Church in America, General Assembly	1986	180	24,000	200
Moravian Church in America				
Northern Province.	1990	98	31,032	86
Southern Province.	1990	55	21,269	56
National Baptist Convention of America.	1956	11,398	2,668,799	7,598
National Baptist Convention, USA, Inc.	1991	30,000	7,800,000	30,000
Orthodox Church in America.	1978	440	1,000,000	457
Philadelphia Yearly Meeting, Religious Society of Friends.	1967	202	(1965) 16,965	(1965) 23
Polish National Catholic Church of America.	1960	162	282,411	141
Presbyterian Church (USA).	1990	11,501	3,788,009	10,308
Progressive National Baptist Convention, Inc.	1991	1,400	2,500,000	1,400
Reformed Church in America.	1990	924	326,850	860
Russian Orthodox Church in the USA, Patriarchal Parishes.	1985	38	9,780	37
Serbian Orthodox Church for the USA and Canada.	1986	68	67,000	60
Syrian Orthodox Church of Antioch (Archdiocese of the USA and CAN).	1988	28	30,000	20
Ukrainian Orthodox Church in America (Ecumenical Patriarchate).	1986	27	5,000	36
United Church of Christ.	1990	6,260	1,599,212	4,813
The United Methodist Church.	1989	37,407	8,904,824	20,774
Total (32) bodies.		142,945	46,829,961	117,372

TRENDS IN SEMINARY EDUCATION
1986-1991

Gail Buchwalter King, Ph.D.
Associate Director, The Association of Theological Schools

More students enrolled in seminaries in 1991 than in 1990, more were women, more were African Americans, more were Pacific/Asian Americans, and more were part-time students.

The opening fall 1991 enrollment in member schools of the Association of Theological Schools was 59,919, an increase of 1.2 percent over the previous year.

The rise in numbers of women, African American, Pacific/Asian American, and part-time students continued the trends of the past 15-20 years. But the number of Hispanic students declined for the first time in five years.

The following tables offer an update for fall 1991 enrollment in ATS member schools. In 1990, one school ceased operations and five new schools were admitted to membership. The 1990 and 1991 data use a consistent school base of 208 schools.

TABLE 1 Enrollments in ATS Member Schools

	1986	1987	1988	1989	1990	1991
Number of schools	201	201	202	202	208	208
Total enrollment	57,335	53,766	55,745	56,171	59,190	59,919
By Nation						
Canada	3,696	3,572	4,024	4,113	4,053	4,647
United States	52,639	52,194	51,721	52,058	55,137	55,,272
By Membership						
Accredited	52,864	52,464	52,129	52,913	54,235	55,123
Not Accredited	3,471	3,302	3,616	3,258	4,955	4,796

Comparisons of Total Enrollment to Full-time Equivalents

The fall of 1991 saw an increase (0.4 percent) in the full-time equivalent enrollment, reflecting the general trend of the last 14 years. That means that more of the students are enrolling for part-time or reduced academic loads.

TABLE 2 Total Enrollments and Full-time Equivalents

Year	Total Persons (HC)	Percent Change	FTE Enrollment	Percent Change	Percent of Total Enrollment
1978	46,460		36,219		78.0
1979	48,433	+ 4.2	36,795	+ 1.6	76.0
1980	49,611	+ 2.4	37,245	+ 1.2	75.1
1981	50,559	+ 1.9	37,254	0.0	73.7
1982	52,620	+ 4.1	37,705	+ 1.2	71.7
1983	55,112	+ 4.7	38,923	+ 3.3	70.6
1984	56,466	+ 2.5	39,414	+ 1.3	69.8
1985	56,377	- 0.2	38,841	- 1.5	68.9
1986	56,328	- 0.1	38,286	- 1.4	68.0
1987	55,766	- 1.0	38,329	+ 0.1	68.7
1988	55,745	0.0	36,802	- 4.0	66.0
1989	56,171	+ 0.8	38,178	+ 3.7	68.0
1990	59,190	+ 5.4	40,847	+ 7.0	69.0
1992	59,919	+ 1.2	41,020	+ 0.4	68.5

Women in Seminaries

More than 30 percent of the students in seminaries in 1991 were women, for the first time since such numbers have been collected. Female representation on administrative staffs has kept up with that trend, but the slow turnover in full-time faculty members has kept representation on faculties behind the pace.

TABLE 3 Women Enrollment

Year	Number of Women	Percentage Annual Change	Percentage of Total Enrollment
1972	3,358		10.2
1973	4,021	+ 19.7	11.8
1974	5,255	+ 30.7	14.3
1975	6,505	+ 23.8	15.9
1976	7,349	+ 13.0	17.1
1977	8,371	+ 13.9	18.5
1978	8,972	+ 7.2	19.3
1979	10,204	+ 13.7	21.1
1980	10,830	+ 6.1	21.8
1981	11,683	+ 7.9	23.1
1982	12,473	+ 6.8	23.7
1983	13,451	+ 7.8	24.4
1984	14,142	+ 5.1	25.0
1985	14,572	+ 3.0	25.8
1986	14,864	+ 2.0	26.4
1987	15,310	+ 3.0	27.0
1988	16,344	+ 6.8	29.3
1989	16,461	+ 0.7	29.3
1990	17,571	+ 6.7	29.7
1991	18,301	+ 4.2	30.5

African American Student Enrollment

African American enrollment continued its steady growth, which has averaged 5.6 percent per year for the past five years. In order to meet the shortage of African American faculty, more of these students need to be encouraged to seek a Ph.D. degree.

TABLE 4 African American Enrollment

Year	Number of African American Students	Percentage Annual Change	Percentage of Total Enrollment
1971	908	+ 12.4	2.8
1972	1,061	+ 16.9	3.2
1973	1,210	+ 14.0	3.6
1974	1,246	+ 3.0	3.4
1975	1,365	+ 9.6	3.3
1976	1,524	+ 11.6	3.5
1977	1,759	+ 15.4	3.9
1978	1,919	+ 9.1	4.1
1979	2,043	+ 6.5	4.2
1980	2,205	+ 7.9	4.4
1981	2,371	+ 7.5	4.7
1982	2,576	+ 8.6	4.9
1983	2,881	+ 11.8	5.2
1984	2,917	+ 1.2	5.2
1985	3,046	+ 4.4	5.4
1986	3,277	+ 7.6	5.8
1987	3,379	+ 3.1	6.0
1988	3,662	+ 8.4	6.6
1989	3,961	+ 8.2	7.1
1990	4,303	+ 8.6	7.3
1991	4,582	+ 6.5	7.6

Hispanic Enrollment

After a huge increase in 1990, Hispanic enrollment declined in 1991. Enrollment remains at its second-highest level ever, however. Given the shifting population and demographics in the United States and Canada, efforts of denominations to reach out to this group will continue to be important to the existing program of theological schools.

TABLE 5 Hispanic Enrollment

Year	Number of Hispanic Students	Percentage Annual Change	Percentage of Total Enrollment
1972	264		0.8
1973	387	+ 46.8	1.1
1974	448	+ 15.8	1.2
1975	524	+ 17.0	1.3
1976	541	+ 3.2	1.3
1977	601	+ 11.1	1.3
1978	681	+ 13.3	1.5
1979	822	+ 20.7	1.7
1980	894	+ 8.8	1.8
1981	955	+ 6.8	1.9
1982	1,180	+ 23.6	2.2
1983	1,381	+ 17.0	2.5
1984	1,314	- 4.9	2.3
1985	1,454	+ 10.6	2.6
1986	1,297	- 10.8	2.3
1987	1,385	+ 6.8	2.5
1988	1,415	+ 2.2	2.5
1989	1,490	+ 5.3	2.7
1990	1,904	+ 27.8	3.2
1991	1,629	- 14.4	2.7

Pacific/Asian Students

The numbers of Pacific/Asian American students have risen faster than those of any other ethnic constituency, during the past 14 years. Last year's increase was smaller than the average during that span, but was still the greatest increase of any ethnic constituency. The determination to provide an educated ministry is obvious in these statistics.

Table 6 Pacific/Asian Enrollment

Year	Number of Pacific/Asian American Students	Percentage Annual Change	Percentage of Total Enrollment
1977	494		1.1
1978	499	+ 1.0	1.1
1979	577	+ 15.6	1.2
1980	602	+ 4.3	1.2
1981	716	+ 18.9	1.4
1982	707	- 1.3	1.3
1983	779	+ 10.2	1.4
1984	1,130	+ 45.1	2.0
1985	1,195	+ 5.8	2.1
1986	1,393	+ 16.6	2.5
1987	1,645	+ 18.0	2.9
1988	1,963	+ 19.3	3.5
1989	2,065	+ 5.2	3.7
1990	2,439	+ 18.1	4.1
1991	2,643	+ 8.5	4.4

IV
A CALENDAR FOR CHURCH USE

1992—1995

This Calendar presents for a four-year period the major days of religious observance for Christians, Jews, and Muslims; and, within the Christian community, major dates observed by Roman Catholic, Orthodox, Episcopal, and Lutheran churches. Within each of these communions many other days of observance, such as saints' days, exist, but only those regarded major are listed. Thus, for example, for the Roman Catholic Church, mainly the "solemnities" are listed. Dates of interest to many Protestant communions are also included.

Many days of observance, such as Christmas and Easter, do not carry the list of communions observing them, since it is assumed that practically all Christian bodies do. In certain cases, a religious observance will be named differently by various communions, and this is noted.

In the Orthodox dates, immovable observances are listed in accordance with the Gregorian calendar. Movable dates (those depending on the date of Easter) often will differ from Western dates, since Pascha (Easter) in the Orthodox communions does not always fall on the same day as in the Western churches. For Orthodox churches that use the old Julian calendar, observances are held thirteen days later than listed here. Ecumenical dates, such as Week of Prayer for Christian Unity and World Communion Sunday, also are included. For Jews and Muslims, who follow differing lunar calendars, the dates of major observances are translated into Gregorian dates. For Muslim observances, the festivals are dated according to astronomical calculations that have been published in Paris, not in the United States, and this could lead to slight variations. Since the actual beginning of a new month in the Islamic calendar is determined by the appearance of the new moon, the corresponding dates given here on the Gregorian calendar may vary slightly. It is also possible for a festival to occur twice in the same Gregorian year. Only 'Id al-Fitr and the 'Id al-Adha are religious holidays prescribed by the texts of Islam. Other Islamic dates are nevertheless key moments in the lives of Muslim believers. Jewish observances begin at sundown of the day previous to those listed below and end at sundown of the last day.

(Note: In the Calendar, "RC" stands for Roman Catholic, "O" for Orthodox, "E" for Episcopal, "L" for Lutheran, "ECU" for Ecumenical.)

Event	1992	1993	1994	1995
New Year's Day (RC-Solemnity of Mary;O-Circumcision of Jesus Christ; E-Feast of the Holy Name; L-Name of Jesus	Jan 01	Jan 01	Jan 01	Jan 01
Epiphany (Armenian Christmas)	Jan 06	Jan 06	Jan 06	Jan 06
Feast Day of St. John the Baptist (O)	Jan 07	Jan 07	Jan 07	Jan 07
First Sunday After Epiphany (Feast of the Baptism of Our Lord)	Jan 12	Jan 10	Jan 09	Jan 08
Week of Prayer for Christian Unity (ECU)	Jan 18 to Jan 25	Jan 18 to Jan 25	Jan 18 to Jan 25	Jan 18 to Jan 25
Week of Prayer for Christian Unity, Canada (ECU)	Jan 19 to Jan 26	Jan 24 to Jan 31	Jan 23 to Jan 30	Jan 22 to Jan 29
Ecumenical Sunday (ECU)	Jan 19	Jan 24	Jan 23	Jan 22
Presentation of Jesus in the Temple (O-The Meeting of Our Lord and Savior Jesus Christ)	Feb 02	Feb 02	Feb 02	Feb 02
Brotherhood Week (Interfaith)	Feb 16 to Feb 22	Feb 21 to Feb 27	Feb 20 to Feb 26	Feb 19 to Feb 25
Last Sunday After Epiphany (L-Transfiguration)	Mar 01	Feb 21	Feb 13	Feb 26
Ash Wednesday (Western churches)	Mar 04	Feb 24	Feb 16	Mar 01
Easter Lent Begins (Eastern Orthodox)	Mar 09	Mar 01	Mar 14	Mar 06
World Day of Prayer (ECU)	Mar 06	Mar 05	Mar 04	Mar 06
Purim (Jewish)	Mar 19	Mar 07	Feb 25	Mar 16
Joseph, Husband of Mary (RC,E,L)	Mar 19	Mar 19	Mar 19	Mar 19
The Annunciation (O) (Apr 01 for L; Apr 08 for RC and E)	Mar 25	Mar 25	Mar 25	Mar 25
Id al-Fitr (Festival of the End of Ramadan, celebrated on the first day of the month of Shawwal)	Apr 05	Mar 25	Mar 14	Mar 03
First Day of the Month of Ramadan	Mar 06	Feb 23	Feb 12	Feb 02
Holy Week (Western Churches)	Apr 12 to Apr 18	Apr 04 to Apr 10	Mar 27 to Apr 2	Apr 09 to Apr 15
Holy Week (Eastern Orthodox)	Apr 20 to Apr 24	Apr 12 to Apr 16	Apr 25 to Apr 29	Apr 17 to Apr 21

288

Event	1992	1993	1994	1995
Sunday of the Passion (Palm Sunday) (Western Churches)	Apr 12	Apr 04	Mar 27	Apr 09
Palm Sunday (Eastern Orthodox)	Apr 19	Apr 11	Apr 24	Apr 16
Holy Thursday (Western Churches)	Apr 16	Apr 08	Mar 31	Apr 13
Holy Thursday (Eastern Orthodox)	Apr 23	Apr 15	Apr 28	Apr 20
Good Friday (Friday of the Passion of Our Lord) (Western Churches)	Apr 17	Apr 09	Apr 01	Apr 14
Holy (Good) Friday, Burial of Jesus Christ (Eastern Orthodox)	Apr 24	Apr 16	Apr 29	Apr 21
Easter (Western Churches)	Apr 19	Apr 11	Apr 03	Apr 16
First Day of Passover (Jewish, 8 days)	Apr 18	Apr 06	Mar 27	Apr 15
Pascha (Eastern Orthodox Easter)	Apr 26	Apr 18	May 01	Apr 23
National Day of Prayer	May 07	May 06	May 05	May 04
May Fellowship Day (ECU)	May 01	May 07	May 06	May 05
Rural Life Sunday (ECU)	May 10	May 09	May 08	May 14
Ascension Day (Western Churches)	May 28	May 20	May 13	May 25
Ascension Day (Eastern Orthodox)	Jun 04	May 27	Jun 09	Jun 01
First Day of Shavuot (Jewish, 2 days)	Jun 07	May 26	May 16	Jun 04
Pentecost (Whitsunday) (Western Churches)	Jun 07	May 30	May 22	Jun 04
Pentecost (Eastern Orthodox)	Jun 14	Jun 06	Jun 19	Jun 11
Visitation of the Blessed Virgin Mary (RC,E,L)	May 31	May 31	May 31	May 31
Holy Trinity (RC,E,L)	Jun 14	Jun 06	Jun 29	Jun 04
Corpus Christi (RC)	Jun 21	Jun 13	Jun 05	Jun 11
Nativity of St. John the Baptist (RC,E,L)	Jun 24	Jun 24	Jun 24	Jun 24
Sacred Heart of Jesus (RC)	Jun 26	Jun 20	Jun 10	Jun 16
Saint Peter and Saint Paul, Apostles (RC,E,L)	Jun 29	Jun 29	Jun 29	Jun 29
Feast Day of the Twelve Apostles of Christ (O)	Jun 30	Jun 30	Jun 30	Jun 30
Id al-Adha (Festival of Sacrifice at time of annual pilgrimage to Mecca	Jun 12	Jun 01	May 21	May 10
First Day of the Month of Muharram (Beginning of Muslim Liturgical Year)	Jul 02	Jun 21	Jun 10	May 31
Transfiguration of the Lord (RC,O,E)	Aug 06	Aug 06	Aug 06	Aug 06
Feast of the Blessed Virgin Mary (E; RC-Assumption of Blessed Mary the Virgin; O-Falling Asleep (Dormition) of the Blessed Virgin Mary; L-Mary, Mother of Our Lord)	Aug 15	Aug 15	Aug 15	Aug 15
The Birth of the Blessed Virgin (RC, O)	Sep 08	Sep 08	Sep 08	Sep 08
First Day of Rosh Hashanah (Jewish, 2 days)	Sep 28	Sep 16	Sep 06	Sep 25
Holy Cross Day (O-The Adoration of the Holy Cross; RC-Triumph of the Cross)	Sep 14	Sep 14	Sep 14	Sep 14
Yom Kippur (Jewish)	Oct 07	Sep 25	Sep 15	Oct 04
First Day of Sukkot (Jewish, 7 days)	Oct 12	Sep 30	Sep 20	Oct 09
World Communion Sunday (ECU)	Oct 04	Oct 03	Oct 02	Oct 01
Mawlid al-Nabi (Anniversary of Prophet Muhammad's birthday)	Sep 11	Aug 31	Aug 20	Aug 09
Laity Sunday (ECU)	Oct 11	Oct 10	Oct 09	Oct 08
Shemini Atzeret (Jewish)	Oct 19	Oct 07	Sep 27	Oct 16
Simhat Torah (Jewish)	Oct 20	Oct 08	Sep 28	Oct 17
Thanksgiving Day (Canada)	Oct 12	Oct 11	Oct 10	Oct 09
Reformation Sunday (L)	Oct 25	Oct 31	Oct 30	Oct 29
Reformation Day (L)	Oct 31	Oct 31	Oct 31	Oct 31
All Saints (RC,E,L)	Nov 01	Nov 01	Nov 01	Nov 01
World Community Day (ECU)	Nov 06	Nov 05	Nov 04	Nov 03
Stewardship Day (ECU)	Nov 08	Nov 14	Nov 13	Nov 12
Bible Sunday (ECU)	Nov 15	Nov 21	Nov 20	Nov 19
Last Sunday After Pentecost (RC, L-Feast of Christ the King)	Nov 29	Nov 28	Nov 27	Dec 03
Presentation of the Blessed Virgin Mary in the Temple (also Presentation of the Theotokos) (O)	Nov 21	Nov 21	Nov 21	Nov 21
Thanksgiving Sunday (U.S.)	Nov 22	Nov 21	Nov 20	Nov 19
Thanksgiving Day (U.S.)	Nov 26	Nov 25	Nov 24	Nov 23
First Sunday of Advent	Nov 29	Nov 28	Nov 27	Dec 03
Feast Day of St. Andrew the Apostle (RC,O,E,L)	Nov 30	Nov 30	Nov 30	Nov 30
Immaculate Conception of the Blessed Virgin Mary (RC)	Dec 08	Dec 08	Dec 08	Dec 08
First Day of Hanukkah (Jewish, 8 days)	Dec 20	Dec 09	Nov 28	Dec 18
Fourth Sunday of Advent (Sunday before Christmas)	Dec 20	Dec 19	Dec 18	Dec 24
Christmas (Except Armenian)	Dec 25	Dec 25	Dec 25	Dec 25

IV
INDEXES

ORGANIZATIONS

This index contains the names of organizations listed in the directories. Statistical information about religious bodies in Canada and the United States is found in the statistical section. Depositories of church resources are not indexed here. Consult directory 16 for this information.

INDEXES

291

INDEXES

INDIVIDUALS

This index contains names of people found in the directories of church bodies in the United States and Canada. Individuals found in other directories are not included. They should be found by looking up the organizatin to which they are related.

INDEXES

298

280.5
Y3
1992